The Experts' Guide
to the K-12 School Market

Edited by Carol Ann Waugh and Corey E. Brady

Internet Monitor

The Internet Monitor
1807 South Pearl St.
Denver, CO 80210.
Phone (303) 698-1467
Fax (303) 744-9865

www.internet-monitor.com

ISBN 0-9675792-2-8

Design: Winter Group
Cover Design Illustration: Dean McCready, Winter Group
Printed in the United States of America
10 9 8 7 6 5 4 3 2 1

Publisher's Cataloging-in-Publications
(Provided by Quality Books, Inc.)

The experts' guide to the K-12 school market / edited by
  Carol Ann Waugh and Corey E. Brady. -- 1st ed.
    p. cm.
    Includes bibliographical references and index.
    "Insights from market leaders &
  practitioners"--Cover.
    ISBN 0-9675792-2-8

    1. Educational publishing--United States.
    2. Education--Authorship--Marketing.   I. Waugh, Carol.
  II. Brady, Corey E.

  Z286.E3E96 2002   070.5
                                QBI33-208

Permissions

The "Man in the Chair" ad is reprinted with permission from McGraw-Hill.

Portions of the article entitled *Relationship Building Through Telesales* article was derived from an article previously published in the School Marketing Newsletter, a publication of the School Market Research Institute. Reproduced with permission.

Portions of the article entitled *Direct Mail Copyrighting* were excerpted from *Streetwise Direct Marketing* by George Duncan, published by Adams Media, Inc. (2001). Reproduced with permission.

"Education is about giving wings to children's dreams."

Paul Houston
Executive Director
American Association of School Administrators

From the Publisher

The U.S. Education market is a large, complex, and challenging one. From its colonial roots in the one-room schoolhouse where children were taught the basics of reading, writing and arithmetic, the K-12 educational system today has evolved into multi-billion dollar industry.

But in all this time, there has never been a "textbook" on how to develop and market educational materials and services to the K-12 schools—until today.

When we at Internet Monitor conceived of this idea in January of 2001, we quickly realized that no single person in the industry could cover all the unique aspects of this market. In order to present a well-rounded, quality book, we saw we would have to ask a group of leaders in the industry to pool their thoughts and expertise.

So, we put together a list of experts and outlined the topic areas we needed to cover in order to publish a comprehensive book. When we started talking to potential contributors, we were quite overwhelmed with their initial reactions. We were, after all, asking them to freely share their knowledge and expertise and spend their precious time writing an article for publication—all in exchange for a copy of the book.

The reactions?

"Yes, what a wonderful idea! I'd love to contribute!"

"Absolutely, and thank you for asking me"

"Wow! I'm honored to be included"

As the initial drafts of the book developed, we encouraged our authors to follow their individual interests in refining their articles. While we knew that this approach might lead both to gaps in the book's coverage and to minor inconsistencies in the advice provided, we were committed to allowing free expression of the experts' voices and ideas. For what we sacrificed in orderliness and simplicity, we were more than compensated in seeing the brilliance and personality of our authors, as they came together to share their experiences with colleagues.

In a tribute to this spirit of cooperation and collaboration among the contributors, Internet Monitor is very proud to publish this extraordinary book. It's a book that will give you the "real" story of how to be successful in the K-12 school market. From how to develop educational products and services that will meet the needs of students and teachers, to how to market and sell these products to schools, this book is a compendium of the best advice from seasoned professionals.

Whether you are new to this industry or an experienced veteran, this book will inspire you, challenge you, educate you and give you new ideas on successful K-12 market strategies.

We applaud all of our contributors and thank them for sharing, caring, and contributing.

Kathryn Kleibacker
Carol Ann Waugh
Linda M. Winter

Other books by the Internet Monitor

i-Tips® 2000: The Insiders' Guide to School & Library Marketing
by Kathryn Kleibacker, Linda Winter & Carol Ann Waugh

For a free subscription to the bi-weekly electronic version of the *i-Tips Newsletter* that updates this book with marketing and product development tips from the experts at Internet Monitor, visit our web site and complete the subscription form at www.internet-monitor.com.

i-Tips® is a registered trademark of Internet Monitor.

Internet Monitor thanks:

Dean McCready, Designer, Winter Group for his eye, enthusiasm and energy in designing and producing this book!

Foreword

Katheen Hurley, Senior Vice President, Marketing & Sales, NetSchools Corporation

This is not only a good book, it's also a much needed book for the K-12 industry. To my knowledge, *The Experts' Guide to the K-12 School Market* is the first book ever compiled for the K-12 education industry that actually puts all the information about our market in one place. And, more importantly, the information provided is not by one expert but by many experts. Collectively, the people contributing to this book have over 900 years of experience in the education industry. If I were a new person entering the education world, this is the one book that I would make sure was on my desk at all times. As a veteran in this field, I will definitely have this book on my desk at all times – I cannot think of a better resource to provide me with information ranging from Trends in Textbook Publishing to Key Market Demographics to State Adoptions to Positioning and Branding, and those are only four of the more than 70 subjects covered!

The need for this type of book became apparent to me in April of 2000 as I began the challenging experience of raising capital for NetSchools Corporation. Even though I have been in the K-12 market for years (which will remain numberless), I was surprised by the breadth and depth of questions posed to me in my various meetings with bankers. However, as I began to answer some of their questions and explain the complexities of the K-12 market, I realized that many of these bankers lacked an overall understanding of the K-12 marketplace. For instance, they lacked basic knowledge of some of the key niche markets that drive our industry, markets such as special education, ESL, home schooling and Catholic schools, to name just a few.

However, this type of experience is not limited to venture capitalists. With the explosion of the Internet and the recent national attention on education, it seems that more and more people are entering the education market who do not have an education background from the classroom or from an education-focused company. While I believe it is wonderful that more people are taking

> *"The man who does not read good books has no advantage over the man who cannot read them."*
>
> *Mark Twain*

an interest in education and ways to improve our educational system, it is also creating interesting challenges because many of these well-intentioned people do not have a thorough understanding of the marketplace. From the private sector, there are new people within the industry whom understand how to run a company but do not understand the nature of schools and school districts. For instance, they may not understand how a school purchases or whom purchase from and why. From the public sector, more and more people running school districts and serving on school boards come from completely different sectors of society. For example, in Cobb County, Georgia, where NetSchools is headquartered, the new superintendent is a retired Colonel from the United States Army.

Today, everyone feels ownership of the educational system, from parents to school boards to community leaders to policy makers. While all these groups have different issues of concern, they all have valid and worthy ideas, and many times their experiences can bring new and positive solutions to struggling schools or education companies. This influx of new people provides us with the opportunity to explain the ebb and flow of the education marketplace and help shape the future direction of our industry.

The brief description above shows why this book is needed. However, I am not recommending it solely for "the new people." I also highly recommend it for the "veterans of the industry." *The Experts' Guide to the K-12 School Market* provides a logistical roadmap to help us navigate this expanding industry and gives us the opportunity to learn and grow together as we tackle the new challenges presented by shifting public policy as well as the ever-changing wonders of high technology.

Finally, the individuals who have contributed to this book are not only experts in the industry, but they are also personal friends. Honestly, who better to give advice on *the role of the school board* than Ann Flynn, Director of Educational Technology, National School Boards Association, or the importance of *database marketing* than Jeanne Hayes, President of Quality Education Data (QED). I can say with complete confidence that this is the first publication in our industry to capture the vast experience of so many experts and incorporate them in one complete, concise book.

On a personal note, I would like to extend a heartfelt thank you to Carol Waugh, Kathy Kleibacker and Linda Winter, who had the vision, wisdom and diligence to put together an exhaustive resource that will benefit the entire K-12 community.

About the Author

Kathleen M. Hurley *is senior vice president of marketing and sales for NetSchools Corporation. Prior to joining NetSchools she was senior vice president of education marketing for The Learning Company. Kathy serves on numerous industry and education advisory boards, including: the Software and Information Industry Association (SIIA), the International Society for Technology in Education (ISTE), the Council of Great City Schools Technology Steering Committee, and the National Catholic Education Exhibitors' Association. She is currently board president of the Association of Educational Publishers. Prior to working for the Learning Company she was the senior vice president of SkillsBank Corporation. Kathy has held various positions with IBM, Mindscape, Grolier, and DLM. Kathy began her career working with learning disabled students after receiving her Masters degree at the Jersey City State College. She also continues to support her undergraduate institution, The University of Dayton, by serving on the school of education's advisory board.*

Table of Contents

Table of Contents

Table of Contents

Introducton

by Corey E. Brady

It is a daunting task to introduce the collection of distinguished professionals who have offered their insights in the articles they have contributed to this volume. In framing their work, however, it may be appropriate to draw attention to three of the overarching themes which—though rarely stated explicitly in the articles themselves—I think underlie our shared experience of the educational industry. These themes are:

- *The value of experience* in a time of change
- *The importance of integrity,* in an environment with powerful dichotomies and political forces, and
- *The intimacy of our industry,* within an exploding marketplace.

Particularly for the reader unacquainted with the authors or unfamiliar with the industry, these themes are worth drawing out.

The Value of Experience

The 72 authors of articles in this book have an average of 10-15 or more years of experience in education and the education market. So, all told, the group can boast about 900 years of time spent studying and working successfully in the industry! As a relative newcomer to the market, I find this number astounding. But to give it a proper scale, consider the number in an historical context.

The world of education 900 years ago—of the early 12th century—was different in certain ways from the one we encounter today. Oxford, Cambridge, and the early European Universities would be founded at this time. The late Medieval Scholastics were beginning to feel the ripples of new ideas that gave birth eventually to the Renaissance. And of course just around the corner (from the historical perspective of today, at least), was the radical education technology revolution of the printing press, which would alter the function of the Universities, change the way that educational disciplines were conceived and held together, and shake the roots of economic, social, and cultural life.

But how much has really changed?

In an environment where the Internet has created similar disruption and opportunity for education in particular and for the world's cultures in general, there is a lot that can be learned from voices of experience. As the most human of endeavors, education—like poetry—expresses its great motifs in every epoch.

Too often we are tempted to take the shininess of the latest technology for something utterly unique and without precedent in the history of education. Experience helps us to understand the context of present innovations and see what long-term impact they will truly have. Great changes have indeed occurred in the last 900 years, but there have also been some remarkable continuities and recurrences in that time.

The Importance of Integrity

In considering the educational issues at the center of recent debates, it is striking to note how often the difference between success and failure, between beneficial and harmful measures, turn upon differences in the application of a key term. It may sound simple, but as members of the educational community we would do well to ensure that the higher senses of the terms are the ones we are striving for.

For instance, in the Standards debate. I am sure all would agree that the goal of raising the standards of education is a higher and more noble one than that of merely standardizing the experience of education.

Or in education technology, it is surely a more worthy goal to contemplate improvements in the applications of software to the experience of teaching and learning, than simply to create more software applications—more products to sell.

As we act as members of the community, we must consider the degree to which our actions, our products, or our examples tend either to the higher or the lower of these kinds of goals. In their chosen fields and across the industry, the authors of articles in this collection are admirable for their consistency in striving for higher goals—both personally in their individual actions, and professionally in their roles within their companies.

The Intimacy of Our Industry

The final general point to make in setting the stage for our authors has to do with the nature of the professional community represented here. Speaking again as a newcomer, I have been deeply impressed by the willingness of established figures in the industry to take members of the next generation under their wing; to teach us what they have learned; and to help us to succeed.

But the industry is congenial not only to new members, but also among its establishment. For evidence of this, one has only to look at professional gatherings such as SIIA meetings or EdNET. Consistently, members of the most intensely competitive companies come together to share knowledge and pool mental resources to improve the quality of education. It's inspirational to see this happening consistently across the industry, and it's an example that encourages emulation.

So if you are attending an educational tradeshow and you identify one of the authors of this collection by his or her nametag, take time to introduce yourself. In speaking with them as with so many others in the industry, you can be sure that you will encounter wisdom, integrity, and congeniality.

As I am sure you'll agree, it's a fantastic mix!

About the Author

Corey Brady *is an educator and a developer of education materials that use Web and network technologies effectively. As an instructional designer and programmer, and later as chief education officer and chief operating officer, Corey helped to conceive, create, and manage the online mathematics curriculum products of Boxer Learning, Inc, which can be found at www.boxermath.com. He is now with Texas Instruments, as manager of product strategy for the TI-Navigator networked classroom solution. Corey can be reached at cbrady@ti.com, and he encourages readers to provide insights and/or critiques via email.*

CHAPTER 1
K-12 Market Trends Overview

Inside this chapter…

The History of American Education

by Judith Beck, Ph.D

Colonial America

The English were the predominant settlers in the New World and brought with them their culture, traditions, and philosophy about education. Patterned on the English model, Colonial American education originally developed as a two-track system, with people from the lower classes receiving minimal instruction and only learning the skills necessary to read and write, calculate, and receive religious instruction. In contrast, the upper classes were allowed to pursue an education beyond the basics, oftentimes attending Latin grammar or secondary schools where they learned Greek and Latin and studied the classics in preparation for a college education.

Religion also played an important role in developing the educational system of the colonial United States. The Puritans, a strict fundamentalist Protestant sect who began immigrating to the New World in 1609 to secure religious freedoms, believed that education was necessary in order to read the Bible to receive salvation. This was also in line with the beliefs of the Protestant Reformers. Their schools made no distinction between religious and secular life and were also used to inspire children to endure the hardships of a life in the New World through religious devotion.

Teachers had some status in the community because they, along with the clergy, had more education than most of the population. Their position was clearly secondary to that of the clergy, but like the clergy teachers had to demonstrate high moral character, and they came under intense scrutiny by the rest of the community. They also had many other duties besides teaching, such as cleaning the school, substituting for the minister, and ringing the church bell.

Requiring School Attendance

The first compulsory education laws were passed in Massachusetts from 1642 to 1648. They were specifically oriented towards a (non-Puritan) segment of the population who were not providing their children with what was considered a proper education. Religious leaders were concerned about the rapid growth of this non-Puritan population and took steps to reinforce Puritan religious beliefs in the community. The first act, called the Massachusetts Act of 1642, made education a state concern. While schools were not yet publicly funded and attendance was not yet compulsory, education was, and all parents were supposed to ensure that their children learned how to read and write, or risk losing of custody of them. This law was amended and strengthened in 1648.

A law requiring the establishment of schools was passed in 1647. Under it, all towns of fifty or more households were required to form a school and pay a teacher either out of private or public monies. In addition, towns of one hundred or more households had to establish a secondary or Latin grammar school to prepare students to enter Harvard College.

Education in the Revolutionary Era

As the American colonies continued to grow and prosper, the European traditions that had previously guided the development of schools and education began to lose some of their influence. Though religion was still an important part of the curriculum, the need to build and maintain commerce, agriculture, and shipping industries led to a different educational focus. As generations were born and grew up in the American colonies, people began to see themselves as separate from their European roots and started to develop their own cultural identity. The American Revolution was the culmination of this psychological movement away from European traditions, resulting in political independence for the thirteen colonies from Great Britain. As the United States of America, the former colonists wanted to establish their independence in both thought and deed and saw education as a means to this end. Education was also seen as the tool that would both establish and promote the growth of concepts such as freedom, liberty, and democracy, to ensure that citizens would learn how to be responsible citizens and to establish the United States as a stable nation for generations to come.

A standard curriculum was difficult to achieve in a country as large and sparsely populated as the new United States of America. However, the development of textbooks provided one means of promoting a curriculum that advocated the ideals of democracy and independence from England. Noah Webster (1758-1853) introduced his first text in 1783: a speller with an emphasis on developing patriotic and moral values as well as teaching children correct grammar and spelling. Webster's "blue books," as they were commonly known, eventually sold over 24 million copies, a staggering number given the population of the United States at the time.

The Rise of the Common School

Public or state-sponsored education was still a relatively novel concept in the United States. Though Thomas Jefferson (1743-1826) had been a strong advocate for state funding of public education, public schools were not universally embraced as a right of the common man. The first public secondary school was established in Boston in 1821 and marked the beginning of the long and difficult struggle to achieve public funding. Horace Mann (1796-1859) was the one of the strongest proponents for public education and the common school. As a lawyer, a Massachusetts state senator, and the first secretary of the Massachusetts State Board of Education, Mann worked continually on behalf of the public to achieve support for public education. Many different groups such as private school owners, taxpayers, rural residents, and members of the upper and wealthy classes opposed him because they felt public schools were not in their best interests.

Over time, Mann was indeed able to improve the quality of the schools in Massachusetts. He published annual reports on the state of schools in Massachusetts and through this vehicle was able to make his views known and influence others. Mann felt particularly strongly about the need for professional training for teachers. Prior to Mann, people with a rudimentary education could call themselves teachers if they so desired. Mann saw the need for setting standards and for educating teachers specifically for their profession. The first normal school for teacher training was established in Lexington, Massachusetts in 1839. Prospective teachers were given courses in content knowledge and in pedagogy or instructional methods. In addition, they were required to practice their teaching skills in a model school associated with the normal school. Thanks to Horace Mann, Massachusetts developed a strong system of state-supported common schools that in turn became a model for the rest of the United States.

In the 19th century in the United States, the *McGuffey Reader* was the most common text used in schools. Far exceeding the scope and influence of Noah Webster's spellers, McGuffey's readers sold over 120 million copies. Though not overtly religious in expression, these readers still had a moralistic overtone with an emphasis on virtuous and upright behavior. The text was designed to foster the development of good citizens.

Compulsory Education

The United States experienced rapid growth during the period from 1865-1920, as waves of immigrants made their way to what they viewed as a land of opportunity. At the same time, westward expansion and the settlement of the western territories increased the need for a common system of education to join together and educate an increasingly diverse population. Compulsory attendance laws helped accelerate this process and provided the means for delivering a common school curriculum.

The gradual institutionalization of child labor laws, along with advances in technology, made many unskilled jobs obsolete and led to a rising unemployment rate among lower class youths. In the highly industrialized eastern portion of the United States, this rising unemployment led to large numbers of children having little to do other than roam the streets and (by implication) cause trouble. Lawmakers turned to the schools to take care of this problem and subsequently developed a curriculum designed both to promote the development of moral values and provide training for jobs.

Compulsory school attendance laws were first passed in Massachusetts in 1852 and quickly spread to other sections of the country. By 1900, 32 states had passed compulsory education laws, and by 1930 all states had some form of this law in place. As a consequence, the numbers of children receiving an education increased dramatically.

As the number of students grew, the need also increased for a more efficient method of administration, and school leaders turned to big business to provide a model for effectively managing their resources. Using Frederick Taylor's model of "scientific management," schools began to cluster together into centralized districts and pool their individual resources. Curriculum became more standardized, and increasingly the county, state, and city governments began to assert more control over the educational process. Typically, a superintendent was appointed to run each district, which was also governed by a local school board formed by members of the community who were elected to their positions. Individual schools had principals in charge of them, as well. Thus teachers, who formerly had assumed responsibility for almost the entire educational process, found their duties more and more clearly delimited and controlled.

The Second Half of the 20th Century: Post-World War II and Beyond

Following World War II, the population of the United States increased dramatically with a post-war baby boom. Higher education also experienced a boom, as the Congress passed the GI Bill in 1944 providing subsidies for returning veterans to attend colleges and universities. Over 10 million veterans took advantage of this opportunity, dramatically increasing the number of people who completed college.

As the numbers of school children grew, the demand for facilities and teachers also rose. As the need for teachers increased, teacher certification requirements were lowered and in some cases almost eliminated—to the point that little or no professional training was required for teachers. Later, however, this trend reversed itself; the teacher shortage became in actuality a teacher surplus in the late 1960s to early 1970s, and teacher certification requirements were once again raised.

More schools had to be built to accommodate the large numbers of school-aged children, and small school districts joined together with other districts to from larger ones that could better bear the burden of increased capital and administration costs. The one-room schoolhouse where one teacher taught all grades (usually grades 1-8), which had been a staple of life in rural America, almost disappeared as a result—it was cheaper to build bigger schools and bus children to central locations.

During the 1950s the major political concern in the United States was the Cold War. Following World War II, the Soviets had moved into Eastern Europe and asserted control over the governments of many of these countries. The United States believed its mission was to prevent the further spread of communism and dominate the Soviets in every aspect of political, social, and economic life. In 1957 the Soviet Union set off a shock wave in the United States with the first successful launch of an artificial satellite

called Sputnik. Almost immediately, politicians blamed this failing on the American educational system, claiming that it was not rigorous enough and that more attention needed to be paid to mathematics and science education in particular. Subsequently, the federal government appropriated millions of dollars for educational reform.

The 1950s were also the beginning of the end for school segregation. In 1954, the Supreme Court heard the case of Brown v. the Board of Education of Topeka. Through this case, the court looked again at the issue of segregation and this time ruled that it was illegal to deny people access to a facility based on their race. However, this ruling did not immediately end segregation. Strong opposition arose in many school districts throughout the country, and schools were often the scenes of violent confrontations when integration was first initiated.

In the 1960s, the political emphasis changed from an external or global focus such as the Cold War to a consideration of internal affairs such as civil rights and President Lyndon Johnson's War on Poverty. When President John F. Kennedy, in his inaugural speech of 1961, asked the American public to consider "...not what your country can do for you, but what you can do for your country," he ushered in a new era, characterized by a consciousness about the real meaning of equal opportunity and a commitment to alleviate conditions associated with poverty.

Both Kennedy and Johnson allocated massive funding to programs designed to break the cycle of poverty, and education was one of the areas receiving these funds. Programs such as Head Start, Job Corps, subsidized school lunches, and Title I began during this time.

The reform movement in education was also characterized by a new curricular emphasis. Teachers were encouraged to experiment and use their creativity to make education more interesting and engaging for their students. In place of the textbook-oriented stay-in-your-seat type of learning that had characterized teaching in the 1950s, students were now allowed choices and offered flexible scheduling, individualized instruction, and non-graded schools.

However, the curriculum reform movement of the sixties did not have the hoped-for results in improving educational outcomes. Test scores dropped, enrollments fell, and public confidence in teachers was eroded. In response, a strong back-to-basics curriculum movement gained momentum, emphasizing reading, writing, and arithmetic computation, along with teacher accountability.

The seventies can be characterized as a time of economic concerns, marked by the 1973 OPEC oil crisis, double-digit inflation, and high unemployment and interest rates. Schools also suffered in this economic environment, as funding was cut for public education.

In 1975 Congress passed PL 94-142, which required a free, appropriate education for all handicapped children. This law required that handicapped children be educated to the best of their abilities and that they be provided with an individualized educational plan, written to suit their specific needs. In this same year, Title IX of the Education Amendments Act took effect, requiring that access to programs (in particular, to sports programs) not be denied on the basis of gender. Prior to the implementation of this law, females had only limited opportunities to participate in school sports, because the funding (if it was provided at all) was not provided at the same level as it was for male sports programs.

The eighties saw an escalation of the criticisms aimed at public education and teachers. In 1983, the national report *A Nation at Risk* was published, presenting a powerful argument that the public school system had failed miserably in educating America's children. As a result of this report, school reform movements gained momentum and a number of states passed laws outlining higher standards and expectations for students.

The educational focus for the nineties was primarily directed at school reform. For example, *Goals 2000* was an effort by the federal government to set standards for American education. Restructuring schools to meet the needs of an increasingly diverse population and greater competition in a world that is rapidly changing in terms of technology has been the focus of most educators in recent years. For the most part, teachers have risen to the occasion, taking on roles of leadership and leading the way into the 21st century.

Conclusion

Many great thinkers and contributors have had a role in developing our American system of education, and there will be more to come in the future. Our system is constantly evolving and changing, and perhaps this is the greatest challenge educators face today. Will the introduction of standards and assessments improve learning? Will technology deliver on its promise? Or is the secret just to lift families out of poverty? Whatever the ultimate answer (if there is one), you can count on the fact that just as in colonial times, American education will continue to reflect the needs and values of our local communities—in fact, this is perhaps the only thing that has remained constant since the 1600s.

About the Author

Judith Beck *taught elementary school for fourteen years. She received her PhD from the University of Oregon in Education in 1992, where her primary area of study was talented and gifted education. Since that time, she has been an educational consultant for a computer company, worked as an assessment specialist for school districts, and taught courses at Oregon State University. Currently she is serving as the field placement & licensure coordinator and the head advisor for the School of Education at Oregon State University.*

Key K-12 Demographics
by Sharon Sanford

The education market in the United States is growing, as evidenced by trends visible at a macro-level. Education marketers can take advantage of these trends by identifying emerging or growing segments of the market, changes in the focus and distribution of funding sources, and product and service needs resulting from the increased pressures for accountability faced by schools today.

K-12 MARKET SNAPSHOT: 2000-2001 SCHOOL YEAR

$375 Billion	K-12 Education Market
52.2 Million	Students
111,090	Schools
89,450	Public
21,640	Non-Public
14,300	Public School Districts
323,559	School and District Administrators
3.4 Million	Teachers and Support Personnel

Education represents 9% of the gross domestic product, with $375 billion being spent on goods and services for the K-12 segment. Education is clearly an important market and one that has received increased attention in recent years. As the academic performance of the nation's students has declined, the cry for school improvement and accountability has increased significantly. Improving our nation's schools has become a priority for local, state, and federal policymakers, along with parents and educators. Funding is at an all-time high, significantly fueled by the federal education budget, which reached a record-breaking $42.1 billion for FY2001. Progressively rising since 1993, the 18% increase in the budget this year alone is the biggest one-year boost in history for the US Department of Education. The federal contribution to education represents 6% of available funds, while 49% come from state funds and 45% from local funds. Federal funding, although the smallest portion, is highly influential, as state and local priorities often mirror federal initiatives. The vast majority of government initiatives are aimed at addressing significant changes occurring in the education environment and the impact they have on the quality of education.

Enrollment

At the start of the 2000-2001 school year, 52.2 million students were enrolled in America's elementary and secondary (K-12) schools. Additionally, there were an estimated 1.5 million children being home-schooled. This represents another all-time high in student enrollment: secondary enrollments are expected to increase by an additional 4% over the next ten years, while elementary enrollments will begin to decline beginning in 2002.

K-12 ENROLLMENT: 1990-2010

	1990	1995	2000	2005	2010
K-8	34.0	36.8	38.1	37.6	37.5
9-12	12.4	13.7	14.9	15.9	15.5
Total	46.4	50.5	53.0	53.5	53.0

Source: NCES 2000

Along with increased enrollment growth, the diversity of the student population has changed significantly in the past few years. Looking out over the next ten years, the number of white students will decline,, while nonwhites will increase. The fastest growing ethnic segments are Hispanics and Asians. By 2010, the Hispanic student population will increase by 32% from its year 2000 level, while the Asian population will go up by 34%

PROJECTED NUMBER OF SCHOOL-AGE CHILDREN BY RACE
(in millions)

	2000	2005	2010	Percent Change 2000-2010
White	33.4	32.5	30.9	-7%
African-American	7.6	7.6	7.3	-4%
Hispanic	7.9	9.3	10.4	+32%
Asian	2.1	2.5	2.8	+34%
Native American	.5	.5	.5	-4%

Source: Bureau of Census, 2000

Nearly 40% of the 52.2 million students now in school are located in only five states. These states are often key in early identification of trends or changes in the education climate, ultimately impacting curriculum and purchasing habits. As an example, the diversity of the student population that is now evident throughout the country was and continues to be most dramatic in these states, all of which are impacted by a large number of immigrants.

Top Five States by Enrollment: 2000-01 School Year

	K-12 Enrollment	% of U.S. Enrollment
California	6,554,949	13%
Texas	4,253,532	8%
New York	3,428,968	7%
Florida	2,674,680	5%
Illinois	2,333,005	4%
Total	19,245,134	37%

Source: Market Data Retrieval Enrollment Report, 2000

Schools and Districts

The majority of K-12 students are educated in traditional school environments—either public schools or Catholic and other private schools. Roughly 90% of these K-12 students attend public schools, while the remaining 10% are enrolled in nonpublic schools. This distribution of enrollment has remained fairly constant for the past decade.

The public school segment operates according to a clear hierarchy, with the district at the core of developing district-wide education plans and administering budgets based on those plans. Today, there are 14,300 districts that control 89,450 public schools. Districts vary dramatically in size and their span of control, with approximately 30% of all districts administering 70% of schools, which in turn educate 80% of students.

Public School Districts

Enrollment Size	Number of Districts	Number of Schools	Enrollment
10,000+	1,088	34,400	24,151,923
2,500-9,999	3,175	26,823	14,622,939
600-2,499	5,513	18,707	7,234,772
Under 600	4,524	6,597	1,254,806
Total	14,300	86,527*	47,264,440

*Excludes state and county schools that do not report to a district. Source: Market Data Retrieval, 2000

In recent years, the trend toward site-based management has taken hold. Although district administrators remain key in establishing curriculum standards and making the final decision on district-wide purchases, schools now operate with greater influence over the decision-making process regarding how and when to implement curriculum and what materials they will and will not use in instruction. Today, 69,072 schools have moved to site-based

management. Within these schools, there are 2.3 million principals and teachers who now have increased influence or are directly responsible for many purchasing decisions. This trend has created greater complexity for the education marketer in reaching the ultimate buyer, but it also offers many more opportunities to influence a purchase.

In looking at enrollment by school level, elementary enrollment represents 52% of public school enrollment, followed by 28% of students in senior high and 19% in middle/junior high schools.

Average school sizes range from 468 students in an elementary school to 824 students in a senior high and 657 students in a middle/junior high school.

Schools by Grade Level: 2000-01 School Year

School Type	Number of Schools	Enrollment (in millions)
Elementary	65,904	28.5
Middle/Junior	13,921	9.1
Senior	18,237	14.5
Total*	111,090	52.2

*Includes combined (K-12), adult, special, and vocational schools. Source: Market Data Retrieval, 2000

As enrollments continue to climb, school districts are now confronted with insufficient space to house the growing number of students. In addition, the average school building in the United States is over 40 years old and the infrastructure of these schools is often unable to accommodate the changes occurring in the instructional process, particularly in the area of technology. Nearly 900 new schools have been built per year for the past four years due to the growth in the number of students or the need to replace existing facilities. In addition, during the current school year, nearly 10,000 schools are involved in significant expansion or renovation projects. The average cost for these projects is $6.1 million. Many more schools are now floating bond issues to cover construction costs in addition to expanding the items included in their capital budgets, providing monies to outfit these new and expanded facilities. Under the US Department of Education's FY2001 budget, $1.2 billion has been allocated for school renovation to provide support to those districts needing emergency repairs in their schools in addition to renovations needed to support special education or education technology.

Personnel

District and School Administrators

There are approximately 165,000 district administrators working in the nation's 14,300 public school districts. These administrators are key in the implementation of education programs and initiatives that cover budgeting, staffing, facilities, curriculum and instruction, guidance and special services, and technology. On average, 17% of these administrators are new to their role each year. Within this group, 15% of the top administrators—the Superintendents—are new to their role in the district. Given the level of influence these leaders have over the educational philosophy and practices of the entire school district, marketers should be aware when these top-level decision makers change.

Principals and assistant principals, who are responsible for the effective running of their schools, now total 123,734. With the growing number of site-based managed schools, these education leaders have increased influence and responsibility for a wide range of purchasing decisions. Much like district level administrators, 17% of principals are new to their school each year.

Teachers

Today there are 3.25 million elementary and secondary teachers, a number that has grown by close to 20% since 1990. Even with these increases, there is still an insufficient number of teachers available to meet the growing needs of America's schools. Much has been written about this teacher shortage, which developed as a result of the sustained enrollment growth previously noted along with the record number of teachers reaching retirement age. In addition, the federal agenda's strong emphasis on reducing class size in grades 1-3 has further increased the need for classroom teachers. The US Department of Education estimates that over 2.2 million teachers will need to be hired over the next decade. Estimates of the number of new teachers entering the profession each year range from 40,000 to 100,000 teachers per year. And of these, one-third will leave the classroom within their first few years of teaching. Clearly the number of teachers entering the profession is dramatically insufficient to

> " The current K-12 education environment exhibits many strong demographic indicators pointing to a healthy and dynamic market for education marketers. "

meet the growing demand. By 2010, the number of teachers needed to staff America's schools will reach 3.3 million.

PROJECTED GROWTH OF TEACHERS

	# of Teachers (in Millions)
1995	2.98
2000	3.25
2005	3.32
2010	3.35

Source: NCES 2000

Additionally, according to Market Data Retrieval's annual census of school personnel, the average turnover rate of teachers is approximately 20% per year. This means that over 500,000 teachers transfer to another school or are teaching for the first time each year.

Today's classroom environment is much more complex than in years past. The diversity of students—with different ethnic backgrounds, varying levels of English proficiency, and other special needs—requires the classroom teacher to provide more individualized instruction and have a wider range of skills. Additionally, although technology is now becoming widespread in schools, teachers are poorly trained to fully integrate these resources into their teaching. The common notion that "new teachers" (those in their first or second year of teaching) equates with "computer savvy" or translates into more effective technology use in the classroom isn't accurate. According to Market Data Retrieval's *New Teachers and Technology 1999* report, new teachers and experienced teachers were on par when asked how well prepared they felt to integrate technology into their classroom instruction. Supporting these findings further, in MDR's report, *Professional Development & Standards-Based Education 2001*, both principals and teachers reported that "integration of technology into the curriculum" should be the top training priority for all teachers.

In Summary

The current K-12 education environment exhibits many strong demographic indicators pointing to a healthy and dynamic market for education marketers. These positive indicators also create a number of challenges and needs for today's schools. Increased enrollments, increased diversity in the student population, the mainstreaming of special needs children, a growing teacher shortage, and the changing instructional process brought on by the availability of technology represent increased demands being placed on today's educators. Both the positive indicators and the impact they have on today's schools provide great opportunity for those marketers who have a clear understanding of the specific needs and challenges of schools today.

About the Author

Sharon Sanford *is the general manager of Market Data Retrieval (MDR)* www.schooldata.com, *a company of The Dun & Bradstreet Corporation and the leading supplier of marketing information and services for the education market in the U.S. The MDR database consists of 250,000+ institutions and nearly 5 million educator names. MDR provides mailing lists, database marketing services, school directories, and trend reports and analyses about the education market. MDR's recent publications include* Technology in Education 2001 *and* Professional Development & Standards-Based Education 2001. *Sharon can be reached at* ssanford@dnb.com *or by calling (203) 225-4719.*

Size, Growth, and Structure of the K-12 Market for Technology and Instructional Materials

by Dr. Robert M. Resnick

Despite trends of change in demographics, shifts in technology utilization, changes in public policy, and developments in teaching strategies, the education market's spending behavior has remained quite stable. Market data suggests that the past continues to be the best predictor of the future. Accordingly, education market vendors will do well to study the high-level national data and position themselves to take advantage of reliable long-term patterns.

TOTAL K-12 MARKET SIZE 1995-2000

($ in millions)

Market Segment	1995–1996	1996–1997	1997–1998	1998–1999	1999–2000	% Avg. Growth
Technology Products: Hardware, software/ CD-ROM, Internet, etc.	$4,000	$4,659	$5,047	$5,161	$5,710	9.4%
Instructional Materials: Textbooks	1,810	1,900	2,000	2,100	2,205	5.1%
Supplementary Materials	1,110	1,210	1,310	1,441	1,585	9.3%
Subtotal Instructional Materials	2,920	3,110	3,310	3,541	3,790	6.7%
Other: Trade books, Book Clubs, Book Fairs, periodicals, tests, etc.	1,210	1,310	1,420	1,548	1,687	8.7%
Total	$8,130	$9,079	$9,777	$10,250	$11,187	8.3%

Source: Education Market Research

K-12 Market Growth Rates

The fastest growing segment of the K-12 market is the technology products niche, up an average of 9.4% per year over the last five school years. It should be kept in mind, however, that approximately half of that revenue total is related to computer hardware and peripheral devices, as opposed to educational content. The educational software/CD-ROM business continues to grow, but not at the high double-digit rate that was common in earlier years. In fact, 1998-99 was a very poor year for technology sales, and particularly for software/CD-ROM sales, up a scant 2.3% overall according to Education Market Research's (EMR) *Technology Buying Trends* longitudinal data. The most recent school year, 1999-00, was a bounce-back year with overall sales up 10.6%.

The next 2 charts break down the Technology Products segment of the overall market.

As most schools have moved to networked computers, the business has evolved from sales of single units and lab packs (of multiple units) of software and CD-ROMs, to sales of higher-priced site and network licenses. The Internet now provides an additional means of distributing educational content, which schools, in turn, distribute to teachers and students via their own networks. In some cases, spending on computers and Internet infrastructure may be slowing purchases of software and CD-ROMs. Spending on Internet content and services, while growing rapidly, is still in its early, embryonic stage.

TECHNOLOGY REVENUES 1995-2000

	1995–6	1996–7	1997–8	1998–9	1999–2000
Hardware	$2,000	$2,392	$2,552	$2,468	$2,735
Software					
Educational Software	$670	$779	$822	$803	$857
Comprehensive Courseware	$330	$353	$378	$404	$424
Distance Learning	$850	$935	$1,029	$1,132	$1,223
Telecommunications	$150	$200	$266	$354	$471
Total Software Revenues	$2,000	$2,267	$2,495	$2,693	$2,975
Total Technology	$4,000	$4,659	$5,047	$5,161	$5,710

On the instructional materials side, total supplementary materials sales have grown around 9% per year, while textbook sales have grown about 5%. Trade books and standardized tests, in the "other" category, have grown faster than textbooks, in the range of 8-9% per year.

All things considered, the textbook market should continue to grow at around 4-6%, while the supplementary market (excluding technology products) should grow at about twice that pace, in the range of 8-12%. Software/CD-ROM sales are likely to grow at a similar pace to the supplementary print products (8-12%), while the overall technology products category will grow even faster (possibly 15-20%) due to spikes related to school purchases of computer hardware, Internet services, and multimedia products.

Market Data Retrieval's historical data on "All Instructional Materials" (AIM) expenditures closely parallels EMR's market growth estimates. The AIM category is formed by combining textbook expenditures with MDR's "All Other Instructional Materials" expenditure category. An inspection of MDR's public school expenditure data over the last thirteen school years, dating back to 1986-87, indicates that single-digit increases are the rule. In fact, ten of the last twelve yearly increases have been single-digit. While there *were* two years of double-digit increases since 1995, this was probably due to increased spending on technology and cannot be relied upon as a long-term trend. In fact, the available data suggests continuity rather than discontinuity. EMR estimates an average annual increase in instructional materials spending of 8.3% in the last four school years, which compares closely with MDR's finding of an average annual increase of 7.6% over the last twelve years. Thus single-digit AIM expenditure increases should be expected to continue as the norm.

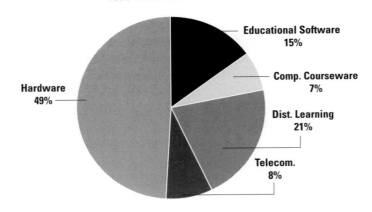

Technology Revenue Breakdown, 1999-2000 School Year.

Educational Software 15%
Comp. Courseware 7%
Dist. Learning 21%
Telecom. 8%
Hardware 49%

The World of Print: Market Size by Grade Level and by Subject.

Taking the estimated dollars spent (excluding technology products) in 1999-00, and spreading them by grade level yields a matrix in which the Pre-K-5 market constitutes about 49% of the total (based on enrollments and spending patterns), and the secondary market (grades 6-12) is about 51%. The following chart shows the estimated market size by grade level for the 1999-00 school year.

K-12 MARKET ESTIMATES BY GRADE LEVEL, 1999-00 SCHOOL YEAR
(Excluding technology sales) ($ in millions)

Grade Level	Est. % of Total	Text Mkt. Size	Supp. Mkt. Size	Total
Pre-K-5	49%	$1,080	$1,603	$2,683
6-8	23%	507	753	1,260
9-12	28%	618	916	1,534
Total	100%	$2,205	$3,272	$5,477

Source: Education Market Research

Alternatively, looking at the market by curriculum area yields the estimates of spending by subject shown in the table below.

K-12 MARKET ESTIMATES BY SUBJECT, 1999-00 SCHOOL YEAR
(Excluding technology sales) ($ in millions)

Subject	Est. % of Total	Text Mkt. Size	Supp. Mkt. Size	Total
Reading	25%	$551	$818	$1,369
Language Arts	12%	265	393	658
Mathematics	19%	419	622	1,041
Science	13%	287	425	712
Social Studies	11%	243	360	603
All Other	20%	440	654	1,094
Total	100%	$2,205	$3,272	$5,477

Source: Education Market Research

Implications for Software

It is also possible to view the software market in terms of sales by subject. Historically, the software market has broken down by subject roughly along the same lines as print materials. Under the assumption that this parallelism continues, and with spending on educational software/CD-ROM (as opposed to business and/or reference titles) in 1999-00 estimated at about $430 million, the following chart shows the spending pattern that would result.

K-12 Market Estimates: Educational Software Sales by Subject, 1999-00 School Year

($ in millions)

Subject	Est. % of Total	Estimated Sales
Reading/LA	37%	$159
Mathematics	19%	82
Science	13%	56
Social Studies	11%	47
All Other	20%	86
Total	100%	$430

Source: Education Market Research

Pupil Enrollment Figures Related to K-12 Market Size

The following chart shows national public school enrollment by grade, Pre-K through 12, and the percentage of total enrollment represented by each grade or set of grades. Since enrollment is highly correlated with unit sales and/or market size, these percentages can also be used to estimate potential unit and dollar sales by grade or grades.

Public School Enrollment by Grade, 1998-99 School Year

Grade	Enrollment	% of Total	% of Total	% of Total
Pre-K	725,180	1.6%	**Pre-K - 2**	**Elementary (Pre-K - 5)**
K	3,442,584	7.4	**24.9%**	**48.1%**
1	3,727,316	8.0		
2	3,681,589	7.9		
3	3,695,789	7.9	**Grades 3–5 23.2%**	
4	3,591,911	7.7		
5	3,519,779	7.6		
6	3,496,637	7.5		**Middle (6–8) 22.6%**
7	3,529,583	7.6		
8	3,480,233	7.5		
9	3,856,100	8.3		**High School (9–12) 28.0%**
10	3,381,772	7.3		
11	3,018,065	6.5		
12	2,723,707	5.9		
Ungraded	661,442	1.4		**Ungraded 1.4%**
Total	46,534,687			

Source: National Center for Education Statistics (NCES), Fall 1998

Consequences for Sales Strategy

Looking at the numbers, it becomes clear that the elementary grades (Pre-K through 5) represent almost half of the total public school enrollment and, by extension, about half of the total revenue in the K-12 market. The middle and high school segments each represent roughly 25% of the total enrollment and revenue. In terms of concentration of students, there are 52,005 public elementary schools, and 13,495 public middle (10,260) and junior high (3,235) schools. Thus it would require four times as many calls (sales calls, catalogs, etc.) to cover the entire grades K-5 market segment compared to the grades 6-8 market segment.

It is possible to estimate unit sales potential by looking at enrollments. For example, if you have a math supplement that is designed for grades 3-5 and intended to be used one per student, Figure 7 suggests that the total unit potential is around 10 million units. Achieving a market penetration of 10% would thus require the sale of 1,000,000 units.

On the other hand, suppose the supplement were designed for grades 6-8. In this segment the enrollment is also around 10 million, but the utilization pattern may be very different. A middle school teacher often teaches five sections of the same class, enabling him or her to share one classroom set of books across five different groups of students. In this likely scenario, the unit potential is 10 million divided by 5, or 2,000,000, so that 10% market penetration would be achieved by selling 200,000 units.

By the same token, if your product is designed to be used one per classroom, its unit potential can be estimated by dividing the grade(s) enrollment by 25 students per class. Thus a video designed to supplement the grades 6-8 math curriculum would have a unit potential of 10 million divided by 25 students per class, or 400,000—and 10% market penetration would involve the sale of 40,000 units. (Of course this may also be true at the elementary level if the school is in the habit of buying one video and sharing it across all classes on the same grade.)

This reasoning tells us that the unit sales potential is, in most cases, higher in the elementary grades than it is in the middle or high school grades, despite the fact that the total pupil enrollment is very similar. On the other side of the coin, secondary school price points are higher, while the cost of goods and marketing costs are lower (fewer schools to cover and more students in each school), giving the secondary school market a higher profitability potential.

Market Size and Projections, 1995-2002

While it would be plausible to point to certain key state adoption cycles, for example, to predict higher instructional materials sales in some future years than others, the chances are that when textbook sales are much higher than normal in some states, supplementary sales may be lower than normal, and the overall market growth will be average. Even if a given year in the next five proves to be an exception, the five-year growth pattern will, most probably, still average out about the same way. All things considered, the odds are very good that total K-12 sales will continue to advance in an orderly year-to-year fashion in the foreseeable future, due to increasing student enrollment, increasing per pupil expenditures, and the strong likelihood that new technologies will augment traditional products in the classroom, rather than replace them. The best predictor of future performance should be the recent past, which has been characterized by 4-6% annual growth in textbook sales, and 8-12% annual growth in supplementary sales. Applying those averages to the key market segments produces the following historical and projected sales for the period 1995-96 to 2001-2002.

TOTAL K-12 MARKET SIZE: HISTORY AND PROJECTIONS, 1995-96 TO 2001-2002

($ in millions)

Market Segment	1995-1996	1996-1997	1997-1998	1998-1999	1999-2000	2000-2001	2001-2002	% Avg. Growth
Technology Products: Hardware, Software/ CD-ROM, Internet, etc.	$4,000	$4,659	$5,047	$5,161	$5,710	$6,509	$7,420	11.0%
Instructional Materials: Textbooks	1,810	1,900	2,000	2,100	2,205	2,315	2,431	5.0%
Supplementary Materials	1,110	1,210	1,310	1,441	1,585	1,744	1,918	9.5%
Subtotal Instructional Mats.	2,920	3,110	3,310	3,541	3,790	4,059	4,349	6.9%
Other: Trade books, Book Clubs, Book Fairs, Periodicals, Tests, etc.	1,210	1,310	1,420	1,548	1,687	1,839	2,004	8.8%
Total	$8,130	$9,079	$9,777	$10,250	$11,187	$12,407	$13,773	9.2%

Source: Education Market Research

About the Author

Dr. Robert M. Resnick *is president and principal researcher for Education Market Research, www.ed-market.com, a market research publishing and consulting firm specializing in K-12 curriculum, instruction, and technology issues. EMR's publications include the annual The Complete K-12 Report, the monthly The Complete K-12 Newsletter, the quarterly Technology Buying Trends in the School Market, and a variety of market segment reports covering the major curriculum areas of reading/language arts, mathematics, science and social studies. EMR also offers custom research and consulting services in areas including market surveys, focus groups, competitive and strategic analysis, and product/market planning. Bob can be reached at bob-resnick@ed-market.com, or by calling (718) 474-0133.*

State Adoptions
by Murrell R. Peddicord

There are twenty-one (21) states that have state adoptions for instructional materials—22 states if the Illinois Textbook Loan Program is included in the count. (The State of Illinois is an "open territory"—a non-adoption state—except for this program.) These states represent 52% of total US student enrollment, and they have had an influence on school districts in the open territories because the instructional materials offered to the adoption states usually represent the most recent edition.

Each state has its own procedures, policies, and timelines regarding adoptions. Some states publish a listing, indicating all the instructional materials that meet their criteria, while other states will only adopt "core instructional materials"—basal programs or collections of materials that meet all of the state's subject matter standards or criteria. The state Departments of Education all have Web sites that identify the people responsible for adoption, and their offices should be contacted for information and the required submission forms, as well as the procedures, deadlines, and samples needed.

The National Association of State Textbook Administrators (NASTA) also maintains a Web site (http://nasta.org). This site provides a listing of all the state adoption administrators as well as a calendar showing each state and its adoption cycle.

Preparing for State Adoptions

While each state adoption is unique, there are some fundamental, shared requirements that need to be addressed in the beginning of the process, especially in the larger states and in states that only adopt core instructional materials. These adoption fundamentals include:

1. *Identifying the funding* source for the adoption so there is some understanding of how instructional materials will be purchased if adopted. Some state governments fund adoptions, while others leave it up to the local school districts to use their own funds for approved purchases.

2. *Correlating the instructional materials* being submitted to the state standards or criteria to show alignment. These correlations should be done in great detail, so that there is no question that the submitted materials meet the state's standards or criteria.

3. *Identifying the key educators* involved in the adoption process at the state level as well as the school district level before the adoption process begins. These people need to be made aware of the instructional materials being submitted.

4. *Identifying school districts* that could serve as pilots or showcases for the instructional materials being submitted. These districts will help to demonstrate the effectiveness of the materials.

5. *Distributing promotional materials* that address the standards or criteria. It is also advisable to provide information regarding the research used to develop the materials as well as the results from pilots.

6. *Carefully labeling the sample materials* being submitted—both on the outside and inside of the shipping carton—so that there is no question about what company has sent the materials and who should receiving them. The subject matter and grade levels covered should also be identified so that there is no confusion for the receiver. You should also review with the state department options to submit technology programs.

7. *Preparing presentation materials* that can be used in meetings with the committees or individuals involved in the adoption process. These presentation materials should be designed to communicate the benefits of the instructional materials or program to different audiences (e.g., administrators or teachers). There should also be a short version and a longer version since the times permitted for presentations can vary.

8. *Participating in exhibits* at the local level as well as the state level. This should be included in the marketing budget and plan for the adoption, so that the instructional materials and the company gain visibility.

ADOPTION STATES AND SUBJECTS 2002 - 2006

State	Bid Year 2002	Bid Year 2003	Bid Year 2004	Bid Year 2005	Bid Year 2006
Alabama	K-12: Career/Technical Ed, Computer Applications	K-12: Math, Health, Physical Ed	K-12: Social Studies	K-12: Arts Ed (Dance, Drama, Music and Visual Arts) Foreign Language, Drivers Ed	K-12: English, Language Arts (English, Handwriting, Speech, Spelling, Dictionaries), Drivers Ed
Arkansas	K-12: Social Studies, AR History 9-12: Drivers Ed, Health, Physical Ed, ESL	K-12: Language Arts: Dictionaries, Language, Grammar, Composition 9-12: Oral Communication, Journalism	K-12: Math, Practical Arts (Business Ed, Career Orientation, Workplace Readiness Family/Consumer Ed) 9-12: Comp Science, Gen. Cooperative Educ.	K-12: Special Ed K-8: Reading 9-12: Foreign Language, Agriculture, Family/Consumer Ed, Trade/Industrial	K-8: Science, Health/Physical Ed 9-12: Science, Health/Physical Ed/Medical Professions
California	K-8: Foreign Language, Math	Health	K-8: History/Social Science	K-8: Science, Visual/Performing Arts, Foreign Language	K-8: Science, Math, Health
Florida	6-12: Lit K-12: Music Agribusiness, Natural Resources 9-12: Safety and Drivers Ed, Int. Science	K-5: Math, inc. ESE 6-8: Math 9-12: Math, Computers Ed/Bus Tech/Tech Ed, Market/Diversified Ed	K-12: Social Stu., All categories and courses, inc. ESE	Computer Ed, Business Tech/Tech Ed, Business. (Accounting, Management, Law) K-12: ForeignLanguage 9-12: Industrial Ed K-12: Visual. Arts, Family and Consumer, Science, Health Ed, including ESE, Health, Science Ed, Market/Drivers Ed, Agribusiness/Natural Resource, Safety and Drivers. Ed/Physical Ed and Dance	K-12: Reading
Georgia	K-8: Eng Language Arts, Reading, Handwriting, Dictionaries	K-12: Foreign Language, ESL 9-12: Eng Language Arts, Dictionaries	K-12: Social Studies, Fine Arts 9-12: Humanities	6-12: Ag Ed, Bus Marketing and Info Mgmt, Comp and Other Info Science, Career Exploration and Career Connect, Family and Consumer Science, Intervention Prog, Tech Ed, Trade and Industrial Ed 9-12: Teacher Ed	K-12: Math
Idaho	K-12: Social Studies, Music, Computer Application Software	K-12: Math, Bus Ed, Tech/Voc Ed, Career Ed, Counseling, Computer Application Software	K-12: Science, Health, Handwriting, Computer Application Software	K-12: Reading, Lit, Computer Application Software 9-12: Drivers Ed	K-12: Eng, Spelling, Speech, Foreign. Language, Journalism, Art, Drama, Computer Application Software
Illinois	5-8: All Subjects	9-12: All Subjects	K-4: All Subjects	5-8: All Subjects	9-12: All Subjects
Indiana	1-12: Social Studies	1-12: Math	1-12: Science, Health	1-12: Art, Music, Bus Ed, Technology Ed, Fam/Consumer Science	1-8: Reading, Handwriting
Kentucky	P-12: Math	P-12: Voc, Practical Living (all Voc areas, Computer Ed, Health/PE, Drivers Ed)	P-12: Arts and Human (Visual Art, Music, Foreign Language, Theater, Dance, Humanities)	P-12: Language Arts (Handwriting, Spelling, Grammar, Writing, Journalism, Speech) Reading/Literature	K-12: Social Studies
Louisiana	K-12: Science, Health, Physical Ed, Computer Literacy	K-12: Foreign Language, Handwriting, Music/Fine Arts	K-12: Math, Computer Science, Computer Literacy	K-8: Language Arts 6-12: Literature	
Mississippi	K-8: Reading 7-12: Technical Ed (Voc) 7-12: Computer	K-8: Handwriting, Spelling K-12: English, Dictionary 9-12: Journalism, Oral Communication	K-12: Social Studies	K-12: Art, Performing Art 7-12: Home Ec, Family/Consumer Science (voc) 9-12: Business Tech (voc), Business Ed (non-voc)	K-12: Math Health/Physical Ed 9-12: Agriculture, Coop and Marketing (voc), Drivers Ed

State	Bid Year 2002	Bid Year 2003	Bid Year 2004	Bid Year 2005	Bid Year 2006
Nevada	K-12: Math, Health 6-12: Language Arts 6-12: Language Arts	K-5: Language Arts/ Reading K-12: Health	K-5: Language Arts/ Reading K-12: Social Studies 9-12: Language Arts 6-12: Language Arts	K-5: Language Arts/ Reading K-12: Social Science, Foreign Language	K-12: Science K-12: Social Studies, Foreign Language
New Mexico	PreSchool-Adult Basic: Language Acquisition, ESL Billing, Mod/Class Language, Reading (Basal, Skills, Other)	PreSchool-Adult Basic: Social Studies, NM History, Arts and Culture, Native Amer History, Library/Ref Mats	PreSchool-Adult Basic: Science, Heath Ed, Physical Ed, AIDS/HIV Ed	PreSchool-Adult Basic: Math, Music, Art	PreSchool-Adult Basic: Language Arts, Spec Ed, NM History, Arts and Culture, Early Childhood
North Carolina	K-12: Social Studies 6-12: Business Ed 9-12: Marketing Ed	K-12: Math, 1-5: Handwriting 2-8: Spelling K-9: Healthful Living 7-8: Exploring Courses (Workforce Development) 9-12: Tech Ed, Trade and Industrial Ed, Health Occupational Workplace Readiness	K-12: Science 7-12: French, Spanish 9-12: Agriculture Ed, German	K-12: Reading, Language Arts, Literature	K-12: Arts Ed (Dance, Theater, Visual, Music) 9-12: Family and Consumer Science, Latin I-IV
Oklahoma	K-12: Languages, Computer Ed 1-12: Health, Physical Ed 3-12: Computer Ed 6-12: Tech Ed 9-12: Bus/Voc, Office, Inst Ed, Coop Voc, Distr Grade, Agriculture, Home Ec, Drivers Ed, Trade/Indus	K-12: Mathematics	K-8: Gram and Language, Spell, Handwriting 1-12: Dictionaries, Remedial Reading 9-12: Creative Writing, ESL, Grammar/Composition, Journalism, Speech	K-12: Science K-12: Computer Ed	K-12: Social Studies, Arts/Music
Oregon	K-12: Math	K-12: Second Language	K-12: Social Science	K-12: The Arts	K-12: English
South Carolina	K-12: Health and Safety 9-12: Math, Science, K-12: Self-Contained EMD Accounting, Driver Ed, Ind Tech, Office systems	K-5: Language Arts Business Administration, Computer Tech	9-12: Language Arts Agricultural Ed, Family and Consumer. Science, Graphic Communication, Office systems	K-8: Social Studies 9-12: Social Studies, Cosmetology	
Tennessee	K-12: Science, Health and Lifetime Wellness 5-12: Family and Consumer Science, 9-12: Agriculture	K-8: Handwriting, ESOL 1-12: Gram/Comp, Eng Handbook, Dictionaries 5-12: Foreign Language 6-12: Integrated Language Arts 9-12: Communication (applied communication, creative writing, journalism, speech)	K-12: Math 9-12: Computer Ed	K-12: Art, Music 1-8: Spelling, 6-12: Theater, Literature 9-12: Business Tech, Business/Office Ed, Marketing Ed, Tech Ed, Health, Science Ed, Trade and Indus, Drivers Ed	K-12: Reading
Texas	1-12: Social Studies (English/Spanish 1-6) Pre-K, Enrichment Economics with emphasis on Free Enterprise	Enrichment: Bus Ed, Agric Science and Tech Ed, Home Ec, Tech Ed/Indus Tech Ed, Marketing, Trade and Industrial Ed, Career Orientation, Health Science Tech 1-12: Health	K: All Subjects 1-5: Math (English/Spanish)	6-12: Math (English/Spanish)	Enrichment: Language, other than English, Fine Arts, PE
Utah	All Subjects	All Subjects	All Subjects	All Subjects	All Subjects
Virginia	K-12: History, Social Science 9-12: English	No adoptions scheduled	K-12: Math, Foreign Language, 6-8: English, Language Arts 6-12: Literature	No adoptions scheduled	
West Virginia	OPEN YEAR	K-12: Social Studies	K-8: Art, Music K-12: Math	K-12: Science, Health	K-12: English, Language Arts

State Adoption
Brief Summary By Subject

Subject	Bid Year 2001 Contract Effective 2002		Bid Year 2002 Contract Effective 2003		Bid Year 2003 Contract Effective 2004		Bid Year 2004 Contract Effective 2005		Bid Year 2005 Contract Effective 2006	
Reading	California	K-8	Georgia	K-8	Nevada	K-5	Nevada	K-5	Arkansas	K-8
	Florida	K-12	Mississippi	K-8	S. Carolina	K-5			Idaho	K-12
	Oklahoma	K-12	New Mexico	PS-AB					Nevada	K-5
	Virginia	K-5							N. Carolina	K-12
Mathematics	S. Carolina	K-8	Kentucky	P-12	Alabama	K-12	Arkansas	K-12	Texas	6-12
	Nevada	K-12	Oregon	K-12	Florida	K-12	Louisiana	K-12	New Mexico	PS-AB
			S. Carolina	9-12	Idaho	K-12	Tennessee	K-12		
			Nevada	K-12	Indiana	1-12	Texas	1-5		
					N. Carolina	K-12	Virginia	K-12		
					Oklahoma	K-12	W. Virginia	K-12		
Art (Includes Visual Performing Arts)	Arkansas	K-8			Louisiana	K-12	Kentucky	P-12	Alabama	K-12
	Idaho	K-12					Mississippi	K-12	California	K-8
	N. Carolina	K-12					W. Virginia	K-12	Florida	K-12
							Georgia	K-12	Indiana	1-12
									Mississippi	K-12
									New Mexico	PS-AB
									Oregon	K-12
									Tennessee	K-12
Social Studies	Tennessee	K-12	Arkansas		New Mexico	PS-AB	Alabama	K-12	Nevada	K-12
	Indiana	1-12	Idaho	K-12	W. Virginia	K-12	California	K-8	S. Carolina	K-12
	N. Carolina	K-12					Florida	K-12		
	Texas	1-12					Georgia	K-12		
	Virginia	K-12					Mississippi	K-12		
							Nevada	K-12		
							Oregon	K-12		
Language Arts	Idaho	K-12	Georgia	K-8	Arkansas	K-12	Nevada	K-12	Arkansas	9-12
	Indiana	1-12	Nevada	6-12	Mississippi	K-12	Oklahoma	K-8	Kentucky	P-12
	Virginia	K-5	New Mexico	PS-AB	S. Carolina	K-5	S. Carolina	9-12	Louisiana	K-8
	Oklahoma	1-12	Virginia	K-12	Tennessee	1-12	Virginia	6-8	Lit	6-12
					Georgia	9-12			Nevada	K-5
					Nevada	K-12			N. Carolina	K-12
Science	Alabama	K-12	S. Carolina	9-12			Idaho	K-12	California	K-8
	Kentucky	P-12	Tennessee	K-12			Indiana	1-12	Oklahoma	K-12
	Georgia	K-12					N. Carolina	K-12	W. Virginia	K-12
	Mississippi	K-12					New Mexico	PS-AB		
	Nevada	K-12								
	Oregon	K-12								
	Texas	6-12								
	Virginia	K-12								

Utah – All Subjects Each Year
PS-AB – Pre-School – Adult Basic
Not All Subjects Listed In Summary – Contact State Depts of Education For Complete Listings

9. Exploring pricing options for components of the instructional materials you are submitting. Prior to submitting a bid in a state adoption be sure discuss this with officials from the state's Department of Education.

Working the Adoption

Once the instructional materials or programs submitted have been adopted, the work really begins. Several strategies have been used and continue to be used because they seem to be effective in reaching the broadest audiences. In addition to deploying a direct sales force, these strategies include:

1. Per Diems. Many companies contract with ex-teachers or administrators for a specific number of days to help work the adoption. They are trained to do presentations and to make sure the instructional materials get to the decision-makers at the local level.

2. Invitationals. Educators from local areas are invited to attend a presentation at a breakfast, lunch, or dinner where an author or a key person presents the materials and describes the philosophy or research that went into their development.

3. Showcases. These are schools that have effectively used the materials presented for adoption. Other schools considering the program can be invited to visit these showcases and speak with teachers that are using the materials.

4. *Briefs.* This information describes the research and documents the classroom effectiveness of the adopted materials.

5. *Direct Mail.* These include mailings to the schools or districts that are adopting the program to get leads for follow-up by sales personnel.

6. *Telemarketing.* Depending on the size of the company and the adopted products, this strategy has been used effectively by some companies.

Conclusion

On one hand, state adoptions represent a significant opportunity to gain market share; on the other hand, they require a significant commitment of time and money with no guarantee of success. Hopefully this article will help to provide some guidelines and information to increase the likelihood that you will succeed in this high-stakes endeavor.

State Department Contacts from AAP School Division NASTA Adoption Schedule
(Updated October 23, 2000)

Alabama
Karen Benefield
Phone: (334) 242-8082

Arkansas
Sue McKenzie
Phone: (501) 682-4593

California
Suzanne Rios
Phone: (916) 657-3711

Florida
Elizabeth Carrouth
Phone: (850) 487-8789

Georgia
Fanette Hilson
Phone: (404) 651-7272

Idaho
Carolyn Mauer
Phone: (208) 332-6974

Illinois
William Lohman
Phone: (217) 782-0734

Indiana
Linda Dierstein
Phone: (317) 232-9120

Kentucky
Carol Tuning
Phone: (502) 564-2106

Louisiana
Jackie Bobbett
Phone: (504) 342-3599

Mississippi
Judy McLarty
Phone: (601) 354-7543

Nevada
Bill Strader
Phone: (775) 687-9245

New Mexico
David Martinez
Phone: (505) 827-1801

North Carolina
Wandra Rule
Phone: (919) 715-1893

Oklahoma
Betty Broadrick
Phone: (405) 521-3456

Oregon
Rex Crouse
Phone: (503) 378-8004, x261

South Carolina
Jim White
Phone: (888) 202-3953

Tennessee
Larry Gregory
Phone: (512) 463-9601

Texas
Edward E. Rios
Phone: (512) 463-9601

Utah
Shelley Kelson
Phone: (801) 538-7783

Virginia
Dr. Beverly Thurston
Phone: (804) 225-2893

West Virginia
Steve McBride
Phone: (304) 558-2691

About the Author

Murrell R. Peddicord's background in educational publishing has included positions as director of marketing and editorial, marketing manager, editor, sales manager, and salesperson. He has helped to build an educational division, rebuilt a sales division, planned and helped to execute successful state adoptions, planned and supervised the development and launching of new products, supervised sales personnel both in adoption states and open territories, and directed and planned mail order and advertising campaigns. He can be reached by mail at 2118 Stonefield Lane, Santa Rosa, CA 95403, by phone at (707) 545-2445, by fax at (707) 545-2445, and by e-mail at Mpeddi2118@aol.com.

The Catholic School Market

by Bret D. Thomas

Catholic schools make up the second largest school system in the United States. Serving nearly 2.6 million students and employing 164,000 teachers in 8,331 schools, Catholic schools have been and continue to be an important and rich component of the American educational enterprise.

As the public school system remains the dominant educational institution serving American youth, its relationship with the Catholic school system can provide an interesting perspective from which to better understand the Catholic school market. Because of strict separation of church and state in America, Catholic schools are legally independent of the public school system. Public schools are supported by taxes, while Catholic schools are financed by targeted federal and state funds, tuition, parishioner contributions, and fundraising. District school boards govern public schools, while each Catholic school has its own board or parish council. Public schools must abide by federal and state regulations governing curriculum, length of school day and year, required staff credentials, graduation requirements, special education mandates, facility management, and a host of other rules and regulations. Catholic school administrators and educators have much greater freedom to make decisions about administration, curriculum, staffing, instructional materials, technology, finances, disciplinary regulations, and students, while adhering to some state regulations regarding curriculum, length of school year and staff competence. Catholic schools can make decisions about educational practices, policies, and products without being constrained by most of the bureaucratic structures that govern the public schools.

Operational Structure

A key characteristic of Catholic schools that presents a substantial challenge to educational marketers is their relative site-based autonomy. No single official church office is administratively responsible for the schools. There is instead a relatively flat and loosely-directed pattern of authority. First, bishops are entrusted with the leadership of education within their dioceses. The United States comprises 175 dioceses. Second, each diocese has an office of education, with a secretary of education and a superintendent and staff who are accountable to the bishop. Third, pastors of parishes have canonical (church prescribed) authority over parochial, or parish-based, schools. Pastors with the advice of parish school boards hire principals, and they retain much of the fiscal responsibility for their school.

Largest 20 (Arch)Dioceses by Student Enrollment

Archdiocese/Diocese	Total Enrollment	# of Schools
Chicago Archdiocese	131,054	336
Philadelphia Archdiocese	119,742	285
New York Archdiocese	110,150	300
Los Angeles Archdiocese	100,618	278
Brooklyn Diocese	72,747	180
Cleveland Diocese	67,436	174
Cincinnati Diocese	59,505	137
St. Louis Archdiocese	58,145	198
Newark Archdiocese	55,909	183
Boston Archdiocese	55,062	176
Detroit Archdiocese	54,734	169
New Orleans Archdiocese	50,579	103
Milwaukee Archdiocese	41,161	156
Rockville Centre Diocese	41,007	78
Baltimore Archdiocese	35,832	97
St. Paul/Minneapolis Archdiocese	34,624	103
Miami Archdiocese	34,128	68
Washington Archdiocese	32,552	110
Pittsburgh Diocese	31,548	119
Toledo Diocese	31,349	101

Source: NCEA/Ganley's Catholic Schools in America Year 2000

Of the elementary Catholic schools, most are parish schools that offer pre-K through grade 8 classes. But there are some Catholic schools that do not come under parish control. There are interparish schools, controlled by several local pastors and school boards; diocesan schools, governed by the diocesan office; and private schools, directed and staffed by religious orders that have cross-diocesan authority and responsibility.

Most secondary schools serve a large cluster of parishes in a diocese, and they are staffed by a combination of sisters, brothers, priests, and laypeople. Others are private schools, owned and operated by religious orders and staffed by members of the religious order and laypeople. Tuition is usually significantly higher at these private institutions.

Religious orders or congregations of vowed men or women constitute another criss-cross pattern of responsibility. They have official canonical status that cuts across diocesan and parish boundaries. For example, orders of teaching sisters or brothers are organized in geographical provinces or unions and may provide personnel to teach in or administer schools. These religious faculty share a charism or educational philosophy particular to their order with the schools in which they serve, thus contributing to the Catholic identity and mission of the schools.

Fundamentally, then, Catholic schools are site managed. They operate with local control and authority that distinguish them on an operational and structural level from public schools. Public schools are organized according to clearly-defined political units that receive the public funds with which the schools are managed. The responsibilities of a public school district superintendent and school board and a diocesan superintendent working collaboratively with a bishop are vastly different. The former have authority to hire, fire, specify materials, and determine curriculum. The latter have the need to persuade Catholic school administrators and educators and the responsibility to support them in their mission of education and evangelization. But purchasing decisions remain primarily a decision of the individual school and its staff. For suppliers of school equipment, textbooks, technology, and building materials this presents a marketing challenge and requires a sales team available to make presentations in individual schools.

Catholic School Type Comparison

TYPE	# OF SCHOOLS	# OF STUDENTS
Parochial	5,127	1,409,828
Diocesan	2,371	751,175
Private order	833	327,097
Total Catholic schools	8,331	2,488,100

Sources: U.S. Department of Education; National Center for Educational Statistics

Educational Funding

Despite language in many state constitutions saying that taxpayers' money may be spent only on public schools, educational marketers will be delighted to learn that federal and state dollars do reach today's Catholic schools in many ways, in many forms, and through many channels.

The Improving America's Schools Act of 1994 reauthorized the Elementary and Secondary Education Act (ESEA), paving the way for government assistance to make its way to Catholic schools. Some states lend textbooks to Catholic school children and transport them to and from school on the same buses that public school children ride. Remedial teachers funded by Title I, who were banished to off-premise, neutral sites by a controversial 1985 Supreme Court ruling, are now back inside many parochial classrooms. Some of the equipment in those classrooms, from computers to cassette players, was put there at government expense—and bears stickers identifying it as government property.

Most federal funds available to Catholic schools come from four sources:
- Title I: Helping Disadvantaged Children Meet High Standards
- Title II: Dwight D. Eisenhower Professional Development Program
- Title III: Technology for Education
- Title VI: Innovative Education Program

Title I of ESEA

Title I is by far the single most heavily funded federal educational program. The main goal of Title I is to provide assistance to educationally disadvantaged students in public, private, and religious schools in order that they may succeed in school and meet challenging content and performance standards. Section 1120 of Title I clearly outlines the rights of nonpublic school students to participate, as well as the obligation of public school representatives to consult with nonpublic school representatives on all aspects of these programs.

The first designation of Title I, Improving Basic Programs Operated by Local Educational Agencies, is aimed at helping educationally disadvantaged children living in areas with high concentrations of low-income families. Title I provides financial assistance to state education agencies (SEAs) for the use of local education agencies (LEAs). These funds provide instructional services in order to meet the educational needs of children who are failing or most at risk of failing to meet a state's challenging content and student performance standards in school attendance areas and schools with high concentrations of children from low-income families. Catholic school students are eligible for instructional services that are comparable to and equitable with those of similar nature for public school students. Services to Catholic school students are provided by public school employees or third-party providers contracted by the LEA.

Title I funding has grown significantly over the past twenty years, from just over $1 billion in 1970 to over $7 billion in the 1998 budget.

Title II of ESEA

The Dwight D. Eisenhower Professional Development Program supports local, state, and federal efforts to stimulate and provide sustained and intensive, high-quality professional development in core academic subjects. This is needed to help students meet challenging state content and student performance standards, to reach the nation's educational goals, and to improve teaching and learning in core academic subjects. Special emphasis is placed on efforts in math and science: the first $250 million in appropriated funds must be aimed at providing professional development in these subject areas.

Training courses under Title II primarily support in-service professional development with a focus on meeting the educational needs of diverse student populations, including females, minorities, individuals with disabilities, individuals with limited English proficiency, and economically disadvantaged individuals, in order to give all students the opportunity to achieve challenging state standards.

In addition to federal professional development programs, Title II includes two other sections: the Eisenhower National Clearinghouse for Mathematics and Science Education and the Eisenhower Regional Mathematics and Science Consortia. These two sections of Title II provide specific emphasis on improving the nation's science and math educational programs by adding extra funds to those areas of education.

Title III, Part A of ESEA

The federal government, through Title III, Part A of ESEA, can assist Catholic schools in their efforts to make educational technology a part of their students' lives. The funding programs from which Catholic schools can benefit include:

- *Technology Literacy Challenge Fund.* Grants are given to states by formula. States then give competitive awards to school districts for a variety of technology resources, including hardware and software, professional development for teachers, and connection to wide-area networks. Catholic schools must receive an equitable share of these funds for their students and staffs in LEAs that are awarded competitive grants by the state.

- *National Challenge Grants for Technology in Education.* In states with formula grants amounting to less than $62 million, this discretionary grant program is available to Catholic schools.

- *Regional Technical Support and Professional Development.* This program sets up regional technical support consortia as technology information resources for Catholic school staffs and administrators.

Title VI of ESEA

Title VI, probably the widest reaching and most effective of federal education programs, benefits Catholic schools on several levels. The program seeks to assist local education reform efforts consistent with state and national programs. Title VI supports a broad range of local activities in eight primary areas:

1. technology related to implementation of school-based reform, including professional development to assist teachers and school officials regarding the most effective use of technological equipment and software;

2. acquisition and use of instructional and educational materials, including library/media services and materials, assessments, reference materials, other curriculum materials and computer software and hardware for instructional use;

3. promising education reform projects such as magnet and effective schools;

4. programs to improve higher-order thinking skills for disadvantaged and at-risk children;

5. literacy programs for students and their parents;

6. programs for gifted and talented children;

7. school reform efforts linked to Goals 2000; and

8. school improvement programs or activities authorized under Title I.

In addition to federal funds, state funding is available to Catholic schools. Thirty states provide a variety of services to Catholic school students and teachers including funds for textbooks, other instructional materials, technology assistance, network and Internet, software, health services, special education, professional development, guidance counseling, and transportation.

Conclusion

Nearly a decade after many educators and educational marketers had written them off, Catholic schools in america are in the midst of an extraordinary revival. Enrollment is up across the nation. Hundreds of new schools have opened. And more than 45% of all Catholic elementary and secondary schools have waiting lists for admission. This resurgent growth has cultivated and sustained a market for school supplies, textbooks, software programs, computers, supplemental materials, and curriculum. Further, this market receives considerable amounts of federal and state aid for just such products.

The quality of academic achievement, social development, and civic instruction offered by Catholic schools provides a compelling argument for their continued operation. In addition, through its religious education, Catholic schools provide a value-added dimension to education. Over and above their educational accomplishments, Catholic schools provide students with a perspective on life that promotes justice, responsibility, charity, and service. Catholic schools take seriously their mission to challenge students to be people of integrity and to live generously in their communities. By providing this alternative to public education, Catholic schools make a unique and significant contribution to American society and provide a viable market to suppliers of educational products.

Summary of State Services Available to Catholic Schools

States	# of Schools	Enrollment	Textbooks	Instructional Material	Technology	Network/Internet	Software	Health Services	Special Education	Professional Development	Guidance Counseling
Arkansas	37	8,510								$	
California	710	251,962								$	
Connecticut	156	44,608	$								$
Delaware	30	13,589						$			
Florida	223	90,070						$	$		
Illinois	298	215,344	$	$	$	$	$		$		
Indiana	20	61,952	$		$	$				$	
Iowa	142	38,698	$	$	$	$	$	$	$		
Kansas	112	29,900	$	$	$	$	$			$	
Main	22	5,083	$					$			
Maryland	179	62,892	$					$			
Massachusetts	259	82,696			$	$		$	$		
Michigan	351	96,816						$	$		
Minnesota	211	55,742	$	$	$	$		$			$
Mississippi	44	10,263	$								
Missouri	293	85,070						$			
Nebraska	123	31,158	$					$	$		
New Hampshire	41	10,036	$					$	$		
New Jersey	441	150,441	$		$	$	$	$	$		
New Mexico	37	8,593	$								
New York	847	302,416	$	$	$		$	$	$	$	
Ohio	524	193,178	$	$	$	$	$	$	$		$
Pennsylvania	715	236,399	$	$	$	$	$	$	$		$
Rhode Island	61	18,255	$		$	$		$			
South Dakota	30	6,545			$	$					
Texas	289	81,004						$			
Washington	88	28,447						$			
West Virginia	33	6,966						$			
Wisconsin	390	81,497			$	$					

Sources: USCC Office for Catholic School Parental Rights Advocacy, *Directory Resource for Catholic School Advocacy*

$ Indicates State Funding

About the Author

Bret D. Thomas, *a former Catholic high school teacher, is the publishing director of Today's Catholic Teacher, a publication of Peter Li Education Group, www.peterli.com, which reaches nearly 51,000 readers in every Catholic school in the US. Bret serves on the advisory council for the University of Dayton's School of Education and Allied Professions and has recently authored a portion of a chapter on the value of Catholic education in I Like Being Catholic (Doubleday, 2000). Bret can be reached at bthomas@peterli.com.*

Homeschoolers: Who Are They—And How Do You Market to Them?

by Maureen McCaffrey

By conservative estimates, there are more than 1.5 million homeschooled children in the United States and Canada.[1] Who are they—or more precisely, who are their parents? The nature of homeschooling tells us one thing: they are independent. It also tells us a few other things: these are parents who care *that* their children learn and care *what* their children learn.

The majority of these parents homeschool for religious reasons, and more than 75% regularly attend religious services. Most are Protestants, and while members of this group have many things in common with each other, it's not always a monolithic group. Catholics and Mormons make up sizeable minorities, and there are a growing number of Jews and Muslims who homeschool as well.[2] If you want to sell to homeschoolers, you must take their philosophy into consideration, or you will have a hard time selling them your product. For example, you aren't going to make any headway with most religious homeschoolers—regardless of what their religion is—with an aggressively evolutionary science text. So don't waste your time and money trying to sell it to them.

Not everyone homeschools for religious reasons, however. There is a secular wing of the homeschool movement as well. One of the first homeschooling families of note, the Colfaxes, who wrote *Homeschooling for Excellence* (Warner Books), fall into the secular wing of the movement. It is an important minority within the market.

These days safety in school is a growing concern to parents and sometimes leads them to homeschool, as does unhappiness with the quality of education provided by the school system. There are also cases where parents feel that schools simply cannot adequately handle children with developmental or behavioral problems, and so they educate them at home.

Most homeschoolers fall into the middle class economically: about 18% have annual family incomes under $25,000; about 44% have incomes from $25,000 to

> **"**The nature of homeschooling tells us one thing: they are independent.**"**

$49,000; 25% from $50,000 to $74,000; and about 13% have annual incomes of $75,000 or more.[3] Homeschoolers are extremely cost conscious in their buying habits.

What Teaching Methods Do Homeschoolers Use?

It is useful, if you are marketing to homeschoolers, to know something about the methods they use to teach their children.

Unschooling

The founder of the unschooling movement is John Holt. His followers publish a magazine called *Growing Without Schooling* and sell books by catalog and on their Web site. *The Unschooling Handbook* by Mary Griffith (Prima Publishing) is an excellent guide for learning about this philosophy and its practitioners. Unschoolers educate by allowing a child to direct his own learning, using his interests and talents as the basis for their teaching.

Textbook Approach

Some homeschoolers use a method based on traditional textbooks. There are any number of companies—largely religious—that cater specifically to the market.

Also very popular among homeschoolers are other methods which open up a world of possibilities to sell books and other educational products.

Trivium

This classical method is based on the Trivium, or three stages, of teaching: the grammar stage, the dialectic or logic stage, and the rhetoric stage. Norton scored a major success with practitioners of this method when it published *The Well-Trained Mind* by Jesse Wise and Susan Wise Bauer in 1999. Subtitled *A Guide to Classical Education at Home*, the book became a hit with homeschoolers and is an excellent reference for those of you who want to market to parents who use this method.

Unit Study and the Charlotte Mason Method

The Unit Study approach uses a particular topic as a springboard to teach many subjects. It is often grouped with the Charlotte Mason method, which seeks to involve children in real-life situations. Charlotte Mason advocates a firm foundation in core subjects, built upon by reading "living books" that make subjects come alive for learners. Homeschooling Today is the magazine for unit studies and Charlotte Mason's literature-based learning. Common Sense Press (www.commonsensepress.com) also publishes books on these approaches to education. If you want to find out more and get a feel for this market, check out both. These methods demand a great deal of supplemental material, including many books, as does the unschooling method.

Anyone who wants to market to homeschoolers ought to arm himself with research and reading materials. Among other things, you'll find out what homeschoolers care about and how other companies market to them. You'll also find companies to whom you can sell your own products or who will publicize your products. A few recommendations:

1. Go out and buy one or two of the many guidebooks available. Two good ones are *The Unofficial Guide to Homeschooling* (IDG Books) by Kathy Ishizuka and *The Ultimate Guide to Homeschooling* (Tommy Nelson) by Debra Bell. Prima Publishing also has a good line of homeschooling books that you should investigate.

2. Get copies of several of the major homeschool periodicals. *Growing Without Schooling, Homeschooling Today, The Link, Practical Homeschooling,* and *The Teaching Home* are good places to start.

3. Go to the following Web sites: www.crosswalk.com (check out their homeschooling section), www.nhen.org, www.hslda.org, and www.nheri.org.

Reaching Homeschoolers

Now that you know who homeschoolers are and how they teach, let's get to the crux of this piece: how to get products to homeschoolers.

It's not always easy. There are not many homeschooler mailing lists available (and homeschooling vendors tend to shy away from renting their names). There are, however, several periodicals including three glossy magazines that sell advertising space. There are also a number of reference books for homeschoolers, some of which review products and/or list suppliers of interest to homeschoolers. Card decks are another available marketing vehicle. Further, there are homeschool vendors who have catalogues and who sell products at homeschool conventions.

Lastly, organizations and support groups abound in the homeschool world. Big and small, many of them sponsor conventions and fairs. Thousands of people attend them each year looking for products to use when they homeschool.

Let's take each of these avenues one by one.

Mailing Lists

As stated above, there are not a huge number of specific homeschool mailing lists available. There are some related Christian lists worth trying. List brokers and owners that you should check with include:

Bernice Bush Company
3 Corporate Park Drive, Suite 200
Irvine, CA 92606
(949) 752-4210

Doug Ross Communications
7400 West Detroit Street, Suite 150
Chandler, AZ 85226
(480) 966-1744

Response Unlimited
284 Shalom Road
Waynesboro, VA 22980-9111
(540) 943-6721

TriMedia Marketing Services
2821 Lackland Road, #102
Fort Worth, TX 761116-4170
(817) 315-2712

There are others, of course, but these will give you a good start: they know the market well and can lead the way for you.

Periodicals

The major homeschool periodicals take advertising and review products. Note that in this market endorsements and word of mouth are important.

The three glossies are:

Homeschooling Today
www.homeschooltoday.com
P.O. Box 1608
Fort Collins, CO 80522
(970) 493-2716 (editorial)
(205) 854-7776 (advertising)

Practical Homeschooling
www.home-school.com
P. O. Box 1190
Fenton, MO 63026
(636) 343-7750

The Teaching Home
www.TeachingHome.com
Box 20219
Portland, OR 97294
(503) 253-9633

Other homeschooling publications include:

Growing Without Schooling
2380 Massachusetts Avenue, Suite 104
Cambridge, MA 02140
(817) 540-6423 (advertising)
blundgren@home.com

Home Education Magazine
www.home-ed-magazine.com
P. O. Box 1083
Tonasket, WA 98855
(509) 486-1351

Home Educator's Family Times
www.HomeEducator.com
P. O. Box 708
51 West Gray Road
Gray, ME 04039
(207) 657-2800

The Home School Digest
www.wisgate.com
P. O. Box 374
Covert, MI 49043

The Link
www.homeschoolnewslink.com
587 N. Ventu Park Road, Suite F-911
Newbury Park, CA 91320
(805) 492-1373

Reviews

Homeschoolers look to several reference books for product reviews as well as to the magazines listed above. The queen of the homeschool reviewers is Mary Pride whose *Big Book of Home Learning* was first published back in 1988. It is now published in several volumes, and Mary updates it periodically. Mary also runs *Practical Homeschooling* magazine. If you have a product for homeschoolers, sending it to Mary Pride for review is a must.

Cathy Duffy's Christian Home Educator's Curriculum Manual is another influential review vehicle. It is in two volumes (for elementary and high school). Cathy also publishes updates regularly. Her address is Grove Publishing, 16172 Huxley Circle, Westminster, CA 92683, (714) 841-1220, www.grovepublishing.com.

As noted previously, Prima Publishing has a homeschool line of reference books. One of their books which is updated every couple of years is Bill and Mary Leppert's *Homeschooling Almanac*. The Lepperts include coupons in their book, which can be a good way to get homeschoolers to sample your products. Prima's address is 3000 Lava Ridge Court, Roseville, CA 95661, www.primapublishing.com. The Lepperts also publish the free homeschooling newspaper, *The Link*.

Card Decks

There are several homeschooling card decks that mail two or three times a year to homeschoolers. Card decks are packages of cards mailed to targeted lists advertising any number of products. They are a very effective way of reaching homeschoolers. Both *Practical Homeschooling* and *Teaching Home* magazines have card decks as do TriMedia and National Response Marketing (7160 Mizer Road, Shawnee Mission, KS 66220).

Mail Order

There are mail order vendors that sell specifically to the homeschool market, many of which are run by families who themselves homeschool. In addition, Christian Book Distributors (POB 7000, Peabody, MA 01961, (978) 977-5060, www.christianbook.com) sells to the homeschool market, as does God's World Book Club (POB 20003, Asheville, NC 28802, (800) 951-2665, www.gwb.com).

The larger companies selling specifically to home-schoolers include:

The Elijah Company
www.elijahco.com
1053 Eldridge Loop
Crossville, TN 38558-9600
(931) 456-6284

Emmanuel Books
www.emmanuelbooks.com
P.O. Box 321
Newcastle, DE 19720
(800) 871-5598

Greenleaf Press
www.greenleafpress.com
3761 Hwy 109 North
Lebanon, TN 37087
(615) 449-1617

Holt Associates
www.holtgws.com
2380 Massachusetts Avenue, Suite 104
Cambridge, MA 02140
(617) 864-3100

Lifetime Books
www.lifetimeonline.com
3900 Chalet Suzanne Drive
Lake Wales, FL 33853-7763
(863) 676-6311

Sonlight Curriculum
www.sonlight-curriculum.com
8042 S. Grant Way
Littleton, CO 80122-2705
(303) 730-6292

Keep in mind when contacting many of these vendors that they usually have small staffs—often family members—and that they are on the road selling at homeschool fairs and conventions during much of the spring and summer.

Where Homeschoolers Gather

The last major way to reach homeschoolers is at their fairs and conventions. Various state and local homeschool groups sponsor these gatherings. The largest state organizations are the Christian ones, but there are more and more alternatives—both religious and secular—springing up every day. Getting your products to homeschoolers using this vehicle is cumbersome but may be worth your effort.

First of all, most conventions solicit exhibitors and people to lead workshops. Of course, they charge most vendors for this opportunity. The homeschool celebrities are invited and paid to speak, but getting to this point is tough. Furthermore, some conventions do limit whom they will allow to exhibit. In particular, the organizers tend to be religious groups who place restrictions in varying degrees on who exhibits. Unless you are set up with reps or you yourself want to spend several months on the road, the convention trail is not necessarily a practical approach. On the other hand, you might consider testing this route at a few conventions or fairs in your area.

There are two other ways to reach convention attendees: by advertising in the convention journal or the organization newsletter, and by having your promotional material stuffed in the give-away bags that most organizations distribute to attendees. Some conventions charge for this placement; some do not. Some use a service to do the stuffing; others do it themselves.

The obvious question is how to find the conventions. If you're interested in stuffing, the first step is to contact the two organizations that do stuffing for a number of conventions. The largest by far is Tim's Great Stuff, P.O. Box 7271, Newark, DE 19711, (302) 737-3672, timsbags@aol.com. They handle conventions all over the country. A smaller company that handles several mid-atlantic conventions is Bag-It, 18 Hudson Avenue, Atlantic Highlands, NJ 07716-1627, BagItStuff@aol.com.

ProServices, a Florida marketing company with clients in the homeschool field, publishes a guide to homeschool conventions each year. Contact them at 2450 Hollywood Boulevard, Suite 202, Hollywood, CA 33020, (954) 923-2246, service1@ix.netcom.com.

Each of the guidebooks to homeschooling recommended in this article includes listings of homeschool organizations as well.

Summing Up the Homeschool Market

What is the most important thing about selling and promoting to the homeschool market? Plain and simple, it is knowing the market. Knowing the market—accepting all its idiosyncrasies and realistically assessing whether your product will fit and whether you can market to its scattered members.

■

[1] Ray, Brian D. *Homeschooling on the Threshold: A survey of research at the dawn of the new millennium.* NHERI Publications, 1999.
[2] Ibid.
[3] Ibid.

■

About the Author

Maureen McCaffrey *is the editor and publisher of* Homeschooling Today® *magazine, www.homeschooltoday.com, a national magazine for homeschoolers. Previously she was vice president of the Conservative Book Club where in the 1980s she helped pioneer their entry into the homeschool market. She is also the president of McCaffrey Communications, a publishing and consulting firm that specializes in the homeschool market. You can reach Maureen at P. O. Box 1608, Fort Collins, CO 80522-1608, (970) 493-2716 (phone), (970) 224-1824 (fax),* publisher@homeschooltoday.com*.*

Distance Learning: New Opportunities in a Changing Market

by Sue Talley, Ed.D.

Nguyen and Suzie in St. Paul, Minnesota smile into the camera that sits on top of their desktop computer. In another classroom, Jose and Marles have a similar camera. They are discussing the differences in the results of their analysis of the water in creeks that run near their schools. This would be interesting even if it were occurring within a single school district, but Jose and Marles reside in San Jose, California. This group of students is also transmitting the results of their analysis in spreadsheets, charts, and graphs to each other over the Internet. Using digital video they are sharing how they gathered the data. Their hypotheses about their results differ, and today they are trying to reconcile their hypotheses so that they can present their results to other students around the country who belong to this same consortium of students in a distance learning science "classroom." Using a virtual whiteboard they are making simultaneous, collaborative changes to a drawing they have developed to explain their hypothesis.

Meanwhile, Mrs. Lamp, Ms. Buffer, and Mr. Gonzalez—teachers in the Colorado Springs school system—are comparing notes with Ms. Jiang, Mr. Perkins, and Mrs. Petranko in New York City. They have already viewed a video case study portraying a dilemma that

most educators face in the classroom today: dealing with conflict resolution. The two groups have separately reflected on what they know and have proposed some possible solutions to the dilemma that was posed to them in the video. Now they are using a text-based online chat facility to share their views with their colleagues to see what similarities and differences exist in their approaches. An expert on conflict resolution in education from the University of Virginia, Dr. House, is also involved in this reflection, and she guides the online discussion. Their discussion will be archived on a Website for others to see and learn from.

In a home in Wyoming, James is learning Japanese. He communicates with his teacher who is in San Francisco and writes to his pen pal in Tokyo. Looking at a digital video clip of Tokyo he is able to see where his pen pal lives and goes to school. James has created a similar video clip for his friend in Tokyo and broadcast it on the Internet to him. They have been communicating in Japanese about differences between life in the United States and Japan. But they are having the most fun tracking the baseball statistics of their favorite baseball teams in each country.

Tantalizing views of the future of education? A future that might materialize, someday? Actually, all of these opportunities exist in the distance learning marketplace today.

A Brief History of Distance Learning

The concept of distance education is rooted in two different formats: the correspondence course and the television course. In both of these types of distance education courses the underlying notion of dealing with distance was to "broadcast" materials from one source to many individuals or groups of individuals. In the correspondence course, individuals were typically mailed materials—either print or videotapes—that they completed at their own pace. To indicate progress in the course, the individual completed a test or did required work that was then submitted to a course proctor.

In a television course, the instructor typically would deliver a series of lectures, much as they might have done in a face-to-face course, except in this format the course was broadcast to the audience over a distance. In even earlier days, this broadcast course may have been done via closed-circuit systems within an education institution.

These courses were offered to individuals who could not attend courses that required them either to drive long distances or to attend during a time of the day when their jobs did not permit an absence from the workplace. The term "distance" referred to the fact that the students were located away from the central "source" of the course. In fact, students often were very geographically remote. Unfortunately, because participants frequently lacked a sense of connection with the instructor of the course, the participant typically had to be highly motivated in order to complete the course successfully.

With the introduction of the Internet these courses began to change. Instructors and students were now able to communicate regularly using e-mail. Students maintained more of a connection with their instructors on a regular basis. With the introduction of other forms of communication such as bulletin boards, this communication took place not only between the instructor and the student but also between all students in the course.

As the Web emerged, many of the distance education courses moved to that medium and other courses appeared rapidly. This format provided an easy method for registering students, distributing course materials, and connecting students with instructors through Web-based communication tools that encouraged dialogue among the participants.

Much of the communication in these courses occurs asynchronously (not at the same time) in such formats as threaded discussion or bulletin boards. A skilled moderator can use these asynchronous tools to encourage the participants to reflect on their reading or experiences. Synchronous (simultaneous) communication occurs also, in chat rooms or MOOs (multi-user object-oriented environments) that allow several participants to communicate concurrently using text. In both of these modes, online courses have an advantage over face-to-face courses because the text of these "discussions" is preserved and can be re-read later. The newest communication format is video. Sometimes this video allows the students to actually "see" one another as if they were face to face. But more frequently, this video is used to share context or course information.

Global corporations were among the first to fully embrace e-learning formats. In these businesses it became clear that face-to-face training was becoming too expensive and was often ineffective because it did not maintain contact between the participants when they returned to their work location and began applying their newfound knowledge. Computer-based training (CBT), while still used, didn't establish the lines of communication that are the strengths of e-learning. With a growing awareness of the importance of human capital it became clear that a company's primary resource is the knowledge

"carried around" by its employees. These employees can share their experiences in e-learning formats, and this information can be archived for other employees to search and then apply to their own situations. This archiving concept led to the development of "knowledge management" systems and processes.

Higher education also actively embraced distance learning because this form of learning grew in popularity just as colleges and universities were seeking a way to reach more students. The number of students able to take advantage of traditional programs was beginning to flatten, and tuition had reached the maximum level allowed in the marketplace. To expand their reach, universities began offering Web-based courses. Eventually this grew into offering Web-based courses and programs that reached beyond the normal geographic boundaries of the institutions. Individuals who otherwise would not be able to participate in these courses or programs because their careers did not allow them to move near the university could now engage in life-long learning. Companies such as Blackboard and WebCT offered the tools for instructors to create online courses, complete with their syllabus and links to resources as well as online communication tools.

Today, Web-based distance learning courses appear in two primary formats. In one format, the students participate in an "any time, any place" manner. In these courses, students can complete the course material at their own pace, and communication occurs primarily with the instructor. The second format is a "cohort" model where all participants in the courses enroll at the same time, similar to a normal educational program. This model typically encourages discussion among and between the participants about the course materials and their experiences and reflections.

Possible Market Segments

There are many market segments in which distance learning is currently being used or where uses are emerging. Predicting the size of these market segments is difficult because distance learning as a concept is changing so rapidly. New technologies add new possibilities. And greater acceptance for e-learning changes both today's regulatory barriers and consumer reluctance. The thinking that participants have to take courses at local education institutions certified by a regional accreditation agency is beginning to change and is opening up market possibilities.

The largest market is the K-12 student market. In the last few years, K-12 face-to-face classrooms have embraced the Web to expand the resources available to them.

Beyond that, though, the market is now moving in the direction of complete online courses. Advanced Placement courses are now offered on the Web, allowing students whose schools cannot otherwise offer these courses to prepare for the AP exams.[1] Collaboratives of schools have joined together to offer courses that they could not offer on their own. The Virtual High School,[2] for example, offers advanced courses in disciplines such as math (calculus, fractals, and number theory), science (meteorology, mechanical physics, and bioethics), and art (music composition). These courses are developed and taught by teachers from the member institutions, who are required to go through training to learn how to teach online.

The concern about teacher competency and the rapidly expanding numbers of new teachers has led to rapid growth in distance learning offerings to teachers and administrators. Projects such as the TEAMS[3] Distance Learning electronic classrooms combine satellite broadcasts with the Web and e-mail to help teachers see and discuss new pedagogical techniques. Connected University[4] provides educators with a convenient way to interact online with their peers nationwide to learn to integrate technology and to improve student learning in their classrooms. Educators using Connected University also have access to other learning resources and to online tutorials to help with technology skills.

With the increasing availability of broadband access to the Web, professional development is beginning to include video case studies. In these cases, educators are either presented with dilemmas that they regularly face or they are shown promising practices. These cases then become the basis for their online discussions with others.

One example of this is the work being done by the University of Virginia on the CaseNex[5] project.

Another area of rapid growth for distance learning is in the homeschooling market. As more parents elect to educate their children at home, they have learned to use the resources on the Web as part of the learning process. Some parents have formed collaborative groups to screen available resources and then recommend courses or Web-based learning resources to others in their collaborative group of parents. One such site is the "A to Z Home's Cool"[6] Web site that lists many distance learning resources for homeschoolers.

Conclusion: Distance Learning is Changing the Way We Think About Learning

While the introduction of the Internet, the Web, easy dial-up Internet accessibility, and increasing broadband access have created the possibility of distance learning, the hardware is really secondary in understanding how distance learning works. To truly understand how to make a distance learning course work well it is even more important to understand the sociology of how learning in cyberspace affects the process of learning.

In the past, we have thought about K-12 education in the context of the bricks and mortar of the learning environment. Teachers taught students within the four walls of a classroom. The teacher was the expert who provided students access to materials for learning. The teacher herself learned new ideas about how to teach through one-day workshops offered in her school building or district.

But when the concept of the four walls is removed and learning is allowed to occur in cyberspace, many differences emerge. Now the classroom is not geographically limited, students have access to experts and peers beyond their classroom walls. Students can take courses that their school is unable to offer in face-to-face form because there is not a teacher available. Disabled students are able to participate, and to participate in such a way that their peers may not even be aware of their disabilities. The resources for learning are no longer

> " The largest market is the K-12 student market. In the last few years, K-12 face-to-face classrooms have embraced the Web to expand the resources available to them. "

found only in textbooks. New materials that may be relevant may appear at any time on the Internet. In fact, students don't have to be in a bricks-and-mortar school building at all to participate in this learning process.

But even these are surface-level changes. The role of the instructor begins to change dramatically in a 24/7 (24 hours a day/seven days a week) environment. Obviously, no instructor can be available all of that time to respond to online communication, so a good online instructor learns to encourage students to help each other in their thinking. The instructor's role is simply to encourage good thinking and to guide students to concepts that may better help their understanding. By giving up the central role and empowering the group to work together, the instructor creates a learning community. The instructor and the group also need to learn substitutes for body language if they are communicating in a text only environment in order to prevent and correct misunderstandings.

Nurturing this learning community is often as important as the design of the Web-based format for the course or the discussion tools. Groups have to create their own culture, particularly if they have never met face to face. These cultural artifacts help the group to establish comfort with each other.

Constructing knowledge together as a group, rather than learning information individually, has been found to lead to deeper understanding of concepts. Even better learning results are produced if this knowledge is then applied, reflected on, and discussed again as a group. Finally, if this knowledge is archived in a way so that it can be retrieved and built on by others, the knowledge can continue to grow rather than simply be transmitted from one individual to a group.

For many years the standard joke among educators was that if Rip Van Winkle entered a classroom today he wouldn't notice any differences. With the introduction of distance learning, Rip Van Winkle is likely to be very surprised!

∎

[1] See for example, APEX Learning at www.apex.netu.com/. APEX offers the 10 most popular AP courses online.

[2] Virtual High School, at www.vhs.concord.org/home.htm. This non-profit organization offers many online courses to member education institutions and their students.

[3] TEAMS, at www.teams.lacoe.edu/. TEAMS was developed by the Los Angeles County Office of Education with funding from the federal STAR Schools project.

[4] Connected University at www.classroom.com. Connected University is one portion of the professional development offerings available from Classroom Connect.

[5] CaseNex, at www.casenex.org. In this project, educators work in local teams and then join other teams using a variety of online communication to share their thinking about the dilemma presented in the case study.

[6] A to Z Home's Cool, at www.gomilpitas.com/homeschooling/methods/DLPs.htm.

∎

About the Author

Sue Talley is a lecturer at Pepperdine University. Her research focuses on the use of online tools for teacher professional development. Currently she is working on online video case studies to be used for professional development. Dr. Talley also teaches in the Online Master's in Educational Technology program and the Doctor in Educational Technology program at Pepperdine. Each of these programs is offered using a primarily online format. Sue may be contacted at stalley@pepperdine.edu.

Standards and How They Are Affecting the Way Schools Teach

by David B. Frost

We have standards for computers, cars, and chemicals; shouldn't we have educational standards for our K-12 students? In a contemporary environment in which 49 states have adopted statewide standards and every major subject matter group has issued standards, the obvious answer would seem to be, "yes." But the answer hasn't always been obvious or yes.

Historically, American K-12 education has not seen an explicit set of subject matter standards for those subjects our teachers have taught our kids. Until the 1980s, most of us proceeded on the tacit assumption that there was a national consensus as to what our students should learn and what they were being taught. In 1983, *A Nation at Risk,* published by the National Commission on Excellence in Education, exploded this assumption. The report exposed many of the flaws and weaknesses in the life of our educational system and suggested that if we did not improve K-12 education in the US, our national security would be in peril.

> "We have standards for computers, cars, and chemicals; shouldn't we have educational standards for our K-12 students?"

Many commentators mark this report as the principal event that prompted the modern standards movement. Thereafter, many standards efforts were initiated, seeking to address the concerns articulated in *A Nation at Risk.* Among them were a number of national subject matter groups that published K-12 subject matter standards.[1] At the same time, almost every state published its own set of K-12 standards, so that today every state but Iowa[2] has adopted a set of standards it expects its students to meet by the time they graduate from high school. Further, most states have developed or are in the process of developing statewide assessments that purport to test whether their students have learned the knowledge included in their respective state's standards.

What *Are* These Standards Anyway?

"Generally speaking, [a standard is] a description of what students should know and be able to do."[3] The standards that most states have adopted may be referred to as academic or content standards, which are descriptions of knowledge and skills that we expect teachers to teach and students to learn. Content standards may be distinguished from performance standards, which describe the acceptable level of performance students must demonstrate to indicate whether and how they have mastered the subject matter, or content standards, they are expected to learn. Content standards consist of both information to be learned and skills to be acquired. In more formal, academic parlance, these two categories are referred to as declarative knowledge and procedural knowledge. For example, in mathematics, a declarative element of the problem-solving process is that a student shall "[understand] the concept of a mathematical proof," while a procedural element of the process is that she/he shall "[construct] algorithms for multi-step and non-routine problems."[4]

Metaphorically, one might appreciate the distinction between declarative and procedural knowledge as the difference between what a football coach knows about the game and what his star running back can do with the football. The coach knows quite a bit about game planning and directing plays on the field (declarative knowledge or information) but is comparatively much less skilled (if at all skilled) at running the ball during a play (procedural knowledge or skill). On the other hand, the running back probably possesses much less information or declarative knowledge about play calling and game strategy than he does about the procedural aspects of successfully running with the football, a skill at which he is quite accomplished.[5]

It is vitally important for administrators and teachers to understand the difference between declarative and procedural knowledge, because of their impact on assessment. With either classroom assessments or large-scale standardized testing, assessments must be able to discern the difference between a student's mastery of information on one hand and her ability to apply a skill on the other. If an assessment does not reveal this distinction, it cannot fully inform teachers or policymakers whether students are learning what we want them to learn, or whether teachers and students are engaged in successful instruction and learning. An assessment that confuses information and skill—one that attempts to measure a student's knowledge about information with a test item concerning skill, or visa versa—simply will not be able to gauge anything meaningful with respect to a student's academic progress in meeting standards.

Who Is Responsible for Meeting Standards?

If all these states have adopted standards; if the school districts in them are aware that their students must learn the knowledge contained in their own state's standards; and if students must take state-mandated assessments, then who is actually responsible for implementing standards in the classroom? Although the process of adopting a set of statewide standards is often resource-intensive, strenuous, and time-consuming, that effort pales in comparison to the work of actually implementing standards-based education in schools.

Among the standards-based issues facing districts, schools, and teachers are:

- Aligning curriculum to standards
- Making instructional time available for meeting standards
- Using classroom materials that are correlated to standards
- Performing regular classroom assessment with accurate record keeping and reporting
- Applying technology appropriately
- Addressing the limitations of statewide assessments
- Tackling issues of accountability

Aligning Curriculum to Standards

Once a school district has adopted its own set of standards or has undertaken to meet its state's standards, the initial task it must accomplish is to ensure that its curriculum is sufficiently aligned with those standards. First, this means that district personnel investigate (or occasionally hire consultants to determine) whether their school district's curriculum covers the knowledge described by a set of standards—is it comprehensive enough, or are there gaps in the curriculum that must be

augmented?—and whether that curriculum includes any redundancies with respect to the standards. A second task, performed less regularly, but of equal or greater importance, is to determine whether its basic instructional practices are consistent with the relevant standards. In practice, many school districts do not grapple with these issues on a systematic basis from the outset. Instead, these issues typically surface as discrepancies between the results of standards-based assessment and the actual classroom instruction that students receive.

Making Instructional Time Available for Meeting Standards

Another issue that is often overlooked, but that makes itself painfully known in the event, is the amount of classroom instructional time required to address the subject matter described in the various standards documents. If schools were to teach all the standards published by the major subject matter groups contained in the fourteen subject areas described above, my colleagues Robert J. Marzano and John S. Kendall report that

> "...educators would have to increase the amount of time available for instruction by about 71 percent. This means that within the current structure, schooling would have to be extended to kindergarten through grade 21—22 years of schooling as opposed to 13. What, then, are educators to do to meet the requirements of the various standards documents? It appears that there are two primary options: (1) increase the amount of instructional time or (2) decrease the number of standards that must be addressed."[6]

Although an increase in the amount of instructional time is a worthy topic for discussion, and although many educators advocate extending the instructional day, given the exigencies of implementing standards in the classroom in the timeframe demanded by current political realities, it is unrealistic to expect widespread expansion of instructional time as a near-term solution to this problem.

Instead, what states and school districts can do is to be very clear about the knowledge they believe is most important for their students to master by the time they graduate from high school, taking into account the amount of time available to their teachers for instruction. In practice this means focusing closely on critical knowledge and letting go of knowledge that might simply be 'nice' for students to know. For example, without recommending which standard should be a priority, one history group has determined that students should "[understand] major developments in East Asia and Southeast Asia in the era of the Tang Dynasty from 600 to 900 CE,"[7] and also that students should "[understand] reform, revolution, and social change in the world economy of the early 20th century."[8] Doubtless, if required to choose between the two, many observers would prefer that students master the latter. Because of the limited availability of instructional time, teachers are forced to make this kind of choice informally; therefore, they and their students would benefit from formal guidance by states and districts.

The need for guided content focus extends into all subject areas: for example, the Third International Math and Science Study[9] characterizes the practice of US mathematics education as being a 'mile wide and an inch deep.' Accordingly, a laser-like focus on identifying the highest priority standards in each subject may serve to limit the number of standards we expect teachers and students to cover in the class time currently available to them.

If states and school districts wish to find out what their own taxpayers and other constituencies believe it is important for their students to know and be able to do by high school graduation, they might be well served by conducting a survey to elicit those views. The results may be surprising. For example, in 1998 a survey asked American adults which subjects they felt were most important for students to learn by the time of high school graduation. The results, in rank order, were as follows: (1) health, (2) work skills, (3) language arts, (4) technology, (5) mathematics, (6) thinking and reasoning, (7) science, (8) civics, (9) behavioral studies, (10) physical education.[10]

Using Classroom Materials that Are Correlated to Standards

Key factors in judging the success of standards-based schools are (1) determining whether their classroom curriculum satisfactorily covers the relevant standards, (2) monitoring whether teachers actually teach that curriculum, and (3) ensuring that classroom assessments address the curriculum.[11] Expressed differently, does the curriculum adequately reflect the knowledge expressed in the standards, do teachers teach it, and do their tests assess

for the content included in the curriculum? If the answer to any one of these questions is no, teachers and students will fall short of teaching and learning their standards.

The importance of curriculum and testing alignment is such that most school districts will not now purchase curricular or classroom materials, nor will states make statewide adoptions of similar content, unless vendors can demonstrate that their educational content is correlated to the relevant standards of a state. Experience has shown that teachers may not have the time or necessary skills to perform such correlations. Consequently, the marketplace has begun to demand that vendors assume the burden of this task. This is appropriate, since vendors have the resources to undertake these correlation tasks;[12] moreover, they can achieve a certain uniformity in their correlations to standards across large areas of content, which otherwise would be balkanized if left to thousands and thousands of individual teachers. Therefore, in order for K-12 content vendors to be competitive, their materials must be correlated to standards as a condition for them to qualify for inclusion on bid lists and RFPs.

Performing Standards-Based Classroom Assessment with Accurate Record Keeping and Reporting

In a standards-based classroom, the practical effects of three factors—assessment, record keeping, and reporting—probably modify teacher behavior more than any other aspects of standards-based reform. Traditionally, in US education, numeric scores are converted into letter grades to represent student performance on specific tests and in subject matter courses. These scores usually are distributed on the basis of a bell curve, along which a few students receive Ds and Fs, most students receive Cs and Bs, and a few students receive As. These letter grades are symbolic references that imply that their recipients performed well on a test or in a course if they received an A and performed poorly if they received an F.

However, if the assumptions undergirding this system are examined closely, the grades to which we are accustomed tell us much less than we imagine. First, different teachers assign different weights to different types of knowledge within a subject area and attribute various values to different types of student performance. Thus an A in one class might translate to a B- in another class. Second, many teachers consider factors other than academic achievement (including effort, attendance, behavior, cooperation) when assigning grades. Third, single letter grades tell students and parents almost nothing about the varying levels of mastery that students may possess concerning the knowledge that teachers expect them to demonstrate on an assignment, on a test, or in a course. Finally, this traditional grading system tends to obscure from view the progress students may be making toward meeting standards.

By contrast, in an authentic, standards-based classroom, grading is closely aligned with the knowledge included in the standards we expect students to learn, because that knowledge is the basis of precisely-drawn scoring rubrics against which student performance is judged. Recall that K-12 standards articulate knowledge that we expect all students to learn at different grade levels and by high school graduation. Therefore, standards-based grading is much less about single letter grades and bell curves than it is about frequently assessing and narratively reporting out student performance (progress) compared with academically designed scoring rubrics.

A sports hypothetical may explain the difference between traditional grading and standards-based grading. Suppose you are training a teenager to become a competitive swimmer. And further, suppose that this swimmer can scarcely keep his head above water at the beginning of his training. According to the traditional grading scheme, our trainee would be given letter grades on his starting dives, swimming stokes, turns, and finishing times. During the course of this training, these single letter grades alone would provide no feedback or guidance to the trainee and his parents as to his progress in mastering competitive swimming, except that if he received a D for one grading period, they would know that he is not doing very well. And at the end of the grading period, because most traditional grading practices would average his performance over time and because his novice performances would have rated no more than D's, the best grade he probably could earn would be a C+, regardless of the quality of his final performance.

> *"By contrast, in an authentic, standards-based classroom, grading is closely aligned with the knowledge included in the standards we expect students to learn, because that knowledge is the basis of precisely-drawn scoring rubrics against which student performance is judged."*

In a standards-based regimen, competitive swimming knowledge would be included in a written standard describing the knowledge necessary to become a competitive swimmer; this most likely would be articulated in procedural terms (skills) for starting at the gun, strokes, turns, and finishing. The swimmer's training progress would be reported in a narrative form, comparing the swimmer's actual skill and performance against the written descriptions contained in the standard, which might provide four rubrics entitled, "novice," "intermediate," "proficient," or "advanced." These progress reports would thereby provide guidance to the swimmer and his parents as to his learning progress. Under this regimen, the swimmer could not "graduate" until he became at least a "proficient" competitor because a standard would require a certain level of skilled knowledge to be attained over time by the swimmer. Further, in spite of his modest beginnings, this swimmer could realistically earn the "advanced" designation, because the rubric calls for a certain level of skill to be attained, rather than a certain average level of skill. The final demonstration of his knowledge might well include a high level of physical performance on the elements of the standard and a fast time for a specified length of swimming (e.g., 100 meters). An instructor wouldn't average the swimming grades of an Olympic swimmer on the basis of his times when first learning to swim competitively; the only real time that would count would be in the final heat of the Olympic event. Certainly, the swimmer would have earned an "advanced" grade according to that rubric.

Applying Technology Appropriately

The widespread adoption of standards-based education in the US has created a large K-12 market for enterprise-wide software for school buildings and districts. This type of software is designed to manage both the adoption of standards and their implementation and to deliver standards-based curriculum resources to teachers' desktop computers. These software suites provide schools a digital platform on which districts may share the work of adopting standards, disseminating standards throughout a district, aligning the standards with curriculum and assessments, and furnishing a template for recording and reporting student performance. One of the benefits for school districts embracing standards-oriented software like this is that its proper use will reveal quite rapidly whether curriculum and assessments are adequately aligned with the set of standards the districts are responsible for meeting.

The successful use of such software by school districts is ordinarily dependent on three questions. First, has the district clearly articulated the purposes for which it wishes to acquire the software? School districts need to be very clear about the reasons they choose a certain type of software, else the software they install will not meet their expectations, and experience shows it soon will fall into an expensive disuse. Second, is it feasible for the district to use the software productively to achieve its purposes? Here, feasibility means whether a district has the resources (money, infrastructure, culture and leadership) to implement enterprise software successfully. This is rarely an easy task across a district. Third, will the relationship between the district and the software vendor be as strong as it should be? School districts should proceed very carefully before choosing a software supplier—salespeople sometimes misrepresent what software can do and the amount of maintenance required to run it successfully, and school districts are not always equipped to sort through the technical and performance claims made by would-be vendors. Once a purchase decision is made, school districts will have made a large investment in a technical product that they may not be able to return to the vendor if it doesn't work out. Vendors should be vetted for customer service with a number of their existing customers (there will always be problems with software, and these customers can provide insight into how the vendor has responded to requests for service in the past). Also, if possible, the software should be test-driven. (Buyers should be afraid of sellers who refuse this request.) Finally, purchase decisions for software should be delayed as long it is practical to do

so. (The longer a district waits, the more robust and feature-laden—and cheaper—the software will be.) Before making the decision to buy software that purports to manage the data generated by standards-based instruction in schools, districts should feel very comfortable with the answers to these three questions.

Addressing the Limitations of Statewide Assessments

Perhaps the most contentious issue surrounding standards-based education is the administration of state-mandated, high-stakes, standardized tests that seek to inform us whether our students are learning what our standards express those students should know and be able to do. Most states either have adopted or are moving to adopt these tests. Furthermore, President Bush has called for the yearly testing of students in a standards-based setting.

Theoretically, such tests should provide to policymakers and school district officials evidence concerning how well our students are learning the knowledge included in state standards, and they should provide teachers, students, and parents timely instructional guidance with respect to the progress students are making in meeting them. In practice, however, most so-called standards-based, statewide assessments do not accomplish these goals.

> " The widespread adoption of standards-based education in the US has created a large K-12 market for enterprise-wide software for school buildings and districts. "

Among the criticisms are these:

- There is little evidence that these statewide tests are properly aligned with the state standards whose knowledge they seek to assess.

- Their practical instructional value to students, teachers, and parents is low because of their timing during the school year (usually in the spring) and because of the long lapse of time between test administration and receipt of the results.

- They deprive students and teachers of valuable instructional time, since the tests require a great deal of time and effort for scheduling and administration.

Because of these shortcomings, these tests fall short of expectations. Many teachers have become quite resentful of them, and there is growing resistance by parents and students to the high-stakes emphasis placed on them. On the other hand, if their political and bureaucratic sponsors could demonstrate that these statewide tests were rigorously aligned with state standards; if they were administered at least twice yearly, as timely feedback for classroom instruction, rather than as on a winner-takes-all basis; and if their results were reported promptly (modern digital technology and bandwidth being what they are, there should be no technical impediment to returning test results within a week after their administration), then these statewide assessments might indeed begin to fulfill their promise.

Tackling Issues of Accountability

Because standards-based education is at a relatively early stage of implementation, there is still a high degree of uncertainty about accountability—about who is accountable, and for what. Ultimately, school boards are politically responsible for what their students are learning (or failing to learn). In a standards-based environment, boards are responsible for choosing the level of adherence to standards. They must choose between a system that is standards referenced on one hand, or one that is truly standards-based on the other. Marzano and Kendall describe the difference between these categories:

> "In a standards-based system, students must demonstrate that they have met the standards at one level before they are allowed to pass on to the next level. In a standards-referenced system, students' standings relative to specific standards are documented and reported; however, students are not held back if they do not meet the required performance levels for the standards."[13]

But irrespective of which system is chosen, operationally, teachers, and students are at the center of the continuing debate about whom we hold responsible for meeting standards, and about what knowledge we should hold them responsible for teaching and learning.

Increasingly, public scrutiny seems to be zeroing in on how well students perform on standards-based, statewide assessments, with a focus on the teachers whose students perform well or poorly. Proportionately, the responsibility quotient appears to be increasing for teachers, but not for students. This trend may be at odds with the factors that education research suggests influence student learn-ing most. One recent study reveals that approximately 80% of what influences learning resides with the student, while only about 20% of learning can be accounted for by teachers and schools (13.5% and 6.5%, respectively).[14] If these data are accurate, then perhaps we should be willing to hold students themselves mostly responsible for their standards-based learning by focusing closely on what personal variables account for it. According to that study, the most influential learning variables are socio-economic status, aptitude, prior knowledge, and interest.[15] Clearly, however, our schools can have more impact on prior knowledge and interest than they can on socio-economic status and aptitude.

There is considerable policy disarray and institutional disparity concerning what knowledge we should hold teachers responsible for teaching and students for learning. The strenuous public debate over standards-based, statewide tests is one clear indication that as a society we do not yet share a national consensus about what it is our students should learn, nor do we agree about how they should demonstrate what they have learned. At a technical level, we also do not share a common view about the level of knowledge that should be taught and learned in the classroom, nor how student progress and performance should be recorded and reported. For example, at what level of granularity should we insist students master the standards: at broad levels of generalization or at detailed levels of description? And how should we inform each other about student performance? Are simple letter grades enough, or do we prefer an extended narrative that extensively describes student performance? Along the implementation continuum of standards-based education there is little general agreement on these questions.

Conclusion

From an historical perspective, the advent of standards-based education is a classic American social experiment. For decades, Americans were rightly proud of their educational progress and accomplishments. Mass education as we have known it has furnished substantive schooling to tens of millions of students. It has served as a vast civics lesson for a wildly diverse population. We hold an almost mystical faith in the power of education. In the US, education is the key to everything we hold dear. It opens the door to literacy, equal opportunity, good jobs, adequate housing, influence, and social recognition—in short, to the realization of the American dream. But for the last couple of decades, Americans have begun to doubt the efficacy of their K-12 educational system. Our faith in it has begun to erode.

In response to the perception that our education system might be failing to live up to our expectations for it, we sought to remedy it in the way William James famously described Americans' penchant for finding solutions to problems--pragmatically. If something is broken, we fix it. That is why the standards-based movement appeals to us. First, if we do not have a common road map for our educational destination, we develop one--a body of standards that explicitly embodies our academic ambitions for our students. Second, we boast standards for a range of other activities in the U.S.; we certainly should establish them for our children's education. And finally, although we won the Cold War, we are now engaged in trade wars with economic competitors who do not share the same democratic and cultural values we possess, therefore we should have education standards the realization of which will ensure our primacy in the world for years to come.

So, as teachers struggle for clarity, as students puzzle about what they are expected to learn, and as parents wonder what the information they receive from their schools means, some of us believe that if we work at this standards business long enough and intelligently enough, our students just might become the successful, world-class learners we want them to be.

About the Author

David B. Frost *is the vice president of new business development at Mid-continent Research for Education and Learning, www.mcrel.org, in Aurora, Colorado. McREL is an applied R&D institution, among whose areas of expertise are standards-based education, professional development, research, evaluation, and educational outreach. Mr. Frost can be reached by phone at (303) 632.5542 or by e-mail at dfrost@mcrel.org.*

[1] National Council of Teachers of Mathematics, Curriculum and Evaluation of Standards for School Mathematics (1989); Project 2061 of the American Association for the Advancement of Science published Science for All Americans (1989) and Benchmarks for Science Literacy (1993); the National Council for the Social Studies published Expectations of Excellence: Curriculum Standards for Social Studies (1994); the Consortium of National Arts Education Associations published arts standards for dance, theater, visual arts, and music (1994); history standards were published (1994); the US Geography Education Standards Project published Geography for Life: National Geography Standards (1994); The National Standards in Foreign Language Education Project published Standards for Foreign Language Learning: Preparing for the 21st Century (1996); the National Research Council published National Science Education Standards (1996); the National Council of Teachers of English and the International Reading Association published Standards for the English Language Arts. During these years and since, new sets of standards from additional subject matter groups and successive editions of standards from some of the groups listed have been published, totaling fourteen sets of standards: mathematics, science, US history, world history, language arts, geography, civics, foreign language, economics, health, life skills, behavior studies, arts, and physical education. For more information, see Content Knowledge: A Compendium of Standards and Benchmarks for K-12 education, 3rd Edition (2000), John S. Kendall and Robert J. Marzano, Association for Supervision and Curriculum Development (ASCD) or at www.mcrel.org/standards-benchmarks/.

[2] Iowa is a curious exception to this virtually universal, state-by-state standards adoption. Although the state itself has not adopted statewide standards, many of its local school districts have adopted their own sets of standards to guide the education of their students. Education has always been a priority in Iowa: its students perennially score comparatively high on standardized math and language arts assessments. Recently, the American Legislative Exchange Council ranked Iowa schools first in the nation. Although not the subject of this article, this phenomenon raises a couple of interesting and interrelated issues. For example, one may wonder whether standards, per se, will ever produce the kinds of academic results we expect of our students, or whether there are other, more powerful influences that may produce such results.

[3] A National Dialogue on Standards-Based Education (Ewing Marion Kauffman Foundation, April 19-21, 2001), Glossary.

[4] John S. Kendall and Robert J. Marzano, Content Knowledge: A Compendium of Standards and Benchmarks for K-12 education, 3rd Edition (Alexandria: ASCD, 2000) p. 49, or www.mcrel.org/standards-benchmarks.

[5] A distinction made verbally by David Braswell, founder of TeachMaster Technologies, Inc., www.teachmaster.com.

[6] Robert J. Marzano and John S. Kendall, Awash In A Sea Of Standards (Aurora: Mid-continent Research for Education and Learning (McREL), 1998) p. 7, or www.mcrel.org/products/standards/awash.asp.

[7] A world history standard as reported in John S. Kendall and Robert J. Marzano, Content Knowledge: A Compendium of Standards and Benchmarks for K-12 education, 3rd Edition (Alexandria: ASCD, 2000) p. 229, or www.mcrel.org/compendium/Benchmark.asp?SubjectID=6&StandardID=14.

[8] Kendall and Marzano, Content Knowledge p. 292, or www.mcrel.org/compendium/Benchmark.asp?SubjectID=6&StandardID=38.

[9] Pursuing Excellence: A Study of U.S. Eighth-Grade Mathematics and Science Teaching, Curriculum, and Achievement in International Context. Initial Findings from the Third International Mathematics and Science Study (Washington: National Center for Educational Statistics, US Government Printing Office, 1997).

[10] Robert J. Marzano, John S. Kendall, and Louis F. Cicchinelli, What Americans Believe Students Should Know: A Survey of U.S. Adults (McREL, 1998), or www.mcrel.org/products/standards/survey.asp.

[11] Robert J. Marzano, A New Era of School Reform: Going Where the Research Takes Us (Aurora: McREL, 2001) pp. 52-53, or www.mcrel.org/products/learning/era.asp.

[12] In practice, something more than a cottage industry (but less than large-scale enterprise) has sprung up to satisfy this demand. Usually, this takes the form of commercial content providers hiring staff, engaging individual independent contractors, or contracting organizations with dedicated expertise to correlate their particular curriculum resources to the subject matter standards relevant to a particular class of customers (for example, high schools in one state or another).

[13] Robert J. Marzano and John S. Kendall, A Comprehensive Guide to Designing Standards-Based Districts, Schools, and Classrooms (Alexandria: ASCD, 1996) p. 160.

[14] Robert J. Marzano, A New Era of School Reform: Going Where the Research Takes Us (Aurora: McREL, 2001) p. 77, or www.mcrel.org/products/learning/era.asp.

[15] Marzano, New Era pp. 68-77 or www.mcrel.org/products/learning/era.asp.

The Schools Interoperability Framework: Overview and Impact

by Timothy Magner

Information management is critical to the success of any school. Whether as complex as the knowledge transfer from teacher to student or as simple as counting the number of students who pass the transom in September, collecting data, organizing it, and reporting out information are key components of operating a school. And with today's emphasis on accountability, the need for accuracy and efficiency are greater than ever.

The methods used to collect, organize, and analyze this increasingly valuable resource have often been slow, labor-intensive, and redundant. Double or triple entry of data, isolated and proprietary software programs, incompatible file formats, and decentralized data collection have all become common hazards of the school information culture.

Both to help overcome the technical hurdles of data sharing and to streamline school administrative reporting, a group of software companies and school systems joined together in 1999 to create the Schools Interoperability Framework (SIF).

The goal of SIF is to help educators maximize their instructional and administrative software investments and more efficiently use staff and faculty time. Educators consistently lament the fact that financial management, administration, library, transportation routing, instructional management, and cafeteria applications do not work together. Through SIF, a public-private partnership of software companies, educators, schools, and associations are working to resolve the challenge of achieving data interoperability in K-12 schools.

The vision of SIF is that accessing data from these operational systems will make it easier for schools and districts to generate reports and help educators analyze data for faster and more accurate decision-making.

> **"Both to help overcome the technical hurdles of data sharing and to streamline school administrative reporting, a group of software companies and school systems joined together in 1999 to create the Schools Interoperability Framework (SIF)."**

The Background of the Schools Interoperability Framework

Since its inception, the Schools Interoperability Framework has grown to an organization of more than 100 software vendors, school districts, and other organizations active in K-12 education. These parties are working together to create a set of rules and definitions that will allow software programs from different companies to share information. This set of rules and definitions is called the SIF Implementation Specification (the Specification).

Using software compliant with the Specification makes it possible to share data without the need for any additional programming by the local school or district and without requiring each vendor to learn and support the intricacies of other vendor's applications.

The Specification is a set of documents developed by SIF working groups, which are comprised primarily of software engineers from K-12 software companies. These documents articulate a set of common definitions for school data and a set of rules for how this data can be shared. The common data definitions are called "data objects."

Data objects cover many types of information utilized in schools. For example, a student's name, address and phone number are part of the "StudentPersonal" data object. By having different software programs understand this common definition of a student, it is possible for them to share this information properly. The Specification currently defines 20 data objects, and additional data objects will be defined as the Specification evolves.

In addition to data objects, the SIF Specification also defines rules for how software programs can share these objects. This set of rules is called the "infrastructure" and uses common Internet and networking communications protocols.

By using open and commonly available means to transport data objects, SIF ensures that all vendors will be able to use the SIF framework and that all school systems will be able to implement it, regardless of what kinds of computers or networks they have. Ensuring that SIF is vendor neutral and software platform independent is an important guiding principal of SIF and the foundation of the long-term viability of the SIF Specification.

The Interoperability Challenge

When developing software, a company often uses proprietary methods of organizing and distributing information within the program. This can work well within a given software application, but it has often made it difficult for software from different companies to work together and to share data. Lack of data sharing has often meant that different departments of the same school or district have had to re-enter the same data many times. This repetition not only takes a great deal of staff time, but it also leads to frequent inconsistencies in data across different programs. Moreover, without standards like SIF there is no consistent, automatic way to update school data—a new phone number in the office, for example, might not be updated in the cafeteria for days or weeks, if at all.

By bringing together over 100 leading software developers, interested school districts, regional education labs, and other concerned organizations, SIF has developed a set of common definitions for school data and a set of rules for how this data can be shared. This combination of common definitions and messaging rules documented in the SIF Specification will make it possible for software applications from different vendors to share data and help eliminate both redundant data entry and data inconsistency.

Because the development of the SIF Specification is an evolving process, it is necessary to indicate both to vendors and to the general public when changes have been made to the Specification. Accordingly, SIF has created a regular process to make changes of various magnitudes and has implemented a numbering scheme to reflect those changes.

For example, the current release of the SIF Implementation Specification is "1.0 r1." The first number

in front of the period ("1") is the number of the major release; the number just after period ("0") indicates the minor release version number, and the "r1" indicates a "revision" or "fix" version. A "revision" or "fix" number is used to indicate that there have been some small text changes to the documentation, but that no substantive changes have been made since the last release. Making a substantial change to the messaging rules or data definitions would constitute a major release and would change the number in front of the period, such as "2.0." A change in the status of a single data object, for example, would trigger a minor release and be written as "2.1."

In summary:

- *Major release versions* address issues that can affect the ways in which applications work together.
- *Minor release versions* address the status of data objects not how the applications function.
- *Fix or revision release versions* address minor issues that were not anticipated and that can be addressed without changing the status of any data objects.

These version categories are telescoped. That is, anything that is addressed in a fix release version will be included in the next minor release version, and anything addressed in a minor release version will be included in the next major release. Thus, fix and minor release versions can be thought of as stops on the way to the next major release.

All major releases of the Specification are formally scheduled; they will occur at regular intervals, and they will generally include more than a change to a single data object.

The Value of Compliance

To provide educators with the confidence that the software applications they purchase will share data without any special programming or significant modifications, SIF is developing the SIF Compliance Program.

The SIF Compliance Program is an ongoing process undertaken by SIF and its members to develop a series of tests that will determine whether a software program has properly followed the rules and definitions of the SIF Implementation Specification. A software application that successfully completes these tests will be authorized to display a "SIF Compliant" logo on its package, on its Web site and in its promotional literature. The SIF Compliant logo indicates that a particular version of the software has been tested and certified to properly communicate and share information with other SIF Compliant software.

Compliance is important for both educators and software companies. For educators it ensures that these SIF Compliant software applications will work together with other SIF Compliant programs without any special programming, or significant modifications to the software. It also allows educators to choose "best of breed" software applications that meet their computing needs, and it allows them to increase the number of programs sharing school data with confidence.

For software companies, the compliance program provides an objective certification that an application is able to share information with programs from other compliant companies. This can be an important differentiator when school districts are making substantial software investments. Adding a new program into an existing SIF implementation saves time and money for the school as well as for the software company by streamlining the implementation and eliminating the need for costly and time-consuming customization.

It is important to note that software programs will be certified as compliant with respect to a particular release of the Specification. The particular release of the specification will be indicated on the logo, as, for example, "SIF Compliant 2.1," which would indicate that a version of the software program is compliant with SIF release version 2.1.

No programs have yet been certified as SIF Compliant, because SIF is still in the process of developing both the compliance processes and the test suites. The compliance testing program is scheduled to be in place by Fall 2001, however, and software programs displaying the SIF Compliant logo should be available beginning in early 2002.

It is important to remember that SIF is not a product. It is a software standard, an industry initiative to develop a technical blueprint for K-12 software that will enable diverse software programs to interact and share data.

The Elements of Interoperability

The SIF Specification is based on a series of technologies that can be used by any company, for products running on any operating system or hardware platform. For sending secure messages, the Specification uses the same technology common on the Internet (HTTPS or secure HyperText Transport Protocol), and for writing data messages, it uses standard Extensible Markup Language (XML), as endorsed by the World Wide Web Consortium (W3C). This combination of technologies is used in many other industries besides education and forms the basis for much of the data transfer that occurs today.

Architecturally, there are four elements that make up a SIF Zone, the logical grouping of software applications that allow SIF to work. These are:

1) *Software Applications*—software programs implemented within a school or district.

2) *SIF Data Objects*—sets of information shared by software applications using the rules of the SIF Specification. The SIF Specification defines the structure of data objects, which are shared through SIF messages and written using standard XML notation.

3) *SIF Agents*—software programs that serve as intermediaries between the software applications and the SIF Zone. The agent publishes messages in response to events and receives messages in response to queries from the other applications via the ZIS (described below).

4) *The Zone Integration Server (ZIS)*—a software program that serves as the central communications point in a SIF Zone. The ZIS keeps track of all of the agents registered in the Zone and manages all transactions between and among agents. It enables agents to provide data, subscribe to events, publish events, request data, and respond to requests, and it manages access control and routing within the SIF Zone.

SIF "works" when a software application, using its agent, broadcasts a message to the ZIS containing information that another software application needs. The ZIS then forwards that message on to the requesting application by means of the receiving application's agent. Thus SIF-enabled software applications and agents do not communicate directly; rather, each application talks to its agent, which talks to the ZIS, which in turn handles all further communication. The role of the ZIS is that of a third-party message handler. This means that the SIF framework is both easily expandable and very reliable and that it is relatively straightforward for software companies to write agents.

The Impact of the Schools Interoperability Framework on Education

For a teacher, the impact of SIF in a school or district will be significant. The ultimate goal of SIF is to provide all school and district personnel with appropriate access to the most correct and timely data available. If a district implements SIF-enabled software, the first benefit they may encounter is confidence in knowing that the data they access—from class lists with parent/guardian address and phone numbers to grade reports and bus schedules—is the most up-to-date available in the entire system. Similarly, if a teacher had formerly been responsible for any sort of data entry, such as entering students into an instructional management system or a grade book program, they may find that all of this data entry has already been accomplished by the SIF-enabled software, saving them time for planning and direct instruction.

These initial benefits of data accuracy and large-scale data entry streamlining will be the most apparent and likely the ones that will directly affect teachers. However, the savings in time and effort necessary, for example, to register an individual new student in the library or cafeteria will also be significant. The real-time efficiency gains for this kind of single-student enrollment will not only help with a teacher's busy schedule, but will have a direct impact on students as well. Not having to hold up the checkout line at the library to get a library card, or not having to produce additional documentation to receive free and reduced lunch can help new students feel a part of a school from their very first day there. Teachers may never have to deal with the nuts and bolts of implementing SIF in a school or district, but the impact of SIF on their ability to be an informed and

effective teacher will be both direct and substantial. In turn, the time saved allows teachers to focus more on their students.

Administrative personnel are under unique pressures, as they strive to fulfill dual roles as both key instructional leaders and heads of school operations. The twin responsibilities for educating children and for managing the staff and resources necessary to accomplish that end are particularly challenging in the face of technological innovations, increased state and federal accountability programs, and municipal funding cycles. Their need for accurate, integrated data to make informed and fiscally responsible decisions has never been greater. Implementing software programs that conform to the Schools Interoperability Framework (SIF) can provide a flexible and robust technology infrastructure to help meet these demands.

Depending upon the number of SIF-enabled applications installed at the school or district, the impact of SIF may include saving time for instructional staff, streamlining administrative tasks, and enabling more efficient and effective management of support staff allocations, facilities planning, and enrollment forecasting.

There are numerous possible benefits extending across the school and district, from providing teaching staff with confidence in the data to which they have access, to sharing data effectively among instructional, administrative, and support software applications to make it possible to be more accurate in both short and long term facilities planning.

SIF and SIF-enabled software applications can give staff access to key data that is reliably accurate and up to date. This will help teachers and administrators to foster, develop, and manage the personnel and resources they have today to nurture and educate our children for tomorrow.

About the Author

Timothy Magner *is currently the director of the School Interoperability Framework (SIF),* www.sifinfo.org, *an organization of over 100 software vendors, schools, and school systems working together to create a technical blueprint that will enable data sharing among software applications in K-12 education.*

Market Trends in Technology

by Anne Wujcik

For more than a decade, the American public has been widely supportive of providing school children with access to technology. Billions of dollars have been spent to acquire equipment, wire the schools, and train teachers. The goals of this effort have not always been clearly articulated, but there is a general sense that children need to be technologically literate if they are to be productive members of society in the 21st century. Business and education leaders have also expressed the hope that technology will begin to transform American education, resulting in improved teaching and learning.

But the goal of transforming education has been elusive. For one thing, the rapid pace of technological change has kept the schools in a constant state of playing catch up. Schools have also had to deal with a changing view of how technology should be used. Early implementations often focused on teaching students about the technology—programming and computer science classes. By the 90s, sophisticated multimedia applications and access to communications allowed the technology to be used to enrich curriculum in all subject areas.

Computers are just beginning to be available in numbers that make possible more intensive instructional use. It took years for technology to effect significant change in business and industry, so it should be no surprise that it has taken time for schools to begin to devise effective strategies for integrating technology into classroom instruction. Teachers have needed time and focused professional development to learn what technology-supported strategies are effective and to devise meaningful technology-based activities that help students grasp difficult concepts, analyze information, and acquire higher-order thinking skills.

At the same time, the clock is ticking. Parents, school boards, and the community are beginning to ask what they have to show for their investment in technology. The increased national emphasis on accountability and "high-stakes" student achievement tests often appear to be in conflict with instructional strategies that focus on

> " ... the goal of transforming education has been elusive. "

creativity, collaboration, and higher-order skills. In fact, however, technology can be applied in many settings and used to support a variety of instructional approaches. If thoughtfully implemented, it holds the promise of helping to deliver truly individualized instruction. The next steps require that attention focus on what technology makes possible that was not possible before. If technology's power can be focused on the real challenges the schools face, significant changes could result.

The K-12 technology market is in a period of transition and consolidation. Many of the emerging trends discussed below are focused on extending the reach and realizing the unique potential that technology makes possible. While the first wave of educational technology often focused on the technology itself and developing the infrastructure, today's focus is increasingly on the use of technology to support improved student learning.

Handheld Technology

A decade-long effort to build up the installed base of computers has brought the national ratio of students to PCs to roughly 5 to 1.[1] It can be argued that until every student has his or her own PC, the potential of technology cannot be realized. Some schools have begun to move toward the one-to-one computing model promoted by a number of vendors. But laptops are still relatively expensive, and there are security and equity issues to consider. One alternative is to equip students with computer-like devices that provide more limited functionality but are also less expensive. Handheld devices, supported by appropriate software, could offer both students and teachers pervasive, personal technology access. Schools could purchase handheld devices for each student and issue the devices like textbooks. Parents could also be offered the option of purchasing them.

Pocket PCs and Personal Digital Assistants (PDAs) have begun to make their way into the school market. Pocket PCs are based on the *Windows CE* operating system, and typically have more processing power, more memory, and more expansion capabilities than the typical PDA. They are also more expensive, in the $500 range. They have the advantage of being able to use scaled-down versions of common application software such as *Word* or *Excel*. The major PDAs use the Palm OS and run the vast library of applications that have been developed for the business and consumer markets. Entry-level PDAs are in the $150-$200 range. Both Palm and Handspring, the major PDA vendors, are working with the developer community to bring education-specific applications to the market.

The next evolution of the handheld device may be the new slate-like Tablet PC. A full-powered, full-featured, Windows-based computer, the Tablet PC is a new concept in mobile computing designed to take advantage of pen-based input. Still just a concept and likely to be too expensive for the education market for some time to come, the Tablet PC may be the laptop of the future.

Wireless Computing

Wireless technology makes possible the "anyplace" connections that once seemed the realm of science fiction. Wireless solutions range from simple mobile computer carts that can be shared among classrooms to implementations of wireless technology throughout a school or district. In some instances, wireless is a solution to an architectural or environmental problem, such as that posed by asbestos, which makes opening walls and pulling wire impractical. But increasingly, wireless technology is seen as a way of empowering teachers and students, increasing access to technology, and facilitating integration into the curriculum. Mobile technology can easily be employed where it is needed, as it is needed.

While typically thought of in conjunction with laptops or handhelds, wireless desktops make it possible for teachers to easily rearrange a classroom space to suit the day's lesson. Laptops equipped with wireless networking cards can tap into centralized school resources or the Internet from wherever the need arises. A wireless network greatly enhances the value of handhelds in the school, allowing students to access instructional resources and teachers to access and update student information as needed.

Wireless technology is also beginning to expand the options available to schools. Texas Instruments has recently introduced a wireless network that connects students' graphing calculators to the teacher's PC. The teacher can transmit information to the students' calculators and view, assess and automatically grade student work in real time.

E-Books

E-Books are digitized versions of texts that can be read on computers, handheld devices, or dedicated e-book readers. While current attention is focused on the consumer market, much of the real potential for e-books lies in the education market. Many college publishers are already offering digitized versions of their textbooks and custom publishing solutions.

Electronic versions of textbooks make possible new ways of delivering content, changing the learning experience. Unlike printed textbooks, with their static content and organizational structure, e-books are dynamic and interactive. Content can be kept fresh and up-to-date through automatic updates. Interactive indexes, advanced search capabilities, integrated analytic tools, and hyperlinks to relevant Web-based resources can make the e-book a unique and adaptive tool, customized for each user and facilitating more engaged, active learning. Since content is digitized, teachers can reorganize and enhance it to match local guidelines or state curriculum standards, and they can develop and digitize their own original materials to be integrated into the mix.

Print and electronic versions are likely to co-exist, at least for the foreseeable future. For one thing, a universal delivery mechanism for e-books is not yet in place. Electronic textbooks should be as portable as their print counterparts. Computer and Internet-based delivery raise significant cost and equity issues, handheld screens are not able to deliver the graphics and layout that textbooks require, and e-book readers are not standardized and are still somewhat expensive. Rights management and copyright issues need to be addressed as well. But the potential is enticing, and already schools and publishers are experimenting with various approaches to delivering more dynamic content.

Online Testing

With the infrastructure now in place, states are beginning to explore the advantages of online testing, often in conjunction with correlations to state standards. While online testing may save some money in terms of the printing, distribution, and scoring of paper tests, the bigger incentive is the hope of improving student performance. Online testing allows for results to be returned immediately and for automatic correlation to required curriculum standards or state-mandated tests, allowing instruction to be more closely targeted to student need.

For example, in an effort to improve performance on its high-stakes Standards of Learning tests, Virginia has released a plan for implementing online Web-based Standards of Learning instruction, remediation and testing in all its high schools by 2003. By coordinating practice test results with instruction and remediation, the state hopes to achieve improved passing rates. Oregon is piloting an online testing program that it expects to expand to all its schools over the next several years. Under the program, students in grades 3 through 10 will take their annual math and reading tests online. And in spring 2002, South Dakota will begin using an online test linked directly to its standards of learning. The computer adaptive test will be administered twice a year to students in grades three, six, and ten. The test adjusts to student performance and, using an artificial intelligence system, determines which grade level a student is testing at in each individual unit, such as fractions or decimals. Twice-yearly testing will allow schools to look at student growth over time and adjust instruction.

E-Procurement

Online procurement services offer schools the ability to streamline the purchasing process and participate in volume buying discounts. Some online procurement systems allow schools to post requests for proposals, invitations to bid, and quotes for services. Others aggregate products from multiple vendors into an electronic catalog that is standardized across suppliers. Catalogs can be specific to districts, listing only those vendors on the district's approved vendor list. Some procurement services allow buyers to join forces and participate in an aggregate buying system with other school districts. The complexities of the systems vary, offering different levels of integration with a district's existing back-office operations.

For schools, the value of any such system depends on the breadth of products included, its simplicity of use, and the ability to customize the service to integrate with existing accounting and other financial systems. Online purchasing can cut down paperwork and facilitate order control and tracking. It can save the district money and facilitate improved resource allocation. On a theoretical level, districts do see the advantages of purchasing from an aggregated source over shopping directly through separate vendor catalogs. But initially schools and districts may opt to purchase online from trusted vendors with whom they have well-established relationships. Schools move slowly on decisions that impact core operations. Districts will gradually scale up their use of online procurement services as their comfort level with the technology increases and as vendors prove their capabilities and stability.

Enterprise Computing

Districts are beginning to adopt a system-wide view of their information technology operations, recognizing the need to integrate administrative and instructional functions. The goal is to use existing information more effectively, to distribute it easily to those constituencies who need or want to know, and to determine those areas where more information needs to be gathered in order to make informed decisions. Ideally, student information of any type would be entered once and seamlessly distributed throughout the district's administrative and instructional databases. Data analysis tools could then be used to analyze student information—for an individual, a class, a school or an entire district—turning isolated bits of information into actionable knowledge that could be used to help improve both administrative and instructional processes. An essential element of this mix is a set of home-to-school communication tools that allows the district to share information with parents on a real-time basis.

Major vendors are now beginning to bring data mining tools and enterprise management systems to market. The schools will also benefit from commercial work on business process engineering, though education-specific adaptations will be necessary. Standards for data interchange, such as the School Interoperability Framework (SIF) and other standards based efforts such as IMS, SCORM, and XML, are an essential component of enterprise computing. Real-time access to seamlessly integrated administrative, financial, curriculum, and assessment data will give schools the information they need to help improve student performance, track and report performance against standards, and ultimately assess the effectiveness of various methods of delivery and instructional techniques.

Outsourcing

Increasingly, schools are focusing their efforts on their central mission of teaching and learning, turning to outside sources to deliver other necessary support services. Many districts already outsource their food services or building maintenance functions. This trend can be expected to increase and diversify, as districts evaluate their core competencies and seek out additional resources in those areas where they lack expertise or cannot cost effectively compete with the private sector. Detroit Public Schools recently signed a five-year contract that outsourced its entire information technology (IT) function to a private contractor. The professional services agreement will provide mission-critical IT services that support Detroit's finance and budget operations, human resources/payroll, food services, transportation, special education, and student information services. Districts are likely to outsource technical support services as they find it increasingly difficult to compete with the private sector in attracting and retaining competent personnel for this important function.

One outsourcing model garnering a lot of attention is the application service provider (ASP) model. In an ASP model, software applications are hosted remotely on the ASP's servers and users access that software in a browser- based environment using computers or Internet appliances. The ASP is responsible for technical support, software maintenance, and product updates, allowing schools to focus on using the applications to meet their educational or administrative needs. Faced with a shortage of technical support staff and increasingly complex software applications, educators are beginning to consider the advantages of the ASP model. While there are still significant barriers to overcome, this trend will continue to develop.

The Ongoing Context

The overall market environment in which these trends are coming to play is one of accountability and standards. While there are concerns about the current emphasis on testing, technology can enable more accurate assessments of what students know, where they are having difficulties, and how teachers might most effectively select instructional materials and develop lessons that match individual learning styles. Vendors and educators alike are looking to technology to provide the means to effectively target instruction, deliver richly varied learning experiences, assess student learning, and correlate all activities and progress to the standards for which the schools are being held accountable. Technology can also lessen the burden of implementing standards-based instruction. In a networked environment with easy access to the Internet, teachers can search for and view standards online, insert them into their lesson plans, find highly correlated materials and include them, and distribute the finished product to students, all electronically. Integrated assessment tools correlated to the standards not only document student progress but also identify strengths and weaknesses, helping teachers fine-tune continuing instruction. When this classroom-based activity is recorded, aggregated, and analyzed in an enterprise-wide instructional management system, the entire educational process can be transformed.

[1] *Technology in Education 2000,* Published by Market Data Retrieval.

About The Author

Anne Wujcik *is managing editor of the* Heller Report on Educational Technology Markets, *the* Heller Reports *Web site, and its* Desktop EdNET *Internet-based information service, all publications of Nelson B. Heller & Associates. Since 1989, the* Heller Report on Educational Technology Markets *has helped education industry executives stay current on the latest strategic moves of key players that are transforming education and the marketplace for technology and telecommunications products. Anne can be reached at* anne@hellerreports.com *or by calling (703) 548-1420.*

The Role of a School Board in the Purchasing Process

by Ann Lee Flynn, Ed.D.

For many people new to the education market, and even for some who have been working with schools for years, the role of the school board is something of a mystery. America's system of locally controlled school governance is both a blessing and a curse. On the positive side, local control allows a community to elect or appoint lay people to make decisions which reflect its vision about the type of educational system it wants to support, to ensure that its students have the kind of skills that will best prepare them to lead productive lives. Unfortunately, the system creates a great deal of frustration for companies anxious to sell products in the education marketplace, since each board operates in a slightly different way and since in the US (as opposed to many foreign countries), virtually no implementation-oriented decisions for education are made at the national level.

There are over 95,000 school board members representing 14,800 local districts in the United States. Those districts represent more than 47 million public school students. A few boards represent districts comprised of only one school building, while other boards cover entire counties. There are boards in districts that serve only grades K-8 and others that are high-school-only districts. To complicate matters, some areas of the country have service agencies that work with a group of local districts—like BOCES in New York—and that have their own school boards in addition to each of the boards of the represented districts. Depending on the item to be purchased, a regional service agency board may be more influential than an independent district's board.

Who Serves on the School Board?

While board members represent all constituencies of the population, a few characteristics can be generalized. There are still more men serving on school boards than women (the ratio is about 60:40), and three-quarters of all board members are between 40-59 years old. In the 1997-98 academic year, a survey found that 7% of board members were African American, 3% were Hispanic, and less than one-half of one percent were Asian.[1] As a rule, board members are not professionally trained educators but lay people with an interest in improving their community's schools. Financial compensation varies across boards, and some individuals are volunteers. In certain communities, board members are elected by the neighborhoods they represent, while in other areas election or appointment occurs on a citywide basis. Some board members see their positions as the first step in what they hope will be long careers of public service, while others have a passion for particular issue and look at their service as an opportunity to promote their personal agendas. Unfortunately, however, in some instances board members have become so focused on their individual issues that they have lost sight of their real reason to exist—to improve student achievement for all children in their districts.

> **"As a rule, board members are not professionally trained educators but lay people with an interest in improving their community's schools."**

The Key Work of School Boards was developed by the National School Boards Association (NSBA) in 2000 to help boards refocus their efforts and engage their communities through a "systems approach" applied to eight critical areas: vision, standards, assessment, accountability, alignment, climate, collaboration, and continuous improvement. Under the framework outlined by NSBA, the budget-setting process is the key instrument available for boards to use to ensure that the district's resources are aligned with its standards and priorities.

Understanding a District's Finances

With more than $350 billion committed to educating the nation's K-12 students in 2000, there is increasing pressure to link academic results with financial data and other contextual factors so that boards can make decisions about how to allocate resources strategically to maximize student achievement. How well a district uses its resources will determine how close it comes to achieving its stated goals. If board members are effectively working in partnership with the district superintendent and other top administrators, then their role in purchasing decisions can be more clearly defined.

Overall, boards have two primary levels of financial responsibility as identified by Steven Pereus in *ASBJ's School Spending* supplement (2000). First, boards must ensure compliance with state and federal laws; and second they must recognize that they serve the community as fiscal stewards by acting responsibly and directing funds to programs that make a difference and move the district toward realizing its vision. In carrying out this dual responsibility, the board acts in ways that affect both the district's budget and its financial plan. For vendors, it is important to understand the difference between these two instruments. It may be useful to think of the budget as the current document that matches revenues against planned expenditures and that keeps the district moving forward on a daily basis. On the other hand, the district's financial plan should have a focus on the future—on where the district wants to go in the long term. According to Pereus, the financial plan should "project the long-term sources and uses of funds, evaluate the effectiveness of programs and departments, and focus financial resources on programs that help attain the district's vision for students."

It's also vital to understand that an important recent shift in school finance litigation is moving the focus from inputs to outcomes, according to Lawrence Picus, the director of the Center for Research in Education Finance at the University of Southern California. In the past, much of the funding litigation dealt with the equitable distribution of funds, or, in other words, with making sure that funds (financial inputs) were appropriately divided on a per-pupil basis. In contrast, districts are now struggling with a more difficult concept, that of finding an acceptable way to define an "adequate education" (the academic outcome). While this issue of adequacy is not a new one, a recent spat of lawsuits suggests that the way funds are distributed will be looked at in light of how effective they are utilized to produce the desired outcome (improved student achievement). Such philosophical shifts in thinking about outcomes versus inputs have the potential to impact a local board's

> " Understanding where a product or service fits into a district's vision and long-term plan is vital to success in school sales. "

thinking about why certain products or services should be approved or where they should be deployed throughout the district.

Although many companies may be unable to devote the time required to understand all the nuances of each district's financial documents or of each state's funding formulas, they should realize that such information can provide the kind of insight that may favorably tilt the scales in closing a "big ticket" deal. Understanding where a product or service fits into a district's vision and long-term plan is vital to success in school sales.

National School Boards Association Purchasing Studies

The National School Boards Association commissioned studies by the Gallup Organization in 1994, 1997, and 1999 to track the extent of involvement of school board members in the purchasing process. In the most recent study, although 97% of the board members surveyed indicated they were involved in the budgeting process in their districts, only 39% were involved in specifying a product brand. However, 90% said they were involved in approving purchase recommendations from staff. So what does this mean for a vendor? It's likely (and appropriate) that board members may not be the group to decide the brand, but it's quite possible they could fail to approve a recommendation if they are unfamiliar with the company or are not aware of a product's potential benefits. According to the Executive Summary of the 1999 NSBA Gallup survey, "When a school board denies a specific purchase request, the main reason is cost, followed by budget cutbacks, and products not meeting the requirements."

The study also found that approximately $20,200 was the average level at which boards were either mandated through state law or by an agreed-upon dollar amount within a district to give the final approval for purchase. This level, however, varies with the size of the district's overall budget. Boards with a budget of $5-$10 million generally require the board to become involved with purchases around $7,450 while those with budgets of $10-$25 million averaged $31,360 before board involvement is required. In 1999, advanced technology items appeared to be the item for which school boards had the most involvement (94%) followed by employee benefits (91%), insurance (86%), and construction management (86%). Not surprisingly, the greatest increase from 1997 to 1999 was in the area of security systems, where eight out of ten board members reported they were somewhat or very involved.

Board-level involvement in cooperative or regional purchasing significantly increased from 1997 to 1999 according to the Gallup survey. Three of four school boards are currently involved in cooperative or regional purchasing arrangements. The greatest increase since 1997 has occurred among school districts with enrollments of 1,000 to 2,500, followed by those with budgets of less than $5 million.

Thoughts from Board Members

Matt Grogger, a retired board member from a suburban Kansas City district shared his perspective on the appropriate level of board involvement in purchasing decisions. "Since the board is a policy-making body, it is imperative that the board only establish policy for the district administration to follow in obtaining quotes and purchasing recommendations. In no case should the board member(s) get involved in the purchase negotiations, even if that board member has professional expertise in that arena. A board member with professional expertise in a specific area can and often will assist the administration in evaluating the bids, but they should not be involved in the actual negotiations. This is particularly true if the board member's firm or employer is bidding on a contract. This would create a conflict of interest for that board member and he/she should remove himself from even discussing the issue with other board members and/or the administration. Some may feel that objective counsel can be provided, but even the appearance of a conflict of interest should be avoided."

According to Bob Hughes, a board member and well-known educational consultant, too much board member involvement around specific purchasing decisions can be seen as an attempt to micro-manage. The results of a National School Boards Foundation Study in 1999, *Leadership Matters: Transforming Urban School Boards* support Hughes's belief. The report clearly suggests that boards should be spending more time and energy focusing on the big picture in their districts. Furthermore, the

decrease in board involvement from 1997 to 1999 in allocating resources to specific line items, as documented in the NSBA Gallup study, indicates that boards have recognized the changing nature of their role in purchasing decisions.

As a member of a suburban Ohio community, board president Martin Horwitz offers a slightly different perspective. He feels each board member acts as a catalyst for change in the district and as they get involved in board work, they usually gravitate to subjects that interest them such as the curriculum, finance issues, buildings and grounds, technology, or athletics. According to Horwitz, "the range of power exerted by a board member will depend on his personality, length of service, leadership role, leadership skills, and expertise. Their behavior might be simple, such as raising a concern at a board meeting and requesting that the administration investigate. Or it might be as overt and heavy-handed as serving as a lobbyist for a group of teachers and principal who are trying to pressure the superintendent for a major policy change. The dynamics of board member interaction with fellow board members, administrators, teachers, staff members, district committees, parent groups, and business and civic leaders can influence dozens of purchasing decisions in a year."

Horwitz shared a list of questions board members are likely to ask as they debate possible purchases in study sessions and committee meetings before making a major decision:

- Are we getting the best value for the money spent?
- How many vendors have we reviewed?
- Who reviewed the vendors or the bid process?
- In this class of goods, services or equipment, do we know the quality of the merchandise?
- Have we checked the reliability of the product or service with other schools?
- Is this the best means to an end? Do we all agree on the merchandise, method, and materials?
- Can some economy be achieved by purchasing a larger quantity, or by acting through a buying consortium?

So What Does Make a Board Say Yes?

Board members in the 1999 Gallup Survey were offered nine possible sources that could be useful for learning about products that might influence their board's purchasing decisions. Hands down, the two activities reported to be most likely to sway decisions were reviewing the district's needs assessment (at 92%), and hearing about the experiences of other districts (at 91%). Other sources of information that board members find useful include: trade show exhibits (82%); sales presentations (65%); visits from sales representatives (63%); online education articles (54%); ads in education magazines or professional journals (51%); direct mail (42%); and television commercials (11%).

Although there's no magic spell to cast that will guarantee a company's products or services will be favorably received by board members, the following is a list of suggestions compiled from various board members. Together they suggest a course of action that a company can follow to stack the deck in its favor:

- Take time to learn about education issues in general and when possible, about the unique challenges facing a particular customer.

- Create a print presence. Make sure that you are placing advertisements in publications and on Web sites that have a board member audience. Examples include the *American School Board Journal, School Board News, Phi Delta Kappan, Educational Leadership, School Administrator, Education Week,* as well as state board magazines and newsletters. When considering advertising in other magazines, ask to see readership profiles by job title to ensure you will reach your target audience.

- Go where the board members go. Develop strategic relationships with key organizations like the National School Boards Association and its federation members in each state, the Association of Education

Service Agencies, and the American Association of School Administrators. Exhibit at their state and national tradeshows, and consider hosting events or presenting sessions when possible. According to the 1999 NSBA Gallup Study, state school board conventions remains the top-rated source of information in purchase decisions(used by 91% of board members).

- Consider your corporate image. Project credibility and stability when dealing with boards. Also, remember board members are not professional educators, and try to avoid using too much education and technical jargon when discussing your product with them.

- Recognize that your company has an obligation to help educate board members not only about your product, but also about your company's industry as a whole. In this regard, supporting industry initiatives in partnership with your competitors can be a win-win for all of the companies involved.

- Approach a district as a long-term partner rather than as a one-time customer. Work at sustaining the relationship after the sale!

As a vendor in the education market, you need to put forth the effort to understand the way school districts are organized and funded, to recognize that the sales cycle in education is longer than in many other industry segments due to those structures, and to develop an awareness of how your products and services mesh with the overall goals of a district. That knowledge will be essential to your success.

[1] The survey was conducted under the auspices of Virginia Tech; its results appeared in a 1997-98 *American School Board Journal (ASBJ)* Virginia Tech survey as cited.

About the Author

Ann Lee Flynn *is director of education technology for the National School Boards Association, www.nsba.org, the nationwide advocacy organization for public school governance. Dr. Flynn provides leadership on issues surrounding education technology to empower education, industry, and policy leaders to improve education processes through productive partnerships focused on finding new ways to work together which can improve the teaching and learning environment as well as increase the market for education-related businesses.*

The School Librarian's Critical Role as Purchaser and Influencer

by Marlene Woo-Lun

What is a School Library Media Specialist?

Far from conforming to the traditional librarian stereotype, today's school librarians comprise one of the most informed and technology-savvy groups of customers for the educational marketer. They purchase not only print materials, but also multimedia and electronic resources, equipment, and technology.

The American Library Association has recognized this change, and together with its members, has created and adopted new official terms for the position ("school library media specialist") and for the facilities that they manage ("media centers"). Although the terms "school librarian" and "school library" are still very much in use, the new terms truly are more representative of the state of the profession today.

According to the National Center for Education Statistics, there were 99,000 school library media centers in the U.S. in 1994. This number has grown—there are 106,400 schools in the U.S. today (MDR), and just about all of these schools have a library or media center. According to Market Data Retrieval, there are 82,000 school librarians/media specialists in the U.S. (In some districts, one librarian has responsibility, and thus purchasing power, for more than one building.)

School librarians have more training and education than the average teacher. In most states, the school library media specialist position requires a teaching certificate as well as a school library media certificate. Many states also require media specialists to hold a master's degree in library science or a related field.

Technology, in the form of Apple IIe's, entered the schools first via the school library. Today, school librarians understand the Internet, the Web, and multimedia. As the first educators to deal with technology, they often serve as technology trainers. They understand the potential for new and different products for use within the curriculum, and they often become early adopters of these products.

Because media specialists work with all of the teachers, they are knowledgeable about the entire curriculum and about the school system as a whole. They understand, encourage, and implement resource sharing. The traditional library book loan has transitioned into database sharing among patrons, students, and teachers.

Rather than teaching a single subject in a classroom, school librarians accomplish a much wider variety of tasks and responsibilities than is generally understood. They hold positions on committees, conduct training sessions, field calls from parents, and run cooperative programs with public libraries. They also manage staffs of library clerks, library aides, and volunteers.

> "...today's school librarians comprise one of the most informed and technology-savvy groups of customers for the educational marketer."

School librarians crave information, information is their business: by nature and by their profession. They are driven to provide information and to help others use information effectively. Thus, they do respond to informational marketing materials. Media specialists listen to vendor presentations. They keep catalogs and product literature for later reference or for sharing with teachers and administrators. For these reasons, they are often the best opportunity to "get your foot in the door" of a school building or district.

They work to stay up-to-date with both print and electronic educational supplementary products by reading professional journals and book and product reviews, and by communicating directly with publishers and vendors. They rely heavily on recommendations from each other. Although they are rather isolated (as there is usually only one media specialist per building), they keep in touch via national and statewide listservs. They also obtain information through their professional organizations, faithfully attending all sessions at conferences and worrying that they cannot attend overlapping sessions. Conference exhibits are important and exciting sources of product information for them, because they often represent their only opportunity to see books and products before purchasing them.

An important attribute of this group of educators is that once they adopt your product and the product proves itself, they will be very loyal customers. They do care about building lasting relationships with publishers and vendors. And not only will they purchase your products repeatedly, but they will also recommend your products to anyone who will listen. Moreover, because the media specialist has done her homework and is very knowledgeable, she will provide good information, even to the extent of helping to distribute your literature and making a contact for you.

School Librarians as Purchasers

School librarians are significant buyers in the K-12 market in their own right. While the average teacher has no budget and spends $600 per year of his or her own money for the classroom, school librarians have annual budgets ranging from thousands to a quarter of a million dollars. Many are responsible for purchasing for collections for several buildings. Because they manage these budgets, school librarians are knowledgeable, experienced purchasers. They know how to obtain and compare product information and are interested in details of the product. And they understand purchase order systems as well as service agreements.

School library budgets cover print materials as well as multimedia electronic resources and equipment. For several years, there was an imbalance as a great deal was spent on multimedia and electronic resources at the expense of the print budget. But now all media is recognized as having the potential to deliver quality educational resources, and the school librarian works to keep this balance of resources for the school.

Not only do school librarians understand how to purchase all media, they also understand how to use print, multimedia, and the Web. They strive to teach and assist students and teachers to use the most appropriate resource for the research or project at hand. Often the school librarian also has the responsibility of technology

coordinator. The school library is often a primary point of access to personal computers and may even incorporate the computer lab.

School librarians are frequent participants in school- or district-wide purchasing decisions for products such as databases and administration systems. They understand, encourage, and implement resource sharing. Thus, they are the prime purchasers for many of the higher-priced products, such as databases, which are meant to be used school-wide. At the same time, media specialists are influencers in the purchase of other school-wide curriculum products because they first help to evaluate and then assist in implementing the product or system.

> " ...their unique and critical role in the schools gives them buying power and influence in purchasing decisions far beyond their numbers. "

The current nationwide growth in educational funding and in the hiring of K-12 educators provides an opportunity for publishers and vendors who understand how to market to school librarians. New schools are being built. Retiring school librarians are being replaced with technology-savvy media specialists. School library positions lost due to Proposition 13 in California have now been replaced and must be filled as soon as possible. This also means that, in addition to new buildings, long-dormant media centers must now be updated with new print and electronic resources as well as with technology and equipment.

School Librarians as Purchasing Influencers

Because school librarians are information specialists, they have many "touch points" throughout the school and the district. Therefore, media specialists also serve as key influencers in purchasing decisions for educational resources.

They strive to be sources of information for everyone in the school (and often throughout the district). In their Information Power guidelines, the American Association of School Librarians urges school librarians to collaborate with teachers to become partners in planning for teaching resources for the curriculum. And in general, today's school library media specialist considers it a responsibility to become an even more integral part of the curriculum.

Partnerships and collaboration provide many opportunities for school librarians to recommend their favorite products. For instance, a teacher might ask the school librarian for information about a history resource. The school librarian would then contact the publisher or vendor for information about the product and convey it to the history teacher. The purchase order for the product might come from the school library, or it might come from the history department. In either case, however, the school librarian will have played a major role in that purchase. A similar scenario can also occur with technology products. A purchase order might come from the technology director, but the product will have been evaluated and chosen by the school librarian or by a committee that includes the librarian.

The school library media specialist is often a key professional development trainer for the school and the district. The variety of topics is wide, including the Internet, Web resources for the curriculum, copyright, reading motivation and literature, and information skills. The consistent, underlying theme is the recommendation of resources for teaching.

In addition, the role of school librarians as a source of information leads to their participating in planning committees, including technology, curriculum, and facilities planning. In this role, they participate in much of the key decision making in the building and in the district.

Based on the responsibilities of school librarians and their knowledge of the curriculum, they are a key first contact for the publisher or vendor, able to understand the potential for your product within the curriculum. They are the information vector from teachers to the publisher and vendor, and also from the publisher and vendor to teachers. They may buy or recommend.

Compared to the number of teachers, the number of school librarians is relatively small. But their unique and critical role in the schools gives them buying power and influence in purchasing decisions far beyond their numbers. They are a key element in the K-12 space and should be a priority for every educational marketer.

About the Author

Marlene Woo-Lun *has dedicated her career to creating and supplying tools for educators. Prior to founding Linworth Publishing,* www.linworth.com, *in 1986, she spent 12 years in the publishing of college textbooks, including Richard D. Irwin, Inc. Today her company publishes a variety of professional development books and journals for the school library and education market. In addition to* The Book Report: The Magazine for Secondary School Library Media and Technology Specialists *and* Library Talk: The Magazine for Elementary School Library Media and Technology Specialists, *Linworth publishes a rapidly growing list of textbooks and professional books. Marlene received her B.S. in microbiology and an M.B.A. from Ohio State University. She is on the board of the Association of Educational Publishers. Marlene can be reached at (614) 436-7107 or at* linworth@linworthpublishing.com.

A View From the Catbird's Seat

by Nelson B. Heller, Ph.D.

Every year, I present a session called "A View From the Catbird's Seat" at our annual EdNET conference, along with the Heller Reports editors, and it's always quite a challenge to "predict" what the educational market trends are from a business point of view. To accomplish this task, I survey not only educators, but also the many companies that participate at the conference on both a national and international basis. It's one thing to read articles about what is going on and quite another to "get into the trenches" and hear the trends from the people who are making them happen.

The school year 2000-01 presented many challenges to publishers for the K-12 education market—both opportunities and threats—some of which will continue in the years ahead as companies struggle with new business models, changing technology, and the evolving needs of educators. This article will outline some of the key issues and trends I see "from the catbird's seat."

What Keeps Us Awake at Night?

Obviously, the Internet has made its presence felt in every business this year. And along with the Internet, there is the coming wireless revolution. And we're starting to see a lot of consolidation—not only within the publishing and entertainment businesses, but also on the buyers' side, as districts accelerate their purchasing power by forming consortiums. Our traditional business models have changed as companies are beginning to deliver content via the Internet, and new accountability and curriculum standards have altered the types of products that schools are interested in purchasing.

Professional development for teachers is becoming more important as a part of the content delivery package, as we recognize that despite years of institutional and industry programs many teachers are still not comfortable with using technology as a means to deliver curriculum. While we think forward to a future when broadband access will be available in every school, we also must realize that there remains a "digital divide" within the educational system. Not only does every student not have a computer for use in school, but many students still do not have access to one at home. How that affects our online product offerings is something we all have to deal with and will be dealing with for many years into the future.

And, of course, globalization, serving our customers on a 24/7 basis, as well as the push for greater return on investment, better results, and accountability. Yes, it's been a challenging year.

What's the Good News?

Our market is probably in the best shape it's ever been. Enrollments are up. Funding is up. Investment is up, even with the chill in financial markets that began last spring.

Enrollments are approaching a post-baby-boom high, with 53 million children enrolled in the US K-12 system.

Total funding for education is now at $714 billion and represents 9% of our country's gross national product. And if our newly inaugurated President maintains his promises, there will be increased funding for education over the foreseeable future. Moreover, this spending is not just keeping up with inflation; it represents a real increase in available funds. For instance, per-pupil spending is expected to increase from $160 per pupil in 2000-01 to $180 per pupil in 2001-02—a 12.5% increase. Spending on instructional technology is expected to increase the same percentage, rising from $8 billion to $9 billion within the same timeframe.

Globalization is Changing Education

For the first time, educational publishers have real-time access to global markets for their products and services. Major governmental commitments from the United Kingdom, Germany, Turkey, Holland, Singapore, Hong Kong, and China are paving the way for more and more of their citizens to get information via the Internet, and a growing number of trade shows (including BETT and WEM) that concentrate on global education continue to expand in both exhibitors and attendees.

Access to Private Capital Has Changed the Competitive Landscape

Education was a hot investment area over the past couple of years as private equity markets began looking at the education market in a new way. Visions of reaching a "pre-consumer" market of students, as well as the teachers and parents—all through offering products and services at home and at school—predominated in the business models of many of the newly funded dot coms. However, we've started to see some backlash from the educators as they grapple with the "profitization" of education. For example, as ZapMe! learned this year, giving away technology in exchange for "student eyeballs" and then peppering them with advertising wasn't a viable business model. And the controversy continues over commercial companies subsidizing schools with payments for putting their ads and products in the school environment.

Furthermore, while private capital has spawned many new innovative educational companies, we are starting to see many failures as well. Some of these companies have simply disappeared from the industry (iMind.com and www.rrr.com are examples this year) and others have been bought up by other companies. Still, the "big, traditional" educational publishers are just starting to jump into the Internet space: Pearson is perhaps the biggest player, not only in the size of its sheer investments and acquisitions, but also in the impact of its new educational portal, www.learningnetwork.com.

Despite all the turbulence in the industry, analysts remain bullish about the potential of applying Internet technology to the education market. How long it will take companies to develop the necessary scalable business models, solve the problems of geography and time, and work out all the bugs, is a matter of speculation. But analysts watch the continued growth in access to technology and are betting that as access expands, so will economic development.

> " Our traditional business models have changed as companies are beginning to deliver content via the Internet, and new accountability and curriculum standards have altered the types of products that schools are interested in purchasing. "

Are You My Partner or My Competitor?

Another change in the education publishing industry is the "partnering frenzy" we've seen in the last couple of years. Prior to the Internet, most companies developed products and took them to market in a very insular way. Of course, they weren't looking for an instant 50% market share either! But in today's environment, companies have recognized that they can't do it all themselves. More and more, the ability to play well with others is becoming a critical requirement for success in an Ed Tech version of "Survivor." The world of the Web moves so quickly that companies have come to understand the need for "specialists," and this is one of the primary reasons for partnering. However, as this trend develops, companies are beginning to understand that partnering is not an "end all, be all" strategy. Some partnerships will flourish and others will wither. In the end, the partnerships that will prove to be the most valuable are the partnerships where each partner brings significant strengths to the other and where both are seriously committed to making the partnership work.

The Quest for an Internet Revenue Model Continues

A few short months ago, a Web site was considered successful if it attracted lots of visitors. Heck, the reasoning went, if you got market share early, you would have to be successful. So lots of money was spent in driving students, parents and teachers to an educational portal. The Problem? Companies are quickly discovering the high cost of converting these people to buyers—generally far more than the profit on a first sale—and the substantial effort to keep buyers buying to the point of profitability. Early on, companies also thought that they could offer good, quality content on their Web sites for free and that enough advertising and sponsorship revenue could be generated to make a profit. Wrong. "Well, that's ok," some say, "we'll change our model to give some stuff away for free and charge a subscription for the really good stuff." Or, "We'll affiliate with a store and make our profits by taking a cut of the revenue." Or...

Let's face it. Educational publishers are still wrestling with this issue. The market is on an early learning curve and only time and experimentation will identify winning business models.

Does Technology Really Improve Learning?

When we think about the enormous investment our country has made in educational technology and the limited gains we have made in the levels of student achievement, one has to question the essential premise of "more technology, higher scores." And, indeed, the press has given us mixed reviews. The over-selling and under-delivering of technology-based and online educational opportunities has had a negative effect on the perception of the promise. As we move forward, educational publishers must participate in the "proof" that technology can indeed improve teacher productivity, enhance student learning, and effectively raise scores on state and national standardized tests. Otherwise, the market might decide to go back to the "tried and true" methods of paper, pen, and textbook.

Now the dramatic stock market reverses of winter 2000-01 are casting a further shadow on e-learning entrepreneurship, particularly regarding raising capital. But have the fundamentals changed? Are school populations or budgets dropping? Is the pace of technological change no longer a serious concern of economic development initiatives at all levels of government? Are educational institutions suddenly comfortable that their graduates may not be technologically literate or prepared with skills that enable a lifetime of ongoing learning? The message we're getting at the Heller Reports from influential stakeholders is a resounding "NO!" The ride's going to be bumpy, but all signs indicate the education technology industry is still at the low end of a hockey-stick growth curve.

About the Author

Nelson B. Heller *is the president of Nelson B. Heller & Associates, Inc., www.HellerReports.com, publisher of two printed monthly newsletters, and two electronic publications that cover business opportunities in the education markets. The Heller Reports also sponsors an annual conference called EdNET: the Educational Technology and Telecommunications Markets, as well as hosting periodic international EdNET Trade Mission programs. Nelson's firm also sponsors the annual EdNET Industry Awards Program that recognizes organizations for using technology to significantly improve education and for expanding the educational technology and telecommunications markets. His firm also publishes market research reports, many jointly with The Peak Group. These include the newly released "Education Channel Partners—A Comprehensive Guide to Channel Options for Selling and Marketing Educational Technology."*

Strategic Planning for the 21st Century
by Dick Casabonne

Prior to 1980, strategic planning for educational publishers was a fairly simple process. There were two things driving demand: state adoptions and state curriculums. And, because most of the students lived in only five states (as is still the case today), demand for curriculum-based materials could be identified by analyzing these five states' curriculum guides and publishing materials that met most of these requirements.

Strategic planning in those days consisted of reviewing the competition, analyzing a company's product line, and updating old materials or filling in the "holes" in the product line.

But with the introduction of computer-based technology in the early 1980's, things became more complex. During the past 20 years, quality strategic planning has become an art and science mixed in with a lot of luck and being in the right place at the right time with the right resources.

Whether you are the president of a small to medium sized educational publisher, or the VP of Strategic Planning for a large conglomerate, the process of building a successful strategic plan is the same:

Determine Where You Are

Understanding the strengths and weaknesses of your company is the first step. Assess your product line. Where are your winners? Your losers? What products are in the pipeline? How do they "fit" into the marketplace? Are they unique? What trends are clearly driving the market now? What trends will drive it in the future? Do you have the "solutions" that will be needed for educators in two to three years?

Another important assessment is your internal resources. Do you have people with the capabilities you need to move forward in the future? Can you get these capabilities from outside resources? Should you "buy" these resources by making an acquisition?

> **"One of the most important elements in developing a successful strategic plan is to understand—in depth—the needs of the K-12 market."**

And what about the competition? Are you gaining or losing market share? Are new competitors coming into play who are introducing new products and services? How will this affect you in the future?

Analyze the Market

One of the most important elements in developing a successful strategic plan is to understand—in depth—the needs of the K-12 market. What are they buying? How are they buying? When are they buying? And most importantly, when is this going to change? It would be unwise, for instance, to think that the state adoption system will disappear. It won't. But the probability of the process changing is quite high. And, the products and services included in the adoption process will also probably change. And that will change what publishers will deliver in the future.

Educational publishers know that change happens slowly in education so that distinguishing between what you can sell this year, next year, and in five years is critical. Developing cutting edge products and services might be fun, but it won't be too profitable until a significant number of schools have the infrastructure to be able to purchase.

Determine Where You Want to Be

Strategic planning also depends on establishing clear and obtainable objectives for where you want to be. Basal and textbook educational publishers generally plan for five to ten years in the future, while supplemental publishers have the advantage of moving quickly to meet emerging trends, so their plans are generally three to five years in scope. In the 1980s, companies had to determine whether or not they were going to develop computer-based products and services. And in the past five years, companies have had to determine whether or not to become part of the Internet revolution. Developing the vision of where you want to be will help you analyze opportunities and challenges you face—if this is where you are today, and that is where you want to be in the future, do you:

- Have the financial resources to get there?
- Have the people and talent you need?
- Have the necessary marketing and distribution strength?

At Harcourt, our mission was clear: grow fast. And in that light, we determined that establishing strong brands was a key element in our strategy. We knew that "Harcourt" was not necessarily a household word. And our overall strategic plan was to provide learning applications and solutions to all people, all the time. We also knew that as the leading provider of textbooks, our strength was in print, and we looked to the future and determined that we needed to leverage this strength by utilizing the new world of the Internet.

Determine Who Can Help You Get There

We also knew, from an analysis of our internal resources, that even though Harcourt is a large educational publisher, that we needed the help and expertise of other companies in order to meet our goals. So, we began pursuing a strategy of developing partnerships—a relatively new approach among traditional educational publishers.

In 1998, we realized that there were too many companies trying to develop "portals" for educators. So we decided to develop a "destination" instead. Since our strength was in printed textbooks, we realized we needed a partner whose strengths were not in print, but in other media. And since our information was 3-8 years old, we also realized that we needed a partner who could update our information with current events. And, of course, we needed a partner who was truly interested in education.

There were several companies that fit our criteria, but in the end we chose to work with CNN to develop what became CNNfyi—a destination resource for 12-to-18-year-old students. This partnership allowed us access to unique media (both video and audio) that we could use to supplement our print products, as well as immediate development of lesson plans to quickly assist teachers to incorporate current events into their classrooms on a daily basis.

We have also developed partnerships with other companies—each having its own unique advantage in either expanding access to new content, repurposing own content for different markets and/or different formats, or continuing to build our brand awareness by accessing other company's established customer base.

Other Things to Think About

Successful K-12 strategic plans for the 21st century will require looking at things in a new way. Our world has changed and while schools may take a while to catch up, catch up they will. Other trends will emerge that will certainly affect the type of products and services educational publishers create, the way companies will deliver these services to the market, and indeed, the very way instruction is delivered to the student.

Some of these trends are obvious. Standards and assessments are already affecting the content of educational products and services whether they are in print, software, or Internet-based. The demand for time-sensitive and current information will pressure publishers to find ways to provide timely updates to back-listed products. The invention of hand-held devices and PDAs will encourage innovation to deliver information in a variety of formats as well as for a variety of screen sizes. The growth of the ethnic populations among students will increase the demand for cross-cultural awareness and sensitivity. The Internet, with its worldwide reach, will open the gateway to an exchange of educational programs and opportunities and strengthen the already-urgent need for educational programs that support collaborative learning.

The Challenge?

Without a doubt, the educational publishing industry is about to embark on the most exciting, challenging, and stimulating era of its relatively short history. Within the last five years, the development of Internet content coupled

> "Without a doubt, the educational publishing industry is about to embark on the most exciting, challenging, and stimulating era of its relatively short history."

with the continued growth of access to that content, has changed the playing field for many publishers.

As of November 2000, there were 407.1 million people online[1] and as of February 1999, there were more than 800 million pages encompassing about 15 terabytes of information that were publicly indexed on the Web.[2] Of this, about 6% of these pages contain scientific or educational content.[3]

Finding a way to utilize the Internet, not only as a means of distributing educational content, but also as a way to link resources together to make something bigger than the sum of its parts will be the strategic challenge of the next decade. Companies who can do this successfully will be the educational publishers of the future.

■

[1] NUA Surveys, www.nua.com/surveys.
[2] "Accessibility of Information on the Web", Nature, Vol. 400, pp 107-109, 1999.
[3] Ibid.

■

About the Author

Dick Casabonne *is president, education and training group at LeapFrog Enterprises. Previously, Dick was senior vice president, planning and business development for Harcourt. He also served as president and chief executive officer of Steck-Vaughn. Dick founded Casabonne Associates, Inc, established 22 years ago to concentrate on educational activities in the school and home markets. A graduate of Brown University, he holds a master's degree in education from Boston University and has taught at both K-12 and college levels. Dick can be reached at* rcasabonne@leapfrogschoolhouse.com.

CHAPTER 2
Developing Educational Products and Services

Inside this chapter...

Creating a Product Development Strategy

by Kathryn Kleibacker

Products are the lifeblood of any company. Whether it's the fashion, automobile, or publishing industry, no marketing season begins without a new line, a new car, or new titles. It's basic economics for any company's growth strategy to follow new trends, capitalize on a bestseller, and replace old products that have declining sales. Publishing in general is a business made up of "backlist" and "frontlist," with all products playing a vital role in a company's business plan.

Although educational publishing shares these basic rhythms, it does have its own idiosyncrasies. Understanding its unique market characteristics, materials sales processes, product evaluation procedures, school budgets, and product life cycles is critical to creating a successful product development strategy.

Defining a Product Growth Strategy

There are several basic product development strategies followed by companies—two of the most common are growth through acquisition and organic growth (through internal development). The acquisition model is the fastest method to increase product offerings and market share; however it generally requires significant capital to accomplish. Organic growth is less costly since it usually depends on existing staff; however, the results are less immediate, usually taking several years to impact sales revenues.

Acquisition has been the leading growth strategy in the textbook and supplemental materials market of late. A few years ago, the school publishing market was dominated by eight major textbook companies and a large number of supplemental materials publishers. In the last four years, however, there has been a seismic restructuring and consolidation in the industry. Besides record-breaking acquisitions by Pearson of Simon &

Schuster's Education Division and Reed Elsevier's purchase of Harcourt General Corp., the industry has witnessed the emergence of private capital investors buying "market share." WRC and Haights Cross, heretofore unknown players in the school market, have acquired a number of small and midsize supplemental publishers and online curriculum providers to build sizable companies. The net result of these changes is a few behemoth educational publishers—now all foreign-owned, with the exception of McGraw-Hill and Scholastic—commanding considerable market share and offering everything, including texts, supplemental materials, testing services, classroom magazines, teacher training.

These companies' sheer size may dominate the educational landscape in the next decade, but the school market is large enough—and diverse enough—to support smaller, well-positioned supplemental materials providers.

> " These companies' sheer size may dominate the educational landscape in the next decade, but the school market is large enough—and diverse enough—to support smaller, well-positioned supplemental materials providers. "

Companies large and small commonly expand product offerings through internal development by adding product line extensions or subject and grade level offerings, or by "repurposing" existing content into other formats (e.g., CD-ROM and online). Generally, this activity occurs as a natural outgrowth of sales and market trend analyses. One recent manifestation of this strategy is "brand extension"—of popular products or proven company names. This strategy offers several advantages, including amortizing the cost of a series, character, or author over more products; building new product sales from an established customer base; and, in some instances, reviving the sales of backlist titles. Current examples of brand extensions include *Time* magazine's launch of the school publication *Time for Kids*, Disney's *Winnie the Pooh* books, educational videos, and software, and Scholastic's *Dear American* series.

The acquisition-based and organic development strategies are not mutually exclusive, of course; and in fact, most companies employ a combination of these growth tactics. The degree to which a company chooses one over the other depends on its overall business goals, its editorial expertise, its sales channels, and its investment requirements.

The only cautionary flag to raise on the subject of formulating any product growth strategy is that you must align your products with appropriate sales and distribution channels. Many a company has learned the painful lesson that it is a mistake to have a high school sales force sell primary grade titles, or to ask library sales reps to carry a line of supplemental materials. This pitfall can be avoided by recognizing some of the special characteristics of the school market.

Unique Market Characteristics

The K-12 education market is unique in that almost all instructional material purchases are funded through federal, state, and local funds. Currently, 93% of a school's funding is provided by state and local budgets; 48% from state agencies, 45% from local government. The federal government contributes approximately 7%.[1] Government funding for schools has its advantages and disadvantages. The advantage is that schools have a regular source of materials funding, so businesses with a quality brand and catalog of products can build a loyal customer base steadily over time. The disadvantage is that because funds are tied to various government agencies, budget appropriations follow the ebb and flow of political agendas.

A second distinguishing feature of the school market is that educational products are not purchased in isolation. They must be correlated to curriculum guidelines established by state departments of education and national guidelines outlined by academic professional organizations for each discipline (e.g., NCSS, the National Council for the Social Studies). Today, there is more emphasis than ever before on products that correlate not only to

SCHOOL SALES CHANNELS AND PROCESSES, BY PRODUCT TYPE

Product Type	Pricing	Target Audience	Sales Cycle	Purchase Approval	Sales Channels
Textbooks	$35 - $50	Students	5-7 Yrs	State Depts of Ed District Offices	Dedicated Sales Reps
Workbooks	$9 - $15	Students	Annual	Teachers Principals	Catalogs Direct Mail
Instructional Software (Standalone and ILS)	Standalone $25 - $125 Site Licenses $1,000 - $20,000+	Classrooms Labs	Annual	District Tech Coordinators	Dedicated/ Independent Sales Reps Dealers Catalogs
Electronic Supplements (Videos, Audio Tapes, Online Subscriptions)	$15 - $75 Online Subs $125 - $2,500	Classrooms Labs Libraries	Annual	District Tech Coordinators Principals Media Specialists	Dedicated/ Independent Sales Reps Dealers Catalogs
Manipulatives (Board Games, Puzzles, Maps, Teaching Aids, Bulletin Boards, Posters, Charts)	$5 - $20	Teachers	Annual	Teachers Principals	Catalogs Direct Mail Dealers
Standardized Tests	$5 per student	Students	Annual	District Offices	Dedicated Sales Reps
Magazines	$2 - $3 per student	Students	Annual	Teachers Principals	Direct Mail
Trade Books (Readers/Reference)	Readers $10 - $25 Sets: $100+ Reference $25 - $75 Sets: $150+	Classrooms Libraries	Annual	Teachers Media Specialists	Independent/ Dedicated Sales Reps Catalogs Direct Mail

national academic guidelines, but also to state standards, and in some cases to district standards. Moreover, schools' product evaluation processes *start* with these standards correlations. If products do not meet these criteria they will not even be considered for purchase.

Materials Sales Process

The process of developing and selling curriculum materials to tap into school funding pools is complex and fragmented. The target audience, type of product, and price point all combine to determine product development, sales, and marketing strategies. Moreover, in many instances, the person sold to (the individual with budget authority) is not the user. This complicates the links between product features, perceived benefits, and selling strategies. Finally, school purchasing procedures are substantially different for products bought at the district and school levels, as the chart on page 66 illustrates.

Product Evaluation Process

The evaluation process is critical to school product sales. Textbooks are traditionally selected by state- and district-wide committees after a lengthy and expensive review process that requires publishers to distribute hundreds of "sample copies" to adoption and curriculum committees. Supplemental material publishers offering trade books, videos, manipulatives, audio cassettes, and software/CD-ROMs, incur expenses to provide "preview" samples of products for review, although not at the same investment level as text publishers. For supplementals, schools will accept "sample reels or disks" of multiple titles, or one or two titles in a set of books for review. These companies are also making creative use of the Internet by providing demo copies and sample chapters online at significant cost savings and as an added promotion vehicle. For teacher classroom materials such as workbooks that are purchased with school funds the evaluation process is less rigorous and formal, but these materials must still meet the requirements of basic curriculum standards.

School Budget Cycles

The education market has specific budget cycles that drive purchasing decisions. Products are evaluated during the school year for purchase in the summer months and use in the following academic year. Schools are either on

a fiscal cycle (usually July to June) or a calendar cycle (January to December). No matter when the actual budgeting cycle begins, however, it is imperative that products are published or released from August through October to take advantage of the evaluation cycle.

August and January are Key Promotion Months. Because the selection process continues throughout the school year, it is also important that publisher catalogs and direct mail pieces are in schools when teachers and administrators arrive. Additionally, many publishers remail (albeit to a more targeted list) in January.

January through April Is the Peak Evaluation and Ordering Period. Depending on a school's and school district's evaluation process, products are reviewed and selection lists are compiled and submitted in this period.

May and June Feature End-of-Year Spending. While orders continue to be placed for next year's products, this is also a time when schools must spend any monies still in their current year's budget. This situation is referred to in school parlance as "use it, or lose it" monies. For if in fact the schools do not spend the budgeted amount, that budget category will be reduced the next year to reflect the prior year's spending level.

Product Life Cycles & Unit Sales

Sales cycles vary by product type, as do their evaluation and purchase approval procedures. Textbooks' life cycles depend on the adoption cycle and length of that adoption, generally 5 - 7 years. Supplemental and library reference materials reach their peak sales typically within 3 - 5 years, although some "classics" survive longer.

Those new to the school market often salivate over the potentially huge, captive, institutional market—3 million teachers, 53 million students, and 110,000 schools. They generally make the mistake of estimating sales projections based on assumptions about possible penetrations of the student, teacher, or school market universes. However, it is unusual for a product to gain more than a 5% - 10% market share since by its sheer size and demographics the market is highly fragmented with hundreds of competing products. There are exceptions, but on average unit sales by product type are confined to the following ranges:

TYPE Textbooks	LIFE UNIT SALES Millions (ideally one per student)
Supplemental Materials	5,000 – 25,000
Trade Books	
Paperback	5,000 – 10,000
Hardback	2,500 – 5,000
Audio Cassettes	2,500 – 7,500
Video Cassettes	1,500 – 2,500
Standalone Software/CD-ROM's	2,500 – 5,000

Creating a New Product Development Strategy

Most companies go through some sort of systematic development planning process. Large companies do this on an annual basis, planning out three to five years and modifying their plan each year. No matter what size your business is, a well thought out development plan sets the framework for the rest of the business—marketing, sales, production, finance, and operations. It outlines how many products you will have, determines their formats, subjects, grades levels, and price points, and by implication it defines who your key competitors will be. In short, the plan becomes the backbone of your business and the filter for evaluating new product opportunities and strategies both internally and externally.

■

[1] p. 63, Simba Information Inc, *Print Publishing for the School Market: 1999-2000*

■

About the Author

Kathryn Kleibacker *is the president of Kathryn Kleibacker & Associates, a consulting firm specializing in new business development for schools and libraries. She is also a partner in Internet Monitor, a company providing school and library publishers online marketing and new product development strategies. Kathy has over 25 years experience in developing award-winning products in print, video, and multimedia. She can be reached at Kathryn Kleibacker & Associates, 16 Wyckoff Street, Brooklyn, NY 11201, or by phone: (718) 858-3459; fax: (718) 858-6022; or e-mail: kkabiz@aol.com.*

Market Research: Identifying Educators' and Students' Needs

by Linda Winter

Here's a story about serendipity...about unexpectedly turning a marketing defeat into a product bonus. A major computer manufacturer was testing new product and service concepts in focus groups at a national education conference. The products in question were, to put it delicately, not testing well. The educators kept saying that they lacked budgeting and planning abilities and as a result, they felt hesitant about committing to larger initiatives. They were unclear about where infrastructure technology was heading. They needed a new generation of planning and evaluation tools. They needed deeper in-house technology planning expertise.

The bottom line? The manufacturer's new "boxes" weren't singing to the focus groups. But the team listened carefully and heard a different tune in the background. What this group of savvy marketers heard was the need for vastly improved professional development for educational technology decision-makers—a service that would help district technology leaders turn needs into plans, complete with costs, estimates for operations, maintenance and support, and forecasts for replacement. The products tested that day never saw the market's light. But a new service concept for professional development was born.

The power of market research triumphs again.

We Don't Have Time for Research: Our Launch Date Is Just 90 Days Away!

In the K-12 market, launch dates rule the calendar and the lives of marketing and product development specialists. The books must be ready for this conference; the software or Web sites ready for that meeting. In the rush to market, too often the critical step of market research is put aside for lack of time. That is, until the product launches with less-than-stellar results. Then comes another kind of rush—the desperate rush to figure out what went wrong, what can be fixed and how the whole unhappy situation can suddenly be "righted."

Whoever coined the phrase, "Somehow, we never have time to do it right the first time, but we always seem to have time to do it over..." could have been talking about product launches, marketing campaigns, new pricing structures, or just about any other school

marketing initiative—particularly when market research is left out of the picture.

Choosing the Research Format: Asking the Right Questions in the Right Way

In fact, there are multiple formats and approaches for education market research. Some can be planned, executed, and completed in two to three weeks. Others require more time and generally will help marketing professional uncover broader, more sweeping market trends, information about brand penetration, and other strategically valuable results.

Of course, like all marketing and product development initiatives, market research yields more productive results when school marketers take the time to establish reasonable research needs and objectives, action plans, and evaluation strategies. When planning market research with K-12 teachers, administrators, technology specialists, school board members, and other "influencers," here are some initial planning tips:

- Even if you operate with an attentive field or inside sales team, a marketing group comprised of former teachers, and the best channel partners in market today, their "intuition" is not the same as research data that's gathered and analyzed objectively. The longer marketing, editorial, and product development specialists have worked in the schools, the more "intuition" they develop. And while these sensibilities are genuinely valuable, objective research adds a valuable component to your planning and decision making.

- The most effective research begins with a specific objective and generates a research methodology that aligns optimally with that objective. For example, testing complex professional development approaches for curriculum products is probably best assigned to qualitative research. Determining personal discretionary spending among middle grade science teachers is a quantitative investigation.

- "One study does not a business make." Too often for reasons of time or resources, publishers are tempted to slap a focus group together, have the editorial or marketing team moderate, and stamp it "finished."

At the other end of the spectrum, a large telephone survey that touches on several issues certainly covers the ground, but in no way can it provide the depth of insight needed for sound strategy. The answer? An integrated set of smaller, better-defined investigations will yield more reliable, balanced information.

- Ongoing research, both qualitative and quantitative, yield the most reliable, actionable and valuable data.

Keep in mind that engaging in research is not an admission that management, marketing, and product development gurus have lost their touch. On the contrary, it's proof positive that they're market-driven, market-responsive, and genuinely knowledgeable about their prospects, customers, and opportunities.

Qualitative Research

The best known qualitative research format is the focus group. Here, a panel of 8-12 respondents, each selected on the basis of a well-defined set of screening questions, convene to spend between 90 and 120 minutes "focusing" on specific issues related to a marketing question, such as product attributes, purchasing processes and preferences, or the evaluation of a marketing campaign or branding initiative. These sessions should all use a consistent "discussion guide" and should be recorded on audio and videotape. It's always helpful to have the sessions transcribed so that your research analysts and your marketing teams can review the discussions in depth. Typically, these sessions take place at dedicated research facilities, where taping is automatic and where there is a viewing room for the client team. Sessions can also be conducted at conferences or trade shows, and the same recruiting processes can be applied.

Focus groups are valuable for uncovering the "why's" behind educators' brand preferences, their purchasing processing and attitudes, and their responses to new and established products alike. A word of caution is in order, however. Focus groups are not mini-surveys. Too often, there is an attempt to "quantify" the results. This is statistically unsound and far too risky. At the opposite end of

> " Keep in mind that engaging in research is not an admission that management, marketing, and product development gurus have lost their touch. "

the spectrum are focus groups conducted to validate "done deals" of company strategy. When the responses contradict a concrete decision you've already made, the only results are frustration and doubt. You could have bought those two outcomes without focus groups.

Other useful forms of qualitative research include one-to-one telephone and in-person interviews with educators, again selected using a pre-defined "screening" process and a consistent discussion guide. Less formal but also helpful are advisory boards and other informal opportunities to gather customers' and prospects' opinions about products, campaigns, or other initiatives. To make this information more useful, it's helpful to standardize the questions you or your staff asks as well as the answer formats. While the information from these sources may not be as comprehensive or objective as formal focus panels or one-to-one interviews, the data can certainly factor into your strategy development process.

Lastly, some publishers and software developers have also employed a valuable research technique that mimics the "market tests" that many consumer goods companies employ. In some cases, they send sample products to educators along with an evaluation form and a small payment. In other cases, they ask conference attendees to take a product sample or a marketing packet and then return an evaluation. These techniques are not optimal when speed counts; but when the objective is an ongoing stream of customer feedback, these customer feedback techniques can be very valuable.

Quantitative Research

Analytical and descriptive surveys, split-run mailing tests, and in-depth database profiling can provide the marketing team with critical insight and understanding of key issues such as the market size, brand penetration, and purchasing plans and patterns. The pre-K-12, higher education, and library markets are all well covered by several database and mailing list organizations, including Quality Education Data, Market Data Retrieval, and Mailings Clearing House. These companies can provide school marketers with mailing addresses, telephone and fax numbers, and in some cases e-mail addresses, selected according to key school demographics such as enrollment, metro status, grade span, and other critical market "selects." This ability to define market niches down to the numbers of buildings, districts and educators will help you define the size, scope, and characteristics of your specific market's universe. Then by working with your market research professional, you can determine the number of questionnaires and completed responses you'll need to make certain your results are statistically valid and reliable.

Again, words of caution are in order. Questionnaire design and data collection are best left to research professionals. Nuances of wording, question sequence, and response rating scales can all impact the ways respondents answer. The client's best approach is to develop a research platform, outlining the topics to be investigated, as well as the key questions and the kinds of information desired. From this type of platform, a better questionnaire will evolve.

It's also important to maximize the data correlations that can result from your quantitative research program. If your study universe is constructed properly, you should have the ability to compare, for example, purchasing patterns for your product or product category among low, medium, and high enrollment districts; or purchases by buildings in urban vs. rural settings. This kind of comparative data can inform your direct sales strategies, your mailing programs, your pricing grids, and all other marcom programs.

Secondary Research

The K-12 market is well covered by its professional publications, the market's data and mailing list companies, the investment community, federal and state governmental agencies, and the many associations to which teachers and administrators belong. Much of this information is available online. In addition, a great deal of market intelligence is readily available from the sales information distributed by professional publications.

For example, in a recent edition of *House of Clues*™, a newsletter published for companies advertising in *Library Journal* and *School Library Journal*, a short article covered the issue of "reach" in business-to-business advertising. The article's primary point was to report on research conducted by Cahners, the publishers of both *Library Journal* and *School Library Journal* showing that "...advertising reaches 86% of the market in the leading publication." According to this study, adding the second-leading magazine delivers "...only 6% more market coverage, and the third magazine just 2% more." If one of your marcom research objectives is to determine which school market publication or publications in which to place your ads, this research is extremely valuable. And that's just one example. Consistent review of the school market's general and discipline-specific publications will uncover important market trends, competitive intelligence, and other valuable insights.

Here's another example from a related market. The April 2001 edition of *Against the Grain*, a publication focused on the specific acquisition needs of college, university, and research libraries, reports on the data from its annual survey of librarians. One of their survey areas was e-books and electronic resources. Their findings? Purchases of e-books grew 40% over year 2000 purchases, with the average budget set aside for e-books coming in at $16,740. Another trend-revealing statistic from these Charleston-based publishers is that 53% of their survey's respondents canceled paper serials in favor of electronic subscriptions. This is the kind of trend that may begin to have significant impact on K-12 purchasing patterns, sooner rather than later. Further, this kind of data can help with strategic planning and forecasting.

Does it replace conducting your own survey of K-12 librarians' plans to purchase e-books? Certainly not; but it can add to the depth and direction and important dimension to your planning efforts.

Online Research

E-mail and Web-based surveys are gaining popularity. They can be created and distributed quickly and inexpensively. Questions can be changed rapidly if researchers find they are not positioned correctly. Responses can be tabulated and distributed in "Internet time." Many companies are also including a customer and/or prospect survey on their Web sites on an ongoing basis, to make customer feedback a consistent component of their marketing programs. This is a strong step in a positive direction.

The only drawback is the anonymity of online survey participants and the difficulty in qualifying them for statistical analysis. Some firms have created online self-screeners with several required fields of data, so that responses can be tabulated using standard statistical methods. In other cases, the data gathered through online surveys is considered as qualitative data—providing "directional" indicators rather than statistically reliable information.

The Discipline of Market Research

Anybody who has ever tried to diet knows that one day of calorie counting and strenuous exercise is—one day of calorie counting and strenuous exercise. Lots of hunger and sore muscles. Not much weight loss. The same is true with market research. Only an ongoing, disciplined program of qualitative and quantitative data collection will provide maximum returns. But done correctly market research will support not only specific campaigns and products but will also inform and improve your entire marketing operation.

About the Author

Linda Winter is an Internet Monitor, www.internet-monitor.com, partner and the president of Winter Group, www.wintergroup.net, an award-winning marketing communications, research, and design firm, focused on the education and library markets. She started Winter Group in 1978. The firm provides a comprehensive collection of integrated services to education marketers, including advertising, sales support and collateral materials, Web site development, custom market research, direct mail, catalogs, event marketing, and exhibit design. Linda received her undergraduate degree from Northwestern University and her M.A. from the University of Denver. She is a co-author of i-Tips 2000, The Insiders' Guide to School & Library Marketing, published by the Internet Monitor. She can be reached at WinterL@wintergroup.net or (303) 778.0866, ext. 12.

Turning Trends into Successful Products

by Lois Eskin

The title of this article might seem to suggest that it is a simple matter to identify trends, or that every trend should be converted into a product by your company. Not so! Yes, there is a lot of market information out there. But not all of it has the same value for determining trends, and not all trends should be translated into products by a given company. The trick is to develop a set of ground rules about what and how much information you need, as well as some questions you should ask to determine whether or not your company ought to jump on a particular bandwagon. Only after these two challenges are met can you begin to think about how to turn a trend into a successful product.

Getting Information about the Marketplace

There are two major categories of market information helpful in searching for trends: primary information or research and secondary information or research.

Primary research is data or information generated by an analyst or researcher specifically for your research purposes. It can be collected using internal sources (such as your sales force, service groups in the company, a development group, a market research department that generates mail or interview surveys), or external sources (such as trade associations, industry consultants, investment banks, or advertising agencies). But the key attribute of primary research is that it is specifically designed to find out what you want to know. Its goals can be to acquire competitive information, forecast market growth, establish product goals, or determine the ideal publishing timetable. The benefits of primary research are: (1) it is very focused on your specific objectives; (2) you can generally be confident about the accuracy and reliability of the results because you know the credentials of the researchers and have supervised the research design, the selection of any survey mailing lists, and the choice of methodology; (3) it can be very useful for studying new markets since it is

> **"**...primary research, say many researchers, should comprise the bulk of the information you use to make market and product decisions.**"**

unlikely that others will have done research on these markets; and (4) you can determine the timing of the data collection and analysis. The negatives of primary research are: (1) it is almost always more expensive than secondary research; (2) it takes a lot of staff time to formulate questionnaires, organize mailings or interviews, and analyze the results; and (3) bias can't always be eliminated when you are orchestrating the research design.

Secondary research is data or information that was gathered for purposes other than your specific goals. It also can be obtained from internal sources (such as sales and marketing reports, financial data, or miscellaneous existing records) or external sources (including government agencies, associations, bibliographies, syndicated services, periodicals, newspapers, or other published sources). The key factor, in the case of secondary research, is that the information was collected for someone else's purposes. It can be helpful to use secondary research before and during primary research to identify sources of additional information or gain insight into the market and research issues that need to be explored further. Here, the major goal should be to provide a broad perspective of the market.

The chief benefits of secondary research are that (1) it saves you money, because the burden of expense is on the original researcher rather than on you; (2) it saves time, because the work is already completed; (3) it is very useful for getting industry overviews. The negatives, on the other hand, are: (1) it may not address your specific concerns, (2) the data is often too general to be useful, (3) the information is only as good as the accuracy and reliability of the data collection and analysis source—it is therefore very important that you know the source of the research, the purpose for which it was conducted, the credentials of the researchers, and so on; and 4) the data may not be current—there is often a long lag time between the collection and analysis and the actual publication of the results in journals or other accessible sources.

Ideally, primary and secondary research should be carried out simultaneously, but primary research, say many researchers, should comprise the bulk of the information you use to make market and product decisions. Some experts go so far as to say that 80% of the research you undertake should be primary research.

Interpreting the Information

Suppose you've collected and/or acquired some market data on what teachers and principals seem to want and need. Now how can you tell whether what they're saying represents a true trend, rather than a mere fad or some idea that's actually past its prime?

When you are asking questions at a particular moment in time, even if you are asking the respondents to project five years ahead, the only thing you can be sure of is that their responses represent their current thinking about the matters under question. If you ask them the same questions again at some point in the future, you can begin to see emerging trends, and if you ask the same questions again and again, you can feel more confident about the trends you identify. In other words, the first time you ask, you're collecting baseline information. You're collecting it so you can compare it to other information, either from other sources or from a different point in time. In order to identify trends reliably, research should be longitudinal; that is, continuous and ongoing. Additionally, it is unwise to rely just on one source of information. The more fingers you see pointing in the same direction, the more likely it is that the direction points to a trend.

Determining if a Market is for You

Suppose you've done your research homework and identified three or four areas that seem to offer promising potential for new products. How do you decide if your company belongs in these markets or not? Business thinkers have come up with all sorts of techniques and tests for helping companies decide whether a particular market, business, or product opportunity is right for them. Some are very simple techniques; others are very

> *"In school publishing, these external forces include enrollments, the student profile, funding, the decision-making process, curriculum trends, and the competition, among others."*

complex. We have used four techniques that are basic and simple to apply, and that have been very helpful to companies we've worked with.

Internal Factors: Your Company's Strengths and Weaknesses

The first technique to think about is how a new product or market possibility matches up with your company's existing strengths and weaknesses. For example, suppose you are a supplementary math manipulatives company and you have collected research information about the reading market. Your data strongly suggests that whole language is diminishing and basic phonics and skills instruction are increasing. "Well," you think, "the reading market is huge and very tempting, and there seems to be a big opportunity for phonics products." Should you go into it?

How would that development possibility take advantage of your strengths as a company? What weaknesses would your company have to overcome? Answering these questions should be part of the risk assessment you make before entering any new market.

External Forces: Opportunities or Threats?

In addition to looking inward at your own company's strengths and weaknesses, it is important to evaluate business opportunities in the light of external forces that may have the potential to affect a market or product entry positively or negatively. In school publishing, these external forces include enrollments, the student profile, funding, the decision-making process, curriculum trends, and the competition, among others.

Each of these forces could present either an opportunity or a threat to you depending on which direction it takes in the future. So you need to do some projecting of future trends. What do you think will happen in each of these areas, and will the future of these forces bring you an opportunity or a threat so far as this new product or market idea is concerned? For example, if funding for immigrant children increases, will this increase or decrease the opportunity for phonics instruction?

If many competitors enter the phonics market, does this represent a threat or an opportunity for your company? Answering these questions is a second important step in assessing the risks of a new market or product possibility.

Barriers to Entry and Barriers to Exit

A third tool planners find useful in thinking about businesses or markets or product lines is the concept of barriers to entering and exiting any market. When you want to get into any new market, no matter what business you're talking about, there are certain common barriers or obstacles that must be overcome in order to get into the market and in order to get out of the market. These include:

BARRIERS TO MARKET ENTRY

- Initial investment costs (e.g., research, plant, staff, prototyping, and building costs).

- High initial unit costs due to small initial market share

- Consumer brand loyalty

- Competitive pressures

- The learning curve

- Government regulations or policies

- Access to distribution channels (including the challenge of finding representation when all available talent is allied with other established companies)

BARRIERS TO MARKET EXIT

- Long-term contracts with existing customers

- Specialized assets to divest (plants, factories)

- Labor contracts, staff severances

- Contracts with suppliers

- Strategic relationships within company

- Long-term arrangements with backers (either internal or external)

- Bargaining power with suppliers

- Image, along with emotional barriers such as pride or loyalty

- Possible government regulations or restrictions

If entry and exit costs are low, the risk of getting into the market is low compared with the risk of going into a market where the entry and exit costs are high. Of course, if entry and exit costs are low, many competitors will want to get into the business; whereas, if entry and exit costs are high, few competitors will want to get into the business.

Market Life Cycle

A fourth way of looking at a market or product possibility is in terms of where it is in its life cycle. Is it an emerging market, a growth market, a mature market, or a market in decline? Each of these life cycle phases has certain characteristics:

MARKET LIFE CYCLE STAGES

Characteristics	Emerging	Growth	Maturity	Decline
Growth Rate	Increasing	Faster than GNP	Equal to or Slower than GNP	Declining
# of Competitors'	Increasing Rapidly	Increasing toward a Shakeout	Stable	Declining
Market Shares	Volatile	Movement Among Top Players	Fixed	Fixed (except for exits)
Customer Behavior	Naïve: Trial and Error	Trial Based on Product Characteristics	Price Conscious; Smart	Price Conscious; Smart
Profitability	Low	High	High	Usually low
Cash Flow	-	-	+	Varies

Can you think of any parts of the educational materials market that seem to be emerging? in growth? in maturity? in decline? Some markets or trends, such as textbooks, have a very long life cycle. Once they hit maturity, they stay there for a long time. Others, such as teaching machines, had a very short life cycle.

It is important to look at your markets and products in terms of their life cycle in order to assess the risks and opportunities inherent in each phase. Obviously, if a market is in decline, it would not seem smart to enter it. On the other hand, if a market is just emerging, you should consider all the risky characteristics of emerging markets before making an entry decision.

Developing Successful Products

Identifying the Competition

Once you've decided a particular product idea is a "go" based on the above tools and whatever other factors you may want to consider, how do you design a product that beats the competition? First, you have to know who the competition is. That may seem obvious. And if we're just talking about the current, direct competitors, these may indeed, be obvious. But you also need to think about who might be your direct competition after you get your new product to market, say, in the next two to five years.

And what about companies that are currently suppliers to yours—might they, one day, become competitors? Then there are your current buyers. Might any of them become competitors? Which school districts and state departments have already published programs? Which might do so in the next two to five years?

In addition, any number of non-profit and consumer organizations publish and distribute (often free) instructional materials. Instructional materials from these kinds of organizations might very well compete with the products you offer or may develop in the future.

> *"Indeed, you must out-market the competition, particularly as a new entrant in a market or product category."*

All of these categories of competitors and potential competitors should be identified as you begin to think about developing your new product, and each should be labeled as either a high, medium, or low threat. The next step is to look at the products produced by the high- and medium-threat companies for the target market and figure out how you're going to beat them. And here's where the genius comes in and where you can use all the creativity you can get, because there really are only a few general ways to beat the competition.

Beating the Competition

First, you can differentiate the product. That is, you can make your product distinct from all the others in the same category or design it to serve the same purpose in ways that make it more desirable in the marketplace. Second, you can charge less for your products or services than your competitors. Third, you can concentrate or focus your efforts on a distinct segment or niche of the market. This strategy may involve issues of differentiation or cost, but its main appeal is that the product concentrates on a distinct market segment or segments. Finally, you can employ a strategy that combines some or all of these three factors but that does not focus on any one to the exclusion of the others.

People often mention out-marketing as one of the ways to beat the competition. You can out-market competitors by creating eye-catching packaging, special promotional offers or premiums, prominent public relations and advertising efforts, and so on. Indeed, you *must* out-market the competition, particularly as a new entrant in a market or product category. Outstanding marketing is essential for drawing in new customers or switching a customer from a competitor to your product. However, it will not sustain the use of your product if the product itself does not add value, cost less, or meet a niche need.

Summary

Even while using all of these techniques, remember also to listen to your intuition. Successful entrepreneurs have the ability to sense a good idea or opportunity when it appears, and these flashes of genius should not be ignored. But then, put them to the tests we've discussed here so you know what you're getting into when you leap into the fray!

About the Author

Lois Eskin *is president of Lois Eskin Associates, a consulting firm for publishers, organizations, and developers of instructional materials for grades K-12. The company specializes in helping clients with management, product planning, marketing, and staff development challenges. Ms. Eskin has over 30 years of experience in corporate educational publishing and in consulting with educational publishers. Lois can be reached at Lois Eskin Associates, Two Horizon Road, Fort Lee, NJ 07024 or by calling (201) 224-8131.*

Accountable Instructional Programs Poised for Success

by Aileen H. Krassner
with thanks to Cynthia Potter

Over the last decade, national and local education agencies have urged greater accountability in the nation's schools to ensure that all students receive an outstanding education. The demand for strong accountability systems has risen in response to the standards-based reform movement as a way to measure the impact of education programs on student achievement. Though some argue that the standards-based reform movement in practice has been more of a "high-stakes, standardized test-based reform movement,"[1] the public at large still supports efforts to raise education standards and to implement better, more comprehensive assessment systems, despite their inherent limitations. Proponents of strong accountability systems believe that student performance and achievement will improve when specific standards for student performance are clearly defined, when all resources available to the education system are aligned to ensure students meet those standards, and when teachers are held accountable for meeting those standards.

Whether one agrees or disagrees with this view, it represents a reality in today's education marketplace. Consider that "49 states now have statewide academic standards for what students should know and be able to do in at least some subjects; 50 states test how well their students are learning; and 27 hold schools accountable for results, either by rating the performance of all their schools or identifying low-performing ones."[2] The publishers who will be most successful in upcoming years will be those who can clearly demonstrate an understanding of and support for national, state, and local accountability systems and who can position their instructional programs in the context of existing and evolving accountability frameworks. Whether they compete in the state-adoption or open-adoption marketplaces, publishers who understand how standards, content, assessment, accuracy, and technology overlap and converge with one another will have a powerful advantage and an opportunity to prosper.

> " ... 49 states now have statewide academic standards for what students should know and be able to do in at least some subjects... "

Importance of Alignment

The 1990s marked the beginning of the standards-based reform movement, when educators began identifying the need for academic standards that would describe what every student should know and be able to demonstrate across the core content areas. Academic associations such as the International Reading Association, the National Science Teachers Association, the National Council for Teachers of Mathematics, and the National Council for the Social Studies, among others, began by drafting broad national academic standards in each of the content areas as general guidelines. States and local school districts took that important work and crafted more specific state and local standards, curriculum frameworks, and benchmarks to identify in greater detail what students should learn and how well they should be able to demonstrate that knowledge and those skills. According to *Education Week*, 49 states indicated in 2001 that they had standards in at least some academic areas.[3]

Standards can guide publishers of instructional materials in two important ways. First, a sampling of national and state standards and standardized test objectives can be used to generate a comprehensive scope and sequence before an instructional program is developed. A scope and sequence identifies key concepts and skills associated with a particular subject area and grade level to create a blueprint for development.

Second, state standards can also be used to create test objectives that assess students' mastery of knowledge, skills, and abilities. Each of the 50 states now has some form of student testing program to measure achievement. The goal of state testing is to measure students' progress toward meeting rigorous academic standards and to give teachers feedback that they can use to improve student learning.

As you can see, the emphasis on standards, content, and assessment shows how important it is to have curricula and instructional materials that align to national, state, and local standards. In fact, alignment is so important that many buyers will not consider the purchase of instructional materials that do not demonstrate strong alignment with their state standards.

Marketing Your Product with Correlations

Keeping up with the ever-changing standards in the 50 states and countless school districts, as well as with the contents of standardized exams, can be a daunting task for publishers. Consider putting your alignment effort to use in marketing your product by creating correlations. A correlation is, in essence, a specialized index that matches the content of an educational product with state or national standards and exams. A correlation may be used as a stand-alone document or may be printed within a program's teacher-support materials. Correlations typically list the particular standards addressed by the product and give references to pages or sections of the material on which each standard is addressed.

How do you most effectively allocate marketing dollars for correlations? First determine not only the audience for which the correlation is intended but also the different types of correlations that are suited for your products. There are three main types of correlations: point-of-use, summary, and adoption form correlations.

Point-of-use correlations are best suited to help teachers in the classroom to select activities that meet a particular standard and to help them develop their own standards-based lesson plans. These correlations might be printed next to each activity throughout a teacher's edition of a textbook, for example. A central strength of this type of correlation is that it allows for extremely specific matches between activities and standards.

Summary correlations can be used to demonstrate how well an instructional program meets the relevant standards, overall. A summary correlation can be used by teachers as an index, but more often it is used by the publisher as a marketing tool. A summary correlation typically lists standards in order, with an exhaustive reference to points in the product where each standard is met. The more examples of matches the correlation has to the standards, the better.

State adoption form correlations are used as part of instructional material submissions to adoption states.[4] Many states require publishers to submit a complete correlation to state standards along with their materials for adoption. This form is a concise snapshot of the best matches between the standards and the instructional program.

> " The publishers who will be most successful in upcoming years will be those who can clearly demonstrate an understanding of and support for national, state, and local accountability systems... "

Other correlations-oriented efforts may also be useful to publishers. For example, supplemental publishers can align their products with basal textbook programs that have already been adopted by several states, to show teachers how their products can enhance the textbook program already in their classrooms. Point-of-use correlations to state standardized exams can also help teachers target knowledge and skills in their curriculum that students will encounter on state exams. Finally, a customized skill database is another option to automate certain kinds of correlations and to evaluate commonalties in standards across a number of states.

Assessment and Test Preparation Components

A successful instructional program not only aligns to standards and curricula but also provides assessments to measure how well a student can demonstrate knowledge and skills in a specific content area. Assessments can take a variety of forms, from traditional diagnostic assessments to unit and chapter reviews to performance-based assessments and the rubrics[5] that guide their evaluation.

Traditional assessments are the staple of any complete assessment package because they integrate with the core program. After a careful examination of not only the content but also the instructional approach of a program, assessment pieces can be created that include simple, content-focused questions. Effective test questions go beyond rote memorization to test higher-order thinking skills. These kinds of assessments can appear in many forms, including multiple-choice, matching, fill-in-the-blank, and short-answer items.

Integrated assessments present other ways to evaluate student learning by furnishing a multidimensional picture of a student's critical-thinking, problem-solving, and communication skills. To develop tasks and scoring rubrics for these types of assessments, a thorough understanding of assessment principles and strong subject-area expertise are required. Examples of integrated examinations include extended-response items such as essays; multistage projects that culminate in a product or presentation; reading inventories; and portfolios.

Test preparation materials for state and national standardized exams and college-entrance examinations are another growing area of demand. Test preparation materials prepare students to perform their best on exams by building their confidence, familiarizing them with test formats and teaching test-taking skills. In the area of specific test practice materials, educators can also use practice test results to gauge student progress and to customize instruction to meet diverse student needs. Publishers should be aware, however, that different states have different rules that define appropriate and ethical test preparation practices. California, for example, prohibits certain kinds of state-customized test preparation materials in an effort to discourage teachers from "teaching to the test" rather than teaching from the curriculum.[6]

It goes without saying that state standardized exams have become very important in the accountability equation. For students, exam results can have the power to keep them from advancing to the next grade level or from earning a high school diploma. Schools and districts that do not score well may be labeled as low performing, may lose monetary incentives, and may risk a takeover or shutdown by the state or district. Consider also that state education agencies are encouraging local districts to

critically view students' test scores as a way of determining the most successful instructional products and approaches.

The market for assessment-based educational materials has always been present, but the emphasis on testing and the amount of money spent on testing are growing. In a survey of 50 state education officials, states reported spending $400 million in 2001 to develop, administer, and score their current testing programs.[7] That number is likely to increase as the Bush administration considers testing children in more grades. A survey by the National Association of State Boards of Education (NASBE) estimates that the President's plan to test students in grades 3–8 every year could cost states from $2.6 billion to $7 billion to implement by the proposed 2004 deadline.[8]

Teachers by and large look for assessments that provide different levels of difficulty to address the needs of a variety of students, rubrics that are specific enough to help teachers objectively assess performance-based projects, and a variety of both traditional and integrated assessment types for use in their classroom. When submitting programs for state adoption, many publishers are careful to include a comprehensive assessment program and state-specific test preparation material as ancillary components to accompany the core program.

In fact, alignment is so important that many buyers will not consider the purchase of instructional materials that do not demonstrate strong alignment with their state standards.

Benefits of State-Customized Products

Publishers who customize educational products for state and local markets can also position their products for success. Publishers who compete in the state adoption marketplace often develop several parallel versions of their products, one customized for the each of the largest states. Because the return on investment is so high if a publisher makes the adoption list, it makes sense to prepare state-customized programs for those states. For example, a publisher may have a "national version" that is sold nationwide with special editions for California, Texas, and Florida.

Publishers submitting programs for state adoption often bundle in many "free" ancillary components to add value and to entice teachers and districts to choose their curriculum program. For textbook publishers, these ancillary products often include workbooks, technology components, state-focused test preparation materials, among other things. Teachers enjoy having many options to teach to a diverse group of learners, even if they are unable to use them all. This phenomenon is not difficult to understand: educators are looking for a "big box" and want to receive what they perceive as the most value for their money.

Publishers may also prepare state-customized products for niche markets and large open territory states,[9] such as Illinois and New York, for stand-alone supplemental programs that enhance the curriculum. State-focused test preparation materials lend themselves particularly well to state customizations.

Accuracy

Educators and the general public are growing increasingly intolerant of errors and false statements that appear in education products. Many states now heavily fine publishers whose instructional programs include factual inaccuracies that may harm student learning. The media has also fueled the increased focus on accuracy with negative news stories that have dramatically portrayed factual errors in textbooks. It is essential that any print- or technology-based program undergo a thorough, independent quality review to verify the accuracy of facts, diagrams and artwork, and answers to assessment questions before the product goes to market.

Inaccuracies can be introduced in a number of ways. First of all, publishers who are preparing a new edition need only introduce 20 percent new content to receive a new copyright. Often, outdated statistics are accidentally left in such programs. Outdated statistics represent one of the most commonly found errors in textbooks. Offering a single answer to a question or problem that has multiple answers, over-generalizing, and presenting incorrect information are other sources of errors. Mislabeled or misleading diagrams and typographical errors (e.g., 1976 instead of 1776) can introduce unintended inaccuracies as well.

Compressed development schedules can make extra quality assurance reviews difficult if not impossible for publishers. However, planning for an independent quality review at the outset of a project will save financial penalties and damaged reputations later on. Look for an independent reviewer who uses content-area specialists, researchers, and innovative technology. In addition, consider requiring your authors to provide sources for their information when they write your instructional materials. Any information you can provide the independent reviewer will provide greater assurance that the instructional program you develop is as accurate as possible.

> " The publishers who understand that providing good content with an attractive design is only the beginning of the story will be the most competitive in the education marketplace of the future. "

Applicability and Technology

Many states are exploring the feasibility of purchasing the delivery and updates to core instructional content and assessment electronically. These states recognize that in just a short period of time, printed materials can become outdated and inapplicable to students' lives. Textbooks can reside in the classroom for six years or more after purchase by an adoption state. With the current emphasis on excellent instruction and student performance, educators are realizing that outdated materials are simply unacceptable.

With the availability of technology and increasing pressure on teachers to improve learning, the demand for aligned technology-based instructional materials and frequent updates is rising. Publishers are responding by creating lesson plans and current-events content delivered to students via the Internet or other electronic devices. They are providing applicable professional development to teachers to get them up to speed on the technology and to integrate content into their classrooms as quickly as possible.

Although it is not a replacement for the printed word, accessible and applicable technology-based content is on the rise. Merrill Lynch has estimated that the e-learning market for grades K-12 was $1.3 billion in 1999 and expects the market to grow to $6.9 billion by 2003.[10] Schools are better prepared than ever to access the Internet—90% of American schools are connected.[11]

Perhaps the greatest indicator that technology is not just a fad is the fact that more and more states have developed technology standards for students—35 states to date. Furthermore, a recent survey found that four states— Florida, North Carolina, Pennsylvania, and Virginia—are using state assessments to evaluate students' technology-related knowledge and skills.[12]

Conclusion

The publishers who understand that providing good content with an attractive design is only the beginning of the story will be the most competitive in the education marketplace of the future. Teachers are looking for instructional tools that are fully aligned to national, state, and local standards. Instructional materials must be factually accurate. They must have built-in assessments that help educators measure program effectiveness, and they must be delivered flexibly enough to accommodate changing current world events and issues. Finally, and perhaps most importantly, publishers must provide all of this information in a way that minimizes the time educators must spend learning and implementing the materials in the classroom. Though the push for account-ability is still building steam, publishers who are mindful of how their instructional tools fit into the landscape of accountability will ultimately be poised for success in tomorrow's education marketplace.

■

[1] Thompson, Scott. *"The Authentic Standards Movement and Its Evil Twin."* Phi Delta Kappan, 82 no. 5 (January 2001): 358. This article includes a well-balanced discussion of the standards-based reform movement.
[2] Education Week. *Quality Counts 2001: A Better Balance.* (January 11, 2001), www.edweek.com/sreports/qc01/.
[3] Education Week. *Quality Counts 2001: A Better Balance.* (January 11, 2001), www.edweek.com/sreports/qc01/.
[4] "Adoption states" refers to the 21 states that purchase or adopt instructional materials on a set schedule for use in the public schools in that state. If a textbook or instructional program passes an extensive review and makes the adoption list, the publisher is virtually guaranteed large profits in that state. The largest adoption states are California, Texas, and Florida.
[5] A rubric is a set of authoritative rules to give direction to the scoring of assessment tasks or activities.
[6] California Board of Education. *"Policy on Preparation for State Tests and the Standardized Testing and Reporting (STAR) Program. (September 2000).*
[7] Stateline.org is a Web site that reports on state and policy issues. Its report *"States Pay $400 Million for Tests in 2001"* is available at www.stateline.org/education.
[8] National Association of State Boards of Education. *"Cost of President's Testing Mandate Estimated As High As $7 Billion."* (25 April, 2001): www.nasbe.org
[9] "Open territory" states refers to states that do not purchase instructional materials through an adoption process. Many of these states purchase materials in all subjects every year.
[10] Merrill Lynch & Co. *The Knowledge Web.* (May 2000).
[11] Education Week. *Technology Counts '99: Building the Digital Curriculum* (September 1999), www.edweek.com/sreports/.
[12] Education Week. *Technology Counts 2001: The New Divides* (May 2001), www.edweek.com/sreports/.

■

About the Author

Aileen Hester Krassner *is the president of Publishers Resource Group, Inc. (PRG),* www.PRGaustin.com, *a full-service print- and technology-based instructional materials developer. PRG specializes in creating superb core, assessment, and ancillary instructional materials across all subject areas and grade levels and in languages other than English. PRG also provides marketing support services, such as correlations, fact checking, state customizations, market research, program evaluation, and more. Aileen can be reached at* akrassner@PRGaustin.com *or by calling (512) 328-7007.*

Applying Educational Technology Research to Help Differentiate Products in the Marketplace

by Jay Sivin-Kachala and Ellen Bialo

Educators have become increasingly sophisticated in their ability to recognize quality educational software products. Especially when districts or schools consider higher-cost Web-based software solutions, they often require competing products to be submitted for careful consideration by district or school technology committees.

Business and marketing professionals in the educational software industry can benefit from what research has to say about effective educational software design in two ways:

- They can use this knowledge to help develop product design requirements that will ensure their company's products will be well received by prospective customers.

- They can use research results to communicate more effectively about the positive design attributes of the software products they market.

In this article, we review several aspects of effective educational software design that can help differentiate products in the marketplace:

- Multimedia capabilities
- Feedback
- Cognitive strategies
- Embedded conceptual change strategies
- Instructional control strategies
- Navigation maps in hypermedia

You'll find that the discussion reflects both research and common sense.

Multimedia Capabilities

Research demonstrates the benefits of video, animation, spoken narration, and still graphics in software designs—when used strategically. Findings from research include the following:

- Video and animation can help students achieve learning goals when motion or action are involved in the skills or concepts to be learned.[1]

- Animation with spoken narration is generally more effective than animation accompanied by explanatory text.[2] However, when providing voiced narration, it is

best to avoid additional unnecessary background music and sound effects.[3]

- Still graphics can enhance learning when what is to be learned has a visual aspect but doesn't involve motion or action.[4]

Feedback

Feedback is the information a software program provides the learner in response to an action the learner takes. The student's action can come in the form of key strokes, mouse moves or clicks, or even inaction—waiting for several seconds without doing anything. (Some sophisticated programs analyze the *pattern* of the student's actions over time in order to determine what to provide next.) The feedback that the software program provides can be via text, sound, still graphics, animation, or video segments—or some combination of these.

Research suggests that feedback that explains why a student's response was incorrect is more effective than feedback that only indicates what was wrong.[5] Another form of feedback that has proven effective with older students is called *adaptive advisement*—based on the student's current level of performance, the program indicates the amount and/or sequence of instruction the student should complete in order to improve.[6] Quality educational software anticipates the likely errors a learner might make and is ready to provide easy-to-follow explanations and advice as to how to proceed—similar to what a good teacher would do.

Cognitive Strategies

Cognitive strategies are the patterns of thinking and approaches to learning that successful learners use. Effective cognitive strategies can be built in to educational software so that even students who have not developed these solid "habits of mind" can have a learning advantage.

Research points to the effectiveness of software that prompts and guides students through several cognitive strategies, including repeating and rehearsing the content to be learned, paraphrasing, outlining, *cognitive mapping* (drawing diagrams of the relationships among concepts),[7] structured note taking,[8] and generating students' own examples to illustrate the concept being learned.[9]

Embedded Conceptual Change Strategies

Conceptual change strategies are sequences of instruction that move students from their faulty preconceptions about a concept to a more accurate understanding of it. Students have been found to benefit academically from software with embedded conceptual change strategies in both science and social studies.[10]

One promising method of stimulating conceptual change[11] consists of the following steps:
- Assess students to identify individuals who have a flawed understanding of the concept.
- Provide a sequence of text-based activities focusing on clarifying the concept.
- Reassess students to identify who still has a flawed understanding of the concept.
- Provide a second sequence of activities to students whose understanding of the concept is still flawed. In this sequence of activities:
  - Represent information graphically,
  - Highlight key text points in different colors,
  - Prompt students to record information on a structured record sheet, and
  - Offer optional reading materials about conceptual change strategy.

Research suggests that when assessing students to determine their misconceptions, having students write justifications for their answers may be counterproductive. According to one group of researchers,[12] writing explanations of conceptual misunderstandings may actually serve to reinforce misconceptions.

Instructional Control Strategies

Research suggests that offering students some control over the rate of presentation, the amount of review, and the sequence of instruction in educational software often results in higher achievement and better student attitudes toward learning than having the software control all instructional decisions.[13]

The following instructional control strategies are supported by research:
- When offering students the option of reviewing an instructional presentation after making errors on assessment or practice items, regularly encourage students to make a self-assessment of their understanding of the concepts presented.[14]
- When giving students control over the pacing and sequence of instruction, a *FullMinus* strategy (providing a comprehensive set of possible instructional experiences and offering the option of bypassing some experiences) may result in superior achievement to a *LeanPlus* strategy (providing a basic program of instruction and enabling students to request additional instruction).[15]

Research suggests caution when designing an instructional control strategy for low-achieving students and students with little prior content knowledge. Such students have been shown to require more structure and instructional guidance than other students.[16]

Navigation Maps in Hypermedia

Research suggests that students using instructional hypermedia can benefit from a navigation map interface that shows the links among the different "pages" of information. Two designs have shown promise:
- Present a navigation map that uses connecting lines to indicate the links among the screens, but don't include text descriptions of the relationships.[17]
- Present a topics map in the form of a graphic representation of the hierarchical structure of the hypertext.[18]

Conclusion

It is, perhaps, surprising but true that many educational software publishers have to yet reflect more than a decade of educational technology research in their software designs. This presents a significant market opportunity for those professionals willing to consult the research on an ongoing basis, translate it into practical software design features, and then communicate to prospective customers about these features.

[1] M. Szabo and B. Poohkay, "An experimental study of animation, mathematics achievement, and attitude toward computer-assisted instruction," *Journal of Research on Computing in Education*, 28(3), 1996, 390-402.

[2] R. Moreno and R.E. Mayer, "Cognitive principles of multimedia learning: The role of modality and contiguity," *Journal of Educational Psychology*, 91(2), 1999, 358-368.

[3] R. Moreno and R.E. Mayer, "A coherence effect in multimedia learning: The case for minimizing irrelevant sounds in the design of multimedia instructional messages," *Journal of Educational Psychology*, 92(1), 2000, 117-125.

[4] D.M. Chun and J.L. Plass, "Effects of multimedia annotations on vocabulary acquisition," *The Modern Language Journal*, 80(ii), 1996, 183-198.

[5] N. Nagata, "Intelligent computer feedback for second language instruction," *The Modern Language Journal*, 77(3), 1993, 330-39.

[6] R.S. Santiago and J.R. Okey, "The effects of advisement and locus of control on achievement in learner-controlled instruction," paper presented at the 32nd International Conference of the Association for the Development of Computer-Based Instructional Systems in San Diego, CA (ERIC Document Reproduction Service No. ED. 330332), October-November 1990.

[7] R.H. Barba and L.J. Merchant, "The effects of embedding generative cognitive strategies in science software," *Journal of Computers in Mathematics and Science Teaching*, 10(1), Fall 1990, 59-65.

[8] D. Armel and S.A. Shrock, "The effects of required and optional computer-based note taking on achievement and instructional completion time," *Journal of Educational Computing Research*, 14(4), 1996, 329-344.

[9] A. Johnsey, G.R. Morrison, and S.M. Ross, "Using elaboration strategies training in computer-based instruction to promote generative learning," *Contemporary Educational Psychology*, 17, 1992, 125-135.

[10] M.S. Jensen, K.J. Wilcox, J.T. Hatch, and C. Somdahl, "A computer-assisted instruction unit on diffusion and osmosis with a conceptual change design," *Journal of Computers in Mathematics and Science Teaching*, 15(1/2), 1996, 49-64; H.J.A. Biemans and P.R.-J. Simons, "Contact-2: A computer-assisted instructional strategy for promoting conceptual change," *Instructional Science*, 24, 1996, 157-176.

[11] Biemans and Simons, 1996.

[12] Jensen, Wilcox, Hatch, and Somdahl, 1996.

[13] D.W. Dalton, "The effects of cooperative learning strategies on achievement and attitudes during interactive video," *Journal of Computer-Based Instruction*, 17(1), Winter 1990, 8-16; M.J. Lee, "Effects of different loci of instructional control on students' metacognition and cognition: Learner vs. program control," in *Proceedings of Selected Paper Presentations at the Convention of the Association for Educational Communications and Technology* (ERIC Document Reproduction Service No. 323938), February 1990; and R. Hannafin and H. Sullivan, "Learner control in full and lean CAI programs," *Educational Technology Research and Development*, 43(1), 1995, 19-30.

[14] Lee, February 1990.

[15] S. Crooks, J. Klein, H. Dwyer and E. Jones, "The effects of cooperative learning and learner control in computer-assisted instruction," paper presented at the Association for Educational Communications and Technology, Anaheim, CA, February 1995.

[16] A. Simsek, "The effects of learner control and group composition in computer-based cooperative learning," in *Proceedings of Selected Research and Development Presentations at the Convention of the Association for Educational Communications and Technology and Sponsored by the Research and Theory Division* (ERIC Document Reproduction Service No. ED362205), January 1993; C. Temiyakarn and S. Hooper, "The effects of cooperative learning and learner control on high and low achievers," in *Proceedings of Selected Research and Development Presentations at the Convention of the Association for Educational Communications and Technology and Sponsored by the Research and Theory Division* (ERIC Document Reproduction Service No. ED362208), January 1993; E.C. Shin, D.L. Schallert, and W.C. Savenye, "Effects of learner control, advisement, and prior knowledge on young students' learning in a hypertext environment," *Educational Technology, Research and Development*, 42(1), 1994, 33-46.

[17] E.E. Schroeder, "Navigating through the hypertext: Navigational technique, individual differences, and learning," in *Proceedings of the National Convention of the Association for Educational Communications and Technology and Sponsored by the Research and Theory*, Nashville, TN, February 1994.

[18] D.S. Niederhauser, D. Salmen, P. Skolmoski, and R.E. Reynolds, "The influence of navigational style on learning from hypertext," paper presented at the Annual Meeting of the American Educational Research Association, San Diego, CA, April 1998.

About the Authors

Jay Sivin-Kachala and **Ellen R. Bialo** *are vice president and president of Interactive Educational Systems Design (IESD), Inc., an educational technology consulting firm in New York City. IESD provides a variety of consulting services related to the marketing, development, and evaluation of educational software and multimedia products; conducts research in the field of education technology; develops print materials that supplement educational software; and trains educators in the use of technology. IESD's clients include software developers and publishers, technology hardware manufacturers, government agencies, non-profit institutions, and school districts. Sivin-Kachala and Bialo can be contacted at (212) 769-0909 or at* iesdinc@aol.com.

Supporting the Teacher Using Guides and Teacher Training

by Vicki Smith Bigham

Successful classroom use of educational products and services is greatly enhanced when teachers receive instruction regarding how to use them. This should be fairly obvious. And educators know the basic principles of teaching, including: break instruction into small pieces, repeat instruction, and allow for practice, among other instructional maxims. But when it comes to training and supporting teachers, all too often effective teaching practices are forgotten, and administrators and companies alike are too quick to adopt the thinking that if you put tools in the hands of teachers, they will figure out how to use them on their own.

What's Wrong with this Picture?

Teacher training and training guides are critical to teachers' appropriate and most effective use of your products and services. School administrators should want to support teachers' comfortable and effective use of products, and your company should want this as well, since effective use will lead to satisfied customers and additional sales in the future.

The National Staff Development Council insists on the importance of training to support teachers in comfortably and effectively using new products.. They further recommend that this kind of support be provided on an ongoing basis. Further, NSDC contrasts "sit and get" sessions where teachers passively learn from those considered experts with staff development that "...includes high-quality training programs with intensive follow-up and support, but also other growth-promoting processes...."

The bottom line is that the importance of professional development should not be underestimated. Several reports substantiating this position can be found on the Web at www.nsdc.org. In particular, the following two recent reports in the specific area of technology-based products illustrate the growing evidence in support of the need for teacher training:

• *Does It Compute?* This is perhaps the first study to document the relationships between student use of technology and higher scores on a national standardized test. The strongest message in this study, though, is the vital importance of professional development.

• *The CEO Forum's 1998 STaR Report* focused on professional development. The message for administrators and teachers is a call to establish long-term technology related professional development plans and proficiency standards. The report stresses that every professional development program should integrate technology as a part of all training components.

Teachers must have ongoing professional development that allows them to experiment with products and services, share best (and worst!) practices, review exemplars of student work, and deal individually and in networks of peers with their conflicts, successes, and disappointments. This is critical for their work with students as well as for their self-esteem and personal growth; and it's also critical in helping your company to get a good return on its development investment and secure its prospects for subsequent sales.

Know Your Audience

So, training is important—for teachers' professional growth and for their successful use of your products and services. But all too many training sessions and guides seem to demonstrate how much is not known or understood about teachers and how they work and what matters to them. If you want to be prepared and successful in delivering training, don't rely on just knowing your content. Whether you are providing training through workshops or with guides, you need to know your audience, too. And you need to let them know that you understand what life is really like within the four walls of their classrooms.

Investigate your audience and focus your presentation or materials on their priorities. Demonstrate how the ideas, plans, and tools that are the focus of your training materials address and support their priorities. Adjust your language according to whether you are presenting for elementary teachers, secondary teachers, special needs teachers, or other kinds of educator audiences.

Maximize the Utility of Your Visuals

Visuals can either add to or detract from training. They are necessary and should be interesting and supportive of points and messages you are making. Mix the visual media you incorporate into your training or training materials and, for face-to-face training workshops, always test your visuals in advance.

For visuals in training, some simple reminders are in order: preview them ahead of time; use them to focus trainees on key points; and hold trainees accountable for some kind of follow-up assignment after viewing.

Teachers like flip charts, and they can be useful training tools in workshop scenarios. They provide an accurate follow-up document of information and a written record of suggestions and ideas. Post them on the walls for reference and to let the trainees see evidence of their ideas and efforts. Use different colors and sizes of markers. But use flip charts only with smaller audiences.

For slides, whether they are transparencies or electronic ones, such as for PowerPoint:

- Limit the number of words per slide, and use large, easy-to-read fonts—it is a good idea to try to make only one point per visual.

- Use graphics for interest and to appeal to visual learners.

- Turn off the projector or move to a blank slide when you are talking about something not directly related to the current slide.

- Reveal relevant information on slides as you speak.

- Selectively use different colors or fonts to make points—but don't overdo it!

- Use upper and lower case lettering.

- Allow time for trainees to read the material on a slide before you speak.

No matter what visual tools you use for in-person training, it is critical to consider your audience to determine the formality of your visuals.

Carry these strategies over into your development of training guides, too. Use templates and consistent formats that make it easy for the teacher to identify the objectives and intended audience for an activity or product, clear steps for accomplishing the task, and the materials needed to do so. Provide examples that relate to themes that are topical for the grade level of the materials. Where reasonable, suggest ways to build a home-school connection. Make liberal but appropriate use of graphics, charts, icons, and other visual images not only to make the pages more visually appealing, but also to cue the eye towards key components, such as content areas addressed or quick tips.

For training workshops or development of guides, the rule of thumb is *break it down*. Break tasks and activities into small, concrete steps. Be clear and provide

---

TIPS FOR SUCCESSFUL TRAINING

For leader-led, in-person training sessions, consider the following suggestions:

- Think critically about what teachers are likely to know prior to the presentation. Build on that knowledge, providing new information that is meaningful to their needs. Avoid telling them what they already know.

- Tie your presentation to educational goals that are expressed by the teachers themselves, referencing how your product or service can help them achieve those goals.

- Connect with your audience. When they pose questions or issues, write them down—on your computer screen, on a flip chart, or on a notepad for your own reference. As you make your presentation, refer to each at appropriate times and reference them to demonstrate your having listened to teachers' input.

- Communicate a strong vision supported by an achievable strategy. Encourage teachers to build on past successes and learn from mistakes as they follow you toward achieving that vision.

- Be concise and clear in delivering your message. The teachers are offering their time to learn your ideas, strategies, and suggestions. They need to perceive the time spent as a wise investment. As a general rule, before you begin each topic presentation consider three points you most want them to retain from your presentation—stay focused on those messages.

- Provide examples or scenarios that illustrate the points you are conveying, along with relevant research and observations or experiences that support your statements.

- Respond positively to all questions. Teachers will draw on their knowledge and experiences to assess the validity and rationale for your ideas and suggestions.

- Celebrate and recognize accomplishments already made among your teacher trainees and in their schools. These might be in articulating vision, creating a plan, sharing a success story from a classroom, showcasing a sample of student work, and so forth. Encourage their sharing and help validate their successes.

examples. Allow time for practice, or suggest methods for practicing skills applying them in the classroom. To achieve these goals, don't be bound by traditional book-based forms. Printed training materials can expand beyond the common booklet to include note cards with a different activity on each, reproducible 2-sided tasks or activities to try, and other similar easy-to-digest formats.

Use visuals to support the content you have to share: this will dramatically increase the impact of your message. Studies show that telling, when used alone, results in 70% recall 3 hours later, and only 10% recall 3 days later. Showing, when used alone, results in 72% recall 3 hours later and 20% recall 3 days later. But a blend of telling and showing results in 85% recall 3 hours later and 65% recall 3 days later.

The Six P's

When planning face-to-face training workshops in schools, you will do well to remember the Six P's: *P*roper *P*reparation and *P*ractice *P*revent *P*oor *P*erformance. As you prepare, keep the following ideas in mind:

1. ***Identify needs.*** Your needs, which might include such things as how you want the room arranged; the needs of your teacher audience, which include considerations to make them comfortable; and the needs of administrators regarding what they want to be accomplished in the session. Don't make the mistake of letting a training session be about your goals alone.

2. ***Learn about your attendees.*** What knowledge are they coming in with? What are their interests and attitudes? What is their preferred time for training (e.g., what time of day or, of week, or of year, what length of sessions, etc.). Be realistic about the objectives for a specific training session. What do teachers need to know?

3. ***Plan your approach to accomplish the objectives.*** Be sure to start on time and work to create a sense of anticipation. If teachers in the session do not know one another, consider an ice-breaker to help them meet one another.

4. ***Plan the training.*** Develop an outline, if that matches your style. Consider what strategies will work best (i.e., working individually or in pairs,

engaging in hands-on activities, incorporating repetition to hammer home key points, etc.). What can you reasonably accomplish in the time you have?

5. ***Plan the application.*** Share with teachers ways they might use their new skills in their classrooms, and help them set goals for their use of new skills. Consider making note cards available during the training and invite teachers to write down their questions to give to you at a break. It may be easier for some of them to use this method than to ask questions in front of the group.

6. ***Have teachers summarize the new skills they have learned.*** They should verbalize or write down an account of the new ideas they have absorbed.

7. ***Physically prepare for the workshop.*** Organize materials. Prepare any necessary publicity or notices. Prepare attractive handouts. And be there early to set up.

Focus on Students and Learning Outcomes—Not on Products and Services

Forget the hype about your product and its features—the jazziest new technology, the end-all tool that will improve the teacher's life. What teachers care about is students and learning. Focus on that. This approach will also help you hone in on the important messages you need to deliver about your products and services. Train teachers with an emphasis on how what they are learning will contribute to improved learner outcomes. Whether you are presenting a manipulative, an online service, an art product, a workbook, or any other educational product, focusing on how it will improve teaching and learning is the key.

Special Needs of Adult Learners

It has been said, "You can lead a course with 'you oughta', but you can't make 'em think!" If your company has a team of people very competent in developing instructional content for students, it may seem an easy task to develop learning content for adults. This is not necessarily true. There are two basic but important concepts of adult learning that are important to consider along with your understanding of the classroom environment and teachers' priorities:

- ***Adults are more concerned than are children about time.*** Teachers have unavoidable time commitments, due to their jobs and their personal lives. They may be tired when they are in your workshop. They may not have had a choice regarding their attendance. They therefore need to perceive time spent in training as a worthwhile investment. And they need your help in being motivated.

- *Adults have more experiences and a richer base of knowledge upon which to draw than do children—and therefore more "unlearning" to do as they abandon old habits and procedures.* Solicit sharing of these experiences in training, and use analogies, similes, and metaphors that work. Allow for choices, discussion, role-playing, group projects, and other similar strategies. Share any experiences or personal anecdotes or frustrations with teaching you have had with trainees. It will contribute to their heeding your suggestions and ideas.

Marketing Your Training Products and Services

Training is the budget item many experts believe is most critical to a school's ability to achieve its instructional goals—but it is often the most ignored and under-funded budget item. Why? As stated at the beginning of this article, there is a tendency to believe that putting products and services into the hands of talented teachers will naturally cause them to make the best use of them. But if teachers don't have time to learn all of the features of a product or to consider a variety of ways to use it, they will not get the most out of the investment the school has made and will not make use of the features your development energies and monies have gone to create.

Be aware that from a cost-planning perspective, administrators must look at the costs of trainers, materials, and substitutes if training is conducted during the school day. It will be appreciated if your training suggestions include creative ways to accomplish ongoing support (e.g., strategies for teachers to support one another, each

becoming an expert on small pieces of what all are expected to know; suggestions for maximizing planning time; models for peer sharing of successful product use; and other support vehicles). Perhaps your firm can provide ongoing support through online or other resources. Training and training guides should provide your best ideas for supporting the ongoing growth of teachers in using your products and services.

Craft your messages about training workshops and guides to inspire change and motivate interest. Here are some to try: "Keep your skills in...up to date." or "Learn the latest about...." or "Come to this workshop and get your hands on...." Statements such as these appeal to teachers' desire for knowledge and mastery and also to their interest in novelty and sensory stimulation. Of course, another motivator for teachers is the satisfaction of seeing students' learning improve.

Schools often use the terms "in-service education," "teacher training," "staff development," and "professional development" interchangeably. However, some of these labels may have special meaning to particular groups or individuals in a school system. Check this out with the market you are addressing.

Conclusion

As Oliver Wendell Holmes said so well, "a mind stretched to a new idea never goes back to its original dimensions." Providing teacher training, whether via face-to-face interactions or in printed or media-based guides, is a wonderful opportunity for you to support the professionalism and professional growth of teachers and to provide resources and strategies to help teachers enhance their work with students. It will be equally effective in ensuring that teachers make the best use of your company's products, enabling you to retain satisfied customers and attract new ones.

About the Author

Vicki Smith Bigham *is managing partner of Bigham Technology Solutions, a Houston-based consulting company working with schools and with organizations developing for and selling to the educational technology market. Vicki has over 25 years experience in public and private school education as a teacher, software developer, school administrator, university professor, and consultant. In 15 years of consulting, she has managed a variety of product development, training, meeting planning, and marketing projects. Contact her at* bighamv@aol.com *or (281) 866-9728.*

Developing Online Education Products

by Corey E. Brady

Educational product development for the Web is still in its infancy as a discipline. But already companies have discovered many of the new operational competencies that the medium requires—new employee skill sets, new productivity and product management tools, and new approaches to design, quality control, and using customer feedback.

The new competencies required extend beyond operational change, however, to affect management philosophy. With very little historic data to guide them, development managers face the challenge of preparing their organizations psychologically and culturally to handle the unique demands of producing products for the Web.

This article emphasizes the management issues in "moving to the Web" over the related operational issues. This is not because the details of Web strategy are unimportant or separated from management philosophy. Rather, the concern is that fundamental management issues can be overlooked, while most operational challenges will quickly call attention to themselves in practice. For instance, many members of a development team will be quick to identify operational differences between the Web and the world of software such as the following:

- Web sites are built of thousands of small files; hence product maintenance and QA balloon in both importance and difficulty.

- Incremental publishing removes the discipline of the single "release date," but developers and products still need closure, and users still need notice about new features.

- Web browser releases can occur more than twice as frequently as operating system releases, and the support for advanced functionality is more tenuous, making it more risky to pursue innovative product features.

All Web enterprises need to confront these and many other concerns. The operational solutions and policies adopted can be expensive and complex, but they are at least concrete, and their effectiveness can be measured. In contrast, reinventing a development team for the Web demands philosophical changes that may be less visible and harder to test. There is little history to refer to, and the online medium itself is undergoing continual redefinition.

To address these subtler challenges, managers of e-learning companies can rely on their instincts; but they will be even better served if they adopt creative ways of benefiting from ideas and "best practices" in fields other than their own. One such approach is analogy, which can allow managers to widen the scope of their search for historical comparisons. To illustrate, this article will focus on two comparative examples:

- first, an analogy across industries, comparing Web development for education and Web development for e-commerce.

- second, analogies within a single industry, comparing elements of educational efforts of various kinds: the functionality of educational products; the workings of product development organizations; and the dynamics of classroom teaching.

E-Learning and E-Commerce

There are certainly many concrete, tactical tips and lessons one can pick up by observing e-business practice outside of education. For example, e-learning companies should be certain to learn about scalability, basic design, technology infrastructures, and so forth, from Web successes and failures outside of education.

But the dot com experience should be mined for more subtle lessons as well—education companies should use it in coming to understand the Internet as a developing medium, with emerging use patterns and standards of interface and etiquette, as well as emerging business models and regulatory parameters. As a rough first step in this effort, consider some analogies between the principal issues facing e-learning and e-commerce enterprises.

The following table indicates one way of comparing features of e-commerce sites or solutions, with features that might be included in educational products and services.

Many educators may find it offensive to compare learning with commerce. But an intriguing relationship of analogy between the two is encoded in our very language. (We say we "don't buy" arguments that we think are

E-COMMERCE	E-LEARNING
Primary Objective: The Purchase.	Primary Objective: The Meaningful Learning Event.
Design Directive: facilitate buying, at any point in the user's experience of the site.	Analogous Directive: facilitate focused learning at any point in the use of the site.
Commerce Feature: provide feedback on purchase (e.g., instant confirmation emails and printable invoices).	Analogous Feature: provide feedback on learning (e.g., instant scoring and printable "report cards").
Site Feature: personalization, interface customization.	Analogous Feature: management and tracking system that tailors the learning experience.
Critical Goal: motivate the add-on purchase (e.g., sell accessories).	Analogous Goal: instill the desire to "find out more" and extend the learning event.
Differentiating Feature: publishing customer reviews.	Analogous Features: providing peer help, facilitating study groups, or promoting teacher community tie-ins.
Tactic: create affiliate programs.	Analogous Tactic: provide correlations to standards, textbooks, or other relevant learning contexts.
Marketing Tactic: provide coupons or free offers.	Analogous Tactic: create curriculum connections with real world problems or current events.
Key Tool: shopping cart, with "one-click purchasing."	Analogous Tool: structured means of planning the learning event for students, with an easy mechanism for creating student assignments.

flawed, for example; and on more abstract levels we talk about the "marketplace" of ideas, and about learning "gains," the "acquisition" of knowledge, and students' "investment" in their education.) So, while the two activities may be very different in spirit, it may be provocative to pursue analogies between them.

For a simple example, consider the first pairing above, between the e-commerce directive to "Facilitate buying at any point" on the site, and a proposed e-learning directive to "facilitate focused learning at any point." Starting from this analogy might provide a means of critically approaching site design and analysis. There are numerous lampooned examples of e-commerce sites that have "dropped the ball" in this way, losing potential customers because of interface gaffs. If teachable moments can be missed just as sellable moments can (and educators will tell you that they can), then this analogy might provide us a new lens through which to examine a site that is in development or being user tested.

Moreover, the analogy can provide ideas for metrics or measurement strategies. For example, a Web reference site might measure search-to-download click-through rates with strategies borrowed from e-commerce sites that measure click-throughs between shopping and purchase. The massive e-business development efforts of the recent past have generated fantastic tools and techniques for measuring the performance of Web sites, so the difficult questions for e-learning companies are likely to be of the form, "What should we measure?" rather than, "How can we measure it?"

The insights gained by analogical thinking may be common sense at one level, but developers and managers often need tools to help them move from the technical details of Web production to the level of usability and interactive design.

As some of the features described in the right-hand column of the table above are developed by online education providers, the lessons learned from e-commerce successes and failures with the analogous features on the left-hand side can be put to good use. To take just one more example from the table, Web publishers seeking to design part of a site that encourages "lateral" or cross-curricular learning should consider the design techniques and experiences of e-business in promoting add-on sales of products.

Great Products, Great Teaching, and Great Organizations

If the first section of this article dealt with what e-learning can gain by comparisons *across* industries with other online efforts, the second section examines how analogical thinking *within* the framework of education can help to identify key issues. The central premise of this section is that the processes and workers that create great educational materials find analogies in the workings of the great educational materials themselves, as well as in the "best practices" of great classroom teaching.

Part of the reason this is true is that all Web-oriented organizations need to be able to *learn* efficiently as organizations—coordinating and adapting their various resources of talent to fit the organization's emerging understanding of the medium and its core competencies within that field of action.

This bears repeating: all Web-oriented organizations need to be wired for learning and evolution (like students). For startups, the need for adaptive development is obvious. But the capacity to adapt may be even more important for organizations that have experience (and habits) in developing for other media. One should never assume that "product is product," or that a simple "port" of a successful networked application is possible. A change in medium or delivery technology can radically alter the user experience and use patterns of even the most familiar and well-understood content. The cell phone provides a clear illustration of the principle: while most users would consider the "content" delivered by a cell phone to be equivalent to that received over a land line, what a profound change has been produced in the application and user experience of that content!

To see how the learning paradigm might provide insight for Internet education companies, consider a critical product design challenge—the Web's unique pressure on coordinating dynamic and interactive on-screen elements. The best online learning products integrate visual, verbal, interactive, and technical dimensions elegantly, to create a harmonious interface and user experience. The lack of some of these aspects, or an imperfect orchestration of them, can spell failure for products that are moving to the Web from other media, or for products produced by development teams new to the Internet.

Thinking analogically about this general issue, two lines of thought emerge. First, it becomes evident that this interoperation among design elements is in some ways similar to a teacher's presenting material to activate multiple learning styles and aptitudes in students. While rather obvious, this comparison can help developers to keep a focus on the user experience and can guide strategic decisions about layout and design.

A second line of thought emerges when the product issue is reconceived as an organizational one. Just as successful products facilitate interaction of on-screen elements, so successful development organizations benefit from cross-fertilization and interoperation between the departments that build these elements. Whereas in more mature media, departments can operate more independently, relying on conventions for interaction between design elements, Web design must be total, organic, and emergent. Collaborative development is inescapable. (Moreover, like collaborative teaching and learning, it's incredibly fulfilling, creative, and fun!) The more balanced the team and its contributions to the overall product design, the more outstanding the product.

On a professional level as a manager, too, it is quite powerful to recognize the parallelism between:

1. the issues that face educators, and

2. the issues that face managers of education companies.

Once appreciated, this parallel allows one to read John Dewey, Howard Gardner, or the *SIIA Effectiveness Report*, for example, as commentaries on organizational dynamics of e-learning companies. It also allows one to replace the potential emptiness of ideas like creating a "good" corporate culture, with more substantive and productive ways of evaluating the work environment (e.g., "Does our company learn collectively?" "Do we allow for appropriate expression and contributions from employees?" or "Do we appropriately and efficiently employ free discourse and discussion?") These can become real, strategic questions, rather than rhetorical ones, in the corporation as in the classroom.

Complicating an Analogy: Points of Contrast

To this point, the discussion has explored how analogies can suggest provocative *similarities* between best practices in different realms. However, an analogy can be equally effective as a tool for highlighting critical *contrasts* between the terms it places side by side. Finally, then, consider just one of the red flags that is raised in the first analogy considered above, where e-learning is considered in light of e-commerce.

Unlike shopping, learning is a deep, reflective activity that requires a calm user in a focused state of mind. For this reason, many of the best practices of Web design from other industries are not applicable in the context of Web-delivered education.

In particular, the kind of "literacy" that the broader Internet promotes is not the kind that educators require. Even the most sober Web experiences outside of education are centered on grabbing data and information, rather than producing and absorbing knowledge. A developer should consider how often he or she sits in front of a Web browser with a "note taking" attitude or with the possibility in mind that they may have a true "eureka moment" while online. The browsing mode is characterized by low investment and low focus. But as every educator knows, student investment and focus are critical ingredients of the teachable condition. The developer's challenge in products, and in supporting services such as teacher training, print and electronic ancillaries, and so forth, is to identify and promote an alternative, even an *opposite* attitude, that will allow the product to succeed.

Here is where the analogy can help out. When a development team seeks to establish a user experience that is counter to emerging conventions, it is particularly critical that the team study those conventions closely. A great deal of media savvy will be required when developers seek to slow student-users down at points critical to learning. The techniques in e-commerce that promote the opposite effects in buyer-users can be turned on their heads.

Conclusion: Basic Questions, High Stakes

In these first years of Web-based learning, some of the most important questions that e-learning companies face will be the most basic ones. Managers of these companies should resist the temptation to focus solely on operational issues; they should also spend energies "pulling the camera back" to consider issues of the online medium itself.

This approach is critical not only to the success of individual enterprises, but also to the success of Internet education as a whole. The early stages of the Web's development are witnessing the formation of "genre expectations" that its audiences will bring to bear on all future productions in that medium. As with all media, there will be a period in which the audience is uncertain about how to "read" what it finds on the Web, but this period will be short. After that period of uncertainty closes, it will be very hard to break through genre expectations to use the medium in a new way. (A recent example of this genre-defining process is television, where educators also initially saw the potential for powerful applications to learning. Now, however, viewers come to their TV's with limited expectations of experiencing transformative educational events. They can be surprised of course, but programs have to work extraordinarily hard to shake viewers out of their attitudes toward the medium as fundamentally non-educational or even anti-educational.) It's inspiring (and sometimes terrifying) to realize that the Web as an educational medium is developing its audience's expectations, semi-permanently, right now.

Now is the time when Internet users will be open to the idea of true learning (knowledge production) on the Web, rather than simply data-transmitting (information exchange). But if the education industry fails to deliver on this potential, users will grow more and more jaded in the face of the information-centered uses of the Web outside of the sphere of education. Genre expectations will solidify, and the opportunity for radical innovation will fade.

By analogy, and for the same reasons, now is the time when larger corporations will be open to ideas for different development models in their Internet products divisions. Generative development environments have a limited time to prove themselves against more formulaic approaches to creating products, but unless they do prove themselves, corporations' expectations will solidify, and the opportunity for radical organizational innovation will fade.

∎

[1] A general caveat: while analogies can be very compelling and powerful tools, they are much better for identifying important questions than for providing complete or easy answers to those questions. In the discussion that follows, it's vital to keep in mind that it is almost impossible to deduce concrete best practices in one realm by studying case histories in another.

[2] Good places to start here are useit.com, creativegood.com, and webword.com, along with any of Jakob Nielsen's articles (including his "Top Ten Mistakes of Web Design" which is still relevant after over five years).

[3] Other surprising and even more potentially offensive analogies have also proved illuminating or effective. For example, some educators have described education in terms of a war upon ignorance and used the analogy to explain or investigate key educational issues.

[4] In some ways, education publishers may actually have more license than e-commerce companies. Students and parents have fewer objections to teaching strategies that involve tricking students into learning than consumers do about deceptive commercial practices. Ironically, this may provide education sites a degree of freedom at the design level that is not available to e-commerce sites.

[5] Again, the newness of the online medium gives this kind of thinking a power that it may not have outside of the Web. In book publishing, for example, the conventions of reading and of page and facing layout are established enough that while analogical thinking may be of academic interest, it is less likely to point insightfully to overlooked principles of design.

[6] Incidentally, this is not the same as call for generalists. The other side of the collaboration coin is a call for individual technical know-how. Web developers across the board should be encouraged to extend the detailed technical knowledge they have of their piece of the product puzzle. In particular, while desktop application developers can allow for a division of labor between the "what" of what the screen will display and the "how" of how this will be accomplished, new media environments collapse these two in the face of unexplored possibilities concerning both what and how. For example, content authors should understand as much as possible about HTML and JavaScript, graphics artists about image compression, Java programmers about the workings of various virtual machines, and Web and database programmers about server communications, configurations, and performance. That way, cross-departmental collaboration can be ad hoc as well as formal, as most members of each department will be able to speak intelligently about the activities and capabilities of their department.

[7] Consider Dewey's "Progressive Education and the Science of Education" or Gardner's The Unschooled Mind, for instance, in this respect.

∎

About the Author

Corey Brady *is an educator and a developer of education materials that use Web and network technologies effectively. As an instructional designer and programmer, and later as chief education officer and chief operating officer, Corey helped to conceive, create, and manage the online mathematics curriculum products of Boxer Learning, Inc, which can be found at* www.boxermath.com. *He is now with Texas Instruments, as manager of product strategy for the TI-Navigator networked classroom solution. Corey can be reached at* cbrady@ti.com, *and he encourages readers of this article to provide insights and/or critiques via email.*

Multimedia Product Development: What Educators Really Want

by Gail Hartman

Remember way back in 1984 when "multimedia" was synonymous with "floppy disk?" Today, of course, multimedia includes any and all applications that combine and integrate text, graphics, video, and sound. Delivery of multimedia in K-12 classrooms includes such formats as CD-ROMs, the Internet, CD/Web hybrids, videodiscs, laserdiscs, distance learning, video conferencing, and the ever-evolving handheld PDAs and e-books.

But no matter how it's delivered, it's still multimedia, and educators want and expect certain things when selecting it for their schools. So what makes an ideal multimedia product? What do educators *really* want and need? This article discusses some of the most common educational and technical elements that educators identify as essential in exemplary multimedia.

Educational Issues: Different Strokes

Every school district in every state buys multimedia for different reasons. Some want it only for remediation and others only for enrichment. Some want products that empower students to create their own multimedia, and others want only drill and practice. Some schools have computers in each classroom, others only in a lab or library.

There are as many different types of multimedia products on the K-12 market as there are educational philosophies and instructional methods, and schools choose those best suited to their own educational styles.

Addressing Different Learning and Teaching Styles

It's a basic and generally accepted fact that every student learns differently and at a different pace. The best multimedia products therefore enable students to move through them at their own pace, providing both visual and auditory cues to address different learning modalities. Beyond self-paced features, however, the instructional approaches that are dominant in the classroom play a significant role in determining the most appropriate multimedia products. There are primarily two camps out there: those educators who support a traditional, teacher-centered approach, and those who support a student- or learner-centered approach.

Teacher-Centered Classrooms

In a teacher-centered classroom, the teacher disseminates all or most information through lecture, textbooks, workbooks, and/or software. Students work alone most of the time, sitting at desks or in front of computers. Subject areas are often taught separately, in assigned slots of time (i.e., 45 minutes of math, then 45 minutes of geography). Assessment is also traditional, relying primarily on pre- and post-tests scored on an A-F letter grade scale.

Teacher-centered classrooms often purchase drill-and-practice, subject-focused, and/or encyclopedia products. Multimedia that focuses on critical thinking and problem solving is often purchased only for use in students' "free time" or with gifted students. Teacher-centered classrooms also purchase many "teacher tool" products to help teachers generate such things as crossword puzzles, worksheets and blackline masters, calendars, quizzes and tests, spreadsheets, slideshow presentations, report card templates, flash cards, and gradebooks.

Learner-Centered Classrooms

In the learner-centered classroom, the teacher's role is more that of a facilitator or guide, steering students to construct their own knowledge and understanding of the world. Students in these "constructivist" classrooms often work collaboratively and are challenged to use "higher-order thinking" as they analyze and synthesize information. Content areas are blended as often as possible instead of being taught in isolation. Teachers may embrace alternative assessment tools (in place of, or in addition to traditional tests and grading systems), or holistic assessments (such as portfolio and performance assessments).

Learner-centered schools often purchase multimedia products that focus on critical thinking and problem solving (e.g., simulations), and that help students make connections to the real world through role-playing environments. They look for multimedia that provide real resources for research, reading, and writing (e.g., concept map tools, online databases, and geographic information systems). Since discovery, experimentation, and communication are key to learner-centered classrooms, multimedia that encourages students to work together or that provides ways for them to communicate with peers and experts outside their classrooms is also highly desired. Such multimedia includes authoring tools, virtual field trips, online science "probeware," Web site building tools, and server-based collaborative environments. Teachers in these classrooms also often purchase electronic portfolios to keep track of students' academic, emotional, and social growth.

Content

It goes without saying that educators want all multimedia products to contain the highest quality content that will enrich, complement, and supplement their existing curricula. They expect highly motivating multimedia to increase student interest, attention, and retention.

Educators look for content without gender, ethnic, or racial biases. Many want multimedia built around common thematic units (e.g., colonial America or weather), or programs that provide opportunities for collaboration among students and/or that provide different views and perspectives on an issue so that students learn to approach subject matter in ways that are rarely found in textbooks.

Thus, content is much more than just factual and descriptive information. In order to be successful in the classroom, content must be based on a real understanding of schools' curricular emphases, how children learn, and how classrooms really work. Educators are quick to dismiss content that fails in any of these respects. "When evaluating a multimedia product for my school," notes one New York high school media specialist, "I can tell within the first minute of playing with it whether or not it was created by people who ever actually taught in a classroom."

> " In order to be successful in the classroom, content must be based on a real understanding of schools' curricular emphases, how children learn, and how classrooms really work. Educators are quick to dismiss content that fails in any of these respects. "

ESL and Bilingual Education

More and more, teachers across the country are looking for multimedia that meets the needs of ESL or bilingual students. One California technology coordinator, who works with a large ESL student population, tells of a very popular student authoring tool that takes the first step toward being a true bilingual product but that leaves the task unfinished. "Students can toggle the menus to read them in Spanish," she says, "but the Help screens are only in English, and the built-in word processor doesn't even let the kids type accent marks or tildes! It's as if the publisher started to create a real bilingual product and then just stopped mid-way."

In addition to being educationally sound and free of cultural stereotypes, educators expect ESL and bilingual programs to include such things as true ESL/bilingual text and audio, spell checkers, help screens, menus, and built-in word processors.

Teacher's Guide and Classroom Activities

Teachers want supplemental guides (in hard copy and/or PDF format) that include technical information—"… written by humans, not techies: we can tell the difference!" notes one Texas elementary school teacher—and suggested classroom activities that complement the electronic content, enabling students to work both on and away from the computer.

The best supplemental classroom activities are written so that teachers can adjust them to fit their own curricular requirements, their students' skill levels, and class schedule constraints. Supplemental activities should also include interdisciplinary connections so that teachers can learn how to cross and blend content areas in natural ways.

Connections to the Web

Educators also want recommendations and/or live links to quality, pre-screened Web sites that help extend the product's content and that will be around for a while. Teachers just don't have the time to peruse the Net for "safe" sites that contain excellent content, written at the appropriate grade level. Teachers also expect multimedia publishers' Web sites to keep their links updated at all times.

Standards Alignment

Aligning multimedia and supplemental products to educational standards was once considered an added bonus; it is now considered mandatory if the product will be used in K-12 schools. All public schools adhere to state and/or national educational standards for language arts, math, science, and social studies. Most follow state (not national) standards for geography and for the arts (i.e., music, dance, theatre, and the visual arts). Additionally, most schools now seek to follow some set of technology standards. Although adherence is not mandatory, The *National Educational Technology Standards for Students* (NETS)[1] are being used quite frequently. Some school district technology coordinators are also crafting their own technology standards for their individual schools.

Assessment

The pendulum of educational pedagogy never fails to swing one way one year, and then the other way the next. The pendulum swung about as far as it could toward standards-based education. While some educators are cheering the testing frenzy that goes along with it, others fear that "...state tests are overshadowing the standards they were designed to measure and could be encouraging undesirable practices in schools."[2] This major controversy won't end any time soon, experts predict.

But whether or not a school lives and breathes standardized tests, all schools know that some form of regular and balanced assessment is critical to continuous measurement of students' growth and progress. Some multimedia has built-in assessment, or scoring/record-keeping functions, including such things as pre- and post-tests and the ability to track how long a student works at a task or how many attempts are made before getting the correct answer. Some multimedia products offer rubrics of learning objectives for teachers to print and complete off-line.

Since teacher- and learner-centered classrooms embrace different types of assessment as described above, many publishers, within their off-line supplemental materials, wisely try to address all variants by offering a wide range of suggestions for traditional and alternative assessment.

Training and Technical Support

The US Department of Education reports that almost "two-thirds of all teachers feel they are not at all prepared or only somewhat prepared to use technology in their teaching."[3] And Merrill Lynch finds that, "almost two-thirds of teachers (65 percent) had never used a computer before being introduced to one in the classroom." The report goes on to say, "These teachers need basic technology training, especially those who are receiving computers and using the Internet in their classrooms for the first time."[4] Many multimedia publishers are addressing this enormous lack of technology-trained teachers by offering training for their products. Some conduct a basic "how to" session for the technology coordinator who then trains the teachers. Others provide more lengthy, customized training, working alongside teachers "in the trenches" and helping them determine the best ways to integrate programs with their own curricula. On-line training, using "virtual workshops," is another option.

In addition to training, teachers also expect toll-free technical support from a staff that can really troubleshoot and fix problems. Far too often, teachers report long wait times on a long distance toll call that eventually leads to a conversation with an operator who has never used the product.

Technical Issues

If teachers acquire new multimedia that requires them and their students to focus on learning the technology instead of the content, they will consistently abandon the product.[5]

Educators want multimedia that is intuitive and easy for students, as well as adults, to learn and navigate through right out of the box or upon first landing on a Web site. They want computer environments that are easy to handle by first-time users and experienced users alike.

GUI Design

A product's graphical user interface (GUI) must contain the following types of elements to be deemed user-friendly in schools:

- Simple, uncluttered screens.
- Age-appropriate graphics that enhance the content, rather than interfering with it.
- Fonts, styles, sizes, and colors that are easy to read.
- Concise text that pays attention to grammar and punctuation and that avoids slang.
- Dialog boxes that have titles so the user knows what the box is meant for and that always offer a way out (i.e., a Cancel button).
- Background and foreground screen colors that aren't too bright or too dark.
- Menus (e.g., drop-down, cascading) that are grouped logically and structured so they make sense, even to the novice.
- Click-and-drag features with visual cues (e.g., a cursor that changes shape, icons that change appearance). While this is most critical for early learning programs, it is a design plus for all education users.
- Shortcut navigation keys.
- Icons that clearly represent what they're meant to represent!
- On-line help (hypertext) systems that actually help users to get answers to their questions easily.

Navigation

Navigation should be seamless. On CDs, for instance, there should be more than one way to move around (e.g., via icons and menus). Web sites should be easy to navigate from any page. All links within and outside the site should work smoothly, all the time. Outside links should open within the site, within a new browser window, or enable students to easily jump back to the page they left, using the browser's Back button or Home page icons/links.

Audio

Audio must sound crisp and clear and must serve to enhance learning. Narrated text should be spoken clearly and slowly enough so that the user can understand what is being said. Often, developers of early learning programs hire children as their audio talent. While this can significantly enhance the product, giving it a fun "kid" feel, it can also hurt the product if the children's speech is slurred or spoken too quickly.

Volume control (as well as the ability to turn off audio completely) is a crucial feature that some multimedia developers overlook. The result is that in some schools, excellent products remain untouched because the schools' computers have no headphones and are located in a central area, like the library. Without volume controls, students can't use the product without disturbing others.

Video

Video clips can make a product come alive, but they must play smoothly, each and every time. Students should be able to pause or stop the video in mid-play without causing the program to crash. Historical video clips are hugely popular because they are one way to bring primary sources into the classroom, but some publishers' Web sites link to other sites that have very slow servers, making the clips virtually useless. If a Web site contains a video, there must be a link to get the free browser plug-in to run it, if one is necessary.

User-controlled

Excellent multimedia enables users to take control of the learning experience—to stop mid-way, bookmark a place, quit at any time (and return later to the exact place they left off), and easily "Undo" a decision.

Non-breakable

Multimedia is given quite a workout in K-12 schools and needs to withstand incorrect mouse clicks and repeated pounding on the keyword. Anyone who has ever watched children at a computer knows that they will boldly click one button after another, without pausing, or will repeatedly click on any part of the screen or a Web site page, at any time, just to see what will happen.

One multimedia publisher tells of using students from a local school to test the durability of each of its products. "A product can be carefully tested for weeks in our QA Department and we'll find a handful of things to fix," an engineer notes, "but once those 10 year-olds get hold of it, we can identify problems that we never even dreamed could have existed!"

Any multimedia product that expects to be used in schools must stand up to each and every click without so much as a hiccup.

Feedback and Reinforcement

When students make an incorrect choice, how does the computer respond? Many teachers balk at feedback that seems punitive (e.g., "Wrong answer!") and look for multimedia that provides only helpful, positive feedback (e.g.," Good try … try again.") so students will feel safe in making repeated attempts.

Teachers also look for positive reinforcement that subtly guides students to the correct solutions by having them re-think facts or situations. For example, if an incorrect path is taken, the program's response might be a pop-up dialog box or audio clip with a question to spur thinking and help guide students back to the correct path without directly pointing them to the answer.

Customization

Educators need and expect options to customize certain parts of multimedia. Most often, products enable the teacher (or student) to turn some features on or off (e.g., printing or audio), toggle between languages, or change skill levels, data displays, RAM configurations, scoring parameters, or the number of exercises a student must work through in each activity. When teachers are given these types of options, they feel that they can better address the needs of individual students.

Repeat Play

If a product is deemed "done" after one play, it inevitably lands in the closet to gather dust. Schools expect products that can be replayed over and over again, so that students are challenged and can learn something new each time the product is used.

Repeat-play school products often cross over into the home (and homeschool) market. Parents who are enthusiastic about extending their children's learning at home will often look to schools to recommend educational and "long lasting" products for them to purchase.

Conclusion

Creating exemplary K-12 multimedia is no easy task. Educational and technical issues must be weighed and balanced to create a product that is engaging, meaningful and relevant, and well-adapted to different learning styles, as well as being technically fit for classroom use.

But when it is done right, the power of well-designed multimedia in the classroom can't be denied. Integrated seamlessly and authentically into a class curriculum, multimedia can meet diverse learner needs and abilities, create multidimensional and multidisciplinary learning opportunities that break down the classroom walls, and motivate students of all ages.

■

[1] International Society for Technology in Education (ISTE) Accreditation and Standards Committee. National Educational Technology Standards for Students—Connecting Curriculum and Technology. International Society for Technology in Education, 1998.

[2] Education Week. "Quality Counts 2001: Seeking Stability For Standards-Based Education," Editorial Projects in Education, 2001 Vol. 20, No. 17, pp. 8,9.

[3] United States Department of Education, National Center for Education Statistics (1999). Fast Response Survey System, Public School Teachers Use of Computers and the Internet, FRSS 70, Washington, D.C., 1999.

[4] Moe, Michael and Blodgett, Henry. The Knowledge Web. p. 104. Merrill Lynch & Co., Global Securities Research & Economics Group, Global Fundamental Equity Research Department, 2000.

[5] Trotter, Andrew. "Preparing Teachers For the Digital Age." Education Week On the Web, 1999 Editorial Projects in Education, Vol. 19, number 4. www.edweek.org/sreports/tc99/articles

■

About The Author

Gail Hartman is the president of Hartman Educational Technology, Inc., www.hartmanedtech.com, a curriculum design and instructional technology firm specializing in K-12 education. Hartman Educational Technology works with multimedia publishers to create innovative, award-winning on-line and off-line educational content, curriculum, teacher's guides, classroom activities, and assessment materials that help teachers successfully integrate technology into the classroom in meaningful ways. Gail can be reached at gail@hartmanedtech.com or by calling (303) 665-2876.

Developing Subscription Products for the Internet: It Is All about Customers and Value

by Becky Snyder

A subscription is a direct partnership—a one-to-one commitment—between the customer and you the publisher. A subscription-based product allows you to create customer loyalty and a more profitable business model. Subscription products that don't attend to these things are destined to sink.

The Opportunity: Higher Return Due to Long-Term Customer Retention and Improving Margins

A subscription business model has the potential to create a much higher return on investment than a model based on a number of single titles requiring the same development effort. This is true whether one is publishing in print or on the Web: higher revenues and lower costs, over time, are the reason.

Subscriptions create a higher life-of-customer revenue stream than do the single titles. Despite the fact that the expected revenue per sale is often lower than what one would charge for a one-time sale of a single product with the same content, total life-of-customer revenue is generally much higher. Of course, this assumes that the customer regularly renews the subscription; and much of this article describes methods to substantially improve the probability of these regular renewals. By customizing and continually evolving a subscription product to meet the needs of your customers, you can achieve a long-term buying relationship with them.

Subscription models also generally demonstrate improving profit margins over time. Initial sales and marketing efforts are required to build the subscriber base, but these gradually become a lower and lower percentage of sales. For a well-established subscription product with good market penetration, a sales and marketing budget of under five percent of sales is not uncommon.

> " A subscription is a direct partnership—a one-to-one commitment— between the customer and you the publisher. "

The Risk: Higher and Longer Cost Investment

The risks involved in starting a subscription product are substantial. At the time of launch, the investment required in the development and sales of a subscription product is usually more than for a single product with equivalent content. As described below, subscription product development requires more extensive planning and more flexible infrastructure and systems, not to mention the continuing development effort necessary to maintain the product. Moreover, while much of your investment comes before launching the product, high costs (both actual and as a percentage of revenue) continue for the first three to five years after launch. Content development continues, the infrastructure and Website evolve, and of course sales costs are high. To obtain greater revenues, profit, and ROI, then, you are wagering that the return from a long subscription relationship will more than offset the higher investment.

Be aware that it is difficult to sustain the needed investment in the face of these continuing high costs and that there will be substantial pressures to reduce the investment. Only if you are confident that you are truly in touch with customer needs and that your product meets these needs can you move forward with confidence.

Publishers of subscription products must keep an eye on value, as defined by the user. When your customer pays for a subscription, they pay for an on-going relationship. To build loyalty, the publisher must be accountable to customer needs in a proactive way. Toward that end, the publisher must create and re-create value daily.

Charting a Clear Course

The steps in developing subscription based products are no different than the steps of any good product development. You define a need, create a plan, develop a prototype, field test, develop, and then deliver.

However, when you develop a subscription-based product your development process is cyclical. While you are delivering your product you are planning and continually adding new content and services. When you develop for the Internet, the development is not only cyclical but the customers expect the cycle time to be daily. For the publisher, this means your work is never done. Once you make the decision to go for it, here are some suggestions for success:

Customize Your Product to Meet Your Customers Need

All personalization efforts require customization. Identify the ways that your subscribers use your product. Think about the problems they are trying to solve. Use those distinctions to divide your subscribers into groups. Most likely you will need to make general groupings of customers. This segmentation of the user base will allow mass customization to meet the needs of these groups cost effectively.

- Create products that are more about the customers and their work than about your content.

- Appropriate their language; use terms and jargon from their practice to describe your product.

- Allow the customer to determine their own settings or preferences.

- Allow the customer to choose what they see and what they do not see.

- Provide content that is relevant and up-to-date.

- Integrate information from all customer activities, including clickstream logs, demographic databases, and transaction analyses in order to personalize your product and to anticipate your users' needs.

If Content Is King, Service Is Queen

Content alone is not enough. The continuing commoditization of information means that publishers have to provide some clearly-articulated added value to justify the cost of subscriptions. One excellent way to add value to content is to offer additional services. With print and CD-ROM resources, customers assume responsibility for

> " Before you begin development of a subscription product you must have a solid idea of who your customers will be, both today and tomorrow. "

navigating through the databases to find what they need. On the Web, customers not only want the content, but also the services, tools, and resources to help them use the information more efficiently and effectively.

Subscriptions should activate a chain of desire and dependence. If the subscription service offers no surprises, or doesn't tantalize or tease, it could be the first thing jettisoned when funds are tight. Don't be an "invisible service." Don't let time march by undifferentiated for the end user. The only thing that should be routine is the accuracy, timeliness, and dependability of the content delivery. In particular,

- Provide access to "special events" online that are relevant to the content;

- Support peer-to-peer interactions for subscribers with common interests; and

- Provide a "look ahead" at new and exciting things on the event horizon for subscribers.

Subscription products get dropped when subscribers realize they aren't using them and that they don't miss them. This reassessment of value happens at each billing cycle. Assuming you have a strong product, this means you must ensure it gets used, early on in the lifetime of the subscription. The best way to do that is to check back with the customer repeatedly and offer user support that is geared to their needs. Don't ask users about satisfaction directly; ask about use and about ways of supporting or improving use.

Know Your Customer, Again and Again

Before you begin development of a subscription product you must have a solid idea of who your customers will be, both today and tomorrow. When you develop a stand-alone product you need to understand the needs of the customer at that given moment, the moment of the sale. In contrast, with a subscription-based product you not only need to know the target customer segments but you need to be able to distinguish one from another and you need to know what they want today, tomorrow, and every day that they subscribe. Understanding and meeting individual needs is required for customer intimacy and one-to-one product development.

First, know what customers want. Ask them directly, creating opportunities to dialog with them. Understand their frustrations and their desires. No buying decision occurs without a need and a desire. And remember: value isn't what you think it is. It's what your customers think it is. Know what they value.

Use Web technology to track preferences and observe behavior as users interact with your content and services online. Look at use data, but also at purchase data. Look at your customer base over time to see how the customer develops over time in interaction with your product. It may be that new and continuing customers have different usage patterns that will help you to further differentiate your products.

Look at your present sales. Understand the numbers, analysis, and statistics. What is your fastest growing product or service? Where are your biggest revenues coming from?

Make your customers a part of your development team. Create an advisory council for each of the different major customer groups.

To create a compelling value proposition, it is essential to get to know customers individually because the concept of value will be different for each one. You must know your customer in order to achieve meaningful, relevant, and predictive personalization of your product or services.

Interact with Your Customers

Interacting with your customer during the subscription year is the first message to your customers that you value the relationship. The interaction can take place in a variety of forums—do not limit communication to your renewal notice. You will want to create cost-effective methods for interacting. You can use your product and the Web as tools in various ways, including the following:

- Throw out product FAQs and talk to your customers directly instead. Real-time chat for customer support can teach you more about what your customer wants and what they are looking for.
- Don't ask for more information than you need. Each time you interact, you can ask one more question,

maybe two. Over time, you'll gather more than enough contact and preference information.

- Great relationships are built on satisfaction. Work towards customer satisfaction.
- Build communities, initiating integrated customer communication strategies. Let users know they are not alone. Support interactions for your customers: kid-to-kid, colleague-to-colleague, and parent-to-school.
- Web-based subscription products can provide a 24/7, 360-degree view of the relationship; use this to your advantage.

Finally, you need to make sure that every interaction teaches you something about that customer. Look at patterns emerging over time within the renewing core group of customers.

Invest in Retention and Renewal

Focus on retention rather than acquisition. Retaining a solid core of renewing subscribers is more cost-effective than marketing to find, attract, and sign on new customers. Having a core of loyal consumers allows you the luxury of the longer view for further product development. And you must continue to develop and evolve your product to retain your customer base. If most of your energy is directed toward repeatedly capturing new customers, you are standing still in a changing market place. Many of the dead dot coms offered us memorable marketing campaigns, but nevertheless failed to create a loyal, repeat-visit customer base. Without a consistent revenue stream, these companies could not dedicate the time and attention needed to continue product and service development efforts.

Think about Context

Once upon a time, Crown Books sold books. It sold them cheaply. But it turned out that the people who devoured books were not looking for cheap—they were looking for choice, and they were looking for ambience. They liked to browse; for them the book store was an activity, not an errand. If you look at today's successful bricks-and-mortar bookstores, you see embedded coffee house partners, such as Starbucks. You see kid-friendly children's sections where parents can safely park their kids while they browse. You see special events that include authors from many niches: travel, psychology, and poetry. You see stationery supplies that are exotic and pricey. Borders and Barnes & Noble aren't selling books; they're selling a customer perception of what it means to be a literate adult, to be a 'reader,' or perhaps even a writer. So too must online vendors think about the larger context of their products. You may be providing a subscription to content, but how is that content used, and what is the environment of use in which those customers think of themselves? Identity is a powerful seducer. Develop services and a context online that sell users an identity or two.

All Aboard

A subscription model is a direct partnership—a one-to-one commitment between the customer and the publisher. Creating value in a subscription is a never-ending journey where each day is different than the next. To make it work on the Web, we must be accountable to the customer's needs in a proactive way to build the relationship and cultivate customer loyalty.

About The Author

Becky A. Snyder *is vice president and publisher for the Schools Division at ABC-CLIO. ABC-CLIO has been a leading publisher of subscription-based products for the education market for 45 years. Prior to joining ABC-CLIO, Snyder devoted 15 years to teaching, curriculum design, and classroom technology integration for the K-12 education system. For more information about ABC-CLIO, visit www.abc-clio.com or call (800) 368-6868. Snyder can be reached at BSnyder@abc-clio.com or at www.abc-clio.com.*

International Publishers/Packagers/Developers: A Source for Product

by Tom Murphy and Dom Miccolis

It is tempting to overestimate the international markets as opportunities for sales or as source of products. Within North America, US and Canadian ELHI publishers have long been sensitive to the prospects of sales of products "across the border" and to opportunities for the conversion of some products to fit one another's market. The export of North American K-12 products to other countries is relatively small, but the import of international products or product concepts has increasingly becomes important for American and Canadian publishers anxious to reach niche markets.

The Sellers

As is true of most aspects of publishing, one has to understand the motives of the international educational players. What they see is a huge well-funded market in the United States, and they want a piece of it. For the most part they are European. Even more specifically, most of the activity is connected with the United Kingdom, although there is some activity in other countries as well. Because of the new European Economic Community (EEC) many of the educational projects undertaken nowadays are multi-language. Thus cooperative projects for innovative programs, like special needs, electronic education, and training, tend to be joint ventures involving an English language partner. For some European companies the unspoken reason to get involved is to be able to indicate to investors or funding bodies that they have products which are sold or at least have potential in North America.

The Japanese have made several unsuccessful attempts to sell English language rights to electronic products. Basically the core problems with Asian products are not connected with the content or the technology, so much as with the substantial cost required to translate and recreate product graphics.

> "Attending a show involves more than buying a plane ticket, overpaying for a hotel room, and pre-registering. You need a guide to the world that each of these shows contain."

The International Basal Scene

While American K-12 publishers in the past (and undoubtedly in the future) have flirted with the idea of converting basal product to sell to the corresponding European market, this has never been seriously attempted. The central reason is the complexity of the European basal system. Each country has a similar subject curriculum, but the introduction of specific topics varies, as do the instructional goals, the sequencing of material, the cultural context of presentation, and the preferred graphic treatment.

Additionally, each country's basal market is essentially a "closed environment." Schools prefer to buy "home grown product" from a well-defined list of instructional publishers.

Not too long ago it was literally true that every child in every school in France was on the same page of their textbooks on exactly the same day. There is more freedom today, but the pacing of instruction remains similar. In many European countries secondary school texts for science courses are one-third the size of an American schoolbook for the same subject, because their approach is closer to an outlined presentation rather than a full-text explanation.

Thus much of the opportunity internationally is in niche markets, particularly with school libraries, rather than in instructional markets.

This doesn't mean that one should ignore the lessons that can be learned from foreign publishers. It has been alert ELHI publishers' knowledge of European or Australian-New Zealand product that has influenced their development of whole language programs, their use of manipulative in mathematics; and their use of cognates in the early stages of a foreign language instruction.

Some Early Niche Successes

The success of several major niche programs in the past does tend to attract publishers' attention. Undoubtedly the best known example of success in exporting K-12 product was the introduction of SRA Reading Laboratories to the United Kingdom in the '70s. The most successful imported series were the BIG BOOKS series brought from Australia and New Zealand and the Cuisanaire rods imported from England. These and other successful imports were highly innovative for their time and were brought to the American market by visionary entrepreneurs like Tom Wright of the Wright Group and Jeffrey Sellon of Cuisanaire North America.

In contrast, today most of the successful imported products/programs are more of the library reference type than instructional and many come from European publishers and packagers.

Localization Pitfalls

It is important to keep in mind the caution that is required in accepting a non-North American new media product. Oftentimes publishers focus on the technical aspect of the CD-ROM or video and perform only a limited review of the content treatment. However, content localization is not accomplished by mere translation. Sensitivity to different cultural nuances is needed. For example, a Swedish CD-ROM recently considered for localization contained cartoon illustrations of a schoolgirl's derriere and a language lesson invloving a child's being asked by a parent to go to the store to buy beer. Such cultural miscues are not likely to receive a positive response by teachers or parents on this side of the pond.

Even technical matters can lead to localization issues if they don't receive careful attention. An example from a German video series: literal translations of narratives on videos often did not fit the available footage, licensing for some patented elements had expired, and archival footage had limitations because of geographic, format, and language restrictions.

The Quest

Staying current with the ever-changing evolution of K-12 instructional materials and school reference ideas is not a simple task. The critical issues are not posted in the *Wall Street Journal*, updated in *Publisher's Weekly*, or featured in Internet chat rooms. Instead, the old-

There are dozens of international book fairs held throughout the year and while all of them are useful, the K-12 publisher will find that these five fairs provide the maximum value in pursuing rights:

FRANKFURT BUCHMESSE (www.frankfurt-book-fair.com)
The Frankfurt Buchmesse is held each October and is the Granddaddy of them all. If you have never been, go! It makes an important statement: publishing is a huge business worldwide. While that is easy to say, Buchmesse makes the statement emphatically and in a theatrical way. All the people with whom you are likely to want to meet will be there.

Going to the Frankfurt Book Fair to "find" new and exciting works and concepts is a waste of time, however. Most of the "good stuff" will be spoken for well before Frankfurt—the Book Fair is the event at which deals are finalized and signed by the publishers and packagers who know how "the game" is played. Instead, what a publisher can find at Frankfurt are the concepts, projects, and products that have not already been "reserved" earlier during the year. A "successful Frankfurt" is the result of investigations, discussions, and negotiations that have been ongoing for months beforehand.

BOLOGNA (www.bolognafiere.it/bookfair/)
Bologna Fiera is held in mid April and is the largest children's book fair in the world. The emphasis is very strongly upon products intended for trade and retail distribution. Additionally, the focus is on the younger end of the children's book market. This fair offers an opportunity to meet and deal with developers and packagers in a less frenetic atmosphere than that of Frankfurt.

BOOK EXPO AMERICA (www.bookexpoamerica.com)
Book Expo America is held in late May or early June, and by the nature of its Chicago location may be the least expensive in terms of travel and time. Originally the focus of the show was booksellers, but increasingly it is becoming the year's halfway point in acquiring or firming up rights sales. At this time, not all the K-12 UK developers and packagers are regular attendees.

INTERNATIONAL READING ASSOCIATION (www.reading.org)
Always a May event, IRA is fast becoming the major English-language rights show for reading developers and publishers. Once upon a time, this show was almost totally a domestic customer show. (It was difficult then to justify the "International" in the name.) Today, however, you'll see a wealth of product from near and far, and increasingly it is a gathering place for rights people. The show rotates to major North American cities.

GUADALAJARA (www.fil.com.mx)
A show to keep a watch on is Guadalajara-Feria Internacional del Libro, held each year in late November or early December. As the educational market grows bilingual, this is an increasingly fertile source for product. However, because every Latin country has localized its language, and because differences in vocabulary and structure between these languages and the Spanish spoken in Europe are great, do not underestimate the cost in modifying product for the US and Canadian markets.

fashioned method of attending international book fairs remains the best way to keep up to date.

As publishers shop internationally for product ideas, they should keep in mind some fundamental differences between North American publishers and their international counterparts. For example, there are dramatic differences even between typical US and UK approaches. Although editorial or full service educational developers in the US are increasingly taking the initiative to create product on either a royalty or a work-for-hire basis, their core business posture remains that of a sub-contractor filling in the gaps to complete a work that they themselves have visualized. The UK developer is a slightly different breed, typically developing the idea from scratch; perhaps publishing a UK edition or licensing a title or series to a full line publisher; often selling translations rights. In essence they act as a co-publisher but usually do not have the resources to market products themselves. While some instructional products are developed in this way, the emphases are clearly upon school and library reference products.

The sidebar indicates a partial list of UK developers that are characteristic of this model.

Buchmesse, chances are that your legs will give out before you finish a complete tour of the thousands of exhibits. If you are a basal browser it would be useful to arrange a visit with your counterparts abroad at a fair or if you are traveling to their city. If you are part of an international company, use a corporate meeting to discuss publishing trends. If you are interested in supplementary and library products, you will want to set up meetings with some of the United Kingdom developer-publishers.

Be aware that attending a fair is only the beginning of the acquisition journey. A fair can be the starting place. But acquisitions can't be achieved through fifteen-minute conversations. Follow-up is required to ensure that both parties are on the same page.

The Basics: Some Typical Deal Arrangements

What follows are some typical arrangements. Of course, keep in mind that deals by their nature often have creative twists and turns.

For new media, the usual arrangement is based on a standard royalty, unless heavy translation or localization costs are involved, which may justify a lower percent age for the seller. The seller will typically negotiate for an advance, but will often settle for a small advance (in the $1,000 range) or none at all. For many sellers, the most important element of an agreement may be the time commitment for the release of the North American edition. Regarding the term of these deals, most sellers will accept a seven-year term, although they will negotiate for five.

For major book products, a consortium of publishing houses (typically three, but sometimes four), is often formed for the purpose. Generally, each member of the consortium will represent a language or geographic territory and will be awarded exclusivity. The funding for the development of the product will usually be spit among the partners; although sometimes adjustments

SOME UK DEVELOPERS AND PUBLISHERS TO CHOOSE FROM:		
Developer/Publishing House	**Contact(s)**	**E-Mail or Website**
Atlantic Europe	Duncan Baird	www.atlanticeurope.com
Andromedia-Oxford	Christofer Collier	Chris.collier@andromedia.co.uk
Belitha Press	Peter Osborne	
Brown Partworks	Ashley Brown; Sharon Hutton	Info@brownpartworks.co.uk
Chrysalis Books	Louise Prettejohn	L.Prettejohn@chrysalisbooks.co.uk
Evans Brothers Ltd.	Britta Martins	Brittam@evansbrothers.co.uk
Marshal Editions	Barbara Marshall	Ellen.dupont@marshalleditions.com
McRae Publishing	Jim and Anne McRae	Mcrae@tin.it
Orpheus Books	Nicholas Harris	Nicholas@orpheus.com
White-Thomson Publishing	Stephen White Thomson	Steve@bexin.co.uk

The Top Five International Fairs

Attending a show involves more than buying a plane ticket, overpaying for a hotel room, and pre-registering. You need a guide to the world that each of these shows contain. If you have never been to the Frankfurt

are negotiated if one or more partners are willing to provide a disproportionate level of resources. A typical consortium includes one house that creates the concept and prototype, one that develops and designs the "mother" edition; and one or two houses who contribute substantial funding in exchange for geographic territory.

The Complexities of UK Packager Deals

There is really no "standard deal" you can strike with UK packagers; rather, there are many different possible variations, depending upon such things as:

- Whether you want to buy the work outright or structure a royalty deal;

- The extent of the rights you will want;

- Whether or not you are inclined to share develop-ment costs;

- Whether or not you want finished books; and

- What the current state of the economies in the UK and US might be.

The first point needs to be settled at the outset of negotiations, as it will significantly impact costs. An "outright buy" will cost the publisher a great deal of money. Packagers enjoy a continuing income stream that results from a royalty deal. However, at the right price many packagers are willing to consider deals of either kind. The choice is largely up to the publisher.

Over the years, the rights question is probably the single most important one in this context. Many of the UK packagers, particularly the larger ones, are heavily engaged in trying to negotiate "co-edition deals" for products they develop. The broader the co-edition rights the packager is allowed to retain, the lower the product cost will be for any participant in the overall project.

If the publisher is willing to settle for relatively narrow distribution rights—for example "US schools and libraries only, English language only, print-on-paper only, exclusivity for only the publisher's particular version of the work"—then the publisher should be able to do well on the cost side of the project. However, the more require-ments the publisher wishes to add by way of rights, the pricier the project will become. The caution here is, of course, that the publisher must be careful not to leave the door open for a competitor to be able to cut a deal

with the same packager for a "similar work" that utilizes some of the same resources as those found in the initial version.

More On Rights

"Picture rights" and "electronic publishing rights" are two areas in particular that can add significantly to the overall cost of the contract. Packagers in the UK prefer to offer graphics on the basis of "one time use" for a particular version of the work, and this is the most economical way for publishers to proceed. If a publisher needs (or more typically just wants), things like "world wide" rights, "re-use" rights, or exclusivity rights for artwork, then project costs will rise significantly.

"Electronic publishing rights" are a serious cost issue. Too many publishers negotiate for electronic publishing rights, for no other reason than the fact that "experts" have told them that they must have these rights. Publishers generally want electronic delivery rights on the off chance that they will be able to "do something" with the work in electronic format going forward. This is a mistake: one should not pursue electronic publishing rights unless there is a clear plan at the outset for some well-defined electronic use of the content. At most, ask that a "right of first refusal" for electronic publishing rights be built into the agreement. The guideline in all of this is "do not pay dearly for rights unless you are absolutely sure you need and will use them!"

The publisher's willingness to share development costs, usually structured as an advance against royalty, is an important bargaining tool. It seems that every single UK packager, no matter what his or her size, is "hurting for cash". Usually, at the signing one third of whatever the agreed-upon cost might be is paid to the packager.

Many, but certainly not all, of the larger packagers will prefer to deliver "finished books." In this way, they are able to add significantly to the profitability of the project through the addition of a "handling charge" for manufac-turing the finished book.

Economic conditions at the time of negotiations are always an important factor. US publishers have been able to cut some very nice deals while the economy in the UK has been in a down turn.

Some Important "Ifs"

There are several issues that can impact a deal, either positively or negatively. Among these are the following:

1. If the publisher can select a project from among concepts the packager is already working on, that can help on the cost side. Such concepts have probably already been identified as attractive co-edition opportunities by the packager, and the more co-edition rights are sold, the lower the project cost will be to each co-edition participant.

2. If the publisher is coming to packagers with a content idea that needs to be developed "from scratch", the publisher must investigate beforehand to identify only those packagers that have demonstrated expertise in the content area covered by the concept. Many of the packagers will claim that they can "do" any content area for any application and for any age, reading, or interest level. That is simply not true!

3. The publisher needs to be very careful that both parties have the same understanding of the complete "terms and conditions" under which the project will be operating before any agreement is signed. Many problems and issues arise from the fact that US publishers assume that because the two parties in the deal are using many of the same words, are all collectively "speaking the same language." That is absolutely not true!

Finally, while the following should go without saying it is often not considered at the outset: the publisher needs to be as sure as possible that the project will be profitable at the agreed-upon cost. Publishers are well advised to keep in mind constantly that product price must be a function of product cost, and that price must be sustainable and competitive in the channel and market being attacked. The publisher/packager environment is littered with both cancelled and completed projects that were driven by enthusiasm and unrealistic expectations in terms of sustainable pricing and unit commitments in a given market, and that were thus based upon unreasonable profitability assumptions.

Know what you are able to pay for the project before you start negotiating. Be firm in this regard, and do not be shy about walking away from a developer/packager who is unable or unwilling to meet your cost expectations.

Summary

It is best to look upon international opportunities as just another possible source for projects. It does not displace domestic sources. It may provide products at the same or at lower cost than you can have the equivalent work done here. Negotiations can be complex and thus require care in drafting.

About the Authors

Tom Murphy *is founder and partner of Professional Publishing Services Company, an educational and reference consulting firm, whose assignments include working with European publishers and the placement of programs or distribution of their titles into the North American market. His e-mail address is* pps2000@optonline.net.

Dom Miccolis *serves as strategic advisor to a North American reference publisher and a media developing company, and sits on the board of directors of a publisher and marketer of education products and online services. His e-mail address is* dmico@aol.com.

Smart Packaging for School Products
by Bill Pflaum and John Magryta

Smart packaging for school products is about three things:
- function
- form
- finances

A Package's Function

"What should this package do?" That is the first question to ask if you belong to a product team charged with deciding on the right package. Packages must do many things. The three most important functions of packages are to protect, to identify, and to hold their contents.

These roles can be performed simply or with great complexity and pizzazz. At the simple end is an Amazon.com shipper for a single book: a pocket of plastic film inside to hold the book in place, a simple corrugated sheet wrapped and glued, your name and amazon.com's on the outside. That's it: protection, identity, and containment.

At the other end of the spectrum is the multicomponent classroom package for a primary grade reading program: colorful boxes, custom designed for each component, fit like pieces of a fine jigsaw puzzle inside a dazzlingly bright master container; hinged flaps with Velcro tabs open and close to provide access and protection; the exterior displays the program's logo and signature graphics. And like the Amazon.com package, it too protects, identifies, and contains.

Between these two extremes are myriad combinations of designs, materials, sizes, colors—and costs.

No Longer an Afterthought

Only a few years ago, product packaging for school products was an afterthought. Educational publishing companies would plan and produce the pupil edition, the teacher edition, and ancillaries, and maybe a CD-ROM. Then, at the eleventh hour, they would scramble to design a package that fit them all. This mad race at the end of the process left everyone panting and no one happy.

Today, package planning is usually on the table from day one. The product team comes together to ask and answer critical packaging questions. The team may be small—perhaps a managing editor, a designer, a marketing manager, and a print buyer. At a large basal textbook publisher the team may have broader representation, with packaging specialists from the design, production, and manufacturing departments playing key roles.

But marketing has to answer the question, "**What do we want this package to do?**"

Protecting the package in transit from warehouse to school might be enough—in that case, the publisher may choose simply to pack books securely in a standard corrugated container with an address label and the publisher's name and logo. This approach works for fill-in products or other routine delivery of already-sold materials.

But there are times when product delivery is not simply a logistical activity. Often, in fact, product delivery can be a critically important marketing event. Take two examples:

> "Today, package planning is usually on the table from day one."

- ***The in-person sales presentation:*** Packages sell products. To paraphrase Marshall McLuhan, the package is the product. At a committee presentation, the package speaks to committee members. Its functional design reveals the care that has shaped the entire curriculum program. Packaging graphics announce the program's visual tone, quality, and features. In these ways, the package provides indispensable support to the sales representative.

- ***Samplers sent without a personal call:*** In the absence of a sales representative, the package guides the prospective buyer to notice distinguishing product features. Carefully thought-out functional design, combined with effective graphic treatments, can separate the successful program from its competitors.

After the sale, packages are often used in the classroom by the teacher and students. Books and other components are stored there when not in use. The design, durability, and graphics of the package continue to support and sell the program's benefits to teachers. If the package breaks down in the classroom or scuffs, cracks, and mars, your product and your company's image will suffer.

A Package's Form

Packages usually are formed from one of five materials:

- corrugated board
- chipboard
- solid bleach sulfate (SBS) or folding carton stock
- vacuum-formed plastic
- vinyl

For school products, corrugated board is the publisher's most frequent choice. With a lithographic printed sheet called a label adhered or mounted to it, corrugated board offers the best combination of durability, flexibility, and presentation. Chipboard and SBS often are used for smaller single-product boxes. Vacuum-formed plastic is used for videotapes, audiotapes, and some CD-ROMs, and vinyl often is used on three-ring binders, folders, or pouches.

Corrugated Packages

As a packaging team member charged with planning the right product for the right price, you will want to understand the basics of corrugated packaging. These basics can be categorized as follows:

- types of corrugation
- types of printing
- types of coatings

Types of corrugation. Corrugated board is made of a fluted inner sheet (called the corrugated medium) with flat sheets (called liner boards) bonded to each side. Corrugated boards are identified by the height, number of flutes per inch, and composition of the medium, and the liner board is described by bursting strength (#150, #200, #250, and so on). The three most commonly used for educational packaging are E-flute, B-flute, and C-flute, shown below.

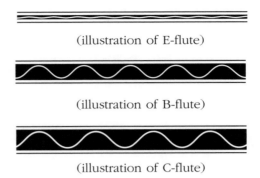

(illustration of E-flute)

(illustration of B-flute)

(illustration of C-flute)

Recent additions to the corrugated industry are F-flute, G-flute, and N-flute, which are designed for better printing; and more intricate designs, which are made possible by the narrow caliper of the board. Your packaging supplier can discuss the advantages and disadvantages of the flute styles. They basically involve trade-offs among appearance, strength, printability, and price.

Types of printing. Printing can be done either directly on the corrugated board or on a separate sheet of paper. The flexographic process is used to print directly on corrugated boards. Flexographic plates, as the name suggests, print with a flexible, raised printing surface. The process most often is used to print solids, type, or multicolor designs. Although newer flexographic technologies permit relatively high resolution, flexographic printing does not have lithography's quality. The main advantage of flexographic printing is its price.

Higher quality graphics are achieved using the lithographic printing process. This is accomplished by printing sheets that are then pasted to corrugated board. The printed sheet, called a label or wrap, is often 70# or 80# coated one-side stock. Reproduction quality can be very high, but the cost generally is higher than flexographic printing.

Gaining popularity is a process called preprint, in which a thin sheet of solid bleach sulfate (SBS) is lithographically printed and laminated directly to the fluting. This results in a higher print grade because of the smoother surface.

Types of coatings. Coatings add strength and protection to the printed sheet and enhance its appearance. Coatings also can be important for classroom durability and appearance. The three principal types of coatings are film lamination, ultraviolet (UV) coatings, and press-applied coatings.

Film lamination is the strongest and most attractive coating option. It is also the most expensive. Various types of film are used, depending on the applications. The film is applied to the sheet after printing and provides excellent luster and scuffing resistance.

Liquid UV coatings are also applied to the sheet after printing. They are applied on a separate press, or in-line, and are dried with ultraviolet lights. UV coatings are scuff-resistant and glossy but can crack at folds and corners. Their advantage is cost: they can be 25% or less of the cost of film lamination. For coating packages, UV is the least often used of the three coatings.

Press-applied coatings are water- or solvent-based coatings laid down when the sheet is printed. They are referred to as aqueous or varnish coatings, respectively. They seal the inks and provide some gloss but little resistance to scuffing, scratching, or cracking. Press-applied coatings are the least expensive of the coatings.

Chipboard and SBS Packages

Chipboard is a gray- or white-faced recycled board used primarily to make slipcases and telescoping boxes (boxes with tops that are slightly larger than their bottoms). The chipboard is wrapped with a lithographic printed label. Chipboard boxes work well for flat products like transparencies, but they are only as strong as the lithographed wrap and are not very practical for intricate designs.

SBS packages, also known as folding cartons, allow printing directly on the relatively thin white board. They can be inexpensive and easy to assemble. However, they are not strong enough for large products, and they don't work well as storage units. SBS is increasingly used as packaging for CD-ROMs instead of jewel cases or vacuum-formed plastics.

Vacuum-Formed Packages and Vinyl Binders

Vacuum-formed packages are useful for videotapes, audiotapes, and sets of CD-ROMs delivered in combination with literature. Graphics are limited to the front, back, and spine inserts. Off-the-shelf standard packages with custom-printed inserts can be a functional choice, but they seldom lend distinction to your product.

Vinyl binders are less frequently used now than in the past, as teachers' shelves have become overloaded with them. However, transparent vinyl sometimes is used to make pouches, allowing the contents' graphics to be seen.

A Package's Finances

"How can we keep the cost down?" everyone asks today. The secret to economy is knowing what you want, knowing how much you can afford, and then planning accordingly. Many factors contribute to cost, including package size, quantity, quality, type of materials used, printing method, and complexity of assembly.

> " The secret to economy is knowing what you want, knowing how much you can afford, and then planning accordingly. "

As you plan for the most economical package, first settle the package's function. Know what you want it to do. This is a point where potential conflicts with sales, marketing, manufacturing, and finance can occur. Address and resolve those conflicts, and make sure that everyone else on the team and up the approval chain agrees. Costs inevitably go up when plans change.

Moving from Plan to Action

When the function is defined and the desired features are locked down, call in your packaging supplier. Describe the package's function, features, and graphic style, along with your budget guidelines. If possible, let the package designer meet with your team, especially members from design, marketing, and manufacturing.

With your product and budget guidelines in hand, the packaging designer will develop a variety of preliminary concept drawings or prototypes. These will show several options that meet your functional and budgetary goals. Your product team should study these concepts carefully, asking for revisions if necessary. There are typically a number of prototype development rounds before final prototype approval.

While reviewing the prototype carefully, ask yourself and other team members whether the package meets your goals: Will it display the product well? How will it travel in and out of the sales representative's car? What will it look like at the sales presentation? How will it stand out on a classroom shelf? Will it hold up during shipping and under regular classroom use?

Make sure you have exact prototypes or dummies of all the products that go into the package. To ensure final fit, and to avoid crises at the assembly stage, make sure the dummies are to exact trim sizes, page counts, and paper specifications. Avoid the humiliation—and cost—of hearing an assembly manager say, "Your package is here, but the books don't fit!"

If necessary, have the designer modify the prototype. Review it once more to ensure that it meets your functional requirements and budget guidelines. After sign-off, the package designer will finalize the package design using a computer-aided design (CAD) system. The CAD system will yield an electronic layout and a strike sheet (also known as a die template, layout, or Mylar layout) to guide the design department in positioning copy and art.

Make sure that everyone—especially design and production—understands the tolerances of the material and printing method you've chosen. Flexographic presses have looser tolerances than lithographic presses, and tolerances in mounting the lithographed sheet to the corrugated board must be considered in the graphic layout. Make sure that these tolerances are allowed for. Don't risk being disappointed when graphics misalign because tolerances were overlooked at the graphic design stage.

When the package is delivered, assembled, and shipped at or under budget, celebrate with your team and your CFO, and wait for sales to begin.

About the Authors

Bill Pflaum *is vice president of The Mazer Corporation, a publishing services company providing full-service development of print and digital products to educational publishers. Mazer's services range from concept creation through writing, editing, design, production, package design, and printing of kindergarten through college materials. Bill founded Mazer's packaging division and headed Mazer's creative services division for over twenty years.*

John Magryta *John Magryta is a packaging consultant for The Mazer Corporation. A graduate of Michigan Sate University with a degree in packaging, John has designed and managed package development for hundreds of educational programs, ranging from single CD-ROM folders to seven grade-level basal reading programs.*

E-Publishing and Digital Rights Management: Hope or Hype?

by Mary Westheimer

In March 2000 when Stephen King's novella *Riding the Bullet* was downloaded by 400,000 people in a matter of days, e-publishing became news, big news. The idea was not new, but now available technology—and interest—coalesced to create a true phenomenon.

Those in the publishing industry had special reason to take notice, and take notice they did. Publishers jumped onto the e-publishing bandwagon with both feet and their pocketbooks, converting thousands of titles that they hoped would sell as wildly as King's novella. Later reason returned, as participants realized that King's star power and the fact that many readers did not pay for the downloads (retailers paid the tab to attract visitors to their Web sites) skewed the apparent commercial viability of e-books. Too, the technology, while it had clearly advanced, had not reached the maturity necessary to sustain a solid market base.

The excitement was not entirely misplaced, however. What this phenomenon told publishing professionals was that there were 400,000 people who knew how to read e-books, or who were at least willing to learn. That revelation quickly added electronic production and delivery to the list of viable publishing options.

In addition to the embrace of a publishing darling such as King and the interest of readers, advancements in technology had indeed brought e-publishing and e-books into the mainstream. Several companies had developed handheld electronic readers, with RocketBook and SoftBook leading the way. Two months before the appearance of *Riding the Bullet*, Gemstar International Group Limited purchased both of these companies as part of its initiative to make this technology more "consumer friendly." (In October 2000, Gemstar would release its next generation reader and new marketing model to a mixed reception.)

One month after this stunning development, Adobe Systems released PDF Merchant and Web Buy, a "lock and key" form of encryption that could be used on the Web. Not far behind was Microsoft, which released its MS Reader LIT format with its usual marketing vigor.

These initiatives as well as others were spurred by the demand of many publishing industry professionals for a way to protect their intellectual property. Developments in industries such as the music business, which was turned upside-down with the advent of Napster and other services that challenged copyright protection as we know it, as well as the blurring of the traditional geographic delineation of rights by technologies such as the Internet, made many publishers leery of putting their material in such an easily reproducible format without some sort of protection. The answer for many is the emerging discipline known as Digital Rights Management (DRM).

What Is E-Publishing, Anyway?

But what exactly is e-publishing? What are its advantages and challenges? First, let's define the term: e-publishing is the digitizing of text, graphics and photographs. In its digital form, an e-book can be downloaded to a desktop, a laptop, a palmtop, a handheld device, or some other sort of computer. The digitized version might be a complete book, a part of a book, supplementary or updated material, or a special edition created especially for an interactive medium.

There are clearly advantages of e-publishing. They include:

- Cost-effective production
- Ability to get material to market more quickly
- Ability to update material more quickly, easily and often
- Ability to repackage material so that it can be sold in parts or in combination with other materials as a new product
- Interactivity, including searchability, bookmarking, and linking.

E-publishing also is of special interest to publishers who want to test materials, even though interest in an electronic document does not necessarily indicate interest in a printed form. It also is an interesting option for publishers who do not want to compete with their traditional channels, such as their distributors, wholesalers and bookstores. They can create new documents or products that can be sold only from their sites. This strategy is not unlike that of computer manufacturers who sell certain models through retail computer stores and other models, with different features, directly.

With e-publishing still in its infancy, many people still think solely of entire books in electronic format. Electronic publishing can take different forms, however. In addition to the well-known full-text presentation, the *granular* approach is most appropriate for large directories composed of many smaller entries. A good example of granular e-publishing is the Audiobook Title Locator, a joint project of the Audio Publishers Association and R.R. Bowker, at www.audiopub.org/titlelocator.html. The locator contains the entire text of *Words On Cassette*, the audiobook equivalent of *Books In Print*. The printed version is available for more than $200 in several volumes, which is impractical if all you really want is to find one particular listing. In contrast, the online version allows a visitor to make one search for less than $2 or buy a book of 10 searches for $15. Industry professionals usually opt for an annual subscription or license, which also is available. The result is a resource that is in many ways more valuable than the original print version, providing more incremental income than the publishers would otherwise enjoy and greater ease of use for readers.

How do you determine what format is best for a particular property? A combination of factors help dictate that choice:

- *Type of information*—Can the information be broken down into smaller parts and the parts be sold for more than that of their sum? Is it more valuable to visitors to be able to search it?

- *Organization of content*—Is the information cross-referenced? Would the ability to find the information more quickly or by more than one criteria simultaneously be helpful? (Imagine the option to find career opportunities by skill requirements and educational requirements.)

- *The audience's comfort level with electronic devices and files*—For a K-12 audience, comfort with computers is likely to be high, unless dealing with special audiences that work better in printed form or those that need to practice those skills.

- *Timeliness of data*—How often is the information updated? A granular approach, which can be handled with a database, can be easier to update. (Actually, all types of electronic documents are easier to update than their printed equivalents, but databases are particularly easy to update.) Using a database or a Web-based interface, there is no need to re-publish an entire section if just one entry needs updating.

- *Likely location of use*—While most educational materials are used in the classroom, electronic devices can be well-suited for field trips or onsite learning, making a handheld reader quite useful. For example, in the world of work, doctors are finding devices such as Palm Pilots invaluable as they do their rounds.

Granular e-publishing is also the basis of initiatives such as Questia and eBrary, which let visitors access the contents of books, journals, maps, periodicals, and other digitally archived materials.

Despite its many advantages, e-publishing is not for every book or audience, especially in these early stages of its development. For instance, large-format art books may someday make sense in electronic format, but currently they do not translate well.

Digital Rights Management's Part of the Equation

Digital Rights Management, or DRM, refers to any technology that specifically protects digital content from unauthorized usage or duplication. Its use is still new and, for surprising reasons, controversial.

Unauthorized copying is undoubtedly a powerful force in the market. "Once material is in bits and bytes, it's especially susceptible to copying," observes Danny O. Snow, CEO of Unlimited Publishing. "Stephen King's electronic novella *Riding the Bullet* survived less than 48 hours before pirated copies started to surface on the Internet," Snow said in comments to National Public Radio, which broadcast excerpts of his commentary on June 3, 2000. The question is whether unauthorized copying represents a net negative or positive to the commercial success of the authorized product.

While many publishers and authors feel that DRM is a necessary protection of their property, not all experts are convinced that the security measures of DRM represent the best approach to e-publishing viability. M.J. Rose (www.mjrose.com), a novelist, co-author of *How to Promote and Publish Online,* and a columnist for Wired.com on e-publishing, believes that the future of e-books is in keeping the price extremely low and not worrying about DRM. "If the price is low enough," she explains, "it's easier for people to buy the book than steal it."

Online marketing guru Seth Godin went so far as to actually give away his book *Unleashing the Idea Virus*, which promotes "infecting" people with an idea in order to create demand. Visitors took him up on his offer, downloading more than 100,000 copies of the entire book within 30 days. During that time, another 300,000 copies were downloaded from other sites or passed along. Remarkably, however, the give-away apparently didn't dampen sales of the $40 hardcover edition of the book, which hit #5 on Amazon.com's bestseller list. Danny Snow's experience supports Godin's. He reported at BookTech East 2001 that "at least 20% of readers who downloaded the first edition of my book for $3.95 subsequently ordered a paperback for $8.95 plus shipping and handling."

Dan Poynter of Para Publishing, known by many as the "self-publishing guru," says DRM is not for his company, either. "My information is so time-sensitive that, by the time it's passed onto someone else, it's out of date. I see the sharing as advertising for the current version," he says. "And when the book or report is forwarded to another person, the present version comes with an implied endorsement or testimonial from the sender. The recipient is introduced to my work and is a candidate for the next edition and all my other work on the subject." Publishers who take these sorts of positions usually make sure purchase information is prominently displayed.

The DRM discussion, as well as the technology that supports it, will continue. Time will be the arbiter of success, and it may well be a split decision.

What Format Art Thou?

Just like VHS and Betamax competed in the early days of videotape, there are still a number of format choices in e-publishing. These issues are starting to sort themselves out with the emergence of OEB ("Open E-Book"). OEB is a free-flowing format based on HTML and XML that is focused on content, while the most commonly used and available format, Adobe PDF ("Portable

Document Format"), is focused on maintaining the original presentation of the document.

Options include:

ADOBE PDF: More than 165 million copies of Adobe free Acrobat Reader have been downloaded, so many people know how to use this technology. It produces a document that looks just like the printed version, maintaining quality and consistency. Publishers are also quite comfortable with this format, because many of them are already using it to produce camera-ready versions of their books for print production. Images are easy to incorporate. Adobe is also currently producing new formats such as its eBook Reader format, which is based on the well-known PDF consistent-format, production-focused approach.

HTML/XML: HTML is easy to read—anyone who has a browser (and browsers are free) can do so. And the tools to create HTML are easy to use and also free. However, HTML cannot be easily protected from theft, and images can be included in .GIF or .JPG (.JPEG) formats only. HTML is the basis of the developing Open eBook standard (the first version uses HTML semantics in XML-based syntax), but XML eventually will offer the flexibility for conversion into a number of formats. Currently encryption is still an issue for HTML and XML.

MICROSOFT READER: Microsoft's OEB-based ClearType technology offers easy-to-read black text on white background. The type size can even be adjusted on the fly. Images can be included sparingly. The format is now available on PocketPC handhelds and on desktop and laptop computers.

RCA REB: There are far fewer dedicated electronic reading devices than Palm Pilots or copies of Adobe's Reader. Two models of the RCA REB have replaced the Rocket eBook and Softbook, which were the most popular types of handheld readers before the company that created them were bought by Gemstar International. RCA REB's format is copyright-protected and OEB-based. The impact of this new reader is still to be determined.

PALM PILOT/PEANUT PRESS: There are more than 7 million PalmPilot users, many of whom read from their Pilots. There are a variety of Palm document formats, including DOC and PRC. Some Palm-friendly formats can be encrypted, but most cannot. No images are possible.

In March 2001, Peanut Press was purchased by Palm, Inc.

TEXT/WORD PROCESSING: Text versions can come in various formats, from RTF (Rich Text Format), to Microsoft Word, WordPerfect, and MS-DOS Text (also known as ASCII) formats. Of all these options, RTF and MS-DOS Text are probably the best because they are the most generic. Almost any word processor can read RTF, and it includes formatting such as bold and italic. MS-DOS Text drops formatting, but can be read by nearly every program. Images can only be included in the higher-end formats. Word and WordPerfect provide more formatting options, but publishers either need to pick a version that everyone has or a "lowest common denominator" format that may not provide the formatting options desired. Too, it is at best difficult to encrypt, or protect, these formats. That means that the pre-keyed text is easy to republish as someone else's material, a real issue in these days of instant global availability.

The Economic Impact of Electronic Books

Not only are there many ways to produce and offer e-books, but the market is also so new that costs to publishers and prices for consumers can vary wildly. The cost to publishers of producing electronic versions of a book can range from nothing to several hundred dollars, depending upon the complexity of the project and the way it is going to be offered. There are several e-book sites that will convert documents at no charge in exchange for 40 to 60% of revenue and ownership of the electronic version. Unlike printed editions, however, once the material has been converted, there are no additional printing costs. For consumers, the low cost of reproduction—and the force of competition—have delivered savings, as many publishers and sites offer e-books at a 33% discount. On the other hand, other publishers charge the same price for electronic versions of books as for printed editions.

Where to From Here?

As e-publishing matures, a few formats will emerge as the "keepers" for publishers, distributors and readers. E-books will likely integrate the benefits of multimedia, of which we caught a glimpse in the "shooting star" lifetime of CD-ROM publishing, taking more advantage of computer capabilities of sound, movement, and interaction.

And despite any and all predictions of its demise, the printed book will not die. Instead, publishers will offer—and readers and educators will purchase—books in multiple formats. Print will share the marketplace with audio, e-books, and perhaps other media choices, with publishers and consumers choosing the mix that is appropriate for their use of a particular property. One thing is abundantly clear, however: e-publishing is here to stay, and those organizations that learn and begin using this powerful medium will ultimately benefit.

About The Author

Mary Westheimer *is CEO of BookZone, a leading provider of Internet hosting, design, development, and promotion services for the publishing industry. BookZone's Web site at* www.bookzone.com *is the Net's largest publishing community. Since 1998, BookZone has offered granular and full-document e-publishing systems, with and without digital rights protection. For more information, contact BookZone at* epub@bookzone.com*, (800) 536-6162, or from within Arizona, (480) 481-9737.*

Protecting Your Intellectual Property Rights
by Lloyd L. Rich

An educational publisher's intangible intellectual property assets (its publishing contracts, copyrights, trademarks, and possibly patents and trade secrets, along with their associated goodwill) may not appear on the company's financial balance sheet, or may be vastly undervalued there. Nevertheless, these are arguably among the most important assets of a publishing company, and it is essential to ensure that appropriate measures are taken to develop, perfect, and manage these intellectual property assets.

This article focuses on means of protecting a publishing company's publishing rights through (1) its contracts with authors, illustrators, photographers and other freelancers who contribute creative material to publishing projects, (2) copyright registration and protection of published products and other copyrightable material and (3) trademark protection for series titles and for other products and services.

Contracts

For any given publishing project there are many types of contracts that may involve the publisher. The most important is the publishing contract between the publisher and the author, as this contract defines the scope of the author's and publisher's interests and governs their respective rights and obligations. However, before the project has been completed there may be other contracts with freelancers such as those for contributing writers who may provide a chapter, preface, introduction, or index for the project; for illustrators and photographers; for cover designers; for project editors; and for other freelancers involved in the development of a particular project.

The publishing contract with the author has traditionally been a written contract; however, this has not always been the practice for contracts between the publisher and freelancers. A written and not an oral contract should exist here, too, for the following reasons: (1) an oral contract can lead to difficulties if the parties have a disagreement regarding the specific terms of a contract or about whether a contract actually exists; (2) the Copyright Act requires that all transfers of copyright ownership and exclusive licenses be incorporated in a written document that has been signed by the copyright owner; and (3) a state law requirement known as the Statute of Frauds requires a signed written agreement for any project that cannot be completed within one year from the effective date of the agreement.

Types of Contracts

There are two types of agreements that the publisher may use with creators of copyrightable material. The first, and usually the preferable one for the publisher is a "Work Made for Hire" contract, under which the publisher has complete control over the creator's work and owns all rights in the work, including copyright ownership. The Work Made for Hire doctrine, which is codified in the Copyright Act, is an exception to the fundamental principle that copyright ownership vests initially in the individual who creates the work. There are two scenarios under which the publisher could be the copyright owner of the creator's work. The first is when the creator of the work is an employee of the publishing company and is creating the work within the scope of his or her employment, and the second is when the publisher commissions a freelancer to create the work. In either case, when the creator's work is prepared as a Work Made for Hire and when it satisfies the specific requirements of the Copyright Act, the publisher and not the individual will be recognized legally as both the creator and copyright owner of the work.

The Copyright Act requirements will be satisfied if all of the following conditions are met: (1) if the work was specially ordered or commissioned by the publisher; (2) if the work fits into one of the nine categories of work enumerated in the Copyright Act–(contribution to a collective work, translation, supplementary work, compilation, instructional text, test, answer material for a test, atlas, or part of a motion picture or audiovisual work); and (3) if there is a written signed agreement between the publisher and freelancer that specifically states that the work was created as a Work Made for Hire. It is also highly recommended that the Work Made for Hire agreement be executed before the freelancer commences with the creation of the work. The publisher should be aware that if the Copyright Act requirements are not strictly followed, the freelancer, and not the publisher, could be recognized legally as the copyright owner of the work, in which case the publisher's rights to exploit the work could be severely limited.

The second type of contract is an "Assignment of Rights" contract. An Assignment of Rights contract is more limited in scope than a Work Made for Hire contract because the creator of the work usually retains copyright ownership of his or her work and may only grant the publisher limited rights to use the work.

The critical language in an Assignment of Rights contract is commonly referred to as the "grant of rights" clause. This clause delineates the scope of publishing and other rights granted by the creator to the publisher. The grant of rights clause may be extremely broad, granting all rights in the creator's work exclusively to the publisher, possibly including copyright ownership. On the other hand, the grant of rights clause may be very limited—for example permitting publication only as a hardcover book with distribution restricted to only North America, while all other rights in the work are reserved by the author.

The crucial point for the publisher to remember is that the publisher will only have the ability to commercially exploit those rights specifically granted by the creator. In the event that a publisher attempted to exploit rights not granted by the creator of a work, the publisher would be at risk for infringing the creator's copyright in the work.

Copyright Protection

Federal copyright law protects almost all types of creative works as long as the particular work meets the standards provided under the Copyright Act. Copyright protection, with some exceptions, is available for "original works of authorship fixed in any tangible medium of expression, now known or later developed, from which they can be perceived, reproduced, or other wise communicated, either directly or with the aid of a machine or device." The "originality" requirement is generally a relatively easy hurdle to achieve because a work will be

deemed original if it was independently created and not copied from another work. The "fixation" requirement will be satisfied once the work has been set in any stable and permanent form, including electronic formats.

Copyright protection automatically exists from the moment of creation for any work that satisfies the originality and fixation requirements. Copyright registration is voluntary and may be accomplished by the copyright owner at any time while the work is still protected by copyright. Registration is available for both published and unpublished works. It is relatively easy to do, and the process can be accomplished by the copyright owner, the owner's agent such as a copyright attorney, or a copyright registration service.

Benefits of Copyright Registration

Although copyright protection now exists independently and regardless of registration, there are significant benefits for the copyright owner to copyright register the creative work. These benefits include deterrence to would-be infringers as well as real legal advantages in the event that the copyright is actually infringed.

Regrettably, however, many copyright owners neglect to obtain a copyright registration for their creative works. The reasons usually given for failing to obtain copyright registration run the spectrum from "It's not required." or "I don't want to spend the $30 registration fee." to "I don't have the time to complete the registration application." or "I forgot." Although the copyright owner may have spent significant time and expense in creating and/or publishing the creative work, the failure to register the copyrighted work, or to register it in a timely manner, may preclude the copyright owner from pursuing specific remedies in the event the work is copyright infringed.

The copyright owner should register a work in a timely manner for two main reasons. First, copyright registration is a prerequisite for bringing a copyright infringement lawsuit. A copyright owner cannot proceed with a copyright infringement lawsuit unless the work has been registered. And though a copyright owner can register

> " The crucial point for the publisher to remember is that the publisher will only have the ability to commercially exploit those rights specifically granted by the creator. "

the work after it has been infringed, this strategy can prove to be very costly and damaging to the copyright owner. At a minimum it can cost the copyright owner a significantly higher registration fee to expedite the registration of the work so that a lawsuit against an infringer can be filed quickly.

The second reason a copyright owner should register a copyrighted work in a timely manner is that this will qualify the copyright owner to receive "statutory damages" (as opposed to actual damages), and "legal costs and attorneys' fees" from a copyright infringer. Legally, registering in "a timely manner" means filing for registration prior to an infringement's taking place or within three months of the publication date of the work. If the infringement occurs prior to the effective date of copyright registration and after the three-month grace period then the copyright owner will not be entitled to receive statutory damages and legal costs and attorneys' fees. The effective date of copyright registration is the date when the Copyright Office receives the completed registration application consisting of the application, fee, and deposit copies of the work.

The significance of qualifying for statutory damages is that in this case the copyright owner can choose to receive statutory damages in a successful infringement lawsuit, rather than having to prove and quantify actual damages. A copyright owner may elect to receive statutory damages rather than actual damages, since proving actual damages may be very difficult or the profits made by the infringer may be very small. The statutory damages that will be awarded are discretionary and depend upon how willful and harmful the infringement was: usually the more deliberate and more damaging the infringement, the greater the award. Furthermore, the legal costs in any copyright infringement lawsuit, particularly attorneys' fees, are extremely high. And if the owner has registered the work in a timely manner, the court also has discretionary power to award attorneys' fees and legal costs to the copyright owner.

The third reason why the copyright owner should register a copyrighted work is that the Certificate of Registration serves as prima facie evidence that the work is original and is owned by the registrant of the copyrighted work. This becomes especially important if it becomes necessary for the copyright owner to obtain a preliminary injunction against a copyright infringer, such

as the immediate cessation of the distribution of the infringer's work. Legally, a presumption of validity only applies if a work is registered within five years of its publication date.

In actuality the benefits received from registering a copyrighted work may be even more important than those resulting from a copyright infringement lawsuit. This is because the great majority of copyright infringement matters are settled outside of court, primarily due to the high cost in time and money involved in such lawsuits. Thus a great deal of the legal value of registration lies in its power as a deterrence. After registration, a copyright owner is in a position to send a "cease and desist letter" to an infringer whose demands would be backed up by the real threat that a lawsuit could be filed immediately under advantageous conditions, since (i) the validity of originality and ownership will be presumed, (ii) statutory damages can be awarded, and (iii) legal costs and attorneys' fees may also be awarded by the court. When a copyright infringer receives a cease and desist letter written from a position of legal strength, they will frequently accede to the copyright owner's demands without the copyright owner's actually having to file a lawsuit.

Trademark Protection

Trademarks are used in publishing for series and periodical titles, for graphic characters, for names of publishing companies and product lines, for Internet domain names, for slogans, and for other products and services. Trademarks do not need to be federally registered in order to be protected, as they may be protected under the common law or state law when registration occurs in a particular state.

Under common law, the ownership and protection of a trademark is automatic once the mark is used in commerce. State law protects a mark once it is used in commerce and registered in a particular state. Trademark rights usually belong to the first user in a geographical area for a particular product or service. Common law or state law protection is probably satisfactory, and may be the only type of protection that is available for a mark that is only used in a single geographic market such as a city or state. Ownership and protection of a trademark will continue for as long as the owner uses the mark in commerce.

The federal Lanham Act governs the federal registration of trademarks that are registered with the Patent and Trademark Office on either the Principal or Supplemental Register. There are important advantages the trademark owner receives from the federal registration of a trademark that are not available when the trademark owner relies only upon common law or state law for protection. Therefore, if the trademark owner has a trademark that is eligible for federal registration but has not already been registered on either the Principal or Supplemental Register, or if there are plans to introduce a new mark, then the trademark owner should consider federal registration of the mark.

Trademark registration requires a filing fee, currently $325 for each class of goods or services for which the trademark owner wants to register the mark. As a general rule, print publishers register their marks in class 16, electronic publishers in class 9 and Internet publishers in class 41 or class 42. Many trademark owners register their marks in multiple classes depending upon the breadth of their product line and the services they provide.

Trademark Protection for the Titles of Works

When a new title is published, the publisher expects the copyright law to protect the creative expression in the work for the duration of the copyright term. Many publishers are under the misconception that the titles of their publications cannot be protected. Generally, the reason for this misconception is that publishers rely only upon their knowledge of the Copyright Act, which does not treat a title as protectable subject matter. Thus, they do not realize that trademark and unfair competition laws will provide protection under certain circumstances. Title protection is important for a number of reasons, including the value of public recognition that particular publications originate from a specific publisher as well as the additional goodwill and value that is added to the publisher's balance sheet through the possession of widely-recognized titles.

Intellectual property law does not protect titles as easily or as comprehensively as it protects the contents of a

> *Intellectual property law does not protect titles as easily or as comprehensively as it protects the contents of a literary work.*

literary work. Although nothing in the Copyright Act specifically precludes protection for titles, Copyright Office Regulations and judicial decisions have made it clear that titles are legally considered to be only the equivalent of short slogans and not to contain sufficient expression to be worthy of copyright protection. At least one reason that courts are hesitant to grant copyright protection for titles is that they fear that by doing so they will prevent a title's use by others for whom it may be equally legitimate and appropriate.

Thus a single title, such as the title of a particular work, may only be protected by unfair competition law and possibly trademark law if the publisher can demonstrate that the title has acquired secondary meaning. Secondary meaning, with regard to literary titles, develops when in the minds of the public, the particular title is associated with a single source of the literary work. Although blatant attempts to deceive may be protected by unfair competition law, it generally is not an easy matter to protect a single title.

Even though a single title cannot be registered under federal trademark law, the common law of unregistered marks has been interpreted by the courts to protect single book titles from a likelihood of confusion. This protection is not confined to situations involving confusion about the authorship of a work: it can also apply if consumers are confused about the sponsorship of a work, or about the affiliation or connection between one work and another. For example, if a second publisher used the title *Gone with the Wind* in a cookbook title, the public might be confused about whether the book was affiliated with or endorsed by the publisher of *Gone with the Wind* or its author, Margaret Mitchell.

Series titles are much easier for publishers to protect under unfair competition and federal trademark law; in fact, federal trademark law actually permits the registration of a series title. The benefits of federal registration, especially preventing the use of a series title by another publisher on competing titles, could make the effort and cost of obtaining the federal trademark registration very worthwhile.

The advantages of registering a mark on the Principal Register are as follows: (1) there is a presumption of trademark ownership and validity in any subsequent litigation involving the trademark; (2) registration usually provides the trademark owner with rights in the mark for a larger geographical area—usually nationwide—than is possible under common law and state law; (3) the scope of protection under both common and state law is usually restricted to the specific products or services for which the mark has been used while the scope of protection for a federally registered mark is usually much broader, encompassing related products or services as well; (4) judicial remedies are more far-reaching and costly to an infringer than those available under common law; and (5) after five years the mark may become "incontestable."

Conclusion

Because of their immense value, intellectual property assets should be managed and protected carefully. The following are some basic recommendations and reminders that publishers should take into account in order to manage and protect their intellectual property:

1. All contracts involving the publishing project should be in writing, even though an oral contract may indeed be valid.

2. A Work Made for Hire contract must be in writing for it to be valid.

3. The publisher must have a written contract with all creators of copyrightable material incorporated in their published products.

4. At the beginning of a publishing project the publisher should negotiate for and obtain all the rights that are essential for the financial success of the project.

5. Register copyrighted works immediately upon their creation or publication.

6. Register trademarks for series titles and publications, as well as for important services.

Disclaimer: This article is not legal advice. You should consult an attorney if you have legal questions that relate to your specific publishing issues and projects.

About the Author

Lloyd L. Rich, www.publishingattorney.com, has 25 years of experience as a publisher and now provides legal services to the publishing community in the areas of copyright, trademarks, contract preparation and negotiations, litigation, and other aspects of publishing law. He also writes the PubLaw Update Newsletter (free subscription available at www.publaw.com) written to help publishers keep up with current legal aspects of intellectual property protection. He can be reached at (303) 388-0291 or rich@publishingattorney.com.

CHAPTER 3
Marketing Plans and Strategies

Inside this chapter…

Developing a Marketing Plan
by Carol Ann Waugh

Because the K-12 education market is large, highly fragmented, diverse, and complex; and because the products and services that schools purchase vary widely (from textbooks and supplementary materials that support teachers and students to paper and other supplies that support the school infrastructure), it's a mistake to look for a universal, one size fits all "marketing plan" for this market. Instead, each and every company must construct its own unique plan to support their goals, their products and services, and their financial capabilities.

The most important thing to understand as you create your marketing plan is the process by which schools select and purchase the materials and services you wish to offer them. Aligning with and supporting this process will ensure that your marketing programs are hitting the right people at the right time with the right message—and this is what differentiates a plan that is effective at returning the maximum revenues from the minimum expenditure.

Understanding the School Buying Process

Site-Based Management
One of the important changes that has occurred in the past 10 years is a shift from districts making the decisions on what their schools will buy to individual schools making that decision. Of the 14,109 public school districts, 10,955 (78%) have given their schools increased decision-making authority.[1] The implications for marketers are enormous. No longer can we send in our sales force to the district and make a district-wide sale. The number of institutions and people within those institutions that need information about our products and services has expanded exponentially. And the number of potential decision makers and influencers involved in the decision to purchase has expanded as well.

Funding
Schools are funded from a variety of sources. The latest statistics are from the school year 1996-97 where

states contributed 48%, local sources contributed 45.4% and the federal share was 6.6%.[2] The majority of these funds are distributed to a school system according to the local government's budget cycle—generally covering a fiscal cycle from October to September of every year. Some federal dollars flow into the schools earlier as Congress has authorized "advanced funding" for some programs. The availability of funds has a major impact on when schools buy.

Product Evaluation
Traditionally, the evaluation and buying cycle begins in late August. This is the time that many teachers and administrators begin the process of collecting information about new products and programs that may be purchased for the following school year. Accordingly, most educational publishers time their new product introductions for the fall of every year and send out their catalogs and marketing materials during the months of August, September, and October. This is the time to develop "awareness" in the market place.

Product Selection
Spring is the time when most educators get together in their "teams" of decision makers and influencers to determine which products and services they will purchase for use in the following school year. This is the time they review demos of products, ask for additional information, and compare the different features and benefits of a variety of choices. Again, many educational publishers target this time of year to send out their spring catalogs and make sales calls on schools and districts.

Product Purchase
Traditionally, June through August are the highest revenue months for educational publishers. This is the time when purchase orders are issued for products to be delivered in time for the opening of school.

> "...it's a mistake to look for a universal, one size fits all marketing plan..."

Other Key Purchasing Windows

There are two other times during the year when publishers can take advantage of purchasing opportunities. One comes in September, as schools realize that some of the products they have ordered did not arrive. (Yes, some companies promise but don't deliver!) Schools scramble at this time to look for replacement products. Additionally, in September, there are many new teachers who are coming into the school system who might also want different materials than were decided upon the spring before.

The other time is in May. As with all government-funded institutions, the axiom of "use it or lose it" holds true for school funding. If for some reason they haven't spent all their money by the end of the school year, they will try to use up their funding so they don't lose it the following year. This is an especially good time to send out "sale" catalogs or promotions. Educators are always looking for bargains, and they see these opportunities as a way to make their left over money go as far as possible.

This is not to say that purchasing doesn't take place all year. It does, especially for smaller ticket items and supplemental materials. But for larger purchases—particularly those concerning technology, the timetable indicated above is pretty ingrained in our educational system. And for new companies entering the market, it is the most difficult thing to understand and to manage. Suffice it to say that selling into the K-12 market is not the same as selling into the consumer market where a "hit" product like the Razor scooter can sell millions within a few months. On the other hand, while market share is usually built slowly in K-12, it pays off dividends for years.

What are the Components of a K-12 Marketing Plan?

Companies who have been in this market for a while have discovered that using a multi-channel marketing strategy is the best approach. In short, this means using every possible channel to promote product awareness and to convert prospects into customers. Depending upon the financial strength of a company, the channels described below can be used to a greater or lesser degree.

PURCHASING POLICIES FOR A SAMPLE SCHOOL DISTRICT*

- Purchases under $300 are processed through purchase orders. While competitive quotes may be obtained, they are not required.

- Informal purchases over $500 are processed by soliciting at least three telephone or faxed quotations. The Purchasing Department tabulates and evaluates the quotes, and then issues an award based upon the lowest and best quote.

- Formal bids for purchase over $5,000 are processed by issuing invitations to Bid or Requests for Proposals to prospective vendors. Sealed bids are opened publicly at the date and time designated on the bid documents. Bids are tabulated by the buyer and sent to the requesting school or department for recommendation. Proposals are evaluated by the buyer in conjunction with the school or department representative.

- Purchase orders are awarded based upon a combination of factors such as: lowest competitive price quotations; best possible delivery; adherence to specifications; quality; and performance consistent with bid requirements.

*This is an example of the actual purchasing policy for one school district in the US. It is important to note that each district has their own "policies" and these may vary widely from district to district.

Direct Mail

For companies selling supplemental materials, this is the channel of choice. It is by far the most cost-effective way to reach a large population of decision makers and influencers. Response rates to direct mail can vary from 1-5%, depending upon the percentage of customers contained in the mailing list. The higher that percentage is, the greater the response that can be expected.

Catalogs are by far the most popular item sent by direct mail, since educators are used to getting these pieces and since they often keep them on file for future reference. Catalogs generate sales for 2-3 years, so they remain an active marketing tool well after the mailing date. They are good for showing your entire product line, introducing new products, and providing incentives to "order now."

Other types of direct mail are also used, including full mailing pieces, post cards, and self-mailers. These mailings can be used to address other marketing objectives, such as announcing a significant new product where the "2 page catalog spread" isn't enough space to fully describe the benefits and features; promoting complex, expensive products and services where the intent is lead generation rather than a quick sale; inviting people to a special event at a trade show; or promoting a specific reference product to a school librarian who needs to know much more detailed information about a product than a short descriptive paragraph in a catalog can provide.

Space Advertising

Because space ads have been proven to increase direct mail response, many companies coordinate their advertising messages prior to the arrival of their direct mail promotions. Increasing company and product awareness is essential to building a presence in the K-12 market. Teachers and administrators also need to feel confident in their purchasing decisions and supported by their suppliers—over the long haul. This is perhaps even more important now that it was even a few years ago. The demise of many of the dot coms who entered the educational market during the past two years has shaken the confidence of many educators. Building brand is one thing. Staying in business is another!

While many educational publishing companies eschew advertising (because of its high cost and the difficulty of tracking responses), advertising can be an important component of your marketing plan—if you do it right, and if you can clearly stand out among the crowd. But this is perhaps the greatest challenge.

Public Relations

The K-12 education market is populated with hundreds of magazines and newsletters devoted to bringing information about new products and services to the attention of teachers and administrators. And these magazines are happy to receive your press releases and feature stories: they are always on the lookout for "newsworthy" information about what works in schools. In addition, almost every newspaper in the country covers the "education beat" since the topic of education touches almost everyone in the country.

Since the opportunity for coverage in the media is huge, most educational publishers devote a portion of

> "Increasing company and product awareness is essential to building a presence in the K-12 market."

their marketing plan to public relations. This includes creating and mailing press releases, establishing contacts with magazine editors to "pitch" stories, and holding special "press events" at trade shows and conferences. Some companies hire in-house specialists for PR, while others use the services of a wide variety of public relations experts who concentrate on the educational market.

Conferences and Exhibits

There are hundreds of educational conferences and exhibits where educational publishers can demonstrate their products and services to teachers and administrators. Choosing the right ones to attend is always a challenge, as more and more of these conferences are announced each year. There are national, state, and local exhibits. There are exhibits by product format (NECC), exhibits by subject specialty (IRA), and exhibits by job function (NSBA). Some exhibits are sold out a year ahead of time, and some have long "priority" lists so that new companies are stuck in out-of-the-way spots. Despite these inconveniences, however this marketing channel has multiple benefits—including meeting potential customers face-to-face, reviewing the competition, developing partnerships for marketing efforts, and generating sales leads for future follow-up.

Thus, while the cost of exhibiting can consume a major portion of your marketing budget, it's an essential component of being a player in the K-12 market.

Third-Party Distribution

Distributing your product through third parties can be an effective way to increase your sales without investing your own marketing dollars. Obviously, these third-party distributors will want a commission or the ability to purchase your products at a substantial discount, but there are many distributors that have been very successful at building up their businesses by marketing other companies' products.

Perhaps the most notable development within this marketing channel has been the rise of the catalog houses that distribute software. Many small companies who had only one or two programs benefited from this type of distribution. Large, well-established companies also saw the benefit of listing their products in these catalogs.

On the other hand, some types of distributors concentrate on specific "niche" markets within the K-12 schools such as special education, ESL, or vocational education, while others specifically target subjects like math, science, and history.

Another avenue—especially suited for technology companies—is the independent dealer or value-added reseller. These companies have established relationships with schools, who depend upon them for advice and product recommendations. If you are a vendor without a large field sales force, these companies can get your products purchased when no other marketing channel can.

Direct Sales

Not all companies can afford to staff and manage a field sales force. But the ones that do make this the major component of their marketing plan. Everything else in the plan is designed to support the field sales people—not to generate revenue directly.

Textbook companies have long established this as their primary marketing and sales tool to the K-12 market. Companies selling high-ticket "technology solutions" are also using this model. In general, the higher priced or more complex your product or service is, the more seriously your company should consider using this marketing channel as its primary channel.

Independent Reps

Another alternative to the cost of hiring, training, and managing an in-house field sales staff is to use the large network of independent reps that call on K-12 schools. These reps are mainly "Mom & Pop" operations that take on several product lines to sell into schools. The biggest issue with this type of representation is their requirement for "exclusivity" within their geographic territory. Companies who are strong direct marketers hesitate when they are asked to pay a 20-30% commission on every sale made in a territory, regardless of source. However, an analysis of sales by zip code can point out

weaknesses in a national marketing campaign (especially within the largest school districts like New York City), and adding these types of reps can be helpful in breaking into specific areas where a "personal touch" is required.

Telemarketing

A third alternative to fielding a sales staff or hiring independent reps is the use of a strong telemarketing approach. In the past, telemarketing was used to follow up on direct mail as a way to generate sales of a specific product. While this approach is still used to some extent, telemarketing has developed as more of a relationship-building device—providing a connection between customers and prospects with a publishing company. And in some cases telemarketing is used as a support channel for a direct sales staff—providing leads and making appointments for sales presentations. Using the telephone as a marketing channel can be an investment that pays big dividends.

> " Web sites are now one of the major ways teachers and administrators are finding information about products and services. "

Web Sites and Internet Marketing

The advent of the Internet has added a new marketing channel to most educational publishers' marketing plans. Some companies have begun developing Internet-delivered subscription products, while others have simply used their Web site to promote their existing products. Regardless of your approach, Web sites are now one of the major ways teachers and administrators are finding information about products and services. While the Internet is still in its infancy, and while revenue and cost saving models come and go, companies who are using this channel to build relationships with customers and prospects are well on their way to adding an important, cost effective, and responsive channel to their marketing mix.

Conclusion: Plan and Measure

Understanding the way the K-12 market selects and purchases products and developing your marketing plan to support this process is the best way to formulate an effective marketing program. The ultimate trick to effective marketing is to "do more of what works and less of what doesn't." However, this assumes that you have the tools in place to measure each marketing channel and evaluate its effectiveness on a continual basis. If you don't measure your efforts, you can never understand what is working, why it's working, and how to "tweak" it so it works better next year!

∎

[1] Market Data Retrieval, 2000-2001 list catalog.
[2] Digest of Educational Statistics, 1999, Department of Education

∎

About the Author

Carol Ann Waugh *is president of Xcellent Marketing, www.xcellentmarketing.com, a consulting company specializing in providing strategic planning and marketing strategies for educational and reference publishers. Her clients range from start-ups to the largest companies in the industry including print, video, and software publishers/distributors; magazine publishers; venture capitalists; supply companies; Internet companies and database publishers. She can be reached at (303) 388-5215 or at cwaugh@xcellentmarketing.com.*

Now Is the Time to Create an Effective Channel Plan!

By Glen McCandless

Channel planning is critical to success in selling to schools, whether you are new to the education markets or a well-established supplier. Yet despite the proliferation of channels and marketing methods, few companies devote sufficient time to the design of their channels or manage them to optimize market coverage and cost-effectiveness.

You may have a revolutionary new product that you passionately believe will "change the world," but your company's profitability will suffer unless you can efficiently and effectively present the product to potential buyers.

You have plenty of options. The latest *Technology Purchasing Forecast,* published by Quality Education Data (QED), lists more than ten sources educational buyers turn to when they purchase software products. They run the gamut from publisher-direct to catalogs and software sales reps. There are dozens of other suppliers that educators rely on when they want to get information about products, or when they need to evaluate or obtain support for them.

Channel planning is not as simple as placing products in catalogs, finding distributors, enlisting strategic partners, or hiring sales reps. An effective channel plan is a reflection of your channel strategy, the blueprint you will follow to take your products and services into the education markets. Your channel plan can also provide competitive advantages.

The word "channel" has multiple definitions. For the purpose of developing your plan, a channel is any resource you use to market, sell, and support your products, as well as maintain customer relationships. As you begin the channel planning process, your goal should be to design a strategic plan that balances the natural tension between minimizing cost and maximizing customer satisfaction while providing significant competitive differentiation.

> "An effective channel plan is a reflection of your channel strategy, the blueprint you will follow to take your products and services into the education markets."

Here are the steps to building a successful channel plan.

Study Your Target Audience

Most companies are quick to tout how terrific their products and services are. Few tout their channels. As with good product development, your choice of channel should begin with gathering information about the buyer's perspective. You must know how potential buyers prefer to find out about, evaluate, purchase, support, and maintain similar products, either by gathering the information from existing reports (like the one from QED) or better yet, through primary research.

Having current, reliable facts about buyer preferences is a critical step because channels are dynamic (witness the rise of warehouse clubs and online distribution). You might miss a paradigm shift if you assume that past or present channels, used by your company or competitors, are what your target customers prefer today, or will prefer tomorrow. The only way to know is to regularly survey a random, representative sample of your customers and potential customers to uncover trends that will allow you to lead the market. It is very risky to make assumptions or base your channel decisions on general observations of the education markets.

Consider Your Competition

Product comparisons are popular ways to position products. Most companies can articulate why their products or services are better than a competitor's. But rarely can they also provide competitive positioning for their channels. Your channel plan should provide meaningful differences that allow you to do just that.

Periodic competitive analysis will give you the intelligence. Then, because product differentiation by itself is no longer enough to be successful, your channel strategy should be adjusted to be better than your competitor's.

What does it mean to be better? Simply put, the closer your channels match buyer preferences, the more likely you are to outsell your competition. Importantly, you should have a plan to promote your channel advantage as part of your total solution.

Evaluate Your Options

There are dozens of categories of resources and marketing methods you could use to reach faculty, administrators, and students. New channels pop up all the time.

There are cross-over channels (those that target home and school markets), outsourced field-sales and marketing organizations, professional associations, direct marketing and telesales services, and OEMs and distributors, to name a few. Any one of these channels might use several methods to reach potential customers. With so many options, systematic evaluation is the only way to put together the right mix for your unique situation.

For each potential channel category, list its strongest attribute. That is, specify which of the marketing, sales, support, and maintenance roles each channel you've identified performs with the highest quality and efficiency.

Factor in Product Life Cycle

The most effective channels for selling and marketing your products and services vary over the life of the product. Many companies market and sell all their products through the same channels regardless of their life cycle stage.

In the earliest life cycle phase, buyers need more support than they do for mature products. Sometimes, for new product categories, much of the effort is educating the audience about product capabilities. Later in the life cycle, when products are better known, some buyers are more interested in easy availability than they are in product information. At that stage, models that combine volume channels with service providers often achieve the right level of efficiency to serve a diverse buying audience.

Take a look at the channel and product life cycle chart below.

Where are your products in the cycle? Do your channels map to the characteristics of that stage? If you have a channel that carries more than one product you offer, make sure that the channel is suitable and has the right infrastructure and cost to match the phases where your different offerings may be.

For example, a new courseware authoring system may move best through direct sales channels or school-specialty VARs during early-adopter and early-majority life cycle phases, but sell more profitably via catalogs in peak or declining phases.

Product Life Cycle Channel Map

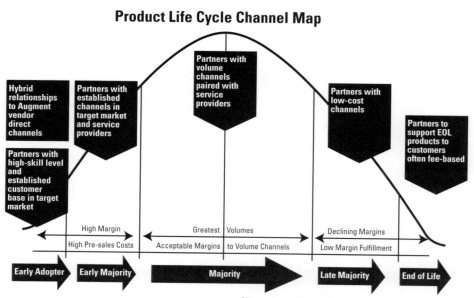

Chart adapted from Channel Strategies, Inc.

Analyze Channel Costs

A winning education channel strategy is the most efficient mix of resources you can commit to get the job done. If you are developing a channel plan for a new company, you'll need to forecast your costs. If you are already in business and want to lower your sales and marketing expenses, you should compare the expenses of operating your current channels to the costs of the options you're considering.

The best approach is to determine the relationship between activities performed by the channels and the resources they consume as a percent of the product cost. Resources required to sustain indirect channels typically include training, advertising support, technical support, management, commissions, and order processing.

On the flip side, you must evaluate the expense savings you could achieve from each channel you are considering. In order to do this, you must understand the steps in the process of getting your products to market and also the cost to support and maintain customers. You should consider expenses for promotion, inventory, financing, ordering, payment processing, installation, and post-sales support. With the right combination of channel resources, you can maximize profitability by lowering your sales, marketing, and support costs.

Create a Channel Matrix

Now you're ready to begin putting together your channel plan. A useful tool to create your blueprint is a channel matrix, a visual aid that overlays channels, methods, and market segments that you can produce with a spreadsheet program. The channel matrix allows you to allocate demand-generation tasks across channels, recognizing that the building blocks of the channel plan are not the channels, but the tasks that must be accomplished.

The channels are either direct (controlled by your company) or indirect (controlled by a third party). The tasks are the methods you can use to reach potential customers, either directly or indirectly. For instance, your company can hire and utilize its own field sales reps, account managers, or telemarketers, and the same methods can be used with indirect channels.

Create your channel matrix one product (or category of products) at time. Begin by listing the various marketing channels or methods down the first column of the spreadsheet. Then, across the adjacent columns, use headings to describe the various tasks required to acquire and maintain customers. Finally, overlay specific market segments, filling in the cells of the matrix. Here's an example of what a channel matrix might look like for a hypothetical product and market:

Sales and Marketing Channel Matrix

Sales and Marketing Tasks

Channels and Methods	Brand Awareness	Lead Management	Initial Contact	Needs Assessment	Sales	Fulfillment	Support	Maintain	Develop Account
Business Dev Exec				High Opportunity Accounts					
Consultants									
Call Center		ALL							ALL
Resellers and Agents				Second Tier Accounts					
Channel Manager					Resellers, Agents, Partners				
Conference Exhibits	ALL								
Direct Mail									
Advertising									
Public Relations									

Your channel plan, depicted by the channel matrix, depends on your thorough understanding of channel costs and customer buying behavior, which you should have if you completed the previous steps in the planning process. When you add a new channel or want to service a new market segment, changes you make to the matrix must reflect all of these important variables.

Recognize, Assess, and Control Channel Conflict

The channel matrix makes it easy to identify potential channel conflict. Channel conflict arises when different channels are used to provide the same sales and marketing function to the same target audience. Conflict is an inevitable result of a multi-channel strategy. And, as you may know, when you add a channel or substitute a new method of communications, your sales reps, distributors, and other channel partners will resist. Their opposition is driven by fear that they will lose revenue or have to compete for customers.

The first step in managing channel conflict is recognizing and communicating its existence. If you already have channels in place and conflict exists, pretending that there isn't a problem can destroy your channel relationships.

Then, you must assess the magnitude of the conflict (or potential conflict) particularly in terms of revenue impact to the affected channels. While some amount of revenue overlap is desirable to maximize coverage, pervasive channel overlaps can cause customer confusion, channel management issues, and inefficiencies that lead to profit erosion.

Finally, you must find ways to control channel conflict by establishing boundaries and guidelines for serving customers, typically based on customer demographics (for example, large districts versus small districts, or community colleges versus research universities), order potential, strategic considerations, geography, and products.

> "...improper selection or utilization of channels and marketing methods imposes high cost and usually leads to poor return on channel investments."

Determine Your Channel Resources and Develop Your Program

An essential component of any channel plan is how you intend to implement, manage, support, and develop your channels. While the channel plan itself may not specify the names of companies and people that will be channel resources for your product, someone will need to develop a prospect list for each channel category on your channel matrix and then recruit. Preferably, the person leading that effort will have channel management experience, as well as a combination of sales skills, marketing expertise, and business acumen. The channel manager will also develop a channel compensation program, channel marketing plan, training program, and other aspects of a solid channel program.

Once the channel plan is implemented, the channel manager will coordinate channel tasks, ensure that relationships are intact, and keep the channel partners informed about their roles in achieving your sales and marketing objectives. In a multi-channel system, it is critical that the channel manager oversee the various hand-offs between channels to ensure that they are smooth and to avoid disruptions and customer satisfaction issues.

The channel manager often assumes responsibility for channel development—that is, helping existing channels perform their duties to the best of their ability and optimizing the channel mix. Maintaining productive channels requires ongoing recruiting and skillful relationship management.

Conclusion: Seize the Moment

While many companies serving the educational markets today use both direct and indirect channels, few companies recognize that improper selection or utilization of channels and marketing methods imposes high cost and usually leads to poor return on channel investments.

"More is better" is the predominant channel philosophy. Decisions to add channels or marketing methods are often made quickly and independently by individuals who lack the experience to understand the impact of such decisions. As a consequence, companies find themselves stumbling over hastily constructed and poorly implemented channel programs, resulting in excessive sales and marketing expenses.

The hasty approach is of particular concern when you consider the dizzying array of products and services being offered to schools. Today's high-tech products cover the spectrum from simple and low-cost to very complex and costly. And while the number of products being offered has skyrocketed, buyers are more savvy, more demanding, and more in control of their purchasing behavior.

The proliferation of catalogs, online stores, and other low-cost, high-volume channels has given educational buyers more control than ever about what they buy, where they buy it, and what they pay for it. Channels that were once a good fit are now delivering lower profitability. And while the capabilities of channel partners for selling and supporting your products are critical, it is also important to ensure that the channels work for you (make money) and meet the needs and goals of your customers.

If you are launching a new company, a new division of your company, or a new product, be sure to invest the time and resources necessary to create a solid channel plan. If you are an established company seeking to increase your profitability and market share and you do not currently have a channel plan, now is the time to develop one. If you have a channel plan, but haven't taken the time to do a thorough analysis, there is no better time than the present.

■

[1] The channel matrix process is based on the hybrid marketing model of Dr. Rowland Moriarty, associate professor at Harvard Business School, and is described in his landmark report, Managing Hybrid Marketing Systems.

■

About the Author

Glen McCandless *is a principal of Focus Marketing, Inc., a firm specializing in the education markets and publisher of sellingtoschools.com, the online resource center serving high-tech education sales and marketing professionals. Leading computer hardware companies, software publishers, and e-learning providers rely on Focus Marketing for strategic sales, marketing, and channel consultation. FMI also provides marketing communications, channel, and sales development programs focused on faculty, staff, and students in the K-12 and higher education markets. For more information, go to* www.sellingtoschools.com/focusmarketing *or e-mail Glen at* gmccandless@sellingtoschools.com

Identity and Branding

by Diane Rapley

We are surrounded with brands every day. Brands—company and product identities—are part of our daily lives. We all have our favorite brands and perhaps our least favorite brands. And we have all heard a few famous brand "stories"—like when Coca-Cola tried unsuccessfully to change its flagship product brand and identity, and quickly switched back again.

But how do we approach branding in the education market? What are some of the factors to consider in developing a brand, and why is branding important at all?

Jane Hrehocik Clampitt, a brand manager with Dupont Corporation, speaking at the 2000 EdPress meeting, defined the major characteristics of a brand as follows:

- Uniqueness (products can be copied, but brands cannot)
- A consistent logo, look, image, identity, and tag line
- A promise to the target audience
- A guarantee of consistent performance
- A differentiator from the competition
- A whole marketing approach
- A reputation
- A key business asset

We often think of a brand purely in terms of the unique logo and typography used for a company or product name, but these additional aspects of brand have implications that play an important role in marketing.

The Power of Brand

Branding helps customers make choices and thus makes their lives easier. When we are surrounded with ten kinds of toothpaste in the grocery store, our brand awareness helps us cut quickly through the clutter and make a selection, without having to spend valuable time comparing the features and prices of competing products. Naturally, features and price are important, but a buying decision is rarely made on features and price alone. In fact, if your customers are evaluating your product only on features and price, with no awareness of your brand and what it stands for, it is unlikely that your product will be the one selected. Brand recognition and brand

attributes—the characteristics your target market associates with your brand—are often the deciding factor in the purchase decision. Psychologically, brands reduce the time needed to make choices and the risk associated with making a purchase. And so one of ours goal as marketers must be to make it easier for the customer to choose our products, by developing a strong brand.

Branding also helps new products enter smoothly into the marketplace. For example, when a company like BMW or Ford introduces a new model of car, our brand associations make it easier for us as consumers to accept the new model, even if it departs from the company's previous direction. Companies invest heavily in promoting brand preference, so that their future product offerings will be more easily accepted. In building our brands, we are trying to build an asset that can be used over a long period of time.

It is important for educational technology companies, in our crowded marketplace, to work at determining brand attributes and establishing brand preference. How do we want our customers to see us? What characteristics do we want our customers to associate with our brands? For example, do we want to be seen as teacher-oriented or student-oriented, comprehensive or specialized, entry-level or advanced, inexpensive or high-end? We have to select our brand attributes carefully, be able to justify them with reference to our products' features and functions, and consistently promote them as part of our brand identity.

But branding involves more than a logo and more than the marketing department. The entire company needs to understand and help build the brand. In order to successfully build a brand, everyone in the company needs to be able to convey the essence and purpose of the brand in any contact with a customer. Many companies work hard at maintaining a consistent brand identity inside as well as outside the company—through internal memo pad stationery, internal PowerPoint templates, and the like—in order to reinforce the brand to employees on a daily basis and instill a consistent "brand story."

Of course, in order to build brand preference over time and generate repeat purchases, product quality must be consistent. Customers must know you have a product they can rely on. But a sense of brand heritage is important also. In our market, there are many new companies, particularly in the Internet space. Our customers are often looking for a sense of where the brand came from. It's important to build the history of the company or the company founders into the brand identity in order to provide a sense of assurance.

Brand Preference and Personal Identity

Jane Hrehocik Clampitt, in her EdPress presentation, makes the point that brand selection always involves a statement by the customer about himself or herself. The kinds of brands we select make statements about our tastes, values, ages, and lifestyles. When developing our brand attributes, it's important to think about how we are asking our customers to see themselves when they select our brand. Do we want them to see themselves as innovators and visionaries? Is our product for people who break the mold? Or do we want our customers to see themselves as careful guardians of well-established precepts? Is one of our brand attributes that our product has been around for many years and is tried and true? Strong brands have unique personalities that we as consumers share in as we associate with them by selecting them; and one of the goals of branding is to create a feeling about the brand in the minds of the target audience. In order to develop a brand personality that is both strong and widely appealing, then, it's important to determine the characteristics of the target audience and how they relate to the brand.

Over time, the customer base becomes a big part of the identity of a brand. Accordingly, testimonials can be very important brand-reinforcing marketing tools. The kinds of customers who use our products say a lot about our brands and help us promote them to new prospects. If we present testimonials from large urban school districts that use our products, other large urban school districts are likely to feel that ours is a product that will meet their needs. Similarly, if we use testimonials from

women superintendents, other women superintendents are likely to respond positively to our brand. The characteristics of the customer become part of the brand personality.

In making this kind of appeal, it's important to begin promoting our brands at the beginning of the typical selling season or decision-making process. When we begin talking to our customers in the early decision-making stages, we are better able to move them forward toward the perception of preferred choice. Customers also need to understand the functional and emotional benefits of the brand, as well as have a sense of its value and utility to them.

> "As brands are built, it's essential also to listen to customer feedback and take note of how our brands are being perceived."

As brands are built, it's essential also to listen to customer feedback and take note of how our brands are being perceived. Our customers may be telling us that some aspect of our brand we think is important is not worth much to them. They may help us identify our strongest brand characteristics and build upon them further. It's important to have an ongoing dialog with customers about how the brand is being perceived, in order to refine and improve it and make it more successful over time. Focus groups and customer surveys can be very helpful in soliciting feedback and discussion on brand strengths and weaknesses.

Visual Elements of the Brand

Much of the physical representation of the brand, of course, comes from the "trade dress"—the logo, typography, and tag line of the product or company name. It's essential that company and product logos and tag lines communicate the spirit of your brand personality. Does your logo look traditional or cutting-edge? Fun or serious? Does it communicate a bargain price point or "expensive-but–worth–every–penny"? Does it reflect the business you are in—books, software, the Internet, or teacher training? Is it age-appropriate for your target market—elementary or high school students or K-12, teachers or administrators or superintendents? Does it look dated or contemporary? Does it fit with your intangible brand attributes?

The visual presentation of a brand identity extends beyond the logo. Our brand identities—the broader "look and feel" of the company image, generally developed from the colors and characteristics of the logo—need to be communicated in our print materials, on our Web sites, in our trade show booths, in our advertising, and in all our communications vehicles. When we look at the Apple Computer brand, for example, we are of course aware of the strong logo. However, the broader attributes of the Apple brand are communicated graphically through more than the logo, through a well-developed "look" that very successfully supports the brand characteristics—clean, uncluttered, innovative, and high-tech, but also friendly and with strong educational credentials. To maximize every opportunity to build brand awareness, it's essential that companies develop and consistently implement a strong visual identity that supports and extends the logo across all marketing vehicles. The goal is that when customers walk by our tradeshow booth or pick up our brochures, they know who we are before they read the company name, just as we recognize Kodak film on the shelf without reading the name Kodak.

As you develop your logo, it's important to survey the field and see what kinds of branding your competitors are doing. Any logo or product name you select will need to be trademarked for your protection, and it's unlikely to pass successfully through the trademark search process if there are similar logos and product names in your market segment or in the educational market in general. Beyond the legal considerations, however, in order to establish a strong brand you will clearly need an identity that differentiates you from your competitors and helps your customers recognize you in a crowded marketplace.

It's important to establish ground rules for the use of your logo and brand identity in a company style guide format. Everyone in the company involved in implementing the brand and identity needs to know not only what typeface and colors to use, but also what guidelines to follow in the numerous implementation situations that arise. How to show the logo on various color backgrounds, for example, or how to display the logo in combination with business partner logos. Many large companies have brand and identity manuals of 100 pages or more, to cover every possible occurrence. This may not be needed in our market, but it does point out the emphasis many companies place on consistency in brand identity.

However, sometimes brands and logos need to change. Times change, fashions in typestyle and colors change, logos become dated, and brands need a new look. But it's important not to abandon the entire brand equity in the updating process. The FedEx logo and the HP logo have both recently been given a new look. Both updated logos capture something new and fresh yet retain important characteristics of the old look, combining the best of the brand heritage with an appealing statement about change and innovation.

Conclusion

Clearly, having the strongest brand in a category is a huge advantage, especially when there is parity in performance. In many product categories, the competing products are very similar. In this case, customers are most likely to select the one with the strongest brand.

To begin developing a strong brand for yourself, think about what you stand for. Define your brand characteristics and your target audience. Review the competition. Work with your graphic design team to develop a range of solutions, until you get the identity that's right for your brand. And then implement it consistently, consistently, consistently!

About the Author

Diane Rapley is currently director of marketing communications for NetSchools, where she is responsible for company identity and messaging, and for print and online communications. Before joining NetSchools, Diane managed her own consulting firm for seven years, working with clients such as The Learning Company, SkillsBank, Computer Curriculum Corporation, Mindscape, and LightSpan. Diane was also vice-president of marketing for the Education Division of Broderbund Software, where she managed the company's initial positioning and marketing efforts to schools.

Partnering for Success: Getting to Win-Win

by Michael Ross

Today's marketplace presents a variety of challenges for the average publisher of intellectual property. It is becoming increasingly difficult to develop and produce innovative product profitably. In addition, once a quality product is produced, bringing it to market presents its own set of challenges. Your existing infrastructure may not be ideally suited to take advantage of all distribution opportunities, or the complexity of the market may require multiple channel strategies. At the same time, original intellectual property, properly developed, is extremely valuable and highly leverageable. Given the vastness and diversity of the market, as well as the need and appetite for products of quality and value, there are many opportunities to develop something once for a specific market and then reuse it in several different formats to reach additional markets.

Many of the problems associated with developing and marketing products can be solved by working with a partner. By finding the right partner, a publisher may be able to develop products more affordably, find efficient ways to reach new and profitable markets, and discover ways to repurpose content for delivery in other formats. In order to find a partner with the right fit—who adds long-term value to your development or marketing program—you need to know what you want to accomplish, be aware of changes in the marketplace, and be prepared to take "yes" for answer. In other words, you have to be ready and willing to share your content and perhaps gamble on exploring unknown territory.

Development and marketing issues are closely intertwined, and many of the criteria used in selecting a development partner are identical to those used in choosing a marketing partner. In exceptional cases, the same partner may be able to play both roles. However, even though the general criteria may be the same, the specific skills, attributes, and expertise you seek in a developer are different from those of a marketer.

Why Partner for Development?

There are many reasons why you may be looking for a development partner. Perhaps you have created a series of profitable books in print and you also want to turn them into e-books. Or you may have a series of CD-ROMs that now need to be Web enabled. These are typical issues facing intellectual property holders who want to migrate their products from one medium to another, yet do not have the in-house expertise to do so.

The need for new technological capabilities is only one possible motive for entering into development partnerships, however. In fact, you may find, ironically, that you need a development partner who is able to provide expertise in an "old" technology, which you, and a large part of the market, have abandoned. For instance, suppose you made a strategic decision in the past not to "chase" an old technology that was moving out of favor in the market. In this case, you may have lost obsolescent skills associated with that technology. Your team may have moved on, but there may still be a substantial niche need in the market that is not being filled and that you no longer have the skills to address. For example, many of us no longer have production teams that know how to work with microfilm, yet there might be an opportunity to repurpose unique content if we did. Many schools and libraries have older technology that won't read certain CD-ROMs with high minimum hardware and software requirements. And some library collections will still purchase microfiche, at premium prices. There are opportunities out there for content providers to partner with developers who can deliver product on older standards.

Translation and localization projects will almost always require partnering. It is unlikely that you will have in-house expertise in putting your products—print, CD-ROM, or Web—into another language. At the same time, there may be large revenue opportunities that you are missing by not localizing your product. In this case, you will want to find a partner who resides in the target market. Only a developer who is part of the culture where the language is spoken will understand all of the nuances necessary to make a successful second-language version of your product.

Potential Pitfalls of Development Partnerships

Along with the opportunities of development partnerships come several pitfalls that you should be aware of, so that you can weigh the costs and benefits of partnering against those of internal development. Through your analysis, you may decide that you need to develop the necessary in-house skills to accomplish, for example, a given technology transfer. In general, if you anticipate having an ongoing need for a skill, you may want to plan to develop it as a new core competency in-house, even if you do decide to partner in the short-term. If you do not develop these skills internally, in the future you may leave yourself open to either paying too much for outside services or giving up part of the market to a more nimble, more cost-efficient competitor. You should be aware of the risks of falling into a long-term "competency trap," and not be afraid to develop skills internally that may be outside the scope of your current core competency. By internally developing new skills, you will provide some insurance against a partner who, for one reason or another, is no longer interested in meeting your business objectives.

Even a good partnership can go south if you choose to rely too heavily on your partner for core, business-critical skills. One of the classic examples is Apple, who in the early days of developing desktop computers outsourced their monitors to Sony. This gave Sony a core competency in producing computer monitors and made Apple totally dependent on Sony for a key system component. The result was that Sony, starting out merely as a component supplier for, and partner with, Apple, ended up being a major competitor in personal computers. In particular, they used their know-how in miniaturization to produce some of the most compelling compact personal computing devices on the market.

At World Book we faced a similar problem when we decided to go into the development of CD-ROMs for consumers. We had deep expertise in producing leading CD-ROMs for researchers, librarians, and scholars, but we had no expertise in producing engaging multimedia that would appeal to a mass audience. In this case, we wouldn't have developed a consumer product if we couldn't partner with a leader in this field. As a result,

"Few business partnerships are meant to last a lifetime."

we entered into a partnership with IBM, who at the time had a variety of award-winning consumer product lines as well as innovative technologies that only a company with IBM's resources could develop and maintain. Although we relied on IBM to provide their state-of-the-art assets and know-how, we never retreated from building new basic skills ourselves. We also made learning from IBM a priority during the course of the partnership. As a result, when the two companies together decided to terminate the partnership to pursue different strategic directions, we at World Book had cultivated the basic skills necessary to develop and improve our proprietary products, either on our own or with a new partner. From that point on we decided to continue developing the consumer products on our own rather than seek another partner. Luckily we had taken on a sufficient number of new skills to ensure that we could produce consumer products that had substantial competitive advantages. By carefully managing our reliance on our partner, we did not fall into a competency trap. And given the increasing dependence of our products and businesses on technology, many of us in traditional publishing have (or will) become technology experts for the same reasons.

Keep in mind that most partnerships, regardless of the reasons for establishing them in the first place, are likely to break up. Business models change; companies get bought. In any partnership, the "divorce" must be anticipated from the beginning. This does not change the value of the partnership. Few business partnerships are meant to last a lifetime. In a development partnership, understanding this may be a matter of survival. For example, at a certain stage in your company's development, you may need a partner to provide crucial innovation in order to extend your product range. You may determine that your future growth depends on this. Given the degree of change in the marketplace and the constant shifts in technology and infrastructure, many of us will need to form a technology partnership simply in order not to fall too far behind. But if you become too dependent on your partner for innovation and technology and ignore the need to acquire new skills and expertise, you are likely to become a weak partner in the short term and perhaps compromise your future in the long term.

What to Consider in your Marketing Partnerships

The size and fragmentation of the education market also opens up many opportunities for marketing partnerships. Most of us will not be able to develop the skills necessary to reach all of the markets for which our products were intended, or for which they may be appropriate. Even though it was originally designed to be an Internet service provider, AOL has become one of the world's most successful marketing companies, precisely because it provides instant access to a huge market that would otherwise be inaccessible to many of its partners. The North American school and library market also requires special skills, often a dedicated sales force, and relationships that need to be nurtured over time. Foreign markets require local expertise and sometimes language skills, as well as cultural knowledge of what works and doesn't work. In short, the market is vast, and you will find yourself in need of a variety of partnerships to even scratch its surface.

If you are a small company with a limited product line, you are unlikely to have the marketing depth to take full advantage of the market. In this case, you will require a partner, even to gain access to the heart of the market for which your product line was developed and positioned. Even if you are a large company with many products and product lines, you may still be unable to exploit all the marketing opportunities available. If you are successful in your primary market, you may not have the incentive to exploit potentially lucrative marketing niches. Whatever your size and marketing needs, you will want a partner who not only has the skills to reach lucrative markets, but who has the interest and will to treat your product as if it were his or her own. Indeed, this is probably the single most important attribute you will want to identify in a marketing partner.

"...the second most important attribute of a good marketing partnership is flexibility on both sides..."

Getting Buy-In

It is not always easy to identify a partner who is going to behave in this way. Sometimes longevity or reputation in the marketplace is not enough. I have seen both big and small companies fail on this very issue. One way or another, your partner must give your product the highest priority and regard your product as proprietary. At the very least, your partner cannot have a product that directly competes with yours. But you must also beware of a partner who is too distracted by other business to give enough attention to your product. If you see signs of this behavior early in the relationship, cut if off quickly. Do not delude yourself that you can get the partner's attention over time.

One way for a partner to increase his stake in your product is to co-brand the product. This gives your partner visible ownership of the product and increases his accountability. If both partners can actually contribute to the contents of the product, the co-branding will have even more meaning and the commitment will be strengthened. In addition, both partners will likely find more marketing opportunities as a result of the collaboration. For example, at World Book we collaborated with Discovery Channel by providing our articles to a variety of Discovery CD-ROMs. These CDs became part of a range of CDs that Discovery was marketing through their traditional direct-to-consumer channels. In the beginning, both Discovery and World Book regarded the relationship as a simple licensing arrangement. But because Discovery had co-branded the CDs with the World Book name, the CDs captured the attention of the World Book sales force. They took ownership over the CDs because they regarded them as proprietary to World Book. As a result, the World Book sales channel was a new, unanticipated opportunity for both partners, and a successful marketing relationship developed.

Staying Flexible

Probably the second most important attribute of a good marketing partnership is flexibility on both sides, along with a willingness to change and adapt to the market. It is critical, of course, to have a written agreement that clearly spells out the terms of the partnership. But once that contract has been signed, the partners must focus on meeting the needs of the relationship rather than the terms of the agreement. It's the relationship that will sustain the partnership, not the contract. So if the original terms of the agreement no longer make sense—

if the signed contract puts either party at a disadvantage or threatens their business model—then both parties must be willing to rewrite the agreement. I have seen many partnerships fail because of an agreement that started out fine for both parties but that became unsustainable for one of the parties, due to changes in the market. You have to decide which you want more: a strong, long-term relationship or strict, principled adherence to a contract. This attitude is fundamental to a win-win partnership. Many people say they want a relationship, but they behave as if they wanted a transaction.

The hardest part of being flexible is giving up control. Some say that they want a relationship, but only under their terms. Controlling a relationship will strain it and ultimately kill it. It is important to demonstrate to your partner that you trust their ability to understand and meet the needs of the new market you have partnered to address. That will mean that you may have to accept the language your partner proposes in marketing materials,

be willing to make adjustments to the presentation of your product, and perhaps abandon long-held views of your reputation in the market, or worst of all, of what you can charge for your product. It is very hard to take a leap of faith and accept someone else's view of what the market will bear. But if you are moving into a new market as a result of the efforts of a partner, let that partner lead the way.

Taking on a partner will require a cultural shift in your company. Whether you are small or large, having a development or marketing partner will change the way you behave. Expectations on each side may not start out being equal, yet it's important to understand clearly, from the beginning, what expectations your partner has of you—and then exceed them. Think of your partner as an extension of your organization, and act under the assumption that your interests are identical. It may not be the road to a permanent partnership, but it's the path to a successful one.

About the Author

Michael Ross is the executive vice president and publisher of World Book, Inc, where he is responsible for World Book's worldwide publishing activities in all media. He joined World Book in 1992 and has had a variety of executive and editorial positions in educational publishing. He began his career as an editor with Time-Life Books. Michael has contributed to a variety of professional journals and has been an active speaker at publishing and technology conferences, including the Licensing Executive Society, the Hammond Organization, PubTech, and BookTech. He is on the board of directors, and is currently president-elect, of the Association of Educational Publishers. He is also on the board of Indraweb, an Internet search portal. Michael has a B.A. from the University of Minnesota, an M.A. from Brandeis University, and a Certificate from Stanford University's Advanced Management College. He is married with three children.

The Pleasures and Perils of Being an Educational Publishing Product Manager

by Carol Farber Wolf

"Plans and develops marketing strategies and objectives to promote titles within educational product line, including advertising, promotion, sales support, packaging and sampling programs, and budget projections. Direct preparation of sales tools and sales support materials, including field manual pages, product kits, competitive analysis, and newsletters. Develops marketing policies and programs, and coordinates marketing and sales promotion with editorial policy and with overall sales and profit objectives. Provides information to sales force regarding product features and competitive analyses. Develops plans for revision of titles; recommends content and marketing changes."

This definition of a product manager (a.k.a. marketing manager), from the Association of American Publishers provides a good overview of the many accountabilities that come with product marketing.

What it doesn't describe, however, is the precarious path the product manager must walk to be successful in all aspects of this role. Product managers can have tremendous influence on the development and sales of powerful market-driven products. They often do so, however, at their own peril. While development gets credit for the final product and sales reps get kudos and bonus payments for the "wins," product managers will tell you they often get a lot of grief. A critical part of ensuring all the pieces are in place to assure a winning product, they work hand in hand with editors to develop product and with sales reps to help train on and present the product. Yet their names are not listed as contributors when the products are published, and they don't receive acknowledgement when sales awards are handed out.

When product managers are asked to define their role, they most often refer to themselves as "tightrope walkers." Their biggest challenge: "Walking a fine line between editorial and sales departments." The rewards:

> **"Product managers can have tremendous influence on the development and sales of powerful market-driven products."**

"Working closely with editors, reps, and customers. When the team pulls together and the product is a winner."

Product management is one of the most critical and perhaps one of the most difficult roles in educational publishing. Perhaps this is because it is a role with very little definition or decision-making authority, yet with a broad range of responsibilities that cut across all functional areas of the publishing company. It demands both breadth and depth of expertise.

Everyone in an educational publishing organization is committed to building a market-winning product. The product manager's challenge is to manage and facilitate good communication between all involved: from finance to inventory, to development, to sales reps, to customers. The center of a complex network, the project manager has to keep information coming in and going out to help keep the process moving in the right direction.

The job becomes even more complex because many projects are often underway at the same time. As different programs in a product line transition through their five to eight year lifecycle, product managers must deal with old standbys that may need a breath of life, current programs still very much in play, and budding visions that won't hit the market for years. Every stage requires product management support to supply varying levels of content, marketing and sales support expertise.

Why Would You *Want* to Become a "Product Champion?"

Given the enormity and demands of this role, who in their right mind would choose to do this job? For most product managers in educational publishing, the role of product advocate was not their first career. In educational publishing, many product managers begin life as classroom teachers. Classroom teaching can also lead to jobs as sales consultants, sales reps, or editors: the common bond is the passion for delivering quality educational materials for our nation's children.

Ask most product managers and they will readily tell you about the many challenges they face, including:

- Staying focused and aligned with key strategic directives,

- Trusting their teams,

- Staying on the edge of change,

- Dealing with the all-or-nothing climate of state adoptions,

- Maintaining influence and input with minimal decision-making power,

- Managing the constantly changing customer needs,

- Anticipating and beating competitors' strategies,

- Balancing travel: staying in touch with the field while supporting the development and sales support events at home,

- Answering a myriad of daily questions from the field, and

- Finding the time to do it all

Despite these challenges most product managers will tell you they love their job. Why? After what you have read so far, you might believe it is because they are masochists. Certainly being intimately involved throughout the entire publishing process creates enormous strain. Yet it is also precisely the reason most product managers come to work every day. One thing you won't hear product managers complain about is being bored!

The job is far-reaching, with input and influence on every aspect of the publishing and sales process. From analyzing the market to developing the product concept, playing it out in print and design, setting the competitive edge in pricing and implementation, creating the sales story, and training the troops, product managers are instrumental every step of the way.

And the job is varied. During the development cycle of a new program product (which takes years), product management responsibilities change focus at each stage. At any one time they can be involved with research and market trends, pre-work and issue setting, marketing plans and product positioning, partnering with development, submission and samples, product launches, sales training, sales support, exhibits, promos, product updates, and campaign updates for product at different stages of development.

It is no wonder that the criteria for finding the right individual are as stringent as they are!

What it Takes to Become a Product Manager

When a company posts a product management position, the description goes something like: "Dynamic, knowledgeable, polished advocate for product line."

Requirements often include the following:

Incisive, objective decision-making ability

The product manager does not get the "final" say on development or sales issues; however, both groups look to his or her expertise to help make critical decisions. Not only must the individual be able to analyze the situation at hand, but they must also be able to quickly form an opinion or take a position for which they can advocate.

Ability to build strong alliances with a variety of different departments

The ability to build relationships is essential to creating a winning product and sales campaign. To explore ideas from the editorial, marketing, and sales departments, the product manager must be a diplomat and a negotiator with the ability to build trust and respect among all groups.

Strong conceptual and strategic abilities.

Determining market and customer needs for future development requires insight and vision. Keeping abreast of current issues is equally demanding. In today's dynamic marketplace, it is easy to become reactive and miss opportunities. Anticipating market trends and competitors' initiatives and delivering a proactive strategy to stay on the cutting edge are cornerstones of the ultimate success of any product line.

Excellent knowledge of content area and of competition.

The product manager must be able to speak confidently about the curriculum and customer profile in his or her area of specialization. More challenging is staying abreast of the strengths and weaknesses of the competition. The product manager must be able to dig deep, read between the lines, and succinctly report useful data.

Having a solid sense of the competitive environment is expected, as the product manager is often the primary source of definitive, accurate, up to date, and insightful information.

Superior communication and negotiation skills.

Since the product manager is the liaison between all groups impacted by publishing decisions, frequent, crystal clear communication is a must. And because everyone is generally running on a fast track, the more telegraphic, the better. It also requires being a good listener to really hear the "why" behind differing points of view. Since the product manager represents so many points of view, the trickiest part of this requirement often is the need for negotiation skills. Being able to deliver clear and honest feedback between the field and internal groups means knowing when to push back and when to demonstrate flexibility. Thus, no matter how well versed her or she is in the company's product and competition, without strong negotiation and communication skills, a product manager cannot be effective.

Creativity and, adaptiveness in problem-solving situations; and a team player in interactions with sales, marketing, and editorial departments.

By now, it should be pretty obvious how important the team is to building winning product. Not every organization adopts a team model; however, an examination of most winning products will show that they are the result of seamless teamwork, which does include honest discussion and disagreement. The powerful product advocate is the axle that keeps the wheels turning smoothly.... And most successful product managers have the battle scars to prove it.

Strong training and teaching skills.

Once a product is on its way, the product manager is the one who sets the training issues and develops the plan. Since most product managers have a background in teaching or field work, this part may seem like a natural. Still, a large part of the training required in this role includes strong motivational skills. While teachers and consultants do a great job at product overviews, the

key here is the ability to see and set the issues, and to develop a message and positioning that will energize the field so they are inspired, knowledgeable, and confident.

Discernment and delegation skills.

The product management job is similar to most high-pressure, high-impact roles. Everything on the to-do list seems to be "top priority." So the ability to discern and prioritize projects as well being able to delegate responsibility to support staff is the only way a product manager can conserve enough brain power and stamina to provide the far reaching support demanded daily.

Product Manager Accountabilities

Most educational publishing companies share a common set of expectations for their product managers. Depending upon the development status of a program, the degree of emphasis on each of these areas shifts over time. But juggling support for different products at different stages of development never changes.

Market Research and Information

Sound research is the foundation of a successful educational publishing plan. Analysis of the marketplace and changing trends help determine what to publish and when. The product manager helps set clear objectives so that research can effectively guide the publishing vision. In addition to asking the right questions, the ability to actively listen and to wisely interpret a wide variety of information is crucial to building product with the right balance of curriculum and customer appeal. And whether you are looking at the overall market or a specific product, ongoing and comprehensive competitive analysis is a must.

In addition, product managers are expected to perform the following functions:
- Conduct both quantitative and qualitative research. With the market research and editorial teams, establish plans for focus groups and surveys to collect accurate data.
- Develop objectives for product-related market research products.

> "Since the product manager represents so many points of view, the trickiest part of this requirement often is the need for negotiation skills."

- Monitor market and curriculum trends, along with enrollment data.

- Maintain a thorough and ongoing analysis of market and competition.

- Establish and maintain advisory groups for field feedback. Coordinate as a core resource for sales feedback and product information to the field.

- Investigate and report on state and federal funding.

- Provide teacher, supervisor, and student feedback with regional support.

- Take part in field and school visits.

- Participate in development and monitoring of efficacy studies.

Product Development

Here's where the product manager's diplomacy and negotiation skills really need to kick in. A common saying in educational publishing is that there must be a "healthy tension" between marketing and editorial functions. Marketers focus on the sales and customer point of view; editors focus on the quality and integrity of the content and pedagogy. Facilitating an open and honest dialogue that brings the team to consensus is the basis of winning formula. The product manager is the advocate to ensure that every product component wows the customer.

On the product development front, specific duties of the project manager include:

- Providing input on product design, manuscript, and presentation to meet market and customer needs and embed product positioning and message into the product.

- Obtain and report regional, teacher feedback for development team.

- Participating in author meetings.

- Helping to secure and train reviewers and advisors.

- Facilitating communication between the field and development.

- Monitoring product customization to meet specific customer needs.

Strategic Planning

Strategic marketing begins with the research to set a clear vision for the program. Although the product manager has great influence on the development process, the ultimate responsibility for how this vision is played out in content and design rests with the editorial and design groups.

In a perfect world, the position and message would be fully embedded in the product and would require virtually no explanation. Reps love product that they can "throw in the door" and that sells itself. Given today's changing and competitive marketplace, however, the reality is that the product manager must position a program for success.

The product manager must contribute to publishing and business plans that respond to market needs with uniquely positioned and differentiated programs. This means he or she must

- Provide analysis of research findings on market trends, customer needs, and competitive environment.

- Participate in development of business plan

- Help with financial analysis

- Prepare sales estimates; market share projections

Marketing

On the strategic marketing front, the product manager must establish product market position and translate competitive edge into an actionable plan that can be incorporated into sales campaigns. This means

- Meeting with regional sales and marketing staff to build plan that addresses market issues,

- Providing effective positioning plans, and sales messages, and

- Support joint ventures and partnerships to bring unique value to customers.

For particular campaigns, product managers must work with field marketing and sales to develop and integrate consistent sales strategies. This can include:

- Providing advice and input on national and regional implementation plans,

- Planning and implementing pricing strategies,

- Preparing sales forecasts, and

- Contributing to the state adoption bid process.

On more tactical levels, the product manager must participate in the development of promotional materials (by providing concepts and copy points), product packaging, and samplers and submission packs. These materials must be consistent with product positioning, make immediate impact and enhance the evaluation process. On a logistical level, the product manager must coordinate field and regional sampling and plan for appropriate prepublication samplers, with the help of the editorial department.

Sales Support

This is the most demanding, most frustrating, and often most rewarding support role that product managers play. Sales is where the rubber meets the road: the research is done, the editorial team has finished the core product, and the sales force is waiting with bated breath: it is "show time" for the product manager. Time to train, to provide the right materials, to answer questions, to help get the program listed in state or large district adoptions, and most of all, to motivate the sales force to win, win, win. Indeed, the first "customer" the product manager faces is the sales rep. Convince the field you have a winner and you are off on the right foot. It is both grueling and exhilarating, and will hopefully confirm that all the sweat and tears—and time and dollars—that brought the organization to this point will pay off in a product that customers will rave about!

The product manager must assist field marketing and sales personnel with effective development of pre-launch, product launch, and campaign product launch plans and campaigns. This means ensuring that product positioning and campaign strategies are consistently delivered.

Sales training is also a critical component to the sales support a product manager is expected to provide. In creating effective training, the product manager should:

- Develop issue-setting workshops and training consultants to present the product,
- Create model presentations or video,
- Plan and orchestrate product line training at national sales meetings,
- Develop product training schools,

> " The product manager must assist field marketing and sales personnel with effective development of pre-launch, product launch, and campaign product launch plans and campaigns. "

- Provide ongoing regional support as requested by sales management,
- Coordinate and develop submission and sampler builds,
- Prepare for road shows, and
- Provide training requested for regional sales meetings,

Finally, the product manager must provide strong ongoing national sales support to all campaigns, by
- Delivering customer service training,
  - Supervising exhibit planning and management,
  - Providing succinct competitive information as well as detailed product analyses,
  - Creating product related review materials, such as walkthroughs,
  - Supporting annual catalog development by providing key copy points,
  - Establishing product information manuals,
  - Coordinating correlations efforts,
  - Providing piloting information,
  - Responding to daily questions from the field on specific sales and product issues, and
  - Repositioning any products in distress.

Administrative

The administrative part of the job is the aspect that most product managers enjoy the least; but it is crucial to the product's success. Administrative tasks include assuring accuracy of information, maintaining product availability timetables, and the universal challenge of doing more with less: budget management. In particular, product managers must
- Manage and mentor their direct reports,
- Monitor and leverage their budgets,
- Coordinate with inventory management and sales,
- Provide sales forecasts and determine print quantities to assure product availability, and
- Supervise national consultants, and help to monitor effective scheduling of their activities.

Conclusion

Regis McKenna, in his book *Relationship Marketing*, writes *"In order to achieve a distinctive position in any industry, the whole company must think about being in the marketing business."* McKenna continues, explaining that *"[m]arketing is …the integration of customers into the company's design, development, manufacturing, and sales processes"*

In an educational publishing company, the product manager is the embodiment of this definition of "marketing." He or she is the point person responsible for building and integrating internal and external relationships to keep the company "in the marketing business."

It is ultimately the product manager who must be sure the company gets close to the customer, "hears" the market's issues, translates those issues for the product developers, facilitates information flow between design, development, manufacturing, and sales, and delivers the message to the customer. And in the end, if you ask any product manager—even if they are not mentioned in the credits or on the sales award—they will tell you that for them there is no greater thrill than when the customers say, "thank you for listening to us!"

About the Author

Carol Farber Wolf *is currently vice president of marketing, Harcourt Supplemental. Prior to that she served as general manager of Summit Learning a division of Steck Vaughn/Harcourt. She has directed marketing and promotion departments for Addison-Wesley, Scholastic, Guidance Associates, and Prentice-Hall. Carol also served as creative director for direct-response marketing companies including Callas, Powell Bloch and Wolf, McCaffrey, McCall Direct, and Synchronal Infomercials. You can reach her at wolfboston@aol.com or (512) 795-3269.*

Data-Driven Decision Making for Education Marketers

by Jeanne Hayes

"Database Marketing is a marketing process that is information-driven and database-technology facilitated. It is a discipline that utilizes relevant factual information that is assembled to enable marketers to develop and implement customized marketing programs and strategies." *Eric Moore, QED Director of Database Operations*[1]

Database marketing needs to demonstrate some convincing benefits to justify its extra use of resources. In truth, however, its advantages are so broad and compelling that most education marketers can find powerful ways to apply its techniques to their programs. The state of the art is constantly improving to meet the specific needs of the education market, but even techniques generically used by the direct marketing community have applications within education. These include

Adding value to the customer relationship while providing a high return on investment.

As education marketers, you are increasingly concerned about margins; learning more about customer retention and loyalty programs for your best customers is worth time and money.

Analyzing transactional data about your current customers.

Educators are a customer set with a relatively high volume of purchases and relatively disparate set of products. You can use the increasing power of Web-based click stream analysis and other tactics to uncover useful patterns.

Selecting Customer Relationship Management (CRM) systems.

In an education market increasingly driven by high-stakes testing and accountability issues, your previously-loyal

> **"In many ways the concept of data mining is at the very heart of database marketing — extracting what you know about your customers through intelligent structuring of the data to provide information that will lead to data-driven decisions."**

education customer may need more reasons to stay with you as a vendor than ever before. Fortunately, e-mail and other direct channels make it possible to build stronger relationships with current customers.

Addressing privacy concerns.

The government-mandated requirement that schools receiving federal funds have some kind of filtering mechanism to protect children is an opportunity for creative software providers. On the e-marketing side, however, the need for permission is in high profile, so it may be wiser to do prospecting through more traditional direct marketing tools.

These concepts can be discussed within the context of an enterprise-wide database system. Three places where data are stored and can be extracted for analysis are:

- Data Warehouse: Where the mountain of corporate data is stored.

- Data Mart: Where departmental data is stored and various external data items can be added. Usually much smaller than a data warehouse.

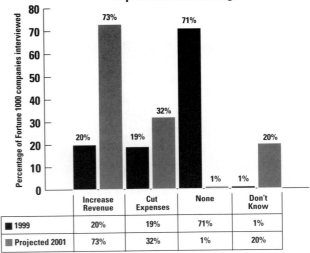

What do Fortune 500 companies expect from data mining?

	Increase Revenue	Cut Expenses	None	Don't Know
■ 1999	20%	19%	71%	1%
▧ Projected 2001	73%	32%	1%	20%

Source: Forrester Research, Feb. 20, 2001, PC Magazine

- Data Mine: Where the data is re-organized for analysis and information is extracted from the data. The data is more richly structured and is no longer just departmental. The data refers to a specific business objective and is analyzed for the purpose of information extraction. Data mining uses statistical algorithms to discover patterns in data. It also analyzes transactions to understand customer behavior.[2]

In many ways the concept of data mining is at the very heart of database marketing – extracting what you know about your customers through intelligent structuring of the data to provide information that will lead to data-driven decisions.

Data-driven decision-making has become increasingly high profile in corporations. Expectations are increasing, as shown by this chart from Forrester Research below.

Despite new applications, the basic principles of database marketing remain fundamentally the same, namely:

- Your best customers contribute a disproportionately large percentage of your revenue and profits. Therefore, it pays to identify your best customers and then monitor their behavior and desires on a continuous basis.

- Your best prospects will share characteristics with your best customers. When you isolate truly meaningful variables, you can create more profitable ways to prospect.

- The more you know about your customers, the more informed your messaging will be and the closer the linkage you will build with them.

The benefits of database marketing are both tactical and strategic. They include:

- Increasing response rates. With database marketing, you have the opportunity to pick the "best 50,000" for a marketing campaign, rather than simply the "next 50,000." Even the rich database selections provided by QED, MDR, and others can be far more powerful predictors of your best prospects when you overlay the characteristics of your own best customers.

- Increasing customer retention and loyalty. When you know more about your customers, you can do more for your customers. If you know that Segment A of your customers buys products three times a year and

has never purchased your new product, you can provide them a value-added offer to purchase this product.

- Optimizing marketing expenditures. Segmentation improves profits. For example, you can target company newsletters to your most important customers in print, while disseminating a less expensive Web-based version for the rest of your market.

- Increasing Profits. If you identify the propensity to buy through profiling, segmentation, and predictive modeling, you can reduce wasted mail and deploy your promotional efforts to greater effectiveness and profit.

Since increasing profits is a worthwhile goal for all of us, let's look at several techniques of database marketing that can make a difference to you right now. We will focus on three techniques: profiles, segmentation, and modeling.

Profiles

One of the quickest and best ways to create baseline information about your customers is to profile them. Utilize purchasing data, demographics and other classifying information to build descriptions of different types of customers. In many cases, you will overlay your customer data with demographic elements from a compiled database to get the richest picture. The basic outcomes of this exercise include:

- Creating a common understanding of your customers among staff. Profiles allow communication of the big picture in a simpler way than do predictive modeling or other techniques.

- Informing product development, especially when you can compare and contrast profiles of new customers with those of older customers, to determine emerging trends and changes in purchasing patterns.

- Refining mailing lists by selecting prospects that look most like your customers, rather than picking prospects based solely on external factors.

- Focusing market research projects. To conduct market research, you need to have some basic understanding of what you know before you even commission a research firm. Furthermore, since drawing the proper sample is critical to the success of a market research project, a profile is an excellent tool to help describe the universe accurately.

School and district characteristics help illuminate the physical environment of the school into which you intend to sell. Since schools are in the business-to-business segment, it's important to understand the underlying characteristics of the institutions in which your buyers reside. Some of the data elements with which you can profile school customers are:

- Sales by product and sales by customer

- Sales for last three years for customers and products

- Categorization of customers by job function

- Student enrollment. Capture enrollment both for the school and for the district to which the school belongs (if it is a public school).

- School type: public, private, Catholic, Early Childhood, etc.

- Grade spans

- Affluence/Poverty of students, via Title I percentage and other metrics

- Title I dollars: Dollars available from federal government for compensatory education based on percentage of children below the poverty line.

- Community affluence Some measures include QED's Education Climate Index™ and Claritas's PRIZM™ Lifestyles

- Student ethnic percentages

- Metro status: Includes urbanicity, membership in Nielsen's Designated Market Area (DMA) or Metropolitan Statistical Area (MSA)

- Instructional expenditures per student

- College-bound percentages

- Geographic classifications

- Technology presence, as measured by number of computers per school, by number of students per computer, or an index such as Technology Measure™

Combining these classificatory data, there are several types of profiles that you can create:

- Product based. What characteristics are common to most purchasers of Product X?

- Cross tabs. What combinations of characteristics are important?

- Cross-product. What other products do purchasers of Product X buy?

SINGLE-PRODUCT PROFILE: PENETRATION BY STATE

State	# of Customers	% of Customers	% of Universe
CA	2,445	48%	28%
FL	532	7%	7%
TX	277	5%	9%
IL	223	4%	5%
All Others	1,626	32%	2%

This profile for a bilingual product shows the company has done exceptionally well in California. Nevertheless, considering the universe of potential customers, there may still be a substantial opportunity for growth in that state.

MULTIPLE-PRODUCT PROFILE: CUSTOMERS BY JOB FUNCTION

Job Function	# of Customers	% of Customers	% of Universe
Remedial Reading	1,677	36%	3%
Reading	1,237	26%	1%
7th Grade	861	18%	4%
8th Grade	924	17%	4%

This profile of customers for multiple senior high remedial reading products shows that the product has been used for on-grade-level instruction in 7th and 8th grades. This data points to promotion opportunities that may have been overlooked. The initial marketing focus may have been on specialist teachers, but the numbers indicate that for the next direct mailing, it may be well worth borrowing, renting, or swapping to get more names of mainstream teachers.

Among the recent advances in presentation techniques, pivot tables in spreadsheets allow you to look at different dimensions of a profile dynamically. For example, you could look at the above data by the additional dimension of dollars spent. Many vendors offer this advanced way to look at data. For instance, QED's advanced database marketing product, The Peak, provides drill-down or data-mining capabilities via an Excel Pivot Table or one of several cube structures, according to Brett Cunningham, QED's Director of Information Systems.

Segmentation

Cluster analysis is a simple yet illuminating analytical technique used to find natural clusters or groupings among data. As a market research tool, cluster analysis is often employed in preliminary analyses to find naturally homogeneous market segments that can be identified and analyzed further with more advanced statistical techniques. Cluster analysis can be used to cluster either individuals or variables into natural groupings. Some common applications include perceived benefits analyses, product positioning, and product usage information.[3]

Segmentation, of which cluster analysis is one technique, divides your customers into groups that share common characteristics or behaviors. The applications can be powerful, allowing you to customize your marketing message, tailoring it to the needs and interests of each of the segments you have identified. In particular, you can

- Create communications vehicles unique to each segment
- Create multiple segmentation strategies
- Create a segmentation matrix as in this example:

SEGMENT MATRIX FOR CHANNEL OPTIMIZATION

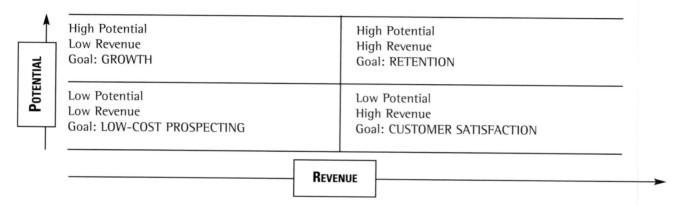

POTENTIAL		
High Potential Low Revenue Goal: GROWTH	High Potential High Revenue Goal: RETENTION
Low Potential Low Revenue Goal: LOW-COST PROSPECTING	Low Potential High Revenue Goal: CUSTOMER SATISFACTION

REVENUE

This chart shows Potential and Revenue as two axes in the matrix to help segment four groups in your market for maximizing channel optimization.

Some criteria on which you can base segmentation analyses include:

- Profit per customer
- Customer longevity
- Customer needs
- Demographics
- Geography
- Behavioral characteristics or patterns

Since segmentation requires a more sophisticated methodology than simple profiling, it must also provide clearer and more precise results to justify the added cost. To be useful, segmentation must be:

- ***Measurable.*** The marketing and sales results must be quantifiable.

- ***Identifiable.*** A significant number of customers must be identified that would have been missed if profiling alone had been used.

- ***Persistent***. The identified segments need to hold up over time so that a sequence of analyses done over time can be meaningfully compared.

Modeling

This third category of techniques for database marketing has improved dramatically as a result of technology advances. Modeling can be conducted more powerfully now that it has become possible to access and process enormous amounts of transactional data, whether stored in a data warehouse or captured through click steam analyses of Web behavior.

The term "modeling" is used to describe any process that uses currently-available data about customers to generate an equation that can predict some future outcome. Modeling techniques typically generate their output in the form of a scoring function that has values for each customer record in the database. Depending on the modeling goal, this score might represent future revenues, response rates, the probability that the customer will buy, or some other unknown that you want to predict.

Examples of effective modeling have included predictive analyses of the following factors:

- ***Customers most likely to defect.*** On the basis of a model, you could put programs in place to help keep customers who are most likely to go to the competition. It costs much more to acquire a new customer than to retain a current customer. Modeling can help you detect those at-risk customers.

- ***Customer Lifetime Value.*** With this kind of model, you could seek to attract customers who are likely to be loyal and profitable. By using a lifetime value model you can focus promotion efforts on customers who will likely become the most profitable.

- ***Channel optimization.*** This type of model could help you to figure out which direct marketing techniques work for which categories of customers.

- ***Prospects most likely to respond.*** Models can help to increase response rates by cutting out unresponsive segments.

Here are three techniques of predictive modeling that can be used by education marketers:

1. CHAID/CART

This is a statistical procedure that is often used when market segmentation is desired. CHAID is most useful when the variable responses are categorical in nature and a relationship is sought between the predictor variables and a categorical outcome measure.[4] CHAID/CART also provides feedback about the most important variables in the equation. Furthermore, marketers using this technique can

- Perform exploratory analyses of data to find conditional relationships

- Build models based on a tree structure using conditional logic to identify smaller segments

- Easily apply the technique to a database

2. Regression Analyses.

This statistical method generates an algebraic equation representing the "line of best fit" for a given set of data.

CHAID Example — Likelihood to Purchase Consistently

Regular customers

| Mean | 49% |
| n | 1199 |

Read as: 49% of customers purchased at least once in each of two years.

Library/Media Center?

Yes

| Mean | 58% |
| n | 865 |

Schools with a Library Media Center were more likely to be regular customers

No<blank>

| Mean | 26% |
| n | 334 |

Grade Span (Building)

Education Climate Index (ECD)

Special Education; Preschool-3; K-6; K-8

| Mean | 39% |
| n | 413 |

4-8 or 7-8; 7-12, 9-12; K-12

| Mean | 76% |
| n | 446 |

Average; Above Average; Below Average

| Mean | 21% |
| n | 266 |

*Segment least likely to purchase

High; Low

| Mean | 46% |
| n | 61 |

The extremes - Very affluent or very poor areas - are more likely to be regular customers.

Middle schools and senior highs were more likely to be regular customers

Education Climate Index (ECD)

Average; Above Average; Below Average

| Mean | 72% |
| n | 327 |

High; Low

| Mean | 87% |
| n | 119 |

*Segment most likely to purchase

Mean: Pct. of cluster that are regular customers
n – Number of school customers in this category

Regression analyses are often used to predict future revenues, response rates, or product usage.

Regression analyses make the most of limited data sets. For example, QED had a client with a small response file of schools that had responded to a Web-based offer for an expensive premium product. To make its marketing programs more effective, the client needed to have a way to predict which schools were most likely to purchase the product. QED used linear regression analysis to score all schools on the database so that their relatively inexperienced staff could request segments easily. The company could then focus their efforts on the creative marketing of the product, rather than on the nuts and bolts of modeling

3. Neural Network Analyses.

A neural net is designed to simulate the workings of the human mind, represented as a network of neurons and synapses. In setting up neural net models, marketers typically begin with one input layer of data, one known output layer of data or recorded behavior, and a number of hidden layers and processes that connect input and output layers. A neural network must then be "trained" by feeding it additional data—examples of new input conditions and the output that results. The neural network "learns" from this "experience." Some of the benefits and drawbacks of neural network models include:

- They performs as well as or better than traditional models

- They can find subtle patterns within data

- They are more complicated than other traditional techniques

- In gathering results from neural models, it is sometimes difficult to ascertain which input attributes have the most impact on results.

Combined Techniques

Each of these techniques can be used individually or in combination. For example, it is common to create a segmentation scheme using a modeling technique to identify the segments. In the same effort, profiles might be used to get a better understanding of the data before building the model or segmentation scheme.

Conclusion: Some thoughts from the SIIA E-Business Division

- Beware of techno-centric solutions. Just because technology makes something possible doesn't mean it makes business sense. The issue isn't how to best build personalization for consumers through data warehousing and other tools. The real issue is how a business can strengthen and deepen customer relationships and build brand loyalty.

- Outsourcing alone isn't the answer. Unfortunately, many database marketers suffer the same problems as any organization trying to get a unified and in-depth view of clients: customer data is fragmented, isolated and often invalid.

- The Internet is just one channel, albeit a very cost-effective and powerful one, to reach your target markets. The real power of personalization lies in the ability to provide a rich, value-added experience at all touch points—call centers, kiosks, retail outlets and even mobile devices.[5]

---

[1] Special thanks to Eric Moore for his ground-breaking workshop presentation on database marketing, which forms the basis for this article.

[2] "Data Mining Beside a Warehouse", Information Discovery, Inc. June 23, 2000. (datamine@ix.netcom.com)

[3] Web Site Examples: Market Strategies/Information & Technologies Division Portland, 1.800.345.8241 (www.MarketStrategies.com)

[4] Web Site: Ibid.

[5] "Connecting with your Customers: Personalization in a Technological Age", Software Information Industries Association (SIIA), May, 2001. Also on Web site (www.siia.net)

About the Author

Jeanne Hayes *is the president of Quality Education Data, Inc. (QED),* www.qeddata.com, *a leading provider of analytical tools and services for education marketers. QED provides marketing campaign consulting and execution, custom market research, industry forecasts, data analysis, mailing lists, conferences and advertising opportunities. Jeanne can be reached at* jhayes@qeddata.com *or by calling (303) 209-9393 x111.*

Software Site Licensing—Myth or Legend?

by George Bigham

This brief primer is an attempt to clarify a chaotic and misunderstood set of topics, both in the corporate world, and in the education technology arena; it therefore may be doomed to failure from its outset…. But here is how the article is intended to work:

Part One establishes some general concepts and vocabulary from the business world. This section also applies directly to schools, in the case of licensing software such as productivity applications, network operating systems, and business office solutions.

Part Two applies the concepts from Part One to the context of licensing instructional software in schools.

Part Three contains some special information and concerns about Web-based instructional offerings. Please note that the author makes no claims that his Ouija Board performs better than anyone else's in predicting the future course of the market. And he is currently looking for some stronger batteries, since there seems to be a flickering problem with the unit—and of course the vendor's technical support line keeps ringing busy….

Part One: Software Licensing in the Real World

Once upon a time, back when TV was only in black-and-white and dinosaurs still roamed the Earth, site licensing did exist. In its purest form, a *Customer* purchased the right to install and use a *Software Product* owned by a *Vendor* on all the computers at the customer's *Site*. This was handled through a one-time transaction recorded in the *Site License*.

At first blush, this model seemed to be a big win-win. The vendor made a huge sale, and the customer got a great price break on the software. But over time problems began to appear with this one-time transaction for the customer. The issues included:

Technical support and training. With a one-time purchase, the vendor was not motivated to provide ongoing support, since there was no ongoing revenue stream. On the other hand, now that everyone at the customer location was using the software, any problem was likely to become very widespread and often critical.

Compatibility. Two of the main categories of software are *Operating Systems* (e.g., Windows, Unix, Macintosh) and *Applications Software* (e.g., word processors, spreadsheets, databases, accounting packages, and so forth). Compatibility issues often arose from combinations between these two categories.

For example, when customers licensed an accounting package and then several years later upgraded to newer computers, typically a newer version of the operating system (OS) would be pre-installed on the new hardware. If the old accounting package was not compatible with this combination of new hardware and OS, then the customer was in a world of hurt. And since the new version of the OS usually was required for the new hardware, this was usually a pretty messy situation. Going back to the old hardware and OS was almost always a bitter pill for the customer to have to swallow.

And at a more basic level, sometimes customers did not purchase any rights to any upgrades to the software —not even to fix problems that showed up with the software after the deal was completed.

While the site license model was no picnic for the customer, across the table on the vendor's side, things weren't looking all that rosy, either. Vendors had to cope with their own emerging issues, including:

No ongoing revenue stream. While the one-time fee for the site license made the sales report for the quarter and year in which it occurred look very good, the vendor received no ongoing revenue stream for the customer's continued use of the licensed software. The expense of staffing for customer and technical support, however, was an ongoing one. And since the incremental cost to the customer of adding new users to the license was often very small, more and more users would be added over time. This increasing number of users of course generated an increasing number of support calls.

No motivation for improvements or updates. Under the site licensing model, the vendor had very little incentive to revise and update the software. A strong retail business, bundling deals, or requests from large, powerful customers could generate an interest in working on revisions. But the typical site license did not allow for or necessitate updates.

Globalization Issues. As the dinosaurs finally died off and color television sets were invented, it became clearer and clearer that there were additional reasons why site licensing needed to be reconceived. Large customers became global operations and they needed versions of the software to support

- other languages,
- other types of hardware,
- 24 x 7 technical support in multiple languages, and
- proprietary networking protocols,
- special security patches, and
- other special requirements.

As a result, the site licensing process had to change to keep up with evolving customer business needs, and change it did. The general nature of the evolution of software licensing has been a growth from a single-transaction purchase toward an long-term business partnership between the customer and the vendor. This arrangement allows the issues above to be resolved in ways that benefit both parties.

But while site licensing has evolved considerably, somehow the terminology has not. And so today, some people still use the term "site license" to refer to what really should be called an "enterprise license," a "volume purchasing license," or some other more accurate term. Let's agree to use "enterprise license" in this article as a kind of generic term, as we consider the characteristics of a successful license. Throughout, it's important to note that the license needs to specify a "win - win" deal for the customer and the vendor over the entire life of their business partnership.

Customer Advantages
Enterprise licenses should provide the following characteristics considered advantages for the Customer:

Money savings. In return for agreeing to purchase large quantities of the software, the customer should be able to negotiate favorable pricing from the vendor and often to lock in pricing for a specified time period.

> " ...it's important to note that the license needs to specify a "win - win" deal for the customer and the vendor over the entire life of their business partnership. "

Technical support and customer service. Often a license will guarantee that the vendor will dedicate an account manager and support resources to the customer in order to provide global and multi-language support 24 hours a day, 7 days a week. Licenses also often involve a commitment by the vendor to close out trouble tickets within a specified length of time. These support and service benefits can be of great value to customers.

Training. The most efficient way for the Vendor to minimize support calls is to train the customer's users and/or the customer's internal support staff. Accordingly, vendors typically make training available both to end users and to customer support staff, either as part of the license or as an added-cost option.

Vendor Advantages
Vendors should realize the following advantages from a well-constructed enterprise license:

Guaranteed revenue stream. Quarterly maintenance payments and new revenue from additional users of the software purchased by the customer keep the vendor's sales reports looking good to its board and its investors.

Economies of scale. The vendor has to meet contractual terms concerning technical support, but as the customer becomes more proficient with the software, vendor resources can be otherwise utilized, as they are less and less frequently needed by the customer.

Quality feedback. The customer, having formed a strategic partnership with the vendor, is strongly motivated to help the vendor improve its product and its support operations. Usually these improvements are incorporated into all versions of the product, not just the customer's version, so this can be a significant, across-the-board benefit for the vendor.

Types of Software
There are different categories or types of software, and enterprise-licensing practice proceeds somewhat differently in each case. Following are brief descriptions of

several types of software with accompanying information regarding their licensing:

Operating Systems

As previously noted, Windows 2000, Unix, and Macintosh OS X are all examples of operating system (OS) software. Most frequently they come bundled with a new computer, so the price paid for the OS is bundled into the price of the computer. A computer without an OS is inoperable and therefore of little value to end-users.

Separate licensing of OS software can occur in a number of circumstances, however. A common example occurs with upgrades. Frequently the vendor of an OS will charge customers for revised versions of the OS. Minor bug-fix versions are usually free and available in the form of "service packs" or "patches" of various kinds. But major changes to the OS are almost always sold.

Applications

Applications are the type of software that is most frequently licensed. Microsoft's Excel, Word, and PowerPoint are all examples of software applications products. These types of software are commonly referred to as "productivity applications," because customers use them to produce documents or data files that are their work product. Web browsers such as Microsoft Explorer and Netscape Communicator can be considered applications too; but since they are currently free, the licenses that support them constitute a different category.

Network-based Software

"Groupware" is the generic term for software that is used by groups of users. E-mail products such as Microsoft Outlook are the most common kind of groupware, with group scheduling products such as Meeting Maker a close second. Technically, groupware belongs to the "Applications" category, but licensing groupware is different enough that it should be considered separately.

Groupware runs over a network and has server components as well as workstation components. So the groupware server application has to be compatible with the type of network on which it is to be installed. And the workstation components have to be compatible with the end-user computers on which they are to be used.

Ten or fifteen years ago, this was more of an issue. The network environment was cluttered with many flavors of Novell Netware, Banyan Vines, Microsoft LAN Manager, AppleShare, and Unix, not to mention proprietary Network Operating Systems (NOSs) from practically every mini-computer vendor.

Currently, Windows NT (and Windows 2000 Professional, its descendant) is the leading NOS, with Novell on the wane, and various flavors of UNIX coming onto the scene. Because all of these NOS products support Macintosh workstations, AppleShare is not an important platform for very many groupware vendors.

E-mail is an unusual case in that Customers can "mix and match" server software and workstation software. That is, customers can license servers from Vendor A and separately license client software from Vendor B. For example, Eudora Pro is an e-mail client that can talk to most types of e-mail servers. Outlook is Microsoft's e-mail client software and Microsoft Exchange is their e-mail server solution.

The ground is shifting somewhat, however. It is becoming increasingly common for e-mail vendors to include other groupware functions in new versions of their products, and group scheduling is almost universally the first functionality added. Part of the motivation for this trend is to give customers an incentive to choose client and server software from the same vendor. In exchange for the larger commitment, the customer receives added functionality.

In considering the world of networked groupware, it is important to note that the term "network" describes both a collection of physical devices, such as servers, workstations, cables, hubs and routers and also a Network Operating System (NOS) that brings that collection of devices to life. Groupware applications will not run without a NOS. And groupware products run best when installed correctly on a healthy compatible network. When something goes wrong, there are lots of places to look for culprits. Besides the groupware product itself, these include the NOS, the server hardware, and other network hardware such as routers, cables, and so forth.

How can the complex interconnectivity of NOS and groupware products affect matters of licensing, and how should it? First of all, as with any application software the quality of a vendor's support, installation, and training should be major criterion for customers in their evaluation process. Second, the jurisdiction of the various vendors whose products are being licensed needs to be clearly spelled out and understood by everyone, and there should be a "Plan B" for every contingency.

The worst possible scenario occurs when the e-mail client support representative is yelling at the e-mail server rep, who is in turn yelling at the NOS person who is yelling at the server hardware technician. The smaller the number of players, the fewer gaps can be expected in support coverage. Most frequently, either the internal IT group or an outsourced company acts as a buffer between the customer end users and all the other players.

Technical support is a very critical component of groupware licensing, and strategies for optimizing resources to achieve quality support on a budget is a topic that could be a whole separate chapter.

Part Two: Software Licensing in the Schools

A simple example of multi-user licensing in the education market would be the "Lab Packs" common among stand-alone instructional software. This is simply a bulk purchase of software for a special price. Disk media, support materials, and teacher training may be part of this kind of purchase, or they might be made available separately.

A more complicated example involves what used to be called *Managed Instructional Systems* or *Integrated Learning Systems* (ILS's). This type of instructional solution consists of

- A number of Instructional Software Units, which are integrated within

- A Student Management System (SMS), which tracks individual student progress through the units, and which requires

- A Local Area Network

When such a system is installed and working correctly, it enables school staff to track data regarding how individual students and classes are progressing through the content. Individualized Study Plans can be generated by the SMS or by teachers, paper worksheets can be printed for students to complete at home, and student progress reports can be generated for parents.

From the discussion in Part One, it should be clear that an ILS is a complex example of a groupware application, and all the usual concerns exist and apply to it. For instance, if a school upgrades its network to a newer version, or purchases new hardware, will the ILS still work? If not, when will there be a revision of it that will? A successful enterprise license for an ILS solution must address these issues adequately.

Distance Learning?

Distance learning has traditionally been defined as an instructional environment in which students and teacher are:

a) at different locations,

b) participating at different times, or

c) both of the above.

This used to mean televised, talking-head instruction, with written assignments completed and then mailed in, to be graded and mailed back.

So, is an ILS a type of distance learning? Most educators would say "No," since teachers and students are present at the same location at the same time. But what happens when the ILS vendor revises the solution so that it can be delivered over the Internet?

What happens is that the Web browser becomes the framework within which the instruction is delivered, and the network cables can effectively get very long, very quickly. Looked at in the simplest possible way, the Internet itself becomes the "(not-so) Local Area Network" for the ILS.

Whew! This is a giant step, as the synergy between the "Distance Learning community embracing the Internet" on the one hand and the "ILS vendors revising their products to work over the Internet" on the other, begins to produce a lot of exciting (and sometimes confusing) new options for schools. This is all going on today at a furious rate, and the challenge to educators to make wise decisions is enormous.

Part Three: Licensing Internet-Based School Solutions

Shakespeare was mercifully unaware of his prophetic abilities regarding technology in the schools when he wrote, *"Oh what a wicked web we weave when first we practice to deceive...."* Well, at least it seems that Web-based solutions are wickedly hard to understand most of the time, and here are some of the reasons why:

Products change frequently. Back in dinosaur days when schools bought a copy of *Meteor Multiplication, Rocky's Boots,* or *Oregon Trail,* they got a box with disks and a manual inside it, and that was the product. Not so with Web-based solutions, especially when today's solution becomes a portal into something else tomorrow.

Vendors change frequently. Dot com startups don't always just go out of business, they also get purchased, usually by other startups. This of course contributes to the product changes noted above, but it also affects vendor relationships with customers, often in unpleasantly surprising ways.

Commercialism. School systems that cannot afford to pay for Web-based commercial-free solutions can sometimes deploy free solutions that feature advertising. Exposing students to advertising at school is a volatile issue, however, particularly when ads are mixed in with instructional content.

Appropriateness. Teachers, other school staff members, statewide textbook committees, PTOs, Intermediate Service Agencies, textbook and software companies, and many others have worked hard to over the years to make sure that students only see instructional material at school that contributes in a positive way to their academic development. This set of tasks has consumed enormous resources even when applied to relatively static instructional material such as textbooks, filmstrips, and software. But trying to police the Internet makes the old dinosaur days look like much simpler and happier times. When current news events and rotating advertising is wrapped around instructional content on the computer screen and is changing from minute-to-minute, monitoring for appropriateness can seem to be an insurmountable task.

Any one of these issues by itself is problematic. But contending with the world of the Internet in schools today means having to deal with all of these issues at once!

About the Author

George Bigham *is a managing partner at Bigham Technology Solutions, a Houston-based consulting company working with schools and with organizations developing for and selling to the educational technology market. He has an extensive background in the education community, with over 25 years of experience in textbook and software sales and training, technology system and network troubleshooting, applications training in schools, database design, and developing training products. Contact him at BighamG@aol.com or at (281) 866-9726.*

CHAPTER 4
Third-Party Distribution

Inside this chapter…

Distribution of Software through Catalogs

by Brenda Raker
with thanks to Sharon Segall

Looking for a way to sell more software? Then partnering with a software distributor may be a solution. Software distributors are defined as companies that purchase and then resell a wide variety of products from other companies. Distribution companies reach out to the market predominantly through catalogs, which feature a wide range of products and/or services. The value they provide to the market is two-fold. For customers who want to work with one company to meet a wide range of product needs, distributors provide one-stop shopping. For software publishers, distributors can account for an average of 20-50% of their total sales.

The challenges that are faced by catalog-based distributors are in many cases similar to the marketing and selling challenges that confront all vendors. There are, however, unique demands to the distribution business. This article will outline both the standard challenges for selling software through a catalog and the unique demands faced by distributors.

There are three distinct categories of marketing challenges that face any company that creates catalogs to promote and sell products:

1) Targeting the audience

2) Developing an integrated marketing plan

3) Creating the catalog

Targeting the Audience

Like all publishers or vendors, distributors must understand the "ideal client profile." Catalogs, which usually range from 32 pages to 250+ pages, are expensive to produce and to mail. It is important that distributors understand the mix in the education market of decision makers and key decision influencers and that the catalogs are targeted to the appropriate educators. Selecting the right lists and using the lists wisely are two important keys to success.

Creating and maintaining an in-house list of current customers will allow distributors to present new materials to purchasers who have already responded favorably at least once to the catalog. This is obviously an important requirement for successful distributors. The in-house database should also serve as the starting point for

analysis of an "ideal client." Are some states disproportionately represented in the customer base? Are there other demographic anomalies? Do more customers come from large or small schools? Are customers more likely to hold certain titles? These are questions that everyone should ask and that are also very important to distributors.

Rigorously analyzing the in-house customer list will provide important insight to the customer base and a means of targeting those educators who match a certain profile in your following campaigns. It may also show where there are surprising gaps in either territory penetration or customer type penetration. This will allow a more tailored approach to materials to reach specific geographic areas or customer types. Of course, keeping your in-house customer database current by rigorous updates is critical. The data should be reviewed on a regular basis to confirm that the contacts identified as customers have indeed purchased recently. And when purchasing patterns have changed, it is certainly time for a call from the sales department!

Using the information from analysis of the current customers, additional mailing lists can be acquired from one of several companies that provide this service. Contacts on this new mailing list would be classified as highly qualified, as they would share the same demographic profile as current customers. These new contacts should be reviewed and watched for movement from a contact status to a customer status. This will allow further analysis and improvement of both the marketing and sales efforts of the company.

Distributors who become extremely good at analysis also create a scheduled mailing matrix which allow them to "customize" the catalogs that are mailed. This tailored approach allows a science teacher to receive a science version of the catalog, a math teacher to receive a math version, and an elementary contact to review a catalog with just elementary products. This "customization," however, still provides for a complete catalog that can be mailed to key decision makers who influence multiple curriculum or content areas.

Developing an Integrated Marketing Plan

For distribution companies, the catalog is the main marketing focus and will either make the company successful if done correctly or hinder the company if done poorly. The catalog, however, should be only one component of a fully integrated marketing plan.

Like all companies, catalog companies need to research the market, determine funding, and outline campaigns that help them best penetrate the market with their products. Obvious components of the marketing plan could be a trade show schedule, advertising plan, special flyers, a Web site, focus group meetings, postcard mailings, fax blasts, e-letters, and box stuffers.

Many companies have found that focus groups are an invaluable resource. They help maintain close contact with customers and they can often be the source of creative ideas for new marketing strategies or product needs. Catalog companies more often than not do not have a direct sales force that can meet with customers face to face. Therefore, focus group meetings provide a forum for gaining an understanding of customer needs and expectations. It is critical to understand the needs of the customer base and the market and to demonstrate this understanding in the catalog. Meeting with a focus group on a regular basis is an important way to seek and receive customer input.

A solid marketing plan will apply the right resources at the right time to influence purchasing decisions. This requires frequent, consistent, and timely communication with customers. Like the practice of alchemy of old, this requires a blend of science and mystery.

Creating the Catalog

A catalog is just another form of direct mail, and the same critical factors that go into creating a successful direct mail piece must go into creating a successful catalog. The most critical challenge is aligning the products, the price, the targeted audience, and the timing of receipt of the catalog. Looking first at the audience, the work that has already been outlined in terms of defining your ideal client provides support for making data driven decisions about the audience for the catalog.

> " A solid marketing plan will apply the right resources at the right time to influence purchasing decisions. "

In addition, the work completed to analyze the market and to prepare a comprehensive marketing plan will provide the data needed to make effective decisions about appropriate pricing and should help in determining how to best present the products. Once product presentation and prices have been identified, it is important to focus on the layout of the catalog itself. A little time here should be devoted to the cover of the catalog. It obviously is the first impression that customers will have about the company and the products it represents. The main goal should be to generate interest and draw customers into the catalog. The catalog cover can feature exciting new products, announce a limited-time offer, or in some other way create a compelling reason for opening the catalog. The back cover also offers a way to focus on key products or offerings and should target a specific customer by including the customer name, not just a title. Use the catalog to sell—the company as well as the products.

Once inside the catalog, copy and design must work together to create a catalog that is "user friendly" and appealing. It is also very important to clearly identify value and benefits to the educators that will be making purchasing decisions. One way to do this is to include testimonials or quotes from satisfied customers. A word of warning, however: please be sure to do the work to find real customers and get their permission to use their testimonials. This will take more time, but the rewards will be much greater.

In addition, make it easy for customers to understand system requirements. Since being assured that the software will operate on the hardware on hand is such a significant issue for the education market, it enhances the value to the customer if finding technical specifications is streamlined and the specifications are easy to interpret.

Obviously, it is important to make it easy for customers to contact you. Make the phone number, fax number, and Web site address a prominent feature of every page. In addition, the order form should be easy to complete and return. All required details for completing an order should be precisely spelled out. Be very exact in this area, for it is very easy to lose the customer's interest if the company is hard to contact.

Work done by the marketing team should also provide information regarding the sales cycle for the education market as it relates to the specific products in the catalog. Recognizing the impact of the sales cycle, it is important to know how long it will take the catalog to arrive once it is shipped and to factor this time period into the planning schedule. It is a good idea to develop a set of contacts who will notify you when a catalog arrives. This will allow the mailing to be tracked and provide verification that the anticipated delivery schedule is indeed correct or provide notice that the schedule should be modified for the next mailing.

Before moving on to unique challenges for catalog distributors, it is important to note that this outline is not intended to be a comprehensive list of challenges that companies must contend with when creating and mailing product catalogs. Many key issues such as frequency of mailings, ensuring that addresses and names in the database are accurate, and having appropriate systems in place to track responses and buying patterns have not been covered. However, this discussion has addressed the key issues for publishers of catalogs: targeting the audience, developing an integrated marketing plan, and creating the catalog.

Distribution Challenges

Distributors of software have some challenges that are unique to distribution. As they may represent literally hundreds of publishers and thousands of products in a single catalog, the complexity of targeting the audience, of developing an integrated marketing plan, and of creating the catalog are all increased. In addition, there are unique challenges for catalog distributors. Key unique challenges are related to vendor relationships, catalog ease of use, and brand name recognition.

Vendor Relationships

Selecting vendor partners and then creating a close working relationship that is a win-win for both distributor and vendor is key to success as a distributor. The completed analysis of the market and the comprehensive marketing plan will provide the data to make good decisions about products that will meet customer expectations and about appropriate pricing.

Creating a positive working relationship with vendor partners will require constant communication and access to data to help the vendor partners understand the distribution market. When you speak with a vendor partner, be ready to discuss sales trends for the company and for similar vendors. Strategies and ideas for helping the vendor partner work more closely with you will also be greatly appreciated. All vendors and publishers understand market fluctuations and experience them directly as well as through their resellers. They will not be surprised when their distribution partner is experiencing similar trends, but they will require special consideration if the distributor is falling behind direct efforts or the efforts of other reseller partners.

Catalog Ease of Use

Since distributor catalogs are often more than 200 pages long, it is very important to make the catalog easy to use. A big part of making a catalog "user friendly" is making it effortless for customers to find the information they need. The catalog design should take into consideration that some customers will want to find products by categories while others may want to look for a product title or a particular vendor. It is critical that the catalog be formatted to allow all customers to search the way they want to search for information.

Determining a format and then standardizing on that format will also help make the catalog user friendly. It is helpful if you provide strict specifications for the vendors to use when describing their products and providing content for the catalog. This makes it much easier for customers to compare similar products and allows the distributor to demonstrate a key value: the ability to source products from a wide range of vendors.

> "A big part of making a catalog "user friendly" is making it effortless for customers to find the information they need."

Brand Name Recognition

Software distributors offer great value to customers who want to simplify their purchasing process by ordering products from a variety of vendors on a single purchase order. However, the distributor must differentiate itself from the other distributors in the market. Obviously, a reputation based on customer service, selection of products, fair prices, timeliness of fulfillment, and knowledgeable sales and customer service staff will provide a powerful position in the market. Key value indicators such as these will be extremely important so that decisions can be made on the value the distributor provides and not only pricing alone.

The distribution of software through catalogs has become a standard part of doing business in the education technology market. Partnering with a distributor can greatly increase the reach of a publisher if the distributor is selected carefully. Distributors must be expert marketers as the demands they face are predominately marketing challenges. In addition, they require competent expertise in merchandising and the management of vendor relationships. Be sure to look for skills in these areas when evaluating distributors. In addition, partnering with a distributor who has a well-known position in the market and a reputation for customer responsiveness will be more efficient and effective. Building a relationship with a solid distribution partner can be very rewarding and profitable. Look around; there are several good ones out here!

About the Author

Brenda Raker *is president of Educational Resources,* www.edresources.com, *the nation's largest source of educational software, technology peripherals and professional development for the education market. Her career in the educational field began in the classroom, where she was a teacher for 12 years. She now has 27 years of diversified experience in the education market and 18 years of experience in educational technology. Raker's expertise encompasses business development, marketing, market and product analysis, direct sales, strategic planning and business alliances. Brenda can be reached by calling (800) 624-2926 or at* braker@edresources.com.

Value-Added Resellers: Your Link to a Successful Sales Strategy

by Lillian Kellogg

The education market can present some overwhelming challenges even for the savvy marketer. It is a complex and fragmented market that presents significant distribution obstacles. It is well noted for its geographical fragmentation, decentralized purchasing, and complex decision-making and purchasing processes. The US K-12 education market remains, however, an attractive and highly sought after market.

The US K-12 market is large, diverse, and growing. It is one of the largest markets in the US, commanding 8% of GNP[1] and second only to the health care industry. It is primarily an institutional market. This means that products and services are purchased by the institution (school or school district) for use within the school community. With the recent school-to-home trend there is a slow migration of products and services from the school into the home. The education market is actively pursued not only for its size—both in terms of population and money spent—but also because it has tremendous additional value and benefit. It is a perfect environment for establishing name identity and long-term brand loyalty with a large audience of current and future consumers.

The distribution challenges stem primarily from the complex funding and organizational characteristics of the education market. The vast majority of K-12 funding distributed to thousands of school districts comes from state and local sources, and as a result, technology planning, evaluation, and acquisition are very decentralized. In addition, federal funding is typically disbursed through formula or grant programs managed at the state or local education agency levels. If your organization wants to "cover" the market, your sales and marketing strategy will have to accommodate over 16,383 school districts, 110,826 school sites,[2] and potentially hundreds of thousands of decision makers—a daunting task for any organization. Thus, small and large companies alike are faced with the problem of creating a successful sales and marketing organization that is affordable and effective.

The education technology sector presents the same challenges and opportunities as does the broader K-12 market. Achieving sales success requires a combination of an understanding of the key local issues—such as

funding sources, technology implementation plans, curriculum objectives, and administration initiatives—with local presence and availability, to allow your product or service to be presented, promoted, demonstrated, and proposed. Value-added resellers are key players in providing this local presence.

Channel Options

Educational technology market resellers fall into four basic categories:

- Value-added resellers
- Direct mail catalog companies
- Online resellers, aggregators, and e-procurement companies
- Distributors

Each of these channel options plays an important role in developing a channel sales strategy. Of course, each should be evaluated for its appropriateness or alignment with your particular product or service. Value-added resellers differentiate themselves from the other channel options primarily in their ability to intimately know and understand their customers and leverage long-term customer relationships. This becomes particularly crucial in the education market. It is widely held that the education market is one of relationships versus transactions. This means that educators prefer to conduct business with known and trusted business partners who have a local presence and commitment not only to the education market in general but a commitment and vested interest in their particular institution as well.

Although there are different ways to represent products to education customers, the most desirable method is through local field sales representation. Considering the vast number of schools and districts, only the largest and most established education vendors can operate a direct sales force comprehensive enough to have sizeable market reach and coverage. Many organizations seek to leverage or supplement their existing direct sales resources with indirect sales resources such as those offered by value-added resellers. Still others look to develop the market primarily through utilizing an indirect sales channel relying heavily on the resources of value-added resellers. As a result, value-added resellers representing a limited number of product lines and offering one or more representatives per state are highly coveted by vendors. They can play an important role for virtually any vendor by providing direct, local access to key customer sales opportunities.

Value-Added Resellers Defined

As previously outlined, there are a wide variety of reseller organizations operating within the K-12 education market. The majority are small-to-medium sized companies or small divisions of larger organizations. Their smaller size is often an asset, as it allows them to remain focused on their geographic and/or vertical solutions, and to build strong customer and vendor relationships. After analyzing hundreds of education market resellers, the following two basic and primary criteria can be used to qualify an organization as a value-added reseller:[3]

1. The ability to deliver services as well as products to education customers.

2. The ability to assist publishers and manufacturers in presenting products directly to customers utilizing a field sales force.

The ability to deliver services can be interpreted in a number of ways. Typically value-added resellers have a particular solution focus, such as curriculum or networking, and their services are oriented toward bringing together multiple products to create a solution. They then provide additional support by helping customers install products, training customers to use products, and maintaining products or upgrading them over time. Alternatively, some value-added resellers may have significant value for customers simply because of their specialized knowledge in a particular area, and their services may come only in the basic form of pre-sale consultation for product selection.

In the K-12 market, no single value-added reseller has a market share beyond 5-10% in its target geography. This low penetration does not indicate that they are ineffective; rather it suggests that customers engage a wide variety of purchasing options for educational

technology products and services. For many vendors this means it may be necessary to take advantage of all channel options to develop a sales and marketing strategy that embraces a majority of the ways customers purchase products.[4]

What to Look for in a Value-Added Reseller

High-quality, education-focused value-added resellers are valuable because of their ability to represent products to established customers and because they possess an in-depth understanding of the education market in general. This understanding allows them to identify products that meet the needs of their customers, match products with available funding, target the appropriate decision makers, and facilitate the order process. The following are some of the key characteristics of high-quality value-added resellers:

1. The ability to understand the value of a product and represent it accurately.

2. The ability to understand what schools want, how they purchase, and who is the decision maker.

3. Insight into the various funding sources that are appropriate to purchase a given product.

4. A sincere interest in representing quality educational technology products.

5. The desire to make money.

Education value-added resellers are as diverse as the customers they serve. We have previously defined value-added resellers as organizations that have the ability to deliver services as well as products and that utilize field sales representatives that have a direct relationship with the customer or end user. They are capable of implementing both "top down" (superintendents and administrators) and "bottom up" (educators) sales strategies. They participate in demand generation activities such as conferences and trade shows, seminars, direct mail, marketing, catalogs, newsletters, Web sites, and other education marketing activities. They typically support the customer in both pre-sale and post-sale activities. They understand the need for and are able to provide professional development services to the education customers they serve. They are capable of

> " Many organizations seek to leverage or supplement their existing direct sales resources with indirect sales resources such as those offered by value-added resellers. "

becoming fully trained and knowledgeable about the products they represent, to professionally present them to education customers. They tend to be "solution-oriented," meaning they provide curriculum and technology products and services that are unique to the education market. And finally, they seek to establish a market niche that differentiates them from their competition.

There are some interesting similarities among successful education value-added resellers. These characteristics include:

1. Longevity in the market: value-added resellers average an education market experience of 10+ years.

2. Key customer contracts: many successful value-added resellers provide products and services through established ongoing contracts with their customers.

3. Face-to-face sales capability: having a direct business relationship with the customer or end user.

4. High-end solutions: the more astute and sophisticated resellers have the capability to represent higher end solutions commanding higher margins.

5. Vendor relationships: successful resellers have developed long and mutually beneficial "partnerships" with their vendors.

Value-Added Resellers versus Sales Agents: What's the Difference?

The issue of taking title to the publisher or manufacturer's product is becoming increasingly important in today's evolving market. This is not simply an accounting matter; rather, it affects many aspects of the relationships between vendors, resellers, and end users. Two contrasting models are as follows:

Traditional Reseller Model. In this scenario the reseller actually orders the product from the publisher, manufacturer, or authorized distributor and physically takes title to the product. The reseller then ships and bills the education customer under the agreed terms. The difference between what the reseller pays the vendor for the product and what it is sold to the customer for is the profit margin the reseller works off of.

> "...close reseller-customer relationships can actually benefit vendors, allowing them to take advantage of resellers' sensitivity to local issues."

Sales Agent Model. The sales agent model is similar to a "manufacturer's rep" program. While this scenario does require sales and marketing activities from the reseller, customers actually purchase products directly from the publisher or manufacturer. A purchase order is issued to the publisher or manufacturer, who is responsible for delivering the product, billing the customer, and collecting the receivables. The reseller is simply paid a commission for generating the sale. Some hardware companies use this model to alleviate the burden of financing large volumes of sales from their resellers. Online publishers typically prefer this model as it allows for them to forge a closer customer relationship, facilitating support as well as accommodating a subscription model.

Some resellers are resistant to a sales agent model and prefer to "own" the customer relationship themselves. They do not want to relinquish the customer relationships they have worked hard over the years to establish. Furthermore, close reseller-customer relationships can actually benefit vendors, allowing them to take advantage of resellers' sensitivity to local issues. In some cases, for example, bids or contracts require that publishers and manufacturers offer flexibility to accommodate local needs. If a reseller has an existing contract that a new vendor can "piggy-back" onto, clearly the vendor has an incentive to modify its policies to allow inclusion of its products.

This issue is an important one for vendors to consider in the development of their channel sales strategy. A sales agent program is typically viewed as a stronger relationship between the vendor and reseller, and sometimes includes some level of geographic exclusivity. A traditional reseller relationship may offer a less dedicated relationship but may allow for more reseller competition to serve the customer's needs.

Addressing the Issue of Exclusivity

Some value-added resellers seek vendor programs that offer them geographic or territorial exclusivity. In this scenario, usually sales credit and/or commission is given to the reseller of record regardless of whether they generated the sale. With this protection, the value-added reseller feels that they can invest more time, energy, and resources into building a market for the vendor, as they are certain of securing commissions on the sales that may occur there. This is simply a return-on-investment consideration for both the reseller and the vendor. Both parties must have a sense of confidence that their increased investment in the business proposition will result in better returns. An exclusive sales program builds very strong relationships between the value-added reseller and the vendor, as they become interdependent on each other to achieve sales and profitability goals and objectives. Exclusive programs are typically considered in circumstances that involve long or extensive sales cycles or process, sophisticated solutions that require a high degree of training, high-end solutions that result in sales in the tens of thousands of dollars or more, or sales programs that require a significant portion of a resellers resources.

Some vendors build a channel strategy that does not guarantee exclusivity but that effectively creates a virtual exclusive environment by limiting the number and selection of channel option resellers.

The "Value" in Value-Added Resellers

Resellers play a variety of important roles for customers:

Technology and Information. Many administrators rely on their resellers to keep them abreast of the latest technology developments and options. In the increasingly political world of education, administrators are striving to make forward-looking and effective investments in technology. Resellers participate in local and regional meetings, technology fairs, and conferences to support the adoption of technology.

Support and Local Representation. Value-added resellers are typically the first level of support for their customers, meaning they receive the calls about defective products and other issues. Well-trained and resourceful resellers can minimize a vendor's own requirements for customer support. Education customers are relationship oriented and enjoy the ability to personally interact with a local sales organization they trust and can rely on.

Aggregation and Customized Solutions. Resellers have the ability to aggregate products and make them available to schools and school districts, minimizing the number of purchase orders a school or school district has

to process. In addition, value-added resellers can combine products to create a customized solution that meets the customer's needs.

Aside from pure sales opportunities, high-quality value-added resellers offer value to publishers and manufacturers:

Expertise and Experience. Resellers usually have a broad and in-depth understanding of their customers. They are able to identify key decision makers within education organizations, and they understand the buying cycle as well as the availability of funding.

Accelerating Awareness. Vendors targeting the education market need to do a wide variety of broad-based and targeted marketing to increase their visibility in the market and generate opportunities, whether selling from the bottom up or the top down. Respected resellers with a long-standing presence in the market can accelerate this awareness by endorsing the product and targeting key customers and influencers.

Leveraging Resources. Resellers can help make a vendor's investment in sales and marketing activities more effective. For example, launching a new product at a state-level technology conference can expose a vendor to many potential customers, but a good reseller can significantly add to this exposure by arranging private meetings and inviting key customers that may spend very little time walking the exhibit floor.

Geographic Coverage. Vendors can "piece together" a network of resellers to cover their target geographies or the entire country with as few as a dozen regional value-added resellers.

Creating Value-Added Reseller Relationships

Successful value-added resellers have established their position in the market by creating relationships not only with their customers, but with their key vendors as well. Over time these business relationships evolve into effective "partnerships" where the value-added reseller and the vendor both feel comfortable in investing their time and resources, knowing that they will receive a targeted return on their investment.

Creating a good value-added reseller relationship requires support and management.

Vendors should be prepared to provide organized support and leadership with clear communication about the expectations and outcomes of working together. A strong business relationship is based upon a solid business proposition. Once the business proposition is understood, value-added resellers can be your link to overcoming the significant education market challenges and barriers.[5]

■

[1] Source: US Department of Commerce.

[2] Source: Quality Education Data (QED), *US K-12 Education Market Overview 2000-2001.*

[3] The Peak Group, *Education Channel Partners.*

[4] The Peak Group, *Education Channel Partners.*

[5] The Peak Group, *Education Channel Partners.*

■

About the Author

Lillian Kellogg *is a managing partner of The Peak Group, LLC. Prior to co-founding The Peak Group, Lillian founded and served as the president for a market-leading value-added reseller in the K-12 educational technology market. Lillian specializes in all aspects of sales and distribution strategies, business plan design and development, and strategic business partnerships and alliances. Lillian brings a high level of proficiency in developing growth strategies including market share enhancement, market expansion, and new market segment penetration. Her experience includes over seventeen years in selling and marketing educational technology as well as publishing industry analysis reports including the "Educational Channel Partners" report. She can be reached at (650) 917-8467 or lilk@peakgroup.net.*

Selling through Parent-Teacher Stores: Established Relationships Are Key to the NSSEA Retail Dealer Channel

by Adrienne Watts

Smart marketers know the power of the local education retailer. With teachers given increased responsibility to specify products and place orders in recent years, parent-teacher stores should be a major component of every supplier's educational sales strategy. Why? Because educational dealers have existing relationships with schools that make them an invaluable resource in the community. Parents, too, are discovering what teachers have known for years: they can trust their local parent-teacher retailer to carry the finest classroom-tested products that are educationally sound and appealing to children.

Parent-Teacher Store Customer Mix

As the name implies, parent-teacher stores attract customers from both the home and the classroom. The 1999 *NSSEA Retail Customer Study* reported that teacher customers spend an average of $448 of their own money on school supplies and instructional materials annually. Nearly 80% of teachers in the study were spending their own money in the stores versus school or PTA funds.

Not only are teachers spending more money, but parents are also expected to send their children to school fully stocked with products from a long list of required supplies mailed to parents prior to the start of the school year. These sales, which traditionally went to the school distributor through a bid for the entire district, are now passed on to parents and given to teacher supply retail stores and discount office superstores. While about 40% of parents surveyed spent under $75 per year on instructional materials; about one third spent between $75 and $199; 23% spent between $199 and $499; and 10% spent over $500.

Product Selection Geared toward Students

Whether it is flashcards for multiplication tables, write-on/wipe-off workbooks for handwriting, or educational software to build critical thinking skills, parent-teacher stores are well equipped for students of all ages, typically carrying over 12,500 different items from 150 vendors. Educational retailers select products based on quality, teacher and parent demand, value, packaging, and price.

Educational retailers specialize in merchandise that is *not* sold by mass-market superstores and that has true educational value to help children learn. NSSEA reports

NSSEA Typical Parent-Teacher Store Stocks

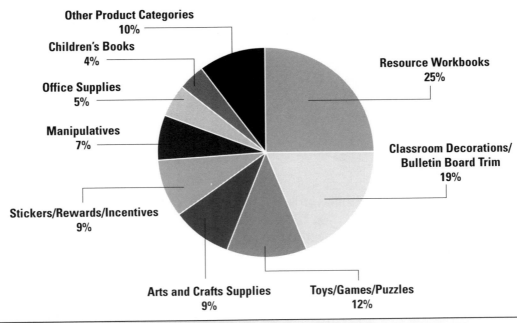

- Other Product Categories 10%
- Children's Books 4%
- Office Supplies 5%
- Manipulatives 7%
- Stickers/Rewards/Incentives 9%
- Arts and Crafts Supplies 9%
- Toys/Games/Puzzles 12%
- Classroom Decorations/Bulletin Board Trim 19%
- Resource Workbooks 25%

that "quality of products" and "variety of products" are the top reasons given by 60% of teachers and parents as to why they shop at parent-teacher stores. Other compelling reasons include convenience/location, level of service, and price. Customers are less concerned with price, however, when shopping at a specialty store devoted to improving teaching and learning.

According to NSSEA, the typical parent-teacher store stocks the following product mix: resource/workbooks, 25%; classroom decorations/bulletin board trim, 19%; toys/games/puzzles, 12%; arts and crafts supplies, 9%; stickers/rewards/incentives, 9%; manipulatives, 7%; office supplies, 5%; children's books, 4%; and other product categories, 10%.

With the increasing emphasis on standards and assessments, parent-teacher stores are an invaluable source for curriculum products correlated to state and local standards. "Educational retailers can tell you the educational standards (national/state/district) that were used to create products in their stores," says Vicki Geske, of The Teach Me Shop in Great Falls, MT. This ensures that parents are buying the products targeted to the standards being tested in the classroom.

"When my daughter was having trouble mastering all the concepts being tested on the SOLs (Virginia Standards of Learning), the teachers at my school directed me to the Teacher's Mart," says Nancy DeBrosse, mother of three in Fairfax, VA. "I went to find workbooks in the areas that my daughter was having problems with, and what I found was a much larger selection, plus I got a lot of help from the salespeople at the store. There are so many interesting ideas at the store to help a parent understand the lessons that our children are learning and achieve better test scores."

Parents Can Shop Where Teachers Shop

Parents who wander into an educational products retail store for the first time discover an abundance of materials they probably never knew existed. Parent-teacher stores offer a wide variety of products for every age, grade, and skill level. They specialize in products that stimulate learning using creativity and fun. According to the 1999 *Retail Customer Study*, over 72% of customers rated the selection of products better at parent-teacher stores than other specialty stores, discount stores, or office supply stores.

Almost 94% of parents visiting an educational products retail store reported that they prefer to shop for school supplies and instructional materials at retail stores; only 6% said they prefer to shop by catalog. Nearly 85% of the parents surveyed made three or more purchase visits each year.

Your Products Will Be Supported by Personalized, Friendly Service

"Educational supply stores can offer one very important aspect that others stores with a workbook section cannot... assistance!" says Lyn Nelson, president of Keys to Learning in Nashua, NH. "When a parent comes into our store and says, 'My child needs help with this or that,' we can advise that parent and help them pick the most appropriate learning tools for their child, based on how that child learns best. There is more to learning than workbooks."

Parents and teachers are comfortable shopping at educational retail stores because many store owners and employees are former or current teachers and know how to advise customers on integrating a variety of educational materials. This comfort level keeps them coming back: over 37% of teacher customers reported visiting parent-teacher stores 3-6 times per year, 27% visited parent-teacher stores 7-10 times per year, 13% reported 11-15 visits per year, and another 13% came to the stores over 15 times in a year.

Another draw for teachers and parents alike are in-store workshops. Educational product stores offer parenting classes, story hours, product demonstrations, book signings by children's authors, and more. Once buyers are accustomed to shopping at a particular store, they are likely to buy new products introduced there or recommended by store personnel.

While most customers surveyed shop for school supplies and instructional materials at discount stores and office supply stores in addition to the parent-teacher stores, 70% of teacher customers rated the level of service better at parent-teacher stores than elsewhere. "Our best asset is our staff of current and former teachers who can guide parents in their purchases," says David Persson, president of The School Box, with ten educational supply stores in Georgia.

Once a relationship has been established and needs are being met through new product introductions, training, and good service, it can be difficult to lure teachers to Web offerings and direct sales. However, most parent-teacher stores don't rely just on walk-in traffic; over half publish a catalog, and increasing numbers are providing online ordering via their Web sites.

Teachers Prefer Retail

Nothing beats the ability to handle and examine a product in person. Retail stores appeal to teachers and parents who want the hands-on experience and want to bring home the product and start using it immediately. Over 92% of teacher customers prefer to shop in a retail store rather than by catalog or online.

"When you need clothes, wouldn't you prefer to try them on in a store rather than go through the hassle of mail order?" says Lyn Nelson. "Teachers can see and touch what items they are interested in. They can read the box or thumb through the book to see if it's appropriate for their students before they pay. I believe it actually saves them time!"

Teachers also prefer retail stores for reasons of product quality. They know that their local educational supply store will have the latest products for their classroom. Further, they feel that if an item is stocked at a parent-teacher store, it is most likely high quality, current, and tested.

NSSEA surveys show that teachers find out about parent-teacher stores mainly through colleagues. Over 65% of teachers surveyed learned about the stores through "word of mouth," while one fourth discovered the store by its sign or by driving by. Only 7% of respondents reported learning about the stores through advertisements, 7% through a catalog, and another 4% through a flyer or mailing.

Why Sell through Parent-Teacher Stores?

Sales through retail stores can be less costly for vendors than selling direct because educational supply retailers bear the majority of operational costs. In exchange for providing shelf and catalog space, performing customer service, and handling product refunds, most manufacturers offer retailers substantial discounts, a catalog allowance or cooperative advertising funds, favorable payment terms, and freight allowances, to help promote their products.

Parent-teacher stores provide much-needed sales support for manufacturers selling to the education market. Teachers like to buy from people they trust, and parents are quickly learning that parent-teacher stores are an invaluable resource partner in their children's education.

While somewhat of a novelty even 20 years ago, 80% of NSSEA member dealer companies have retail operations. Over 1,000 parent-teacher stores are listed on the NSSEA roster. According to the *NSSEA Market Definition Study*, retail and catalog sales of school equipment, instructional materials, and school supplies amounted to $6.169 billion in 1996, the last year figures were available. For additional resources and assistance with marketing your products through parent-teacher stores, visit our Web site at www.nssea.org.

About the Author

Adrienne Watts *is vice president of marketing for the National School Supply and Equipment Association,* www.nssea.org. *Since joining NSSEA in 1987, Adrienne has worked on a wide variety of publications, marketing campaigns, membership drives, and fundraising efforts. She is responsible for directing the promotion and marketing efforts for all NSSEA events and services. In addition to serving as Director of NSSEA's Education Excellence Foundation, she works with NSSEA leaders to develop programs to increase the profile of the school market.*

Education Market E-Commerce: Consolidating a Fragmented Market
by John Politoski

Online marketers are flocking to the education sector, and for good reason—schools purchase a staggering volume of products, schools are infamous for their antiquated and inefficient purchasing systems, and schools offer a link to students and parents (consumers) that many marketers covet.

The Internet has changed almost every aspect of our modern world, and the education market is no exception. The Internet has altered the way we do business, and it is also beginning to affect the way schools do business. Business-to-business companies offering online e-integration and e-procurement services are slowly changing the school's traditional purchasing landscape. Industry leaders who have provided many of the school supply products predict a rapid adoption of the e-procurement model once schools see other school districts successfully utilizing these services. Hence, many of the traditional school supply companies have added an e-procurement component to their business. Today, schools have significantly increased options for products, services, and information. It won't be long before we see a grand shift in school purchasing.[1]

There are four primary categories into which we can group the various companies targeting this market:
- Traditional companies migrating to e-commerce
- Purchasing and e-procurement system providers
- Aggregators and e-integration companies
- Home market, school-to-home, and fundraising companies

Traditional Companies Migrating to E-Commerce
The Internet has opened up several new avenues of distribution opportunities. There are an increasing number of companies active in the online purchasing market. Many are in the process of transitioning their traditional reseller or direct mail catalog operations to the Web, but a significant number of companies have been created over the past two years to capitalize on the advantages that Web-based purchasing offers to the education market. Virtually all companies that operate in this category are national in their ability to serve the education market.

Previously, e-commerce initiatives in the K-12 market focused almost exclusively on individual purchasers, but substantial inroads to the much larger institutional expenditures are now being made. Companies addressing this category include educational materials publishers and manufacturers, traditional field resellers, direct mail catalogers, and online resellers.

Many online resellers are similar to traditional catalog companies except that their catalogs are only available online and they have e-commerce capabilities. Unfortunately, most schools and districts have been slow to adopt e-commerce: while they seem to understand the benefits of pricing and delivery efficiencies, most have been stalled by their requirements for controls and paper-based signature approvals and by their legacy accounting and procurement systems. Still, the Internet is viewed as the best prospect for more efficiently selling and marketing to the highly fragmented and decentralized school market.

Online resellers are positioned between direct mail catalogers and e-procurement channel players. They are similar to direct mail catalogers in that they can represent thousands of products from hundreds of vendors. The key differentiation is they typically rely solely on their online presence to generate sales and do not print or mail a catalog. Similar to e-procurement companies, they offer e-commerce and procurement capabilities, but usually do not offer the comprehensive management of the entire procurement process that e-procurement companies offer. These organizations need to develop purchasing contracts and online strategic and marketing alliances in order to compete with their channel counterparts.

Publishers and manufacturers are also utilizing the Web to sell directly to schools. Apple Computer (www.apple.com) is an example of a manufacturer has been relatively aggressive in implementing e-commerce with its institutional customers. Competing in a business with ever-decreasing product margins, Apple ultimately replaced its network of sales agents and urged customers to order online, reducing both its internal and external cost of sales. Teacher Created Materials (www.teachercreated.com) is an example of a historically "non-technology" company that is slowly but surely growing its online sales via e-commerce with a very reasonable investment.

Purchasing and E-Procurement System Providers

The basic marketing message of e-procurement/online procurement organizations is that they can significantly cut costs of procurement, funneling the savings back into schools and classrooms. This will allow schools to spend more money on products and less on the purchasing process, thereby increasing their total effective buying power. It is estimated that schools purchase as much as $144 billion in products each year. Furthermore, it is estimated that a paper requisition costs anywhere from $100–$175 per requisition, with schools processing approximately 25 million purchase orders per year.[2] It doesn't take long to see the cost savings that could be generated by streamlining the requisition process.

Lamar Alexander, former US Secretary of Education, and chairman and co-founder of Simplexis, states "School business officials struggle with an arcane set of state laws and local bid regulations that sometimes make their work virtually impossible." Simplexis has developed a Web-based procurement system to help reduce the delays and high cost of paper-based processes, generating volume discounts for the country's 16,000 school districts. His company's goal is to save its customers a combined $10 billion by 2005.

Just as the business-to-business commercial market developed on the heels of business-to-consumer, e-commerce in the education market is growing beyond credit card purchases by parents and teachers and now addresses the highly customized needs of education institutions. Epylon (www.epylon.com), Simplexis (www.simplexis.com), and Kawama Commerce (www.kawama.com) have taken an approach that focuses on the institutional customer, rather than a traditional approach that focuses on products. These companies are not simply selling products—they provide services to schools to budget, track, and more efficiently procure goods and services. Traditional educational materials and supplies resellers have also migrated to the Internet offering similar services. School Specialty is a good example of this with its JuneBox (www.junebox.com) division.

These companies are shaping the next generation of the school supply market. In a market segment that has been mired in traditional tactics and processes on both sides of the transaction, these competitors are positioned to produce change rapidly. They provide one-stop shopping by aggregating thousands of catalog products online, enable buyers to send quotes and bids electronically to suppliers, and offer industry related news, event information and product reviews. They enable cooperative purchasing and facilitate the sharing of best practices among community members. Typically, these companies provide all of this free of charge for educational institutions and make money on the transaction while still saving the education customer money. At the same time, they reduce customer acquisition and processing costs for suppliers by aggregating a very fragmented customer base. Currently, these companies are competing to acquire customers, and it is likely that just a few will dominate the market as it requires a very significant investment and a high level of volume to meet profitability expectations.[3]

There has been a steady trend in the education market towards decentralization and site-based decision-making. More and more products and services are being selected by the users at the building level, including classroom teachers. This trend is projected to amplify as increased options become more readily accessible.

E-Procurement systems offer comprehensive management of the entire procurement process. They cover the requisition process from requests for quotations to order input management, and from electronic purchase order generation to delivery tracking and integration with schools' and vendors' back office systems. The objective of their model is to provide the widest possible variety of products from the widest possible selection of vendors for customers' purchases.

These Web-based school purchasing systems are designed to streamline traditional paper-based processes, enhance school purchasers' ability to cost-effectively see related items being purchased, and help secure better prices.

Potential education customer benefits include:

- Ability to streamline and simplify the purchasing process, saving time and money

- Reduction in overhead by lowering processing costs

- Up-to-date, competitive pricing

- School participation in aggregate purchasing with other districts

- More efficient utilization of staff

- Ability to research contracts and suppliers online

- Assistance in complying with local laws and regulations

- Tracking of current and historical orders and shipping status

- Ability to conduct online quoting and bidding

- Ability to integrate with accounting systems that are electronic, allowing streamlined financial systems

Potential vendor benefits include:

- Efficient and cost effective ways to reach the large, fragmented school market

- Ability to expand sales "reach" to a nationwide network of schools

- Improved order management, leading to reductions in operating and processing costs and increases in revenue

- More time for the sales force to focus on new business

- Shortened sales and payment cycles

- Inexpensive ways to test new product lines

- Inexpensive ways to liquidate clearance items

- Reduced cost of goods

- Reduced fulfillment errors

- Electronic processing of RFPs and RFQs

- Standardization of specifications for bid documents and contracts

The value of these e-procurement organizations lies in their potential breadth of school district coverage, their understanding of the K-12 market, their scope of services offered to their customers, their existing and growing relationships with school districts, and their comprehensive product lines.

Aggregators and E-Integration Companies

Aggregators and e-integration companies are a new and quickly emerging segment of the channel. The proliferation of online products and services has created opportunities as well as challenges for schools, school districts, and post-secondary institutions. These companies have been created to address these challenges, utilizing their technology and education market expertise. Education is currently looking towards utilizing online products and services to meet all aspects of the business of education, including administrative functions, curriculum, content, applications, tools, professional development, and communication services.[4]

These companies are aggregating a variety of solutions and bringing them to the education market as a single solution, utilizing state-of-the-art e-integration technologies. An excellent example of this new class of channel partner is VIP Tone, Inc. (www.viptone.com). The company offers both an integrated industry-tailored portal and the outsourced management of the IT infrastructure to streamline content management. They ease administration of complex equipment and networks, and they offer one source for billing and customer care. Their Web-based portal services connect users, applications, content, and infrastructure in one secure place. VIP Tone uses the tag line "connecting all the dots," meaning the company brings together an assortment of critical education online applications into one fully integrated, turnkey solution.

Home Market, School-to-Home, and Fundraising Companies

While there is a growing concentration of companies focusing on the institutional customer, there are still a wide variety of companies that focus on the individual purchaser.

While met with less frenzy than at its introduction, Internet e-commerce is still attractive for its ability to economically aggregate consumers—specifically, special interest groups, and vertical market segments.

Teachers are widely targeted, and various resellers have stated their propensity to spend an average of $500 per year on classroom materials and supplies alone. With approximately 3 million teachers in the US, that makes for a $1.5 billion market segment. In addition, many companies work with teacher unions and associations to target teachers as consumers and offer various products and services ranging from discounted computers to financial services.

Parents are also highly coveted for their spending on educational products and services for their children, as well as for their general expenditures as consumers. SmarterKids (www.smarterkids.com) has one of the highest profiles in selling education-oriented products to parents, but everyone from Amazon (www.amazon.com) to individual publishers and manufacturers is looking for a piece of the action. Increasingly, companies competing for a portion of these expenditures offer online services like tutoring, test preparation, and homework resources.

Historically, many companies have attempted to penetrate the retail market by leveraging their success with schools, but very few have succeeded. Apple Computer (www.apple.com) has never managed to parlay its significant success and leading market share in the K-12 market into any considerable retail market share. In fact, most K-12 brands—including market leaders like Pearson, Sunburst, and Tom Snyder Productions—are almost unknown in the home market, where they are replaced by consumer brands like Penguin Books, Disney Interactive, and Hasbro.

Scholastic (www.scholastic.com) is one exception to this rule. Scholastic has had great success in leveraging its relationship with schools and has effectively turned schools, teachers and PTA/PTOs into its distribution system.

The school-to-home segment of the market has been very volatile in 2000 and 2001 as many companies have failed or had to modify their business models significantly. Many companies initially planned to offer a variety of free resources and services to schools and thought that they could leverage the relationship with schools by attracting advertisers looking to reach schools or e-commerce companies looking to sell to schools or parents. In general, these revenue plans went unfulfilled as companies mistakenly treated schools like consumers. Schools have complex budgeting, decision making, and authorization processes and are changing very slowly to become more efficient and effective in their purchasing.

Fundraising has long been a robust segment of the education market. Many believe that this segment can drastically and rapidly expand through the use of e-commerce as a mechanism to more easily reach schools and significantly expand the products offered. Fundraising companies, such as Schoolpop (www.schoolpop.com), make a wide variety of products available while actively attracting new purchasers to e-commerce through their grassroots marketing campaigns. Savvy e-commerce fundraising companies have recognized the need to conduct traditional sales and marketing activities such as direct mail, events, family nights, and school site signage. The schools themselves become part of the sales and marketing process, as they are motivated to promote the fundraising to parents to maximize the volume and their school's proceeds.[5]

■

[1] The Peak Group, *Education Internet Marketplace Report.*
[2] Source: National School Supply and Equipment Association statistic
[3] The Peak Group, *Education Internet Marketplace Report.*
[4] The Peak Group, *Education Channel Partners.*
[5] The Peak Group, *Education Internet Marketplace Report.*

■

About the Author

John Politoski *is a managing partner of The Peak Group, LLC. Prior to co-founding The Peak Group, John served as general manager and vice president of marketing for a market leading value-added reseller in the K-12 technology market. John specializes in all aspects of marketing strategies, including market plan design and development, channel development, direct marketing, market research, and industry analysis. His accomplishments include the development of the second largest educational technology products reseller catalog nationally. John is the author of numerous reports and presentations annually, and he can be reached by calling (408) 927-5879 or at johnp@peakgroup.net.*

CHAPTER 5
Sales Strategies

Inside this chapter…

Developing a Sales Plan, It's Something You Need

by Pat Walkington

Everyone agrees that it is important to have a sales plan, and in every situation a sales manager is likely to encounter, a well conceived sales plan is a critical component for success.

Yet many companies do not take the time to develop a plan. This results in a business environment where there are frequent ad hoc responses to immediate concerns. In addition, without a plan the company lacks a fundamental strategy and focus to direct activity. Since the sales lead time for most companies is between 3 and 8 months, long-term goals are essential—without them, months can go by quickly and quarterly sales targets can be missed. In fact, many companies miss an entire school selling season completely.

A well developed sales plan can help a company:
- Plan for needed resources
- Attract funding
- Recruit the best sales candidates
- Clarify a company's thinking
- Increase the chances of success

It is extremely useful to develop at a minimum a three-year sales plan. This allows the company to determine what it can reasonably expect in terms of revenue, growth, and profitability. In addition, investments in programs like building an inside sales force can be rationally justified, in spite of the fact that at the outset the cost-of-sale may be higher than desired. However, over a three-year period the sales and profitability of a well-implemented program should more than justify the expense.

In general, a sales plan should include the following six components:
- A company overview
- An Evaluation of the market opportunity
- An Analysis of the company's current sales programs and process
- A Definition of company's sales goals and tactics
- An Evaluation and selection of appropriate sales channels

- A financial plan that includes program costs and a profitability analysis.

The remainder of this article explains how to go about writing each part of the sales plan.

Providing a Company Overview

The company overview begins with a financial analysis of the business, including overall profitability. It also includes a situational analysis of the current sales program and sales history. Lastly it includes a definition of the company's core competency.

Financial Analysis

Review the company's income statements for the current and previous years. Is the company currently profitable? Are revenues reaching target and costs being held to target? In a comparison to a year ago, how fast are revenues growing? How fast are costs growing? What are sales and marketing expenses as a percent of sales and how fast are these expenses growing relative to revenues and relative to total costs?

Situational Analysis of Current Sales Programs

Review how the current sales program is working. Are sales meeting company expectations? How do they compare with the previous year? How much revenue is there in the later stages of the company's sales pipeline? (According to one company's six-stage categorization scheme, "later stages" would include stage 4: "company selected," stage 5: "final approval given," and stage 6: "order received/shipped.") Is this pipeline healthy enough to meet quarterly expectations even if some account slippage occurs?

For example, when the author joined Broderbund Software in 1996, the company was already well established in the K-12 market. However, sales in the K-12 market for that fiscal year were not meeting company expectations. In fact, they were well below FY'96 levels. The division was emphasizing third-party products and new products, but core products were not receiving much focus. It was assumed that the market already knew about these products. By reviewing the current sales program, it was possible to adjust the strategy to focus more on selling the established brands. This resulted in a 50% increase in sales the following year.

If the company is new to the market, the size of the market and reasonably-projected demand for the product will need to be considered in lieu of a sales history. (See below for these elements.)

Defining the Company's Core Competency

Defining the core competency helps the company focus on what it does well and identify new markets. It also helps the sales team position the company's products and services, relative to competitors, in their customers' minds.

A core competency is a skill or trait that:
- Is prized by customers,
- Is extendable into future products and services,
- Is seen as somewhat unique, and
- Can help the company to expand into other markets.

For example, The Learning Company spent a great deal of time identifying and developing its core competency. The company did not want to be viewed by its customers as an "edutainment" company. It also did not want to be viewed as a company, which developed "textbook-like" products. Rather, it did want to be known as a company that developed high quality educational products that made learning fun for kids.

Evaluate the Market Opportunity

In developing a sales plan, a crucial component is the market opportunity. In order to evaluate this opportunity, it is first necessary to understand the K-12 market in general and identify the opportunities for selling the company's products and services to that market. It is also important to segment the market and to define the actual target market.

Market Size and Selling Opportunities

Two key elements of understanding the market are market size and selling opportunities. Briefly stated, the size of the US K-12 public school market is as follows:

- 14,349 districts and administrative units
- 89,000 public school buildings
- 52 million students
- 3.4 million teachers

For K-12, one key to evaluating selling opportunities is to know what percentage of the market is centralized as opposed to decentralized. In a centralized district, purchasing decisions are made at the district level for all of the schools in the district. In contrast, in a decentralized district purchasing decisions are made at the school building level. This distinction is very important because it may influence a company's choice of distribution channels.

> "226 districts control 25% of all spending, and the three states with the greatest number of these top districts are California, Florida, and Texas."

Another key to selling opportunity is that student enrollment drives spending. 226 districts control 25% of all spending, and the three states with the greatest number of these top districts are California, Florida, and Texas.

It is important to determine what is being spent in the major product categories like textbooks, technology, and supplementary products, and to project an average growth for the three-year period of the sales plan. A good source of information for evaluating market opportunity is *The Complete K-12 Report, Market Facts & Segment Analyses 2001*, by Robert M. Resnick, Ph.D. This report can be obtained through Open Book Publishing, Inc. in Darien, Connecticut. (Dr. Resnick's article in this book can also provide a good starting point.)

Here's how a company can assess the market opportunity for its products and services:
- Determine how much money is potentially available for your products or services.
- Identify how many companies this money is divided between.
- Determine what percentage of this funding your company can reasonably expect to capture.

Segmenting the Market

Sales to the education market are complex and often involve more than one decision maker. Some decision makers control larger sales decisions than others.

Segmenting the market provides an opportunity to target the more lucrative part of the market by identifying "where's the purse?" and "who holds the strings?"

Where's the Purse? Of the money that's available for your product category, focus on the top districts. Clarify who your product is designed to help and consider which funding sources are targeted to the same needs.

Who holds the Strings? Within the top-funded districts you have identified, determine who makes the decision for the type of product that your company offers. Profile top customer districts to identify patterns and generate ideas on how to best penetrate other top districts.

Analyze the Company's Current Sales Programs and Sales Process

This section of the sales plan takes an in-depth look at the current practices of the sales organization and asks some key questions about each. The table below provides a starting point for this internal analysis, but it should be noted that additional topics can be added to this section and that these topics are not arranged in any particular order:

Develop Sales Goals and Tactics

There are three major sales goals for any company. In some cases these could be considered marketing goals as well. These are:

1. Maximizing revenue from existing customers
2. Focusing on retaining customers
3. Targeting and reaching new customers

A well developed sales plan needs to address how each of these areas will be serviced by the sales channels. The following is a checklist of tactics to help achieve these goals:

For Existing Customers

- Have current customers been identified and profiled? Is a plan in place to call on these customers and inform them about new products/services?
- Has a customer loyalty program been developed?
- Are programs in place to detect and analyze customer dissatisfactions?
- Have the sales reps or customer service reps talked to customers who haven't ordered recently?

TOPIC	KEY QUESTIONS
Current revenue targets by quarter	Are the sales reps meeting quarterly targets? Are these targets realistic?
List of sales reps, resumes and territory assignments	Are sales reps qualified to close sales, which require the customer to make a change in his or her behavior? Does the sales rep have existing relationships with key customers? Does the sales rep have a track record of meeting and or exceeding quota? Are territory assignments realistic?
Compensation Plans	Are the sales reps being rewarded for closing sales? Does the commission rate increase as more sales are made?
List of current customers	Who are the sales reps selling to? Are they accounts from the top districts and states? What is the average order size?
Sales Process	What is the process for selling the company's products? Has the process been developed such that each stage or is well defined? Is each stage measurable such that the sales rep can effectively move the account from one stage to another? What is the length of time between stages? What is the average length of time to complete a sale from beginning to end?
Sales System / Infrastructure	Is a sales system/infrastructure in place that enables sales reps to update and report on sales progress? Does the system allow for the remote syncing of data? Does it have account management as well as inside sales management capabilities? Can reports be easily developed and revenue tracked in a variety of ways?
Sales Leads	How are leads obtained and handled?

For New Customers

- Have top target states been identified?
- Has a market opportunity analysis been conducted to estimate the amount of funding available for the company's products in its target states and districts?

Other Considerations

- Has a realistic three-year revenue forecast been completed, taking into account past product sales, new products in development, and market trends?
- Have sales goals been identified and documented?
- Has a territory coverage plan been developed before field sales or inside sales staffing is in progress?
- Is a sales system in place with a well defined sales pipeline? (Sales Logix, Goldmine, and UpShot are among the more commonly used systems.)
- Has an effective compensation plan been developed?
- Have the right channels been selected, based on the goals of maximizing margins and profitability? (Channels can include field sales reps, inside sales reps, resellers, direct mail, and the company's Web site.)

Select Appropriate Sales Channels

In planning appropriate sales channels, it is important to look at the most cost effective and profitable way to cover the territory and achieve the desired revenue goals for years one, two, and three in the plan. In addition, it is important to determine from the market opportunity analysis where the money will most likely be available.

One important variable to consider in selecting appropriate sales channels is the average order size. For example, if the average order size is under $1,000, a direct mail program may be the best approach to achieve sales, along with a reseller channel. If the average order size is $1,000+, an inside sales program could be considered, if the company has some brand awareness in the market, and if the product features and benefits can be easily demonstrated in a catalog or over the Internet, or at regional and state tradeshows. If the average order size is $5,000 or greater and the sale requires face-to-face contact with key decision-makers, field sales reps should be considered.

Develop a Financial Plan Including Program Costs and Profitability Analysis

The financial plan is based on the overall revenue target and the breakdown of this target by channel. Unit sales targets for each channel are derived from these targets for net revenue to the company. Subtracting the cost of goods from net revenue then gives the gross margin for each channel. A certain amount of staffing will be required by each channel to reach its target. Each channel will also have other associated costs, such as inside sales infrastructure, postage for direct mail, and travel for field sales reps. Subtracting these costs yields the net profitability of each segment of the sales program.

The profitability analysis allows a comparison between channels and provides the justification for the investment in the sales program as outlined. This analysis may be critical in gaining approval for an expanded sales program from the company's top management.

About the Author

Pat Walkington is the co-founder of LanierWalkington, a full-service marketing, sales, business development, public relations, and advertising firm. Lanier-Walkington develops strategic sales and marketing plans for clients and provides integrated marketing and sales solutions to help companies increase their sales and profitability in this market. Prior to LanierWalkington, Pat Walkington was the vice president of the school divisions of Broderbund Software, Inc. and The Learning Company. She is a co-founder of Making It Happen with Deb deVries and Kathy Hurley and serves on the board of directors for the Math/Science Network, an organization aimed at helping prepare young women for careers in math and science. Pat can be reached at (415) 564-2364 or at pat_walkington@phc.net.

Tips on Selling to Niche Markets
by Charles Blaschke

Over the last three decades Education TURNKEY Systems has monitored federally-funded niche markets such as Title I and special education, and most recently the E-Rate; we have helped officials formulate policies conducive to technology use in such niche markets and have helped over 100 firms enter or expand their penetration into these markets. While these niche markets, such as the rapidly growing special education niche market, offer great promise for some vendors, some pitfalls do exist; below are suggestions on how companies can adjust their strategies to minimize pitfalls and effectively sell to these niches.

Develop In-Depth Knowledge about the Niche

Several of the largest niche markets such as special education, Title I, and E-Rate, are rather complex; serious vendors must develop an in-depth understanding of the legal framework and the principles underlying these programs and how the programs operate. If such knowledge does not exist or cannot be acquired internally, then sales staff need to be trained from the outside. Sales staff may have to "acquire the language of the niche," all of which have often-used acronyms as well as verboten phrases (e.g., "students with disabilities" rather than "handicapped students").

"Unlearn" Traditional Marketing Advice

Some textbook marketing lessons do not apply to niche marketing. For example, rather than targeting sales on high wealth schools, the opposite should occur in Title I oriented selling. In 1999, for every one new computer purchased by a high wealth/low poverty school, two and a half computers were purchased by schools with 75% or more poverty, and almost half of the funds used came from federal sources. Also, rather than targeting districts with large Title I funding, companies should focus on those districts with recent and unexpected increases in Title I funding. These districts are much more likely to purchase hardware/software related products. This year, fewer than 500 districts nationwide will receive 80% -90% of the overall $700 million increase in Title I funding. Virtually all federal education funding targets high poverty schools and districts; and in most ESEA programs a large percentage of their formula funds are based upon district Title I allocations. In fact, last year the "digital divide" between high and low poverty schools virtually disappeared, if one considers only the ratio of students to computers, although the divide still exists with respect to access to Internet and online services.

Position Products and Services to Increase Buyer "Comfort Level"

Most of the key decision makers in niche markets are administrators, such as special education district coordinators, principals, and technology coordinators. While instructional products should be positioned as "research-based, proven approaches to increasing student performance," positioning should also increase the "comfort level" of these administrators in several areas. For example, the pricing options should accommodate niche funding and budgeting policies and processes such as the following:

- Under certain conditions a district can purchase a high-ticket instructional configuration using one or more ESEA funding sources under a lease/purchase arrangement; in this circumstance, new policies allow federal funds to be used to pay for not only the principal but also the interest;

- If a principal is offered the option of a school-wide license for an instructional configuration where the price is the same regardless of the number of teachers or students who use the system, then he or she may be able to use IDEA special education funds to purchase the program and have it used by non-special education students under new "incidental use" provisions. Principals can mention this in responding to disgruntled parents of non-special education students who feel that federal funds are not being used to help their child.

Even though many district federal programs are operated autonomously from district regular operations, these program administrators often want to be assured that the instructional configuration "fits within the district's overall curriculum and meets district/state standards."

Don't Assume District Officials and Principals are Aware of New Flexibility on Allowable Uses of Federal Funds

During the first 25 years of ESEA, federal categorical programs such as Title I and special education PL 94-142 (and later IDEA) were rather inflexible regarding use of funds. As a result, many state and local officials were guided in their decisions by an "audit mentality." Since the ESEA reauthorization in 1994, however, legislative amendments and a general "loosening" of strict interpretations have provided a much more flexible legal framework for not only Title I but also IDEA. (The 1997 "incidental use" provision mentioned above is one very significant flexibility provision.) Even though federal officials and congressional leadership have strongly encouraged districts to take advantage of new flexibility provisions, many local superintendents and even coordinators of federal programs are not aware of these flexibility provisions and in some cases where they are aware, they are not taking full advantage of them. A 1999 GAO report found that a major barrier to increased flexibility at the local level were state Departments of Education which in 25 states have actually discouraged districts from taking advantage of new flexibility provisions such as commingling of funds in school-wide programs and from transferring "unneeded" federal funds from one program to another.

Consequently, when approaching these individuals, vendors should not assume that basic policy and procedural awareness exists. Indeed, one of the most effective means of getting through to such coordinators (as noted, below) is to make them aware of flexibility changes in federal programs. For example, in a recent letter developed for a firm's direct marketing campaign, the opening sentence informed the reader that now he or she," as a principal in a school-wide program can commingle Title I and IDEA funds for purchasing a student information system which will make life easier...." The letter drew an unusually high response rate. Opportunities for educating buyers about program opportunities abound. For another example, during Year 1 and Year 2 of the E-Rate, the majority of school technology officials responsible for E-Rate were not aware that they could use the so-called BEAR process (initiated in August 1998) to request refunds for purchases of eligible products made before discounts were known and applied. The majority were furthermore unaware that these refunds could then actually be used to purchase ineligible products such as software, staff development, and hardware for student and teacher use. Vendors who can supply this kind of information to school officials will have an enormous advantage.

Use Consultative Selling to Reach Niche Market Decision Makers

A key to successful consultative selling is providing fresh and useful information to district administrators of federal programs. Many vendors complain that it takes ten to twelve phone calls to get through to a large urban Title I coordinator. One sure way to get immediate attention is to tell whoever answers the phone that you would like to make the Title I coordinator aware that they will be receiving an increase in federal funding next year of approximately x amount. This type of information is usually posted on USED's Web site, but it can be two to three months before final funding amounts are sent to the states and then, to the districts. That lag time can represent a valuable opportunity for vendors.

Beware of hidden politics when calling on district administrators, however. "Dropping the name" of the district superintendent or the name of the Director of Special Education Programs may actually backfire, since in many districts such niches represent "encampments" of an overall feudal system in which bureaucratic turf battles with Title I often occur. If a vendor is seeking districts that are likely to receive E-Rate refunds, it is much safer and effective to have a principal or other decision maker who wishes to purchase its product but doesn't have the money, to contact the E-Rate office to determine whether any E-Rate refunds are available for purchasing. A vendor who "calls cold" directly to an E-Rate office, is walking through a "political land mine."

If a vendor provides new information about funding increases or other items noted above, the likelihood is high that these individuals will call back later about updates, etc., which can lead to a long-term professional relationship.

Vendors Have to Be Prepared to Move Quickly to Take Advantage of Targets of Opportunity

Vendors have to be flexible in several respects to take advantage of opportunities. One such opportunity occurred early in January this year when USED announced that 380 school districts and others, who had applied 14 months earlier but had been denied funding, were being allocated approximately $220 million under the 21st Century Community Learning Center grant program. Concerned that the new Administration might attempt to reduce the almost 100% increase in funding for FY 2001 when it took office, the Clinton administration decided to fund these highly-rated proposals that had been turned down for funding in May 2000. Several firms that had the flexibility to deviate from their overall sales plan were able to take advantage of this situation, and many of the districts receiving "unexpected funding" decided to resurrect their after-school proposals with products and services from these vendors.

Successful selling also requires good timing in these niche markets. For example, the funds allocation process and hence the purchasing cycle have changed dramatically over the last couple of years in Title I and special education due to increased congressional use of "advanced funding." In 2000, districts received 60% of their Title I funds in July or August with the remaining sent out a week before Thanksgiving. For this coming school year, only 25% will be allocated this summer with 75% withheld until after October 1. Many firms which have marketing and sales plans based upon traditional K-12 purchasing cycles and who are not able to reschedule and reallocate budgets to accommodate the change in the major purchasing cycle, will miss this year's cycle, which is likely to be October/November 2001 through February/March 2002.

Take Advantage of "Funding Uncertainties" That Can Generate Sales for Vendors

In most federal programs there has always been a funds allocation dilemma between "things" and "people." For vendors of "things," the major competitor for the federal dollar is teacher salaries. During the last two decades federal budget uncertainties have arisen and have impacted purchasing patterns. For example, in the mid-1990s Speaker Gingrich led the newly elected

republican Congress to rescind about 30% to 40% of federal education funding in mid year; many districts were "burned" when they found out there wasn't enough Title I funds, for example, to cover the last three months of Title I teachers' salaries. A similarly uncertain situation exists today with respect to the FY 2001 budget for class size reduction (CSR)—$1.6 billion to cover the salaries of 40,000 recently-hired and soon-to-be-hired teachers. The current Bush proposal which will be passed by Congress would consolidate these funds with other related ESEA programs such as Title II and Title V with an amount for FY 2002 several hundred million dollars below the $1.6 billion level. In the FY 2001 budget there is a provision that any district with 10% or more of its teachers not being certified may use more CSR funds than the 25% upper limit for staff development; indeed all such funds could be used for staff development rather than for hiring new teachers whose salaries in subsequent years may have to be "picked up" from local resources. Hence, vendors providing professional development services could take advantage of this uncertainty by encouraging districts to use much more funds for purchasing staff development from them than for hiring teachers.

Creative Financing Assistance is Critical to Closing Large Sales

A central aspect of consultative selling is the ability to assist potential customers or clients in financing their purchases from multiple federal funding sources and in justifying the use of various funding sources for certain components of an overall technology-based solution. Many of the above tips on selling come together at this phase building upon the knowledge about funding flexibility and what is now justifiable and allowable. With the significant growth in niches such as special education, whose per-student funding is rising from approximately $450 per student five years ago to between $1100-$1400 this year), several targets of opportunity should be rewarding for vendors in the immediate future.

About the Author

Charles Blaschke is president of Education TURNKEY Systems, www.edturnkey.com, a company providing a subscription Technology Monitoring and Information Service (TechMIS) to over 50 technology vendors. TURNKEY also works with company sponsors to fund its National Survey of Technology Use and Expenditures in Special Education. For more information, contact Charles Blaschke at cblaschke@edturnkey.com.

What Makes an Excellent Education Market Sales Executive?

by John Meeker, Ph.D.

An excellent sales executive for the education market is easy to find. What's the big deal? All you need is someone who walks on water, whose heart-rending speech can bring grown men and children to tears, and who motivates field-hardened salespeople to accomplish what they never thought possible, year after year. Easy!

Well, just in case you haven't yet found the perfect sales executive, here are a few other ways to identify this extraordinarily important member of your company's management team.

Why Is It So Hard to Find the Right Sales Executive?

More than any other leader on the executive team, the sales executive must exercise multiple skills to be effective. In addition to meeting or exceeding sales objectives, he or she also needs to demonstrate excellent interpersonal skills, superb management ability, and exceptional strategic talents.

Each of these skill sets is intensely demanding. What makes the matter even more difficult is the diversity of the skills required—they are not logical extensions of one another. It's unusual for any one person to have had the constellation of career experiences necessary to be fully equipped to perform the range of responsibilities required of a sales executive.

It isn't that many individuals don't have some of these skills. The scarcity of individuals in whom these three difficult skill sets coalesce is what makes top sales executives few and far between.

Adding to the difficulty and diversity of the skills required, the sales manager must be able to work effectively with three distinct groups of stakeholders or constituents: customers, company managers and sales representatives, and the company's executives and board/investors. Even as the necessary skills are different from each other, each constituent audience requires the sales manager to perform a very different role as well.

For example, customers need to feel genuineness, trustworthiness, and to some extent, even friendship with the sales executive.

Company managers need a sense that the sales executive can deliver the assigned quota. The sales organization needs to feel that quotas are achievable and fair, and that sales representatives can count on the support of "their boss."

The third constituency is the company's executives and its board or investor group. To succeed here, the sales executive must frequently perform tasks that require abilities quite different from interpersonal and management skills. For example, the board or investors typically think in highly quantitative terms using an array of analytical tools. The sales executive must portray field experiences and management wisdom in language that is cogent and useful to these critical decision makers.

As illustrated by the following chart, the three critical skill sets are valued very differently by the three constituencies with whom the sales executive interacts.

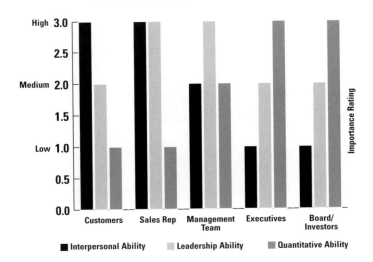

How Constituents Value Sales Executive Skills

Source: Meeker & Associates, Inc.

So, What Are the Criteria that Determine an Excellent Sales Executive?

While walking on water may not be a formal requirement, there are eight essential criteria that do define the successful sales executive. Depending on a company's immediate and long-term needs, these criteria will be weighted differently. But strength, if not excellence, is required in each.

The criteria may be grouped into three categories:
1. Industry expertise
2. Management expertise
3. Strategic capabilities

Industry Expertise

1. Passion for education

To be successful in this industry, a sales executive must feel and demonstrate passion about education and children. The education "market" or "industry" is different from other markets because the key players are essentially mission-driven. Teachers, administrators, and even many support staff are motivated principally by a sense of purpose and the desire to make a difference in the lives of children. A sales executive who is anything less than passionate about making a difference with children will be perceived by prospects as "just a vendor." Without sensing such passion from the sales executive, the prospect is likely to remain a prospect rather than becoming a devoted customer.

2. Knowledge of the education market

Leading a successful sales effort in the education market demands an accurate understanding of the many cycles and timing milestones that influence educators' buying decisions. In addition to these decision-making cycles, the sales executive must also understand how trends in public policy and changes in funding sources affect purchasing decisions. Educators face many over-lapping challenges such as standardized objectives, high stakes testing, etc. The sales executive must appreciate these sufficiently so that the sales organization can respond appropriately to customer needs and recognize opportunities for sales.

3. Building relationships through listening

Listen! Listening is the cornerstone ability of successful communication. This is true whether meeting with customers, sales representatives, management team members, or investors.

The common presumption is that a successful salesperson, and even more, a sales executive, is a "silver-tongued orator" who can motivate through powerful speeches and make the sale with clever "closes." Not so.

Educators make purchases. They do not like to be "sold to."

It is the case in most industries, but especially so in education, that sales are built on relationships. Trust, along with all the other ingredients of a relationship, is the basis of an education buyer's decision in favor of a product and a company.

There are many dimensions to establishing and growing a relationship with a customer. Listening is the essential underpinning that allows the relationship to develop.

The importance of this criterion—building relationships through listening—is emphasized here because so many education customers state how infrequently representatives of companies really do listen. Whether it's the regional sales rep or the national sales manager, building a relationship is hindered when salespeople start "selling products" rather than listening. As a relationship develops and the salesperson begins to understand customer issues from the perspective of the educator, solutions can be presented that the buyer will welcome.

Modeling listening skills is the most effective way to train sales reps to listen and ultimately achieve sales. Thus, the behavior of the sales executive sets the tone for the entire organization.

As with all relationships, whether romantic, parent-child, or business, creative listening establishes understanding, trust, and friendship. And purchasers like to buy from friends.

Management Expertise

4. Compensation plan expertise

Sales executives face two challenges in developing and implementing compensation plans. First, the plan must provide incentives for representatives to sell and to exceed quotas. The key here is not only to give financial rewards, but also to creatively shape compensation to engage the different motivational "hot buttons" of individual reps.

Second, compensation plans can be used as strategic tools to achieve goals other than simply producing revenue. Depending on the company's objectives, particular products may merit some difference in sales incentives. Incentive payments can also be used to accomplish other strategic business objectives.

The sales executive needs to be an expert in the wide variety of compensation approaches that can be designed to meet a broad range of company objectives.

5. Recruiting exceptional talent

Sales executives tend to recruit sales representatives who have an established sales track record and a "rolodex" of long-term relationships in a territory. This approach can result in a reasonably satisfactory sales force, but not always a great one.

The most outstanding sales executives target not just "the usual suspects." In addition to hiring people with proven sales track records, the objective should be to build a sales force comprised of individuals who have consistently excelled in their chosen endeavors across the board. The dimension to capture is not necessarily competitiveness, but excellence at whatever the individual has been passionate about, whether in academics, arts, human services, politics, or sports.

Being a successful sales rep should be only the price of admission to an interview. The outstanding sales executive seeks to recruit sales representatives who consistently outperform their peers throughout their lives.

6. Team and infrastructure building

Excellent sales executives build teams of people, and they also work to create the essential infrastructure needed to support those teams in multiple ways. Moreover, they recognize that the sales organization is one of many company teams that together are responsible for customer enthusiasm, company profitability, and individual sales quota performance.

Building an effective infrastructure means creating and/or refining the operational resources throughout the company that are necessary to support the sales organization. Essential components of the sales infrastructure include:

- Recruiting;
- Sales training;
- Shared objectives between related functional units, such as customer support, technology services, and marketing;

- Reporting systems that are accurate and timely;
- Accurate accounting for and prompt payment of incentives and expenses.

WORDS OF WISDOM FROM THE MASTERS

David Benoit, Sylvan Learning Ventures

"Help your team to recognize that they are not selling a commodity to schools but building a consultative relationship. More so than any other business, success in education sales is dependent upon developing and maintaining the trust of customers."

"Salespeople need to see their role as requiring that they can serve as a resource to the district, avoiding being 'labeled' as strictly a vendor."

Deb deVries, NetSchools

"Most salespeople spend too much time telling prospects about their company/products and never enough time listening to their prospects."

"If someone tells you to do something and they are wildly successful, it's best if you imitate or do it even if it's awkward."

Sheila Fernley, Voyager Learning

"Who Wants to be a Millionaire...get as many lifelines as you can, even if you never need to use them."

"Develop processes and templates that define the sales steps and provide the tools to sell your solution."

Tom Fitzgerald, Gateway

"Help your customers find their money sources."

Jeanne Hayes, Quality Education Data

"Be sure to limit requests for your salespeople to do non-sales activities. Don't distract them."

"Don't ever select an employee because their resume 'looks right' without having a gut connection to the candidate—your customers will probably have the same reaction."

Brenda Raker, Education Resources

"Get to know your sales team as individuals. Learn what each of them needs from you in order to be successful and motivated."

"Balance hard work with fun. Team meetings should provide opportunities to learn, but they can also be opportunities to have fun."

Steve Salmen, Co-Nect

"In the world of consultative sales, there are two absolute characteristics of a great sales person: patience and persistence."

"The challenge in sales management is finding the balance between discipline, advocacy, and service."

Strategic Capabilities

7. *Forecasting accuracy*

The essential quantitative skill sales executives need is forecasting accuracy. Sales executives must be able to translate an ocean of individual field experiences and anecdotal encounters with customers and reps into a highly reliable forecast.

Other company managers base crucial decisions on the sales forecast, including what products and services are to be available to customers and when. Pricing and procurement are contingent on accurate forecasts. Financial decisions made by chief financial officers are inextricably linked to the sales forecast. The chief executive officer

decides about strategic alliances or acquisitions based in part on forecasting. And board members and investors sift through forecasts very carefully as they decide whether or not to make substantial financial investments.

Sales executives are expected to make quota. However, the professional sales leader becomes most valuable to the management and investment process when he or she not only makes quota but also accurately forecasts when and how much revenue will be booked.

If the sales executive anticipates a shortfall, it is critical that he or she present an accurate revised forecast to company management as soon as possible. Although making quota is the number one responsibility of a

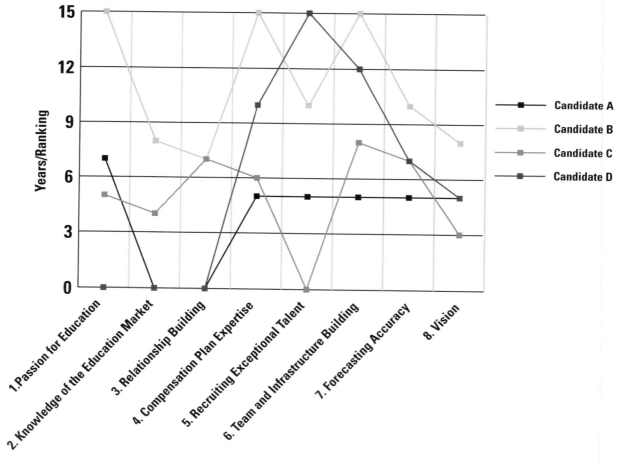

Position Criteria Matrix

Source: Meeker & Associates, Inc.

sales executive, the ability to foresee when expected numbers cannot be achieved—and to understand and explain the reasons why—can be invaluable to company decision makers.

8. Vision

In designing company strategy with other managers, executives, and investors, the sales executive plays an efficacious role by sharing his or her vision of the point on the horizon that the company should aim for. In this role the sales executive is a team member working in concert with others who also are staring at the horizon trying to determine the most appropriate long-term targets.

Being competent to discuss the state and direction of the entire education industry is also essential because the sales executive may have the opportunity to represent the company with high-level education leaders. For example, the sales executive may meet with state education department leaders, political executives such as governors or even, given our current political climate, the president. Chief executives and other senior management people from major companies or investment banks may also merit a "sales call."

How to Hire an Excellent Sales Executive

When recruiting a sales executive, the company's current needs together with its long-term strategic goals should shape the search. In addition, there are two dimensions to consider in evaluating any candidate.

First, candidates' backgrounds and prior experiences should be measured against the criteria described above. Meeker & Associates, a professional executive search firm, typically performs a quantitative analysis to compare candidates on various criteria important to the client company. As illustrated below, no single candidate is likely to fulfill every criterion at the highest level.

This comparison can be instructive in highlighting candidate strengths that may be of particular value to the client company in making a hiring decision. But the quantitative analysis is only half the equation.

For any company hiring a sales executive, it is also absolutely essential to engage intuition or gut instincts. Selecting the best candidate requires a dual process. Quantitative analysis alone is sterile. Hiring based solely on personal feelings also risks missing the mark.

Hire the best candidate based on how his or her track record stacks up against your company's criteria plus your gut instincts informed by years of professional experience. Target those who excel in all their achievements and those who are persons of the highest integrity.

Working with an excellent search firm is a good idea, too. There are several of us!

About the Author

John Meeker has an extensive background in executive recruiting, education leadership, and corporate management. His business experience includes responsibilities in educational technology and telecommunications corporations, as well as in entrepreneurial private and public companies throughout the United States. His firm, Meeker & Associates, Inc., conducts searches for sales and marketing executives, technology management, and corporate executives. Clients include industry segments in publishing, software, telecommunications, and Internet delivery of educational and corporate training. John can be reached in Minneapolis, Minnesota, at john@johnmeeker.com or by calling (952) 921-3262.

Sales Meetings With Flair!
How to Plan and Present Meetings that Will Be Remembered

by Priscilla Shumway

Sales meetings! Depending on what your experience has been with them, the mere mention of those two words can either strike fear into the hearts of your sales team or pump them up for a jammin' good time! What is the difference? What are the ingredients that go into designing and hosting an effective and fun sales meeting? From needs assessment to budgets, and from location to agendas, proper planning is the key to success. Your sales meeting is the time to motivate, train, and focus your team so that what they have learned will be of lasting value and result in increased sales for the company.

Meeting Objectives

Why have a meeting? That is the central question that must be answered before any meeting is held. Furthermore, this question must be answered by all parties involved—marketing, sales, operations, and company leadership. Is the objective to sell more? To learn about new products? To reward people for a job well done? To learn about price changes? To present new company policies? If you try to address all of these in one meeting, your team will walk away overwhelmed. Choose two or three clear objectives and then achieve them!

Needs Assessment

Getting buy-in from all parties who attend the meeting will go a long way towards ensuring the success of the event. Not only will you be sure you have focused the sessions on what is of value to the attendees, but you will be able to confirm that the expectations of upper level management are addressed as well. The more buy-in that you get up front, the more likely you will get the results you want. The central question to ask all parties involved is, "What does a successful meeting look like to you?"

There are a variety of ways to conduct needs assessments, from e-mail surveys to phone interviews. No matter what process you choose, be sure you are timely and thorough and that you actually use the results to guide your planning.

If you choose a written survey of some sort, whether it be e-mail or snail mail, keep your survey short enough to be completed in ten minutes. Include mostly questions with quantitative responses (e.g., "On a scale of one to five, please rank the importance of the following topics."), providing areas for further comments if the respondent has the time. Also, consider offering some form of prize or incentive for returning the survey. For example, each respondent could receive a free laser pointer at the meeting. This approach will increase your response rate and give you better buy-in.

Needs assessment can also be conducted in other formats, including:

- Phone interviews (keep them short—10 minutes at most)
- Focus groups
- Assessment grid (see sample on page 192)

The topics that you include in an assessment grid can include issues that you have gathered from upper level management, sales managers, and your planning team. Listing these on the grid will let these stakeholders know that you have listened to their concerns, and still provide an opportunity for all participants to vote on the importance of these topics. It is important to let everyone know the results of the needs assessment so that they understand how the majority voted and therefore why the agenda shaped up the way it has.

Now it is up to you to include these topics in the agenda, allowing adequate time and preparation for each. This is critical: if "Funding Sources" has been voted number one but you spend the least amount of time on it at the meeting, the participants will wonder why you bothered to ask them for their opinions, and they may be unwilling to respond the next time. "I don't have time to answer this," they will say. "It made no difference during the last meeting!"

It's the Budget, Stupid!

In setting the budget for the event, consider how the company is doing financially. Are you trying to exercise fiscal restraint and pass that message on to your team? Or have you had a stellar year that you want to celebrate and reward the troops for? Work with your CFO and your marketing team to come to an agreement on budget. All things flow from that—the theme you choose, the venue, meals, prizes, events, guest speakers—all depend on the budget that is set at the earliest planning meeting.

Once the budget is set, keep to it! There is nothing worse than having to cut corners to meet the budget, or remove events at the last minute. Worse still is coming in over budget and going back to accounting with unexpected bills. Getting budget approval for next year's meeting will be twice as hard.

Location, Location, Location

Look back at your objectives and your budget for the meeting. These will help you to determine the location, size, and theme of your meeting. For example, if money is tight, you might consider looking for hotels near major airports that have adequate meeting rooms.

On the other hand, if rewarding top salespeople is the objective, then you might consider a cruise or resort location. Off-season rates can make it possible to treat staff to a normally pricey retreat. Tacking a sales meeting onto the beginning or end of a major show or convention is another way to cut costs. Chances are, your staff needs to be at the convention anyway, so airfare is already booked. However, you also need to consider time away from families and the general fatigue that occurs with these big shows.

Agenda

Now you are ready to tackle the agenda. The location you have chosen, the objectives that have been identified, and the needs assessment results are all key ingredients. If one of your objectives is to reward top sales staff and do some team building activities, then it's important to factor in free time for golf, spa appointments, or an evening cruise.

The planning team should draw up a first draft of the agenda and send it to all sales managers and upper level management, if appropriate. One person needs to be the point person for all changes and revisions. As the agenda begins to take shape and once the upper level management has agreed to the time, dates, location, focus, and objectives, you can begin to line up presenters.

The initial format of the agenda will go a long way towards planning for the overall needs of the meeting.

Provide presenters a planning grid with spaces for them to indicate their needs for handouts, AV equipment, and supplies. This way, you turn the responsibility over to the presenters for communicating their needs at the earliest possible time.

If breakout sessions are to be involved, a separate sheet for each breakout room should be created. These planning grids can then be used to work with the hotel staff to ensure that your set up is complete.

Once the agenda is completed, a shortened version (showing only the first two columns of the chart on page 194) should be sent to the participants along with their invitation. Keeping participants informed helps create buy-in, increases the learning curve, and heightens their excitement.

Invitation

How you invite folks to the meeting can set the tone for a huge success or a dismal failure. In these days of e-mail, the personal touch can get lost. E-mail is an efficient way to communicate details of logistics, changes, updates, and so forth. But there is nothing better than receiving an invitation in the mail to begin to build the theme, enthusiasm, and focus of a meeting. Stationery that reflects the theme or location, brochures from the resort, or confetti in the envelope can all help to get folks pumped up. Fun and inexpensive premiums that support your theme are also fun to include in the invitation. For example:

THEME	PREMIUM
Leading the Way in Technology	Toy compass
From Buzz to Bucks	Play money
Setting Our Sights on Success	Sun glasses
Sailing Ahead in 2002	Sun visor with logo
Winning the Internet Gamble	Pair of dice or playing cards

Participants should be instructed to bring the premiums to the meeting, and activities can be planned to include them. For example, a product scavenger hunt with the toy compass could be a fun way to get new product questions answered. An evening dinner cruise with the sun visors could hold this twist: using colored markers, you can place different colored stars under the brims of random visors. The people with the stars win a variety of prizes on the cruise. The fun activities that are planned during the "off-line" time help keep folks motivated and involved.

Use the invitations as an opportunity to let folks know what to expect, to get them excited about the meeting, to set the tone, and to advertise the theme. How the attendees perceive the meeting before it starts will affect their level of energy and involvement during the meeting. Include statements and cues like:

- Business casual
- Prepare to have fun
- Expect to meet new folks and network with your peers
- Lots of new helpful product information
- Time to relax and share ideas
- Give you time to pump up for the new selling season

Include an abbreviated agenda with the invitation. But the invitation is meant to be welcoming, not overwhelming: any pre-reading or company policies should be sent under separate cover. In the right context, appropriate pre-reading can be helpful in getting folks prepared for new material and can help to communicate the seriousness of the agenda. It also can enhance new learning and increase retention.

Room Set Up

OK, so you have your budget approved, your needs assessment completed, the location selected, the agenda set, the invitations sent out, and a head count completed of who will be attending. Now is the time to determine room set up. Depending on the objectives of a session and the number of people who will be attending, different room arrangements will be required. For example, the best set up for fostering discussion is round tables of 4-6 people. This allows high participation, good control by the presenters, and maximum sightlines for all participants. Round tables also allow for mixing up the groups, which helps with networking. But be sure that you only set the chairs in half rounds so that no one is sitting with their backs to the presenter.

Music can help to set the tone, keep people involved, and get people re-energized. Playing music at breaks can also serve as a means for letting them know when break is almost over. Be sure to use music that is not copyrighted, however!

Always visit the site and every room that will be used beforehand. Consider the ambient lighting (especially if AV equipment is to be used), look for adequate electrical plugs, and be wary of rooms containing posts or pillars that will obstruct views. Check on costs for rental of screens, power strips, extension cords, flip charts, projectors, microphones, and CD/tape players. Depending on the meeting location, it may be cheaper to bring these supplies from your office. Hotels usually allow you to bring your own AV equipment, but most will not allow you to provide your own food.

Openers and Energizers

There they are: a captive audience who has come because you invited them. They are excited to be there because you have set the stage for a fun and valuable meeting. Now, build on this foundation. Openers and icebreakers are brief opportunities to:

- Mentally involve and challenge your participants
- Facilitate networking
- Relieve stress and energize a group
- Engage learners with resources such as brain teasers and music

---

SAMPLE ASSESSMENT GRID

On a scale of 1-7, (one is low and 7 is high) rate the importance of the following topics to be included in the sales meeting.

	1	2	3	4	5	6	7
Funding sources	❏	❏	❏	❏	❏	❏	❏
New product training	❏	❏	❏	❏	❏	❏	❏
Company policies review	❏	❏	❏	❏	❏	❏	❏
New educational legislation	❏	❏	❏	❏	❏	❏	❏
Marketing events and programs	❏	❏	❏	❏	❏	❏	❏

An assessment grid can help meeting planners to prioritize topics for sessions.

Nametags are a must. Unless you are a small group who know each other well, nametags help avoid embarrassment of new staff who may not be familiar with everyone. Even for the presenters, it is helpful to have nametags. It's best to use first names, with 1/12 inch letters. You may want to identify participants by department or region as well. And encourage folks to wear them at all events, especially large group gatherings.

Avoid having each participant stand and introduce themselves to the group. Instead, have them introduce themselves in smaller groups—for example, to their table or team. Then, build in many chances for small group discussion, so that folks will get to know one another over the course of the meeting. Change the teams at the beginning of each day and use a new opener. Some ideas for openers or icebreakers include asking participants to:

- Introduce themselves to their team and share one of their greatest challenges in selling a particular product.

- Share what their top objective is for the sales meeting.

- Write down one question they need answered on a post-it note, share it with their team and arrange the notes on a group flip chart. For this one, the meeting facilitator should review several entries with the whole group.

- Share a tip for selling the product that is to be discussed. Post the tips on flip charts that can be hung around the room.

- Tell a story about a mentor or coach who was important in their lives. List common mentoring characteristics on a flip chart.

- Tell what their first job was and how it helped to prepare them for their job today.

- In teams, write a quiz question on an index card, based on the topics that have been presented in the meeting so far. The teams then trade their cards and try to "stump the chumps."

Breaks

Allow adequate time for breaks. Half-hour breaks and 1-1/2 hour lunches allow sales people time to make calls. You can work with this need rather than against, even giving a prize for anyone who closes a sale during the meeting. Having said that, it is also important to get people back from breaks on time, and it is up to the meeting facilitator to enforce the start and end times of sessions. If you say you are going to start at 8:30 and then delay until 8:40 so that stragglers can arrive, you send the message that being late will be tolerated. Instead, start right on time, and offer incentives for being punctual.

For example, at one meeting, each time a participant got back from break on time, they were given $10.00 in play money. If everyone from their team arrived back on time from break, each member got an extra $10.00. At the end of the meeting, the participants with the most money could "purchase" a variety of prizes such as gift certificates, golf jackets, books, and music CDs. A grand prize of a weekend for two at a hotel chain also went to the highest money winner. The same basic concept can work using playing cards—the person with the best poker hand at the end of the meeting is the winner.

MONEY-SAVING TIP

Most large printers such as Kinkos have nationwide offices that can help you save money on shipping handouts. Here's how: you can arrange for an e-mail account at the office closest to your meeting hotel. Then, all presenters can e-mail their handouts to Kinkos, where the copies can be made and delivered free of charge to your hotel.

Break foods should be served at the back of the room if possible. This allows folks the opportunity to warm up their coffee or get a snack without having to leave the room. It also keeps folks in the room so that they are less likely to be late. And as the saying goes, "The brain can absorb only as much as the rear end can endure"—it gives participants the chance to stand up while a presentation is going on, without interrupting.

Meals

If your meals are intended to be working sessions, be sure they are interactive. Do not have a guest speaker take up the entire meal hour. Instead, schedule in group discussions, Q&A, ice breakers, and free time. Meals also need to be a time when participants can relax and process the day. Do not underestimate the value of informal interactions. Unstructured conversation time is often when the most learning occurs.

SAMPLE PRESENTER PLANNING GRID

Time	Presenter	AV needs	Handouts	Supplies
8:00-8:30 Continental Breakfast				Food in back of room
8:30-9:15 Kick off and introductions	J. Jones CEO K. Hart VP marketing	LCD, computer, Screen, music	Meeting manual	Name tags, markers
9:15-10:00 Product announcements	C. Smith product manager	LCD, computer, screen, Internet	Slide handouts	Flip charts
10:00-10:30 Break				Refresh coffee

Materials/Handouts

The American Society for Training and Development (ASTD) did a survey several years ago and found that the majority of meeting participants never go back and refer to their training materials after the session is over. To combat this, try to make your meeting materials as useful and user friendly as possible. View them as a job aid, and consider their format. Instead of three-ring binders with tabs for every session, could you provide all handouts on a CD? Could you create accordion file folders, portable file boxes, or a Web site with downloadable files?

Meeting Planners

Aghast? Dumbfounded? Overwhelmed? Depending on your budget, your objectives, and the size of your meeting, it might be wise to hire a professional meeting planner! A planner can take care of important details, such as:

- Travel
- Incentives
- Budget and costs

- Site location
- AV equipment
- Invitations, programs, and signage
- Event guides
- Food and beverages
- Team-building activities
- Speaker selection
- Registration

But working with a meeting planner is for another article in another book!

Good luck. Sales meetings that are well planned can turn the concepts and information that are presented at the meeting into actions and values that make a difference in the company. They provide an opportunity for the company to demonstrate that it cares about its employees, that it attends to their needs, and that it values their presence and input. So, whatever the business goals of your meeting, prepare to have fun!

About the Author

Priscilla Shumway is business development manager for NetSchools Corporation, www.netschools.com. As the former principal in New Learning Presentation Systems, a national training and consulting firm, she specialized in powerful presentations, educational software, professional development, and learning styles. Priscilla has also co-authored several teachers' guides and training manuals for popular educational software titles. She has facilitated sales meetings and trained sales agents for such clients as The Learning Company, IBM, Northwest Vermont Board of Realtors, Houghton Mifflin, and the South Carolina Department of Education. Priscilla is also a national trainer for the Bob Pike Group.

Hiring and Managing Independent Reps

by Linda Lee

For a small company, a new company, a company with a product line that does not have great critical mass, or a company whose product line is not a simple "box" sell, an independent sales rep force can be the most cost-effective and efficient method of reaching customers.

Making the Decision to Sell through Independent Reps

Selling through independent sales reps can provide a middle ground between direct mail or telesales strategies on one hand and a full staff of in-house reps on the other. To determine whether independent reps are right for you, consider the following:

Independent reps versus direct mail or telesales.
Independent reps shine in selling a product line that is not inherently easy to understand or that is multifaceted. For example, a niche product that has very specific uses and therefore a very targeted customer base (i.e. a multiple phased reading program); a product that requires training or technical advice or support to utilize (e.g., a subscription to an Internet curriculum site, or software application program); a product that has multiple uses and crosses over multiple disciplines/curriculum areas (multimedia packages or kits that contain both technology and books); or a product that is best understood through a live demonstration.

In other words, if your product cannot be described in a half-page or less in a catalog, having a sales rep call on your customer will probably result in increased and larger sales than a direct mail or tele-marketing promotion.

Independent reps versus in-house reps.
Independent reps can be more cost effective than in-house reps, particularly when selling a product line that does not have great critical mass or that has limited new releases each year. Having a sales rep make a personal call on your customer is costly, whether you utilize an independent rep or in-house rep. If you choose to

support an in-house rep on your payroll, you must figure a minimum of $100K in costs—this would include salary, benefits, travel expenses, base salary, commission, etc. Unless an in-house rep can generate $500K in sales in a given territory, you should probably consider using an independent rep as an alternative.

Here's why. An average sales rep, whether in-house or independent probably has a maximum of 176 days a year in which to make sales calls. This calculation is based on the fact there are an average of 20 business days in a month, less four days a month a sales rep would need to spend on administrative tasks, multiplied by 11 months (eliminating personal and school vacation periods). At maximum, the rep might be able to make 3 sales calls a day in person or perhaps 8-10 calls a day by phone. The sustainable maximum for calls of any kind probably lies somewhere in between these figures, so you should estimate a rep's capacity at about 880-1,000 customer calls per year. If you have a small product line, or a product line that has limited new releases each year, the numbers will work against a strategy based on in-house reps. To make $500K in sales on 1,000 customer calls, the average order value for the rep has to be fairly high. Thus, if your product line consists of only a few hundred titles or less, an independent rep is probably the most cost-effective method of reaching your customer.

> "Having a sales rep make a personal call on your customer is costly, whether you utilize an independent rep or in-house rep."

Hiring an Independent Rep

As in anything else, finding the right person to do the job is the most critical factor. Given the time it takes to interact with an independent sales rep, as well as the administrative costs of supplying materials, tracking sales, and paying commission, I would offer the unorthodox advice of leaving a territory unmanned rather than simply filling it with a body—especially if the independent sales rep is only one of several channels to reaching your customer. Many companies use a variety of sales channels, including a combination of direct mail, resellers, telemarketing, and independent sales reps.

Where art thou?

Perhaps the most effective way of finding a sales rep is to run a query on your customer database to identify your largest customers in the territory you are proposing to cover with the new rep. Then simply call these customers and ask them for the names of the most effective sales reps that service them. Not only will this give you information "straight from the horse's mouth," but it will also give you an important opportunity for dialogue with your customers. You will find out what services they most appreciate and what their primary concerns and needs are, and all this will help you to form a relationship with them that is closer to a partnership.

Alternatively, there are industry associations, such as the NSSEA, which hold national and regional conferences, as well as publishing newsletters that you can subscribe to and advertise in.

The single most important thing to remember, however, is that any sales rep you hire should be knowledgeable of the specific industry your product falls in. A good book sales rep often makes an ineffective media sales rep, and vice versa. When hiring a rep, the most important asset they bring is their collection of personal contacts, and you need to be sure that these contacts are useful for the industry you are in. This is not to say that a good book rep might not learn to sell media well, but whenever possible, you should try to secure a rep who is not only comfortable with the territory you wish to have covered, but is also experienced in your industry segment.

Whither shall I send thee?

Defining the right territory for an independent rep is another key issue. The defined territory must be workable both from the standpoint of size as well as order potential. Giving a territory to a rep that is either too large or small geographically will be counterproductive to their performance for you. An independent sales rep is generally responsible for paying all of his or her own travel expenses, and if the assigned territory is too large, the rep may not make an effective number of face-to-face contacts, because of the expense of doing so. Also, each territory should be evaluated and studied for "best buying practices." No two are alike—which is both the beauty and curse of our collective United States!

In territories that are very centralized (i.e., where state buying consortiums exist), an independent rep is most effective, since they can form valuable personal relationships with the primary buyers. Purchases made on this level are usually large and require repeated interaction with the customer before a sale can be closed. As often as not, these sales are motivated by the personal relationship between rep and buyer; thus a good independent sales rep will not balk at paying expenses to make these calls — the dollar potential is usually motivation enough.

In territories where purchasing is done more on a site level, geographic assignments must by necessity be smaller. As described above, there is only so much time in a day for a rep to travel from one building to another, so offering too large a territory will mean that many sites are left uncovered or ineffectively covered. Large cities are often covered in this manner: for example, you may have one sales rep for the entire state of New York, with the exception of New York City, which may be covered exclusively by another rep.

Defining the right territory, then, involves a careful calculation of size and dollar potential. I have seen some organizations that have two tiers of reps. The first tier is for large, centralized customers, where a single rep might cover many states (as much as one-third to half of the country) but might only have 50-100 centralized customers. The second tier is for more localized regions, in which reps might only cover one city or a few counties, most of which can be reached by car or in a day trip. These reps might handle several hundred accounts at one time.

How Now Brown Cow?

How you compensate your reps, of course, is the key to how well they will commit to your product line. As in so many other aspects of life, money talks! Independent sales reps are usually responsible for their own expenses, including, but not limited to, travel, mail, telephone, and entertainment of customers. Each industry has standards, and in the media industry a standard commission would be 20% of sales brought in. Although this commission might vary from industry to industry, you should count on paying at least 15%.

There are many different theories about how to determine whether an independent rep will be paid commission on a given sale. In the best arrangements (i.e., best for the producer/publisher), commission would only be paid on sales that can clearly be identified as having been generated by the rep. In our contracts, for example, purchase orders must bear a sales rep's name in order for them to receive credit. This is often impractical, however, as purchasing agents or clerks generating a purchase order are not the people responsible for making the decision about a sale, so may neglect to mention the rep's name on the purchase order.

Other approaches to commissioning include automatically giving credit for all sales within a defined territory to a rep whether or not their name was indicated on the sale. The danger in this policy, of course, is that you could be paying 20% commission in that territory on sales that might have come in over the transom anyway, regardless of interaction with the sales rep.

There is no simple answer on this point, and perhaps policy in this area should be made on a rep-by-rep and territory-by-territory basis. For example, if you set up a rep with a large, centralized-customer-based territory, tracking orders by having a sales rep's name on the order can be fairly simple. Usually in these cases, their relationships with their customers are so strong that customers will go out of their way to be sure the rep's name is mentioned on the order. And even if this fails, the rep can identify specific accounts that should be coded to their credit, making tracking simpler. This approach also works well for reps assigned to small but very well defined territories (e.g., the City of New York).

If your rep attends many trade shows, however, a tracking system becomes harder to implement. Perhaps the fairest method in this case would be to use a combination—for example, a 20% commission on defined accounts, with a smaller override (2-5%) for the rest of the territory. The most important thing to remember, though, is that whatever model you choose, an agreement should be reached in conjunction with your sales rep. If reps do not feel they are being fairly compensated or feel at risk of not being compensated for their work (because sales cannot be easily traced back to their efforts), they will quickly lose motivation to focus on your products.

Managing an Independent Sales Rep

Keeping an independent sales rep both motivated and focused on your product line is probably the most important goal of all. Your independent sales reps are unlike other employees: as a rule they will carry more than one line, and their loyalties must therefore be more

carefully cultivated and maintained. They do not receive extra company benefits as employees do, and as a rule, they will act like water in a river, flowing where the course is easiest. This is not a negative commentary; it is simply human nature. Therefore, the primary job in managing an independent sales rep is motivation—and the key words to remember are:

Team Support. Although not employees, the most effective independent sales reps feel that they are an integral part of your team. Each and every staff member should treat a sales rep's inquiries and needs with respect and urgency. When a rep is on the road and needs an answer for a customer, he or she should have an inside contact to whom they can turn to get an answer or resolution to a problem as quickly as possible. Supporting a sales rep's needs should be an organization-wide mission, endorsed by product development, by marketing and sales, by finance, and by everyone else, all the way through to fulfillment. It is important for a sales rep to have key contacts in each of these departments, who in turn have been instructed to focus as much as possible on helping a rep do his or her job effectively. Using the water analogy again, if a rep finds the inner workings of your organization smooth sailing, they will be motivated to visit your waters most often.

Communication. Keep your reps as well informed as possible. This should include not only up-to-date information about product releases, stocking issues, and personnel issues, but also a general sense of the company's activities. We generate a quarterly newsletter as well as sending monthly email updates about the home office, so that a rep feels as connected as possible to what is going on in the office. Having prior knowledge about potential product release problems, or about any other problems, can help them do a more effective job of representing your company well. Remember that a rep's most important assets are their relationships with their customers, so helping them to maintain credibility with them is very much to your advantage.

Another aspect of good communication is providing your reps with the most effective marketing materials possible. Providing catalogs, concise product information sheets, samples, and so forth helps to make their jobs easier. Some companies limit the amount of materials they provide to reps—a practice I find can be very counter-productive. Again, as water flows the easiest course, if a rep is supplied all the aids they need to make an effective presentation or proposal, yours is the product line they will push.

Empowerment. While it is important to set out very clear-cut sales policies, sales reps also need a certain degree of freedom to do their job well. As previously stated, each territory, district, and state in the educational market differs—there are few standards that hold across the board. Therefore, requiring sales reps to stick to "one size fits all" sales policies is often defeating and can limit their abilities to make a good living. Companies are often wary of giving too much discretion to a sales rep, fearing they will "give away the farm." This is not often a concern, however, since at a basic level the rep's interests are aligned with the company's—the higher the purchase price on a sale, the more commission the rep will receive. When you first hire a rep, and for the first year or so that they represent you, it is important to have strict guidelines and policies in place, any deviation from which must have your prior approval. After you have established trust in a rep and he or she has proven to you the level at which they can perform, the best way to get more out of the relationship is to allow a degree of freedom and creativity in your sales policies, to allow the rep to adjust to meet customer needs. Again, these relationships are a rep's most bankable asset, and in the educational market, they are often very long standing. So while it's important to maintain sales standards, thought should always be given to ways you can empower your rep to do the best job for both you and their customers by giving them a certain degree of flexibility.

Summary

A good independent sales rep force can be the most cost-effective way to reach your market. However, since they are not company employees, special care must be taken to keep reps motivated and focused on your product line. Their time is precious, and you can only convince them to put your product line on the top of their list if you make their job as easy as possible—by providing them the best in support, marketing materials, and information. Showing them respect for their trade through empowerment and flexible policies will further increase their loyalty to you and motivate them to give your product line their utmost attention.

About the Author

Linda Lee *has over 12 years of experience in the educational multimedia arena. She began at Weston Woods as director of operations, advancing to the post of vice president. In 1995, she took a position as general manager at Churchill Media, where she was responsible for restructuring the company as well as managing the field sales rep force. When Churchill Media was sold to SVE, she followed, taking a position as special sales manager, where she was responsible for the management of all sales, sales staff, marketing initiatives, new business, and new product development. In 1997 she rejoined Weston Woods after its purchase by Scholastic Inc., as vice president and general manager. In addition to this position, she also served for two years as vice president and general manager of Scholastic's School Technology division, which has now been folded into their Education Group.*

Watch New Business Skyrocket Using Outbound Telephone Marketing
by Cheryl D. Cira

Year after year, school marketers have continued the quest for an increasing percentage of new business. In this effort, they have tested a variety of marketing media, including industry trade shows, space advertisements in targeted magazines, and special public relations events to increase publicity, direct mail blitzes, and telephone campaigns. All are valid ways to generate new business and increase the company's overall customer base.

Using the telephone to generate new business continues to increase in popularity among companies targeting the school market. While educators are extremely busy during the day, they are still quite accessible by phone during planning or preparation periods, as well as before and after school. Administrators at a district level often have office hours and are quite receptive to taking calls.

When to Use Telephone Marketing

School marketers typically implement telephone campaigns to generate leads in three situations.

When Time Is of the Essence.

A company can coordinate, refine, and implement a telephone lead-generation campaign in just a matter of days. School marketers that are launching new products or services later in the school year have often opted for this approach instead of direct mail, solely on the basis of time constraints.

With mailings, it can take weeks, and often much longer, to organize, write, print, coordinate, mail, and receive feedback. Are there enough brochures in stock? Does a special copywriter need to be hired to write the cover letter? Will special envelopes or business reply cards need to be printed? How long will it take before reply cards are returned or calls are received? All of these issues must be addressed when doing a mail campaign. In contrast, telephone campaigns can be implemented quickly and refined as needed. Depending upon list requirements, most telephone campaigns can be up and running in less than a week.

> **"Depending upon list requirements, most telephone campaigns can be up and running in less than a week."**

Telephone lead-generation campaigns are also useful in situations when an inside or outside sales position unexpectedly becomes vacant and coverage is needed immediately. Special telephone campaigns have also been implemented in response to opportunities created by the unexpected release or availability of federal or state funds.

Finally, telephone marketing has also been used when setting last minute appointments for dinner presentations or per diem workshops. Educators who have received invitations in the mail to a dinner conference and have not taken time to RSVP will often say yes if they are personally invited to attend with a phone call.

When the Product's Cost Per Item Is High.
School marketers often use the telephone to generate leads for the more expensive educational materials, products or services. There are situations when doing telephone lead-generation work can be compared to trying to find a needle in the haystack. If took an hour to locate the needle and the value of the needle was just $9.99, a savvy marketer might want to reconsider generating leads by telephone. On the other hand, if it took an hour to produce a lead, but that same lead were worth $900, the telephone would be a cost-effective method of generating leads, whether the company were being billed on an hourly or on a per-lead basis.

Most school marketers use direct mail or card deck promotions to announce and sell less expensive ancillary materials such as educational poster packages, flash cards, audio cassettes, felt boards, or math manipulatives. For these products, the cost per item does not justify the expense of a telephone campaign. In contrast, the more expensive textbook programs, software packages, or workshop programs warrant an array of marketing tools that quite often does include outbound telephone qualification and follow up.

When the Product is Complex. Having a live voice to verify information, answer questions, and confirm details can be a critical part of the sales process. In situations when a product or service cannot be explained adequately through a brochure, space advertisement, or postcard deck mailing, it is common to initiate interest and qualify leads via the telephone.

Examples of complex programs or services for which telephone lead-generation campaigns have been successful include:

- a five-part interactive software program targeting special needs students
- a non-traditional modular elementary science program
- advanced placement textbook programs

After the initial telephone calls have been placed and the lead has been qualified, follow up calls are placed at a later date by either an inside or outside sales force. Additional contact, via telephone or a personal visit is essential in closing the sale. These follow up calls or visits address specific concerns, promote additional features, advantages, and benefits important to the teacher, and determine where the educator is in the decision making process. Specific content and editorial related questions can also be discussed in great detail during follow up calls. In some cases a sales representative or consultant is needed to provide a complete onsite presentation of the program.

Working with the Gatekeeper

One of the greatest hurdles in speaking with any contact, be in at a school or district level, is getting past the gatekeeper. A lead-generation call into a school can be a win-win situation or end in disaster, and the outcome is determined by the caller's ability to listen well and ask the right questions, all in the first sixty seconds of the telephone call.

If the call is handled properly, a school secretary can be a mine of information. Oftentimes this gatekeeper can verify planning and preparation times, provide insight into which curriculum materials are currently being used and updated, and at the very least, provide enrollment and contact information.

> *"...a leads generation call is another valuable method of building a sales relationship."*

Being sensitive and respectful of this person's time is of the utmost importance. Fire drills, last minute assemblies, unannounced visitors, and even fights in the hall are distractions that make a school secretary difficult to speak with and to reconnect with. The job of the educational account representative is to professionally refocus the gatekeeper's attention and to obtain the information necessary to be prepared for a call with a decision maker. This reconnaissance work also involves doing a customer profile, which includes the best time and method of contacting decision makers. Throughout the call, however, the account representative must be courteous and not sound "scripted." A secretary often enjoys adult conversation.

An Interactive Brochure

Using the telephone to generate leads is quite similar to promoting a product or service using an interactive brochure. Ever hear of the interactive comic book where the reader can program the adventure for a different experience and outcome each time? A good lead-generation telephone call should work the same way, as each school and purchasing situation is different and should be handled differently.

While telephone scripts are essential when launching a new campaign, once the decision maker is identified and qualified, the core of the telephone conversation should be responsively adjusted to meet the educator's specific needs and concerns. If each telephone call is treated generically and a script is read verbatim, it will come across to the contact that way. The product will not seem appropriate for the individual needs of the contact, and the sale will often not be made.

Customer profiling techniques can help callers to obtain the big picture and service the customer properly. A telephone script prompting canned "yes" and "no" answers will not enable an account representative to obtain an accurate portrayal of the prospect's needs or address unexpected problems and concerns. In short, a leads generation call is another valuable method of building a sales relationship.

Database Management in Support of Leads Generation

A strong contact management system is imperative to a successful leads generation program. Database management and manipulation can often be an overused phrase, but the method and concept behind the words is tried and true.

Going back again to the idea of the interactive brochure and that each telephone leads generation call should be unique, it is essential for educational account representatives to have the proper tools to track and document each telephone call.

A customized contact management system is essential to a successful leads generation program, allowing the caller to record in real time how, when, where, and by whom the purchases are being made. In a perfect world, purchasing decisions would be made either at the school by a principal or a teacher, or at the district level by a curriculum coordinator or a committee consisting of appointed teachers from within the district.

However, in a growing number of states nationwide, there are county offices or centers, supervisory unions, subdistricts, and school clusters that are involved in decision making and purchasing processes. For example, within larger school districts such as Boston or Philadelphia, there are often subdistricts to help manage the decision making process. Within the Boston Public Schools, there are ten subdistricts, also known as clusters, each consisting of between 7 and 12 schools. Each cluster has the authority to make its own decisions relating to curriculum materials.

In other states, such as California, Florida, and Maryland, the county offices play a large role in the decision making process. In the state of Vermont, there are supervisory unions that oversee 5-6 school districts and can play a role in the final decision making process. All of the specifics related to purchasing decisions that a caller learns should be documented in the company's contact management system to facilitate successful follow up.

> " A customized contact management system is essential to a successful leads generation program. "

Customer concerns and other pertinent details should also be tracked, as well as the documentation of local happenings within each school. Callers can refer back to these details when making follow up calls.

For example, if a teacher seems rushed and confides to the account representative that she has been extremely busy and preoccupied due to upcoming tests, this should be documented and can be used conversationally with the secretary or gatekeeper the next time contact is made. If a principal mentions that the girl's basketball team is in the regional finals, the caller should make a note of this and share it with the person who will be doing the follow up. Personalizing a call makes all the difference in the world. Being respectful of holidays is also important. Catholic school teachers, for example, don't want to be contacted during Holy Week.

Recognizing the power that extensive, personalized information can provide, a growing number of companies targeting the school market are arming their field representatives, inside sales staff, and customer service departments—anyone that has any type of contact whatsoever with the customers—with an all inclusive contact management database. These databases are designed to track and monitor any type of contact with the customer—from accounting to shipping.

Oftentimes, lead generation campaigns call on existing customers in an effort to cross-sell additional products, services, or support materials. These existing customers may have questions related to back order items, billing concerns, or the availability of stock. If the caller has access to a rich contact management database, he or she will e better able to represent the company well, by answering the questions most important to the customer at the moment—whether or not these are related to the campaign itself.

All-inclusive contact management databases include information on everything from mail drops, documentation of incoming calls to customer service, sales visits or presentations, sales orders, back order items and returns. With direct access to all of this information, an educational account representative can conduct a more effective lead-generating campaign while also supporting the company's reputation for superior customer service.

A Win-Win Situation

There are more than 110,000 public, parochial, and private schools nationwide containing over 52 million K-12 students. With additional federal funding and grant monies being awarded to schools over the next few years, the sales potential and opportunities within the school market have never been better.

In this climate, the telephone will continue to increase in popularity as a sales tool. Mergers and acquisitions within the educational publishing industry are requiring outside sales forces to do more and more with less, with individual reps assuming larger and larger sales territories and broader and broader product portfolios. Sales reps do not have the time to spend tied to the telephone making lead-generation calls or personal sales visits to schools simply to see what curriculum materials are being updated. And direct mailings can only target an entire school audience generically, without the charm and effectiveness of personalization.

Telephone leads generation provides a win-win situation, offering a means to contact more educators cost effectively and address individual needs and concerns immediately. You are just a phone call away from watching your new business sales and bottom line skyrocket.

About the Author

Cheryl Cira is the president of Marketing Dimensions, Inc., which has specialized in the areas of school marketing consultation and teleservices since 1993. Telephone marketing services include leads generation campaigns, follow up to mail in requests, exhibit or Web site leads, market research surveys, and overall sales support in territories not covered by an outside sales force. You may contact Cheryl by mail at 748-A Greencrest Drive, Westerville, Ohio 4308, by telephone at (614) 890-1510, or by e-mail at mktgdim@aol.com.

Relationship Building through Telesales

by Gerry Bogatz

We all have an image in our minds of "telemarketing." Whether it's the irritating calls you receive at home during dinner or the rows of pushy salespeople with headsets, you probably don't get a warm fuzzy feeling about it.

Well, think again. There is another kind of telemarketing, or "telesales," in which the goal is to sell products by building relationships. The success of educational marketing in particular lies in building strong, long-lasting relationships with prospects and customers. With this approach, potential purchasers view sales representatives as consultants and friends, and they grow to trust and depend on them and their products. As a result, relationship-based telesales helps establish a solid, loyal customer base that will continue to grow and flourish over time.

Telesales in the Educational Market

To be successful, your telesales campaigns must be tailored to meet the very special needs of the education market. Thus, the necessary preparation for telesales representatives includes:

Understanding school buying cycles and how they impact school purchase decisions. The best offer will not be acted upon if there's no money to be had, so be sure to plan your telesales campaigns for times when you know educators are planning their purchases.

Knowing who the decision-makers are and what messages will attract them. Understand the challenges that face educators today and offer them solutions. Knowing how to segment your target audience and tailor your message specifically to the needs of each group of educators will greatly increase your chances for success.

Understanding the current trends in the marketplace and how they impact the success of your product or service. Analyze trends to understand what dollars are available in a particular state or district; how standards are being implemented in that state; who in the school or district is empowered to make buying decisions; and what the competition is doing to meet the needs of educators.

Effective telesales representatives must be fully aware of all of these issues to be successful. This knowledge will allow them to draw educators into personalized conversations about their situations and get them to respond positively to sales presentations.

Establishing a Relationship

The hardest part of building a relationship with a customer is getting the relationship off the ground. Our first inclination when we pick up the phone and realize that there is a salesperson on the other end is to hang up. The key to keeping people on the phone is starting a conversation with them—building a rapport from the first moment and keeping it going throughout the phone call and into the future.

This requires bright, enthusiastic telephone representatives who are not only knowledgeable about the product or service they are providing, but who also understand the educational environment as a whole. The first part of this statement is obvious. Clearly, sales representatives must have a high level of product knowledge in order to provide a consulting service to the educators they are calling, much as a sales representative visiting in person would. But a salesperson must also know what questions to ask educators to draw them into a conversation and make the link between their needs and the products being sold.

What characteristics must a good telesales representative have? We at MarketingWorks have found that the following are among the most important:

- Excellent oral communication skills;
- The ability to handle rejection well; and
- The ability to project excitement and friendliness over the phone

If you provide your educational telesales professionals with the right training and if they begin with these personal characteristics, you will be able to depend on them to get key referrals to other educators, to respond to e-mail and Internet inquiries in a friendly and professional manner, and to be the face and smile behind your customer service. Be sure they are available throughout the school day, in all areas of the country, to answer customer questions and to build your customer base with expert consultative support. The right person for the job is the one who knows what questions to ask to draw an educator into a conversation and establish a relationship early by making that critical link between an educator's needs and the product you are selling.

Maintaining the Relationship

Once a relationship has been established, either with an interested prospect or a committed customer, the goal is to maintain it and use it to generate future sales. One of the most important aspects of any relationship is continuity. In particular, continuity of salespeople is essential to cultivate the solid relationships with your customers that will keep them coming back again and again. A prospect who has a meaningful exchange with one salesperson one week but then receives a call from a different person the next week is likely to feel confused and even betrayed. In this case, the sense of familiarity and developing loyalty that the prospect has felt toward the initial salesperson (and, by extension, the product) is diminished.

A successful relationship also depends on good and accurate information. A salesperson who makes effective notes after a conversation about the school reforms taking place in a particular educator's district knows right where to pick up with the next phone call. He or she can then inquire about progress with reform efforts and add value to the conversation by continuing the discussion about how the company's product can meet the educator's specific needs. In contrast, picture a salesperson who makes a second call to a prospect but doesn't remember what information he has sent to the prospect after the first call. He is clearly less equipped to manage the next conversation and ask appropriate follow-up questions. Good information and a record of relationship histories allow the salesperson to create a rapport with the customer much as two people who work together on a daily basis create a working relationship.

> " ...sales representatives must have a high level of product knowledge in order to provide a consulting service to the educators they are calling... "

Database Tracking

The ability to keep track of information about prospects and about the educational environment in their schools, districts, and states is also clearly key to fostering customer relationships. By tracking this information in addition to the details of each customer interaction, reps can maintain a broad knowledge of their customers and tailor their offer to best meet the particular needs of each one. For example, a customer's school size and location, the grade level and subject(s) taught, the kind of decision-making authority they have, and many other variables will all affect the best way to present a product's benefits. In addition, the database should be used to rank prospects by how likely they are to purchase, to track past orders, and to record responses to various marketing devices and forms of contact. All of this information can help sales representatives and managers use their resources in the most efficient way possible and maximize their chances of making sales.

While keeping track of each customer relationship is important to any tele-sales effort, the data should also be used in the aggregate to develop targeted marketing and telesales campaigns that build the customer base effectively and efficiently. By analyzing the information in the database, you will better understand who your customers are and what your customer profile looks like. You will also learn the districts, states and regions in which you have strong penetration, so that you can target the prospects that are most likely to turn into new customers – starting with schools and educators that "look" like your customers. In short, data analysis will help you spend your valuable telesales dollars in the most effective way.

Growing Your Customer Base

A base of satisfied customers plays a critical role in building the positive reputation necessary for the growth of any educational product. Strong customer relationships depend on sales representatives who can meet all the needs of your customers, including needs for post-sale customer service or even ongoing product training. If educators are not given sufficient after-the-sale support, they will look for other ways of solving their problems, and your product will end up back on the shelf, gathering dust with all the others that never get used. On the other hand, if you do provide good support, you will create long-term friends who will look to you for help in their current needs as well as their future ones.

For example, suppose Company A offers a professional development workshop, among its other products. And suppose the company establishes a good customer relationship with School B, resulting in a sale of the workshop. Suppose, further, that the salesperson solidifies the relationship with strong follow-up to make sure the school was satisfied with the workshop and to find out what other needs its educators may have. Perhaps the principal isn't in need of other workshops at the moment, but she may well call the salesperson—whom she remembers as both helpful and knowledgeable—the next time she is dealing with a teacher training issue.

Whether the next contact between Company A and School B is initiated by the principal or by the salesperson, the salesperson can offer other products or supplementary training materials that the principal can use to support the initial workshop. The bond that has been created through the sale of the first product leads to repeat sales down the line. This is why telesales can be so effective in increasing the average order size and the frequency of the orders you get from your customers.

In addition, satisfied customers like to share their positive experiences with friends and colleagues. This type of networking is one of the most effective ways to grow market share, and it relies heavily on the relationships that you have developed with existing customers. Referrals provide salespeople and prospects with an automatic bond (the referrer) and are an excellent strategy, because the likelihood of a sale through a referral is much higher than through a cold call.

To illustrate, consider the example of a new classroom periodical, still relatively unknown among the educator community. For this magazine, a direct mail campaign might fail because of a lack of recognition for the product.

"A base of satisfied customers plays a critical role in building the positive reputation necessary for the growth of any educational product."

On the other hand, a targeted telesales campaign can create a small but satisfied base of customers, and the program may succeed as these happy educators start telling their friends and colleagues about this great new resource. The salesperson will obtain names of prospective customers from the existing ones, or new prospects may even call in on their own. To increase the success of the campaign and grow the customer network, the company can enhance the referral mechanism by adding incentives—for example, educators who refer colleagues might be rewarded with a free gift.

Lastly, it is important to recognize that while a strong direct mail campaign may be critical to a successful marketing effort, direct mail on its own is likely to be less effective than it can be when followed up by a telephone campaign. Assuming it reaches and is opened by its addressee, a strong mail piece can provide an entry point for a potential relationship with a potential customer, but it rarely establishes that relationship. Moreover, typical direct mail response rates in the education market are below two percent, but can be as high as five or even ten percent when they are complemented with targeted telephone follow-up. Again, the personal contact and resulting relationship makes a difference. A friendly and informed voice on the phone can bring attention to the mail piece, confirm its message, and offer more information, essentially bringing the mailing to life.

Always remember, the folks on the phones cannot be stereotypical telemarketers, who are in constant danger of insulting their audience the minute there's a deviation from a prepared script. Rather, telesales personnel in the education market must understand and speak the language of educators and address their needs. They become the "face" of your company, and their interactions with your customers and prospects have both immediate and long-term consequences for your business. The result of relationship-based telesales done in the right way is a base of satisfied customers who are likely to continue purchasing your products year after year and to refer them to others to whom you can also sell.

Affording Telesales

When comparing telesales with direct field sales, the number of contacts possible clearly favors telesales. A field rep can make four to six calls on a very good day. In contrast, a telesales rep can make contact with anywhere from 10-25 decision makers a day, depending on the accessibility of the people in the schools and the complexity of the product being sold. That's not to say that some field sales support may not be needed to help build relationships and close sales, particularly for very expensive and very complex products. But clearly, telesales can be a cost effective approach on its own, and it can always be used to support (and reduce the required size of) a direct sales team.

About the Author

Gerry Bogatz *is president of MarketingWorks, Inc., a firm that provides telesales and marketing services for companies that want to increase their sales in the education marketplace. Clients of MarketingWorks include Educational Testing Service, Turner Learning, U.S. News and World Report, The LeapFrog School House, and Gruner + Jahr. For more information on relationship building through telesales in the education market, call Gerry Bogatz at MarketingWorks, Inc. at 1888-MWORKS4.*

Effective Sales Collateral

by Linda Winter

Printed selling. That's precisely what a book titled *Sales Idea Book* published in 1949 called sales collateral. Back then, marketers referred to these essential sales support materials as "bulletins." I'm still oh-so-fond of that terminology, because it carries a sense urgency, import, and brevity. It also has a "Just the facts, ma'am" ring to it.

In developing sales collateral for 21st century educators, we would all do well to think in terms of preparing "bulletins" about our products and services. What makes effective sales collateral? We begin with market's usual suspects: features, functions, and benefits. These form the core of effective sales support copy. What turns these elements into tools that can be vital to the selling process? Strong, descriptive visuals. Clear, easy-to-read design. And oh yes, information that's pertinent to the educators you are attempting to persuade.

Where to Start

While we're all tempted to begin with product or service descriptions, it's smarter strategy to begin in an educator's shoes. Your direct sales team is a great resource here. They know what the first questions teachers and administrators typically ask. They know what moves educators from curiosity to genuine interest and from there all the way to a purchase order. So that's the sequence that should guide your collateral development.

Typically, here's the way information should be organized:
- Special offer or discount details, if appropriate
- The primary benefit
- The supporting benefits
- Key features and functions that contribute to the primary benefit
- Technical requirements or specifications
- Examples of successful use in classroom, library, laboratory or other teaching and learning situations
- Pricing and ordering information
- Contact information

Sales collateral is also an appropriate venue for educator testimonials, short-form case histories, and cross-selling to other related products in your line. And depending on the depth of your competitive intelligence, this is great place to offer comparisons with other products, as long as your facts—and we do mean facts—are correct.

Sales collateral is also a place to support corporate identity and positioning. However, a word of caution here: product sheets are not brochures for displaying corporate capabilities or services. A short positioning line or statement of scope, your corporate logo, Web site, telephone number, and address will do it. Save the rest for the corporate brochure you've been working on in your spare time!

What about the Visuals?

Here's the stage where a strong graphic designer is vital. The techniques of typography, balance, visual flow, and informational design are their specialty. Nevertheless, you must provide direction, ample product information, and insight into your particular sales priorities and objectives.

Typically, you'll want to display one dominant product visual per page. If your collateral piece is multi-page in format, you may want to consider a "spread visual" that runs across the center spread. It's also important to include callouts that describe key product features or functions. Also mandatory are captions for each visual. Even if the title of your collateral piece is the product's name, the product photo should include that name in the caption, along with a re-statement of the primary and most compelling benefit.

Supporting photos are also important. They add impact, visual relief, and valuable product information. Again, captions are a must. Callouts may not be appropriate for supporting photos, since they are "busier" visuals and the key word here is "supporting" not competing with your lead image.

Accent photos, particularly those showing students and teachers in the process of using your products, are also important. Why? Because this is one more subtle way you communicate with educators and demonstrate that you understand their world, their challenges, and their aspirations.

A Word about the Words...

Copy for sales collateral should be factual...persuasively factual. We recommend a well-crafted balance of descriptive copy mixed with "bulleted" lists of features, functions and benefits. Subheads should provide summary benefit statements—the "beefier" the better.

The litmus test for copy? It should provide enough information to turn your prospects into effective salespeople. Why do we say this? In many instances, educators do not make buying decisions in isolation. They work in committees and teams to review information and select products for review and trial. Your sales collateral materials should help your prospects sell your products and services to their colleagues.

Wherever possible, copy for sales collateral should also help educators understand how they can use your products or services. If yours is an instructional technology product, provide valuable hints about integration with curriculum and/or alignment with applicable standards. If yours is an administrative product or a supplemental curriculum product, offer specific information about how it's used and how various school constituencies will benefit.

Finally, don't forget to ask for the order and provide clear ordering information. In many cases, sales collateral materials are left behind following a visit from a sales consultant, or they're sent in response to an inquiry resulting from an ad or a direct mail piece. Remember that phrase, printed selling? Collateral materials are first and foremost sales materials, and it's vital that they include a compelling call to action.

Some Design Dos and Don'ts

Don't Use

Long lines of type

Most sell sheets are sized 8-1/2" x 11", to be read vertically. It's tempting to use one wide column of type. Avoid that temptation, because readers will avoid that copy. Instead, use two parallel columns of type. It's easier on the eye and more scannable.

Terminally cute bullets

Little butterflies. Characters' faces. Things with wings. They can all be appropriate as design accents, but as bullets, they're distracting. Simple color is a better option.

Big areas of reverse type

Areas of solid color are strong design elements. They can guide a reader's eye to important visuals or copy sections. Large areas or blocks of copy reversed out of dark solid colors are generally harder to read, particularly when the type is 12 points or smaller. Use this reverse technique for short headlines or subheads or for special offer or "New" banners. Don't use it for copy blocks, unless you really don't want that particular information to be read.

Loopy type

Two years ago, the font of the moment was Chili Pepper, cute for menus, and maybe even for packaging. For headlines? Probably not. This year, it's grunge type that looks like its creator was a candidate for remedial penmanship. Choose type for sell sheets based clarity, impact, and readability. Leave the fads to the skate-boarding ads.

Do Use

Serif type for body copy

It's simply easier to read. 'Nuf said!

A coordinated family of type

You don't have to use just one font for the entire sell sheet. In fact, a piece can benefit from a unique combination of fonts. You can create a compelling design using sans serif for headlines, serif for body copy. Choose a font with a strong italic iteration for captions. The watchword is selectivity, however. Your sell sheets are not type soup.

Borders

Patterned or solid color borders can work to frame the information and images inside the sell sheet. If you're producing a series of product sheets, borders can help to organize and identify them.

Descriptive visuals

If your product is packaged uniquely or packaged with teacher guides, supplemental materials, or other add-ons, use supporting visuals to display these materials. If yours is a software or online product, use as many screen captures and short descriptions as possible. This gives educators a more concrete picture of what the product is and how it works.

Subheads

They provide visual "breathing room" and they give you the opportunity to emphasize important benefits. They're vital in sell sheets, because they function as organizing elements.

Packaging Sell Sheets...

It's always an organizational challenge. Should you size sell sheets to "stagger" inside a pocket folder or should you produce each sheet as a full-sized insert? There's no right answer to this one. Instead, it's a question of presentation. If there are more than four or five sell sheets in a pocket folio, it's generally best to find other ways to organize the materials, since your prospects may never take the time to "reorganize" the contents. Spiral binding, Wire-O, and other fastening devices may be better options.

Mandatory Elements...

Designers will protest, but we're firm believers in including your logo, telephone number, and Web site address on every single page (or spread for multi-page versions) of your sales collateral. Often educators photocopy these materials to pass them along, or they fax them to colleagues. You want your contact information to make the trip.

Vital usage information should also be part of your list of "must include" information. If your product is designed for a specific grade, grade span, discipline, computer platform, or other defining niche, be sure that information is included as part of a prominent lead in or flag. It helps educators "place" you, eliminating wasted time on their part—and wasted marketing efforts on yours.

Printed Selling...That's What It's All About

Your direct sales team and product managers all have valuable input for sales collateral. While ads and direct mail are the domain of "marketing," sales collateral is by and for the sales team. It's their voice to the customer before they arrive and after the meeting has ended.

After your first drafts of sales collateral pieces are developed, don't simply run them up any flagpole. Run them by some customers, some prospects, and of course, your sales team. Fix the messages that are confusing. Strengthen the benefits that resonate with them. Eliminate the information that's simply not relevant. Then and only then will you have achieved printed selling!

About the Author

Linda Winter *is an Internet Monitor, www.internet-monitor.com, partner and the president of Winter Group, www.wintergroup.net, an award-winning marketing communications, research, and design firm focused on the education and library markets. She started Winter Group in 1978. The firm provides a comprehensive collection of integrated services to education marketers, including advertising, sales support and collateral materials, Web site development, custom market research, direct mail, catalogs, event marketing, and exhibit design. She is a co-author of i-Tips 2000, The Insiders' Guide to School & Library Marketing, published by The Internet Monitor. She can be reached at WinterL@wintergroup.net or (303) 778-0866, ext. 12.*

CHAPTER 6

Direct Marketing

Inside this chapter...

K-12 Direct Mail Secrets

by Scott Knickelbine

E-mail shme-mail.

Despite the enthusiasm about electronic channels for school marketing, good old-fashioned snail mail is still one of the most effective tools for reaching educators with your sales message. Why?

It's accessible. Despite the enormous strides that have been made in the last couple of years in getting schools connected to the Internet, the fact is that in many schools educators have only very limited access. And the technophobes don't look at their e-mail at all, no matter how well connected the school may be. Direct mail reaches everybody—if it's done right.

It's universal. The K-12 market is one of the very few for which the available data is nearly exhaustive. If you decide to target, say, 3rd grade reading specialists in Title I schools, you can go out and get the names and addresses of nearly every last one of them. That's not currently true about e-mail addresses—and, given the sensitivity regarding unsolicited e-mail in most school districts, you're not going to see comprehensive e-mail lists available for a long while.

It's forgiving. If you mail an offer to a school's technology coordinator, and you misspell her last name, she'll probably still receive it—with luck, she'll even read it. And if she's moved on to another school (an increasingly likely event, with turnover rates reaching 30% annually at some schools), the secretary will probably pass your piece on to the new technology coordinator. With e-mail addresses, however, even a single character out of place means your message will wind up in oblivion. And given that many school e-mail addresses still look like "susan.smith@mis.linclnhi. spencer.k12.ca.us," avoiding typos requires a minor miracle.

We're not trying to "dis" e-mail marketing here—it's an exciting development, and one that's certain to become more important in future years. We would encourage you, however, not to overlook the tried-and-true benefits of direct mail in generating prospect leads and boosting sales to schools.

We've been involved in scores of direct mail campaigns over the years, and we've talked to and surveyed hundreds of educators about what they pay attention to when they open their mail. Here are some of the approaches we've discovered to make your direct mail efforts more profitable:

The Strategy

Before you plunge into creating a direct-mail package, its important to think carefully about what you want the mailing to accomplish. There are many things you can attempt to do with direct mail—everything from reminding customers of a product upgrade to closing a multi-million-dollar district sale. But not everything works equally well.

One of the principles to keep in mind is that unless your price point is fairly low (under $100), even your most motivated prospects are going to have to create a consensus among colleagues, administrators, and others in order to purchase your product. Having created this consensus, they will then have to work the purchase into the budgetary process or go after a grant. The result is that direct mail packages usually cannot result in immediate sales. (One exception: mailings designed to snap up unencumbered budget dollars at the end of the school year.)

School purchases tend to be collegial, time-consuming affairs. For that reason, mailings designed to establish or further the sales process will tend to be more successful than mailings that seek an immediate sale. Your best bets are mailings aimed at identifying interested prospects and warming those prospects up.

On the other hand, if you've got a product—or an accessory or add-on—at a price point below $99, you

> **"**...mailings designed to establish or further the sales process will tend to be more successful than mailings that seek an immediate sale.**"**

certainly do have a shot at a direct sale. Because these products can be purchased with discretionary dollars—or from teachers' own personal funds—the dynamics begin to look more like the consumer market. You can make these sales year round, with almost instantaneous turnaround.

The Offer

It's surprising how many people in K-12 marketing tend to overlook the importance of the offer in their direct mail packages or relegate it to an afterthought. That's unfortunate, because direct-response research indicates that the offer is the element that has the greatest impact on prospect response.

In keeping with what we have said about strategy, the most effective offers are those which your recipients are actually in a position to accept immediately. That usually means offers that don't require an immediate purchase commitment.

Offers of information packages, demo disks, and videos work especially well in the education market. Remember that educators must build consensus to purchase most products. So they not only need to be convinced that you've got what they want, they also need the tools to convince others. That's why educators tend to place a high value on offers that give them a thorough, hands-on understanding of your product.

> " ...educators must build consensus to purchase most products. "

As we mentioned above, offers that encourage an immediate purchase tend to be most effective for sub-$99 price points. In those cases, limited-time discounts, two-for-one specials, free gifts, and other consumer-style sales incentives can be very effective. For more expensive products, however, special pricing or packaging offers will only be successful during certain times of the year—generally May and June—when educators have the money at hand and need to make purchase decisions right away.

The List

The quality of your list is also an important factor in determining the level of response to your direct mail campaign. Don't scrimp here. While direct mail can be cost-effective, it's rarely cheap. Sending pieces to the wrong people—or worse, to nonexistent people—can inflate your costs, decimate your response rates, and dramatically reduce the return on your direct-mail investment.

K-12 marketers are fortunate to have several choices of high-quality lists available for rental. Quality Education Data and Market Data Retrieval are the two biggest; both are excellent firms that work year-round to ensure their lists are up-to-date and accurate. Usually, these firms can offer you the universe of names for any job title or demographic select you want. These lists tend to be costly—particularly the more you pile selects on top of each other. But they're almost always worth it, especially if you need to reach educators outside your current customer base.

Other sources of lists include magazines that target educators. These can be somewhat less expensive than going to one of the big education data sources, and they can be a good buy if the publication is read primarily by the market you're trying to target. But because these lists are based on subscription records, they're often not as up-to-date. Also, demographic selects are often not available, and data is often self-reported and not subject to verification.

There are plenty of other brokers who make lists of educators available, often at a very low cost per thousand, but you need to proceed with extreme caution when using them. Remember that the turnover in schools is very high, and many of these lists are often years out of date. You're likely to squander the money you've saved buying a cheap list on sending thousands of pieces to people who may never receive them.

How about when you're mailing to a house list? This ought to be the data you have the most confidence in, but using home-grown mailing lists can have hidden—and disastrous—pitfalls. Unless you're personally in charge of your company's MIS operations you need to make sure you understand how your database is structured and how the data query that generates your list is written, to make sure things are done right.

For example, we know of one company that recently did a mailing to current customers of a particular product, presenting them with a limited-time offer to upgrade that product. The mailing fell flat—response was very disappointing. After some head-scratching about what was wrong with the offer or the creative, the marketing manager finally checked out the list itself. It turned out that the query had been written improperly. In fact, very few of the names who received the upgrade offer actually owned the product in the first place!

Here's one further complication that can arise with house-lists in the K-12 market: Unless your product is only for personal or classroom use, your prospects may be individuals, but your customers will be schools. Your database needs to be able to update every prospect at a school to "customer" status whenever anybody at that school buys.

The Package

Once you've got your strategy, offer, and list identified, then—and only then—is it time to start thinking about what goes in the package itself. The form of the package needs to be driven by your goals and target market. However, as a general matter, a package does need to have a certain bulk to be opened and taken seriously. There's a reason that the venerable "five-piece mailing" is still the standard for direct mail; it's been tested for decades, and remains the most reliable format. Typical components in the five-piece format include:

Cover Letter

We list this one first, because it's probably the most critical element in the package. If you've done your job in getting your mailing to the right readers with the right offer, you'll have your prospects hungry for more information. That's where your cover letter comes in. No matter how attractive the enclosed sales literature may be, if the cover letter does not feel like personal communication the entire package always gets less attention. Be sure you use a direct, emotional appeal.

Don't make the assumption that cover letters have to be short to be read. If you've gotten your prospect to read the letter at all, it's because he or she is very interested in your offer and wants to be convinced to act on it. Don't disappoint this desire—use as much copy as you need to position your offer and make a compelling case. It may go against our intuition in this message-saturated age, but studies show that packages with long cover letters—four pages or more—are typically more effective than those with short letters.

Four-Color Literature

The literature piece in your package serves two functions. Most obviously, it gives readers more information about your product—what it looks like, what it does, what benefits it conveys. Just as importantly, however, it provides a sense of legitimacy for your offer. It makes the product seem real, and it makes your company seem substantial.

Having said all that, the literature insert in the package does not need to be bulky to be effective. A one-page flyer can be as effective as a multi-page brochure, as long as it sticks to a powerful presentation of the offer and its benefits. In fact, you ought to avoid the temptation to overload the package with literature, or insert massive catalogs, particularly if you're mailing to a cold lead. Your literature must clearly and directly support the offer as laid out in the cover letter and reflected in other package pieces. If your prospects have to hunt for what you're trying to pitch to them, your response rates will suffer.

Lift Letter

This small, single-fold note inserted in the package has been a mainstay of direct mail for the last 40 years, and with good reason. Because it differs in size, format, and content from the rest of the package, it's often the only piece a reluctant reader will pay attention to. The lift letter is so called because it usually takes the form of a short personal letter to the reader. The tone should be more direct and intimate here than in the rest of the package. In K-12 direct mail, the lift letter is a good place to put a short testimonial from a satisfied customer.

> "There's a reason that the venerable "five-piece mailing" is still the standard for direct mail; it's been tested for decades, and remains the most reliable format."

Response Mechanism

Your offer needs to be tied to a clear call to action; the reader needs to know exactly what to do to take advantage of the offer. Certainly you need to include your toll-free number and Web address (and it's important that both of these be coded so you can track response). However, readers will generally also expect to see either a bounce-back card or an order form included in your direct-mail package.

As you develop the response mechanism, you should keep a number of things in mind. First, this is a high-visibility area of your package; make sure your offer and your call to action are completely and compellingly restated there, in a highly visible manner. Second, anything you can do to make it easier to for prospect to respond will improve the success of your campaign. That means creating a response form that's simple and quick to fill out. Have the prospect's name and address inkjetted on the form if possible. And by all means use a business reply mail indicia on the envelope or bounce-back card; if the mailing is too small to justify it, have the response mechanism pre-stamped.

Envelope

K-12 direct mail shares an important characteristic with its business-to-business counterpart. In both cases, there's usually a secretary sorting the mail, someone who often is under direct orders to throw away junk mail. How can you keep your piece from being culled? Use plainer envelopes, with cues like "The Information You Requested is Enclosed" or "Time-Dated Material" or "To Be Opened Only by Addressee." Also, use bulk mail stamps rather than a bulk mail indicia on the envelope to reduce the junk-mail look.

Don't go overboard in this, however; one experiment with a pseudo express-mail envelope yielded many angry calls from teachers who were called out of class to receive the delivery, only to find out it was just a direct mail solicitation.

A word about overall design for K-12 direct mail packages: Keep the glitz to a minimum. Obviously, good direct mail packages need to be eye-catching and have compelling content. But educators see themselves as professionals, and are turned off by packages with too much superficial gloss or those that look like junk mail.

Maintaining a Focus on Benefits

Put your benefit statement up front. There's a big temptation to try to cram your mailing package full of wonderful facts about your product. Don't do it. Even if your prospects understand why your product's features are important to them—and they may not—they can still fail to make the intuitive, emotional connection that will hold their interest and move them to action.

The fact is that most mail packages make a perilously short journey from the in-box to the recycling bin. You're only going to have a few seconds to convince your reader to take the time to read your mailing. Once you've crossed that hurdle, you've got maybe another minute to grab and keep that reader's attention long enough to get them to act.

So identify the most compelling benefit of your offer, and focus on it. Make it clear how your product or service will make your prospect's life easier, more successful, or less expensive. Be sure your key benefit is reflected in every headline, every photo, and every piece of art. You may have space to fill in some additional details or benefits of your offer, but never let the reader's attention stray from the big pay-off.

When to Mail

When should you mail? It depends on what you're selling. Products with bigger price points that need to be worked into the budget, or that are central to the curriculum, need to be promoted twice—once in late winter, when educators are researching purchases for the coming year, and then again in the April – June period when funds are actually being encumbered. Products that are more peripheral or less costly or that are purchased throughout the year—particularly those products paid for by teacher's personal funds—should be promoted in the August – October period, when teachers are "stocking up."

The worst times to mail are November and December (when schools are too wrapped up in holiday events and vacations to pay attention), and late June and July (when nobody's around to receive the mail). If you must mail late in the year, be sure you feature a high-value, limited-time offer—something along the lines of "Save 75% when you order before December 31." But without a can't-refuse offer and a firm deadline, most mailings between Thanksgiving and New Years will be ignored.

The Follow-Up

Once the response to your direct mail campaign starts rolling in, your work as a marketer has only just begun. Be certain your lead database is set up to gather the information that comes in on the response mechanism. Also, make sure your inbound phone staff is trained on the package and knows the importance of getting source data from every prospect who phones in.

Obviously, your first goal will be to pursue all those sales opportunities. But in your zeal to move product, don't let the rest of the data you've gathered languish unanalyzed. Keep track of what offers, lists, packages, and mailing dates have been most productive. And cross-link that data to large, comprehensive databases so you can determine which demographics are most predictive of sales. By taking this last step, you'll ensure that future mailings will be even more profitable.

About the Author

Scott Knickelbine *is a partner at Lownik Communication Services, Inc., a full-service marketing communications firm specializing in the needs of the K-12 market. Before joining LCS, Knickelbine was vice president of marketing for Advantage Learning Systems, Inc. Knickelbine is the author of nine books, including the Addy- and Bronze Quill Award-winning* <u>The Seven Deadly Sins of Marketing</u> *(Metis Press, 1998). He may be reached at* <u>scottk@lcs-impact.com</u>. *The Lownik Communication Services, Inc. Web site is at* <u>www.lcs-impact.com</u>.

Selecting Responsive Mailing Lists
by Bob Stimolo

A Brief History

Not too long ago, the major educational mailers all maintained their own lists. Most were compiled from state directories published by state departments of education. That's how Dr. Forrest Long, founder of Roxbury Press and a Professor of Education at New York University compiled his lists. The year was 1928, prior to the invention of the computer, so Dr. Long maintained his lists on addressograph plates.

As other school marketers learned of his lists, Long began renting them as a favor. Over time, as his list business grew, he added a lettershop and service bureau. Eventually he began to compile lists for market sectors more loosely related to the education market, including health care facilities and churches. Today, Dr. Long's company is known as Mailings Clearing House. It's located in Sweet Springs, Missouri, and is still owned and operated by the Long family.

In 1968, about 40 years after the founding of Roxbury Press, Herb Lobsenz founded Market Data Retrieval (MDR). Lobsenz had been employed by Xerox Education Publications and had conducted research that involved the collection of school expenditure data. This project led him into the business of renting school data.

In 1982, MDR implemented an agreement with what is now the Weekly Reader Corporation to take over the compilation of their teacher names. MDR made these teacher names available on the list rental market and, for the first time in history, school marketers could rent from a comprehensive list of classroom teachers.

Prior to the agreement with Weekly Reader to make their teacher names available, MDR purchased a company called Curriculum Information Center (CIC) that compiled the names of district level administrators. The person who was responsible for the CIC database was Jeanne Hayes. Hayes left CIC and MDR in 1980 and, with some help from National Business Lists, founded Quality Education Data (QED) in Denver, Colorado. QED marketed a database of schools to compete with MDR, but with a twist. They were the first to offer in-depth technology selections.

Shortly after Hayes left MDR, John Hood was hired from Baker and Taylor to replace her. He rose through the ranks to become second in command at MDR. In 1990 Hood left MDR and joined CMG Information Services (CMG). Although CMG had been primarily a college list compiler, Hood developed a K-12 database that included teacher names to compete with MDR.

In 1992 Hood added what he called the District Demographic Index (DDI) at CMG, which was the first "off-the-shelf" regression model in the school market. In 1993 CMG introduced their "Teachers Who Respond" file, which was the first shared-response database in the school market. Today CMG is known as MSGI Direct.

When QED offered its teacher-by-name file in 1997, the school market had three sources for lists of teachers by name and four sources for lists of schools and key administrators. Over 70 years after Dr. Forrest Long started maintaining his addressograph plates, a range of highly accurate and up-to-date databases now exist for school marketers.

The Difference Between Compilers, Brokers, and Managers

In the education market, list compilers are companies that research school directories and then mail and telephone school districts and buildings in order to create a file of schools, school demographics, and administrators and teachers by name. The compilers know their files and products better than anyone else.

The compiled files available for the school market are the most sophisticated in existence. Schools and teachers can be selected by over 70 different selection criteria—an overwhelming range of options.

Compiled files enable marketers to target schools based upon building characteristics and demographics. This information includes the size, grades taught, public or private status, size of budget, and much more.

Response files are lists of known direct mail buyers. Often they are customer lists that school marketers make available for list rental, also known as outside lists. There are approximately 200 outside lists available to school marketers.

List brokers are professionals whose job it is to know all the list sources available in a given market. Based upon a broker's years of experience and relationships with clients, he or she should be able to recommend multiple list sources that have a track record in the marketplace. A list brokerage typically uses both compiled files and response files in any given mailing. List brokers often give their clients the advantage of combining important information about school demographics with the responsive lists of direct mail buyers.

List managers are professionals who help rent a company's list to other mailers. Typically, the list manager markets the list and manages production and billing. The list owner approves all rentals, after reviewing promotion samples and mail dates, to eliminate competitors. In addition to providing extra revenue, many companies who rent their lists find this to be a source of information about what products and offers succeed with their lists.

(e.g., special education, title programs, and magnet programs); presence of certain technologies (e.g., computer types, VCR's, cable TV, networks, and telecommunications); and much, much more. One of the challenges when working with compiled files is understanding which criteria to employ when developing database marketing strategies because there are so many from which to choose.

A simple example of a database marketing strategy is to invest more promotion in schools that are larger or that spend more money. For instance, one might choose to mail a piece to 100% of the appropriate personnel in large or high spending schools and to 50% of personnel in medium-sized or medium spending schools, while sending only one piece per school for small or low spending schools.

A company's actual sales history can also be used to help refine a database marketing strategy. For example, matching a customer file to a compiled file then makes it possible to send more promotion to the buying districts and schools than to prospects.

> **"A simple example of a database marketing strategy is to invest more promotion in schools that are larger or that spend more money."**

Database Marketing

A compiled file offers a number of selections that enable mailers to employ database marketing strategies. This means that promotion investment can be controlled by selecting districts or schools based upon demographics. These demographics include census data about the community in which the district or school is located.

Census data may include the median household income, the percent of the population that has a single head of household, or the ratio of college graduates to the rest of the population. In addition, data about districts and schools may be gathered from federally funded programs, such as the percentage of students qualifying for free lunch.

In addition to demographic data, there are many district and school characteristics that may be selected. These include school type (public or private); grade span (K-3, 4-6, K-6, K-8, K-12, 6-8, 7-9, 9-12); school enrollment; expenditure per pupil; presence of certain programs

Personnel Selection Strategy

In addition to a database marketing strategy, a personnel selection strategy can improve the performance of a promotion. First, identify which buildings to mail. Then determine how much to invest. Finally, select the individuals to receive the mail.

When selecting personnel, there are two levels of decisions to make. First, you must choose the appropriate job function. This could be a district-level or building-level administrator (e.g., a curriculum coordinator or school principal); or it could be a classroom teacher by grade level or a teaching specialist (e.g., a reading teacher or special-ed. teacher).

After the appropriate job functions have been identified, choose a list type by ranking your options in order of performance potential, from most to least responsive. Most responsive is the house file (customers and inquiries), as well as the most recently updated names to compiled files (new names). In addition, there are direct mail buyers that match the compiled files, outside lists (the customer lists of other school marketers), and the balance of names from the compiled files in that order, from most to least responsive.

Compiled Teacher Names

Updating and keeping the names of teachers and educators current is a challenging task. About 20% of the universe of teachers moves each year. They enter and leave the profession, change schools, and change grades and subjects taught. Most of this movement takes place between the end of one school year and the beginning of the next.

TEACHER MOVEMENT

	Public	Private
Stayed in the Same School as Last Year	86.3%	82.3%
Moved to a Different School	7.2%	5.8%
Left the Teaching Profession	6.6%	11.9%

Most movement among teachers is not finalized until late summer. Thus, list compilers can't begin the process of updating teacher names too early or they will miss much of the movement. The ideal compiled teacher file would be a real-time snapshot of the universe right after schools open in the fall. But as a practical matter, this is impossible to accomplish.

There are too many schools, too many teachers, and too much movement to be able to capture a picture of the universe at any one point in time. If the various compiled files were compared with one another, we would find that they all contained most of the same schools. The greatest discrepancies among these files would be the teachers by name. If all of the teachers by name from the same grade or subject were selected from two compilers, it would not be unusual to find that only half (50%) of the teachers were the same while the other half was unique to each compiler.

This represents an opportunity for the school marketer. For example, assume that the Department of Education says that for a given grade or subject there are 100,000 teachers. Two compilers have 50,000 of these names in common while 50,000 are unique to each compiler. The total quantity available to a mailer using both sources is 150,000—an increase of 50% over the mailer who uses only one source.

Hotline Selections

In list parlance, "hotline" is the term given to the names most recently added to a list. When most consumer marketers test a new list, they ask for a 6-month or 12-month hotline select. This means they want only those names added to the file over the last 6 or 12 months.

Why do they ask for this select? Because years of testing have shown that recency lifts response. The theory is that if the hotline doesn't pull, neither will the rest of list. Consumer mailers have sung the praises of hotlines for decades. But the pulling power of the hotline concept and its application to compiled databases is a relatively recent discovery in the school marketplace.

GENERAL RESPONSE CHARACTERISTICS—BEST TO WORST

Current Customers	Most recent buyers on your house file.
Previous Customers	All older buyers on your house file.
Recent Inquiries	Inquiries over the last year.
Database New Names	Teachers new to the profession, new to the school, or new to the job.
Most Recent Direct Mail Buyers	Other companies' customers, including response databases and outside lists who purchased within the last 6 or 12 months.
Other Direct Mail Buyers	Other companies' customers, including response databases and outside lists who purchased prior to the last 6 or 12 months.
Other Teachers in Buying Institutions	The remaining teachers after removing customers, inquiries, new names, and direct mail buyers in schools you do business with.
Other Teachers in Non-Buying Institutions	The remaining teachers after removing inquiries, new names, and direct mail buyers in schools you do not do business with.

Those school marketers who have tested and measured the results of mailing hotlines consistently give them high marks as good performing lists. As a general rule, they represent the most productive portion of a list. The

consumer market technique of testing a new list by first trying the hotline portion has application in the school market. It's a good way to experiment with a new list.

Hotlines also represent an opportunity to expand mailings. In most cases, the hotline portion of a list has the least number of duplicate names when merged with other lists. Even fewer duplicates occur when the hotline portions of two lists are combined. As a result, a hotline can represent a good opportunity for adding productive mail volume.

It is interesting to know how many teachers the department of education reports there are in American schools. However, the marketing universe is not defined by that number. Rather, the universe for marketers is defined by the quantity of names that can be mailed to successfully. Thus, hotlines offer a potentially productive alternative worth investigating.

Remailing

Today's successful school marketers do not limit themselves to one list source, as this would eliminate too many additional opportunities. Multiple sources are used in order to maximize productive mail volumes. In addition, marketers find that rather than mailing once each year, promotions should be mailed as often as they prove productive. A direct marketing rule of thumb states that if a given mailing delivers a certain rate of response, the same mailing to the same list mailed four to six weeks later will generate about half the rate of the first mailing.

For example, assume that a marketer's return on investment (ROI) analysis identifies a required response rate at 1%. Then assume that mailing to a given list selected delivers 2%. Mailing to the same list a second time four weeks later should deliver half the original response rate or the required rate of 1%. Keep in mind that for any mailing, some lists will be very productive, some marginal, and some not productive at all. Identifying the most productive lists and remailing them is a way to enhance a mailing campaign's productivity.

There are several approaches that may be used to identify the more productive segments of a list. One technique is called regression modeling. An evaluation of districts, zip codes, or school buildings can be created using census tracking data, sales history, or both. A weight is assigned to each element in the model and then the lists are arranged from best to worst. The performance of a list from the first drop can determine where to establish a cut-off, and the mailing can be resent only to the higher-ranking portion of the original list.

Simpler techniques can be used as well. Certainly customers can be mailed more frequently than prospects to deliver an improved return on promotion. By the same token, more recent customers perform better than older ones and can be mailed productively more often.

List Cost versus Response

Some marketers think that mailing lists are like printing paper—they buy them by the pound and the cheaper the better. Actually, the fact is that the list selection has the greatest influence on the success or failure of a mailing.

Some mailers attribute 80% of their success to the combination of list and offer. Only 20% of their success is credited to package format, timing, and copy and art. Yet, even the most expensive list represents less than 15% of the promotion cost.

In light of this cost-benefit analysis, it simply doesn't make sense to choose lists by price. Rather, it makes much more sense to choose the best lists for your purpose, regardless of their expense.

INFLUENCE OF VARIOUS PROMOTION COMPONENTS ON RESPONSE RATES

Component	Influence on Response up to
List	1000%
Offer	500%
Package Format	100%
Timing	50%
Copy and Art	30%

Tracking List Performance

Tracking sales back to the list source is one of the challenges to succeeding in the school market. Most institutionally-funded sales are submitted on school purchase orders that do not reference the list from which the order originated.

However, often between 10% and 20% of orders are typically received with an accompanying response device. List performance can be evaluated by estimating the sources of untrackable sales according to the ratios observed among trackable sales.

Sometimes the trackable response is too low to be statistically significant, however. In this case, lists should be evaluated based upon their performance over several campaigns.

Catalog mailers have found that they can improve the amount of trackable response from 10% to 20% to as high as 60%. They accomplish this by ink jetting a department or room number into the return address in both the address area and on the catalog order form. The school purchasing office includes this department or room number when it addresses the purchase order.

The order entry people can then look for this number on the incoming purchase orders and record it as the source code.

Tracking response by list is a fundamental component of the list selection process. Knowing what has proven successful in the past provides valuable input in helping to determine which lists and selection criteria to employ in future mailings.

All school marketers are better able to track when the entire organization understands the importance of this function. In particular, strict discipline in order entry procedures goes a long way to improve tracking and analysis.

About the Author

Bob Stimolo is president and founder of School Market Research Institute, Inc., a full service direct marketing agency. SMRI provides consulting and creative services, mailing lists, and printing and mailing services to firms who market to schools through the mail. Bob has accumulated over 30 years of experience in direct marketing to schools and has helped plan and execute thousands of promotion campaigns. He is publisher of School Marketing Newsletter and co-author with his wife, Lynn, of Marketing to Schools: A Textbook for the Education Market. Bob is the official school market consultant of NSSEA and contributes a regular column to their newsletter, Tidings. You can reach Bob at SMRI, PO Box 10, 1721 Saybrook Road, Haddam, CT 06438; phone (800) 838-3444; fax (860) 345-3985; or e-mail rstimolo.smri@snet.net. Visit the SMRI Web site: www.school-market.com.

Developing Effective Offers

by Fred Johnson

Veteran direct-marketing guru Richard Benson states[1] that the "offer" is, at the very least, the second most important factor in the success of any direct marketing effort (if not the most important) superseded only by "list" or target audience. The prime purpose of an offer is to induce the recipient to "act now"—to order —and to order today. Successful direct marketing campaigns give their audiences reasons to "do it now," reasons "not to delay." Offers are also used to get attention. In today's highly competitive media environment, this is critical to success.

Here are a few factors to consider when developing effective offers:

1. Product. Is it an appropriate match to the interests of the prospects being targeted in the marketing campaign? Is it configured or packaged in a way that reflects their needs?

2. Price. Is the price consistent with likely perceived value? Is the price competitive in the marketplace? What incentives have been applied to attract attention and motivate immediate action? A discount? Free goods? Premiums? What rationale is used to establish credibility for the price incentive?

3. Time and Terms. For how long is the offer good? Is there a way to get inertia working in the effort (e.g., an automatic annual update or a standing order)? What payment options are allowed? Open invoicing on the purchase order? Payment by credit card? Installment billing?

4. Reducing Barriers to Action: Guarantees and Other Conditions of Sale. Is there a guarantee to reduce the risk for the buyer to say "yes"? What, if any, conditions are defined in the guarantee? Is the offer simple to understand? Are there frictionless paths to taking action?

Product

The first decisions to be made in developing an effective offer relate to the product—choosing which products to promote to whom and then positioning and packaging them. The closer the match of the product to the interests and needs of the prospect, the greater the likelihood of success. This sounds obvious, but is often overlooked.

Positioning and packaging derive from two factors:
1. knowledge of how a prospect is most likely to use the product, and
2. an effort to reduce the ordering decision as close as possible to a simple "Yes/No".

In this light, consider offering products meant to be used together as a single purchase option—a package that can be defined as a "program." Also, consider offering student materials in a multiple-copy pre-packs of 6 or 10 or more copies.

These approaches yield a number of positive outcomes:
- Because you show you understand how the educator is likely to use the product (i.e., you've clustered books for small group instruction into 6-packs, or books for whole class instruction into 10-packs than can be easily multiplied for variable class sizes), he is more likely to respond positively to your offer.
- Because you've reduced the number of decisions the buyer must make, you've increased the likelihood that he will actually make one (more about this below),
- Because you've aggregated components into a program or pre-pack, you've increased the dollar value of the anticipated transaction.

Configuring or positioning products in ways that minimize complexity and reduce the number of decisions a buyer is being asked to make will improve response. There is an old axiom that "the more choices you give a person, the less likely they are to make one." The best offer is one that can be reduced to a simple "Yes or No" proposition.

A common mistake is to offer a product in advance of your ability to deliver it. Product development and sales staffs often pressure marketers to "get this product in the catalog to be mailed in August" even though the product is unlikely to be deliverable until the following April. This can have two bad consequences: many back orders will be cancelled if a product isn't received by a certain need date, and payment can be delayed for larger orders of which the unshippable product is only a part.

Don't give your prospects a reason not to act. Examples of this error include options to "send for more information" (except when used in a purposeful two-step transaction as discussed below), or notes to "watch for this new product, available in four months."

Pricing and Price-Related Incentives

Expressing prices at just under the nearest hundred has historically enhanced perceived value in all kinds of transaction environments. Education is no different. It is better to price a book at $5.95 than $6.00, or a software license at $3,795 than $3,800. This "supermarket" pricing will almost always out pull pricing that uses "rounded up" even numbers.

Discounts

Discounts can be powerful motivators to act, especially when combined with time limits. Moreover, their power is significantly enhanced when there is a credible reason for offering them. For example, buyers understand when prices are discounted as the size of their orders goes up (and sometimes they demand that this be true).

The proposition, "Purchase the whole program and get it for less than the sum of the prices of all its components" is not only credible but also it makes the purchase decision easier for the buyer. It obviates his need to examine all the components and make multiple decisions about which to include or not.

Another example of a discount used to encourage higher order size is, "If your order totals $500, deduct 10%, if your order totals $1,000, deduct 20%."

Buyers also find "pre-publication" discounts credible. Early purchase commitments reduce risk for the seller and reward buyers. They help sellers make better manufacturing decisions and get cash flowing to them sooner to recover development costs.

Discounts can be expressed in terms of "percent savings" or "dollar savings." The more powerful offer is the one that communicates the biggest perceived savings. On higher ticket items discounted at 10% or less, the dollar savings usually have more impact. (For example, on a $395 item, "Save $30" is more powerful than "Save 7%.")

On lower priced items, even small percent savings may have more impact. (If a product is regularly $24.95, "10% off" is more powerful than "$2.49 off.")

Free Goods

Offering free product is often a powerful incentive. It is most natural when the free product drives a larger transaction or future orders. Good examples are the "first title free" in a series of products being sold in a continuity program, or "first issue free" in a subscription offer. The free product serves as a trial or sample of what's to come.

Another example is the offer of free supporting ancillaries to drive sales of core products. Basal textbook publishers have historically offered teacher editions, software, and supplementary materials free to secure adoptions of their core student books.

Free copies are sometimes offered to increase order size (as in, "Buy 10 books, Get two free"). The advantage is that the buyer perceives the value at the list price, but the actual cost to the seller is only the fraction of that which is his manufacturing cost.

While offers of free goods can be powerful, it's important to consider the possible negative impact they may have on sales of your product. Every copy given away is one that could potentially have been sold. This is why marketers often choose a "free good" which is not their product, but someone else's. In these cases the goods are referred to as "premiums."

Premiums

A premium can be almost any item with natural appeal to the target prospect. The item should have a high perceived value to the prospect, but a cost acceptable to the seller in the margin calculation of the transaction. Education marketers often assume that only "educationally related" products can be effective at motivating teachers. This has proven not to be true.

In fact, teachers respond best to items that have primarily personal, rather than institutional appeal, although school marketers often try to choose items that can be rationalized as useful in the classroom as well as at home. Examples are electronic items, books, and desk accessories. Classic users of premiums are the student book clubs, which offer them to teachers to motivate their activity as sales agents to students and parents.

An important rule in building offers with premiums is to "sell the premium first, then the product." The premium operates to command attention. Once secured, this attention can then be led to the product. Bob Stimolo (author of the preceding article) has significant experience in the application of premiums to direct marketing offers and has written extensively on the subject (see Chapter 6 of his book noted in the recommended reading for this article).

Free Freight

Shipping and handling charges represent an important income stream to marketers, often contributing to margin over actual cost. Offering not to include these charges on a shipment is an effective discount. This kind of offer is especially popular with commissioned sales representatives because often it's a discount that has no negative impact on their personal earnings. It can be effective when applied by a sales rep when securing very large orders for "commodity like" products—orders that may otherwise go to a more generous competitor. It is less effective in direct marketing because it draws attention to something that is often overlooked by the customer. In any case, it should be used with care and restraint.

Time and Terms
Limited Offers

"Limited" is a powerful word in offers. The terms "available for a limited time" or "in limited numbers" can be used in combination with incentives to motivate action.

Specifying that an offer is good "for a limited time only" can have dramatic impact. Discounts and premiums are most often tied to "act promptly" requirements. It's important, however, for education marketers to take into account institutional budget cycles when defining offer expiration dates. Fall offers with short cut-offs can be effective at securing unspent funds from the new budget year which started the preceding July 1. However, spring offers which seek to get orders from the upcoming budget will fail if the expiration date is set in advance of the availability of funds for purchase.

"While supplies last" limits may be applied to discounted annual products nearing their update time, or to titles going "out of print." It can be especially powerful when applied to premiums, as in "the first 100 respondents will get an autographed copy of (famous author X's) new book."

Inertia—Making It Work for You.

When products can be offered successfully on a subscription basis, paid for in installments, or purchased under standing orders—all with automatic shipping and billing—the result is a very attractive transaction pattern. Marketers should try to establish these models wherever products lends themselves naturally to them.

Periodical products are traditionally sold by subscription, and annually-updated reference works are traditionally sold on a "standing order." These approaches are being innovatively applied in other ways today, as software licenses or Internet services are subject to annual "renewal" or "upgrade and maintenance" offers.

Any offer with can result in an "automatic" commitment to future shipment and billing is a powerful builder of longevity in customer relationships. Customers willing to make these commitments are treasures to be treated with the greatest care and respect by education marketers.

Two-Step Transactions

While the objective in every marketing effort is always an order, for sizeable transactions or complex products, this often can be accomplished only in stages, and education marketers need to be patient. In these cases, two sets of offers need to be developed. The first offer has the objective of securing an action preliminary to an order—granting permission for a sales representative to call, requesting further information, asking for a sample or demo copy of the product. The second offer has the objective of closing or supporting the closing of the sale. In these cases, the same concerns about offers need to be applied to the second stage in this two-step transaction process.

"On Approval" offers are an example of a two-step transaction. The offer reduces risk to the prospect by limiting the commitment to a "free, no obligation trial" of the product for a limited time (usually 30 days), with the understanding that an invoice will accompany the shipment, but that payment will not be required if the product is returned within the allowed trial period. In these cases, sellers are counting heavily on the power of the product itself to make the sale. Shipment inserts reminding these conditional customers of the benefits of the product and the attractiveness of the original offer will improve "conversion rates" (i.e., the percentage of orders which are retained and paid for as opposed to returned). The more qualified the prospect (e.g., recent customers), the higher the conversion rate may be expected to be.

Payment

Education marketers typically derive most of their business from institutions. To be effective, they must offer to ship and bill any school or library on an "open account" basis when the order is received on a purchase order, or other media containing a purchase order number. Many however are able to tap the significant pool of purchasing power represented by teacher use of personal funds to acquire goods for school use. In these latter cases, response can be dramatically increased by offering to accept credit card orders—the more cards honored, the better the response.

Reducing Barriers to Action
Guarantees – Be Generous, Inspire Confidence

Knowledgeable marketers to educational institutions are comfortable making the most liberal of guarantees: "If for any reason and at any time you are not satisfied with this product, return it to us for full credit or refund. No questions asked."

The reality is that so few institutions will do this that there is no significant risk to the marketer who offers the guarantee. At the same time, it defines great confidence on your part in the product and provides one more reason for the buyer not to delay a "yes" decision. Marketers to teachers at home assume risks in guarantees akin to consumer marketers.

Make It Easy To Respond

Offers to "Call Toll Free," "Fax Toll-Free," or "Order Online" increase the likelihood your audience will take prompt action when deciding to buy. Establishing toll-free phone lines for voice and fax is easily accomplished and relatively inexpensive. Establishing a Web site that allows for online ordering is more complex, but vendors

of Web design services and publishers of off-the-shelf e-commerce software are making it easier for sellers to accommodate buyers who prefer using the Internet.

Offer Testing

Testing is the first article of faith of direct marketers. One of the great advantages enjoyed by direct marketers is their ability to try approaches with limited risk to see what works, and then to improve the productivity of their investments by increasing spending on the things that work, while avoiding those that don't.

The most frequently tested variable in direct marketing is the "list" or target audience. That topic is the subject of the preceding article. Offer is the next most frequently tested variable, as it is the variable next in importance. Successful direct marketers make testing an ongoing part of their marketing plans.

Reading Test Results

Testing in educational marketing can be challenging, given the difficulty of tracking response.

Educators responding to campaigns targeted to them at home and buying from personal funds will often use the order form included in a campaign. In these cases marketers can often track responses not only to a given campaign, but also to segments of the campaign— subsets of the lists mailed and variations in the creative or offer.

Educators responding to campaigns as influencers of institutional purchases more often do not use order forms, but rather requisition items they want and secure approval for their purchase by authorities who execute the decision using "purchase order forms" unique to the buying institution.

In these cases, tracking can be done using a number of tried and proven methods:

1. including in each product number a prefix which designates the campaign or campaign segment, a prefix which will appear on any purchase orders using product numbers

2. preserving a copy of the addresses mailed in each campaign test segment, and comparing addresses on the orders from the campaign to see which match the various segments.

3. including a department number as part of your address which respondents will be asked to use when sending you their orders.

Careful attention to tracking code details in order entry is necessary to successful data gathering for response analysis. It will pay handsome dividends to those who undertake it. Any of the offers discussed in this chapter can be the subject of a test, and should be—to determine how it impacts action from the customers you want to reach.

Summary

To close, here are a few guidelines for building an effective offer:

1. Know your objective(s). Among the possibilities are

- Act Now
- Order Now
- Order More
- Order Often
- Order Regularly

2. Keep it simple. Make it understandable fast.

3. Promote it redundantly. Readers must see the offer to respond to it. Consider presenting it on the outer envelope, on the order form, on catalog or brochure covers, and in the footers of every catalog page spread.

4. Be sure it's credible. If an offer sounds too good to be true, (even if you intend it that way) it may depress response. The more believable the reasons for making a decision to buy, the more successful the offer.

Educators behave like the consumers they are. They respond to all the traditional offers devised by direct marketers in the consumer market. Don't assume because they are educators that they will be motivated to buy an educational product only by your presentation of the product's features and benefits—important though they are. Building effective offers into your campaigns will dramatically enhance your likelihood of success.

■

[1] Richard Benson *Secrets of Successful Direct Mail* (1987), The Benson Organization, p 153.

■

About the Author

Fred Johnson *is a veteran of 40 years experience marketing education and entertainment products—a publisher of audiovisual media in the '60s and '70s, a marketing consultant to print, music, and video businesses in the '80s, the president of a supplementary materials publisher in the '90s, and a consultant in strategic planning and business development. His associations include Times Mirror, the Center for Humanities/Guidance Associates, Scholastic, Time-Life, Harcourt Brace, Scott Foresman, Silver Burdett, Henson Associates, Cherry Lane Music, Lorimar Video, NASCAR Video, Unapix Entertainment, Sundance Publishing, and Haights Cross Communications.*

Direct Mail Copywriting

by George Duncan

In true direct marketing tradition, we begin this article with a disclaimer. No one can teach you how to write. Whether writing is a talent or a skill is beyond me, except to say it's likely a little of both. But, as guitar pickers say to colleagues who want to learn a tune, "I can't teach ya…but I can show ya."

First let's address the question of grammar and usage when writing to teachers because it's an exception to the usual rule. Conventional wisdom around direct mail copywriting to most markets is "keep in mind, this isn't the Great American Novel. It's writing for dollars. Ms. Grundy or Sister Mary Elizabeth won't be around to rap your knuckles if you split an infinitive. And if your copy reads more clearly that way, go ahead and split it! Not sure which punctuation is best after a statement? Use an "em" dash—like that—and to heck with it."

But what if you're writing to Ms. Grundy or Sister Mary Elizabeth? Ah, now that's another matter! Like the professional proofreader who was unable to read the daily newspaper—he had to compulsively "proof" it—teachers are in a similar spot. They're much more sensitive than most to grammatical mistakes, errors in punctuation, and so forth. So, while you still want your copy to flow, you probably don't want to take quite as many liberties in writing to teachers as you might with a general consumer letter.

The point of grammatical license in sales copy is that you want your writing to be crystal clear to the reader, whatever it takes. You want the reader to move smoothly from the outer envelope teaser to the order form (or telephone, or Web site). Any major interruption in the reader's train of thought, such as an awkward phrase or sentence, even if grammatically correct, and chances are you'll be derailed. So copywriters sometimes overlook strict grammatical rules in phrasing and punctuation if it makes the point more clearly or emphatically. In writing to teachers, however, that same tactic could well cause the distraction!

Good copywriting also has a rhythm that helps move the reader along. Alliterations in text, short statements and comments, use of contractions ("you'll" instead of "you will," for example), use of italics for emphasis (sparingly!), and rising and falling inflections, all contribute to a sort of iambic pentameter for copy that makes reading more of a pleasure, and less of a chore.

Headlines and Teacher Benefits

The first thing to consider in your letter or brochure is the headline. The headline is critical in determining the success of a mailing piece. It focuses readers' attention on one quick benefit or promise (or two) and gives them a reason to spend their valuable time reading this material. Put more forcefully, it's what determines whether readers will or will not spend time reading your material! If the headline doesn't make it, you don't make it.

Headlines also help close out other random thoughts and provide a context for what is about to follow. As to length, worry more about whether your headline has captured the essence of your product than about its length, although shorter is better.

Unlike most consumer direct marketing targets, teachers have two primary interests: 1. themselves, and 2. their students.

For themselves, teachers mostly want products that make their lives easier. Curricula and aids that make it easier to teach. Beyond that, what they want most is for students to *respond positively* to the material. If you can make either or both of those claims, you should at least get a hearing.

As much as possible, you should position benefits headlines in terms of the students, as in, "XYZ software makes mathematics come alive for your students…" and/or in terms of the teacher's job, as in, "…and makes teaching, class preparation, and research a joyful new experience for you!"

This assumes you're mailing directly to teachers. But what if you're mailing principals or district administrators? Then the benefit headline can be made in terms of their teachers, like this one for a K-6 substance abuse curriculum: "Help your teachers respond to students' fears, concern and confusion over alcohol and drugs, their use and misuse!"

Even a catalog has—or should have—headlines at the top of a page or at the introduction of a particular product category. For example, "A biography program that provides role models for students." Then, in a product subhead, "Invite Abraham Lincoln, Cochise, and JFK into your classroom!"

Sell Benefits, and List Features

Like everyone else, teachers tune in to station WIFM—"What's In It For Me?" Benefits are far more significant to us than dry features. Benefits get past the mind's gatekeepers with greater reliability than do features and all the other image flotsam and message jetsam that bombard us every day.

However, don't leave out the features—they often provide the basis for the more rational justification a buyer can use to justify a purchase instead of acknowledging the emotional appeal of the benefits.

For example, in the catalog copy example above, the heading, "A biography program that provides role models for students" is the benefit: providing role models for students is what the product will do for you—or them. In the subhead, "Invite Abraham Lincoln, Cochise, and JFK into your classroom!" Abe, Jeff Chandler (just kidding!), and JFK are the features.

Another way to think of it is that features are expressed in the language of the seller (a sports car's air suspension), while benefits are expressed in the language of the buyer(a smoother ride). The great Roman orator, Cicero, who knew a thing or two about persuasion, said: "If you wish to persuade me, you must think my thoughts, feel my feelings, and speak my words."

Or as a copy chief I once worked with put it, "Tell me about my lawn, not your grass seed." That remains about as succinct a way to remember the differences between features and benefits as I know.

> "Benefits get past the mind's gatekeepers with greater reliability than do features and all the other image flotsam and message jetsam that bombard us every day."

Starting to Write

Begin writing your package at the beginning—with the envelope teaser—because that synthesizes the major benefit and often flags the offer in a single phrase. Then rough out the headline on the letter and on the brochure, so that those key messages are coordinated to project a common theme, but not in the same words.

Next, write the opening. "I am writing to you about..." or "I want you to know about..." are not openings. The reader, frankly, doesn't care what you want. She cares about herself (albeit as a teacher with a desire to help students). Direct mail is almost universally written in the second person with "I" and "we" used as sparingly as possible.

Most letters and brochures succeed or fail in their first sentence. The surest way to lose is to begin talking about yourself and your organization.

Going back to the XYZ software example, consider the following opening:

"For you as a teacher, XYZ software is like having a team of crack assistants at your side. One to prepare your lecture notes, another to create overheads, a third to write your exams, plus a tireless researcher who never even stops for coffee."

Or how about this, for Internet monitoring software depicted as a friendly Labrador retriever named BESS:

"Wouldn't you like to give your students the opportunity to travel all over the world, to visit famous libraries and museums, to get research information right from the experts and even correspond directly with our government leaders? Now you can, safely and conveniently, with BESS at each student's side."

"Give your students _____" (Fill in the blank) is a key phrase in selling to teachers.

Finally, it's a good idea to write the order form immediately, because that spells out, succinctly, what you'll be asking the prospect to do when you've convinced him or her that he or she can't survive another day (happily and successfully) without your product.

Sell the Offer—and Date It

In direct mail, you sell the offer, not the product. The free trial, the no-risk 30-day preview with money-back guarantee, the limited-time, half-off deal, the free premium.

It's much easier to sell a 30-day trial or a free examination than it is to sell the product itself. You'll discuss payment terms later.

You support the offer basically with benefits, product information, and "reason why" persuasions, urging the prospect to "act now!" You support that in turn with testimonials, research, and/or test results ("classroom tested!"), and then wrap it all in a credible guarantee and a call to action (*i.e., ask for the order!*).

You'll want to date your offer. An expiration date (4-6 weeks from the drop date is best) helps to keep your mailing from going up between the lamp and the tape dispenser for "later." It's also helpful to "merchandise" the offer by referring to it at several points throughout the letter. For example, "When you send for your free demo (30-day no-risk trial, etc.) you'll quickly see…"

Sell Copy

From the offer preview, get right into the benefits your reader will realize when she tests, previews, and examines your product. In consumer direct mail you stay in second person throughout the letter. With a teacher, however, you also want to frequently reference "your students" to remind her that she's really buying this for them, not herself. You're talking to her (one person, not a group or market) and about her (not you), and so you talk about your company and your product only in terms of what they will do for her and/or her students.

Use Subheads to Introduce New Thoughts

You want to avoid eye-glazing, mind-numbing, wall-to-wall copy, so use subheads to introduce new thoughts and to move from one part of the letter to the next.

Write in short sentences.

And short paragraphs.

Present a list of benefits or features in list form,

- Each item
- Preceded by
- A bullet

instead of in a linear paragraph.

Use words of one syllable as much as possible. *The New York Times* is written to a ninth grade level, for clarity. Your reader is trying to quickly extract the key information he needs, often by just scanning your letter. Which is another good reason to use subheads…bulleted lists…and…ellipses.

The Guarantee

Mitigating risk is an essential function of successful direct mail. No one wants to make a mistake. Especially not an expensive mistake. Relieve that fear with your guarantee. By law you must refund legitimate requests up to 30 days anyway, so why not make a virtue of necessity? Some worry that a guarantee might somehow cast doubt on the product. But the guarantee speaks not to your product, but to you as an honest and fair businessperson your prospect can trust.

Still, try to avoid the rather abrupt "Money Back Guarantee" or "Full Refund If Not Satisfied" kind of thing. That's negative. A Free (or Risk-Free or No-Risk) 30-day Trial is the same thing, expressed in positive terms. "Examine it, try it, use it for a full 30 days without risk." That's an invitation, not a warning.

The Call to Action

Even after all that, you can't assume the reader will do what you want her to do, right away. But that's what she must do. So spell it out. Ask for the order! Does she detach and complete a reply card, call a toll-free number, complete a questionnaire, check a box, punch out a token? What? Is there a postpaid or self-addressed reply envelope to use?

Ask her to do all this right now because that expiration date will be here before she knows it. Because she really wants to try this, but if she lets it go till "later," she'll forget.

The P.S.

Punctuate the call to action with the signature, then add a P.S. After the headline and first sentence, the P.S. commands the highest readership in the letter. Use that important space to repeat a key benefit, or add a twist or another idea to something you've already said. Also, repeat your call to action here, in slightly different words.

Interactive Copy

In direct mail you want to use words that invite the prospect into the world of your product. Words that help her imagine herself using the product or that project the results of using the product in the classroom.

- *Learn, discover, try, explore, test, find.* These are words that invite the reader into our proposition and set the stage for action.
- *Free, new, now, announcing.* These are words that promise something new. Why is every packaged product on the market "new and improved?" Because people are naturally drawn to the latest and newest.
- *In addition...furthermore...what's more....* These are phrases, sometimes called the "bucket brigade," that help move the reader smoothly from paragraph to paragraph to order form.

The Last Word

Having said all that, copy and creative are only about 10% to 20% of the success of a direct mail campaign. The list and the offer do the heavy lifting at 40% each.

Well-written copy will always enhance the results of any offer, but the right offer to the right list at the right time will likely survive even mediocre copy. On the other hand. if you brought Claude Hopkins back from the dead he could not save the wrong offer to the wrong list. Always test your lists and offers first, before you put additional time and money into testing copy and format.

Further, all copy and creative is a compromise with time. Some top writers agonize over every word and phrase and revise, revise, revise through sleepless nights, while others do a first draft, polish it once or twice, and let it go—often because with the press of deadlines and a heavy workflow they have no choice. Which you are will depend on who you are, and nothing said here will change it.

Good luck.

About the Author

George Duncan *is an award-winning direct mail writer and consultant, frequently numbered among the top direct mail copywriters in the country. He started Duncan Direct Associates in 1976, providing a full range of direct marketing services to a national roster of publishers, software developers, and marketers of business-to-business and consumer products and services. He is the author of* Streetwise Direct Marketing, *published by Adams Media. He can be reached at* duncandirect@pobox.com, *or (603) 924-3121.*

Turning Your Catalog into a Top Performer

by Linda Winter

Catalogs are the marketing staple in K-12 education. Librarians save them for years and typically file them by name, rank, and serial number. Teachers often hold them for one or school years, and administrators have been known to clip those delightful little routing slips to their covers and actually circulate them among colleagues and staff.

Seasoned school marketers will tell you with their last gasps that if you do nothing else in terms of school marketing, a catalog is a must. It's more than a promotional vehicle for educators. It's a planning tool and so much more…and for this reason catalogs—whether 'filled with hundreds of products or only a few—are anchors for most school marketing programs.

Here are some important design and organizational tips that will help you in writing and designing education catalogs and in evaluating the work produced for you by your own marketing team or by outside creative and production vendors:

Production Economics

While it's necessary to plan in 4-page sections, 16-page signatures are the most economical. In many cases, 16- or 32-page catalogs are more economical in terms of printing than are 12- or 28-page books. The bottom line? Think in 16s rather than 4s when you're producing a larger book. 8 1/2" x 11" is a more economical size for printing than larger or "unique" sizes. However, because postage for "flats" continues to rise, many education catalogers are looking at smaller sizes, such as "digest" (5 1/2" x 8 1/2") and "Slim Jim" (6" x 11"), because they can be mailed at lower commercial rates. Always make certain your printer's equipment specifications are clear prior to production of camera-ready art, and work with your printer in advance. Frequently, a simple change to 8 1/2" or 8" for width and 10 1/2" for depth can save a surprising amount of money.

Covers

Catalog covers function at multiple levels. Like outer envelopes for direct mail promotions, the cover's first job is to hold the educator's attention long enough to persuade her to take one or more critical actions…opening the catalog, saving the catalog, leafing through it, and ultimately deciding to place the order. In focus groups, copy tests, and post-mailing surveys, educators note that a single dominant image is the most memorable and "relate-able." That no doubt mirrors many marketers' call center experiences, as educators call in to place an order from "…the panda catalog" or "…the molecule catalog."

Other visual techniques for the cover will strengthen your catalog's selling power as well. The "series" approach works exceptionally well, in which all of your catalogs use the same design "template" with updated information. The image or images, verbiage, dates, phone numbers, logos, and so forth always appear in the same position on the cover. Copy and images change, but the layout remains consistent. Thematic approaches also work well. If yours is a math product line, you may want to devote your catalog covers to graphic interpretations of equations. Literature product lines lend themselves beautifully to "art" covers or examples of your illustrators' work. And of course, educators always give high marks to covers that visually feature students using the products being merchandised.

Key Selling Pages

The front cover, inside front cover, and center spread are prime catalog real estate, followed closely by the back cover and the last left-hand interior page. These are the pages where your new products, your best catalog offers, your best sellers, and other supporting offers should be featured prominently.

Visual Organization

Color, solid bars, and clear folio organization can help educators use your catalog to buy. If your product line is organized by grade span, subject area, or product category, color can function as a key organizing element. Remember to use your color-organizing scheme in your table of contents and if possible, on your order form as well, to help educators find what they're looking for and then translate that "find" to an actual order.

Design Consistency

In catalog design, clarity supersedes creativity. Orderly pages that become "familiar" from the first spread forward function better. Product titles should receive consistent typographic treatments. The column formats should be consistent from section to section. Section organizations should be parallel. Prices and technical information should appear in the same relative places for each product, series, or bundle. Special offers should be featured in each spread and should be featured in the same visual area of the spread.

Introductory Pages

If your catalog includes merchandising information for several different product categories, it may be valuable to use section introductory pages. These provide a visual break and give you an additional opportunity to merchandise "best buys" in the section that follows. Introductory pages also give you the opportunity to make important curriculum and/or classroom integration points. You can highlight specific curriculum standards that your products meet or feature a mini-case study, showing how your products are used in classrooms, libraries, or computer labs.

Testimonials

Educators believe their colleagues far more readily than they believe us marketers. Testimonials, complete with attributions, are valuable additions to any catalog for the school market. From a graphic standpoint, again, a consistent treatment using boxes, borders, bursts, shaded backgrounds, oversized quotation marks, or other techniques will call attention to the testimonial and provide more immediate recognition on a page.

Photography and Imagery

In copy and concept test focus groups, educators consistently prefer detailed visuals depicting products. This is particularly true when products are bundled or are provided in "kit" form. Photos or illustrations that show the contents of the entire kit are stronger selling images. In addition, when a product has special features that can be visually represented, call-out captions are particularly helpful and persuasive.

One important additional note with regard to visuals concerns accurately portraying diverse student and faculty populations. While this may seem a cliché, it is vitally important to show ethnic and gender diversity in your marketing materials. Educators are beyond sensitive to this point—and rightly so. By including students and teachers of all origins, you are making an important statement…a statement that also expresses your insight into contemporary classrooms.

Icons

They're helpful. They save space. They provide visual interest and rapid communication. "They" are icons, and when used appropriately, they provide important buying clues for your customers and prospects. Simple, recognizable characters or images work best. Color combined with simple verbiage also serves to provide important information without detracting from a more important selling message. A word of caution is in order, however. While your catalog designers may instantly recognize icons and their meanings, your prospects may not. So, every two or three spreads it's helpful to repeat the legend that describes your icons, to make sure that the information is clear and usable for your readers.

Ordering Information

Once per spread, your 800 number, Web site, and fax number should appear, and these mandatory elements should appear in the same place on each spread. Typically, they're designed into "footers" that run along the bottom of the page.

Order Forms

They're essential. That's the bottom line. Many school marketers complain that the order forms are never received. Nonetheless, educators report that they use these forms to plan and organize their orders, and they often send along your order forms to their building or district purchasing offices. In designing your order forms, use informal testing. Once you create a format that captures all of the information you need from customers, try giving it to several people both inside and outside your organization and asking them to complete it. Have them tell you what worked, what was confusing, what was repetitive, and so forth. For reference, also look at the order forms used by established K-12 direct marketers. These formats can be excellent launching pads for your catalog's order form template.

Curriculum and Grade Span Charts

Educators use and appreciate charts that organize your products by curriculum standards, by pedagogical precepts, by grade span, by reading level, and by other real-world classroom applications. Moreover, this kind of graphic information helps them "sell" their purchasing recommendations to their colleagues and supervisors. These charts, while they take up a page or so of catalog real estate, are also excellent vehicles for demonstrating your thorough understanding of an educator's needs and curriculum requirements.

A Few Words about the Copy

Product descriptions within a catalog should be short and concise, but detailed enough to give educators the information they'll need to order or request a preview. A mix of running copy and bulleted descriptions typically works best, unless all text descriptions are short (50 words or less). Copy needs to be designed for readability …not as another "graphic." This is particularly true in longer, more descriptive product merchandising.

Typography

Serif fonts for body copy are generally easier to read. For headlines and subheads, sans serif fonts can work well; however, it's best to save the novelty fonts for true graphics and illustrations, rather than using them in the working text of the catalog. Italic type works well for photo captions and is often ranked as more highly read than body copy describing product. Irrespective of the fonts you choose, though, beware of large blocks of reversed copy (white type on a dark background) and type that is placed over "screened" images. Both of these techniques make the copy hard to read…and if it's hard to read, chances are educators simply won't!

Don't Forget the Layout Stage

In today's desktop publishing whirlwind, it's relatively easy to produce several pages of what looks like finished catalog design in a rather short period of time. If it looks finished, it must be finished, right? Wrong! Layouts and proofs are essential parts of the catalog development process. Look at the pages individually. Look at them sequentially. Order from them. Hand them to your customer service representatives for review. The layout of a catalog can mean the difference between a tool that performs well with educators, and one that well…flops.

Catalog design is part art, part science, part analytics, and part intuition. It's also a core component of a successful school marketing program. When school starts in the fall, and when educators return from winter break, your objective is to make certain your catalog is one that's used, shared, and ordered from. Happy designing….

About the Author

Linda Winter is an Internet Monitor partner and the president of Winter Group, an award-winning marketing communications, research, and design firm focused on the education and library markets. She started Winter Group in 1978. The firm provides a comprehensive collection of integrated services to education marketers, including advertising, sales support and collateral materials, Web site development, custom market research, direct mail, catalogs, event marketing, and exhibit design. Linda received her undergraduate degree from Northwestern University and her M.A. from the University of Denver. She is a co-author of i-Tips 2000, The Insiders' Guide to School & Library Marketing, published by the Internet Monitor. She can be reached at WinterL@wintergroup.net or at (303) 778.0866, ext. 12.

CHAPTER 7

Space Advertising

Inside this chapter…

Why Advertise?

by George Halo

Doing business without advertising is like winking in the dark; you know what you're doing, but nobody else does. Advertising works, provided the correct message is placed in a visually appealing presentation and targeted to the right audience.

Critics of advertising claim that advertising is an inexact art and that it is difficult to determine its effects on a company's customers. According to this school of thought, money spent on advertising may well be spent elsewhere in product development or sales expenses where the need is more urgent.

Howard Reed, Publisher Emeritus, of *Curriculum Administrator* magazine, was the first space rep in the 1950s to sell advertising to David Packard, of Hewlett-Packard fame. Here is the story of their meeting, in Reed's own words:

"There was a great company in Massachusetts several decades ago that was the envy of every electronic test instrument manufacturer in the world. It led in sales and in quality of product and service, but did not advertise heavily.

"At about that time, a man named David Packard headed a small company that also made fine instruments, but it was comparatively new and unknown. At his tiny Palo Alto office, I showed David the classic ad run by McGraw-Hill, then the leader in business publishing. He studied it carefully and soon said, "We'll buy six pages." Within a year or two, Hewlett Packard became the electronic industry's largest test instrument advertiser and producer.

"Years later, I saw David at a convention, and recalled how much his initial purchase of advertising space had meant to me. He answered by saying that advertising helped make his salespeople more efficient. Customers knew and respected H-P products and the company long before a salesperson appeared, so when he or she arrived, closing was easier."

Branding, Branding, Branding

You may be familiar with the three very important words in real estate: Location, Location, Location. Location is key to the valuation of real estate property. A condo in New York is going to fare ten times better in the market than one in a small town like Cranford, New Jersey. Well, advertising too has its own language and its three words—Branding, Branding, Branding. In some respects, they are very similar: advertising for branding seeks to create location, location, location for products and companies, in the minds of educators.

Brand as defined by Random House College Dictionary, is (1) kind, grade, make or model as indicated by a stamp, trademark or the like (2) a mark made by burning (3) any mark of infamy, stigma. Although definitions two and three are pejorative in connotation, they capture some of the essence of branding. To brand is to burn an image into the mind of the market, altering that market fundamentally and giving it new "marks"—new reference points and new categories. Your main mission in advertising is to inform or persuade school administrators or teachers to learn about your products and to purchase them. Through this act, your product becomes branded in their minds through repeated exposure, during the long selling cycles in the K-12 education market (sometimes as long as 12 to 18 months). Advertising burns your marks into educators' minds so that they will recall your company's name and products when they're ready to buy.

Another key to effectiveness in advertising is to use mystery to develop interest and familiarity, over time. Remember the recent computer virus known as "the love bug?" Most of us were on alert for viruses at the time. Our information defense systems were deployed. Then we got an e-mail that said, "I LOVE YOU" in the subject line. What happened? We said, "Somebody out there loves me! Who is it?" And Bang! In spite of our caution and our defenses, we were taken in. There is an incredible untapped need for love out there.

"I don't know who you are.

I don't know your company.

I don't know your company's product.

I don't know what your company stands for.

I don't know your company's customers.

I don't know your company's record.

I don't know your company's reputation.

Now—what was it you wanted to sell me?"

MORAL: Sales start **before** your salesman calls—with business publication advertising.

McGRAW-HILL MAGAZINES
BUSINESS•PROFESSIONAL•TECHNICAL

So how do you capture that need as an advertiser or marketer? You need to create mystery around your brands as to why buy. And then allow the educator to fall in love with your brands. Teaser ads are very effective to help create suspense around a product launch. But it is also important to get educators involved in the product design process at the start to cement these love affairs and turn them into positive buying experiences. Don't let your customers feel that they have been duped by the promises implicit in your advertising!

Why Education Companies Love the 360-Degree Brand

The myth that schools are poor and don't have technology dollars to spend was dispelled years ago. Billions of dollars are being spent every year. American industry is responding to the education market in a big, big way. As a result, brand advertising has increased its value in a crowded market where it's both critical and difficult to capture mind and share of market. Building brand equity has become the cornerstone reason for advertising and keeping brand messages in front of key school administrators during the various buying and planning segments of long purchasing cycles.

The challenge for educational marketers is to build the 360-degree brand. This term is a code word for pervasive advertising that the educator can't ignore. To achieve it, you really need to think about all the points where an educator may come in contact with your brand offline and online. Many companies recognize the importance of integrating print advertising with trade show appearances, direct mail promotions, sales support programs and Web advertising. The most important level of integration is to create messages online and offline to dovetail with one another.

Compaq Education provides us with a great example. They have been running spreads offline in such education journals like *Curriculum Administrator* with the recent creative headline, "Not too long ago, a room full of wired kids was a bad thing." The headline grabs the attention of the school administrator to see a collection of students depicted inside the computer as learning via

instructional technology. The second page of the spread carries direct marketing copy to sell various personal computer, laptop, and server models. A Web banner online screams across www.educatorsportal.com, an education news Web site for school administrators, to direct you to their Compaq Virtual Learning Village. Once you get there, they will collect your e-mail address if you subscribe to their e-mail newsletter. Similar marketing themes coincide in their trade show booths and direct mail efforts.

The Wedding of Booth Traffic and Space Advertising

More than most other industries, education suffers from a plethora of conventions, conferences, symposiums, seminars, and meetings about meetings.

In 1993, a market research study offered an explanation for the fact that some convention booths are always crowded with customers and prospects while their competitors' exhibits have barely a soul. Exhibits Surveys, Inc. of Middletown, New Jersey conducted this report, and the results were released by McKellar Publications.

The reason for a booth's being busy or not, the research says, appears to relate to how much advertising a company does in key publications. In fact, the report gives an explicit correlation between the amount of space used by successful exhibitors with the number of people who pick up literature at their booths:

- Six-time, four-color page advertisers hand out their literature to 55% more people than non-advertisers.
- Twelve-time, four-color page advertisers average 100% more literature requests than non-advertisers.
- For every four pages of advertising, a company experiences about a 40% increase in individual literature requests.

The research also offers interesting data correlating advertising to overall booth traffic:

- Total booth visits increase for six-time advertisers by 45% over non-advertisers.
- For every four pages of advertising, there is a 30% increase in booth visitors.

> " Brand advertising has increased its value in a crowded market where it's both critical and difficult to capture mind and share of market. "

The above third-party research shows a direct correlation between booth attendance and advertising activity. Many trade magazines in the field publish special conference planners and/or produce ShowPacks where they can distribute literature for you. Taking advantage of these venues, Brother International conducted one of the most effective campaigns in memory. To tie their space ads together with their show booth; they included free ten-minute calling cards imprinted with their logos in 1,000 ShowPacks that were distributed from *Curriculum Administrator's* booth. Administrator attendees created a mob scene at the booth to grab the ShowPacks and obtain the free calling cards. And every time they used the cards, they heard a brief Brother commercial about the company's family of products for the education market.

Should Educational Marketers Advertise in a Down Economy?

When times are great, it is quite easy to justify the cost of advertising. Sales are flying high and dollars are rolling in. Advertising is seen as an important contributing factor to the company's success. If the economy turns sour, however, advertising becomes the luxury item no company can afford.

Howard Reed has another one of his famous stories to share on this subject:

"John opened a hot dog stand on a busy highway and erected dozens of costly and attractive signs north and south. The farthest sign read "10 miles to the World's Best Hot Dog." The second sign was the same except that the distance was reduced to nine miles, then eight, and so on, until the last sign read "100 yards to the World's Best Hot Dog."

"John built a fabulous business and grew rich. One day, his son, fresh out of college, told him the country was in a recession and his business was bound to suffer. Following his son's advice, John took down all the signs to save money. Soon the business failed. On the day he closed his stand for the last time, John proudly told his wife, "How smart our son has become. He said business would get worse, and it did!""

Would John have gone out of business had he continued his advertising? Think of your own situation. Is today's economy causing you to reduce your company's advertising effort?

Even if a large school district's budget is slashed 20% from $20 million to $16 million, there are still $16 million left for you or your competitors. Somebody is going to get the business, and intelligent and aggressive advertising and selling can get you a bigger piece of that pie. Smart advertising is even more critical to a company's survival in an economic recession, and companies that advertise effectively often rebound quicker than their competitors when times improve.

"Every Brand Has a Unique Personality"

David Ogilvy, the famous advertising executive of the last century, coined those famous words in his book *Ogilvy on Advertising* in 1985. His book is a great resource to check out for any advertising or marketing executive. In particular, his views on branding are important for educational marketers to consider.

In Ogilvy's analysis, the sales process can be divided into seven steps:

1. Establish contact
2. Create awareness
3. Arouse interest
4. Build product preference
5. Make specific proposals
6. Close orders
7. Keep customers sold

While personal sales contacts can best make specific proposals and close orders, trade advertising can effectively assist in each of the seven steps of the process. Here are some examples:

Establish contact. Reaching a key decision-maker through advertising wins you half the battle since many administrators can hide behind voice mail and e-mail systems.

Create awareness. You can announce new district volume purchase plan as a price advantage)

Arouse interest. Bell Atlantic once generated 300 business reply cards from a single black-white-page ad with a business reply card for their free E-rate booklet.

Build company preference. Pioneer advertised with informational pieces to help them dominate the market for laserdisc players in K-12 education.

Build brand preference. Apple Computer was very successful in the mid-1980s in building strong grass roots awareness among teachers for Apple IIs.

Keep customers sold. You can use ads to reinforce purchases made by school buyers as the right choices.

Advertising may never be a science where you invest a set number of ad dollars to yield a specific return on your investment. However, advertising can provide low-cost exposure to educators throughout the selling process and enhance your sales performance in the education market. Since purchasing cycles are long in education, holding the hands of educational buyer every step of the way is essential to your company's success. Advertising is one ingredient in your sales and marketing recipe and can make a good campaign in the same way that good cheese makes a good pizza. Certainly advertising and the pizza man have one goal in common—both need to deliver results.

About the Author

George Halo *is national sales manager with* District Administration, *formerly* Curriculum Administrator *magazine, the leading curriculum and technology magazine serving the K-12 public education market. He has sold advertising for several education trade publications for 14 years. He lives with his wife, three daughters, and two dogs in Linden, New Jersey. He is a direct descendant of Captain James Lawrence who was fatally wounded in the War of 1812 and who gave us the US Navy motto: "Don't Give Up The Ship!" A rare lithograph of this famous battle, depicting Lawrence's death on board the ship, hangs on George's office wall to motivate him. He tries to live up to his ancestor's creed daily. He can be reached at his Cranford, NJ office by phone at (908) 276-1432 or by e-mail at* GHALO5212@aol.com.

Stop-In-Your-Tracks Visibility with Specialty Promotions

by Marilyn Schutz

What Is a Specialty Promotion?

Spe-cial-ty (spesh' ∂l t_), *adj.* a product of a special kind or of a special excellence.

Pro-mo-tion (pr∂ m_' sh∂n), *n.* the act of furthering the growth or development of something.

A specialty promotion can be like the deepest décolletage at the party. It gets a lot of attention and it can work to initiate a long-term relationship. While the K-12 education market is a lot less provocative, marketers are increasingly looking for ways to distinguish their products from the growing number of often-similar products with which they compete. "Most forms of product differentiation can be offset or copied by competitors in a very short period of time," says integrated marketing pioneer Don Schultz; thus one of the ways companies can distinguish products is through the innovativeness and customization of their communications with customers.[1]

One publisher comments, "Marketers in just about every industry have experienced the same thing—incredible competition, information overload and waning effectiveness of traditional marketing elements."[2] K-12 education has not been immune to this phenomenon.

Enter specialty promotions. In K-12 education, specialty promotions may take a variety of formats. These may look like magazines, newsletters, special reports, or books. They may be videos, audio tapes, or CD-ROMs. They may be multimedia kits, downloadable intranet or Internet newsletters, or two companies' products bundled together. What all specialty promotions represent are unique modes of communicating with a targeted audience in pursuit of marketing goals and in support of an integrated plan. They creatively use media to build and sustain relationships with identified groups of customers and prospects. They are customized and designed to set themselves apart from standard media. Specialty promotions are intended to reach smaller, more targeted audiences defined by interest areas, position, geography, and so on. Effective specialty promotions are relationship building in their focus, and they create value for the customer. They can be customized communications with the help of a periodical publisher. They can be developed internally.

Or they can be developed with the assistance of external resources.

According to an MPA survey in 1999, marketers are increasingly looking at custom communications as direct marketing vehicles "that enhance the ongoing relationship between themselves and their customers." Technology is the driver. It has allowed marketers and media organizations to identify, segment, select and attract smaller, more attentive and focused audiences for their audio, video and print vehicles. One direct mail specialist for the publishing industry says, "Targeted marketing coupled with custom publishing changed the rules of marketing by proving that it's more important to reach the people who count than to count the people you reach."[3] And the way to reach them is through customized communications that soar above traditional venues.

Gaining Attention Requires Increasing Effort

"As the number of message senders increase and the number of messages they attempt to send multiplies, the confusion in the marketplace grows," notes Don Schultz.[4] And educational research confirms this reality. In one 1998 telephone survey of K-12 educators, 61% of teacher respondents said that they received too much mail, too often, getting an average of 40 pieces per month. And only 19% said they had received a memorable piece of education-related direct mail in the preceding 12 months.[5]

As marketers, we know that it takes six to 10 contacts before we can make a sale. So what do we do? A customized specialty promotion can often be the glue that binds an entire marketing program or initiative together and gets the stop-in-your-tracks attention we need.

"How Will a Specialty Promotion Impact My Sales?"

The tendency in educational marketing is to measure all media by their direct production of sales. By this definition, marketers should give up everything but direct mail and salespeople. But the building of relationships is also critical, and relationships are central to the concept of specialty promotion. Don Schultz notes that "the marketer must be truly interested in developing customers and prospects. Short-term, get-rich-quick approaches simply won't work in a truly integrated program. Building trust may be more important than gaining market share. Building a relationship may be more vital in the long term than increasing profits in the short term. The critical ingredient is the long-term relationship built through various forms of communication."[6] Specialty promotions are not necessarily trackable in themselves. They are value-added components of your overall marketing plan. You should devise ways to assess their effectiveness before undertaking them, but direct, immediate sales are not likely to provide the most appropriate measuring stick.

NINE GOOD REASONS TO GIVE SPECIALTY PROMOTIONS THE NOD

Any form of custom communication requires a commitment of dollars, time and human resources. That's why many marketers have turned to trusted publishers or to outsourcing professionals to help them brainstorm, develop—and often distribute—these pieces. Not only will these professionals undertake the creative development of custom promotions; they'll often be able to find appropriate partners with whom to share costs as well.

The reasons to embrace specialty promotions as an ongoing part of marketing and sales plans are many and compelling: A specialty promotion offers the opportunity to:

1. Drive brand awareness.
2. Control your marketing message, without competition, in what you consider an optimum environment.
3. Target that portion of your database related to what it is you sell.
4. Initiate dialog and interaction with customers.
5. Reinforce the perceptions of current customers toward your company.
6. Develop long-term relationships with prospects.
7. Establish your company as an innovator in a particular area.
8. Direct customers to your Web site.
9. Support your sales staff in its ongoing interaction with customers.

A "Win-Win"... Both Marketers and Educators Benefit from Specialty Promotions

Specialty promotions are not new in the K-12 marketing arena. However in the last decade the availability of technology to more carefully define audiences, the desire to build relationships with customers, and the need for companies to distinguish themselves from other providers of competing products and services, have all turned marketers' attention toward more customized communications. Here's a look at some K-12 examples of specialty promotions that have benefited all involved—true win-wins.

A textbook company regains its lead and changes the way its category is sold.

In 1990, D.C. Heath & Company was no longer the leading elementary mathematics publisher; rather it was number three. However, it was developing a new program (*Heath Mathematics Connections*) which would align with the new National Council of Teachers of Mathematics (NCTM) standards. These standards were somewhat controversial at the time, not necessarily dovetailing with many of the existing state standards. For instance, they did not mirror Texas's standards. In a bold move, D.C. Heath chose not to enter the Texas math adoption. Instead, it focused on developing a math program that would use the new NCTM standards as the backbone of its curriculum. To kick off a two-year marketing effort, D.C. Heath, with the help of periodical publishing professionals, set out to create a special promotion that would be the centerpiece of its marketing effort. *Making The Case for Math,* a special report in magazine format, was the result.

This teacher-friendly piece used the language of the classroom to interpret what the new standards meant in terms of everyday teaching and learning. It included interviews with real teachers and laid the groundwork for what teachers should expect. Contributors to D.C. Heath's new program wrote many of the articles. Keith Garton, director of marketing at D.C. Heath at the time, and now publisher of Time School Publishing, says, *"Making the Case for Math* became a very powerful marketing tool. We received thousands of requests for copies. NCTM itself requested thousands. Teachers were invited to send us their comments, and D.C. Heath editors responded to each of the hundreds of letters received. This was important to us in strengthening our relationships with educators." Further, the piece was presented in workshops as a workbook to assist school districts in writing the language for their own curricula based on the new standards.

D.C. Heath waited one year to sell its program. But in the interim it told educators, through *Making the Case for Math,* as well as in workshops and through salespeople, "Wait to purchase your math program. Wait until you find one that reflects the new standards." The end result was that hundreds of districts delayed their purchasing decisions, and D.C. Heath was the first publisher to market with a series based on the new NCTM standards. The company regained its number one position in the next two years.

A technology company makes up for lost time and relies on the credibility of a trusted ally.

Technology & Learning Magazine offers marketers the opportunity to sponsor a value-added CD-ROM, *The Best of the Best*. It provides demos of the winners of its Annual Software Awards of Excellence. The CD-ROMs are polybagged and sent to *T&L*'s 80,000 circulation as well as distributed at targeted technology conferences. Most recently, Apple Computer sponsored the awards to achieve a number of marketing goals—to support the software developers with which it worked and wished to work; to reaffirm its commitment to the K-12 market; and to align itself with excellence in education technology. *Technology & Learning* publisher, Jo-Ann McDevitt, points to the high market acceptance of this promotion not only from Apple, but also from subscribers. Said one technology educator, "This is just what I've needed to show teachers some of the newest software on the market. It will give us the chance to discuss what will be useable in their classrooms." A state technology director added, "What a great tool! If possible, I'd like 25 more copies. I'll be sharing it with my county technology coordinators at our next meeting. One item on the agenda is connecting with resources and tools to support the integration of technology tools with instruction. Software shopping is high on our list of things to do."

Companies look to an established voice to educate the communities they serve.

Cable In the Classroom magazine created and customized *Better Viewing,* a parent guide, for two major cable operators—Media One and Suburban Cable. Advertising director Nina Bohn says, "The companies wanted to help people, especially parents, understand that TV could be used effectively if managed correctly. This was a powerful way to support media literacy and to build relationships with their customers. And it was a hands-on tool for parents confused by offerings available to their children." Publications were customized for each of the operators with a logo on the cover and a dedicated news page. Operators distributed the guides to customers directly at community events and as part of their marketing packages.

A telecom giant provides critical information to an important market while gaining exclusive visibility in its region.

In the late 90s, telecoms aggressively pursued K-12 schools, offering them a variety of technology products and services, including Internet access. Ameritech, the leading telecom in Illinois, Wisconsin, Michigan, Ohio, and Indiana, demonstrated its commitment to K-12 education by providing customized copies of the fall issue of *The Big Deal Book of Technology* for three consecutive years. The publication reached 55,000 administrators and technology coordinators in the five-state region. Understanding that school and district budgets were increasingly tight, Ameritech wanted to provide a resource which would give educators access to grant opportunities, free materials and equipment, Web sites, and training programs without having to develop these resource itself. It also wanted to strengthen its relationships with state educational organization such as the Michigan Association of School Administrators, Illinois Computing Educators, Buckeye Association of School Administrators, and so on. It turned to *The Big Deal Book* to create a customized version for each state. The customization took the form of Ameritech and non-profit logos on the cover, an introductory letter from both state organizations on page one, and six pages of ads presenting the company's products, services, and special programs offered to educators and parents.

The publication was partially supported by ads from non-competitive companies. Ads ran as two-sided, perforated pages that could be used as direct response vehicles. Marketers benefited from the significant distribution added to the nationwide distribution, and participated in a vehicle that provided both a long shelf life and a direct-response medium. Ameritech gained an innovative branding opportunity, a stick-out-in-the-crowd, value-added premium and a relationship-strengthener with an important identified market. In addition, it received valuable research from a mail-back questionnaire.

Regional educators responded enthusiastically. A Wisconsin technology coordinator wrote: "In two recent years we spent $225,000 annually to upgrade technology. We have one more 'big' year ahead of us to get ourselves into the 21st century. *The Big Deal Book of Technology* is an invaluable contribution to that goal." And a Michigan principal wrote, "I put the book to use the minute I opened it. Our technology committee loves it!"

A textbook company introduces a new program, applauds its current customers, reaches out to new prospects and keeps its sales staff wanting more.

When Open Court Publishing sought to introduce a new reading program, it created *Success Connections: Linking Authors, Educators, Students and Resources*. This was a series of eight-page, 11" x 14" newsletters that presented interviews with the authors of the new program and spotlighted the stories of educators who had achieved significant classroom success with current Open Court programs. The newsletter also included a pullout poster and hands-on ideas for classroom use. Issues of *Success Connections* were sent to identified customers via mail, hand-delivered by salespersons to customers and prospects at schools, and used in workshops. Salespeople found using the voices of customers to communicate with their prospects to be a strong and sought-after sales-support tool.

Where to Start in Creating an Excellent Specialty Promotion

You want to distinguish your products and services from all the others available out there with an innovative, eye-catching, why-didn't-I-think-of-that customized communication. Here are twelve questions to explore. Before proceeding, you should determine:

1. What specific marketing issues/problems it will solve.
2. What group of customers or prospects you want to reach.
3. What kind of relationship you want to build with your customers. (Do you want to generate leads, generate sales, build brand awareness, provide information, or introduce new products or services?)
4. Whether this promotion will dovetail with your current marketing plan or serve as the centerpiece to a new program.
5. Who are the best brains to brainstorm with, both inside and outside of your organization. (Ask them about their experiences—the positives and the pitfalls.)
6. Whether to execute your objectives from scratch or to seek an alliance with another organization to meet your goals.
7. How you want customers to respond and what kind of information you want from them.
8. Whether you have sufficient internal resources (time, money and people) to commit to the promotion. (Who will actually execute the promotion and drive it forward?)
9. How you will pay for the promotion. (Are you able to tap current budget categories? Are you able to partner with other departments, subsidiaries, or marketers to help absorb costs?)
10. Whether it's more cost effective to turn to outside resources.
11. How the outcome will be assessed.
12. What internal cooperation will be needed to ensure success.

■

[1] *The New Marketing Paradigm*. Don Schultz, Stanley Tannenbaum, Robert Lauterborn, NTC Business Books, Lincolnwood, IL 1994. p 19
[2] *Something To Shout About* by the Custom Publishing Council, Magazine Publishers of America, October, 1999.
[3] *Something to Shout About*.
[4] *What Educators Think of Your Mail*, Marketing Projects, Inc., June 1998
[5] Schultz, Tannenbaum, and Lauterborn, p.44.
[6] Schultz, Tannenbaum, and Lauterborn, . p. 154.

■

About the Author

Marilyn Schutz is president of Marketing Projects, Inc., an Illinois-based marketing communications organization. The company works with publishers, associations, and corporations seeking to reach educators, students, and parents with a wide range of marketing activities including qualitative and quantitative research, focus groups, sales support, catalog and direct mail development, school outreach programs, Web content development, and advertising sales. Marketing Projects, Inc. also publishes The Big Deal Book for K-6 Educators and The Big Deal Book of Technology for K-12 Educators (www.bigdealbook.com), as well as a biweekly, e-mail newsletter for administrators and teachers. Marilyn can be reached at maschutz@aol.com or by calling (800) 650-0034.

Stand out from the Crowd:
Creative Ways to Get Your Marketing Message Across

by Jo-Ann McDevitt

Education professionals respond to marketers who demonstrate a commitment to meeting their needs. Print advertising is one way to communicate this commitment, but it's not the only one. To get your message across with the greatest impact, you sometimes need a more dramatic approach. Converting prospects into loyal, long-term customers often requires a more focused and controlled strategy than traditional advertising offers. As you develop your marketing strategy, consider printed inserts as part of your marketing mix. They can be cost effective, increase sales, and even save you money. Inserts comprise a broad range of innovative marketing vehicles and creative materials. This article will introduce a number of them for your consideration.

The Power of Marketing with Inserts

Research shows that inserts are the most cost-effective method of putting literature into the hands of prospective buyers. A survey by Cahner's Research found that inserts received 58% higher "Remember Seeing" scores than regular full-run ads. One computer software advertiser used three catalog inserts in a leading computer publication during a two-year period and charted a 400% increase in sales.

Another company found that inserts ranging from 8 to 20 pages generated a 43.6% overall rate of removal (the rate at which readers took the catalog out of the publication for future use). When the company calculated the cost of advertising versus the cost of direct mail, they found that it cost an average of only $2.80 per respondent to distribute the catalog via magazine advertising versus $10.40 for direct mail.

READERSHIP RESPONSES TO INSERTS VERSUS TRADITIONAL TYPES OF PRINT ADVERTISING.

Advertising Readership Median "Noted" Scores

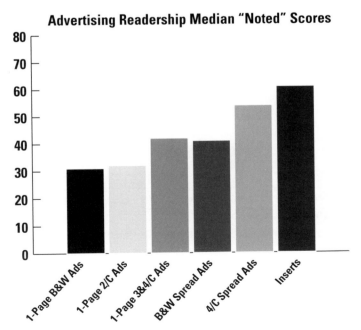

Source: ACT Reports, Technical Publishing Co.

WHEN TO CHOOSE AN INSERT

Here are situations when you should consider an insert for getting your message across with the most impact:

You have a new product launch. You need a creative way to demystify, unveil, or simply explain your new product or technology.

Your company is changing course. You want to explain that change at length.

You are a new company entering the education market. You want to show that you are a serious entrant in the field.

Your company is celebrating a milestone or event. You need an environment to showcase your achievements or show how the product you've developed revolutionizes the industry.

You need to boost sales from existing customers. You want to maintain customer loyalty even after the sale is made in order to validate that they have made the right decision by doing business with you.

You want to promote new partnership initiatives with other companies in the market.

You want to create awareness and change market perceptions. You need a venue to generate visibility and influence the opinions of the education audience.

You want to promote your trade show activities.

You need to improve your company's image or achieve a new level of visibility in the market.

Your management has just set an extremely aggressive sales goal.

You haven't advertised in quite some time and you want to let everyone know you're not only alive, but on top of the world.

Readership studies have also found that inserts have a higher readership response rate than any type of conventional ad (as measured by "Noted" scores in surveys).

The remainder of this article suggests ways of using various types of inserts to make a one-of-a-kind impact on your audience.

Types of Insert

The most effective types of inserts can be grouped into two categories:

- Supplements, and
- Pre-printed inserts and outserts

Supplements

Supplements use common magazine formats to present ideas and products to readers, in a setting that disposes them to accept your message.

Custom Supplements. These can be a great way to establish a dialogue with your customers, to create and maintain relationships, and to deliver your message to your targets. Just like any magazine, a custom supplement has a glossy, heavy stock cover and a distinctive design with editorial features written by recognized writers. It can be polybagged with a magazine or distributed as a stand-alone. The topic of the editorial is typically a "hot button" in education. It can have an editorial focus that relates to the products of the sponsoring company, but this does not have to be the case. There are a number of ways a supplement can reach your target audience. It can be distributed to magazine subscribers or to mailing lists of customers or potential customers, or it can be distributed at trade show booths at major education conferences.

Special Advertising Supplements. Often referred to as "advertorials", special supplements provide a way for your company and products to gain visibility in a single-theme editorial environment. You get exposure to the magazine's audience in an exclusive section clearly marked with your company's name.

Benefits Supplements Offer You

Supplements of either type offer you a range of benefits, including:

- Excellent exposure
- An opportunity to build goodwill and provide an educational service for readers.
- Long shelf life
- A use as collateral for sales team
- Timely
- Targeted circulations
- The ability to coordinate messages with key meetings and conventions

Pre-Printed Inserts and Outserts

Polybagged or tipped into a publication, pre-printed inserts give you another means for additional exposure and impact. Some examples are:

Catalogs. Your company catalog—or a condensed version of it—can be tipped into a magazine or polybagged. Note: you cannot have a postal indicia on material inserted in a magazine. If it's polybagged, you will pay an additional "ride along" fee—at the third-class postal rate.

Brochures. This is a multipaged piece of product or company collateral that showcases your company or a particular product line.

BRCs (Business Reply Cards). Inserted next to your ad in a magazine, these can provide an efficient call to action response mechanism for special offers.

Posters, Wall Charts, Calendars. Educators love them, especially if they provide useful tips and creative ideas for the classroom. These items are often polybagged (if they are 25% editorial and align with the host magazine's content), but they can be inserted as well. They are displayed in schools for several months and are often used again year after year.

CD-ROMs. Polybagged with a magazine, a CD-ROM sampler is an effective "gift" for giving educators first-hand demo experience with your products and company. A CD can provide a product sampler, demonstrations, or materials to support professional development or training.

Customized Classroom Materials. These, too can be polybagged or bound in a magazine. They offer a unique way to distribute teaching aids for classroom use labeled with your company's name, giving you vast exposure to teachers and students.

Cover Wraps. This is a cover "outside" the magazine cover on lighter paper stock printed with your advertising message.

French Gatefolds. Here, the magazine cover splits down the center, which opens up to your ad or marketing message.

Post-It Notes. You can attach a 2" x 2" sticker with an additional message.

Pop-Ups. This is a four-page insert with a sample "pop-up" between pages two and three.

Bellybands. These six-inch paper bands which wrap around a publication with your company's advertising message are a great way to get noticed at a trade show and draw traffic to your booth. Bellybands also can be mailed to the entire magazine circulation.

So How Do You Pay for These Great Ideas?

Often you need creative financing to fund these special projects and ideas. Funding sources can be allocated from a variety of departmental budgets, including:

- Advertising
- Product Management
- Marketing
- Corporate Communications
- Partner Co-Op Programs

These suggestions are proven ways to maximize your visibility in the market place and boost sales. But they are just a starting point for your marketing campaign. With imagination and creative thinking, the possibilities are endless.

RED FLAG ALERT

Postal regulations apply if you have a supplement polybagged and mailed with a publication as a "ride along." Publishers must follow post office regulations to qualify as second-class postage. The phrase "supplement to the magazine" should be printed on the cover and there should be an editorial well of at least 25% that fits with the editorial content of the host magazine. Also, magazines should adhere to the guidelines of the American Society for Editors and Publishers. These guidelines specify that advertising sections and sponsored sections should be clearly identified as such on each page.

About the Author

Jo-Ann McDevitt *is publisher of* Technology & Learning *magazine and of the Web site,* techLEARNING.com. *Owned by CMP Media, the Technology & Learning Network offers a variety of creative marketing opportunities for education technology companies. For more information on the magazine, the Web site, or Technology & Learning events, please visit* www.techLEARNING.com.

Assuming Leadership and Creating Mind Share: Special Reports and Custom Publications

by Marina Leight

Marketing is in the process of reinventing itself. Hundreds of books and articles have been written about the converging roles of marketing, sales, and public relations. Companies are encouraged to have "focus," create positioning, and integrate their strategies. What does this mean to the company doing business in the education market, and what strategies lead to results with educators?

To succeed in selling to the education market, your company must identify ways to create "entrance points" for initiating contact with decision-makers. Special reports and custom publishing create an excellent point of entry. Technology is a growing budget item for universities as well as the K-12 market. Information technology decision-makers need information and spend time reading articles, magazines, and even advertisements to better understand infrastructure, curriculum, hardware, and software. In this environment, special reports and custom-published pieces can play a particularly influential role. Because they provide information in a neutral way and can be shared amongst many decision-makers, these publications can both help decision makers to learn about key issues and support the sales efforts of vendors.

"Technology is transforming choice and choice is transforming the marketplace. As a result, we are witnessing the emergence of a new marketing paradigm—not a "do more" marketing that simply turns up the volume on the sales spiels of the past, but a knowledge and experience-based marketing…"[1]

When Regis McKenna, who has written and lectured extensively on the social and market effects of technological change, said this a decade ago, he set the stage for what he called the Age of the Customer—a phenomenon that has been renamed over and over during the '90s as the Information Age, the Experience Economy, the Digital Era, and so on. As a technology company doing business in the education market, you should be helping educators understand the transformational nature of the times we live in. It is also important to realize that custom publications can be used to build a relationship with readers by demonstrating an understanding of the special dynamics that characterize the education space.

The Dynamics of the Market

How does a market behave? A marketplace by definition is made up of buyers and sellers. Big business has already figured out that education is big business, but the education community itself is still coming to terms with the idea that it is a consumer of technology. "Partnership" means different things to businesses and their education customers. Businesses that use special reports and custom publishing in this market to clearly define what their company means by partnership will have an advantage in selling to educators. Businesses that simply invest in traditional sales collateral and bulk mail as a means to boost revenues miss out on opportunities for creating a long-term impact. Education executives need information and resources to base their decisions on; they do not readily adopt the latest and greatest gadgets or services that technology has to offer. Education is a wonderful place to be innovative, but marketing professionals must be aware that marketing on "Internet time" and expecting Internet-time results will be disappointing.

"Education institutions want the companies to slow down, while the companies feel nothing but pressure to keep moving ahead. The bottom line is that the education community needs to get beyond the denial and admit it is a market so it can behave like one," says Peter Stokes, executive vice president for Eduventures.com.[2]

Many education executives are part of the "public sector," which makes them answerable to different constituencies. They spend tax and/or grant dollars, which makes them accountable to taxpayers, parents, foundations, and federal and/or state agencies. Special reports need to remember that the bottom line in education is the student. This can present a challenge to marketing, advertising, and public relations teams. Your marketing and positioning must address the educator's bottom line, which is not only composed of dollars and cents, but also of student achievement and the educational experience.

The digital education marketplace is very young. It is still in a developmental stage with a lot of activity in the market. Companies are entering and exiting the space at a phenomenal pace. This is good news for companies who strategically integrate their marketing strategies to address the dynamics of selling to educators.

Even though this is a time of great innovation and entrepreneurial spirit, the educational arena is complex and burdened with day-to-day administrative functions like student management, busing, food, and athletics. In the minds of many administrators, this complexity is only compounded by the addition of technology and the need to learn how to use it effectively. Accordingly, companies should use the extra space that custom publishing offers by showing education executives not only the "new things" they can do but also the old things they can "stop" doing by deploying new products or services. As companies work toward helping educators transform education, their marketing strategies should also be reflective of an appreciation for the field of education and a passion for learning.

Another point to make about this market is that the education community is not traditionally known to be quick in adopting new ways of doing things. To illustrate this, Clark Kerr said in the Carnegie Commission's 1994 Policy Perspective:

"Taking, as a starting point, 1530, when the Lutheran Church was founded, some 66 institutions that existed then still exist today in the Western World in recognizable form: The Catholic Church, the Lutheran Church, the parliaments of Iceland and the Isle of Man, and 62 universities..."[3]

Eliot Levinson, CEO of the BLE Group, a Washington, D.C.-based management consulting firm and the co-founder of LearnCity, a Web-based accountability solution, recently compared the education market both to an oil tanker and to lemmings. In his column, "Tech From the Top," he wrote, "Introducing new products into education is like turning an oil tanker—the process is slow and usually accompanied by inertia and resistance. Conversely, once a critical mass of school systems adopts a new method for doing things, the others follow like lemmings running into the sea."[4]

In order for your company to come out a clear winner in this market, you must take a leadership position. Special reports and custom publishing, when used well, are effective in educating the market and will gain market share for your company.

Building Relationships and Educating the Market

The high level of activity and excitement in the education technology arena creates confusion. Special reports give the private sector an opportunity to clarify uses of technology in carefully crafted editorials. They also provide opportunities to share successes, demystify technology, and help educators begin to develop technology strategies for their jurisdictions.

American Business Media reported in a white paper that "when done right, custom publishing can be very profitable and can actually help build a strong relationship between the customer and the corporation."[5]

Building relationships with the education community and creating a better understanding about technology are key roles that a special report can play. Lewis Rhodes, former associate executive director of the American Association of School Administrators, said, "The fragmented use of technology in schools today undermines the ability to understand and create value."[6] However, when a company takes the time to provide information in a non-sales-oriented manner, a basic foundation for a relationship is created. Educators are not looking to be sold, they are looking for solutions, and they are looking for partners. A custom-published piece can be used as a bridge for the kinds of relationships your company needs in order to do business in education. Additionally, this type of collateral can solidify relationships by offering a platform to elevate and draw attention to a particular project or to highlight the leadership and efforts of a particular education executive.

The Buzz: Creating or Building a Brand

Branding is about creating singularity and differentiation. Custom publishing gives you the room to build that impression and reinforce it. What makes your company, product, or service strong, unique, and the best choice? Your investment in this type of marketing also provides an opportunity to create new categories in the market, positioning you as a leader.

At the same time, you are also providing supportive, anecdotal information to help drive funding for technology projects in the education market. There is a lot of confusion and misunderstanding about the benefits of technology for schools and universities. The more information provided to the academic space (especially research-driven data), the more likely funding will occur for technology oriented projects.

In *The 22 Immutable Laws of Branding*, Al and Laura Ries describe the law of publicity. "Today brands are born, not made. A brand must be capable of generating favorable publicity in the media or it won't have a chance in the marketplace."[7] Use your special report to create this kind of critical buzz and publicity. In 1976, Anita Roddick of the Body Shop built a company around natural cosmetics that were environmentally friendly. She boomed the company by generating an enormous amount of press.

Education technology marketing teams have the best of both worlds, working in a market naturally attracting media attention. Between education being a top domestic issue and the role technology is playing in transforming education, there has been no better time for a well-crafted special report to capture attention.

Position your company as first. Be the first to measure results, the first to show impact, the first to turn a low-performing school around, or the first technology project on a university campus, and watch the media sit up and take notice of you. The media wants to cover what is edgy, new, or about to happen; everybody likes to hear about the next "new thing."

The Bottom Line is Always the Bottom Line

At first, outsourced custom publishing projects might appear expensive to a company. In actuality, however, the quantitative and qualitative economics make sense.

From a quantitative perspective, take an à la carte look at what is involved in the production of a custom-published piece: there is editorial content (the hiring of writers), a creative design element, the production unit (cost of paper, printing and someone to facilitate the project), postage costs, list rental or insertion costs and other hidden staff costs. Moreover, outsourcing complex projects like this makes it more likely that it will:

1. Actually get produced. (These are notoriously the kinds of projects that take the back burner and don't get done.)

2. Come in on time and on budget.

3. Incorporate an editorial perspective that will resonate in the market.

Since it is a published product, creative feedback mechanisms can be built in. Independent reader surveys can be conducted or special Web sites can be created to measure the piece's impact and effectiveness.

An American Business Media Association's white paper suggests another value for this type of publishing. It argues, "Corporate publications are also an excellent way to perform market research directly with customers in the form of reader response cards, information requests from readers and subscription forms. One publisher cites an example where an issue of a publication he produced continued to receive about 50 inquiries per month, even three years after the original publication. Another publication received more than 6,000 responses from dozens of countries."

Finally, in your cost-benefit analysis, remember that this type of piece will have multiple uses for your company. It will be used for public relations purposes (creating a buzz), it will position your product (a marketing function), and it will be used to create dialogue, build relationships and educate the market (supporting your sales team). Since all three groups within your organization will benefit from the piece, portions of all three budgets can be combined to pay for its production; everybody's budget is maximized.

From a qualitative perspective, people spend more time reading special reports than advertisements—your special report's message will be reviewed carefully and thoughtfully. Additionally, these types of publications are frequently passed around (pass-along rates of eight times are not uncommon); they are used to share ideas and build support for technology projects. The piece will generate an audience that becomes engaged in the concept of what you are presenting. It will capture the audience that is already predisposed to your message and the word of mouth in the market will follow.

A Checklist

There are many ways your company can capitalize on the power of a published special report or custom piece. Consider sponsoring a piece that covers topics around your company's products and services and position a corporate profile or fresh creative along with it. Or use the piece to highlight success stories from your company.

As your marketing, sales, and public relations teams begin to brainstorm the use of a special report or custom published piece for your company, they should consider the following questions:

- How can this piece differentiate us in the market?
- What are the successful applications of our product or service that we believe can be replicated across the country? The world?
- Who are the education leaders that could be highlighted?
- Would a before-and-after format be effective? Or a sequential story?
- How about a "makeover" format (a story where your company really transformed a campus or classroom)?
- What type of publicity opportunities could the piece support?
- How can this piece inspire action?
- How does our company make a difference for education executives?

In Conclusion

Education executives use a variety of resources to become educated about technology. When decisions are being made in boardrooms, classrooms, district offices, or the president's office, a stand-alone informative piece that can be read, passed around, shared, and used as presentation material will further build the case for technology in education. You will build a competitive advantage for your company and secure your role as a leader in this market space through the use of a special report or custom-published piece.

[1] Regis McKenna. *Relationship Marketing*, Addison Wesley, 1991.
[2] Victor Rivero and Michele Norman. *"Visions 2001"* Converge, January 2001.
[3] Clark Kerr. *Policy Perspective*. Carnegie Commission, 1994.
[4] Eliot Levinson and Barbara Grohe. *"Tech From the Top"* Converge, May 2001.
[5] Lee Clontz. *Custom Publishing and Advertorials as Brand Extensions: Partnering With Advertisers*. December 1998.
[6] Victor Rivero and Michele Norman. *"Visions 2001"* Converge, January 2001.
[7] Al Ries and Laura Ries. *The 22 Immutable Laws of Branding: How to Build a Product or Service into a World-Class Brand*. Harper-Collins 1998.

About the Author

Marina Leight *is the publisher for* Converge Magazine, *an award winning national publication designed to foster and inspire leadership for technology in education. Converge's parent company, e.Republic has specialized in public sector technology topics for nearly twenty years through its publications, conferences and research division. Prior to joining Converge, Marina worked as the executive director for Government Technology's executive forums managing strategic relationships and facilitating dialogue between private and public sector executives. Marina can be reached at* mleight@convergemag.com *or (916) 363-5000.*

CHAPTER 8
Public Relations

Inside this chapter…

Reviews and Awards

by Charlene F. Gaynor

"The only thing worse than being talked about is not being talked about." More than 100 years after he said it, Oscar Wilde's catch phrase still brings sweat to a marketer's brow. That's because in today's competitive marketplace, grabbing your 15 minutes of fame is an imperative. Creating or building brand equity means getting recognized—preferably in a positive way.

The most direct, efficient path to positive recognition is thrusting your product before the public in one of two ways: by entering it for consideration in prestigious awards programs; or by submitting it for critical review in widely read publications. The awards route is, by far, the safer of the two. Because you prepare the entry, you have some control over how the product gets presented. And if your product doesn't win, there's no risk of negative publicity, as there is with reviews. (No reputable awards program releases its list of losers.)

Both strategies have the potential to generate quantifiable sales as well as priceless publicity. Indeed, good press is literally priceless—and unlike paid advertising, it doesn't carry the stigma of self-promotion. Both awards and reviews can provide intangible benefits as well—like affirmation of a job well done or actionable feedback from the market. Using awards or reviews effectively as part of an overall marketing plan calls for one part skill, one part mechanics, and one part serendipity. Here are some guidelines to keep in mind.

Awards: Lifting Spirits and Sales

Because the financial boon that awaits the winners is so substantial, many publishers reorganize their production runs to coincide with the calendar for the big awards. The value of a mention from the Oppenheim Toy Portfolio judges on The Today Show or of a Caldecott award from the American Library Association is arguably beyond calculation. Being named an Oprah Book Club selection is said to guarantee a book's place on the bestseller list. (Each of these distinctions now generates a special display in most bookstores, too.) "These awards are like the Oscars," says Bob Harper, formerly of Carus Publishing and now president of the LeapFrog Learning Club. "They can generate big sales."

This is true, too, of awards that don't have a high profile among consumers, but that are nonetheless highly respected in the education community. When a product is mentioned as an award winner in a top educators' magazine, for instance, the contact person listed can expect his or her telephone to start ringing with interested customers on the other end of the line. And in an environment of increasingly well informed consumers, these accolades can have a double impact—influencing both direct sales to teachers and librarians, and "referral" purchases by parents who follow their lead. Marketers so value the iconic power of an award logo to set their products apart from the pack that some actually have created their own ribbon-and-stamp designs just to emit that "winning" illusion.

Winning a prestigious award has intangible internal benefits, too. For instance, it can be a great boost to the morale and motivation of your creative staff. Moreover, even a disappointing outcome can have its rewards, in the form of feedback. Comments from judges can provide invaluable insights to guide future product development. For example, one entry for the Association of Educational Publishers' Distinguished Achievement Awards for Instructional Materials received rave reviews for its content. But one of the judges—a teacher—knocked it out of the running because the product was just slightly too big to fit inside a standard student desk. This sent a clear and valuable message to the product development team.

Which Ones...

Of course, there are many awards to choose from. The time and expense of applying make it important to pick the right ones. So how do you decide? First, do the obvious: weigh the expense and the labor involved in applying against the chances that you would win. One way to form an opinion of the award's stature is to examine the list of judges. The most established awards generally will be judged by the greatest concentration of industry heavyweights. Check to see who's involved: are these the names you hear mentioned or see regularly in the trade press? Also consider the process the judges will pursue in making their decisions: how thorough a review do they make?

Pay careful attention to the categories and criteria. Do the criteria named as the most important in judging entries match the priorities that you identified in developing your product? A reputable program balances strict criteria with fair and flexible judging. Before you submit, don't be afraid to call up and ask questions that can help you understand the program philosophy. For example, if an entry is submitted in the wrong category, will it be disqualified or moved? Finally, ask to see a list of previous winners. If your competitor's name is on the list, go for it.

Finally, consider the "reach" of the award. New prizes constantly present themselves, especially in fast-growing areas. But if and when you win an established contest, it can yield a good return without much added work by publicists to "spin" its significance. The main thing is that you pursue the kind of recognition that will support your larger marketing goals. Kati Elliott of KEH Communications offers this example: "Companies that want to gain visibility outside their niche should consider an award in a larger category—for instance, the New York Festivals, which cover a variety of awards from television and print advertising to software programs." So, if you're trying to attract new investments or you're considering going public, an award from outside your current industry may be just the thing. On the other hand, if you are looking to establish a brand position within your niche, a different choice might be appropriate.

...and When?

For a company whose product is just hitting the launch pad, awards, and reviews are particularly important (more on reviews, below). Of course, marketers will want to make individual contacts, putting the product on the desks of top individual "influencers" (recognized media, scholars, and other important individuals within the education community). But consider the greater efficiency of the award approach, which provides you the opportunity to present your product to assembled groups of experts who actually have set aside time to evaluate it.

A new product generally will collect evidence of its effectiveness through beta launches and pilot studies. But that route to success stories, based on both anecdotes and hard data from school customers who pioneer the product, is an evolutionary process that often develops very slowly. According to Kathryn Allen, vice president of sales and marketing at LeapFrog SchoolHouse,

"Awards are a way to show potential customers immediately that a product is recognized as important." For her company's *Leap Into Literacy Center*, awards presented exactly this kind of immediate momentum during the first year of its operation. For a sales force, particularly, awards help to distinguish a new product from the many others vying for educators' attention.

No matter where your product is in its life cycle, though, remember that your job doesn't end once the winners have been selected. If your product does win, be sure to do the follow-up required to leverage the value of that compliment. Of course, for a skilled and intrepid marketer, this is where the fun begins. A sales force's enthusiasm over the award will only be further stoked by imaginative marketing materials. Touting even an obscure win will help persuade customers of its importance. And over time, an award that is promoted consistently within an industry will acquire status. (Think about J.D. Powers in car manufacturing, or *The Golden Lamp* in educational publishing.)

Reviews: Capturing Fame or Using Feedback

Attention, control freaks: reviews can be hazardous to your health. Pitching to the media is a crapshoot. So if you require absolute control over the outcome, don't even go there. On the other hand, remember that just as an award emblem is a picture worth many words, reviews also carry a unique complimentary value. A write-up in a respected educator or parent publication comes directly to the mailboxes of potential customers. And a good review can be very persuasive; after all, readers choose the publications they subscribe to, and most often respect the opinions of the writers featured in those publications.

Typically, the block-and-tackle functions of public relations—creating media kits, writing press releases, and developing relationships with the media—are handled by PR professionals. And with good reason. Making a successful pitch to the press can be a time-consuming process. Much like sales, it takes communication, persistence, and a basic understanding of the customer's (i.e. the editor's) needs. But as a rule of thumb, Warren Buckleitner, editor of the *Children's Software Revue*, advises publishers in pursuit of positive press to keep things simple. Make sure your press materials contain the key information. And skip the gimmicks and give-aways.

"Instead of a fancy T-shirt," he says, "put your energy into sending a second, or even third, mailing."

Whether reviews reflect favorably or not on your product, they can serve an important purpose in your overall marketing plan. Good reviews have all the residual benefits of a prestigious award, including sales and morale building. They send a cost-free, bias-free snapshot of your product directly to your customer. And they have legs—that is, the good news lives on for as long as your item remains in print (or online). Unfavorable reviews are equally useful. Objective feedback can be helpful in product development. And if it calls to the fore an interesting debate—competing educational approaches, for instance—the "buzz" of controversy can help position your product. (For example, Frank Wang of Saxon Publishers, with tongue firmly and proudly in cheek, refers to his back-to-basics math materials by their detractors' label, "drill and kill.")

With a relatively untested product, it may be a good idea to work your way up the visibility ladder, starting with solid publications that have smaller circulations. That way, should your product receive a negative response, you will have the opportunity to retool it before moving on to a bigger spotlight. A less-than-glowing assessment actually can be an opportunity, particularly if it comes from an experienced product reviewer or teacher whom you respect. According to Charlene Blohm of C. Blohm & Associates, negative reviews have helped her clients discover some of these basic but retrievable marketing mistakes:

- The name doesn't accurately describe the product.
- The directions aren't clear.
- Customers can't tell from the packaging what it is.
- Using it isn't easy.
- The product doesn't deliver on its educational goals.

Most evaluators try to criticize constructively, especially when a product is in its field-testing phase. But even when a product already is in distribution and is placed for evaluation with a classroom teacher or professional reviewer, it's worth the extra effort on your part to glean as much useful feedback as you can. Also, a healthy respect for the power of the media is prudent, but don't let a negative critique stun you into silence. Similarly, don't think that reviews are written in stone. If you note any inaccurate information in a review, send a cordial e-mail questioning or correcting it. Blohm's advice is, when and if you do connect with your critic, remain courteous and attempt to understand his or her point of view. Think of the occasion as a learning opportunity that can influence future development.

Conclusion

There's no doubt that awards and reviews can be an effective, cost-efficient way to raise your product's status and its sales. Awards and reviews serve different purposes, and you should pursue both. While an award pins a feather in your cap for all to see, a review in a respected publication provides more detailed feedback, often specific to your customers.

So, after reviewing the dos, don'ts, and other tips included here, take a look at the awards and media contacts listed in the K-12 Industry Resources section of this book, and consider what these sources of recognition can do for you and for your product.

Author's Note: This article was written and edited with assistance from Eileen Fisher. The Education Product & Company Awards and Educational Media Contacts (see the K-12 Industry Resources section at the back of this book) were compiled by Edward P. Hamilton.

About the Author

Charlene F. Gaynor *is executive director of the Association of Educational Publishers (AEP), www.edpress.org, which supports the growth of supplemental publishing and its positive impact on learning and teaching. Members include print and digital publishers, educational foundations and associations, and the education trade press. In her former life, Charlene was publisher of Learning Magazine, senior editor of new magazine development at Meredith Corporation, and a reporter, writer, and editor at The Milwaukee Journal. Charlene can be reached at (856) 241-7772 or at cgaynor@edpress.org.*

Press Kit Tactics for Tech and Start-Up Companies

by Leslie Eicher, APR

A press kit (also called a media kit) is an information package that provides journalists with the material they need to learn about your organization and cover your stories. Information in your kit should always be "newsy" rather than promotional. Press kits that "sell" instead of "tell" make reporters suspicious and lower your chances of gaining media coverage. As a rule, media kit materials should copy the style of a news release: straightforward, clear, and with few adjectives.

What you place in a media kit depends on the story that you're presenting to the press. Here's a list of the items that are generally included:

- A press release on the story you want reported in the media

- Background information (fact sheets, timelines, histories, achievements, or descriptions)

- Biographies of key personnel

- A question-and-answer sheet that addresses inquiries reporters are likely to make

- Photographs of your product or personnel. (These photos should have captions that are easy to remove and that explain or identify their subjects.)

- Other visual aids such as diagrams, slides, or samples

- Past articles about or by your company (to help to inspire ideas and prevent duplicate articles)

- Additional materials (annual reports, review copies, product sheets, white papers, brochures, newsletters, or other publications)

Some public relations practitioners routinely send out unsolicited press kits to the media, but journalists warn that this practice may end up costing you, wasting both time and postage. Reporters deal with loads of e-mail, telephone calls, press releases, and press kits on a daily basis. They're likely to either throw away your kit or file it under "I'll get to it when I have the time." Having a journalist express interest in your story and then sending them the press kit ensures that the kit really will be read.

However, it does make sense to send unsolicited background information if you are introducing a revolutionary new product or rounding out a pitch letter. You can also send updated press kits to media contacts who regularly cover your company in order to ensure that they always have the most accurate information. In each case, you will have to decide how comprehensive your press kit needs to be. As mentioned earlier, the decision to ship a simple fact sheet with your news release or send the whole kit-n-caboodle depends on the story and what you think the reporter will need.

Despite these limitations, you have a myriad of ways in which you can use your press kit. Take it to trade shows, hand it out at media conferences, distribute it in response to breaking news, and send it to reporters preparing to interview you. In fact, it's a good idea to have a press kit ready for any situation in which the media will need to know more about you and your story.

Now that you've figured out what a press kit is and how to use it, you have another challenge: selecting the medium in which your kits will appear. Technology has given the public relations practitioner the choice of three basic press kit formats: print, Web-based, and CD-ROM. The optimal approach would be to have a combination of two or all three of these formats.

Print Press Kits

The most traditional form of the media kit is printed material placed in a folder. Although some believe that digital press kits will make the printed kit obsolete, print has one major advantage. That is, no special equipment is required to view the information, so reporters can flip through them any time, any place. This factor should keep printed kits around as a popular alternative for some time to come.

One major point to remember when creating a printed press kit is to avoid overkill. Shifting through a pile of papers can be overwhelming, and journalists often complain about receiving folders overflowing with information that is of no use to them. Only include data that pertains to the story you want covered. For example, don't include old releases unless they provide a history relevant to the current story.

Although print materials do not have the multimedia capacity of digital formats, you can use the theme of your story or company to add a creative element. For example, Disneyland has sent out press kits in which Goofy presents a fake business card reading "Goofy—Press & Publicity."[1] And when Eastman Kodak introduced its Advantix brand, the company distributed press kits accompanied by a suitcase-sized product kit containing an Advantix camera, film cassettes, and more. Kodak then arranged press events that featured colorful photo sets and on-site processing so reporters could test the equipment and see the results immediately.[2]

However, don't think you must rely on gimmicks or elaborate folders to attract media interest. Reporters are primarily interested in the story, not stunts. Attention-grabbing tactics should be balanced with the core objective of facilitating media coverage of your story (as with the Advantix example). Many attempts to be "clever" have been met with confusion and irritation by editors and producers. A newsworthy story and useful information are worth a thousand tricks.

Finally, always put some form of identification on your press kit folder. Remember that journalists will have a pile of media kits on their desks. Some companies use custom-printed folders emblazoned with their company name and logo, while others purchase pocket folders from supply stores and add visuals themselves. A line or two describing what your company does will also help busy reporters keep track of your media kit and why they requested your information.

Internet Press Kits

An increasing number of organizations are creating online press kits so journalists can access company information 24 hours a day. The online press kit may also be called a Web site's media room or pressroom and is typically placed under the "About Us," "Company Information," or "News" sections of the Web site.

An Internet press kit saves you a great deal in postage and printing expenses. Information can revised quickly and efficiently without having to discard reams of outdated papers. In addition, potential employees, investors, and other members of the public can easily learn more about you.

These online kits contain the information usually put into paper-based kits. However, they can also include archives of your old news releases, high-resolution graphic files for downloading, news of service or product upgrades, and more. Reporters will be able do as much or as little research as they need, and unlike a printed media kit, the online kit will not lead to information overload, provided its Web pages and hyperlinks are well organized.

The most exciting thing about Internet press kits is their vast potential for multimedia and interactivity. E-mail news releases can contain links to your online pressroom, and instead of static text and images, you can include animation, audio clips, and video clips. Add video and audio news releases, corporate videos, clips from previous interviews, demo clips, or anything else that can be used to illustrate or clarify your story.

Several services exist to help you with your video and audio production. Examples are Video News Wire (a branch of PR Newswire) and Medialink (which also provides audio and digital photo production). You can find similar services in your geographical region or on the Internet. Look at a broad range of work samples, discuss the details of prospective providers' services, and get an idea of their track record for customer satisfaction before making a selection.

No matter what you place in your online press kits, always ensure that the Web pages contain up-to-date information, download quickly, and are easy to read and navigate. Since you can't be sure what type of computer or word-processing program reporters will be using, place your downloadable information in PDF or flat text files.

Some companies require that journalists complete a profile or register for a password before accessing the pressroom. Their goal is to generate a list of media contacts to whom they can send news updates, tailor future releases, and pitch story ideas. But this is a risky proposition at best. Harried reporters on deadline need

> "...don't think you must rely on gimmicks or elaborate folders to attract media interest."

information quickly and may decide to move on to another, more accessible, site rather than spend time registering. Many resent having to submit information because they see no real reason for the registration requirement. After all, why would you be granting the media access to information that you don't want the public to know? Other reporters prefer to keep a low profile while collecting data, and some may even enter false information.

The best approach is to give the media unlimited access to your online pressroom. Use regular opt-in methods such as offering news updates, newsletters, discussion lists, or white papers as incentives for joining your contact list.

CD-ROM Press Kits

The press kit on compact disc contains many of the best features of both the printed and the online kits. You can mail or hand out the CD to the media, but you still retain all the interactive and multimedia features of a Web site. In fact, you can even provide hyperlinks from your CD press kit to your Web site.

As with the Web media kit, the CD's multimedia capabilities allow you to be creative as you wish. For example, the lumber company Trus Joist, McMillan (TJM) used an illustration of a town map as their CD press kit's main interface. Seventeen locations led journalists to different sections tailored for their specific editorial needs. A building trade editor could go to "the Neighborhood" to learn about the company's use of engineered lumber in housing and light-commercial construction while a real estate writer could get data on affordable housing and alternative building materials from "the Town Hall."

The reporters were able to tell which section suited their needs because pop-up windows describing each section appeared whenever the cursor moved over them. The CD also provided a search function, an inventory of stock photos and illustrations, and downloadable text documents.[3]

Your CD-ROM, like your Web site, should be organized so that the media can control the amount and type of information they access. And, as with a Web site, you

> **"The best approach is to give the media unlimited access to your online pressroom."**

must plan for easy navigation and reading. You also have to decide what you will place on your CD; you'll want to put in everything that is useful without turning the kit into a sales piece or a simple reproduction of your Web pages.

Since journalists will be using both Windows-compatible PCs and Macintosh computers, it's best to have a CD that runs on both. Also, bear in mind what the CD's minimum requirements will be. This includes processing speed, memory, video and audio cards, the computer software needed, and the CD-ROM drive speed. Then, test the CD on different configuration combinations to see how it reacts.

Creating a CD press kit may require writers, photographers, graphic designers, computer programmers, multimedia developers, and much more. If you do not have the resources or time to create the CD yourself, you can pay a multimedia service to create it for you. As with video and audio producers, examine both work samples and the service companies themselves before settling on one.

Screen print your company name and logo onto the CD so that the editor can easily identify it. And remember to make the CD's jewel case a part of your presentation. The inserts can be used for illustrations, general descriptions, contact information, and so forth.

Rules for All Types of Press Kits

A few principles hold true for all press kits, regardless of their format.

Prepare them in advance so that you're ready for sudden events such as a breaking story or an unexpected media query. CD-ROM press kits in particular can take months to compile.

Always make sure to include a business card or contact information. Give the reporters your URL, mailing address, telephone number, and e-mail address. It's especially important to include telephone numbers since reporters on tight deadlines will need to get in touch with you as quickly as possible.

If the press kit was requested, send an accompanying cover letter reminding journalists that they're expecting it. The cover letter should establish or reinforce rapport, so be business-like but friendly. A very formal letter will make you seem pretentious and can turn off the recipients. Also, follow up by phone or email to see if reporters actually received the press kit and have all the information they need.

Keep ease of use foremost in your mind. Although it can be tempting to simply pack your kit with information, exercise restraint. Make sure each sheet in your printed kit has a clear heading and limit the quantity of layers in your CD-ROM or Web pages.

Conclusions

The press kit has been a stalwart media relations tool for decades, and your imagination is the only limit on its originality. However, the substance of your story and supporting materials is the true key to attracting the media's attention. Although technological advances have created diverse formats, the kit's purpose remains the same: to provide reporters with easy access to research materials.

■

[1] Theresa Blackburn, *"Disneyland's 'Goofy' Press Kit."* Tactics May 1997: 10

[2] Thomas L. Harris, *Value-Added Public Relations*: Chicago: NTC Business Books, 1998

[3] Tony Harrison, *"Issue Highlights. Hands On: Firm Management Sidebar"* Tactics September 1996. Retrieved May 17, 2001 from the World Wide Web: www.prsa.org/tacfiles/seprom96.html

■

About the Author

Leslie Eicher, *a 15-year PR veteran, has made a career of communicating information regarding the products, services, goals, and positions of her clients. Specializing in the education market, Eicher's experience runs the gamut of strategic planning, positioning, media relations, employee communications, crisis planning, and new product launches; and her clients have included companies such as Jostens Learning, Turner Learning, Dell Computers, Computer Curriculum Corp., and NCS Pearson. Her work on employee relations programs during layoffs, mergers, and acquisitions has won numerous public relations awards. Leslie can be reached at leicherpr@aol.com.*

Writing a Press Release

by Catherine L. Wambach

What is the goal of a press release? To get a reporter's attention! Press releases are not read by teachers and administrators; the educators read the magazines, newsletters, and online announcements that reporters, analysts, and editors write. So the first lesson in writing a press release is to appeal specifically to the needs of reporters. They appreciate clear writing, correct spelling and grammar, modest use of industry jargon, and the appropriate writing style. A well-written press release allows the reporter to use the copy as is, without a lot of edits and style changes. Members of the media use the *Associated Press Style Book* and *The Chicago Manual of Style* as references for style, punctuation, and grammar guidelines. Any press release writer should read both of these handbooks and keep them nearby when composing a release.

A good press release communicates the news efficiently and quickly. Reporters receive hundreds of press releases in a week and even in a day. They will read releases that look newsworthy, that fit their beat, or that succinctly impart interesting information. The best press releases present the most important information first—in the headline, the sub-headline (directly below the headline), and the lead or first paragraph. For example, if you are composing a press release to announce a new product and an award received for an existing product, you should start with a headline that identifies the new product and indicates its key benefit for educators. In a sub-headline you can report on the award. Your lead paragraph can then provide information on the significance of the new product. And in the body of the release, you can use a paragraph subhead to draw attention to the news about the award, which you might discuss in detail in the third or fourth paragraph.

In lead paragraphs, avoid long company descriptions such as, "award-winning, industry leader based in New York with offices in Los Angeles and Chicago today announced…" This deflects attention from the news.

Reporters are more likely to read a release beginning with a short company description such as, "education software developer," followed immediately by the news. If your company is well known, you can omit the description in the first paragraph entirely. A descriptive company paragraph at the end of the press release will be sufficient in this case.

Promote User Benefits

Writing a press release is a comprehensive writing task that requires information gathering, thoughtful planning, drafting, editing, and then more editing. The greatest error a writer can make is to focus the news on the company, as in, "We did this and it is important." Instead, the focus should be on the reader, the market, or the user—in this case, educators. One thing to remember is that the media report on news, trends, and interesting case studies. Unless the press release is intended for financial markets only, the news should be about how the product or service meets the *needs* of educators—saving time, increasing achievement, or helping them to succeed.

> "Editors and reporters say that they prefer a short one-to-two page press release with supporting documents."

Successful press release writing is based on the "pyramid format" of delivering information. At the apex, state the most important news and give a hook about why the news is important. Then support the news with a second level of information, such as market research, trends, or product data (e.g., what differentiates it from competing products). A third level might provide a quote from a company executive or industry luminary who is familiar with the product or occurrence. This third level supports the second level and so on. A fourth or fifth level should clearly state pricing, availability, system requirements, and contact information for orders or inquiries.

Editors and reporters say that they prefer a short one-to-two page press release with supporting documents rather than a three-or-four page release containing all the details. A press release should include enough information to support the news story but should leave room for a reporter to interview a company executive or industry source for more details.

The press release closes with a company description. This boilerplate paragraph may be used in all press releases. It includes the location of the corporate headquarters and offices, the stock symbol if the company is publicly traded, and one or two sentences that position the company in the market.

Be frugal with descriptive adjectives and adverbs extolling the accomplishments of the company. Remember, the best press release is one that a reporter can use directly. Very few articles include subjective praise about a company. Reporters have limited space to fill and they must make every word count. Press releases should be written with the same restrictions. A poorly thought-out or written press release reflects negatively on a company. And they may not do it intentionally; reporters adopt attitudes towards companies based on multiple impressions, one of which is the press release.

Press Release Tactics

As mentioned earlier, the lead paragraph should tell a reporter the primary news. Before the lead paragraph, the headline and subhead should give the reporter the heads-up on what the release is about. Therefore, the headline and subhead must indicate the benefits of the news for educators. Reporters can more quickly grasp the news content of releases written in this manner.

Below are three examples of press releases written for companies known by the education media.

Example One: Product Release

The example below is an abbreviated new product launch press release from Macromedia. The release immediately imparts what is the product, what it does, and for whom. The lead paragraph identifies an education trend and benefit: using multimedia in the classroom and making it easier for teachers to do so.

Headline: New Project-Based Multimedia Curriculum from Macromedia

Subhead: Projects Help High School and Middle School Educators use Multimedia in Classroom

Lead paragraphs:
*San Francisco, Calif.—April 27, 2001--*A new curriculum guide from Macromedia, Inc. makes it easier for high school and middle school teachers to use Web multimedia with their students in several academic disciplines—including Writing, Social Studies and Earth Sciences. *Project-Based Multimedia: Step-by-Step Projects for Integrating Multimedia into Your Classroom* is the first curriculum guide in the new Macromedia Web Design Series.

Macromedia developed the new book series in response to teacher requests for cross-curricular instructional materials and project ideas that teach Web design skills. Priced at $20, the printed curriculum guide and accompanying CD is available at www.macromedia.com/education.

Example Two: Tradeshow Release

This example shows an abbreviated tradeshow release about enhancements to an existing product, DiscoverySchool.com. It also features secondary news about results from an educator research survey.

Headline: DiscoverySchool.com has New Core Curriculum Tools For K-12 Teachers

Subhead: Teachers Pick DiscoverySchool.com as Top Education-specific Commercial Web Site

Lead paragraphs:
Special to F.E.T.C.—Orlando, FL (January 10, 2001) -- In response to teacher demand, DiscoverySchool.com has added two powerful new features to its premier online education destination: Custom Classroom and Worksheet Generator. A third new feature, Lesson Plan Creator, will debut this fall.

With anytime, anywhere access to DiscoverySchool.com tools, teachers can easily create their own K-12 puzzles, quizzes and other core-curriculum materials. Some of this content is based on Discovery Channel programming—a trusted educational resource that brings the world into the classroom.

The new Custom Classroom application lets educators create a convenient personal account for saving puzzles they create in Puzzlemaker, and quizzes they create in Quiz Center. Custom Classroom, which launched in September, already boasts over 50,000 registered users.

Example Three: A Case Study Press Release

Writing a case study press release on a customer's application involves a different writing style from news releases. The case study story is about users. It is often longer than other types of press release. The company and products are referenced insofar as students and teachers use them, but they are often not mentioned until deep in the copy. A good case study press release identifies an industry problem and presents a solution that users have achieved by applying the company's products.

Reporters seek good case studies that provide readers with potential solutions to their everyday education problems. The case study press release example below led to two feature articles and a cover story. The educators profiled in it received hundreds of e-mails from readers.

This example release describes ideas for redefining the high school shop paradigm by teaching multimedia in regular curricular subjects. It addresses an industry trend of meeting the needs of low-performing students. Examples of students using Web design software bring home the company messages.

Headline: Digital Safari Academy Narrows the Digital Divide

Subhead: California High School's School-Within-A-School Combines Multimedia With Academic Learning

Body of the Release:

Concord, Calif. (January 2001)-- At the Digital Safari Multimedia Academy, students who normally wouldn't dream of taking technology classes let alone expect to have high tech careers are actively working and collaborating on multimedia projects.

"By working on multimedia projects in academic classes, students can sharpen their basic academic skills and acquire new competencies for succeeding in the information age. These include teamwork, creativity, online research, and entry-level Web-design skills that companies value," said Ted Maddock, director of the Digital Safari Multimedia Academy at Mt. Diablo High School in Concord, California. "Macromedia Web solutions empower students to find and express their own voice— by letting them use the images, words, animation and sound they need."

Vocational Training With Multiple Exits

"The business community needs labor with multimedia, computer and collaborative skills," said Maddock. "Our job as educators is to balance the demands of the marketplace with the emotional and intellectual needs of the students."

Mt. Diablo High School is the most economically disadvantaged school in the district. Seventy percent of the students are minorities and many speak English as a second language.

"These are kids who—more than most—are at the mercy of economics," said Maddock. Completing a two or four-year college degree seems unthinkable when there doesn't seem to be any way to find or earn the money for tuition and books.

The Digital Safari gives these students hope, and marketable skills. Students leave the program with a digital multimedia portfolio to present to prospective employers, experience in working on a team, and entry-level multimedia skills that companies value.

The day after graduating from the academy, one young man started a $33,000-a-year design job at a graphic design firm. "And he wasn't what you'd call an academic superstar," said Maddock.

Unlike the old-style vocational training, school-to-career programs like Digital Safari offer multiple exit points and paths to success. "Vocational high school training once meant students studied auto mechanics or some other trade, went on to an apprenticeship, and wound up with a low-paying job for the rest of their lives," said Maddock. "After completing Digital Safari in High School, they can go as far as a master's degree in multimedia at higher ed schools like California State Hayward. And students have the groundwork for a variety of high-tech career options."

School-Within-A-School

Over 1,400 students attend Mt. Diablo High School, and 120 are enrolled in the Digital Safari Multimedia Academy program. "The Multimedia Academy is part of a restructuring model we've been working on for several years," said the high school's principal, Louis Suarez. "Kids learn at different rates and in different ways. Some students, who are lost in an urban, comprehensive high school setting really blossom when you reduce the size of the learning environment."

The benefits become apparent within a year or two, according to studies cited by the U.S. Department of Education. Students experience a greater sense of belonging and fewer discipline problems. Crime, violence and gang participation decrease. Absences and dropout rates fall, while graduation and postsecondary enrollment rates head upward.

Digital Safari, now in its fifth year, received start-up federal funding earmarked for school restructuring. The Mt. Diablo Unified School District has since obtained a grant from the U.S. Department of Education Smaller Learning Communities Program to develop and implement additional school-within-a-school models.

Professional-Standard Tools

Academy students learn computer-based multimedia production skills along with the core academic curriculum. Their multimedia projects are designed for their academic classes.

The program uses professional-standard hardware and software. "If we are going to call ourselves a vocational program, we need to use what people see when they walk into a job," said Maddock.

Students use Macromedia Director as their primary interactive multimedia authoring tool, and Macromedia Dreamweaver as their main Web authoring tool. They also work with Macromedia Flash, SoundEdit 16, Freehand and Extreme 3D. The students work on 30 Apple Macintosh computers, including G4 towers and high-end iMacs.

In the last three years, the academy has won 10 awards at the California Student Media and Multimedia Festival, a statewide event open to all K-12 public and private schools.

Teachers Become Co-learners

Officially the academy has four teachers, but unofficially it's more like one hundred twenty-four. Technology is changing too fast for teachers to be experts in everything. Instead, they present the big picture and function as project managers. "You must be willing to learn the new features along with your students, and be willing to let students teach you something all the way," said Maddock. "We're still teachers—but we're also facilitators, coaches and, most importantly, co-learners with our students."

As a 25-year teaching veteran, he admits this co-learner paradigm surprised him at first. "Our kids are quite capable of self-direction and collaborative learning," he said. "If you had asked me ten years ago, I would not have pushed for this style of learning."

Rather than teach every single multimedia skill to every single student, academy teachers develop student consultants—or narrow-slice experts. When introducing Macromedia Director, for instance, the instructor starts with a simple demonstration for everyone on how to make a ball, how to change the color, and how to provide navigation features.

Sooner rather than later, a student will want to incorporate sound. Instead of stopping the entire class, the instructor pulls aside a small group of students who want to learn about sound. This initial cluster of students becomes the narrow-slice experts on sound—and they teach others.

Multipurpose Classrooms

Classes take place in 90-minute blocks of time. Facilities consist of three classrooms and a 30-by-60-foot state-of-the-art technology lab with flatbed scanners, a large-format laser printer, digital still cameras, digital video cameras, digital recording equipment and video editing equipment. On half of the lab is for classes, with 20 computers and production equipment. The other half is for collaboration and individual work with a conversation pit, worktables and 10 computers.

Project teams typically consist of four students. For an earth science project, juniors used Macromedia Director to create "Universal Tours." During the eight-week project, teams choose 12 stops in the universe and design an interactive tour package. "They can surf the rings of Saturn or play basketball on the moon, but everything developed in each stop must be scientifically accurate," said Maddock.

Changing People's Lives

When Principal Suarez arrives at school at 7:00 a.m., he is often greeted by academy pupils wanting to get an early start on their day's work. They cajole the principal into unlocking the computer lab for them.

A former truant hones his Web site—while sophomores look on enviously. He's working on his senior e-business project for his economics class.

Each student workgroup designs an e-commerce product or service. Using the Internet and the telephone, they research expenses for office space, advertising, equipment, salaries and employee benefits. They prepare a budget, conduct competitive analysis and write a marketing plan. Simultaneously, they design a fully functional Web site for their business, which must be up and running before they can receive a grade.

"The academy definitely changes people's lives," said Kamela Jones, a graduating academy senior headed for the University of California Santa Cruz and a major in computer science. "We work together like we're a family. We respect people for their special abilities and gear our projects around their skills. We learn how to do things other people don't know how to do."

Conclusion

Press releases are effective tools for communicating a company's product announcements, strategic marketing messages, awards, and customer success stories to reporters. Good press release writers think like reporters. They research and analyze the facts, determine how the news benefits customers, and synthesize to show the relevance of the story to trends and current events. As with most good writing, thinking and developing the press release angles typically takes longer than actually writing it.

About the Author

Catherine Wambach is the president of Wambach & Company, Inc. a public relations and marketing firm specializing in education and eLearning markets. Clients such as Macromedia, Discovery Channel, Lightspan, and Encyclopedia Britannica tap Wambach & Company to launch new products, reposition existing ones, and develop lasting media relationships. Catherine may be reached at cwambach@aol.com or by calling (505) 281-5324.

Addressing Complex Issues beyond the News: Shaping Op-Eds and Trade Articles for National Publication

by Sheppard Ranbom

Placing articles in education trade publications and op-ed pieces in major dailies can be an effective method of explaining complicated issues and drawing attention to new approaches that can help improve education—particularly when you feel that your message will not be communicated adequately through regular news coverage. Publication in these venues can provide instant visibility for your ideas among educators and policymakers, opinion leaders, and the public. But the competition for space and editorial requirements demand that writers target pieces to the requirements of each publication, meet a high threshold of news value, speak directly to the audience, and present provocative new ideas in compelling ways.

Too often, those who are not used to writing for publication focus too much on their own products and programs without placing their work in a larger context. The publication's editor automatically will reject "articles" that are merely disguised ads. The challenge of publishing articles is to take the high ground and not be a self-serving promoter for your organization or product. Like good news stories, feature articles and op-ed pieces should:

- Identify the controversy around the issue;

- Present interesting data to provoke interest, challenge current belief, and prove a point;

- Draw attention to surprising or counter-intuitive aspects of the subject;

- Make the issues real by providing specific examples that make the point;

- Enable readers to see themselves in the story;

- Make a case using colorful language; and

- Present newsworthy information that ties in with big stories in the news, if possible.

In addition, the pieces should be written for or bylined by the most persuasive messenger available—the one who has the most name recognition, most impressive title, or most relevant experience to attract and convince the readership.

Op-Ed Pieces

Most of the nation's daily and weekly newspapers have space for commentary articles in their op-ed sections (literally, the page "opposite the editorial page"). Writers submit their op-eds to daily and weekly newspapers to express their positions on particular topics. These short and insightful essays, usually on timely issues or linked to local or national events in the news, are always in demand.

Before you start writing, you can call the op-ed editor to see if they are interested in your topic and your perspective before you invest the time in preparing and drafting a piece. In most cases, however, they will be noncommittal and will ask to see the piece before making any judgment.

Once you have written an op-ed you believe is compelling, submit it and then follow up with the appropriate editor. Some papers may invite you to write an op-ed on an education issue if they are aware of your particular expertise. During the conversation, explain why your views would be of value to their readers.

Most daily and weekly papers have an op-ed review process that can take from one to ten days. Many larger papers will require "exclusivity," which means they will consider your piece only if you agree not send it to any other paper. You should be aware of any exclusivity clauses before you call or send a piece to other papers, but you can shop around for the best newspaper to publish your op-ed, depending on its topic, or submit a piece to another paper if it is rejected by your first choice.

You should include a one-page "pitch" letter with your op-ed explaining why your opinion should be published, why it is current and relevant, and how your information will be of interest to the paper's readership. A final suggestion: don't get discouraged easily. Good writing is hard work. If your column doesn't make it into your local paper, consider submitting it elsewhere or redrafting it as a letter to the editor, which can also be an effective way to voice your opinions.

Framing the Argument

The biggest challenge in writing an op-ed piece is creating a focused argument on a topic that will appeal to a broad range of readers of a publication. An op-ed gives an opinion and tries to convince the reader to adopt a certain point of view. It needs to take a definite position on an issue and make the best case possible. An op-ed can present a problem in a new context that is memorable and distinctive, bring the most important facts to bear, sort through myths and fallacies, offer a solution, or show why the author has more credibility on an issue than those who may oppose him.

Suppose that your organization or corporation is about to release a new technology application that helps educators and policymakers address achievement gaps among student populations. Your op-ed piece would probably best begin not by focusing on the technology but perhaps by summarizing why traditional approaches to address the problem have failed. It could then paint a tantalizing picture of an entirely new way of doing business that is now being used in the local community with proven results.

Other factors—such as timing and the purpose for placement—should be taken into consideration as well. Perhaps you are trying to draw attention to a research-based approach to improving reading and literacy. In this case, you might want to place your piece in a major daily newspaper from a textbook adoption state, focusing it on why the selection of a particular book or approach will be ineffective unless the state also invests in professional development. To make your point, you might include anecdotes that reflect some of the lessons learned from your program's implementation. And you might time the release of the op-ed to coincide with the release of national or state test scores in reading or the announcement of a new statewide reading initiative.

Tips and Hints

The point of these examples is that you need to bring the best information and thinking you have to bear to make your case. Following are some tips in preparing op-ed pieces:

Be brief and to the point. The standard length for most op-eds is about 700 to 900 words, but some newspapers may want more or fewer words to fit specific spaces on their op-ed pages. *USA Today*, for example,

requests 500-600 word pieces, but *The Chronicle for Higher Education's* "Point of View" section runs longer pieces, usually about 1,200 words. *Education Week's* Commentary page uses pieces of 1,500 words. Some newspapers, such as the *Los Angeles Times* and the *Washington Post*, have weekly "Outlook" sections in their Sunday editions that use essays of 1,500 words.

Have a forceful lead. Make your strongest, most compelling point first, and support and back up your arguments. There are different kinds of leads for different kinds of pieces. You may want to debunk some commonly held belief with a surprising fact that opens the door to your argument or localize or humanize the piece with a brief anecdote that epitomizes a current situation or a new approach to addressing a problem. The lead may vary by topic, the publication's style and readership, an upcoming event, and the data and information you have to work with.

Express a clear of view. The piece should be original and shed new light on an issue from a distinct perspective.

Be timely and topical. By giving your opinion piece a topical slant or "hook," your chances of seeing it published will increase.

Identify the controversy. Find ways of showing where your viewpoint fits in with the larger debate in the field and how it may advance the argument.

Discuss issues that people and your community care about. Innovative ways to teach students, or insightful advice that helps parents and opinion leaders address challenges they face may resonate well.

Use punchy, colorful language. It's not enough to make your point—you have to make it stick in the minds of your readers. The piece should paint vivid pictures to get your point across and use real life examples and analogies to bring alive the issue you are discussing with the reader. On the release of its report, *What Matters Most*, for example, The National Commission on Teaching and America's Future noted that every child has "a right to a caring and competent teacher." In response, the report and op-ed pieces vividly argued,

When it comes to widespread change, we have behaved as though national, state, and district mandates, could, like magic wands, transform schools. But all the directives and proclamations have been so much fairy dust… On the whole the school reform movement has ignored the obvious: what teachers know and can do makes the crucial difference in what children learn. And the ways schools organize their work makes a huge difference in what teachers can accomplish.

Spokespeople for the Commission also made a colorful point about the need for better qualified teachers: "We spend more money to license those who groom our pets than we do to evaluate the skills and knowledge of those who educate our children."

Express strong opinions. The piece should demonstrate the courage of your convictions and show that you can support your point of view with persuasive arguments and compelling facts. Be passionate about the topic you choose to write about, because if you don't care about it, neither will anyone else.

Articles for Trade Publications

Articles for trade publications typically include many of the elements of an op-ed piece. Their purpose might be to inform, inspire, educate, or convince. But articles for trade publications are more often written for an audience of educators and policymakers who have some specific expertise in the field. Therefore, their focus needs to be more specialized and their content more rich and detailed.

PUBLICATIONS AND REQUIREMENTS FOR SEVERAL TRADE JOURNALS

American School Board Journal. Published by the National School Board Association. The editor (2001) is Sally Banks Zakariya (*editor@asbj.com*). Address: American School Board Journal, 1680 Duke St., Alexandria, VA 22314. Phone: (703) 838-6739. Fax: (703) 549-6719. ASBJ looks for non-scholarly news and feature articles. Professional writers should query with story ideas or to be put on the journal's list for on-assignment stories. Articles should focus on the needs and issues of school board members and administrators. They like writing based on personal experiences and/or specific events. Text should be 1,250 to 2,500 words. See also *www.asbj.com/writersguide.html*.

Educational Leadership. Published by the Association for Supervision and Curriculum Development. The editor (2001) is Marge Scherer. Address: Marge Scherer, Editor, Educational Leadership, ASCD, 1703 N. Beauregard St., Alexandria, VA 22311-1714 (note: send two copies of manuscripts). Educational Leadership wants brief articles that are practical with descriptions of programs, proven solutions, and research results. They also take opinion articles if they combine debate with examples. Issues have themes, check guidelines online for latest version (*www.ascd.org/readingroom/edlead/guidelin.html*). Articles should be aimed at leaders in curriculum, instruction, and supervision. They prefer manuscripts to query letters.

Education Week. Send to: M. Sandra Reeves, Commentary Editor, Education Week, 6935 Arlington Road, Suite 100, Bethesda, MD 20814-5233. Phone (301) 280-3100. Fax (301) 280-3200. E-mail *ew@epe.org*. A Commentary piece for Education Week is halfway between an article and an op-ed. A Commentary piece should deal with a policy issue or have implications for policy. It should be written in journalistic style, with personal experiences used as examples to support a larger point (as opposed to being the whole story). Commentaries generally range from 1,300 to 1,700 words although they have printed a few that break 2,000 words.

Phi Delta Kappan. Send to: Pauline B. Gough, Editor, 408 N. Union, P.O. Box 789, Bloomington, IN 47402-0789. Phone: (812) 339-1156. Kappan is an academic journal and thus more technical than the other publications described here. A Kappan article must be both well-researched and well-written. The journal is read mainly by academics and policymakers, so the articles tend to be more theoretical and address longer-term implications. Many articles relate to new research or to analyses of policies. Pay close attention to your references. Feature articles run from 1,500 to 5,000 words. (See also *www.pdkintl.org/kappan/kedguide.htm*.)

The School Administrator. Send to: Editor, The School Administrator, AASA, 1801 N. Moore St., Arlington, VA 22209-1813. E-mail *magazine@aasa.org*. The School Administrator is published for superintendents, principals, and other school leaders. The magazine likes articles focusing on actual real experiences, school system practices, effective, policies, and successful programs. Articles should not only say what was done but how policies were put into place. Some, but not all, of the articles each month relate to that issue's theme (see *www.aasa.org/publications/sa/ed_calendar.htm*). Feature articles range from 1,500 to 3,000 words, while focus articles (instructive how-to pieces on school management) run from 750 to 850 words and guest columns (op-eds) average 750 words. (See also *www.aasa.org/publications/sa/author-guidelines.htm*.)

Before writing for a magazine or trade publication, check to make sure they take outside submissions. Generally, newspaper publications like *Education Week* have their own staffs and print material developed in house (except for "Commentary" pieces and op-eds). For other publications you should check their Web site and/or request a copy of their guidelines. *Phi Delta Kappan, Educational Leadership (ASCD), The School Administrator*, and *American School Board Journal* all accept outside articles. See their requirements on page 268. If a publication has regular theme issues, shaping your article around an upcoming theme will increase your chances of being accepted.

Framing the Issue

Your topic should combine an interesting angle and a consistent point of view suitable to the audience with valuable information that speaks to key issues in the field. How you should frame the issue will vary by publication. Publications for teachers such as *Instructor* or *K-8 Education* as well as subject-specific publications such as *Social Education* or *The Science Teacher* include how-to articles that show teachers how to cover a specific topic. You can introduce your product as an activity around a larger lesson or even focus on your product, so long as the lesson has an instructional goal beyond familiarizing students with the product.

Query the Editor

Before writing the editor, determine the publication's readership (this is easy in a field with publication titles like *The School Administrator* and *Instructor*) and consider what they would be most interested in reading. Read several issues of the publication and pay attention to topics, themes, length, and format. Pick ideas and concepts that would fit in.

Send a short query letter or call to see if the editor would be interested in your piece. Your query should present the topic and identify why it is important—give a sense of the depth of information and knowledge to be discussed, and discuss information that is directly targeted at the publication's readership. You also need to identify the author's unique or special expertise about the topic. As with editorial page editors, trade publication editors are likely to be noncommittal until they actually see the piece.

You may want to find a prominent person in the magazine's readership to co-write the article. An article bylined by a software executive and a school board member is more likely to interest the *American School Board Journal* than one by the software executive alone.

Write the Best Piece Possible

Even if an editor expresses interest in topic from your query letter, he or she can still reject the final article. Following are some suggestions and issues to consider before writing a feature article:

Answer key questions. How does the product, service, or initiative address key problems in the education field? What are the key challenges in education your efforts will help solve? Why is this important or different? What does the research say? What makes your idea, concept, or product different from previous ones?

Address controversy. What do people on both sides of the issue say? How can your work help educators resolve this controversy?

Identify the implications for policy and practice. A piece should discuss the scope and real-world applications of an innovation. Readers should know how many people have benefited and how. Does the product or approach work in all circumstances or just in particular settings? What are the implications for others? What are the policies that would enable the innovation to flourish? What changes in practice are required?

Include resource information. You may want to identify books or resources that the reader can refer to for more information.

Be aware that articles for education publications frequently take a long time to be accepted and even longer to appear in print. Wait at least a couple of months before contacting an editor to see what happened to your manuscript. Even so, an article should be sent to only one editor at a time, except under highly unusual circumstances. Moreover, if your article is not accepted by one publication, you should not submit it elsewhere without rewriting it around the new publication's audience and themes.

After You Are Published

The value of getting placement is not only to have your ideas injected into the mainstream audience of a particular field. Reproductions of the articles can be sent to key audiences you want to influence. Copies of the article can be included in press packets and sent to funders or people who might be influential in advancing your work. You also can use an article in one publication to show others that you are a respected authority in the field.

About the Author

Sheppard Ranbom *is president of CommunicationWorks, LLC, a Washington, D.C.-based public affairs agency in the education field. The firm's clients include many of the nation's leading nonprofit organizations, corporations, foundations, colleges, and government agencies and commissions. A former staff writer for* Education Week*, Mr. Ranbom has edited a national education news syndicate for daily newspapers, written and edited many authoritative reports on education, ghostwritten scores of op-ed pieces placed in some of the nation's leading daily newspapers, and shaped hundreds of education and social policy issues for media consumption and public debate. Sheppard can be reached at (202) 955-9450 x 315.*

Working with Editors

by Charlene Blohm

"Be pleasant, persistent, professional, but not pushy," is how one magazine editor summed up her requirements for a successful public relations person. In today's competitive marketplace, it is a truism that the public relations professionals who are best at forging relationships with magazine editors are the ones who will get their products written about most frequently.

Does it take years of experience to develop these relationships to the point where you can successfully place products for clients on a regular basis? The answer is yes and no. The quality of the relationships will certainly change and deepen over time, but with a few basic rules and simple professional etiquette, you can become effective in a remarkably short period of time.

Who is the Customer?

This is the most important question to answer initially. Viewing the magazine editor as the customer will put the relationship into the proper perspective from the start. The job of the public relations person is to "sell" the editor on the client's product. All aspects of the public relations process should lead toward this goal. Just as there are stages to the sales process, there are stages to achieving successful product placement or editorial coverage.

The first step is to do the product homework. It is important to be able to discuss the product comfortably without relying on a scripted product description. Understanding why the product was developed, what specific educational needs it addresses, and why all the features and benefits are important to the product and the end user should be of primary concern. It is vital that the PR person be able to differentiate the client's products from its competitors. Editors are savvy about products, but they cannot always distinguish which features make the product different from the competition. The best PR professionals take responsibility for making the editor understand how the client's products outshine others in the category. That said, one way to earn an editor's respect is to let her know when her questions have outstripped your ability to answer them. It is never offensive to offer to connect an editor with someone at the client company who has more detailed product

knowledge, and in fact this is often a smart strategy. Furthermore, if an editor is interested enough to follow up in this way it usually is a sign that she is considering giving the company editorial coverage.

The second step is to understand which publications are appropriate for the client's product. If there is not a good fit between the product and the publication's editorial platform, pushing for placement wastes everyone's time and gets your relationship with the editor off to a bad start. In fact, one of the biggest pet peeves for education editors is that many PR folks do not take the time to research whether or not the magazine platform and its audience are appropriate for the product.

Knowing the right person at the magazine to start with for your product pitch is also important. Frequently, it is more productive to start lower on the editorial masthead than with the Editor in Chief. In contacting a publication for the first time after a simple press release, it can often be more effective to begin with someone lower on the ladder. A less senior member of the staff may be able to give the product more attention.

Basic Business Etiquette, or "What *Was* Her Name?"

It is amazing how much can be accomplished through the practice of simple business etiquette. Taking the time to spell an editor's name correctly is sometimes enough to send PR folks to the top of her call-back list. Saying please and thank you, and being appreciative of an editor's time and saying so are all things that will improve her impressions of your clients and their products.

The next tactic is to find out what the editor's preferred mode of communication is. It is important always to respect the editor's time and attention by getting to the point quickly. When leaving voice mail, it is wise to speak slowly and distinctly. Also, it is always a good practice to spell your first and last name and to leave your contact information twice. On a garbled voice message, "Tracey," "Stacie," "Gracie," and "J.C." all sound the same.

E-mail is quickly becoming the leading mode of communication for most business people. While e-mail etiquette is still evolving, there are some basic practices that should be used. You should carefully review every single e-mail you send for accuracy and spelling before you press the "send" button. Sloppy e-mails will quite often be deleted immediately. E-mail may be cheap and fast, but it is also easily disposable. With just one click, an e-mail and its information can be gone.

Easy-to-scan e-mail messages with paragraphs and subheads will make it easier for the editor to acquire complete product information quickly. Also, avoid attachments. You can't assume that everyone is using the same word processing software as you are. The best protocol is to copy and paste press releases into an e-mail rather than attach extra documents. If this not possible or if it seems too cumbersome, it is also acceptable to send an editor a hotlink to your client's Web site.

There is one final piece of business etiquette that can make the difference between getting and not getting a product mentioned. The smart PR professional makes sure she is as accessible as possible. Sometimes there are emergencies that require editors to make quick substitution of products just before a magazine goes to press. Being quickly accessible by voice, fax, and e-mail can result in a surprise product placement. Editors quickly learn whom they can turn to in a pinch for an additional press release, product photo, or substitute product. A PR person's failure to be accessible has lost more than one customer their product placement.

Dealing with the Deadline Devil

Editors live with deadlines. It is the nature of the magazine business. Helping an editor successfully meet deadlines with good story ideas and accurate, timely information will make her a friend for life. Be familiar with the editorial calendar. Understand where the opportunities are for industry stories and pitch them accordingly. If an editor says to call back in two months, it is best to take the hint and not hound her. Finding out the lead times for the production cycle and planning accordingly will also yield good results. One situation to avoid at all costs is being inaccessible to an editor when she needs answers—forcing her to contact your client directly. This can result in unpleasant questions from the client like, "What am I paying you for?" It is a good idea to return all phone calls within 24 hours. When an editor is calling, it usually means that a deadline is looming.

Again, this presents an opportunity for the smart PR person to shine by responding quickly.

Developing a reputation as a "go to" person can also yield exciting rewards for a PR professional. The ability to bring unusual or "out-of-the-box" ideas about other ways to promote a client's products through sponsorships, giveaways, grant programs, or other editorial tie-ins will result in greater frequency of contact with editors, which usually leads to more frequent product placement.

Building the Relationship

As in any profession, there are both mediocre and good PR professionals. Those who are the most successful understand the need to be prepared to discuss more than just the individual product they are promoting. Bringing something else to the conversation is always a plus. Using conversations with an editor as opportunities to share information about what is happening in the marketplace or about issues affecting the quality of education will leave the editor with the impression that you are someone she should stay in contact with—always a good thing in public relations.

National shows and conferences provide the opportunity to spend time with editors in a collegial atmosphere. Editors quite often attend several conferences a year. For example, an editor of a middle-school math journal might attend the conferences held by the National Council of Teachers of Mathematics (NCTM), the Association for Supervision and Curriculum Development (ASCD), the National Middle School Association (NMSA), and perhaps one of the technology conferences, such as the Florida Educational Technology Conference (FETC). All of these shows feature events that provide opportunities to further develop relationships with editors. Many public relations professionals sponsor events for their clients at these conferences and invite editors. If the conference sponsor is also the owner of the journal for which the editor writes, there are usually sessions at which you can meet the editors to learn more about their processes for article submission and development. Understanding the challenges that an editor faces will help immensely in crafting a strategy for successful product placement.

There is always the option of scheduling an individual meeting with an editor during a conference. These conferences are extremely busy, though, so it is a good idea to start planning appointments several months in advance. Giving your undivided attention to the meeting without allowing interruptions is an important courtesy to the editor. If you are constantly looking over her shoulder during the meeting, she will inevitably come to the conclusion that you consider her as a mere distraction until a better prospect comes along.

Conferences also provide the opportunity to treat editors to lunch or dinner. But no one likes to be pounded with a message while eating. It is a smarter strategy to use the time to build a friendship, to get to know the editor as a person, and to establish a personal bond so that the next time you have the opportunity to connect, the exchange builds upon a friendlier foundation. Enjoying a pleasant evening together makes the person, company, and product more memorable for the editor. As a follow-up to each meeting, a hand-written thank-you note will put the accomplished PR professional at the top of the editor's list. Everyone likes to feel appreciated, and thanking an editor for her time and interest is simply good manners.

Some Final Thoughts

Good PR professionals always keep the communication with editors consistent with the type of product they are promoting. Sending a fun press release for a fun product or an elegant press release for an elegant product will ensure that your message is received with the appropriate tone. Similarly, quality counts: if the press release is substandard, editors will assume that the product is as well. The oft-quoted maxim that "perception is reality" is definitely in play here. The presentation and follow-up to the message is as important as the message itself. This cannot be overemphasized. The words and actions of a PR person can determine the success or failure of editorial placement independently of the quality of the product or the client company.

The combination of a pleasant personality, an understanding of the editorial process, and simple professional etiquette is one that is hard to beat in the educational marketplace. Learning to stand out in the crowd is relatively simple. Editors appreciate good public relations when done properly. It makes their jobs easier when they can depend on the PR community to keep them abreast of late-breaking news and products that will interest their readers. The development of solid relationships with editors will yield positive results for PR professionals and their clients for years to come.

TOP TEN RULES FOR PR SUCCESS

1. Know who to call and when to call them.
2. Have enough product knowledge to describe your product well.
3. Understand the publication before you call to pitch your product.
4. When you send a press release or product, follow up within 4-5 days.
5. Don't make promises you can't keep.
6. Be aware of deadlines. Get your materials in on time.
7. Always return phone calls. Being accessible can make you successful.
8. Be honest when you can't answer questions, and find the editor someone who can.
9. It is your responsibility to help the editor understand your product.
10. Remember your manners.

Author's Note: This article was written and edited with assistance from Annie Galvin Teich, who is also experienced in the education market. Prior to joining C. Blohm & Associates, Inc. Annie was the publisher of *Learning* magazine.

About the Author

Charlene Blohm *heads C. Blohm & Associates, Inc., an independent public relations and marketing firm that specializes in educational publishing. An experienced consultant, she has worked with a wide range of companies whose products have included computer software, search engines, portals, satellite and cable programming, reading programs, supplemental learning resources, trade books, and school supplies. Her professional experience includes marketing, advertising, and public relations positions with TI-IN Network and the University of Texas Institute of Texan Cultures, and such newspaper positions as managing editor, columnist, and reporter in Texas and Montana. You can reach Charlene at (210) 656-2324 or at charlene@satexas.com.*

Getting Press Coverage

by Susan McLester

Editors in the education press enjoy a friendly rivalry that allows us to argue on panels and among ourselves about the merits of a particular curriculum product, the wisdom of a company's marketing strategy, or the implications for schools of an emerging technology or piece of legislation. Sometimes our viewpoints are even diametrically opposed. In one area, however, we're in unanimous agreement (at least 98% of the time). And this is in the area of public relations.

I know this because I happen to be a member of an exalted secret society for education journalists. Okay, well I guess, everybody pretty much knows about the EDIT group—an acronym for Eat, Dance, Imbibe, Talk—and all right, I guess it's not really that exalted either *per se*. EDIT members convene at conferences around the nation to share the lowdown on trends and other hot conference topics relevant to our publications. Fairly adept at multi-tasking, group members often exchange information while engaged in other activities, such as contests to see who can gulp down the biggest spoonful of horseradish without taking a slug of Red Hook. Whatever the task, topic, or setting, however, an ongoing discussion of public relations people and strategies is a given at these sessions. As an EDIT member in good standing, I believe I may take the liberty of speaking for us all as I offer tips on the best ways to deal with the press to get the coverage you need.

Be Likable

Barbara Streisand was pretty much on the money with that "people who like people" thing—especially when it comes to dealing with editors. If you are pleasant to speak with, to deal with, and to be around in general, we are much more likely to spend time with you and the product(s) you represent. A smart PR person works at developing trusting, ongoing relationships with editors and fostering open, honest communication that will ultimately benefit both parties. Editors can provide valuable feedback on products that might come in handy for later versions or updates, and PR people can help out editors by making them aware of trends, or rounding up a list of competing products or success stories that will help us bring useful information to our readers.

Do Your Homework

Know the publications you're working with. Know what departments they run, and pay attention to what topics they've covered recently and are about to cover. Call for a media kit to see what articles are planned, or go to the Web site and print it out. Design your pitches around the editorial calendar, when possible. However, even if you don't see a place your product might fit in, send news of it anyway. Most editorial calendars are "cast in quicksand" in order to be flexible and responsive to the market.

Know Your Own Competition

Even though you may feel there "really is no competition" for your product, it is nevertheless wise to spend some time studying those offerings that editors might consider your competition. Companies with large, multi-featured products, such as school management packages sometimes even put together a feature-by-feature chart to help editors get a handle on how it stacks up component-wise, against similar offerings. (Of course, expect us to be skeptical of any evaluative components to your chart.) Beware of claiming "the first" or "the only" when describing your product. Editors, especially those who've been around a while, usually have a pretty good idea of what's already been done, so an inaccurate claim can seriously undermine your credibility.

Don't Give Us Assignments

We've all had PR people call up and ask, "Have you covered us in the last year?" or "Here's a press release. How would this fit into your magazine?" It is the PR person's job to do this legwork, not the editor's. Another mistake is not having a PR agenda. Editors appreciate the opportunity to ask questions, but booking up a time slot, or a lunch, and then asking us what we'd like to talk about is not the best approach. Tell us what you think is relevant to our readers; we may not know enough about what you're doing to ask the right questions.

Don't Cry Wolf

We know it is the job of the PR person to keep in contact with editors, but taking up time with persistent phone calls or demos when there really isn't any news can do more harm than good for you in the long run. If your CD is now available for Macintosh as well as Windows, please do send an announcement, but don't hold a press conference. I can't count the number of times I've heard editors say, "I like that PR group, but they never have any news." Pretty soon, no one reads your e-mails anymore.

Don't Ask Us to Compromise Our Integrity

I know policy differs from one magazine to the next, but be aware of how a publication operates. For instance, at *Technology & Learning*, we would never consent to sending you pre-published editorial copy for your approval. If your product is being evaluated, you'll have to trust the professionalism of our writers. "Running it by you" first would be the quickest way for us to lose credibility with our readers. Similarly, respect the policy of magazines that keep a strict barrier between advertorial and editorial —don't insist on coverage simply because you're advertising in an issue.

Know Which Editor Does What at the Magazine

Find out which editors cover news and legislation, application stories, software and Web products, and hardware and emerging technologies. Getting a press release into the right hands can really boost your chances of getting coverage. Also, find out each editor's preference for receiving information—is it voicemail, e-mail or snail mail?

Do Send Review Copies, Web Passwords and Usernames

Software that is sitting on the shelf in and editor's office is much more likely to be reviewed than programs we need to research and contact others to send us. Similarly, if a Web site's password is ready-to-hand, we can visit it at our leisure rather than spending time trying to get a hold of someone who can provide us with one. Also, be sure to send a press release with a product or

> " ...respect the policy of magazines that keep a strict barrier between advertorial and editorial. "

Web announcement, so we know what to expect. If the product comes in a school version, with a teacher's guide or other materials, be sure to send us that version, or at least give us a heads up that one is in the works.

Do Respect Our Time at Conferences

For most editors, industry conferences and trade shows are like Mr. Toad's Wild Ride. We're running from booth to booth, from convention center to hotel suite, from dinner to press event. My experience is that 15 minutes is usually enough time to understand what a product is about and to ask the important questions. Most helpful to us is knowing what general category the product fits into, seeing a quick demo of it, and finding out who to contact for follow-up information once we've had a chance to test drive it ourselves back in the office. Don't insist on an hour-long meeting during a two-day conference when there are 25 other companies we need to cover. One incident, a legend among EDIT members, involved a company that first spammed all editors at all magazines with requests for demos and lunches, then rounded up the same huge group for dinner at a good restaurant, and next kept them waiting—foodless and drinkless—for 40 minutes until the company representative showed up. The nightmare continued when, after a few glasses of wine, we discovered "plants" at our tables who turned on the hard sell while the salmon entries chilled down to an arctic temperature. That PR firm dropped a load of money and committed a lot of time, only to have things backfire. Everyone avoids them now.

Don't Overwhelm

We know you're excited about your product, but beware of coming on too strong. More than once, an editor has stumbled, glazed-eyed into an EDIT meeting, muttering "The horror! The horror!"—and has had to be "talked down" over a platter of chicken fingers, or fried artichoke hearts. The most common tale is that of being "trapped like a rat, outnumbered and grilled" by an aggressive squad of clean cut, corporate evangelists, who want to show you every detail of their product and then demand to know right then and there where and how you'll cover it. Sometimes information needs to "steep" a bit and be shared with other staff before we know exactly how we'll use it. It's best to step back a bit and follow up later with these specific questions.

Know that a Picture Really Is Worth 1,000 Words

It can be good to know how a product was conceived and sometimes even what the vision was behind it, but a demo will have the greatest impact if you spend most of the time actually showing the software or Web site. A lengthy PowerPoint explanation of the company's marketing strategy can be informative in the right circumstances, but at the end of a long day, it can also induce the jungle sleeping sickness.

Let Us Hear from You When Things Go Right, Too

If we print the wrong price, the wrong news, or the wrong contact information, do let us know. But similarly, if you're delighted with the coverage, tell us about that, too. Everybody appreciates positive feedback.

Be Aware of Our Deadlines

Most of us have a three- or four-month lead on printed content. Please be sure to get relevant press releases to editors as soon as possible. If your product won't officially be launching until after a press deadline, suggest that we sign a non-disclosure agreement and get us an advance copy. This will allow us to help you out by covering your product immediately after you announce it.

Write a Clear Press Release

The importance of this cannot be overstated. Because editors may see hundreds of press releases in a week, they are likely to read the title and subtitle, and perhaps skim the first paragraph. All of the main pieces of information should be included up front; otherwise, the release is likely to end up in the circular file. Incredible as it may seem, some press releases lack even the most basic who, where, and what. Editors are not likely to put in much time trying to "crack the code" on these.

Be Helpful

Press suites at conferences that let editors visit several companies in one room are great time savers. And small conveniences—such as mailing press kits to our offices so we don't have to schlep a heavy briefcase, supplying pens and tablets, and having a Coke or some water handy—are also always appreciated. On an ongoing basis, you can help us out by posting high-quality graphics and other screen shots in an easy-to-find place on your Web site—along with pricing information and other basics about your products.

Bottom line, put yourselves in our shoes. We need you and you need us. Let's make it fun and productive for both sides.

About the Author

Susan McLester is editor-in-chief of Technology & Learning, the national magazine sponsoring SchoolTech Expo. She has been an editor for T&L for eight years, is an experienced classroom teacher and has written about technology in education for a variety of publications including Newsweek, Home PC, and Parenting. McLester writes a weekly column on education technology for the Los Angeles Times, has talked about technology on Microsoft NBC's The Site and other television programs, and has been a judge for numerous software contests.

The Demo Suite—Demonstrating the Value of Your Products

by Kati Elliott

Merriam-Webster's *Collegiate Dictionary* gives the following definitions for the term "demonstrate:"

1. (a) To prove or make clear by reasoning or evidence; (b) to illustrate and explain, especially with many examples;

2. To show or prove the value or efficiency of to a prospective buyer.

When determining whether or not to hold a demo suite, answer these key questions:

- Are you trying to prove to the media the power of your product by reasoning or evidence?

- Are you trying to show the value of your product to prospective buyers?

If the answer is "yes" to either question, and if you have determined that your exhibit presence does not provide a suitable environment for intimate conversations with potential customers or the media, it is time to plan a demo suite. In order to pack the most into your demo suite, follow the PAC rule—Planning, Atmosphere, and Communication. If you have thoroughly addressed all three of the PAC components, you are on your way to having a successful demo suite. But leave out one and you could have a disaster.

Planning

Holding a demo suite—whether for media appointments, customer appointments, or both—is an expensive undertaking for a company. Consider the following questions in making the decision to hold a demo suite:

- Will the demo suite pay for itself in either articles about a product or purchases by key customers?

- Did you begin planning early enough to attract the right people?

- Is the story compelling enough to compete with other demo suites or conference sessions?

- Does the demo suite provide something unique that can't be accomplished through your booth?

The following discussion will help define the implications of each of these questions to help you in planning for your demo suite.

Will the Demo Suite Pay for Itself?

To determine whether a suite will pay for itself, you will need to determine your definition of financial success. Everything we do, from sales to marketing to public relations, needs to directly increase sales for the company. If your company is not making money, it cannot afford to continue to create high-quality educational programs that benefit teachers and students. The following chart indicates the average cost of hosting a two-day suite, along with its potential benefits.

COSTS

SUITE NEEDS	COST
Room Rental	$400
Catering	$2,500
Signage	$300
Postcard Invitations	$500
Equipment Rental	$3,000
Give-aways	$500
Decorations	$250
Travel for Product Developer	$500
Hotel Room for Product Developer	$700
Shipping to and from Suite	$300
Total	**$8,950**

BENEFITS

SUITE APPOINTMENTS	FINANCIAL BENEFITS
Media	1 article at $500 for column inches
Media	1 article at $1,000 for column inches
Media	1 article at $1,000 for column inches
Media	1 article at $3,500 for column inches
Customer	No Sale
Media	No Article
Customer	Sale at $25,000 for school district
Customer	Sale at $1 million for state-wide purchase
Customer	No Sale
Media	1 article at $3,000 for column inches
Total	**$1,034,000**

In this scenario the demo suite has more than paid for itself. This suite was successful because the company holding the suite paid close attention to the PAC rule.

Did You Begin Planning Early Enough to Attract the Right People?

Generally speaking, a demo suite should be planned three to six months prior to the convention and demo suite dates. For a company exhibiting at a convention, it is recommended that this company coordinate the demo suite space with the organization sponsoring the conference. The exhibits coordinator will have an understanding of the meeting space available and will most likely be able to place your demo suite in one of the convention hotels.

If you know your way around the city where your demo suite will be held, have two hotels or locations in mind before you contact the exhibits coordinator. If you know what you want, the likelihood of your getting a good location is better than if you leave it completely up to the exhibits coordinator. If you don't know the city well, find someone who does. Ask your local salespeople to describe the city and identify key locations near the convention center. Being centrally located in a convention hotel is critical to attracting people to your suite. If people have difficulty finding your suite, or if they have to travel a distance to get there, it is unlikely that they will attend.

Once you have picked the location, conduct a site visit. This will help you to determine the amount and kind of signage you will need; allow you to sample the food the hotel or convention center can provide; and give you a chance to build a relationship with your on-site contact. If you need an Internet connection in the suite, be aware that this often needs to be ordered a couple of months prior to the service date. Your on-site contact can put you in touch with the best providers of Internet connections, equipment rentals, flowers, and other services you may require.

Once you have chosen the location for your suite, it is recommended that you create a task list to guide the next phase of your planning. With a list of tasks in hand and a timeline for their completion, you can assign responsibilities to the appropriate staff and make sure that everything is completed in a timely fashion. You should involve the product development, marketing, sales, and public relations departments in the planning of the demo suite. If all staff members know their responsibilities and the objectives of the demo suite, you are more likely to succeed.

Also, it is highly recommended to conduct a review of the suite's performance, after the conference. Make a list of the things liked by all involved, those things that did not work, and those things everyone wished had been thought about before the demo suite took place. This kind of re-cap will give you concrete notes for the next demo suite.

Next up, you will need to develop your invitation list and the invitations themselves. If your demo suite is being held during a highly engaging convention, it is recommended that you send out invitations six to eight weeks prior to the convention dates. In order to do this, you need to create invitations, determine the products you will promote, and get invitee lists from your salespeople two or three months before the demo suite dates.

Is the Story Compelling Enough to Compete with Other Demo Suites or Conference Sessions?

Educational conferences are the number one place to meet with the media and potential customers to share product news. Because of this, the competition for visibility at these conferences is fierce. To fare well, you need to be sure that your news is compelling enough to warrant a demo suite. If you are introducing a new product or service that changes the way individuals teach or learn, and if you can express this effectively on your invitation, your story will be compelling enough to draw people to your demo suite.

One approach to articulating the nature of a product or service and its value for schools is to have a key product developer on hand to discuss the philosophy behind the product. Also, any educators who were involved in the development or testing of the product can help provide evidence for its need to a board audience.

Does the Demo Suite Provide Something Unique that Can't Be Done in the Booth?

Although education conferences are a great venue for getting access to a large number of people who have an interest in your market, it is a very expensive proposition just to exhibit at a convention. Adding the cost of a demo suite is only recommended if you realistically believe your demo suite will garner benefits beyond its costs. If you are able to schedule appointments in the demo suite and fill up your days there with potential customers and media, and if a suite allows you to have conversations that could not take place on the show floor, then it can be a positive venue for achieving the outcomes you desire.

Atmosphere

Determining the image you will portray in the suite is another key step in planning a successful demo suite. This image should be consistent with that of other marketing materials and should reflect the personality of both your company and the product you are showing in the demo suite.

A good recent example of setting atmosphere in a demo suite was provided by the Internet education company, Classroom Connect. The company set up a rain forest in a demo suite to announce its MayaQuest program to the media. They used plants supplied by the hotel where the suite was located and displayed stuffed animals commonly found in the rain forest to set the stage for their announcement. The rain forest atmosphere immediately focused the attendees' attention on the product, while it also allowed for an intimate discussion of the company's products and services. The company held a drawing at the end of the demo suite press period, which allowed them to give away the stuffed animals displayed and have further, follow-on discussions with those individuals who won.

> "Determining the image you will portray in the suite is another key step in planning a successful demo suite."

As you decide upon your company's personality, determine how this translates to the invitations, the food you will serve, the location of your demo suite and the follow-up materials you will use.

Even if you do not want to decorate your demo suite extensively, a few key elements can set your suite apart from the others:

- Flowers and greenery give the suite a homey, comfortable feel and add a fresh scent to most hotel rooms.

- Displays of food and drink that are out of the ordinary help to differentiate your suite from the others. Finger foods allow individuals to eat even while they are taking notes. And don't forget to have something for vegetarians!

- If you have a restroom attached to your demo suite, a lighted candle provides a calming effect for those individuals who use it.

- A box of tissues is an added bonus for those media and potential customers who get hit with allergies while traveling.

- Mints are always welcome.

- A small medicine box can provide needed relief to someone who has discomfort, such as a headache or a blister during your meeting.

A comfortable demo suite, stocked with supplies appropriate for the meetings, will help your attendees feel comfortable and allow them to focus on the product you are showing.

Communication

Clear communication—both internally and externally—will allow you to have a successful and cost effective demo suite.

To communicate internally, make sure all parties involved in the suite know their responsibilities. Also, assign the schedule to a single individual. That way you will not overlap appointments.

Department by department, here are some further suggestions to help you prepare your team to use a demo suite to its fullest:

Sales representatives. If you are planning on using the demo suite for potential customer meetings, make sure your salespeople know the results you expect and how they can meet those outcomes. Let them know how many customers can meet comfortably in the suite at one time. Have each salesperson supply you with an invitation list. Other things to consider include:

- Equipment needed to demonstrate the product

- Product developers and/or beta testers that could be on hand to discuss the product and learning outcomes

- Times the suite will need to be manned for appointments

- Dates for invitation mailing, scheduling, and other preparatory tasks.

- Theme of the demo suite
- Person assigned to keep the schedule for the suite
- Materials you will have on hand to assist sales people (e.g., PowerPoint demonstrations, fact sheet, brochures, theory papers, and so forth).

Once you send the invitations, confirm that your salespeople will call their key customers to schedule appointments. Regular follow up with your sales people will help to ensure that they are filling the demo suite with appointments.

Marketing. Your marketing staff is your link to materials for your suite. They should create your invitation; the materials available for use during your meetings; and any follow-up material you will use after the meetings. It is very important to supply marketing with a realistic timeline so they can get materials done on time.

Public Relations. If you are scheduling media appointments in the demo suite, several calls will need to be made. Keeping a calendar to mark when the media are available to schedule appointments will help to assure you get on their schedules at the appropriate times. The media are constantly working under deadlines and you must accommodate these deadlines when trying to schedule their time. Once appointments have been scheduled, it is important to confirm them as the event approaches.

And Finally, the Planner. Ongoing communication with the hotel staff is important for getting what you want. Confirmation of Internet connection installation, equipment rentals, catering, set up, etc., is important to making sure your demo suite is conducted smoothly. An organized schedule, with communication back to all people scheduling appointments is important to a smooth transition between appointments.

Lastly, provide yourself sufficient time to break down the room and package up materials for shipping. A stress-free planner makes for a smooth event.

About the Author

Kati Elliott is president of KEH Communications, Inc. (www.kehcomm.com). KEH Communications specializes in education public relations and marketing services. KEH Communications provides each of its clients with a robust public relations plan that is individualized to meet their needs. Kati Elliott, a former editor for an education magazine and a long-time account representative at a mid-sized public relations agency, formed KEH Communications with the goal of helping companies to be successful in education. Kati can be reached at (410) 975-9638 or kati@kehcomm.com.

CHAPTER 9

Conferences and Exhibits

Inside this chapter...

Developing a Trade Show Strategy

by Peggy R. Lanier

Tradeshow participation is one of the most expensive yet rewarding marketing activities for any size or type of education company. The key to understanding and maximizing the tradeshow experience is to put yourself in the place of the attendee.

Think Like Your Customer

Try to remember how you feel when you attend a tradeshow. Do you go with an agenda, or do you want to stop and speak to every vendor on the show floor? What makes one vendor showcase inviting and another one tedious? How much material and information do you want to take away from your visit to the show floor? Do you really just want to gather up free "goodies?" Do your feet hurt? Do you find in general that company representatives understand your job, your needs, and your budget? How much of the information that you gather do you throw away when it comes time to pack up your suitcase for the long trip home? If the material does make it home, to whom in your school or district do you distribute it? Once you're back at your office or school, do you remember whom you spoke with during the show? Yes, this is a lot to think about, but the point is that all of these issues and more should be considered as your build your company's tradeshow strategy.

The Big Picture Is a Lot of Small Dots

Tradeshow strategy is just one component of your overall marketing plan. It should support and integrate with other marketing strategies and tactics to create a more cohesive whole. Tradeshow strategies fall into several different categories, including:

1. awareness building and brand extension,
2. lead generation,
3. product demonstrations, and
4. onsite sales of products or services.

> "Getting the most out of your tradeshow investment begins several months or even a year before the tradeshow starts."

In addition, tradeshows provide an excellent opportunity to obtain competitive information, develop relationships with other companies to form partnerships, meet with current or prospective distribution and sales organizations, recruit and interview prospective employees, have company sales strategy meetings, and speak with the press regarding your company and its products. Understanding the various aspects of the tradeshow will help you to pinpoint the places in your overall plan where tradeshows can be the catalyst to connect all the marketing "dots."

What's the Best Show to Attend?

This question is often asked and easily answered. The best show to attend is the show that delivers the targeted results you have identified as important to your company. No single show is the right fit for all companies. Small shows can sometimes deliver a better overall response than larger shows: it all depends on what you are seeking. For example, one company attended a small targeted show with only 300 attendees, which resulted in 58 highly qualified contacts. That may not sound like a lot, but when you consider that most leads take roughly six to eight months to move into the "qualified" category, it was an excellent outcome. For another company, larger conferences provided more brand awareness and allowed them to deliver their message to hundreds of prospects in only a few days. If they had been looking for qualified prospects, these larger shows might have been deemed failures, but they were not because they had a different goal for those events—to expose as many educators to their product as possible. As with all marketing activities, the key to determining whether tradeshows meet their objectives is to have well-defined goals.

You Need to Know What You Want

Regardless of your individual tradeshow strategy, the best basis for determining if a show is worthwhile is to know what you want out of the event. Having a clear picture of the results you expect from the show will help you to commit funds and personnel to the tradeshow with confidence in your decision. The show history is the only way to know what can be expected from each individual tradeshow. You must do your homework and know who attends, why they attend, what buying power or influence they have, and how many people you can expect to show up each year. If a tradeshow is in its first year, take a cautious approach—attend the event, but just walk the floor. This way, you can minimize your risk and still determine if it is worth your investment to attend the following year.

Once you know who your target customer is, locating the right show for your product or service is easy using the Internet. Most education magazines and newsletters list shows of interest to their readership. In addition, several publications have online schedules of shows available for no charge. Some of the most popular Web sites for locating education tradeshows are:

1. Peter Li Publications, at www.peterli.com

2. *T.H.E. Journal*, at www.thejournal.com

3. *eSchool News*, at www.eschoolnews.com

Once you have identified shows that appear to attract buyers who match your products and services, use the following matrix to help you identify the best shows for your needs. You will need to visit each show's Web site and look up the following information:

process is to determine when you can submit proposals for presentations. The proposal for presentation is the first step in obtaining a speaking slot during the conference portion of the tradeshow. Most education tradeshows have a conference agenda that includes topical sessions presented by peers. For example, the Florida Education Technology Conference (FETC) features over 300 presentations. A teacher or panel of teachers gives each presentation to an audience of teachers. The peer-to-peer nature of these presentations builds credibility for the products or programs that are discussed, as well as for the teacher-presenters themselves. It is extremely important that you develop positive relations with your customers and help them submit proposals for presentations at the events you are attending. The more help you can give an educator to make a presentation a success and a positive experience, the more devoted they will become in advocating your company and your products. You may want to offer them a small stipend, or offer to pay for the cost of a substitute teacher so that your lead advocate can attend and present.

The proposal for presentation is usually submitted online, six to nine months in advance of the tradeshow or conference. Competition for the limited number of speaking slots is intense, so you need to develop a catchy title and timely content, and find a presenter who is an engaging public speaker. Having a speaker who resides in the state or area where the conference is being held is always a very good thing! Submit as many

TRADESHOW NAME				
Who Attends?	What Influence?	How Many Attend?	What Geographic Area?	How Many Leads Do You Expect?
Collect this information from the tradeshow's Web site.	Do they make or influence buying decisions?	Collect this from the tradeshow's Web site, or contact the management.	Collect from the tradeshow's Web site. No one gets to talk to all the attendees.	What's the minimum you would be happy with from this show?

Once you have charted all possible shows, you need to consider staffing, budgets, booth space availability, and most important of all, your strategy for lead follow-up.

Planning, Planning, and More Planning

Getting the most out of your tradeshow investment begins several months or even a year before the tradeshow starts. The first step of your initial planning

proposals for presentations as you can to increase your odds of getting several different speaker slots. Only as a last-ditch effort should you submit a proposal for presentation using a company spokesperson or paid presenter. These presentations are usually not granted speaking time, since conference organizers see them as a commercial activity.

Sponsorships

The next step in planning your tradeshow strategy is to identify any special promotional opportunities you may want to take advantage of during the show. There are a variety of sponsorship opportunities, including conference-bag advertising, hotel door drops, daily conference flyers, meals, breakout sessions, computer rooms, and so on. Talk to each show manager to identify the special events that are available and their costs. Virtually everything is negotiable, so don't feel obligated to pay the first price that is quoted, but recognize that the show management needs to have companies cover the cost of these items!

Booth Themes and Events

Once you've secured your speaking sessions and know which promotional activities you plan to sponsor, you're ready to start planning your pre-conference marketing activities. Remember, it is your responsibility to drive the conference attendees to your booth. Merely having a booth—regardless of how big or impressive—is rarely enough to get the walkthrough traffic you desire. You must design an event that will entice even the most skeptical prospect to your space. And don't forget, educators love free stuff!

Here are a few examples of successful events at tradeshows.

- Create a booth environment that has the look and feel of an element of your product or service. Send out a pre-conference postcard inviting attendees to come to the booth for a free gift or product sample that coordinates with the look and feel of the booth/product.

- Organize an off-site event and provide free transportation to and from it. However, make sure you have notified the show management and received their approval for the activity before taking people away from the show. They usually allow these types of activities only after show hours.

- Take advantage of a sporting or other event in the city where the show is being held and invite key prospects and customers to attend. Send a "goodie" bag beforehand that will give them hints as to what the event is, but don't tell them until they arrive at the show and visit your booth.

The Demonstration

One of the most successful tradeshow activities is the in-booth demonstration. Educators will take time from their hectic schedules to sit through a group demonstration of products they already own or those that they intend to purchase. It is important to create an environment in your booth where attendees don't feel trapped and can enter and exit easily. Also, make sure that the chairs or benches are comfortable and that your sound system works properly. Remember, your prospects can leave as they want, so motivating them to stay in their seats throughout the presentation is a must. One technique is to give away a free product or service at the end of the demonstration for anyone who has completed a lead card. This works well in keeping their attention through to the end of the presentation. Make each presentation no more than 10-12 minutes long and vary the content throughout the hour. Have a large clock or sign that lets passers-by know what is to be demonstrated and when, and stick to your schedule. If no one shows up for a presentation, give it anyway for the practice and go to the next scheduled event as shown on your sign. Nothing irritates customers more than making their way back to the booth to find that the presentation is not being given as advertised. Careful planning and practicing of your in-booth presentations is essential.

> **"One of the most successful tradeshow activities is the in-booth demonstration."**

After the Affair

Pre-planning how you will respond to the leads you acquire is the single most important step in building your overall tradeshow strategy. After all, what's the use in doing all the lead-generating activities if follow-up is lacking? Here are a few things to keep in mind when determining how to follow up.

Prospects forget you quickly. Your lead follow-up plan needs to go into action the day after the tradeshow is over.

Use the electronic lead collection devices, but customize the response card for your products and services.

Get as much information as possible on your lead card. Design the card to capture all the critical information, plus info such as the best time to call, what current products the prospect is using, when they intend to buy, who controls the budget, and of course the all-important phone number and e-mail address

Create a way to identify hot prospects, and code the lead card so these leads can be passed directly to a salesperson. E-mail or fax them back to your office the day of the show so follow-up can begin immediately.

Send the conference's pre-registered attendee list to your salespeople a few weeks prior to the event, so they can see who is attending. Then, just before the tradeshow, canvass your salespeople and ask them to identify any key prospects who will be attending the show. Each person at the show should know who these people are and respond to them if they come to the booth.

Tradeshow lead tracking should be made a budget priority to help justify the company's continued financial commitment to these important marketing events.

In Conclusion

Successful tradeshow strategy development should result in increased brand awareness for your company and products, improved relationships with your customers and the press, and an abundance of qualified leads for your sales team. By carefully planning and implementing this important component of your overall marketing plan and strategy, you will help to assure your organization's continued success and prosperity.

About the Author

Peggy R. Lanier *has helped education companies build effective marketing and sales strategy for over two decades. She has knowledge and understanding of all facets of marketing including strategy, tactical implementation, advertising, public relations, tradeshows, marketing research, and corporate identity, branding and logo/brochure design. At companies including IBM, McGraw-Hill, Computer Associates and other major and smaller education organizations, she has led marketing departments to achieve their goals. Peggy is currently co-founder of LanierWalkington, www.lanierwalkington.com, and she can be reached at planier@home.com or by calling (619) 260-0974.*

On With the Show:
Exhibits—Where Marketing and Design Meet to Greet

by Linda Winter

Thinking about trade shows and marketing through exhibits? It's expensive. Every decision you make has real cost implications. Plusher carpet? That costs more. Hiring an exhibit company to manage set-up, teardown, and exhibit maintenance? It's less expensive to do it yourself. Or is it? Theater-style product demonstrations? Premiums and give-aways to draw traffic? The battery on your calculator is burning up and your head is spinning.

In the education market over the last few years, we've all witnessed a new sophistication on our conference show floors. Interactive, theater-style product demonstrations presented by product experts who are wired for sound. Elaborately-costumed characters beckoning teachers in for a free gift and short sound byte. One large computer manufacturer regularly brings in troops of jugglers and acrobats to entertain and provide new product information as they wobble. Recently, at the annual conference of the National Science Teachers' Association, NASA arrived with a mock-up, walk-through space command center, complete with special effects.

It's show time, and the price of entry for exhibitors is going up.

Maximizing Impact, Controlling Costs.

A decade ago, the McGraw-Hill Laboratory of Advertising Performance reported that the average cost of contacting and closing a sale with a qualified trade show prospect was $334, compared to the $1,384 cost estimated for completing a sale through on-site, in-person selling. We suspect that while the numbers have changed today, the gap hasn't narrowed much at all. And the costs of fielding a direct sales staff that calls on districts and reaches individual school sites has grown beyond the reach of many of the school market's smaller and even mid-size companies.

Conferences continue to represent superior marketing and selling opportunities. The challenge is to achieve your objectives and control your costs...all while taking full advantage of the on- and off-the-floor opportunities that every national and regional education conference provides.

Here are some quick tips that will make your conference investment more productive:

Establish real objectives for each conference venue, in terms of number of leads, number of appointments, number of press contacts, and so forth. This kind of focus leads to better results.

Assess conference attendance and targeting each year. Some national shows lose their cachet. New events crop up. Regional conferences grow in prominence.

Assume that a pre-show promotion is a "fixed" cost – as much so as shipping for your booths and literature or hotel rooms for your staff. Pre-show promotions build traffic, serve as door-openers for your sales staff, and give your show initiative cohesion.

With the above three guidelines as the backbone of your conference planning, it's easier to control costs and maximize your marketing impact. For example, if your objective is to gather 400 leads for your new software product, then your pre-show promotions, your booth graphics, your press focus, and your literature should all be concentrated on this objective. It can save you money across the board.

Exhibit Design and Configuration: There's a Solution Here Somewhere

There simply is no single "right" solution for exhibit design. The number of shows you attend, the space dimensions you reserve, your technology, display, and presentation requirements, the number of staff you assign to "work" the booth, your capacity for do-it-yourself set-up and tear-down—all of these factors form the foundation of your booth's "design program." Professional exhibit design firms are expert at taking your program of functions, needs, selling style, and product line characteristics and using those as a launching pad for creating an exhibit that will drive traffic and results.

Does that mean you have to hire a costly exhibit design specialist? Yes and no. If you consistently use a 10' x 10' space and have simple display and literature distribution needs, you can work with an exhibit house to purchase or lease modular, portable units that are lightweight, inexpensive to ship, and simple to set up. Once you've settled on the base "unit" you can manage individual exhibits on your own. Our advice, however, is to spend the time and money needed with an exhibit professional, even if your needs are modest. Why? There are so many add-ons, unique configurations, and options for materials, display units and lighting that a professional's "eye" and experience can add tremendous value.

At the other end of the spectrum, if your conference strategy follows a "go big or stay home" mentality, exhibit designers can make your booth look and function better and can save you money in the long run. Professional exhibit designers know their way around sight lines, storage, lighting, traffic flow, creating visual "arrival" across a crowded room, and designing space for multiple interactions...ranging from casual walk-throughs to more intense, higher-level conversations with key customers and top prospects.

Professional exhibit designers will typically require—that's right, require—clients to complete a detailed "program document," outlining all of the functions that will need to occur within an exhibit space. It's a time-consuming, laborious process, but the more completely you answer these design-programming questions, the better your exhibit will look and function.

The Design Process

Thanks to the wonders of computer-assisted drafting, your exhibit designer can show you early booth concepts in full dimension. This is the time and the place to look at as many options as you can. Experiment with different shapes of units, fixtures, and display devices. Consider the visual impact at long, middle and close range. Build in flexible merchandising options for graphics so the base structure can be easily adapted to a succession of show themes, product launches, and other key marketing events.

As the design process unfolds and after you've selected a basic booth configuration, your exhibit professional will work with you to map traffic flow, literature distribution, product demonstrations, larger theater presentations, signage, and storage. You or a trusted representative

should be involved in this design phase from beginning to end. It's vital to assure that your booth meets your needs, not the designer's. Further, fabrication costs will be estimated on the basis of the specifications developed. Your full participation translates to fewer surprises on the bottom line.

After all the traffic drawings, construction blueprints, swatches, and display layouts are complete and approved, construction begins. During this phase, you can relax—temporarily. You may want to involve your marcom team in creating graphics for displays and so on, but there's no pressing need to check particleboards as they're being cut. That is, not until your trial run set-up. This is a mandatory step—not optional in the slightest. Here, your booth should be set up completely on the exhibit firm's floor. Test the lights. Open the cabinet doors. Sit on the benches. Walk through the entryways. Run the monitors and the microphones. Make sure each literature rack, backlit poster, and shelf you've specified is included and is functioning perfectly. At the same time, re-confirm shipping items. This includes the number of crates, assembly instructions, labeling, spare parts, and power cords. Make sure it's all there and accounted for.

> "Visuals for booth displays need to be bold, descriptive, and compelling."

Whenever possible, at Winter Group, we prefer to have a representative of our exhibit firm's staff on site for the set up of a new booth. Every large exhibit has its own set of nooks and crannies and idiosyncratic features that require specialized know-how. Once this maiden voyage is out of the way, there's much smoother sailing at subsequent conferences.

Graphics, Collateral, and Giveaways: A Few Quick Tips.

Graphics are a key element of booth design. But they're different from your ads, your brochures, or your direct mail pieces. Lots of verbiage means less readership and less impact. We like the seven-word rule. More than that and you need to call for rewrite.

Visuals for booth displays need to be bold, descriptive, and compelling. If your focus is a new product launch, you may want all of your graphics to highlight specific components and benefits of the new product. If your show focus is a price promotion for your entire product line, your graphics should emphasize that—not the hundreds of delicious benefits each of your products offers. Color, background, the texture of materials—all of these can help frame your visuals and the messages of your copy. Here again, the "eye" of the built-environment designer is of tremendous value.

Collateral materials are another matter. Simple product and promotion flyers are effective and less expensive than complicated services or product brochures. However, it's important to note that at many education conferences, your most current catalog or catalogues should be made available. As many administrators and teachers alike have told us during focus groups, they expect to pick up current catalogs on the show floor...and in fact, that's part of the reason they're attending!

Giveaways are effective in most markets...but in the education market, their impact is remarkable. Educators flock to booths to get the "stuff!" Remember earlier in this article when we spoke about pre-conference promotions? Your pre-show mailer, program ad and other promotions should highlight the "free stuff" you're giving away. It draws traffic, creates buzz, and helps you to open conversations with your booth visitors.

If you're an education conference veteran, as many of us are, you know that typically, the busiest booths at any show—from technology conferences to math meetings—are the booths that sell the teacher "stuff." The pencils,

the buttons that say, "Love your teacher," the magnets... you get the picture. We're not salmon, and we don't want to swim that hard upstream, so at Winter Group we counsel clients to pay attention to the market's message. If they want that "stuff," well, we'd rather they spend time in our booth getting it from us, so that we get a chance to talk to them, understand their needs, and sell them our stuff!

What does all this have to do with booth design?

When you know that educators come to pick up literature and they put you on their dance cards based on the "stuff" you're giving away, it makes sense to design your booth to accommodate these needs. Then your design program can set aside more intimate space for product demonstrations, quieter conversations, and the real work of introducing prospects to your products and selling. Even in a 10' x 10' booth, you can create a "give-away" kiosk and a product demonstration area...it just demands good spatial design.

Exhibit marketing is a fact of life in the education market. Good design, thorough planning and yes, some cool free stuff can make any event more productive and profitable. You'll reach your objectives for leads, sales, and prospects so that when you arrive back at the office, you can follow the next rule of trade shows: responding to all leads in five days or less. But that's another article...

About the Author

Linda Winter *is an Internet Monitor partner and the president of Winter Group, an award-winning marketing communications, research, and design firm focused on the education and library markets. She started Winter Group in 1978. The firm provides a comprehensive collection of integrated services to education marketers, including advertising, sales support and collateral materials, Web site development, custom market research, direct mail, catalogs, event marketing, and exhibit design. She is a co-author of i-Tips 2000, The Insiders' Guide to School & Library Marketing, published by the Internet Monitor. She can be reached at WinterL@wintergroup.net or at (303) 778-0866, ext. 12.*

Myths and Misperceptions of Sponsorships and Events

by Deb deVries

So…is this like party planning? I don't remember that one in the list of "P's" of business…product, planning, positioning, people, profitability…party planning? Well, call it whatever you like, but in the school market the category of sponsorships and events can be an integral component of the marketing plan. For purposes of clarity, let's agree on some definitions:

Sponsorships: the payment or sharing of expenses related to all or specific activities of a conference, meeting, or organizational function—usually made in cash but sometimes in kind.

Events: specific activities scheduled separately from or in conjunction with a conference or meeting. Usually sponsored by a vendor, these events are determined either by the organization or sometimes by the vendor.

Also, for clarification purposes, the sponsorships and events addressed in this article are specific only to organizations and associations within the school market. Nevertheless, while the article does not address sponsoring an event or function within a school district, on a general level the same principles apply! (And if a company were to identify a large opportunity within a school district, working with them to identify some sponsorship opportunities might make a lot of sense!)

While the concept of sponsorship and event marketing is fairly common in the corporate and private sectors as a primary marketing vehicle to promote brand recognition and image, there are lots of myths and misperceptions regarding their role in the school market. In an effort to dispel these mistaken ideas, the following represents some of the more common truths and falsehoods communicated regarding sponsorships and events:

"Sponsorships Are a Way of Showing Support for Organizations and Associations"—*True*

Most organizations have a list of functions and benefits they provide to members. Some have an annual conference with a hall for exhibitors. These conferences are money-makers for most organizations, and they frown on those vendors who won't exhibit. Other organizations do not have exhibits but may have scheduled meetings throughout the year. Most organizations are very familiar with the needs and desires of vendors for access to their constituents. A great deal can be learned about the membership of an organization through their Web site and other vehicles, but at a basic level most organizations base their sense of vendors on their willingness to support the organization's functions and activities. Said differently, "If you won't support our organization efforts, why should we support your company by buying your products?"

Not all sponsorship opportunities are obvious or explicitly listed as options for vendors. If your company has determined that a certain organization appears to be a good match with your target market, the best approach is to schedule time with its key officials and ask about the organizations needs, explain your company's position, and determine together whether there are some areas of synergy. It may be out that of that discussion a number of opportunities arise, in addition to the "regular" sponsorships (receptions, breaks, etc.), such as helping to publish a document, assisting in an organization program by providing or supporting speakers, and so forth.

"There Is No Way to Sponsor *Anything* Without It Costing a Lot of Money."—*False*

While it is true that you can spend a lot of money by sponsoring events, you don't have to! Naturally an opening reception will probably cost more than a coffee break, and sponsoring a keynote speaker may cost more than providing a session leader. But sometimes the more expensive option will get you more return for your money because of the high visibility of the event or initiative. One strategy is to share the expense of the event or initiative with another vendor (ideally, one that is complementary to your company, or at least not a competitor). It may be that sharing the recognition does not diminish the value your company receives, and this sharing strategy may allow you to sponsor more events).

"Only the 'Big' Companies Sponsor Events."—*False*

While it does appear that at certain conferences and meetings the same big companies are always sponsoring the events, the school market landscape has changed significantly, and many smaller companies are now sponsoring organization and association conference and meeting events and initiatives. It never hurts to ask—even when you know a company has sponsored the same thing for years. Things change, and you may find the spot has become available. Also because of the volatility of the industry many "big" companies have found themselves teaming up with smaller companies. Moreover, initiating a conversation about sharing a sponsorship can be an excellent way to start a business discussion about partnering on a larger level.

"You Never Get Your Money's Worth out of Sponsoring."—*False*

You can always get your money's worth out of sponsoring by leveraging the experience—working before the event to contact attendees, matching up company representatives with attendees and the event's program, attending the event and networking with participants, determining what (if any) materials will go home with the participants, and following up afterwards. If your sponsorship is for an initiative rather than an event, discuss all the opportunities to promote it both within the organization or association and in your company's own promotional materials and Web site. Sometimes an initiative has a longer lifespan than an event and therefore provides a longer marketing opportunity for your company. A number of organizations and associations are implementing longer-term partnership relationships, hoping to work with a few companies who pledge larger sums of money for overall recognition and visibility. These organizations include FETC and COSN. There are obvious benefits to the organization and association for working with a few sponsors who commit to the majority of dollars—including knowing the dollars up front they have to work with and being able to rely on consistent quality in the functions and events they offer. For the vendor, being one of the primary sponsors affords more marketing opportunities as well as the

chance to be promoted at all of the organization's functions and events rather than only one.

"An Event or Sponsorship May Be the Best Way to Get in Front of a Customer."—*True*

All organizations and associations have membership lists, and all have some standard ways to communicate with that membership—including Web sites, regular mailings and newsletters, and conferences and/or meetings. Most companies who work with organizations and associations do take advantage of some or all of these means communication and yet never get really up close and personal with the customer! Working with an organization and association to identify opportunities that may include sponsorship of an event or function makes a lot of sense if it guarantees you a customer audience. Most organizations and associations have occasions where subsets of their membership meet, and there are usually opportunities to get involved in those settings. For example, AASA has special meetings for rural/small school district superintendents, suburban school district superintendents, women school district superintendents, and state-level school district leadership. Sometimes the best opportunity to get to know someone is at a more social occasion, which can provide a basis for following up later.

"What Happens Before the Event May Be More Important than the Event Itself."—*True*

Every organization and association will provide conference and meeting sponsors with an agenda and an attendee list. These pre-conference items can be very beneficial in getting maximum value from your sponsorship. Meeting times can be made prior to the conference or meeting with key attendees, a letter of introduction can be sent with company materials inviting attendees to sponsored event, and sessions of interest to company representatives can be identified. Often seeing the agenda may prompt a vendor to suggest a speaker or identify additional resources for the conference or meeting planner. While it is best to ask, most conferences or meetings are open to this kind of vendor participation, and it can

> " ...initiating a conversation about sharing a sponsorship can be an excellent way to start a business discussion about partnering on a larger level. "

provide a great opportunity to learn first hand about the organization and association and get to know its leadership.

"Once You Sponsor an Event You May Never Have to Do It Again."—*True*

It is often thought (mistakenly) that once you have sponsored an event that you will have that sponsorship each year unless you specifically ask to be removed. Most organizations will give the current sponsor the right of first refusal on continuing to be the sponsor. But the continuation of sponsorship should be reviewed against the marketing plan goals and objectives to determine if it still makes sense to do it. For example, NetSchools Corp. decided to cosponsor the opening reception at NECC, 2000 with Hewlett-Packard Co. This expense represented a significant portion of the marketing budget for NetSchools, and yet when evaluated against the goals of launching a new relationship and product in the corporate headquarters city with an audience of key customers and influencers, the decision was easy. Since the goals and variables were different the subsequent year, the opportunity to sponsor the opening event was declined.

On the other hand, it may be determined that a particular event is important to the overall marketing plan and needs to be repeated annually. These decisions need to be reviewed against the marketing plan to ensure that maximum benefit is realized.

"You Don't Need to Sponsor an Event after You're Established in the Market."—*False*

While you may not think you need to sponsor an event or function if you are well known, the very fact you are well known may be the goodwill created and perceived support you have provided by sponsoring in the past. Sometimes the reason for sponsoring is to thank attendees. Sometimes the reason is to help the organization move in another direction or to launch a new initiative that would be better accepted with the established vendor name attached. In every case, understanding the needs of the organization and association will help determine whether an established vendor should continue in a sponsorship role.

"Organizations and Associations Have No Idea How Tight Things Are Right Now."—*False*

These are interesting times we are experiencing: lots of consolidation, merging, investing, and buying…and yes, some companies are disappearing completely. The organizations and associations representing our constituents are well aware of what is going on in the market; in fact, some school districts have experienced the volatility first hand. Many vendors who sponsored at significant levels in the past either aren't around or have had to cut back in the number of their sponsorships or the level of their support. While this is not an ideal situation to be in from an association's perspective, they do understand that budgets get negatively impacted and plans may need to be changed. Your ability to communicate the bad news gracefully is enhanced if your relationship with the association has developed over time. And while sharing sponsorships with other companies may not be the desired format for either the association or the vendor, it may enable an event to go on and be paid for!

"Most of the Time Attendees at Events Don't Even Know Who Sponsored the Event."—*Unfortunately this can be True*

It is sad and surprising the number of events that are sponsored at conferences and meetings where the sponsoring vendor did not send a single representative! Usually the sponsor is recognized in both printed materials as well as verbally during the proceedings. And while the attendees may make the connection between the event and the vendor, it is much more powerful and beneficial for the vendor to attend the event in as large numbers as possible. The event provides a natural networking opportunity, as attendees want to thank you and are positively inclined toward you. The follow up that may occur after an event is much easier if a live connection has been made. As part of your sponsorship your company may be able to provide literature or premiums during the sponsored event or to include them in registration materials. Be sure to inquire about the possibilities; but remember that most people are not crazy about picking up loads of materials at a reception. You may be better served by either mailing to attendees after the event referencing your sponsorship or providing something complementary to the event like a picture, bag, or memento.

Well, maybe it is party planning after all. For any great party you have given or attended the following guidelines applied:

- Know your audience and pay careful attention to their needs and desires

- Do your homework beforehand and prepare upfront

- Be a visible host or hostess

- Make sure everyone has a good time and network with all guests

- Follow up afterwards

And never, never run out of food or drink!

About the Author

Deb deVries *is the director of marketing programs and development for NetSchools Corporation. NetSchools' products and services transform education by ensuring accountability to standards and equity of access resulting in student achievement. Deb has held sales and marketing leadership positions in many educational technology companies including Control Data, MECC, The Learning Company, and Connors Communications. She resides in St. Paul, MN with her two daughters and her husband, Nizar.*

Where Educators Gather: Marketing at Conferences

by Kay Englund

Meetings. Conferences. Conventions. Educators—teachers, media specialists, principals, school board members, and others—gather with their professional peers every year at local, regional, and national conferences. They meet for a variety of reasons such as to continue professional development or to update their credentials, to learn about the latest educational technologies, to find out how other schools and districts are handling budget cuts or legislated mandates, and, of course, to mix and mingle with new and old friends. Conferences may be organized by education associations, vendors, or government agencies. Most of these events include participation by vendors whose products or services are of interest to the group attending the conference.

Should your company be participating in educators' conferences?

The advantages are obvious. You can introduce your company and its products to hundreds or even thousands of prospective buyers—in person—in a couple of days. You can schmooze with current customers and potential business partners. You can check out the competition.

What's the price tag? There is often more than one level of participation for vendors to choose from, with different costs attached. Before deciding whether you want your company to have a presence at a conference or convention, answer these questions:

- What are your company's goals for attending a conference?
- Which conference or conferences best fit your goals?
- What level of participation will be most cost-effective?

First, Determine Your Company's Goals for Attending a Conference

Decide what your company needs to gain from participating. Gather your company's senior management team to determine why you are investing in this effort. It will be very difficult to justify the expense of implementing a plan to attend a conference if the management team does not support your marketing goals for the conference. Once determined, your goals will drive your strategy. For example, your goals might include one or more of the following:

To obtain X number of sales leads. If this is your goal, the sales team should be on hand at the conference to meet with educators and listen to their questions and concerns.

To launch a product into the education market. Company management and your product development team will be key players in the effort to position your product where you want it in the marketplace.

To learn about the competition.

To conduct strategic meetings with potential partners.

To conduct market research.

To see and be seen. Sometimes companies are conspicuous by their absence. To be a player in this market, you must show up.

To gather your company sales team for a training session. This can be a cost-saving strategy if the sales team is national and if they will be attending the conference anyway. By adding a couple of days to their stay, you can conduct training in conjunction with the conference.

To recruit new personnel. This is a small industry; as companies merge and change their focus, excellent candidates often attend conferences to promote themselves.

To find distribution partners. Many deals are struck at conferences because key industry leaders gather there.

To look for companies to acquire your company.

To look for companies to buy.

To meet with the press. Education reporters attend education conferences, making these events excellent venues for presenting your message and demonstrating your products.

To reward customers. Hosting customer receptions and inviting a mix of current and potential customers can be very effective.

To expose potential customers to your products and services.

To look bigger than you are. Even a very small company can make a big splash at a conference with creative marketing techniques.

To distinguish your company from others in your field. Plan messages and activities that call attention to what makes your company unique.

To position your company as a key player in the market. Vendors can choose to invest money to become key sponsors of conferences. Sponsors are assured of premium positioning for their name and/or advertising in the meeting program guide, on the show floor, at coffee breaks, on signage throughout the conference hall, at opening receptions—everywhere!

Second, Find the Conference that Meets Your Needs

When you've determined your company's goals for participating in an education conference, plan to attend those conferences that will give you the maximum return on your investment. There are a number of places to obtain timely information about upcoming conferences in the educational marketplace. Three excellent resources are located on the Web:

Peter Li Education Group's Educational Meeting Calendar (http://pleg.solveinteractive.com). This is probably the most comprehensive, updated calendar of educational events. It also includes links to the sponsors' Web sites.

Internet Monitor (www.internet-monitor.com). This site offers a comprehensive list of links to professional education associations, most of which sponsor meetings and conventions for their members.

THE Journal (www.thejournal.com/conferences). This site offers direct links to educational technology conferences scheduled nationwide. In addition, for each conference listed on the Web site THE provides a detailed "planning page" that includes the following information:

- Show name
- Location
- Day and month of the show
- Organization sponsoring the conference
- Web site where you can obtain registration, vendor, and program information
- Target audience
- Primary attendees (teachers, trainers, school administrators, school board members, tech coordinators, business executives, product developers, and so forth)
- Number of attendees expected
- Number of vendor booths
- Contact name
- Contact phone number
- Contact e-mail address

About 50% of educator conferences occur in the first three months of the calendar year. This is when educators are learning about new products and services available and are beginning to plan and budget for the purchases they will make for the next school year. In addition to annual education association conventions, almost every state has an educational technology conference highlighting the accomplishments of key educators who are striving to integrate technology into their curriculum.

How do you decide which conferences are right for your company? In assessing the value of participating in any conference, consider these factors:

Who will be attending? If the audience is primarily teachers, is your product one that teachers will readily embrace and see value for in their classrooms?

If the audience is primarily technology coordinators and principals, do your materials explain the technical requirements for using your products? Do your solutions fill the building-wide needs of their schools?

If the audience consists of district staff, school board members, superintendents, or state department of education officials, are your materials and demonstrations presented in a way that relates to their system-wide point of view?

If your audience is curriculum coordinators, does your product information include integration strategies?

Who are the other vendors and exhibitors? Conferences and conventions present an excellent opportunity to learn about your competitors and see how they are positioning themselves in the marketplace.

What are your business development goals? Key industry leaders attend conferences. Strategic meetings at conferences can be extremely productive in developing relationships that lead to product development partnerships, acquisitions, and mergers.

Third, Decide Your Level of Participation in the Conference

Once you've determined what your company hopes to gain from attending a conference and which conferences will be most worthwhile, you must decide how much to invest in participating. Your level of involvement can vary significantly depending on your needs, and the size of the conference, and what you want to accomplish through participating. For example, you can use your presence at the conference to build your company's image or further other business goals by:

- Conducting focus groups
- Setting up key industry meetings to be held during the conference
- Hosting an industry reception
- Hosting a customer reception
- Gathering customers at a luncheon to make an announcement
- Meeting with the news media
- Renting a hotel suite for hospitality or to conduct appointments
- Meeting with an executive recruiter
- Exhibiting at the conference
- Sponsoring the conference

Many individuals and companies are available to help you plan and implement these types of activities if you do not have sufficient in-house staff or expertise.

To Exhibit or Not to Exhibit

Exhibiting at an educator trade show or convention can be an excellent investment or a big waste of money. A company in start-up mode may find it valuable to attend a conference to conduct market research, meet with potential or established partners, and gain a better understanding of the education marketplace, but not to exhibit. This really depends on the goals you have set.

If you do plan to exhibit:

Reserve booth space early. The competition for booth space has gotten fierce at many national shows and new companies may need to wait a year or two to obtain a booth. This is where key partnerships can offer the opportunity for a small, new company to gain access by "renting" a 10x10-foot space within a larger company's booth. Or by being granted time to present product demonstrations in a partner's theater or viewing area.

Get your hotel reservations in immediately to secure a spot in the conference hotel or very nearby.

Have a booth designed with graphics that display your messages. Your exhibit should be flexibly sized to fit a 10x10 or a 10x20-foot space—or larger, if your budget permits.

Offer a drawing or run a contest to entice people to stop at your booth and fill out lead cards.

Provide give-aways that support your theme or draw people to your Web site.

Choose a company uniform for the personnel who will staff the booth.

Use your booth space to demonstrate and present your product.

Planning Effectively for Conferences and Trade Shows

To get the most benefit from your company's presence at a conference or trade show, follow these steps:

1. List your conference goals.
2. Determine the messages you want to deliver at the conference. Identify the number one message that booth visitors should remember.
3. Determine what experience visitors should have in your booth.

4. Select the vehicles you will use prior to the conference to promote your presence there: mailings to the pre-registration list or calls to key educators to invite them to an event, for example. You may encourage educators to submit "call for speaker" forms to the conference organizers asking that your company provide a speaker or member of a panel on the conference program.

5. Determine how you will market your company during the conference.

6. Determine strategies for following up on leads generated at the conference. Many companies do not think this through prior to the meeting and valuable contacts and leads are lost as a result of poor planning. Your sales team must receive the leads immediately with as much information as possible about the needs of each potential customer.

7. Develop a timetable for accomplishing all actions. Remember to make reservations early if you plan to host a dinner or other event in conjunction with the conference.

8. Determine and produce the marketing materials needed to execute your strategy.

Who from your company should attend?

Determine the personnel who need to be present to accomplish your goals:

- Conference manager
- Marketing staff
- Public relations manager
- Vice president of sales
- Sales team from the region or from around the country
- CEO, President
- Director of Strategic Partnerships
- Director of New Business Development
- A customer or someone who uses your product and can speak knowledgeably about it—vendors often hire educators to work in the booth to present products to their peers.

Pre-Show

There are numerous ways to promote yourself at a conference or education trade show. Notifying customers or potential customers ahead of time about the booth location and any special promotions or demonstrations you've planned builds momentum for a successful event. Obtaining the conference pre-registration list is extremely important to effectively promote your company's presence and activities. To get the attention of conference attendees in advance of the conference, you can use mailers, fax blasts, advertisements in educational publications, announcements on your company Web site, and telemarketing campaigns.

A very effective pre-show tactic is to send special invitations to targeted individuals that you want to visit you at the booth or attend a special presentation during the conference. These invitations can be either e-vites or mailed invitations, but they should go out two weeks before the event. For crucial meetings, a phone call is a more personalized way to secure an attendee's time and schedule a meeting.

Other pre-show tactics include arranging for sponsorships offered by the convention, including: branding on registration bags, e-mail kiosks, registration areas, badges or lanyards, or at breaks or lunches.

At the Show

This is the time to showcase your company and products and communicate important messages to the audience. Remember, you'll have to compete for the attention of the conference attendees.

Make your company and its products memorable. Greet your audience with a "room drop"—for a fee, the conference organizer will arrange to deliver your promotional materials to the hotel room of every registered conference attendee. Create hands-on product demonstrations that allow individuals to develop their own personal, lasting experience with your product. Having gifts, holding raffles, or passing out fun and useful items—such as pens, calculators, and other unique classroom items—will increase the number of visits to your booth. If you plan to offer special prizes, promote them ahead of time to attract additional booth traffic.

Lead cards should always be filled out at the booth. Lead cards capture the name, contact information, and interests or needs of booth visitors. They can be used as raffle tickets, entries for prize drawings, or simply to collect follow-up information from people who express interest in your products. The booth staff should be given the goal of securing a given number of leads per day at the show.

Breakfast or dinner meetings during the conference allow you to meet and mix in a more personal way with potential or existing customers and clients.

Sponsoring the conference allows you more opportunities to make your presence visible if you are prepared to invest at a higher level. Sponsors are given options to advertise throughout the conference, including on banners outside the convention hall, in the programs and exhibit guides and other special show publications, on promotional signage in the convention hall, at the airport, in transit vehicles, in the hotel, and outside the convention center. Sponsors also command prime booth space and booth location.

Post-Show

After the conference, be sure to contact any prospects or valuable leads your staff has collected. Following up in a timely fashion will help your company stay fresh in their minds. Send a thank you card for stopping by your booth, send a letter, make a phone call or drop an e-mail, but follow up! If the prospects filled out lead cards, you should be familiar with some of their interests and may be able to set up a meeting or product demonstration on their premises after the show. With these leads, you can also build interest lists to use for marketing promotions later in the year.

Finally, as soon as you've unpacked your display cases back in the office, summarize your company's experience at the event and deliver a report to your management team. Prepare to use what you've learned this time to make your next conference even better.

About the Author

Kay Englund *is the president of Englund Consulting, a firm that has designed sales and marketing strategies for the education market since 1996. Her clients have included Target Stores, Mervyn's California, The Learning Company, Houghton Mifflin Interactive, Linworth Publishing, Pepperdine University, Aha!interactive, The LearningStation.com, NetSchools, and HiFusion. You can reach Kay at* kay@englundconsulting.com.

How to Work a Tradeshow Exhibit

by Cathy Jackson

After planning and staffing hundreds of tradeshow and conference exhibits, a school market veteran was enjoying the rare experience of being an attendee, in the guise of a "mystery shopper." Decked out in comfortable, soft-sole shoes and loose-fitting khaki pants, and holding a burlap tote bag and a program describing the corporate exhibitors, the mystery shopper blended well with the other attendees and was ready to critique the sales effectiveness of the corporate exhibitors.

Targeting four companies, the mystery shopper set out to explore how exhibit "staffers" met people, qualified leads, and made sales. To look authentic, the mystery shopper displayed a badge *proving* his position as a technology consultant from a school district. Well prepared and rehearsed, this conference critic was ready to evaluate how well these exhibitors measured up to a criteria list that included:

- Making first contact,
- Listening,
- Qualifying and disqualifying,
- Displaying product knowledge,
- Giving product demonstrations,
- Demonstrating competitive knowledge, and
- Gaining commitment.

What can we learn from the examples these companies provided?

Bait and No Hook

Bypassing the crowds at one exhibit giving away a car, the mystery shopper walked the perimeter of the massive booth display to scope out the exhibit staffers. An impressive theater-style demonstration caught his attention because of the animated presenter. Walking to the far side of the thickly carpeted exhibit he discovered waist-high podiums holding literature and laptops for one-on-one demonstrations. After sauntering around in the exhibit for ten minutes with no one approaching, the mystery shopper got someone's attention by standing behind a person getting a one-on-one demonstration of curriculum software. The exhibit "staffer" then quickly asked for a name, school name, and position. Just when

the mystery shopper thought the staffer was going to ask effective qualifying questions, however, the staffer's turn came up to do the theater-style presentation and he handed the critic a brochure and asked him to stick around for the presentation.

It was clear that this company's objective for exhibiting at the conference wasn't to sell. They did an outstanding job of drawing in attendance, and their presenter was energetic, knowledgeable, and engaged her audience. All this company needs now is to train the staff on the importance of taking advantage of the tradeshow as an opportunity to uncover needs, find buying influencers and decision makers, and gain commitments from qualified prospects to take the next step in the sales cycle.

Disqualifying

The critic moved on to the next exhibit, where the staffer actually asked about interest, school size, technology being used, and what issues would keep the school from using this technology. This was much better. After getting this information, the staffer demonstrated that he was very knowledgeable and enthusiastic about the company's products and services. He spent at least 15 minutes with the critic, even after being told that the school didn't have any money. At every moment, our critic expected to be "disqualified" or be asked for a commitment to take the next step (e.g., make a future appointment or get a decision maker's name). Instead, the staffer concluded the visit by merely requesting that the critic fill out a lead form that collected contact information and went into a drawing for a prize.

Know Your Product

A major computer manufacturer's exhibit was like an island, open on all sides to the public. Walking around the exhibit and observing from a distance, the first thing that attendees noticed was that the staff looked tired and abused. After all, it was late afternoon and these poor souls were dragging. After a few minutes, our mystery shopper managed to make eye contact with a staffer. The staffer bravely asked if he could answer any questions, so the critic asked about any special solutions that his company might have for education. Describing the company's hardware products, the staffer also mentioned a curriculum package. This proved disastrous because he didn't know a thing about it. Unable to recruit help, he simply gave up, handing the critic a brochure. The mystery shopper left the booth without being asked to give a name, a job title, or any other information. For the company's sake, it's a good thing the mystery shopper wasn't a serious and qualified buyer.

A second visit to this exhibit didn't improve. This company is recognized as a leader in computer hardware and network solutions. If they plan on exhibiting at future educational conferences, it's recommended that they crystallize their position on education, train exhibit staffers on the products to highlight, and train all staffers on how to meet people, qualify them, and gain commitments from them.

Know Your Competition

Strolling to the back of the convention center, the mystery shopper noticed an exhibit that wasn't getting much action. It was hard to tell from the front of the exhibit exactly what the company did. A casual walk around to the back of the exhibit revealed a billboard-like sign listing their entire product benefits list. (Maybe this is why the exhibit wasn't getting much attention from the attendees.) Although there weren't any other customers in the exhibit, nobody approached the mystery shopper. Giving them the benefit of the doubt (maybe these guys had been in retail and been trained to let the shopper look around a little before initiating a conversation), the critic made the first move by asking the open-ended question, "What does your company do?" The staffer responded with a joke, and conversation was off and running. He told our critic about his products but when asked how his curriculum solutions differed from the other companies, he responded by saying, "There is so much out there it's hard to keep up with competitive products."

This staffer never asked the mystery shopper for a name, but when asked for his business card he reciprocated by asking to scan the attendee badge. Walking away thinking that the VP of sales of this company probably wouldn't be too pleased with this interchange, the critic looked down at the staffer's card. Lo and behold, he was the VP of sales!

Earning the Right to Ask

One company at the show positioned itself like a large "warehouse" for everything "computer," so the exhibit was like walking around a department store. Selected items were mounted on the walls and visitors were free to just browse around without interference from staffers. It's a good thing, too because no staffer in that exhibit was going to bother the mystery shopper! These clever, energetic staffers were working hard to create a carnival-like feel in their exhibit. They actually had customers doing somersaults to earn the right to a give-away!

The staffers were very upbeat and positive and could have easily asked questions that would give them new qualified prospects (after all, they had earned the right to do so by giving away stuff). But while the exhibit succeeded in creating energy, it failed to direct that energy toward any specific goal.

By this point in the experiment, just getting staffers to ask for a name had become our critic's standard of success. (Forget about asking whether our critic could make decisions about technology at his school—this wasn't going to happen). At the end of the day, our mystery shopper left the exhibit floor shaking his head about the number of opportunities being lost at the show.

The Ideal Sales Call

There are telling statistics of why you *could* and *should* be selling more at your tradeshow events. Tradeshow Weekly's *1999 Data Book* reports that:
- 86% of show attendees make or influence buying decisions.
- 85% are not called by salespeople prior to the show.
- 75% leave the show making a purchase (where "making a purchase" can also mean committing to take the next step, e.g., making an appointment).

How much time would it take you to make this many contacts in another way? Here's some math to think about. Let's take some numbers from a national educational conference and calculate how many potential contacts you could make while exhibiting.

> ### SAMPLE NATIONAL EDUCATIONAL CONFERENCE
>
> | | |
> |---|---|
> | 15 | Hours Exhibiting |
> | 8,000 | Attendees |
> | 370 | Exhibitors |
> | 25 | Minute visits per attendee per exhibit |
> | 533 | Visitors per hour |
>
> The above is equivalent to 106.6 visitors per exhibit staffer (if there are 5 staffers in an exhibit). This also indicates how important it is to quickly dismiss visitors that do not meet your qualifying criteria.

The act of visiting a conference exhibit also pre-qualifies a prospect as someone who has an interest or need. At the show, you have access to buying influencers and decision-makers in a friendly and fun environment. You also have technical resources at your disposal and your executive management on hand to meet key customers. All this adds up to an "*ideal sales call*."

Essential Skills for Exhibit Selling

Making First Contact with Visitors

Make sure visitors step into your exhibit and feel comfortable speaking with you.

- Present a professional appearance
- Look alert and ready to greet visitors
- Look willing to do business—enthusiastic, approachable, and active
- Face the aisle even when speaking with colleagues
- Keep a smile on face
- Maintain eye contact
- Use the visitor's name to keep their attention and increase rapport
- Use a positive opening question
- Make people feel comfortable
- Introduce yourself by name and use the company name in conversation
- Give visitors your business card

Listening

Use effective listening skills in a noisy, distracting exhibit.

- Face the speaker, making sure he or she can hear you
- Maintain eye contact
- Encourage speaker to continue talking by using verbal signals like "I see," and "uh huh"
- Use friendly gestures like smiling and nodding your head
- Lean forward to encourage the speaker to elaborate
- Paraphrase and demonstrate your understanding
- Take notes of important details

Qualifying and Disqualifying

Learn how to quickly qualify and dismiss visitors that don't meet your qualifying criteria.

- Quickly assess whether visitor is qualified
- Ask open-ended questions
- Get the "vital information" (i.e. name, address, phone, and e-mail)
- Use a lead card to capture information
- Gain understanding of the school's needs and the timing of their purchases
- Classify the visitor as a decision-maker, buying influencer, or just an information gatherer
- Ask for referrals to decision makers or colleagues
- Gracefully dismiss a visitor when he or she is disqualified as prospect
- Control the conversation
- Tactfully avoid sensitive topics
- Ask for next step and how to follow up

Displaying Product Knowledge

Create value and differentiation by knowing your products and services.

- Know your products and services
- Use exhibit staff resources
- Match your product's capabilities effectively to the visitor's needs
- Take action to coordinate future resources and solve buyer's problems

Giving a Product Demonstration

Build value in your solution by matching your product demonstration to your visitor's needs.

- Demonstrate benefits to qualified prospects
- Focus on unique or superior features

- Keep your demonstration simple and involve visitors
- Use a small public-address system with a lapel microphone (for groups)
- Deflect questions you are not prepared to demonstrate
- Do not make negative remarks about the competition
- Position your product as value to the customer
- Remember, the time to buy (or take the next step) is right now
- Defer demonstrations to their scheduled times

Demonstrating Competitive Knowledge

Differentiate your products and services from the competition.

- Know how to differentiate from competition
- Be up-to-date with competitive information
- Don't "knock" the competition

Gaining Commitment

Advance the sales opportunity to the next step in your sales cycle.

- Ask for a commitment to take next step in the sales process (i.e., make an appointment)
- Ask for a commitment to buy

Doing an Instant Replay to Improve

Engage in ongoing learning and self-improvement.

- Self assess your effectiveness with the visitor
- Think about what you might do differently

Conclusion

How important is it to be "selling" at tradeshow exhibits? Phenomenally important! After all, a ton of money is poured into these events every year to attract your prospects and customers—and they are all in one place at the same time.

What a great opportunity to meet prospects, qualify opportunities, build relationships, and get appointments and commitments for the next step in your sales process! Maybe that's it—companies don't see exhibiting as a selling event. Companies go to great lengths and huge expense to draw in crowds (e.g., the drawing to win a car just to get a name that was easily available from the conference sponsor). Theater-style presentations with grand prizes given away for sitting through a demonstration are the standard. Entertainers, actors, and even models are hired to give the best performances. Expensive colorful brochures, CDs, and trial software are given out freely and without hesitation or reciprocation of even a name.

How many times have you heard exhibitors say, "We only exhibit because our customers expect us to be there," or "We aren't trying to sell anything!" or "We are only here because our competition is here," or how about "Our objective is creating market awareness." (What are the chances, by the way, that the shareholders of these companies would approve of these statements?)

Or, look at it another way: these companies are making serious investments to develop leading-edge technology solutions that will hopefully someday help our nation's kids get the best education in the world. So what are they doing just standing around at the tradeshows, when so much can be accomplished there in so little time?

In our mystery shopper's opinion, it will take more than large prizes, rich hospitality suites, entertainers, and free give-aways to make both corporate and educational dreams a reality. It will take earnest and well-trained salespeople to ask the right questions, discover the needs, present the solutions and get the commitments needed to sell their solutions. When this is done we all will be a step closer to a better world for our kids!

About the Author

Cathy Jackson, *founder and principal of Sales Champions, combines 20 years of real world experience with practical, proven, and powerful sales tools and skills development that drive business growth and sales excellence. Sales Champions works with Fortune 500 companies, small businesses, and entrepreneurs and specializes in educational information technology companies. Cathy can be reached at cathy@saleschamps.com or by calling (828) 749-2449. Visit their Web site at www.saleschamps.com.*

Handling the Hardware for Successful Road Shows

by George Bigham

Author's note: The editors warned me that most people find reading about hardware pretty boring. As a practicing geek I found this very puzzling, but I am following their instructions to make this chapter as entertaining as possible.

Oh, and one more thing—if you are the trade show coordinator for Apple, Compaq, Hewlett-Packard, Sun, or one of the other major hardware vendors, *please stop reading this article right now*...You already know more than I do, and I'd rather not be embarrassed, thanks.

Do You Really Need to Ship It?

If you are a software company or a Web-development house whose products run on any generic Windows workstation, check with the hosting locations. In many cases hardware can be rented more cheaply than it can be shipped.

For example, San Francisco is a strong union town when it comes to trade shows. By the time your company has paid the shipping charges, the unloading from the truck charges, the schlepping it into the hall charges, and the setup charges...well you get the idea. Especially when the other half of the charges start kicking in at teardown.

Even typically exorbitant hotel audio-visual department equipment rental rates begin to look good by contrast in this situation. And bear in mind that you can usually negotiate with those folks.

This is not to say that you should avoid locations where road shows are expensive to put on. Just make sure you and your managers are aware of those costs ahead of time and are reasonably certain the return will be worth the investment. If costs are significantly lower in a nearby suburb or sister city and your customers can be induced to go there to attend your event, consider those alternatives whenever possible.

Many years back, a small Houston company was selling remote data processing services to a national meeting of past, current, and potential customers. This was in the days when computers were mostly bigger than refrigerators, and so shipping and setup was even more of a challenge than it is today. And in this case the customers all knew what the hardware looked like anyhow. So the trade show planner set up all the company's equipment in their lobby at headquarters in Houston several weeks before the event and had a professional photographer come over and take a large-format photograph. At the trade show, setup consisted of unrolling the 3' x 8' photograph and taping it to the drapes. Then the company reps put a phone and a modem in the front of the booth, poked a hole in the photograph, and ran the telephone line through the hole. Since the real equipment was at the other end of the telephone line back in Houston, they could still do live demonstrations.

The moral of this story is that the hardware that never leaves the building never is late arriving, never gets broken, never gets stolen, and never falls on your foot, either...

If You Have to Ship Hardware, Get It There Safely, in Plenty of Time, and Insured!

Your event starts on a Monday at a hotel, so your crew will be setting up on Sunday. Do you ship the gear to arrive Saturday? No! Ship it to arrive on Friday afternoon, allowing an extra day for weather, equipment breakdowns, and other acts of Murphy to occur without disrupting your schedule.

Do you ship it the cheapest way? No! Use a carrier with whom your company has an ongoing relationship. And when in doubt, use Federal Express—they almost never lose anything.

Hotel Security Is an Oxymoron

(This is mostly true, but not always; in any case it is very difficult to assess ahead of time how good a hotel's security is, so it is safer not to rely on it unless you know for sure that you can.)

So, the hardware arrives on Friday afternoon. Who is responsible for its safety until your crew (including your-self—you do lead from the front, right?) shows up on Sunday at 10am for setup? You should have known the answer to this question before you shipped the equipment, of course. And the meaning of the word "responsible" is extremely variable in this context.

Scenario 1: The equipment cannot be found and you cannot prove to the hotel staff that the equipment ever arrived on their property. No receipt ever got to you. It is Sunday, and your shipper's office is closed. Your office is also closed.

Scenario 2: The gear has arrived on schedule Friday afternoon at the hotel's receiving dock—and you can prove that, because the shipping receipt found its way into your slot at the front desk. And guess what? There is an illegible signature on the receipt, presumably put there by some hotel employee. But the hardware is nowhere to be found on the property Sunday morning, and no one at the hotel knows anything about the situation.

Scenario 3: The hardware has arrived and you find it on Sunday morning, but some of the cartons are torn and crushed, and a few are missing. You can put together about half of the systems you need from what is available and working.

Now given any of these scenarios, and even assuming that on Sunday morning you can locate someone at the hotel with a) any knowledge of the situation, and b) any authority or power, do you honestly think that the hotel's having said they were responsible means that the assistant manager on duty is going to send a crew out to a nearby computer store in a truck and buy replacement hardware for you? Not very darn likely.

Or maybe the hotel will just rent you equivalent hardware from their audio-visual department? Oh, but now you learn that the AV department is a separate business from the hotel—it just happens to be co-located in the hotel for ease of operation. Getting help in this scenario is therefore only slightly more than not very darn likely.

A final note about hotel security. Many hotels have a large, locked cage in which valuable goods are stored. Always inquire about cages or other secure storage areas and use them. But never trust that they are secure. It seems as though every staff member knows where the keys to the cage are stored.

Send Someone Ahead...and Get Them a Suite!

In many cases it is a reasonable business expense to fly someone out to arrive at the hotel on Friday before the equipment, install them in a large enough suite, and have them tip the bellmen to haul all the hardware up to the suite. They can fly on a cheap "Saturday-night-stayover" fare in many cases, and if the suite has multiple bedrooms and bathrooms it can be used during the conference both for sleeping rooms and meeting rooms. Don't forget that you may need the suite for equipment storage at teardown as well.

Palletize, Palletize!

If the computer gear is all stacked on a pallet that is then surrounded with many yards of plastic cling wrap and then steel-taped, it is unlikely to disappear from the hotel. Pallets are just too big to move. Of course this may come around to bite you at setup when your crew has to break down the pallets so the boxes can be moved to the setup area, but at least you will have boxes with which to set up!

Uniformed and Armed Off-Duty Police Officers Are the Best

Generally you will need two shifts, one from 6pm to midnight, and a second from midnight until you or a team member show up in the morning. If your computer rooms are connected by retractable walls, open up all those walls and lock all the doors except the one where the security guard is stationed.

Let the agency doing the hiring know if Internet-surfing computers will be available so that any geek-type officers can sign up for duty and have some fun. And make sure that they and the hotel room service staff know that charges incurred by these security officers for food and beverages while they are on duty go onto your bill. But you can let them know that coffee and sandwiches are more appropriate than steak and lobster.

Electricity is Power

It is never a good idea to assume that hotel power is wired correctly, especially when line testers can be purchased for under $5.00 at any home or building supply store. Hotel electricians are always moving electrical power from one location to another as different events set up and tear down. Make sure your area has clean power.

If your hardware is powered by transformers (laptops, for example), then it will be much less vulnerable to transients, spikes, voltage surges, and so forth. However if something serious enough happens to break the transformer you will be glad if you have packed some spares.

Another tip: sleeping computers use a lot less power than active ones. Computers, monitors, and printers manufactured since about 1998 all have a "sleep" mode to enable energy conservation. This means that when turned on and left idle, they go to sleep after a fixed period of time (usually 15-30 minutes). A sleeping device consumes between one-fifth and one-tenth the current of an active one. But hotel electricians tend not to understand this.

So, it is Sunday evening, and all 150 of the computers are set up in all five of the labs in the hotel separated by air walls. Everything looks fine, and all the machines are asleep. Then, on Monday morning, attendees rush into the labs and start keyboarding and mousing and Web browsing and printing and...and...and.... The lights go out and the computers don't work any more. Darn, don't you hate it when that happens! Guess what? These computers needed more power than the hotel electricians thought.

To prevent this, you can have the electricians read the labels on the computers, monitors, and printers. By law these labels are required to show the maximum power consumption that the unit is rated for. Then make sure they do their math correctly, and supply you at least the required amount of power.

Sometimes when power is brought into a computer lab via the back service doors a security breach is created because those doors cannot be locked. Your best option in this case is to chain and padlock the doors so that human bodies cannot get through them, unless of course the doors are emergency exits. A second choice is to turn off all the gear at the end of the day, disconnect the power, and lock the doors. If the room is not in use, it is usually permissible to lock even emergency exit doors. But if you take this approach, be sure to assign someone to show up in the mornings in time to unlock doors, reconnect power, and turn on all the computers.

Hotel Networks and DHCP Servers

The network is the property of the hotel or other hosting building, and your use of it is contingent on being a courteous guest. If they are already running their own DHCP server, you should not put up one of your own. If you try, certain things will happen for sure, and in this sequence:

1. the network will get all messed up;
2. the hotel network guru will discover that *your* DHCP server caused the problem, and
3. your computers will be off the network very soon after.

There are a lot of special considerations about how your geek has to get along with the hotel geek, but that is all secret stuff and you aren't allowed to know about it. It is best to bring your own geek along, however, if at all possible. If you do, the next item will probably be their responsibility...

Bring Backup Software on CD

Always bring several sets of backup CDs with the correct versions of the operating system software and any application software that is needed for your event. If a computer gets dropped and its hard drive is damaged, it may be possible to regenerate it by reformatting the hard drive and reinstalling everything. Hard drives are very inexpensive these days, and it is usually pretty straightforward to purchase a replacement drive and install it.

And if you do end up having to rent or buy replacement computers, they will be useless unless you can configure them to run the software needed for the event.

It also true that Murphy prefers easy targets of opportunity. So the probability of needing your backup CDs is minimized by being sure you have brought them along.

If Hotel Rental Rates Are Too Extreme, Buy Gear Locally Instead

There have been situations where the hotel geek person had such high daily rental rates for Ethernet hubs and cables that it was less expensive to take a taxi to the nearest computer store and buy new gear instead. Be sure to do a good reality check on hotel rental rates. And if you do purchase locally, be sure to save the boxes to ship the equipment home in at the end of the event.

Special Considerations for Laptops and Handheld Devices (Palms, Pocket PCs, Etc.)

The smaller the item the higher the probability of its being stolen. A common trick of thieves is to come into the room, casually place some product literature on top of one of your laptops, wait until no one is looking, and then pick up the literature with the laptop underneath it and take off. This is difficult to defend against unless the devices are chained down to tables using special locking security devices available for that purpose.

Use Special, Custom Shipping Containers If Needed

If there are going to be a number of road show events it sometimes is both convenient and economical to have special locking shipping containers constructed. Anvil and Halliburton make stock-sized locking cases, some with wheels, which come filled with foam. You can use a utility knife to cut custom openings in the foam for your equipment. Buy all the cases at the same time and specify that all locks take the same key, or purchase units with settable combination locks.

Working Smoothly with Hotel Staff

There should be a lead person on your team and a lead person on the hotel staff team. All transactions should be from lead person to lead person, unless those leaders agree on specific delegations of authority. Any other arrangement brings chaos, complaints, and lots of negative energy, all of which detract from the effectiveness of your event. Usually extra hotel staff help can be hired for setup and teardown, but these arrangements must be made ahead of time. Don't forget to tip these workers and to let them know up front that this will be happening if things go well—and don't forget to make a note of those tips as they are paid, so you will have records for your expense reports.

Communications Strategies for During the Event

Most hotel staffs use walkie-talkies to communicate amongst themselves. It may be prudent for your company to invest in some Motorola Handi-Talkies or similar devices. Your team does not want to be on the hotel staff frequency (nor do they want you to be), but it is smart for your primary hotel contact to have one of your radios so you can talk to them.

Because hotels and convention centers are full of elevators, power cables, telephone and computer wiring, and lots of other stuff, wireless communication can be tricky, and you may need to experiment with frequencies to find the best local solution. But at least your local radio network is a point-to-point one, unlike cell phones, which have to reach out from inside the hotel to a cell-phone antenna somewhere else. Cell phones are almost never reliable enough to be used for this purpose, and even if they did work, the cell phone bills for a single event would be more than the cost of walkie-talkies.

Bring plenty of batteries for the radios. Buying batteries at hotel gift shops is expensive!

Working Smoothly with Your Shipper

Be friendly with and respectful of the workers that show up with the truck. Be appreciative of their good work. Make sure that their unloading activity is coordinated with the work of the hotel staff and of your team, and ensure that all local union rules and hotel cultural rites are complied with. It is also a good idea to make sure the unloading crew has access to water and/or soft drinks and that they know where the restrooms are.

If they are late because their plane was delayed or because there was bad weather or a traffic accident, see if they would like you to order them a sandwich from room service. If you like their work, ask them what you need to do to make sure this same crew will show up to help you at teardown and loadout.

These last two points are especially important on the front end of your event. You will get great effort and good cooperation from workers by tipping heavily up front, and you can taper off on the tips as the end of the event approaches. But don't stiff anyone, OK?

Sometimes a Dedicated Vehicle Makes Sense

There have been situations where the number of events and the extent of the hardware requirements were such that the best solution was to contract with an Audio-Visual company to have a van full of gear driven around the country to event locations. If this is a good solution for you, make doubly sure that the vehicle has appropriate alarm systems and that the contractor has all the necessary insurance.

One of the advantages of this approach is that you have the same unloading and loading crew at every event; they usually will help with setup and will become very proficient after working several events.

Don't Forget the *Tape*!

Good tape is hard to find. And I don't mean duct tape either. 3M Scotch Extreme Packaging Tape is in the Office Depot Catalog (item #200-400-791) but is not stocked in their retail locations. This is bi-directional filament tape, and a single roll is 50mm wide by 50m long (that's 2" by about 50 yards). At teardown when the gear is repacked there should be two complete circles of tape around every box or case.

Order tape well ahead of time and ship more than you think will be needed. If your equipment is not taped securely into its cardboard cartons or cases for return shipping it is much more likely to be damaged or tampered with.

Special Considerations for Teardown and Loadout

Be sure you have enough bodies, whether they are colleagues, or hotel staff. And if they are hotel workers, make sure you have make arrangements in advance for them. Be sure they have the tools and supplies needed to do their job. Good tape can only be cut with a knife, by the way…

Your responsibilities for the event are over only when you have received signed receipts from the shipper(s) for all your gear. Sometimes the trucks don't show up on schedule and you will need to temporarily store packed equipment in a safe place overnight. You may be glad you have that suite, since Murphy usually sees to it that the hotel's next event is already in progress and all the rooms at the hotel are booked.

Make sure that you or one of your responsible colleagues has enough flexibility in their itinerary (and in their plane ticket) to stay over an extra night. Of course, there will be times when the FedEx truck shows up at 5:45pm to get your gear, giving you just enough time to get on the last flight home (or to your next destination) at 8:00pm. Acting professionally in this circumstance requires that you refrain from hugging the driver.

And in Conclusion…

Remember the 9th Beatitude—"Blessed are they who expect nothing, for they shall not be disappointed." No irreverence is intended here, but you should expect that at least one thing will go wrong at an event and be emotionally and mentally sturdy enough to cope with it. And once you have those signed receipts from the shippers, appropriate medication can usually be found in the lobby bar…

About the Author

George Bigham *is a managing partner at Bigham Technology Solutions, a Houston-based consulting company working with schools and with organizations developing for and selling to the educational technology market. He has an extensive background in the education community, with over twenty-five years experience in textbook and software sales and training, technology systems and network troubleshooting, applications training in schools, database design, and developing training products. Contact him at BighamG@aol.com or at (281) 866-9726.*

CHAPTER 10
Internet Marketing

Inside this chapter…

Developing an Internet Strategy

by Carol Ann Waugh

By this time, only 6 years into the age of the Internet, many educational publishing companies have tried many different models to take advantage of this growing phenomenon—and with mixed results. Only a short three years ago, most traditional publishers were sitting on the sidelines, unsure about what to do or how to do it. Then, all of a sudden, the educational market was "discovered" by the venture capitalists, who foresaw the benefits of serving the fragmented school market by offering "scalable" products and services online, as opposed to in print and through fixed media. As these firms funded more and more pure plays in the dot com world, pressure was brought to bear on traditional publishers as their executives (and their stockholders) asked "What's your Internet strategy?"

By the end of 2000, we started to see some failures take place among the venture-backed dot com companies who thought that "getting traffic" was the measurement of success. We saw companies whose business model relied on advertising to schools begin to realize that this might not be the best approach for the education market. We also saw many companies "giving away" valuable content without having a sense of when to begin charging for it.

Early in the game, we all watched a relative newcomer to the education market called Family Education Network. They were a newsletter-based company who quickly capitalized on the parent market by offering quality online content for parenting. They branched out to cover students and schools and as a result of their partnerships with other key players, they succeeded in attracting substantial traffic to their site (70 million page views per month in July 2000), eventually resulting in a valuation of $129 million when the company was sold to Pearson.

Encyclopedia Britannica is a good example of a company who decided first to charge an online subscription fee for access, then to offer their content for free (revenue to come from licensing this content to other Web sites), and

recently, to go back to a subscription-based revenue model. Scholastic also began as one of the first educational Web sites to offer its content on a fee basis; but after a year or so, they decided that the "free content" model worked better.

The question everyone is asking these days is "Is anyone making any money?" No one seems to be willing to step up to the plate and say "yes," but this is hardly surprising. At least not surprising to the companies who have been suppliers to the education market for a period of time! We know several things about our complex market:

> **"...many teacher training institutions have still not incorporated the Internet into their teacher training curriculum."**

Educators Are Slow to Change and Adapt to New Things

Teachers are taught how to teach in a University setting. They are taught how to develop lesson plans. They are taught how to deliver curriculum. They are taught how to manage a classroom. And even though the Internet was available as early as 1995, many teacher training institutions have still not incorporated the Internet into their teacher training curriculum.

Besides the issue of a new teacher's education, the school system is mainly populated with older teachers—teachers who have already spent a great deal of time developing their lesson plans for traditional classrooms. Teachers who are familiar with traditional educational materials like textbooks, workbooks, videos, and manipulatives. Teachers who may or may not have access to computers at home or at school. Data from all the research that has been done has shown these teachers do not feel completely comfortable with incorporating "technology" into their classrooms.

So it's not a surprise that many companies have been feeling a bit of frustration in introducing their new Internet-based products and concepts to this market.

The Digital Divide Still Exists and Will Continue to be a Barrier for the Foreseeable Future

Let's face it. Not every child has access to a computer on a daily basis at school. And many do not have one at home, either. This is a critical issue when it comes to selling Internet-based programs to schools. Educators are concerned that all kids have equal access to educational information. How can you provide a "solution" that will only work for half of the kids in a classroom? Sending homework assignments through e-mail or posting them on a teacher's Web site only works if all the students have access. The much touted "school-to-home connection" is something that everybody talks about as a "good idea," but in reality there is much resistance from teachers who, after spending a day in school and a couple of hours at night grading homework aren't looking forward to answering e-mail from their students or their students' parents. As a result, companies are beginning to understand that Internet solutions need to be backed up by off-line solutions as well.

Market Penetration into K-12 Schools Takes Time and Patience

Regardless of the "killer app" that might be developed for school use, it will take time to penetrate the market, and since few products—no matter how innovative, effective, or inexpensive—ever attain a 50% market share (20% is more realistic even for a great product), companies who have built their hopes and dreams on a quick and deep market penetration will not simply be disappointed: chances are their money will run out and their businesses will fail.

Selling Annual Subscriptions on a Per-Student Basis is Difficult

Traditional school budgets set aside for the purchase of educational materials are not fashioned to accommodate a yearly subscription model. There is only one area of the school that is used to purchasing annual subscriptions— the school library. One other area that could be considered as having some budget for annual, recurring expenditures is the Technology Department, where money is spent for hardware maintenance contracts. Schools are used to paying for materials on a one-time basis and reusing them every year. This is how text-books, media, and software have been sold to schools for many years. Even software companies, who broke new ground with pricing by adding site licensing to the school's vocabulary, licensed the software for an unlimited time. For companies now selling online subscriptions to schools, the unanswered questions are how to price a subscription product on a cost-effective basis for a school and how to find money for annual subscriptions within the traditional school budget.

Advertising to Teachers and Students Remains a Controversial Topic

Chris Whittle broke the mold in 1989 when he introduced the concept of free educational content supported by advertising. In exchange for free technology (television sets, VCRs, etc.), schools would subscribe to Channel One—a news program geared towards middle and high school students. They had to promise that their students would watch the news program, thus guaranteeing an audience for Channel One's advertisers. In the early years, schools were desperate for "free stuff" and the company grew quickly. However, in recent years, their market penetration has stalled at 12,000 schools serving 8 million students. ZapMe! tried to copy this model for developing an Internet-based service—free technology in exchange for "student eyeballs"—but quickly realized that schools were not happy with the concept of selling access to their students for advertising, even with the bonus of getting free stuff. ZapMe! has discontinued its educational business model and changed its name to rStar Networks, and it now provides and manages satellite-based networks for large-scale deployment across corporate enterprises, educational systems, and common interest groups.

So What's an Educational Publisher to Do?

With all these substantial barriers to developing a profitable Internet strategy, should educational publishers invest in the Internet at all?

The answer is an unqualified yes. But your strategy probably cannot be to "spin off your dot com company, go IPO, and make millions."

There are three Internet strategies that educational publishers should be pursuing now.

1. *Using the Internet as a low-cost marketing and information tool* and making it easy for teachers and administrators to get more information, communicate with the company, and order online.

2. Looking at cost savings benefits of reducing overhead, cost of product, cost of fulfillment, and direct marketing costs.

3. Building up a permission-based database of prospects and customers in order to communicate with them electronically, now and in the future.

As the Internet matures, broadband access becomes universal and all teachers and students have Internet access on a 24/7 basis, other possibilities will open up, including the delivery of streaming video and audio; creation and delivery of customized textbooks and workbooks; online teacher training for products and services; and student management systems that can track students from birth to graduation, regardless of their physical location. These ideas are all in the developmental stage but will take years, if not decades, to fully develop.

Conclusion

It's difficult to play the "realist" in this gung-ho market—but companies who understand the specific nature of the K-12 education market can and have developed strategies that work to meet their objectives. Setting realistic objectives is the key.

About the Author

Carol Ann Waugh *is president of Xcellent Marketing,* www.xcellentmarketing.com, *a consulting company specializing in providing strategic planning and marketing strategies for educational and reference publishers. Carol has more than 25 years of experience in marketing to K-12 schools and libraries. She developed her first Web site in 1996 and currently is the Webmaster of three sites. She can be reached at (303) 388-5215 or at* cwaugh@xcellentmarketing.com

Essential Elements of an Educational Web Site

by Kathryn Kleibacker

Although the concept of a Web site is only a few years old, users and reviewers of educational online services and content providers have already established basic criteria for Web site evaluation. This is in part due to the need to weed the "good from the bad" as Web sites have popped up in staggering numbers, and in part as an effort to set guidelines for a new content delivery medium. The essential elements of a Web site described below are based on an analysis of hundreds of Web sites, comments culled from a number of user focus groups, the results of a 1999 EdNET Customer Survey, and Web site evaluation instruments used by various industry magazines.

Access and Time Impact Web Site Usage

With the phenomenal growth of computers and Internet access in U.S. schools, Web developers need to be cognizant of the fact that even in the most sophisticated, technologically advanced schools, not every child has access to a computer at home, nor do teachers have ample time in the school day for extended online searching. In the future, even if access to a computer or online services is not an issue, classroom time will always be a precious commodity for teachers. This means providing classroom Web offerings that are relevant, easy to use, correlated to the curriculum and contain information at a variety of skill and learning levels.

"Free" Isn't Always a Plus

An interesting finding of the 1999 EdNET Customer Survey was that contrary to popular thinking, free information on the Web isn't always valued by teachers. Teachers commented that many times, using free content can mean that they "do the work" to make it meaningful. This further underscores the value that teachers place on materials that save them time. The study indicates that educators do value the added editorial efforts companies are making to tailor their sites to school needs and that they are willing to pay for this service. This business model is being validated in the marketplace, as pay-per-view and subscription-based pricing are becoming common and accepted pricing structures.

In contrast, advertising models—which offer free access to content in exchange for the presence of banner ads and Flash billboards—have not fared as well for school-oriented sites (or for many consumer sites, for that matter). For educators, this debate echoes the one concerning Whittle's *Channel One* venture. In both cases, some administrators and school boards have viewed advertising as a necessary evil that can save them money; but generally, it's frowned upon. And it's a definite "no-no" on any pages designed for student use.

Home Page Advantage

Internet users—students and teachers alike—are very impatient. This no doubt is either the result of fatigue from wading through a flood of sites to find the answer to a question, or the impact of the overwhelming array of information coming at users at Internet speed. Whatever the reason, Web sites' Home pages and first links, must immediately assure users that they are "in the right place" to meet their educational needs. Depending on the product and service, the kind of information that should be prominent at first glance can include:

- The company's name, logo, and tag line

- The target audience segment (e.g., students, teachers, administrators, or parents)

- The products offered (organized by brand, by series title, and by formats)

- The subject areas addressed (e.g., reading, math, professional development, or reference)

- The grade spans addressed (e.g., primary, elementary, K-3, or K-12)

- An "about us" section (including company address, e-mail contact information, sales force information and contacts, etc.)

- A site map, with an index to sub-pages on the site.

Traditionally, this information is prominently displayed either at the top of the page or on the left-hand side bar (and sometimes in both places, just in case).

Make it Easy to Use

A Web site's copy and overall navigation should be as direct and simple as the elements that make up its Home page. Losing your visitors in a tangle of Web pages with no way back "home" is a sure way to lose them as return visitors to your site. Here are several tried-and-true components that can help to make sites user-friendly:

- *Meaningful and straightforward menus*. Avoid using 8-point type, hard-to-read fonts, unusual icons, or awkward or esoteric phrases.

- *Instructions that are easy to find and understand.* Make effective use of headlines, subheads, and bulleted phrases. Avoid putting everything on the Home page; instead, add click-through buttons when you need to provide more detailed information.

- *Simple registration procedures*. Avoid having visitors fill out detailed log-in forms as their first experience on your site. Give users a real incentive to submit that information by offering them a timed "free" demo or an online premium in return.

- *Printing choices and formats.* Provide several options for printing documents and articles, ranging from simple page-print functionality, to downloads in PDF format (particularly for longer documents or ones that feature photos, graphs, or illustrations).

- *Online and offline support.* Include a "contact us" button on the Home page, and at top or bottom of every page. Provide postal address, 800 number, fax number and e-mail contact information.

Content is King—But Not Just *Any* Content

Content accuracy and credibility are major concerns of educators in general; and even more so for online information. Since the Web is an unregulated, uncensored global library of information (and often, of misinformation), educators critically scrutinize the source and the quality of the content they find there. Even with increasingly good filtering programs, it is important for information providers to assure users that the information on their sites is accurate, authoritative, and up to date.

In particular, there are several things educators say they look for when considering whether or not to use a Web site. These criteria include:

- Brand name familiarity

- Company reputation

- Signed articles, teacher's guides, and lesson plans (indicating the author's name and affiliation and providing a standard bibliography)

- Data citations (giving source information, including publication date, page numbers, and so forth)

It must have been frustrating for experienced producers of educational materials to see so many new dot coms spending so much on marketing in an attempt just to establish their brands. But as time has shown, educators weren't dazzled by the hype.

Keep Searching Simple

Searching is the very essence and lifeblood of the Web. After all, the Internet was created to share vast amounts of information! However, it can be extremely frustrating and time consuming to everyday folks and non-professionals to try to create a satisfactory search "string" that will pluck a cherished bit of information or a desired fact from the trillions of pages and millions of sites that make up the Web. Add to that the disturbing trend among major portals like AOL, Excite, Yahoo and AskJeeves, who are selling preferred placement in their search engine results to the highest bidders. One hopes that educational Web providers will avoid this new practice, where a query about say, Albert Einstein would rank a Web site offering celebrity posters (a paid-for-placement search result) higher than sites that contain Einstein's biography and summaries of his research.[1]

Sites with extensive databases of materials like magazines, newspapers, and encyclopedias, or subject-specific resource centers such as *Gale's History Resource Center* or ABC-CLIO's *American Government* need to take particular care to streamline searches and search results. Many now offer more sophisticated search capabilities and helpful results pages. For example, one of the more user-friendly research sites for K-12 students is *World Book's School Online (see research example on following page)*. There, a typical search query for Abraham Lincoln, yields a results page that lists topical materials organized by format, number of hits within each format, and percentage-based relevancy rankings.

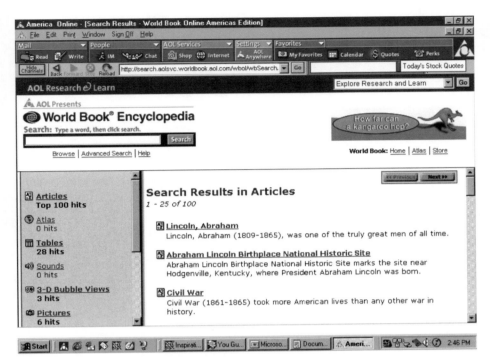

SAMPLE SEARCH RESULTS PAGE FROM WORLD BOOK ONLINE

Without question, the most useful and effective search capabilities for educational Web sites are those that offer searches correlated to the curriculum by subject and topic. The more sophisticated sites also break these search results down by grade level, saving everyone substantial amounts of time—and increasing user satisfaction.

Building a Base of Repeat Visitors

Taking care to incorporate all of the elements outlined above will increase the likelihood of repeat visitors—and loyal customers. The Web provides an opportunity to create a real-time, ongoing relationship with your users. Take advantage of this unique and powerful capability, as any "retailer" would, by:

- *Refreshing your content* (changing some Home page features daily, weekly, monthly, and adding information about new products)

- *Updating your offerings* (eliminating links to Web pages and sites that no longer exist, and removing outdated articles)

- *Promoting special discount offers*

- *Offering personalized and customized features for students and teachers*

The basics of good product development don't change just because the medium does. It's happened with film and television and software—and now the Internet. In the end, it's not the medium, but the message.

[1] San Francisco Chronicle, Business Section/Technology: *Searching for Profits*, June 18, 2001.

About the Author

Kathryn Kleibacker *is the president of Kathryn Kleibacker & Associates, a consulting firm specializing in new business development for schools and libraries. She is also a partner in Internet Monitor, a company providing school and library publishers online marketing and new product development strategies. Kathy has over 25 years experience in developing award-winning products in print, video, and multimedia. She can be reached at Kathryn Kleibacker & Associates, 16 Wyckoff Street, Brooklyn, NY 11201, by phone at (718) 858-3459, by fax at (718) 858-6022, or by e-mail at kkabiz@aol.com.*

Relationship Marketing and the Internet

by Roger C. Parker

"How much income did your Web site contribute to your firm's bottom line profits last year?"

Most educational publishers, if they're honest, will answer: "I don't know." Others, with even greater candor, will respond: "Nothing!"

Most Web sites fail to live up to their potential as cost-effective marketing tools. The costs of this failure are staggering; outside of a handful of success stories, many companies spend hundreds of thousands of dollars each year creating and maintaining Web sites that succeed only in forfeiting millions of dollars in lost revenues and missed opportunities.

Why Web Sites Fail

There are many reasons for this failure. Most boil down to the fact that many Web sites are over-designed from the point of view of appearance but under-planned from the point of view of content and goals. Symptoms of Web sites that waste money include:

Slow speed. Too many Web sites are characterized by large, slow-loading graphics that take agonizing amounts of time to download, and—after downloading—fail to reward visitors with meaningful content. A large logo, or picture of a distributor's office or warehouse, isn't a sufficient reward for a 30-second download. And, since many educators are still accessing the Internet with a dial-up modem from home, a slow-loading home page can result in their "clicking" to another site.

Failure to engage: Most Web sites are written from a first person, ("I," and "we") rather than second person ("you") point of view. These sites stress features (e.g., "We've been in business since 1989") rather than translating them into benefits (e.g., "Our experience translates into time and money savings for you.") Educators who visit your Web site want more than "brag and boast" advertising.

Failure to capture e-mail addresses. Unless you capture the educator's e-mail address, you will get one and only one chance to sell them. It's essential to gain permission to contact them in the future, considering that the casual visitor may never again return to your site.

Out of date content. Web sites should be considered constant "works in progress." They are never "finished." New content must constantly be added, and old content reviewed and removed on a continual basis. However, keep in mind that educators like some consistency in a Web site designed to help them teach in the classroom situation. Nothing can be more frustrating to a teacher than to plan a lesson around the Web site content, only to return a few weeks later to find the content missing!

Failure to follow up. How many times have you sent an e-mail requesting information to a Web site but had to wait weeks for a response? Long delays, inappropriate or "canned" responses, and even complete failure to respond still occur.

"One-size-fits-all" mentality. Visitors to your Web site have different information needs, depending on whether they are first-time prospects, recent buyers or long-term customers. Your Web site should offer different information depending on the visitor's position in the "customer relationship cycle," described below.

All of the above problems are symptoms of a lack of planning. Without a goal or purpose statement, backed up by the publisher's positioning statement and a review of the publisher's position relative to the competition, there can be neither Web site purpose nor an easy way to measure its success or failure. In contrast, successful educational Web sites begin with a creative brief that describes the site's goals. The task of identifying these goals is best approached through an understanding of the relationships between customers and companies that Web sites can help to create and cultivate.

The Goals of Relationship Marketing

The basis of relationship marketing is a desire to replace customer acquisition with customer retention. The marketing and advertising costs associated with customer acquisition can bankrupt most firms, as the investment community has discovered during the past few years. It costs far more to acquire a new customer than to retain and sell again to an existing customer. Advertising, sales, and travel expenses quickly mount up when you "churn" your customers, constantly replacing old ones with new ones. Churning customers is like running on a spinning treadmill or filling a leaky bucket with water; you never get anywhere or have a chance to rest.

Past customers represent the best prospects for present and future sales, but until now, it has been difficult for most vendors to keep in contact with past customers. Catalogs and newsletters have been used as customer acquisition tools, but in print these are expensive to produce and mail. Moreover, they are often out of date by the time they arrive in the customer's or prospect's mailbox.

E-mail and the Internet offer a whole new approach to customer retention, enabling you to keep in constant touch with your customers and prospects without expensive graphic production, without expensive printing, and without expensive mailing. E-mail and the Internet permit you to immediately communicate, in color, as much information as appropriate without expensive production costs.

The starting point for understanding how to put this powerful new tool to work begins with an understanding of the five-stage customer relationship cycle.

The Five-Stage Customer Relationship Cycle

The starting point for creating a customer-centric Web site is to examine the first possible stages that exist in most customer/vendor relationships and to analyze the customer's differing information requirements at each stage. In order, the stages of the cycle are: awareness, comparison, transaction, reinforcement and advocacy. Let's take a closer look at each stage.

The Awareness Stage

At the awareness stage, educators are encountering your Web site for the first time. These educators may be new to teaching or may be seeking alternatives to their current educational suppliers. The awareness stage is a time of mutual introductions. You have two primary goals at the awareness stage. One is to introduce your company and describe your company's product and service offerings and the benefits you offer. Your second goal is to capture the educator's e-mail address and obtain permission to contact them again via e-mail in the future. This second goal is crucial: unless you capture an educator's e-mail address, you're relinquishing control of

the relationship and you may never gain another opportunity to market to him or her.

The Comparison Stage

At the comparison stage, both you and your Web site visitor learn more about each other. Your primary goal is to position your company relative to the competition. You want to answer the question: "What makes you the preferred vendor?" Instead of merely describing your company's offerings, your goal should be to compare your company to your competition and show why you are the preferable alternative. The starting point is to identify your local and distant competition and describe what you do differently. Your secondary goal is to find out more about your visitor's interests and needs. By analyzing the pages that your visitors access and the amount of time they spend on each page, you can identify their areas of greatest interest.

The Transaction Stage

At the Transaction Stage, your goal is to motivate past or present educators to make an immediate purchase. This is where most sites begin. But, asking for the sale too early is wrong. It's wrong because before committing to a purchase, educational institutions will typically research the market and decide which vendors appear the most competent and professional. Vendors must first demonstrate their competence and competitive advantages in the Awareness and Comparison Stages before asking for the sale. To the degree that you have learned about your market's needs and concerns, you will be better able to custom tailor your offerings at the Transaction Stage. Transactional motivations work best when there is a strong incentive to act right now. Few things succeed like deadlines, limited availability, and, of course Free gifts! Your Transaction Stage content will succeed to the extent that you communicate Act Now! Immediacy.

The Reinforcement Stage

The reinforcement stage, which most vendors ignore, occurs immediately after a transaction. Your goals at the reinforcement stage are to express appreciation for the buyer's purchase and pre-sell them on their next purchase. A simple e-mail thanking the customer for their purchase "primes the pump" for the next purchase. An even better approach is to send your customer an e-mail directing them to pages of your Web site that add value to their purchase by showing them "insider tips" about how to maximize the value they enjoy from their purchase. This kind of "pump priming" can also include offering special savings on accessories and supplies that can help the buyer make the most of their purchase.

A customer satisfaction survey is one of the most effective ways you can communicate your appreciation and professionalism. A customer satisfaction survey is a tangible expression of your concern. This not shows you care but also helps you identify actual and potential problem areas in your firm's delivery and fulfillment divisions.

The Advocacy Stage

The advocacy stage is the final stage of the customer relationship cycle. Your goal at the advocacy stage is to convert previous customers into advocates for your firm, providing them the motivation and tools they need to act for you in this capacity. When educational institutions discuss their vendors, you want them to recommend you as the preferred vendor based on a combination of your pricing, your competence, and your professional approach to the relationship.

The five-stage customer relationship cycle represents a major departure from the approach taken by most "one size fits all" Web sites. It reflects a long-term view of customer development rather than the typical "get what you can while you can" Web site attitude that begins and ends at the transaction stage. It requires taking a long-term "nurturing" view of your firm's relations with your customers, rather than the typical short-term "harvest" approach. The long-term approach requires more investment at the start, but once set up, it scales easily to greater size without major increased investment.

Components of a Successful Relationship Marketing Program

There are four key elements to a relationship-marketing program based on the above five-stage customer relationship cycle. These include:

- E-mail
- Incentives
- Premium Content
- Cookies

E-Mail and Incentives

E-mail is the "engine" that drives the relationship marketing program. E-mail sent to visitors to your Web site who register their e-mail address advances visitors from the awareness stage through the comparison, transaction, reinforcement and advocacy stages. In many ways, e-mail is a silver bullet that can help your firm develop a uniquely differentiated marketing program.

But to succeed, visitors must register their e-mail address and must explicitly give you permission for you to contact them in the future. Never send unsolicited e-mail! Unsolicited e-mail, colloquially known as "spam," is an irritant that can quickly and permanently poison an otherwise promising relationship. Although printed "junk mail" that appears in a prospect or customer's postal mail box rarely arouses anger, unsolicited e-mail is generally considered an unwanted invasion of priority. You <u>must</u> gain permission if you want to send future e-mails to your Web site visitors.

How often should you send e-mail? The answer depends on how frequently you update your Web site.

In order to obtain the e-mail addresses of your Web site visitors and gain permission to contact them in the future, you must provide visitors with an incentive. It's not enough to include a registration form on your site and ask visitors to submit their e-mail addresses. You have to provide a reward, or incentive, for their sharing this valuable personal data with you. Information is, by far, the most successful registration incentive. Information simultaneously pre-sells visitors on your competence and is valued far more than shallow discounts or other short-term incentives.

Premium Content

Premium content is the key to a successful relationship marketing program. Premium content refers to information that is distributed electronically to site visitors that register their e-mail address. Premium content information is not available to casual, or unregistered, Web site visitors. There are several ways you can distribute premium content information:

- ***Unlinked pages.*** One of the easiest ways to distribute premium content is to place it on pages that are not otherwise accessible to visitors to your Web site. When visitors register their e-mail address, an e-mail is automatically sent to the visitor. This e-mail contains links to the pages containing premium content.

- **Password protected pages.** An alternative is to include premium content on pages that cannot be accessed without first entering a password. When users register, you can send them a return e-mail that contains a password to allow them access to these pages.

- **Attachments.** Yet another approach is to send your premium content as an attachment to the e-mail acknowledging the visitor's registration. This typically is done using Adobe's portable document (PDF) format. One of the advantages of this approach is that the attachment can be fully formatted (e.g., it can be presented as a multi-column publication containing photographs and formatted using type-faces not available on the recipient's computer.) To read the document, visitors would open it using Adobe Acrobat Reader, a free software program already installed on most computers and also available as a free download from the Adobe.com Web site.

Cookies

Cookies are the final tool the Internet offers you. Cookies are small files that your Web site inconspicuously downloads to your visitor's computer. Cookies can help you to "recognize" visitors when they return to your site. Thus, they permit you to provide repeat visitors with different content, depending on their stage in the customer relationship cycle and the particular products or services they have expressed an interest in and/or purchased.

The above four elements place you in the driver's seat and permit you to customize your Web site visitor's experience. They replace a one-way "one-size-fits-all" approach with a Web experience that is custom-tailored to your visitor's needs. At each stage, visitors encounter the information they need.

This approach places a premium on providing useful information rather than focusing on presentation and on gratuitous or merely decorative design elements like Web site colors, typeface, or layout. Instead of competing on subjective grounds such as whether a green background or a yellow one is better, your Web site can justify itself on the basis of quantifiable metrics including:

- What percentage of your site visitors are registering their e-mail address.

- Whether you are retaining your customers or losing them to the competition, forcing you to replace them with new ones.

- Whether you are gaining business from word-of-mouth referrals.

Developing a Relationship Marketing Program for Your Web Site

Information is the key to a successful relationship marketing program. The success of your program will be determined by the value of the information you provide. This requires you to "get inside the mind" of your customers and prospects and identify their information needs. The potential pitfall you face is the tendency to be myopic, providing information that satisfies your own needs rather than the needs of your customers and prospects.

Web site visitors are selfish. They don't care about you or your business, except insofar as your business can help them save money, order the most appropriate products, and use those products as efficiently as possible. Prospects and buyers are also risk-averse; they want to avoid expensive mistakes. What they want from your Web site is confidence that you know your products, that you can help them make the right choices, and—most of all—that you appreciate their business.

The starting point for creating an effective relationship marketing program is to ascertain your market's information needs at each stage of the customer relationship cycle. Then, divide this information into "open content"—(which any visitor to your Web site can access), and premium content (which visitors can only access after registering their e-mail addresses). The easiest way to do this is to use a form similar to the information development worksheet shown on the following page. You can also download copies of this worksheet at www.gmarketingdesign.com.

Note that the information development worksheet makes it easy for you to separate open content, premium content, and information delivered via e-mail for each stage of the customer relationship cycle.

A FIVE-STAGE INFORMATION DEVELOPMENT WORKSHEET

STAGE OF CUSTOMER DEVELOPMENT	OPEN CONTENT	E-MAIL	REGISTRATION INCENTIVE	PREMIUM CONTENT
AWARENESS Goal: Introduce your business and your offerings to prospective buyers.				
COMPARISON Goal: Set the business apart by emphasizing your business's unique competitive advantages.				
TRANSACTION Goal: Encourage purchase (or repeat purchase) right now.				
REINFORCEMENT Goal: Express appreciation and pave way for follow-up sales, i.e., upgrades, supplies, etc.).				
COMMUNITY Goal: Encourage word of mouth referrals and provide customers with tools to sell their coworkers.				

Closing Ideas and Tips

Experienced relationship marketers have found that the following ideas help them gain the most from their relationship marketing initiatives:

- *Include multiple registration forms.* Do not expect top results from a single e-mail registration form. Include multiple registration forms on your Web site. Place one on your home page, but include additional forms at strategic locations throughout your site as well. Better yet, include a registration form at the bottom of each page. Your responses will increase to the extent that you offer multiple ways of getting to your registration forms.

- *Make registration quick and easy.* Respect your visitor's time by making it as simple as possible for visitors to register their names and e-mail address. Response rates go down as the amount of information requested goes up. Avoid the temptation to add registration fields involving position, firm, mailing address, phone, fax, and intention to buy information. This information will come later as you set up a dialog with registered visitors.

- *Keep e-mails short.* Do not use e-mail to tell your whole story. Rather, use e-mail to "tease," or drive, visitors to your Web site where they can find the whole story. Once they're there, they will encounter other pages of your site. If you provide too much information in your e-mail, visitors may not be motivated to visit your site.

- *Personalize your e-mails.* When setting up your e-mail program, include fields for visitors to provide their first name. E-mails personalized with the recipient's first name are far more likely to be read than those that either don't have a salutation or begin with a generic "Dear Customer."

- *Use a benefit-oriented subject line.* When sending an e-mail announcing updated Web site content to your customers and prospects, provide a subject line that offers a benefit, (e.g., "New Resources for Black History Month") rather than a generic one like "We've Updated Our Site!" Which would you rather read? Which promises the most benefit?

- *Commit to consistency.* Consistency is far preferable to inconsistency. Never promise more than you can deliver. It is better to promise a quarterly or bimonthly e-mail newsletter and deliver it on time than to promise a monthly e-mail newsletter that doesn't appear on time. Customers and prospects will judge your relationship marketing program by both its content and its on-time performance.

Conclusion

For too long, educational publishers interested in customer retention have had to put up with the high costs and delays associated with printing and mailing catalogs and newsletters. Frequently, these were outdated before they arrived in the mailboxes of customers and prospects.

All this has changed. E-mail and the Internet permit vendors to pinpoint their marketing activities, sending customized information to customers and prospects depending on their position in the five-stage customer relationship cycle. More important, time-consuming printing and mailing processes have been replaced with instantaneous communications. Minutes after new content has been posted on your Web site, customers and prospects can receive an e-mail directing them to it.

Those vendors who take advantage of relationship marketing on the Internet will enjoy a major advantage over their competitors who continue to play the "churn" game, constantly trying to acquire new customers to replace old customers they have lost.

About the Author

Roger C. Parker is president of Guerrilla Marketing Design as well as an author, consultant, and seminar presenter with more than twenty years of hands-on marketing experience. Roger's 24 books have been translated into over 37 languages. His latest book is The Streetwise Guide to Relationship Marketing on the Internet (Adams Media). Roger's clients include Apple Computer, Hewlett-Packard, Microsoft, and Yamaha. Visit www.gmarketingdesign.com where you'll find dozens of downloadable forms to use when setting up your own relationship marketing programs. Roger can be reached at (603) 742-9673 or at Roger@gmarketingdesign.com.

Internet Portals: Who Will Be the Market Leader?

By Kathleen Kauff

There is little consensus on how to define the term Internet portal. From academic articles to trade stories, published pieces on Internet portals frequently offer varying definitions of the term. And the ambiguity does not stop there. It spills over into understanding the mission of portals, as well as their evolving roles.

At their inception, the primary goal of Internet portals was to act as a starting point for Internet users by providing structure to the Web's chaotic array of information and resources. They did so by aggregating or pointing to third parties' online content and by making this content easily accessible by organizing it in subject or topic area directories. Today, though, Internet portals' goals are shifting dramatically. While still providing a directory to Internet resources, portals now strive to cultivate a community of users and to increase the amount of time these users spend on their sites by offering proprietary content and a myriad of services, including free communication applications and personalization tools.

There's Clarity in Numbers

Despite the absence of universally accepted metrics for evaluating Web performance, it's clear that Yahoo! and Microsoft's MSN dominate as the two leading general interest portals. Yahoo! claims to reach the largest worldwide audience, offering a network of free services to more than 192 million individuals each month. For its part, MSN boasts more than 50 million surfers each month. Its instant messaging service has somewhere in the ballpark of 30 million users, and its free e-mail service has an impressive 100 million accounts, according to *BusinessWeek* magazine.

Another major player is America Online, which is the largest Internet access provider and also serves as an Internet portal. AOL's paid membership has raced passed 30 million, and its subscribers are clearly hanging around and using AOL's content and tools once they've logged onto the Internet. According to *Upside Today*, AOL subscribers spend 70 minutes daily on the service, which is up from 64 minutes in 2000.

But What Does this Mean for Education Portals?

Top-tier portals and the brands they've created resonate loudly with teachers. AOL, for example, offers a compelling, easy-to-use educational Web site, AOL@School, which features dependable technology, high quality content, and experiences tailored for both teachers and their students. Moreover, the content and experiences America Online serves up on its flagship service and on AOL@School address both the professional and personal needs of teachers, something most educational portals do not do.

MSN is also poised to gain market share among educators and their students. With substantial funding, an unmatchable commitment to research, formidable legacy systems, and powerful brand, reach, and partnerships, MSN offers premium services and content, including the recently launched Encarta Class Server, which promises to help teachers manage curriculum standards, lesson plans, assignments, and assessment.

If you are currently marketing, developing, or considering developing an educational portal, you should be tracking and analyzing these services and their marketing strategies, just as you would your traditional competition inside the educational industry. Among other things, your marketing platforms should clearly distinguish your site from these sites by highlighting your site's unique benefits and strengths. You should also seriously consider the resources you'll need to compete with these formidable opponents. The portal business is not for the meek, as the competition is fierce and portals are easy to imitate, which is evidenced by the burgeoning of educational portals over the past few years. From bigchalk.com, a privately-held, Internet pure-play, to Learning Network, a member of the Pearson plc family, to NetDayCompass, a not-for-profit site launched by NetDay, education portals are being developed with both public and private funds and by organizations both inside and outside the education industry.

Lots of Activity but Little Creativity

This dramatic growth of education portals is not surprising, given the potential $700 billion K-12 school market and the increase in equity funding (education portals alone attracted $458 million in private funds in 2000, according to Eduventures). Furthermore, the perceived ability to leverage the school-to-home connection and consequently tap into parents' wallets has provided another compelling reason for companies to launch education portals. According to a January 28, 2000 article in *BusinessWeek Online*, "the business of education is in a period of dramatic transition, and investors now have a laser-like focus on the role technology—and especially the Internet—can play in delivering educational services." The wave of funding and the education Web sites that have resulted from it provide both an opportunity and a challenge for educational marketers.

Not surprisingly, the increase in funding has produced, among other things, high-profile deals and well-funded product launches. This has led to a significant increase in press coverage of the education industry, which savvy marketers will exploit to strengthen their brand and to expand their customer base. On the other hand, the increased competition demands that you strategically position your site so that it can rise above the fray. You must ensure that your site unfailingly delivers distinctive content and applications that meet your customers' needs. It's your responsibility as a marketer to understand your customers' existing and evolving needs, to uncover unmet needs, and to guarantee that product development is guided by these needs. Many companies have failed to do this well and appear to have followed the same erroneous approach in developing their education portals. This has resulted in confusion for the uninitiated user who will have a difficult time discerning the differences among these education portals. Many of these portals appear to have used the same third-party technology solutions and make similar product promises, thereby further eroding their distinctiveness. Moreover, while their interfaces and designs may be different, these portals often contain the same uninspired applications and content.

Some of the companies creating these Web sites were caught up in the once-prevailing wisdom that they had to have the first-mover advantage to dominate the market.

> ❝ It's vital that you fully grasp and internalize your site's mission, which will ultimately result in smarter product development choices. ❞

Sites were launched with faulty technology, weak or insufficient content, and little consideration given to users' existing and evolving needs. These companies further exacerbated their problems by eagerly and thoughtlessly joining in on a game of me-too product development and rushed to imitate each other's tools and content.

For example, many education sites began adding assessment and Web site creation tools, which presumably were intended to exploit the school-to-home connection. Although these tools are theoretically both useful and appropriate, they do nothing to help users differentiate one site from another. And the short-term, reactive thinking behind their development is flawed for a number of reasons, including the low or nonexistent switching costs in the portal category and the absence of a long-term strategy that is essential to become a market leader. Education portal developers need to stop imitating the same generic, and often substandard, set of tools and begin creating tools and applications that add distinctive value for their users.

It's vital that you fully grasp and internalize your site's mission, which will ultimately result in smarter product development choices. Consequently, these choices will result in a more effective allocation of resources, which will ultimately strengthen your brand and distinguish you from your competition.

Begin by Knowing Your Product

Many education Web sites claim to offer one-stop shopping for teachers, students, and their parents—a colossal undertaking. Among other things, they promise to make sense of the Internet and to find and provide the best educational content it has to offer. Most fail to deliver on this promise.

It's critical that you understand your site's strengths and weaknesses, what it actually delivers and to whom, and the direction it's headed. It's also critical that you understand the difference between an education portal and an education destination site and position your offering accordingly. Do you expect teachers, students, or parents to use your site as a launching pad to the

Internet, or are you expecting to serve most of their educational needs with proprietary content and resources? Are the majority of your links pointing outward to the Web or inward to your site? Do you have a reliable Web search engine? And if you do, does it deliver relevant, streamlined results? Does your content lean heavily toward one of your three user constituencies or toward a particular subject area or grade level?

Answering these questions honestly will help you determine whether your site is a portal or a destination site. If, for example, most of your links point back to your site and your site does not feature an effective Web search engine or subject directory, you've probably got a destination site. Harnessing the power of the Web and its content is, and will remain, the hallmark of a portal, despite its evolving role and the abundance of services it may offer. If your site does not do this, it's not a portal: stop claiming that it is, figure out your competitive advantages, and begin focusing on its true strengths and unique offerings.

Finally, if you are going to position your site as a portal, you should truly care about how the term is defined, both by you and—more importantly—by your users. Given the term's overuse and shifting meaning, users who visit your site will come with their own definition of a portal and be either delighted or disappointed by the experience, depending upon what your site offers. As a marketer, you know it's essential to meet or exceed your customers' expectations and deliver on your product promises.

Is It Really a Good Idea to Give Away a Service or Product?

The value of any product or service is based on what customers are willing to pay for it. Furthermore, if your expenses exceed the cost of goods sold, you don't have a sustainable business—somebody has got to pay. Profitability has become *de rigueur*, and out-of-control customer acquisition and retention costs are no longer acceptable. Impressions, traffic, and click-through rates are virtually meaningless nowadays, unless they can be directly tied to conventional measures of profitability.

> "Impressions, traffic, and click-through rates are virtually meaningless nowadays, unless they can be directly tied to conventional measures of profitability."

Companies are visibly wrestling with whether they should embrace a subscription model, drive revenue through advertising, sponsorships, and ecommerce, or fashion a combination of these four potential revenue streams. Scholastic jettisoned Scholastic Network, its subscription-based site for teachers, and relaunched Scholastic.com, a free Web site for teachers, kids, and parents. The new Scholastic.com includes an abundance of teacher tools, lesson plans, and classroom-ready materials, as well as online activities for kids and education information for parents. Britannica.com went from a for-fee service in 1995 to a free service in 1999. Now Britannica is switching back to charging for its services and plans to launch BritannicaSchool.com, a K-12 subscription-based service that will feature the encyclopedia, curriculum materials, and other educational tools. DiscoverySchool.com recently announced plans to launch in 2002 a subscription service for parents and children who are looking for help with schoolwork. These companies are not alone, as the dot com landscape is littered with companies looking for the right balance among advertising, e-commerce, sponsorships, fee-for-content, and subscriptions.

The resounding message here is that, like other industries, the education industry is seriously scrutinizing the financial outlook of its Web sites. That's not to say that companies may choose not to have a Web presence. Having a Web presence is now a prerequisite for any viable company. It's the missions of these Web sites—and in turn the resources allocated to them and the revenue expected from them—that are under the microscope.

With that in mind, if you have not done so already, you should begin dissecting your revenue model and ensuring that it fits with both your company's and your site's stated purpose and mission. For example, do you expect your Web site to be a revenue producer, a cost saver, or both? If you plan to treat your Web site as a sales or distribution channel, will you evaluate it with the same financial rigor as you do traditional channels? Is your revenue model based on charging for premium online content or tools that cannot be easily replicated, or on or some yet-to-be proven advertising model that faces the strong possibility of being rejected by educators? Will the cost for content or services be based on use, or will you affix a regularly-scheduled fee for all or part of your content and applications? The bottom line is that your Web strategy, especially its revenue model, needs to fit with your company's mission and to hold up under careful examination in order for you to become an online education market leader.

Who Will Survive the Shakeout?

Now that the dot com frenzy has begun to subside, companies are returning to a more rational way of doing business and measuring their results. This is not to say that the pace has slowed, however. In fact, the competition in the education portal war has never been fiercer. It's just that profitability matters again and strategic long-term thinking is a must.

Two or three education portals will capture the lion's share of the market and the second-tier portals that survive the shakeout will serve niche markets. Sites such as Learning Network, bigchalk.com, and Lightspan are investing heavily in both product development and marketing in order to become market leaders. But in order to win the education portal competition, both dot coms and established companies will have to adhere to their stated missions and make decisions consistent with them, differentiate themselves from their competitors, and develop long-term competitive advantages. Regardless of its size, your company will need to act both quickly and strategically if it is to be a worthy competitor.

About the Author

Kathleen Kauff *is an independent educational consultant specializing in strategic marketing and product development. Kathleen recently moved to Denver from New York City, where she had spent fifteen years in the publishing industry, including major stints at Facts On File, where she was the director of direct marketing, and at Scholastic, Inc., where she served most recently as the Scholastic Internet marketing director. She can be reached at* kkhome@mindspring.com.

Establishing Requirements for Your Web Site

by Laurie Swiryn

Web development is not an event; it's a process. Because many companies do not understand this basic statement, the Internet is full of Web sites that actually drive business away rather than solving real-life business problems.

This article will outline the steps you should take to ensure that once you decide to develop a new Web site your efforts will result in a successful online initiative— one that will benefit your customers as well as your employees.

The first step many companies take when they decide to develop a Web site or to engage in a "Web makeover" is to call a Web developer. Do not make this mistake. If you do, you will be skipping the first and most important step of all: establishing your Web site's requirements.

Only after you have a firm understanding of your Web site's purpose, audience, content, and desired functionality should you even consider contacting a Web developer.

The Big Picture

Think about the future of your Web site from the very start. Avoid thinking that you can always build a better site "later" or that now you just want to implement something "quick and dirty." Instead, implement scalable technologies from the start so you can upgrade your Web site and its features without losing a significant portion of your initial investment.

Your Web site is one of your company's most important assets. It is your 24-hour-a-day representative. Everything about your site, from design to functionality, contributes to your company's image on and off the Internet. It is critical that your Web design, functionality, and informational content all work together to correctly convey your company's image. The quality of your Web site in all respects should be equal to, if not greater than, the quality of your products and services.

First impressions really do count! Visitors who don't see what they are looking for within the first couple of seconds are not likely to stay on any Web site. A visitor will stick around if they get an immediate feeling that the information they are looking for can be found on your site. Remembering that your competition is only a click away, you must never lose sight of the fact that people will come to your Web site for information that may be available elsewhere. If they don't find it fast (studies show that usually means within 54 seconds), they'll click away. And second chances on the Web are difficult and costly to attain.

Information on your Web site must be current. Studies demonstrate that 72% of the population uses the Web to research products and services. Disseminating out-of-date information can be very damaging when you consider that 97% of teachers in the US today report that their schools have Internet access and 87% are comfortable with using the Web.

To enable continuous revision, a basic requirement of any Web site is that your non technical staff be able to update easily it themselves. In particular, it is reasonable to expect that your Web site come complete with easy-to-use content editing tools that non-programmers can use on a daily basis to immediately affect your Web site content. Your marketing, sales, and PR departments will want new information posted immediately. They cannot afford for their content to be "queued" for action—they know that if a visitor finds that the site does not have fresh and accurate content, they will surely look to the competition.

Furthermore, your Web site must be convenient for your visitors to use. Many companies sacrifice their Web visitors' convenience for the "bells and whistles" of "sexy" technology that serves no practical purpose. Unless one of your main goals in building the Web site is to entertain your visitors, you are best advised to keep it simple. Simple can be elegant.

Determine the Purpose of Your Web Site

Before you build the site, give careful thought to its purpose. How does it fit into your overall business plan? Why are you developing a Web site? What are you trying to accomplish online?

Think about ways your Web site can help you offer *new products and services* as well as offering existing products and services *in a new way*. Brainstorm about all of your options before settling on your purpose. Some examples include selling online, increasing offline sales, building membership, strengthening brand, advertising, educating, reducing costs, providing customer support and demos, entertaining, and attracting investors. And if you are setting out to create a Web site that is as good as or better than your competition's sites, study those sites carefully!

Interview your customers and co-workers who will regularly visit your Web site to identify their needs. Get them to talk about the benefits and deficiencies of your existing Web site. Carefully map intended features of the new site to problems and inefficiencies expressed in these interviews. Plan to implement forms, user registration, e-commerce, or searchable database of products, services, or information only when you can clearly identify the compelling real-world problem that those features are solving. (If you don't have a Web site yet, you can use interviews and focus groups to help determine what the Web site should accomplish.)

Many companies forget that a well-designed Web site can provide them with valuable information by way of Web site visitation logs. Think about what kind of information you want to glean from your Web server on a daily, weekly, and monthly basis. Examples include referrer information, search engine keywords used, exit page information, time spent on Web site, kinds of searches launched from the Web site, most popular products viewed or sold, number of unique visitors, number of sales, average order size, and number of shopping carts left abandoned. Although collecting usage data is not likely to be your primary reason for developing a Web site, you would be foolish overlook the possibilities of turning this information into a valuable asset.

Once you have established all of the items on your "wish list," prioritize them. Double-check to be certain that each feature will provide an important benefit to either your visitors or your company internally, and remove all the "fluff." Then, once you can fully articulate the Web site's purpose, never let it out of your "site."

Create a Site Hierarchy

One of your first tasks will be to create a flow chart representing your new Web site. This important yet simple step will help you define the site's purpose in detail. It doesn't have to be a fancy document. It can even be hand-drawn, but it needs to include as many section and sub-section names, page and sub-page names as you anticipate requiring. Make sure you indicate which sections or pages will require special features such as forms, user log-ins, searchable databases, e-commerce capabilities, secure servers, and so forth. Include all of the "wish list" items and future modules you can think of in your initial site hierarchy. This makes it easier for everyone involved in the project to get a good understanding of each party's vision.

Focus on Your Visitor's Experience

Your Web site is all about building and maintaining relationships, and as we all know, repeat customers are the key to profitability. Yes, you want a return on your investment from your Web site, but don't try to get it by compromising your Web visitor's experience. Fortunately for the marketer, studies show that user experience is most positively affected by getting desired results, rather than being dazzled by technological glitz. Examples of technologies that are commonly used but that don't support the purpose of most of the Web sites we see today include splash screens, pop-up frames, plug-ins, lengthy animations, and large sound and graphics files.

Don't let your desire to "push" your visitors in certain directions cause them frustration. Think about it: you're annoyed when a pop-up window appears even before the URL you are visiting is fully loaded or when you attempt to view another page. You hate it when even after you have closed browser, the annoying pop-up comes back! Don't do these things to your visitors.

Instead, find friendly ways to entice your visitors to fully experience your site. Lead them gently by employing fixed positions to create familiarity (e.g., keep your menu bar in the same position on each page); implement two-click navigation principles (allowing movement from any page in your Web site to any other page with a maximum of two clicks); and provide intelligent error handling on forms.

Don't insult your visitors by requiring them to register or log in before they can find out about your products and services. You wouldn't stand guard at your office or store door belligerently asking for a password before allowing visitors into your place of business, would you? So, don't do it on the Web!

Determine the Content of your Web Site

Now that you know why you are building a Web site and what the general scope of the site will be, you need to determine what kind of content you want to make available.

People who visit your Web site will be looking for more information than they can get by calling and asking for your brochure, or catalog. Think about ways you can provide customers, employees, and sales representatives with added value. Where appropriate, provide online product demos, sample book pages, related quizzes and activities, product pictures or sample screen shots, product reviews, related lesson plans, and links to valuable Web sites that add value to your products or services.

Make sure a visitor on your site can easily locate your contact information from any page in the Web site. You've already got them on your site—why would you want to make it difficult for them to figure out where they are (or where you are!)?

Features, Features, Features!

Forms. Think about the kinds of information you are likely to want to collect at your Web site. How many forms do you require? Look for a solution that will allow your non-technical staff to create surveys, questionnaires, and other feedback forms on the fly, because you will find many, many uses for intelligent forms on your Web site. Make it very easy for your visitors to tell you who they are and what they want!

"Cookies" and Visitor Tracking. If you do not want to alienate your customers or instill fear and uncertainty in them, don't use cookie technology! Cookie technology is annoying and unreliable, especially in school and home settings where many users share computers. Instead, look for a Web solution that provides anonymous visitor tracking as well as persistent visitor tracking without using cookie technology. To obtain individual information about your visitors, try implementing an opt-in registry of users with a database on the server side to do necessary visitor tracking and site personalization.

Online Databases. Whether you are going to sell products online or not, if you have lots of products (more than 100), you should consider organizing the information about them into a database. Find someone to help you set up the database schema so that it can work well for you internally as well as on the Web. Give exhaustive thought to how to categorize the data, including which fields you want visitors to be able to search by, and which combinations of fields and categories will best enable your Web visitors to quickly find the information they want. Other situations that may require online databases include store/dealer/rep locators, site personalization, visitor registration, product reviews and order/inventory tracking.

If you are going to sell online, think about what can you do to encourage your customers to return often to buy online. Make ordering secure and easy. Implement secure server technology and triple-check your developer's e-commerce experience and knowledge. Accept purchase orders, credit cards, and Web-generated faxed or mailed-in orders. Offer incentives like free shipping, discount coupons, product promotions, and so forth.

Web Environments

Test, test, test your Web site for all conditions. Consider the typical environment your audience will come from (including computer configuration, connectivity, and experience level). For example, if your visitors will largely be coming to your Web site from school locations, you will want to be certain that the Web site you develop will look good and run efficiently on older computers with slower connectivity than if your audience is largely coming from corporate environments.

Selecting Your Web Developer

At last, you're ready to talk with the Web developers. Insist on working with a team that has a track record in your industry with verifiable references. Require a demonstration of live Web applications they have built that are comparable in scope to what you are trying to accomplish. The Web developer should begin the conversation by asking you about your purpose, content requirements, audience and expectations for a development partner. With your answers to these questions, the developer will be able to help you decide on a set of features and technologies.

Supporting a Web site that has been cobbled together with several third-party solutions can be a nightmare. If you are experiencing problems with your Web site, you will want to have a single number to call for help. Partner with a single source to design, develop, deploy, host, and maintain the operational components of your Web site and avoid a frustrating future of making separate calls to your ISP, Web developer, DNS host, e-mail server, your hardware service center when something goes wrong.

Since your Web site is actually a software product, it should be developed by software engineers, human interface designers, and graphic artists, and it should be managed by an experienced product manager. Even if your company has an in-house programmer or programming staff, don't be fooled by thinking that your current staff can take on the additional burden of developing a new software product. Take the time to calculate the real costs of existing and additional programming, design, network administration, and project management staff, and you will discover that you'll save money in the long run by employing the "best people" for the job.

Checklist for Selecting Your Web Development Partner

In comparing the bids of different Web development companies, consider the following.

1. Look for a company that has been in business for more than a couple of years. The Web development industry is volatile. A company that has sustained their own business for several years can likely sustain yours.

2. Get a minimum of three relevant references (clients for whom the developer has done similar work). Call those references! Ask about the initial development process as well as the ongoing relationship and services being provided.

3. Test those relevant Web sites on different computers at several times of day. Try searching, ordering, and filling out a form. Make note of any part(s) of the site that are difficult to use or confusing. (Red flags should go up if this is not a very short list!)

4. Call the Web firms you are considering hiring at 7 am, at noon and at 5 pm. Do they answer the phone? Do they promptly return your calls?

5. Gather at least three Web development proposals (make sure each company has received the same set of requirements). Be leery of developers who require extra time to prepare a proposal or who outright miss the deadline. This kind of behavior can provide a glimpse into what it's going to be like to work with that company.

6. Pay careful attention to the proposals you receive. Proposals should be comprehensive and easy to read. You should get the feeling that the company is responding to your particular needs by suggesting the best way to accomplish the tasks, offering options, and planning for the future, not just generically responding to your RFP.

7. Look at the price for the services only after you have a complete understanding of the value of your mission critical Web site and the track record of those responding to your RFP.

Conclusion

If you begin building your Web site before you have done your homework, you will surely pay the consequences. It costs more to do it wrong. Finding the right development partner and technologies to implement will be easy once you have firmly established your Web site's requirements and determined its purpose. Even if your budget is constrained, you can plan to bring services and additional features to your site through a phased implementation strategy. This approach will be possible if (and only if) you start by implementing time-tested, scalable technologies that will enable you to upgrade your Web site and its features without incurring major re-development costs.

About the Author

Laurie Swiryn is vice president of education markets at Cuesta Technologies, a 6-year-old Web engineering firm that specializes in developing Web applications for companies that service the K-12 market. An educator by degree, Laurie has worked for 25 years in education, as an elementary school teacher, a technology trainer of teachers, and most recently as the catalog manager and Web editor for one of the largest resellers of educational software in the country. Her experience there in catalog production, direct marketing, and online catalog development provided the perfect segue to her current position at Cuesta. Laurie can be reached by calling (888) 932-9004 or laurie@cuesta.com.

25 Tips to Build a Successful Web Site and Web Team

by Valerie C. Chernek

With the newness of the Internet comes the freedom and responsibility to carve out a successful Web site for your educational publishing business. Successful Web publishing requires diverse talents. Whether you choose an in-house team, go outside, or combine them, these tips will guide you. There are many aspects to consider when you put together a Web development team. Remember this: to get the right mix, it's not so much about the technology as it is about *people, knowledge,* and *attitude.*

The Team

1. Choose a manager with experience.

In today's world success means addressing complex issues fast! Find a seasoned manager who has Web experience, who knows best practices on the Web, and who can appreciate the diverse talents it takes to be successful. The question is, who has the right skill set? The answer: someone who will manage a team from the seemingly intractable Web design process through to the actual development of HTML and other programming languages. Someone who understands the importance of back-end data collection and who is familiar with marketing and public relations.

In your search, focus on the higher-level skills. It takes several kinds of talent to plan, create, produce and promote a successful Web site. And let's face it, the person who manages people well, and more importantly, understands the educational customer, is rarely the same person who understands the ins and outs of CGI forms, Javascript, Flash, cascading style sheets, and frames.

2. Look in-house before going outside.

A Web site should be a fundamental program for your business. And this requires a dedicated staff. Experienced marketers and project managers are usually good Web managers. These professionals understand the customer, the competition, the business, and, hopefully, how to motivate and manage an assorted group of talent.

It's all about managing people and reaching the variety of potential customers in the K-12 market. You must engage teachers and administrators and convince prospects that your product or service is the right choice.

The person you select as a leader must be fully aware of how to collaborate with many thinkers and deploy Internet technologies that will best suit the end user.

Look inside the company for a solid marketer who commands good communication skills, follows industry trends, negotiates well, and is good at managing and motivating various personalities. Look for someone who fully appreciates a functional Web interface and powerful editorial content. Look for someone who can create user experiences and make meaningful connections with educators. And remember...content is king!

Once you've selected your Web leader, look for experienced information technology (IT) professionals, programmers, and at least one graphics artist to include on your team. The ultimate goal of the Web team leader is to integrate the technology, the marketing, and the company's overall strategies.

3. If necessary, find a good Web development firm.

It is important and cost-effective to have at least the key players in-house. Building a Web site is not only a great challenge, but it can truly enhance organizational learning among the team...experience that cannot easily be achieved by going outside the company.

Organizational learning helps everyone grow with the project, giving all team members an opportunity to shine. Moreover, Web projects are typically high-profile work— they can provide a showcase for organizational learning skills, which can be attractive for both the Web team and the company as a whole.

In-house staff members, however, may not have the expertise to create e-commerce sites and back-end databases, host multiple servers, or write consistent and fresh Web copy. Depending on your site requirements, then, you may also need to look outside for more talent.

Start your search locally to find firms in your geographic area through recommendations from other companies. Research in local newspapers to explore articles about new Web firms or successful Web projects. Start with three firms and conduct in-depth interviews. Local firms may not always be the right answer depending on the size of your business and your project, but they are a good place to start.

4. Focus on relationships.

A good Web development firm should help you realize a return on your Web investment. To get there, you have to create chemistry between your in-house team and their staff. Finding the right chemistry takes some extra time, so allow for it in your planning. Talk with each firm officially just about the work. Then meet in a casual setting and talk about other Web experiences and move the conversation into other areas to find out more about the team. Bring someone along from your organization but outside the team to observe the dynamics of the group. Test out concepts. See how eager the firm is to understand your business and the intricacies of the K-12 education marketplace. Finally, it's a good idea to suggest that the firm be willing to help your team learn new Internet approaches and techniques…especially if your team is fairly young. Most companies don't take this opportunity to "tap" into the knowledge and expertise of an outside development group to strengthen their in-house team. When it works, everyone grows!

5. Check the references.

Remember, lots of people "talk a good game." Ask for, and contact each firm's references. Pose specific questions about their ability to meet timelines, fulfill expectations, provide ongoing service, solve problems, and be flexible. And make sure the firm doesn't have the habit of sending senior people to pitch the firm who then abandon the project once the contract is signed.

6. Put the budget in the right hands.

There are lots of decisions to make when you create a Web site. There can also be hidden costs. Remember, whoever owns the budget makes the final call. Marketing managers do not necessarily own the Web budget—even though they manage the site. Budgeting issues can cause difficulties in the partnership if they are not addressed ahead of time. Other departments that hold budgets for the Web site could include IT and Sales.

7. Develop requirements.

Talk with the outside Web development firm about the types of documentation they will use to communicate the site design with you. In general, "visual" documents work best for communicating design requirements. Define your requirements in written form, and have

thorough discussions about design expectations in several sessions.

8. Learn what makes each team member click.

Communication is the key. If members of your team do not easily comprehend large text documents, you may want to consider diagrams, flow charts, storyboards, or other pictorial layouts. This ensures that each member of the team is receiving the information necessary to produce their best work and achieve the intended goals for the site.

9. Compromise—every Web site project is a learning experience.

Designing a successful Web site with an in-house team or an outside Web development firm is challenging and involves accommodating different opinions and ideas. You must be able to compromise, "let things go," and "go with the flow" on occasion. There are no hard and fast rules.

The Plan

10. Clarify goals and expectations.

Web projects get complicated. Start out with a specific set of expectations—your Web manager should already have these. Show examples of Web sites that you really like. Involve all team members to set a theme and articulate goals for your site. The list could include intended revenue, number of leads generated, increased customer loyalty and other long-term effects. Each person should be clear about expectations before actual production begins.

Share and discuss the site plan with the team. Site plans should include information architecture, interface design, content creation, forms for data collection, programming and scripting elements, production timelines, benchmarks, privacy statements, and time for quality testing.

11. Navigation is a key element.

Discuss your navigation ideas and goals in depth because navigation can oftentimes be "open" to interpretation. Start with simple branching diagrams of "known" sections of your site. Navigation questions should be formulated and addressed in keeping with the site plan.

12. Graphic design is very important.

Graphic design can be an ongoing problem for Web managers because it is difficult to keep a balance of "flash and form." Set high expectations for your graphic designers. Do not compromise your Web site's look and feel. Pay close attention to the selection of fonts, type size, headers and subheads, as well as to the choice of pictures and graphical branding representations. But be wary of too much glitz. Sometimes designers build Web interfaces to show off their Photoshop or Shockwave skills, rather than doing what best supports customers' needs and their browsers' capabilities. Web managers must make the intentions of the site and the users' capabilities clear and meaningful to designers.

13. Don't overbuild and be aware of "scope of work" creep.

Overbuilding is another common mistake. Programmers and technical staff on the team will innately want to deploy the latest technologies. Internet Service Providers (ISPs), your Web hosting firm, your management—and you—will all want to try new tricks and applications. This is fun stuff...so be forewarned. Be prepared for scope creep. It happens subtly, and your budget, time, and resources will all be affected.

14. Establish review cycles and benchmarks.

Benchmarks could include revisiting the contract with the Web development firm, reviewing deadlines and scope of work, revising goals, discussing problem situations and solutions, and reevaluating launch dates.

15. Test your site.

Someone will miss something that your customer will find. Test different browsers, proofread all copy, test download times, check monitor resolutions, test form submissions, hammer on e-mail forms, check printing formats, and try the site with operating systems. Call your friends and ask them to test the site as well.

The Outcome

16. Give your site some time.

Allow some time (that is, days and weeks) to let your site "sync in" to ensure that all the components work in harmony with each other. Ask your customers for feedback and offer them something *FREE* in return. Your Web site lives and breathes.

17. Evaluate the "finished project," but keep in mind that this is just the beginning.

You will not achieve perfection on your first Web site—or your fifth. Expect this and move on.

18. Use meta tags effectively.

Learn the basic rules about search engines and meta tags. Make sure your programmers are in fact taking advantage of meta tags in your site's title and keyword descriptions. A rule: page titles should be no more than 67 characters long, descriptions should be under 200 words, and keyword lists should take at most 1000 characters. Also, look at your graphics and assign alternate text tags (alt tags). This is helpful for disabled viewers.

19. Position yourself with search engines.

Gone are the days of being phenomenally successful with the search engines. But do spend some manual time at least once a quarter submitting your site to at least the top 10 search engines. You may also have to consider some "paid-for" submissions. This does not necessarily guarantee a top position on the list, but it does mean that your site will be viewed with higher consideration. You pay to play in the search engine game!

20. Play up the site launch.

Build excitement within your company and among your customers. Send e-mail announcements, have a celebration at a user conference, mail a postcard, and send a press release. Remember, attitude goes a long way...especially with your sales and customer service staff. And a *Top Tip*: alert *everyone,* especially your customers, that your site is going to change—before it actually does.

21. Recognize the value of e-marketing and customer service.

The Internet provides a cost-effective method for performing a lot of business functions. You must look at it as a productivity tool that can boost the effectiveness of doing business. Collect email addresses, asking visitors to sign up for an informative e-bulletin that will give them added value. Build a customer loyalty program. Cut down on postage and fulfillment costs. Ask customers for feedback on new product ideas. But always make sure that your e-mails are brief and that they actively help your customer solve a problem.

22. Direct mail plus your Web site make a great pair.

You won't succeed unless you align online and offline marketing programs. Do not count on direct mail reaching high response rates alone or search engines putting you at the top of their lists. Traditional approaches work well alongside new Internet technologies. Explore new programs. Drive targeted leads to a Web site that provides a solution to a customer's real pain, and then *measure the program*.

23. Use your log files.

Log files can help you correlate an online experience to user's expectations and behaviors. Get familiar with reading user logs. Investigate how much time visitors spend on the site. What paths do they typically take? What are the top three pages visited? Did a visitor hit your form but leave before completing it?

24. Read, read, read!

There are loads of good, informative books and Web sites that will help you learn how to improve your Web site...but you've got to be willing to take risks, test concepts, and occasionally fail.

25. Don't take criticism to heart. Take what you've learned and apply it!

Building a solid Internet team and Web site will be rewarding, challenging, frustrating, and intense, but in the end it can ultimately bring you much success in your business and your career.

About the Author:

Valerie Chernek *is the director of Internet marketing for Maryland-based educational publisher Achievement Technologies, Inc. Valerie has 20 years experience in marketing, public relations, and Internet marketing. She has created several Web sites for companies including SkillsBank, The Learning Company School Division, Pointe Technology, Making it Happen, SkillsTutor and Achievement Technologies, Inc. at www.achievementtech.com. Valerie is the Web manager behind the popular Classroom Flyer e-newsletter, which reached 30K+ educators. Contact her at vchernek@achievementtech.com, or (410) 992-4818.*

Bibliography

Here is a list of additional resources recommended by the contributors to provide greater coverage of many topics in the book.

Access to Resources and Services in the School Library Media Program: An Interpretation of the Library Bill of Rights. www.ala.org/alaorg/oif/accmedia.html

Add-A-Form. A free Web forms generation tool. www.addaform.com

American Association of School Librarians. *Information Power: Building Partnerships for Learning.* ALA Editions, 1998.

Baltimore County Public Schools. The Process for Identifying Quality Library Resources. www.bcpl.net/~dcurtis/libraryfacts/plan.html

Bartram, Sharon and Brenda Gibson. *The Training Needs Analysis Toolkit:* Human Resource Development Press, 2000.

Bayan, Richard. *Words That Sell: A Thesaurus to Help Promote Your Products, Services, and Ideas.* NTC Publishing Group, 1987

Bell, Debra. *The Ultimate Guide to Homeschooling.* Tommy Nelson, 2000.

Bly, Robert W. *The Copywriter's Handbook: A Step-By-Step Guide to Writing Copy That Sells.* Henry Holt, 1990.

Buckingham, Marcus and Curt Coffman. *First, Break All the Rules: What the World's Greatest Managers Do Differently.* Simon & Schuster, 1999.

Carlaw, Peggy and Vasudha Kathleen Deming. *The Big Book of Sales Games: Quick, Fun Activities for Improving Selling Skills or Livening Up a Sales Meeting.* McGraw Hill, 1999.

Catholic Education Network. www.catholic.org

The Chicago Manual of Style, 14th Edition. The University of Chicago Press, 1993.

Cohen, William A., *The Marketing Plan.* John Wiley & Sons

Collison, George, Bonnie Elbaum, Sarah Haavind, and Robert Tinker. *Facilitating Online Learning.* Atwood Publishing, 2000.

The Condition of Education 2000. U.S. Department of Education, National Center for Education Statistics. NCES 2000-062, 2000.

Connor, Gary B. and John A. Woods. *Sales Games and Activities for Trainers: Easy-To-Use Games, Activities, and Exercises to Teach and Learn How to Sell.* McGraw Hill, 1997.

Craighead, Donna, PhD. and Vicki Bigham Smith. *The Customers Perspective: The EdNet 99 Survey of Buyers and Managers of Educational Technology.* The Heller Reports, 1999.

Customer Relationship Management (CRM) Forum, www.crm-forum.com

Dance, James. *How to Get The Most Out Of Sales Meetings.* National Textbook Co Trade, 1992.

De Bonis, J. Nicholas, and Roger S. Peterson. *AMA Handbook for Managing Business to Business Marketing Communications.* AMA, NTC Business Books, 1997.

Dewey, John. "Progressive Education and the Science of Education" (1928), in *John Dewey on Education,* ed. Reginald D. Archambault. University of Chicago Press, 1964.

Distance Learning Resource Network. www.dlrn.org

Duffy, Cathy. *Christian Home Educators' Curriculum Manual, Elementary Grades.* Grove Publishing, 2000.

eBooks N' Bytes. www.ebooksnbytes.com

Education Market Research. *The Complete K-12 Report, Market Facts & Segment Analysis.* Education Market Research, 2000.

E-Learning, Putting a World Class Education at the Fingertips of all Children. US Department of Education. December 2000, or www.ed.gov/Technology/elearning/index.html

Electronic Media for the School Market: 2000-2001 Review, Trends, & Forecast. Simba Information, 1999.

Evans, Philip and Thomas S. Wurster. *Blown to Bits: How the New Economics of Information Transforms Strategy.* Harvard Business School Press, 1999.

Farmer, Lesley. *Partnerships for Lifelong Learning. 2nd ed.* Linworth Publishing, Inc., 1999.

Fast Company Magazine. www.fastcompany.com

Felker, Gail. "How to Start Homeschooling in 8 Easy Steps." *Homeschooling Today.* January/February 2000: 15-19.

Fibre Box Handbook (Revised Edition). Fibre Box Association, 1999.

Fuller, Bruce. *Crank 'Em Up!!!: Brilliant Sales Contests and Bright Ideas to Turn on Your Team and Turn Up Results.* Self Counsel Business Series, 1997.

The Gallup Organization. *National School Boards Association Purchasing Study.* National School Boards Association, 1999.

Gardner, Howard. *The Unschooled Mind: How Children Think & How Schools Should Teach.* Basic Books, 1991.

Gemberling, Katheryn W., Carl W. Smith, and Joseph S. Villani. *The Key Work of School Boards Guidebook.* National School Boards Association, 2000.

Gerald, Debra E. and William J. Hussar. *Projections of Education Statistics to 2010.* U.S. Department of Education. National Center for Education Statistics. NCES 2000-071, 2000.

Gladwell, Malcolm. *The Tipping Point: How Little Things Can Make a Big Difference.* Little Brown & Company, 2000.

Glatthorn, Allan A. "Curriculum Alignment Revisited." *Journal of Curriculum and Supervision* 15, no 1 (Fall 2000): 26–34.

Gratz, Donald B. *"Higher Standards for Whom?" Phi Delta Kappan.* 81, no. 9 (May 2000): 681–687.

Hagel III, John and Arthur G. Armstrong. *Net.gain: Expanding Markets Through Virtual Communities.* Harvard Business School Press, 1997.

Hagel, John III and Arthur Armstrong. *Net Gain: Expanding Markets Through Virtual Communities.* Harvard Business School Press, 1997.

Hamel, Gary. *Leading the Revolution.* Harvard Business School Press, 2000.

InfoWorld Magazine www.infoworld.com

International Literary Market Place. R.R. Bowker. (Published Annually).

The Internet School Library Media Center. http://falcon.jmu.edu/~ramseyil/selection.htm

Ishizuka, Kathy. *The Unofficial Guide to Homeschooling.* IDG Books Worldwide, Inc., 2000.

Janal, Dan. *Dan Janal's Guide to Marketing on the Internet: Getting People to Visit, Buy and Become Customers for Life.* John Wiley & Sons, 1999.

Johnson, Doug. "The Why, What, How, and Who of Staff Development in Technology: The Growing Importance of Library Media Specialist's Role in Helping Create Technology-Savvy Educators." *FETConnections*, Summer 2001.

Johnson, Steven. *Interface Culture: How New Technology Transforms The Way We Create & Communicate.* Basic Books, 1997.

Kanter, Rosabeth Moss. Evolve!: *Succeeding in the Digital Culture of Tomorrow.* Harvard Business School Press, 2001.

Kim, Amy Jo. *Community Building on the Web.* Peachpit Press, 2000.

Kirkpatrick, Donald W. *Evaluating Training Programs: The four Levels:* Berrett-Koehler, 1998.

Kleibacker, Kathryn, Linda Winter, and Carol Ann Waugh. *i-Tips 2000: The Insiders' Guide to School & Library Marketing. 2nd Ed.* The Internet Monitor, 2000.

Kohn, Alfie. *The Schools Our Children Deserve: Moving Beyond Traditional Classrooms and "Tougher Standards"*. Houghton Mifflin, 1999.

Kremer, John and J. Daniel McComas. *High-Impact Marketing on a Low-Impact Budget*. Prima Publishing, 1997.

Langer, Judith. *The Mirrored Window, Focus Groups from a Moderator's Point of View*. Paramount Market Publishing, Inc., 2001.

Leadership Matters: *Transforming Urban School Boards*. National School Boards Foundation, 1999, or at www.nsba.org

"Leadership" in *Education Vital Signs,* supplement to *American School Board Journal,* December 1999.

Leppert, Mary & Michael. *Homeschooling Almanac* 2002-2003. Prima Publishing, 2001.

Levinson, Jay Conrad, Mark S. A. Smith, Orvel Ray Wilson. *Guerrilla Trade Show Selling: New Unconventional Weapons and Tactics to Meet More People, Get More Leads, and Close More Sales*. John Wiley & Sons, 1997.

Lewis, Hershell Gordon. *On the Art of Writing Copy: The Best of * Print *Broadcast * Internet * Direct Mail,* 2nd Edition. AMACOM, 2000.

Loertscher, David. *Taxonomies of the School Library Media Program*. 2nd ed. Hi Willow Research and Publishing, 2000.

Look Sharp: Tips for Web Design and Graphics. T&L Magazine, February 98

Lynch, Patrick J. and Sarah Horton. *Web Style Guide: Basic Design Principles for Creating Web Sites*. Yale University Press, 1999.

Magazine Publishers of America. www.magazine.org

McCaugheym Jr, Donald G. *Graphic Design for Corrugated Packaging*. Jelmar Publishing Company, 1995.

McKenna, Regis. *Relationship Marketing*. Addison-Wesley, 1993.

Miller, Robert B., Stephen E. Heiman with Tad Tuleja. *Strategic Selling*. Warner Books, 1987.

Miller, Steve. *How to Get the Most Out of Trade Shows*. NTC Publishing Group, 2000.

Modahl, Mary. *Now or Never: How Companies Must Change Today to Win the Battle for Internet Customers*. HarperBusiness, 1999.

Montana State Library. Collection Development Policy Guidelines for School Library Media Programs. http://msl.state.mt.us/slr/cmpolsch.html

Moore, Geoffrey A. *Crossing the Chasm: Marketing and Selling High-Tech Products to Mainstream Customers*. HarperBusiness, 1999.

Moriarty, Rowland and Ursula Moran. *Managing Hybrid Marketing Systems*. Harvard Business Review #90605.

National Catholic Educational Association, www.ncea.org

National Center for Education Statistics. *School Library Media Centers: 1993-94*. U.S. Department of Education, 1998.

National Staff Development Council. www.nsdc.org

Newsom, Carrell and Bob Carrell. *Public Relations Writing: Form and Style*. Thomson Learning, 2000.

Nykamp, Melinda. *The Customer Differential: The Complete Guide to Implementing Customer Relations Management*. Amacom Publishing, 2001.

Ohanian, Susan. *One Size Fits Few: The Folly of Educational Standards*. Heinemann, 1999.

Online Publishing News www.mmp.co.uk

Open e-Book Forum www.openebook.org

Papert, Seymour. *The Children's Machine: Rethinking School in the Age of the Computer*. Basic Books, 1993.

Parker, Roger C. *Publisher 2000: Get Professional Results*. Osborne McGraw-Hill, 2000.

Parker, Roger C. *Streetwise Relationship Marketing On The Internet* by. Adams Media Corporation, 2001.

Parker, Roger C. *Web Content and Design for Designers - Web Design as Relationship Building* [E-Book: Adobe Reader]. Waterside Productions, Inc.

Pereus, Steven C. "The Financial Plan," in *School Spending: The Business of Education,* supplement to *American School Board Journal* (2000): 12-15.

Picus, Lawrence O. "Adequate Funding" in *School Spending: The Business of Education,* supplement to *American School Board Journal* (2000): 8-10.

Pike, Bob and Robert W. Pike. *High Impact Presentations:* American Media Inc., 1995.

Pike, Robert W. *Creative Training Techniques Handbook: Tips, Tactics, and How-To's for Delivering Effective Training* Lakewoods Publications, 1994.

Plans to Purchase Survey. T.H.E. Report.

The Power of the Internet for Learning: Moving from Promise to Practice. Web-Based Education Commission, December 2000, or www.webcommission.org/report

Preece, Jenny. *Online Communities: Designing Usability, Supporting Sociabilty.* Wiley & Sons, 2000.

Print Publishing for School Market: 2000-2001 Review, Trends & Forecast. Simba Information, 1999.

"The Pros and Cons of Outsourcing" *iMarketing News,* June 2000

The Publishing Law Center. www.publaw.com

Report of the Web-based Education Commission To the President and the Congress of the United States. US Department of Education, 2000.

Resnick Ph.D, Robert M. *The Complete K-12 Report: Market Facts & Segment Analyses.* Education Market Research, 2001.

Ries, Al and Laura Ries. *The 22 Immutable Laws of Branding: How to Build a Product or Service into a World-Class Brand.* HarperCollins Publishers, 1998.

Rose, M. J., and Angela Adair-Hoy. *How to Promote and Publish Online.* St. Martin's Press, 2001.

Rosen, Jerry and Eileen Klockers. *Performance-Based Sales Training* Human Resource Development Press, 1997.

Rosenberg, Marc J. E-Learning: *Strategies for Delivering Knowledge in the Digital Age.* McGraw-Hill Professional Publishing, 2000.

Rosenoer, Jonathon, et.al. *The Clickable Corporation: Successful Strategies for Capturing the Internet Advantage,* Free Press

School Planning and Management Magazine. www.spmmag.com

Schultz, Don E., Stanley Tannenbaum and Robert Lauterborn. *The New Marketing Paradigm.* NTC Business Books, 1994.

Schwartz, Evan I. *Digital Darwinism: 7 Breakthrough Business Strategies for Surviving in the Cutthroat Web Economy.* Broadway Books, 1999.

Schwartz, Evan I. *Webonomics: Nine Essential Principles for Growing Your Business on the World Wide Web.* Bantam Doubleday Dell Publishers, 1998

Seybold, Patricia B., Ronni T. Marshak (Contributor), Jeffrey M. Lewis. *The Customer Revolution.* Crown Publishing, 2001.

Shapiro, Carl and Hal Varian. *Information Rules: A Strategic Guide to the Network Economy.* Harvard Business School Press, 1998.

Sivin-Kachala, Jay and Ellen R. Bialo. *2000 Research Report on the Effectiveness of Technology in Schools,* 7th ed. SIIA, 2000

Smith, Ellen Reid. *E-Loyalty: How to Keep Your Customers Coming Back to Your Website.* HarperBusiness, 2000.

Snyder, Thomas D. and Charlene M. Hoffman. *Digest of Education Statistics, 1999.* U.S. Department of Education. National Center for Education Statistics. NCES 2000-031, 2000.

Sokora, Walter G. and Paul J. Zepf. *IoPP Glossary of Packaging Terminology.* Institute of Packaging Professionals Press, 1998

Standards for Electronic Publishing, An Overview, a report for the NEDLIB Project. Mark Bide & Associates, 2000. Available online at www.kb.nl/coop/nedlib/results/e-publishingstandards.pdf

Stimolo, Bob and Lynn Stimolo. *Marketing To Schools: A Textbook for the Education Market*. School Market Research Institute, 1998.

Strategic Memorandum. Channel Strategies, Inc. 1996.

Technology & Learning Magazine media kit.

Technology Purchasing Forecast. Quality Education Data. www.qeddata.com

Terreri, Malinda A. *Better Sales Meetings In 3 to 30 Minutes*. Hutch Graphics, 1998

Thompson, Scott. "The Authentic Standards Movement and It's Evil Twin." *Phi Delta Kappan*. 82, no. 5 (January 2001): 358–362.

Today's Catholic Teacher www.catholicteacher.com

Trout, Jack and Al Ries. *Positioning: The Battle for your Mind*. McGraw Hill, 2001.

United States Catholic Conference. http://nccbuscc.org/education

United States Distance Learning Association. www.usdle.org

US Copyright Office. http://lcweb.loc.gov/copyright

US Patent & Trademark Office. www.uspto.gov

Van Buren, Chris, and Jeff Cogswell. *Poor Richard's Creating E-Books: How Authors, Publishers, and Corporations Can Get Into Digital Print*. Top Floor Publishing, 2001.

Vaughan, Tay and Scott Rogers (editor). *Multimedia: Making it Work* by Tay. Osborne/McGraw-Hill, 1998.

Walch, Timothy. *Parish School: American Catholic Parochial Education From Colonial Times to the Present*. Crossroad Publishing, 1996.

Web-Based Education Commission. *The Power of the Internet for Learning: Moving from Promise to Practice*. Web-Based Education Commission, 2000

Weisgal, Margit B. *Show and Sell: 133 Business Building Ways to Promote Your Trade Show Exhibit*, AMACOM, 1996.

Wellins, Richard S., William C. Byham, and Jeanne M. Wilson. *Empowered Teams*. Jossey-Bass, 1993

Wise, Jessie & Susan Wise Bauer. *The Well-Trained Mind*. W.W. Norton & Company, Inc., 1999.

Youniss, James, and John Covey. *Catholic Schools at the Crossroads*. Teachers College Press, 2000.

Youniss, James, John Covey, and Jeffrey McLellan, eds. *The Catholic Character of Catholic Schools*. University of Notre Dame Press, 2000.

Zinsser, William. *On Writing Well*. Harper & Row, 1985.

K-12 Industry Acronyms

AAAS	American Association for the Advancement of Science
AACE	Association for the Advancement of Computing in Education
AAESA	American Association of Educational Service Agencies
AAP	Association of American Publishers
AAPT	American Association of Physics Teachers
AASA	American Association of School Administrators
AB	Assembly Bill
ACEI	Association for Childhood Education International
ACORN	Adolescent Coordinated Resource Network
ACT	Agencies Cooperating Together
ACT	American College Test
ACYF	Administration for Children, Youth and Families
ADA	Average Daily Attendance
AECT	Association for Educational Communications & Technologies
AEL	Appalachia Educational Laboratory
AEP	Association of Educational Publishers
AFDC	Aid to Families with Dependent Children
AFT	American Federation of Teachers
AIDS	Acquired Immune Deficiency Syndrome
AP	Advanced Placement
APE	Adapted Physical Education
APP	Alternative Payment Program

AR	Administrative Regulation
ASAP	Alternative School, Accelerated Program
ASCD	Association for Supervision and Curriculum Development
ASHA	American Speech Language & Hearing Association
ASP	Applications Service Provider
ASTD	American Society for Training & Development
AV	Assessed Valuation
AV	Audio Visual
AVEC	Adult and Vocational Education Council
AWOL	Absence Without Leave
BAPC	Business & Administrative Policy Committee
B/B	Bilingual/Bicultural
BD	Behavior Disorder
BEAR	Billed Entity Applicant Reimbursement
BETT	British Education Technology Tradeshow
BIA	Bureau of Indian Affairs
BOCES	Board of Cooperative Education Services
BODY	Better Opportunities for Disadvantaged Youth
BTTP	Bilingual Teacher Training Program
BVMGT	Bender Visual Motor Gestalt Test
CA	Chronological Age
CAC	Community Advisory Committee
CAO	Chief Administrative Office

CARE	Children's Academic and Recreational Enrichment	CSR	Class Size Reduction
CASE	Computer Assisted Software Engineering	CSSF	County School Service Fund
CASE	Computer Assisted Special Education	CTIIP	Classroom Teacher Instructional Improvement Program
CASTS	Computerized Accounting and Student Terminal System	CUE	Computer Using Educators
CBO	Chief Business Official	CWA	Child Welfare and Attendance
CBT	Computer Based Training	DAC	District Advisory Committee
CC	Children's Center	DARE	Drug Abuse Resistance Education
CCA	Common Core of Data	DATE	Drug, Alcohol, and Tobacco Education
CCAB	County-Wide Community Advisory Board	DCH	Development Centers for the Handicapped
CCL	Community Care Licensing	DECA	Distributive Education Clubs of America
CCR	Coordinated Compliance Review	DHHS	Department of Health and Human Services
CCSCO	Council of Chief State School Officers	DI	Direct Instruction
CDM	Career Decision Making	DID	Division of Innovation and Development
CDP	Child Development Program	DIS	Designated Instruction and Services
CDVE	California Directors of Vocational Education	DOL	Department of Labor
CEC	Council for Exceptional Children	DOVE	Data on Vocational Education
CETA	Comprehensive Employment Training Act (now JTPA)	DRC	District Representative Council
CFRP	Child Family Resource Program	DSS	Department of Social Services
CH	Communicatively Handicapped	DTLA	Detroit Test of Learning Abilities
CHDPP	Child Health and Disability Prevention Program	EAS	Educational Assessment Service
COE	County Office of Education	ECIA	Education Consolidation Improvement Act
COG	Committee on Guidelines	EDFN	Education Finance Statistics Center
COLA	Cost of Living Adjustment	EDS	Educational Services
COMPED	Compensatory Education	EDY	Educationally Disadvantaged Youth
COP	Certificate of Participation	EEC	European Economic Community
CPPC	County Policy Parent Council	EEPCD	Early Childhood Program for Children with Disabilities
CPS	Child Protective Services	EESA	Educational for Economic Security Act (a.k.a. Eisenhower)

EHA	Education of the Handicapped Act	GAAP	Generally Accepted Accounting Principles
EIA	Economic Impact Aid	GAAS	Generally Accepted Auditing Standards
EIEA	Emergency Immigrant Education Assistance	GAGAS	Generally Accepted Governmental Auditing Standards
EL-HI	Elementary - High School		
EPA	Educational Paperback Association	GAO	General Accounting Office
EPS	Exemplary Program Standards	GASB	Governmental Accounting Standards Board
EPSDT	Early Periodic Screening, Diagnosis, and Treatment	GATB	General Aptitude Test Battery
		GATE	Gifted and Talented Education
ESEA	Elementary & Secondary Education Act	GED	General Education Development
ESL	English as a Second Language	GNP	Gross National Product
ESSA	Elementary School Science Association	GPO	Government Printing Office
ET	Effective Teaching	GUI	Graphical User Interface
ETC	Educational Technology Committee	HEW	U.S. Department of Health, Education and Welfare
ETC	Effective Teaching - Coaching		
FAPE	Free Appropriate Public Education	HGHL	Healthy Generations, Healthy Learners
FAQ	Frequently Asked Questions	HH	Hearing Impaired
FAS	Fetal Alcohol Syndrome	HS	Head Start
FBG	Federal Block Grant	HSA	Health Services Act
FBLA	Future Business Leaders of America	IA	Impact Aid
FDCA	Family Day Care Association	IAED	International Archive of Educational Data
FES	Fluently English Speaking	IASA	Improving America's Schools Act
FETC	Florida Educational Technology Conference	IDEA	Individuals with Disabilities Education Act
FFA	Future Farmers of America	IEA	International Association for the Evaluation of Education Achievement
FHA	Future Homemakers of America		
FLCIC	Foreign Language Curriculum Implementation Center	IEP	Individualized Educational Plan
		IEU	Intermediate Education Unit
FLTIC	Foreign Language Technology in Curriculum	IFSP	Individualized Family Service Plan
FTE	Full-time Equivalent	IGE	Individually Guided Education
GAAFR	Governmental Accounting, Auditing and Financial Reporting	IMC	Instructional Materials Center
		IMS	Instructional Management Systems

IQ	Intelligence Quotient	MPA	Magazine Publishers of America
IRA	International Reading Association	MRT	Migrant Resource Teacher
IRCA	Immigrant Reform and Control Act	NABE	National Association for Bilingual Education
IRL	International Reading Literacy	NABT	National Association of Biology Teachers
ISTE	International Society for Technology in Education	NAEP	Natinal Assessment of Educational Progress
IT	Information Technology	NAESP	National Association of Elementary School Principals
ITPA	Illinois Test of Psycholinguistic Abilities	NAEYC	National Association for the Education of Young Children
IWEN	Individual With Exceptional Needs	NARC	National Association for Retarded Children
JPA	Joint Powers Agency	NARMC	National Association of Regional Media Centers
JTPA	Job Training Partnership Act		
LAB	Northeast and Islands Laboratory at Brown University	NASDSE	National Association of State Directors of Special Education
LAN	Local Area (Computer) Network	NASSP	National Association of Secondary School Principals
LCC	Local Coordinating Council	NBA	National Braille Association
LCI	Licensed Children's Institution	NCEA	National Catholic Education Association
LD	Learning Disability	NCES	National Center for Education Statistics
LEA	Local Educational Agency	NCREL	North Central Regional Educational Laboratory
LEP	Limited English Proficient		
LEPS	Limited English Proficient Students	NCTE	National Council of Teachers of English
LES	Limited English Speaking	NCTM	National Council of Teachers of Mathematics
LH	Learning Handicapped	NDEA	National Defense Education Act
LIPS	Leiter International Performance Scale	NDN	National Diffusion Network
LRE	Least Restrictive Environment	NEA	National Education Association
LSH	Language, Speech, and Hearing	NECC	National Educational Computing Conference
McREL	Mid-Continent Regional Educational Laboratory	NES	Non-English Speaking
MDR	Market Data Retrieval	NFES	National Forum on Education Statistics
MHS	Migrant Head Start	NMSA	National Middle School Association
MOO	Multi-User Object Oriented	NPS	Non-Public nonsectarian School

NSBA	National School Boards Association		PL	Public Law
NSDC	National Staff Development Council		PPVT	Peabody Picture Vocabulary Test
NSTA	National Science Teachers Association		PQR	Program Quality Review
NSH	Non-Severely Handicapped		PREL	Pacific Resources for Education and Learning
NSPRA	National School Public Relations Association		PS	Program Specialist
NTE	National Teachers Exam		PSAT	Preliminary Scholastic Aptitude Test
NTN	National Transition Network		PSIG	Preschool Incentive Grant
NWREL	Northwest Regional Educational Laboratory		PT	Physical Therapy
OCD	Office of Child Development		PTA	Parent-Teacher Association
OEC	Outdoor Education Center		QED	Quality Education Data
OERI	Office of Educational Research and Improvement		R&R	Resource and Referral
OH	Orthopedically Handicapped		RAM	Random Access Memory
OIE	Office of Indian Education		RAVEC	Regional Adult Vocational Education Council
OJT	On-The-Job Training		RFP	Request for Proposals
OMB	Office of Management and Budget		RISE	Reform of Intermediate and Secondary Education
OSEP	Office of Special Education Programs		ROC/P	Regional Occupation Center/Program
OSERS	Office of Special Education and Rehabilative Services		ROI	Return on Investment
OSHA	Occupational Safety and Health Agency		RS	Resource Specialist
OT	Occupational Therapy		RSP	Resource Specialist Program
PAC	Parent Advisory Council		SAC	School Advisory Committee
PASS	Performance Assessment for Self-Sufficiency		SAFES	State Agency/Federal Evaluations Studies
PCI	Personal Computer Interface		SASS	Schools and Staffing Survey
PDA	Personal Digital Assistant		SALT	Society for Applied Learning Technology
PDK	Phi Delta Kappa		SARB	School Attendance Review Board
PDP	Professional Development Program		SAT	Scholastic Aptitude Test
PET	Parent Effectiveness Training		SAT	School Appraisal Team
PH	Physically Handicapped		SAVI	Self-Assessment Validation Instrument
PIAT	Peabody Individual Achievement Test		SB	Senate Bill

SBE	State Board of Education	UK	United Kingdom
SCD	State Development Center	UR	Unit Rate
SCORM	Sharable Courseware Object Reference Model	URL	Uniform Resource Locator
SDE	State Department of Education	USED	United States Education Department
SDL	Severe Disorders of Language	VEA	Vocational Education Act
SE	Special Education	VEC	Vocational Evaluation Center
SEA	State Education Agency	VH	Visually Handicapped
SED	Severely Emotionally Disturbed	VICA	Vocational Industrial Clubs of America
SEDL	Southwest Educational Development Laboratory	WAIS	Wechsler Adult Intelligence Scale
SERVE	Southeastern Regional Vision for Education	WEM	World Education Market
SH	Severely Handicapped	WIP	Written Instruction Plan
SIEA	Stanislaus Industrial Education Association	WISC-R	Wechsler Pre-School and Primary Scale of Intelligence
SIF	School Interoperability Framework	WRAT	Wide Range Achievement Test
SIIA	Software & Information Industy Association	WWW	World Wide Web
SIP	School Improvement Program	XML	Extensible Markup Language
SITAC	State Instructional Advisory Committee	YEDPA	Youth Employment and Demonstration Projects Act
SOLH	Severe Oral Language Handicap		
SPI	Superintendent of Public Instruction		
SSC	Scope, Sequence and Coordination Project		
SSPI	State Superintendent of Public Instruction		
SSR	Support Service Ratio		
TIC	Teachers in Computers		
TIC	Technology in Curriculum		
TIMSS	Third Internatinal Mathematics and Science Study		
TMR	Trainable Mentally Retarded		
TPC	Technological Planning Committee		
TUPE	Tobacco Use Prevention Education		

Federal School Funding

Here is a sample budget calendar tracing fiscal year 2002 from its initial planning stages to its conclusion. The timeframes in this calendar may serve to clarify the progression of the budget process. In this context, fiscal year 2002 is treated as a normal year, although the normal process may not be what is actually followed.

The Federal Budget Process and Its Implementation in the Department of Education

Source: US Department of Education

Calendar Date	Action	Explanation
Spring 2000	1. Allowance letter issued by OMB to Department.	Following transmittal to the Congress of the FY 2001 President's proposals, OMB specifies budget authority and outlay ceilings for FY 2002 and the out years (FY 2003-2011). This sets the stage for a typical budget formulation process which has similar elements each year.
May 2000	2. OUS (Office of the Under Secretary) staff begin to develop FY 2002 budget and legislative recommendations.	Assistant Secretaries are asked to submit their budget and legislative priorities for FY 2002 to the Under Secretary.
June 2000	3. OUS submits preliminary FY 2002 budget recommendations and the priorities of the Assistant Secretaries to the Secretary.	Secretary makes preliminary decisions on new initiatives and total dollar levels. Requests issue papers as appropriate.
July 2000	4. Budget staff (in OUS) work on the Mid-Session Review of the President's FY 2001 budget.	Final Mid-Session Review, released by OMB in July, results in revised ED budget authority and outlay ceilings for FY 2001-2010, affecting FY 2002 budget development.
	5. OUS staff develop issue papers and submit final FY 2002 budget recommendations to the Secretary, along with the Assistant Secretaries' recommendations.	Formal briefing sessions are held for the Secretary involving OUS, Assistant Secretaries, and other senior staff officers. Secretary makes final decisions
August 2000	6. OUS prepares FY 2002 budget submission to OMB.	Budget submission includes detailed justifications, budget authority and outlay estimates for FY 2000-2011.

Calendar Date	Action	Explanation
September 2000	7. FY 2002 budget request submitted to OMB.	ED submits budget request to OMB in early September, along with a transmittal letter from the Secretary covering highlights and major issues
October 2000	8. ED responds to detailed questions concerning FY 2002 budget submission.	OMB staff request answers to analytic questions to enable them to make recommendations to the Director of OMB.
	9. ED revises FY 2001/2002-2011 budget request to OMB.	Purpose of revisions is to take into account congressional action on the FY 2001 appropriation. Enactment of significant program legislation might also prompt ED to reconsider the request to OMB.
November 2000	10. Actual FY 2000 obligations and expenditures certified.	Treasury Annual Report issued. Data serve as basis for 2001 and 2002 estimates in the President's 2002 budget.
	11. Baseline budget prepared.	Baseline budget estimates the costs, adjusted for inflation and other uncontrollable increases, of continuing current year (FY 2001) policies and programs in the budget year.
November/December 2000	12. OMB Passback.	OMB apprises agencies of its decisions on the FY 2002 budget. The OMB passback contains not only funding decisions, but program policy changes, legislative direction, and personnel ceilings.
	13. Appeals of OMB Passback.	Although the OMB passback represents final decisions, agencies can appeal levels to the budget examiners, the Director, or the President, depending on the nature of the issue.
December 2000-January 2001	14. Preparation of President's FY 2002 budget materials.	ED prepares a variety of materials to explain and justify budget as part of the presentation stage of the budget process. These include materials for the printed President's budget, detailed justifications for the Congress, and an information packet for the public.

Calendar Date	Action	Explanation
February 2001	15. Submission of FY 2002 budget to Congress.	President's request for FY 2002 is presented to Congress and the public. By law, this must be done each year after the first Monday in January but not after the first Monday in February.
	16. CBO reports on fiscal policy and budget priorities.	The Congressional Budget Office submits (February 15) its report on the President's FY 2002 budget and budget alternatives to the Budget Committees. The report suggests different ways of directing spending to achieve varying impacts.
	17. Committees submit views and estimates to Budget Committees.	The process established by the Congressional Budget Act, and modified by Gramm-Rudman-Hollings, requires authorizing committees to report estimates of funding levels for programs under their jurisdiction to the Budget committees within 6 weeks of the President's budget transmittal. ED witnesses frequently asked to testify in hearings held by the authorizing and Budget committees.
February-March 2001	18. House appropriations hearings.	House appropriations subcommittees hold hearings on FY 2002 request and FY 2001 revisions (supplementals or recisions), if any are proposed.
March-April 2001	19. Senate appropriations hearings.	Senate appropriation subcommittees hear testimony on FY 2002 request and FY 2001 revisions.
April 2001	20. Senate Budget Committee reports FY 2002 concurrent budget resolution.	April 1--Senate Budget Committee reports resolution, which contains targets for total levels of budget authority and outlays, and provides reconciliation instructions to committees on how to achieve those targets. Accompanying report gives general breakdown for budget functions; e.g., education and training; and discusses discrepancies among levels suggested by other committees.

Calendar Date	Action	Explanation
	21. Congress completes action on FY 2002 concurrent budget resolution.	April 15--Includes basis for allocating BA and outlay targets for appropriations action. Budget Committees in each House inform appropriations subcommittees of amounts contained in totals for activities in subcommittees' jurisdictions. House and Senate totals must be equal, but amounts for individual functions may differ. The allocation process dividing discretionary totals among the appropriations subcommittees is established in section 602(b) of the Congressional Budget and Impoundment Control Act of 1974, as amended; consequently the allocations are commonly known as "602(b)'s."
May 2001	22. New authorizing legislation must be reported.	Committees must report any legislation that would authorize new budget authority by May 15. ED staff and OMB will have been working on President's legislative proposals so that the proposals associated with the February budget can be sent to Congress prior to Committee action.
June 2001	23. House appropriations mark-up and floor action on FY 2002.	Appropriations action begins in the House, which may begin consideration of appropriations bills May 15 even if a concurrent resolution has not yet passed. The full House Committee on Appropriations marks up the subcommittee version of the bill. Subsequently, the full House votes on the bill and amends it on the floor if necessary. Reports sent to the floor along with the bill explain levels and often provide policy guidance. The House Committee must report its last regular appropriations bill by June 10. Floor action is supposed to be finished by June 30.

Calendar Date	Action	Explanation
	24. June 15--Congress completes action on reconciliation bill.	While this date is contained in the law, final action can occur any time. A reconciliation bill makes the changes in the laws governing taxes, mandatory, and entitlement spending that would be necessary to carry out assumptions made in the Concurrent Budget Resolution. In the Department of Education, these changes most often involve student loan programs, which are entitlements.
July 2001	25. Mid-Session Review of the President's FY 2002 budget.	The President submits to Congress (July 15) revised estimates of his FY 2002 baseline budget and proposals based on new economic assumptions. Estimates cover FY 2001-2011, and determine agency ceilings for development of the FY 2003 budget.
	26. Senate appropriations mark-up and floor action on FY 2002.	The full Senate Committee on Appropriations marks up the subcommittee bill. Often, the Administration formally appeals the House level to the Senate. As in the House, an explanatory report accompanies the Senate bill to the floor where the full Senate may amend the bill before passing it.
August 2001	27. Conference action on the FY 2002 appropriations bill. This could occur any time after passage by the Senate, in August or September.	Representatives of the two committees meet in conference to compromise on the differing provisions of the FY 2002 House and Senate.
	28. FY 2002 appropriations bills are enacted.	A conference bill is reported to House and Senate floors which usually accept Conference advice.
	29. Continuing resolution.	If no appropriation has been passed by September 30, Congress must enact a continuing resolution providing temporary funding for Federal programs that require annual appropriations. A continuing resolution has been required for all but 3 of the last 20 fiscal years.

Calendar Date	Action	Explanation
October 2001	30. Start of FY 2002.	Federal fiscal year runs from October 1, 2001, through September 30, 2002. Amounts appropriated on a forward-funded basis for large State grant programs become available on July 1, 2002, for school year 2002-2003. Most other FY 2002 funds are apportioned by OMB and allotted by ED at the beginning of the fiscal year, or as needed for obligations based on operating plans. This budget execution stage relies heavily on the policies and dollar levels proposed by the President and approved by Congress in justifications, bills, and various reports.

Federal Funding Charts

FEDERAL FUNDING BY STATE 2000-2002

	2000 Appropriation	2001 Appropriation	% Change	2002 Request	% Change
Alabama	$ 549,467,814	$ 624,614,748	14%	$ 664,688,812	6%
Alaska	$ 179,181,580	$ 211,979,043	18%	$ 236,915,654	12%
Arizona	$ 652,676,456	$ 748,905,089	15%	$ 833,877,839	11%
Arkansas	$ 321,703,457	$ 366,130,547	14%	$ 390,698,552	7%
California	$ 3,827,196,590	$ 4,549,449,018	19%	$ 4,931,904,182	8%
Colorado	$ 370,282,855	$ 426,296,978	15%	$ 461,208,291	8%
Connecticut	$ 287,295,735	$ 339,142,009	18%	$ 369,966,645	9%
Delaware	$ 85,735,787	$ 100,253,120	17%	$ 105,288,936	5%
District of Columbia	$ 114,640,586	$ 129,848,476	13%	$ 138,611,292	7%
Florida	$ 1,581,611,741	$ 1,838,399,749	16%	$ 1,982,792,690	8%
Georgia	$ 821,236,045	$ 984,946,332	20%	$ 1,078,971,554	10%
Hawaii	$ 132,043,273	$ 160,612,806	22%	$ 169,225,387	5%
Idaho	$ 149,011,363	$ 174,524,583	17%	$ 185,865,446	6%
Illinois	$ 1,276,464,392	$ 1,477,774,989	16%	$ 1,590,946,252	8%
Indiana	$ 588,009,058	$ 673,037,077	14%	$ 725,343,316	8%
Iowa	$ 305,590,676	$ 345,413,490	13%	$ 366,909,356	6%
Kansas	$ 296,111,073	$ 342,969,236	16%	$ 370,240,043	8%
Kentucky	$ 506,996,366	$ 569,326,636	12%	$ 603,155,137	6%
Louisiana	$ 647,937,545	$ 739,382,375	14%	$ 776,777,699	5%
Maine	$ 155,133,835	$ 175,515,772	13%	$ 185,683,351	6%
Maryland	$ 463,761,303	$ 548,856,285	18%	$ 597,032,152	9%
Massachusetts	$ 675,561,571	$ 787,689,113	17%	$ 846,165,218	7%
Michigan	$ 1,091,393,304	$ 1,244,903,172	14%	$ 1,325,624,423	6%
Minnesota	$ 467,481,969	$ 535,219,087	14%	$ 575,607,493	8%
Mississippi	$ 441,133,274	$ 494,904,327	12%	$ 517,886,655	5%
Missouri	$ 596,240,071	$ 683,658,433	15%	$ 730,116,500	7%
Montana	$ 158,336,540	$ 181,644,605	15%	$ 197,950,097	9%
Nebraska	$ 190,806,074	$ 223,688,114	17%	$ 241,265,187	8%
Nevada	$ 126,529,727	$ 156,161,479	23%	$ 169,548,136	9%
New Hampshire	$ 114,294,562	$ 133,778,902	17%	$ 140,532,317	5%
New Jersey	$ 762,124,027	$ 900,940,154	18%	$ 978,328,229	9%
New Mexico	$ 330,884,647	$ 376,353,371	14%	$ 411,707,198	9%
New York	$ 2,613,956,084	$ 3,069,622,688	17%	$ 3,276,381,614	7%
North Carolina	$ 743,259,804	$ 871,451,979	17%	$ 946,883,425	9%

FEDERAL FUNDING BY STATE *(Continued)*

	2000 Appropriation	2001 Appropriation	% Change	2002Request	% Change
North Dakota	$ 117,910,518	$ 141,550,335	20%	$ 155,164,581	10%
Ohio	$ 1,162,653,385	$ 1,306,739,170	12%	$ 1,387,619,042	6%
Oklahoma	$ 450,207,200	$ 526,948,383	17%	$ 560,904,049	6%
Oregon	$ 335,536,498	$ 386,667,443	15%	$ 415,123,552	7%
Pennsylvania	$ 1,280,604,828	$ 1,451,380,676	13%	$ 1,542,449,523	6%
Rhode Island	$ 133,718,578	$ 155,217,934	16%	$ 164,914,431	6%
South Carolina	$ 438,490,828	$ 507,687,887	16%	$ 548,557,178	8%
South Dakota	$ 133,066,735	$ 160,276,461	20%	$ 175,113,124	9%
Tennessee	$ 581,665,744	$ 657,561,261	13%	$ 699,022,600	6%
Texas	$ 2,486,815,057	$ 2,872,873,404	16%	$ 3,093,631,256	8%
Utah	$ 247,609,306	$ 284,199,152	15%	$ 299,532,782	5%
Vermont	$ 92,591,401	$ 106,487,801	15%	$ 112,422,923	6%
Virginia	$ 649,592,965	$ 766,819,897	18%	$ 825,537,273	8%
Washington	$ 570,977,741	$ 662,825,012	16%	$ 711,424,660	7%
West Virginia	$ 258,381,746	$ 289,547,843	12%	$ 302,276,215	4%
Wisconsin	$ 532,500,703	$ 600,166,887	13%	$ 643,931,017	7%
Wyoming	$ 86,826,320	$ 102,133,079	18%	$ 109,460,345	7%
American Samoa	$ 17,474,966	$ 19,199,697	10%	$ 20,773,228	8%
Guam	$ 31,483,237	$ 33,673,576	7%	$ 36,845,664	9%
Indian Tribe Set Aside	$ 172,001,598	$ 191,254,517	11%	$ 208,467,235	9%
Marshall Islands	$ 1,874,080	$ 2,018,508	8%	$ 2,096,218	4%
Micronesia	$ 4,887,692	$ 5,094,089	4%	$ 5,271,799	3%
Northern Mariana Islands	$ 11,608,389	$ 12,419,826	7%	$ 13,183,865	6%
Palau	$ 1,388,270	$ 1,479,590	7%	$ 1,557,300	5%
Puerto Rico	$ 979,099,488	$ 1,113,916,399	14%	$ 1,161,513,099	4%
Virgin Islands	$ 30,548,863	$ 33,453,148	10%	$ 36,448,580	9%
Other	$ 146,653,680	$ 449,370,242	206%	$ 228,402,382	-49%
Total	$ 32,580,259,000	$ 38,028,356,000	17%	$40,585,743,000	6%

Source: Department of Education

FEDERAL FUNDING BY STATE – RANKED HIGHEST TO LOWEST

	2000 Appropriation	2001 Appropriation	% Change	2002 Request	% Change
California	$ 3,827,196,590	$ 4,549,449,018	19%	$ 4,931,904,182	8%
New York	$ 2,613,956,084	$ 3,069,622,688	17%	$ 3,276,381,614	7%
Texas	$ 2,486,815,057	$ 2,872,873,404	16%	$ 3,093,631,256	8%
Florida	$ 1,581,611,741	$ 1,838,399,749	16%	$ 1,982,792,690	8%
Illinois	$ 1,276,464,392	$ 1,477,774,989	16%	$ 1,590,946,252	8%
Pennsylvania	$ 1,280,604,828	$ 1,451,380,676	13%	$ 1,542,449,523	6%
Ohio	$ 1,162,653,385	$ 1,306,739,170	12%	$ 1,387,619,042	6%
Michigan	$ 1,091,393,304	$ 1,244,903,172	14%	$ 1,325,624,423	6%
Puerto Rico	$ 979,099,488	$ 1,113,916,399	14%	$ 1,161,513,099	4%
Georgia	$ 821,236,045	$ 984,946,332	20%	$ 1,078,971,554	10%
New Jersey	$ 762,124,027	$ 900,940,154	18%	$ 978,328,229	9%
North Carolina	$ 743,259,804	$ 871,451,979	17%	$ 946,883,425	9%
Massachusetts	$ 675,561,571	$ 787,689,113	17%	$ 846,165,218	7%
Arizona	$ 652,676,456	$ 748,905,089	15%	$ 833,877,839	11%
Virginia	$ 649,592,965	$ 766,819,897	18%	$ 825,537,273	8%
Louisiana	$ 647,937,545	$ 739,382,375	14%	$ 776,777,699	5%
Missouri	$ 596,240,071	$ 683,658,433	15%	$ 730,116,500	7%
Indiana	$ 588,009,058	$ 673,037,077	14%	$ 725,343,316	8%
Washington	$ 570,977,741	$ 662,825,012	16%	$ 711,424,660	7%
Tennessee	$ 581,665,744	$ 657,561,261	13%	$ 699,022,600	6%
Alabama	$ 549,467,814	$ 624,614,748	14%	$ 664,688,812	6%
Wisconsin	$ 532,500,703	$ 600,166,887	13%	$ 643,931,017	7%
Kentucky	$ 506,996,366	$ 569,326,636	12%	$ 603,155,137	6%
Maryland	$ 463,761,303	$ 548,856,285	18%	$ 597,032,152	9%
Minnesota	$ 467,481,969	$ 535,219,087	14%	$ 575,607,493	8%
Oklahoma	$ 450,207,200	$ 526,948,383	17%	$ 560,904,049	6%
South Carolina	$ 438,490,828	$ 507,687,887	16%	$ 548,557,178	8%
Mississippi	$ 441,133,274	$ 494,904,327	12%	$ 517,886,655	5%
Colorado	$ 370,282,855	$ 426,296,978	15%	$ 461,208,291	8%
Oregon	$ 335,536,498	$ 386,667,443	15%	$ 415,123,552	7%
New Mexico	$ 330,884,647	$ 376,353,371	14%	$ 411,707,198	9%
Arkansas	$ 321,703,457	$ 366,130,547	14%	$ 390,698,552	7%
Kansas	$ 296,111,073	$ 342,969,236	16%	$ 370,240,043	8%
Connecticut	$ 287,295,735	$ 339,142,009	18%	$ 369,966,645	9%
Iowa	$ 305,590,676	$ 345,413,490	13%	$ 366,909,356	6%
West Virginia	$ 258,381,746	$ 289,547,843	12%	$ 302,276,215	4%
Utah	$ 247,609,306	$ 284,199,152	15%	$ 299,532,782	5%

FEDERAL FUNDING BY STATE – RANKED HIGHEST TO LOWEST (Continued)

	2000 Appropriation	2 001 Appropriation	% Change	2002 Request	% Change
Nebraska	$ 190,806,074	$ 223,688,114	17%	$ 241,265,187	8%
Alaska	$ 179,181,580	$ 211,979,043	18%	$ 236,915,654	12%
Other	$ 146,653,680	$ 449,370,242	206%	$ 228,402,382	-49%
Indian Tribe Set Aside	$ 172,001,598	$ 191,254,517	11%	$ 208,467,235	9%
Montana	$ 158,336,540	$ 181,644,605	15%	$ 197,950,097	9%
Idaho	$ 149,011,363	$ 174,524,583	17%	$ 185,865,446	6%
Maine	$ 155,133,835	$ 175,515,772	13%	$ 185,683,351	6%
South Dakota	$ 133,066,735	$ 160,276,461	20%	$ 175,113,124	9%
Nevada	$ 126,529,727	$ 156,161,479	23%	$ 169,548,136	9%
Hawaii	$ 132,043,273	$ 160,612,806	22%	$ 169,225,387	5%
Rhode Island	$ 133,718,578	$ 155,217,934	16%	$ 164,914,431	6%
North Dakota	$ 117,910,518	$ 141,550,335	20%	$ 155,164,581	10%
New Hampshire	$ 114,294,562	$ 133,778,902	17%	$ 140,532,317	5%
District of Columbia	$ 114,640,586	$ 129,848,476	13%	$ 138,611,292	7%
Vermont	$ 92,591,401	$ 106,487,801	15%	$ 112,422,923	6%
Wyoming	$ 86,826,320	$ 102,133,079	18%	$ 109,460,345	7%
Delaware	$ 85,735,787	$ 100,253,120	17%	$ 105,288,936	5%
Guam	$ 31,483,237	$ 33,673,576	7%	$ 36,845,664	9%
Virgin Islands	$ 30,548,863	$ 33,453,148	10%	$ 36,448,580	9%
American Samoa	$ 17,474,966	$ 19,199,697	10%	$ 20,773,228	8%
Northern Mariana Islands	$ 11,608,389	$ 12,419,826	7%	$ 13,183,865	6%
Micronesia	$ 4,887,692	$ 5,094,089	4%	$ 5,271,799	3%
Marshall Islands	$ 1,874,080	$ 2,018,508	8%	$ 2,096,218	4%
Palau	$ 1,388,270	$ 1,479,590	7%	$ 1,557,300	5%
Total	$ 32,580,259,000	$ 38,028,356,000	17%	$ 40,585,743,000	6%

Source: Department of Education

FEDERAL PROGRAM FUNDING

	2000 Appropriation	2001 Appropriation	% Change	2002 Request	% Change
ESEA Title I--Grants to Local Educational Agencies	7,941,397,000	8,601,721,000	8%	9,060,721,000	5%
ESEA Title I--Capital Expenses for Private School Children	12,000,000	6,000,000	-50%	0	-100%
ESEA Title I--Even Start	150,000,000	250,000,000	67%	250,000,000	0%
ESEA Title I--Reading First State Grants (proposed legislation)	0	0		900,000,000	
ESEA Title I--Migrant	354,689,000	380,000,000	7%	380,000,000	0%
ESEA Title I--Neglected and Delinquent	42,000,000	46,000,000	10%	46,000,000	0%
ESEA Title I--Demonstrations of Comprehensive School Reform	170,000,000	210,000,000	24%	260,000,000	24%
Subtotal, Education for the Disadvantaged	8,670,086,000	9,493,721,000	9%	10,896,721,000	15%
Impact Aid--Basic Support Payments	737,200,000	882,000,000	20%	882,000,000	0%
Impact Aid--Payments for Children with Disabilities	50,000,000	50,000,000	0%	50,000,000	0%
Impact Aid--Construction	10,052,000	12,802,000	27%	150,000,000	1072%
Subtotal, Impact Aid	797,252,000	944,802,000	19%	1,082,000,000	15%
State Grants for Improving Teacher Quality (proposed legislation)	0	0		2,600,000,000	
Class Size Reduction	1,300,000,000	1,623,000,000	25%	0	-100%
Eisenhower Professional Development State Grants	335,000,000	485,000,000	45%	0	-100%
School Renovation Grants	0	1,200,000,000		0	-100%
Safe and Drug-Free Schools--State Grants	439,250,000	644,250,000	47%	644,250,000	0%
Educational Technology State Grants (proposed legislation)	0	0		817,096,000	
Technology Literacy Challenge Fund	425,000,000	450,000,000	6%	0	-100%
Choice and Innovation State Grants (proposed legislation)	0	0		471,500,000	
Innovative Education Program Strategies State Grants	365,750,000	385,000,000	5%	0	-100%
Fund for the Improvement of Education--Demonstrations of Comprehensive School Reform	50,000,000	50,000,000	0%	0	-100%
Education for Homeless Children and Youth	28,800,000	35,000,000	22%	35,000,000	0%
Indian Education--Grants to Local Educational Agencies	62,000,000	92,765,000	50%	92,765,000	0%
Goals 2000--State and Local Education Systemic Improvement	458,000,000	0	-100%	0	
Immigrant Education	150,000,000	150,000,000	0%	0	-100%
Special Education--Grants to States	4,989,685,000	6,339,685,000	27%	7,339,685,000	16%
Special Education--Preschool Grants	390,000,000	390,000,000	0%	390,000,000	0%
Special Education--Grants for Infants and Families	375,000,000	383,567,000	2%	383,567,000	0%
Subtotal, Special Education	5,754,685,000	7,113,252,000	24%	8,113,252,000	14%
Vocational Rehabilitation State Grants	2,338,977,000	2,399,790,000	3%	2,481,383,000	3%
Client Assistance State Grants	10,928,000	11,647,000	7%	11,647,000	0%
Protection and Advocacy of Individual Rights	11,894,000	14,000,000	18%	14,000,000	0%
Supported Employment State Grants	38,152,000	38,152,000	0%	38,152,000	0%
Independent Living State Grants	22,296,000	22,296,000	0%	22,296,000	0%
Services for Older Blind Individuals	15,000,000	20,000,000	33%	20,000,000	0%
Protection and Advocacy for Assistive Technology	2,680,000	2,680,000	0%	2,680,000	0%
Subtotal, Rehabilitation Services and Disability Research	2,439,927,000	2,508,565,000	3%	2,590,158,000	3%
Vocational Education State Grants	1,055,650,000	1,100,000,000	4%	1,100,000,000	0%
Vocational Education--Tech-Prep Education	106,000,000	106,000,000	0%	106,000,000	0%
Adult Education State Grants	424,500,000	470,000,000	11%	470,000,000	0%
English Literacy and Civics Education State Grants	25,500,000	70,000,000	175%	70,000,000	0%
State Grants for Incarcerated Youth Offenders	14,000,000	17,000,000	21%	17,000,000	0%
Subtotal, Vocational and Adult Education	1,625,650,000	1,763,000,000	8%	1,763,000,000	0%

FEDERAL PROGRAM FUNDING *(Continued)*

	2000 Appropriation	2001 Appropriation	% Change	2002 Request	% Change
Federal Pell Grants	7,944,000,000	9,192,000,000	16%	9,582,000,000	4%
Federal Supplemental Educational Opportunity Grants	621,000,000	691,000,000	11%	691,000,000	0%
Federal Work-Study	934,000,000	1,011,000,000	8%	1,011,000,000	0%
Federal Perkins Loans--Capital Contributions	100,000,000	100,000,000	0%	100,000,000	0%
Leveraging Educational Assistance Partnership	40,000,000	55,000,000	38%	55,000,000	0%
Byrd Honors Scholarships	39,859,000	41,001,000	3%	41,001,000	0%
Total	**32,580,259,000**	**38,028,356,000**	**17%**	**40,585,743,000**	**7%**

1. *Preliminary estimate pending completion of action reauthorizing the Elementary and Secondary Education Act.*

2. *This program is proposed, along with selected categorical programs, for consolidation into a new State grant program in the reauthorization of the Elementary and Secondary Education Act. It is expected that the proposed new program will allow flexible funding at the State and local levels, including funding for activities similar to those currently supported.*

3. *Of the amount for School Renovation Grants in fiscal year 2001, a portion may be used for Part B of the Individuals with Disabilities Education Act and/or for technology activities related to school renovation.*

4. *Funds are provided under the ESEA Title I Demonstrations of Comprehensive School Reform.*

5. *This program is proposed for consolidation under Bilingual and Immigrant Education State Grants. State allocations will be determined after completion of action reauthorizing the Elementary and Secondary Education Act.*

Source: Department of Education

Index

A

B

C

D

E

K-12 Industry Resources

Consultants

Irene A. Barnett
14785 Cool Valley Ranch Road
Valley Center, CA 92082
(760) 751-1233
FAX (760) 751-8846
barnetti@connectnet.com

Bigham Technology Solutions
8045-B Antoine #101
Houston, TX 77088
Contact: Vicki Smith Bigham
bighamv@aol.com
Contact: George Bigham
bighamg@aol.com

CCA Consulting
www.cca-consults.com
888 Worcester St
Wellesley, MA 02181
(781) 237-8950
FAX (781) 237-8930
Contact: Carole Cotton
carole@cca-consults.com

Odvard Egil Dyrli
40 Barstow Lane
Tolland, CT 06084
(860) 872-4876
Dyrli@uconn.edu

Education Market Research
www.ed-market.com
PO Box 940418
Rockaway Park, NY 11694
(718) 474-0133
FAX (718) 474-0133
Contact: Bob Resnick
bob_resnick@ed-market.com

Education TURNKEY Systems, Inc.
www.edturnkey.com
256 N Washington St
Falls Church, VA 22046
(703) 536-2310
FAX (703) 536-3225
Contact: Charles Blaschke
cblaschke@edturnkey.com

Educational Technology Marketing
45 Carmel St
San Francisco, CA 94117
(415) 566-8265
(415) 566-9358
Contact: Diane Rapley
dianerapley@compuserve.com

EduExecutives
www.eduexecutives.com
4105 E. Broadway, Suite 203
Long Beach, CA 90803
(562) 438-3868
FAX (562) 438-3857
Contact: Karen Fasimpaur
karen@eduexecutives.com

Eduventures.com
www.eduventures.com
20 Park Plaza, Ste 833
Boston, MA 02116
(617) 426-5622
Contact: Chris Curran

ELHI Publishers Services
301 S. Perimeter Park Drive, Suite 116
Nashville, TN 37211
(615) 369-3544
FAX (615) 369-3550

Focus Marketing
www.sellingtoschools.com/focusmarketing/
P.O. Box 4421
Alpharetta, GA 30023
(828) 681-0203
FAX (828) 684-3197
Contact: Glen McCandless
focusmarketing@sellingtoschools.com

Gill Fishman Associates
www.gillfishmandesign.com
955 Massachusetts Avenue
Cambridge, MA 02139
(617) 492-5666
FAX (617) 547-2501
Contact: Gill Fishman
gfa@gillfishmandesign.com

Grunwald Associates
www.grunwald.com
1793 Escalante Way
Burlingame, CA 94010
(650) 692-3100
FAX 419-730-7431
Contact: Peter Grunwald
peter@grunwald.com

Guerrilla Marketing Design
www.gmarketingdesign.com
PO Box 697
Dover, NH 03820
(603) 742-9673
FAX (603) 742-1944
Contact: Roger C. Parker
roger@gmarketingdesign.com

Lanier Walkington
www.lanierwalkington.com
170 San Pablo Ave
San Francisco, CA 94127
FAX (619) 260-0975
Contact: Pat Walkington
(415) 564-2364
pat_walkington@phc.net
Contact: Peggy Lanier
(619) 260-0974
planier@home.com

Lois Eskin Associates
Two Horizon Rd
Fort Lee, NJ 07024
(201) 224-8131
FAX (201) 224-8131
Contact: Lois Eskin
loiseskin@aol.com

Kate Kauff
612 Milwaukee St
Denver, CO 80206
kkhome@mindspring.com

Marketing A La Carte
104 Dundee Drive
Cheshire, CT 06410
(203) 272-9061
FAX (203) 272-9059
Contact: Lynn Scott
marketing.alacarte@att.net

Marketing Projects, Inc.
www.bigdealbook.com
3800 N Wilke Rd, Ste 3000
Arlington Heights, IL 60004
(800) 650-0034
Contact: Marilyn Schutz
maschutz@bigdealbook.com

MarketingWorks, Inc.
www.marketingworksinc.com
33 South Delaware Ave.
Yardley, PA 19067
(888) MWORKS4
FAX (215) 321-4249
Contact: Gerry Bogatz
gbogatz@mktgworks.com

McCaffrey Communications
PO Box 1608
Ft. Collins, CO 80522
(970) 493-2716
FAX (970) 224-1824
Contact: Maureen McCaffrey
publisher@homeschoolingtoday.com

Dominic Miccolis
10699 East Willow Road
Stockton, IL 61085
(815) 947-3541
FAX (815) 947-3641
dmico@aol.com

The Peak Group, LLC
www.peakgroup.net
101 First Ave
Los Altos, CA 94022
(650) 917-8467
FAX (650) 917-8461
Contact: Lillian Kellogg
(650) 917-8467
lilk@peakgroup.net
Contact: John Politoski
(408) 927-5879
johnp@peakgroup.net

Murrell Pedicord
2118 Stonefield
Santa Rosa, CA 95403
(707) 545-2445
FAX (707) 545-2445
mpeddi2118@aol.com

Professional Publishing Services
4 Ivanhoe Lane
Westport, CT 06880
(203) 227-7266
FAX (203) 226-9971
Contact: Tom Murphy
pps2000@optonline.net

Marilyn Rosenblum
150 Croton Lake Rd
Katonah, NY 10536
(914) 232-6291
FAX (914) 232-6936
maralynr@aol.com

Ruppelt Consulting
14445 Phelps Road NE
Bainbridge Island, WA 98110
(206) 855-1427
FAX (206) 855-1431
Contact: Tina Ruppelt
tinarup@aol.com

Sales Champions
www.saleschamps.com
PO Box 742
Saluda, NC 28773
(828) 749-2449
Contact: Cathy Jackson
cathy@saleschamps.com

Scanlon & Associates
23211 West Sageview Ct, Ste A
Valencia, CA 91354
(805) 297-5898
(805) 297-5869
mcscanlon@aol.com

School Market Sales Management
82 Calvert Ave West
Edison, NJ 08820
(732) 549-3832
Contact: Art Stupar

Rondi Shouse Consulting
5659 Keith Road
West Vancouver, British Columbia,
Canada V7W 2N4
(604) 921-9610
FAX (604) 921-9694
Contact: Rondi Shouse
rondi@istar.ca

Techera, Inc.
www.techera.com
127 McCosh Circle
Princeton, NJ 08540
(609) 924-5133
Contact: Al McIlroy
al@techera.com

Linda Unger Associates
38 Old Coach Rd, Ste 7
East Setauket, NY 11733
(631) 751-8174
Contact: Linda Unger
lcunger@earthlink.net

Ann Watson Consulting
75 Millstone Road
Deerfield, IL 60015
(847) 940-8420
FAX: 847-940-8726
Contact: Ann Watson
annwatson@home.com

Wayside Software
www.waysidesoftware.com
102 Rainbow Drive #52
Livingston, TX 77399-1002
(678) 797-0964
Contact: Lin Marten
lin@waysidesoftware.com

Bonnie Williams
273 Carrollwood Dr
Tarrytown, NY 10591
(914) 631-2635
bonbonw@earthlink.net

Winter Group
www.wintergroup.net
1807 South Pearl Street
Denver, CO 80210
(303) 778-0866
FAX (303) 744-9865
Contact: Linda Winter
winterl@wintergroup.net

Xcellent Marketing, LTD
www.xcellentmarketing.com
1163 Vine Street
Denver, CO 80206
(303) 388-5215
FAX (303) 388-0477
Contact: Carol Ann Waugh
cwaugh@xcellentmarketing.com

Developers, Packagers & Brokers of Educational Products

Bigham Technology Solutions
8045-B Antoine #101
Houston, TX 77088
Contact: Vicki Smith Bigham
bighamv@aol.com

Creative Media Applications
www.cmacontent.com
1720 Post Road East, Ste 214
Westport, CT 06880
(203) 256-4979
FAX (203) 256-4983
Contact: Barbara Stewart
bstewart@cmacontent.com

Design 5 Creative
www.d5c.com
180 Varick St, 15th Fl
New York, NY 10014
(212) 747-8899
Contact: M.E. Morganteen

Entrex Software
www.entrex.com
405-3939 Quadra St.
Victoria, BC, Canada V8X 1J8
Contact: Leanne Wedster
lwebster@entrex.org

Hartman Educational Technology, Inc.
www.hartmanedtech.com
724 Ponderosa Ct.
Louisville, CO 80027
(303) 665-2876
FAX 303-665-3915
Contact: Gail Hartman
hartman@earthlink.net

Interactive Educational Systems Design, Inc. (IESD)
33 West 87th Street, Suite 2A
New York, NY 10024
(212) 769-1715
FAX (212) 769-0212
Contact: Ellen Bialo
iesdinc@aol.com

Kleibacker & Associates
www.internet-monitor.com/kleibacker.html
16 Wycoff St
Brooklyn, NY 11201
(718) 858-3459
FAX (718) 858-6022
Contact: Kathryn Kleibacker
kkabiz@mindspring.com

Mazer Corporation - Interactive Media Services
529 Main Street, Suite 212
Boston, MA 02129
(937) 264-2600
Contact: Scott Hamilton
Scott_Hamilton@mazer.com

Pinnacle Education Associates
www.pinnacleeduation.com
1705 West Northwest Hwy, Ste 150
Grapevine, TX 76051
(817) 424-0907
Contact: Joanne Rodriguez

Professional Publishing Services
4 Ivanhoe Lane
Westport, CT 06880
(203) 227-7266
FAX (203) 226-9971
Contact: Tom Murphy
pps2000@optonline.net

Publishers Resource Group, Inc.
www.prgaustin.com
307 Camp Craft Rd
Austin, TX 78746
(512) 328-7007
Contact: Aileen Krassner
akrassner@prgaustin.com

Victory Productions, Inc.
www.victoryprd.com
55 Linden St.
Worcestor, MA 01609
(508) 755-0051
FAX (508) 755-0025

Visual Education Corporation
www.visedcorp.com
14 Washington St
Princeton, NJ 08543
(609) 799-9200
FAX (609) 799-1591
rlidz@visedcorp.com
Contact: Dick Lidz

Product Packaging & Manufacturing

Color Film Corporation
www.colorfilm.com
770 Connecticut Avenue
Norwalk, CT 06854
(800) 882-1120
FAX (203) 854-3526
Contact: Nelson Winget (Ext 503)
nelson@colorfilm.com

Mazer Corporation - Creative Services
www.mazer.com
6680 Poe Ave
Dayton, OH 45414
(937) 264-2600
Contact: Bill Pflaum
bill_pflaum@mazer.com

Educational Mailing Lists & Brokers

Fairfield Marketing Group Inc.
830 Sport Hill Rd.
Easton, CT 06612-1250
(203) 261-5585
FAX (203) 261-0884

Mailings Clearing House
www.mailings.com
601 E Marshall St
Sweet Springs, MO 65351
(800) 776-6373
Contact: John Hood

Market Data Retrieval
www.schooldata.com
1 Forest Parkway
Shelton, CT 06484
(203) 926-4800
FAX (203) 926-0784
Contact: Sharon Sanford
ssanford@dnb.com

MSGi Direct
www.msgidirect.com
187 Ballardvale St, Ste B110
Wilmington, MA 01887
(800) 677-7959
Contact: Thomas Smith

Quality Education Data
www.qeddata.com
1625 Broadway, Ste. 250
Denver, CO 80202
(303) 209-9400
Contact: Jeanne Hayes (Ext 111)
jhayes@qeddata.com

Peter Li Education Group
www.peterli.com
2621 Dryden Road
Dayton, OH 45439
(800) 523-4625
FAX (937) 293-1310
Contact: Rosemary Walker

School Market Research Institute
www.school-market.com
PO Box 10
Haddam, CT 06438
(800) 838-3444
FAX (860) 345-3985
Contact: Bob Stimolo (Ext 125)
school.market@snet.net

Wilson Marketing Group, Inc.
1194 W. Washington Blvd.
Los Angeles, CA 90066
(800) 445-2089
Contact: Mike Wilson

Wujcik & Associates
810 S. Alfred St., #1
Alexandria, VA 22314
(703) 519-3557
Contact: Anne Wujcik
annewujcik@aol.com

K-12 Card Packs

Art Educators
Mailer: Prentice Hall Direct
(www.phdirect.com)

Early Childhood
Mailer: Prentice Hall Direct
(www.phdirect.com)

Ed Hotline
Mailer: Prentice Hall Direct
(www.phdirect.com)

Educators-At-Home
Mailer: Prentice Hall Direct
(www.phdirect.com)

Elementary Educators
Mailer: Prentice Hall Direct
(www.phdirect.com)

English Teachers
Mailer: Prentice Hall Direct
(www.phdirect.com)

"Extracurricular" Fundraising Pack
Mailer: Media Services
(www.mediaservices.org)

High School Science Teachers
Mailer: Media Services
(www.mediaservices.org)

Guidance & Counseling
Mailer: Prentice Hall Direct
(www.phdirect.com)

K-8 "Essentials for Principals"
Mailer: Media Services
(www.mediaservices.org)

K-12 Educators "The Heavy Hitters"
Mailer: Media Services
(www.mediaservices.org)

Librarian's Technology & Software Pack
Mailer: Media Services
(www.mediaservices.org)

Math Teachers
Mailer: Prentice Hall Direct
(www.phdirect.com)

Music Educators
Mailer: Prentice Hall Direct
(www.phdirect.com)

New Teacher's Welcome Pack
Mailer: Media Services
(www.mediaservices.org)

Pre-K-4 New Teachers
Mailer: Media Services
(www.mediaservices.org)

School Administrators
Mailer: Prentice Hall Direct
(www.phdirect.com)

School Librarians
Mailer: Prentice Hall Direct
(www.phdirect.com)

Science Teachers
Mailer: Prentice Hall Direct
(www.phdirect.com)

Secondary Educators
Mailer: Prentice Hall Direct
(www.phdirect.com)

Social Studies Teachers
Mailer: Prentice Hall Direct
(www.phdirect.com)

Special Educators
Mailer: Prentice Hall Direct
(www.phdirect.com)

Sports & Coaching Educators
Mailer: Prentice Hall Direct
(www.phdirect.com)

Resellers & Distributors

Academic Distributing, Inc.
www.academic-wholesale.com
12180 East Turquoise Circle
Dewey, AZ 86327
(800) 531-3277
FAX (800) 441-5015

Cambridge Development Laboratory, Inc.
www.edumatch.com
86 West Street
Waltham, MA 02451-1110
(781) 890-4640
FAX (781) 890-2894

ClassroomDirect.com
www.classroomdirect.com
2025 1st Avenue North
Birmingham, AL 35203
(205) 251-9171
FAX (205) 226-0021

CCV Software
PO Box 6724
Charleston, WV 25362
(800) 843-5576
FAX (304) 346-4292
Contact: Sheila Dubman
sheila@edumatch.com.

**Carolina Biological Supply
Company**
2700 York Rd
Burlington, NC 27215
(800) 334-5551
(800) 222-7112

The Douglas Stewart Company
www.dstewart.com
2402 Advance Road
Madison, WI 53718
(800) 279-2003
FAX (608) 221-5217
Contact: Jack Bahlman
jbahlman@dstewart.com

Edudex.com
www.edudex.com
PO Box 8197
Princeton, NJ 08543-8197
(877) 301-3100
FAX (609) 720-1234

Educational Resources
www.edresources.com
1550 Executive Dr
Elgin, IL 60121-1900
(800) 624-2926
FAX (847) 888-0792
Contact: Brenda Raker
braker@edresources.com

Epylon Corporation
www.epylon.com
645 Harrison Street, Suite 200
San Francisco, CA 94107
(415) 593-2900
FAX (415) 593-2929

Journey Education Marketing
www.journeyed.com
1325 Capital Pkwy, Ste 130
Carrollton, TX 75006
(800) 874-9001
FAX (972-245-0502)
Contact: Alan Fishler

JuneBox.com, Inc.
www.junebox.com
W6316 Design Drive
Greenville, WI 54942
(800) 513-2465
FAX (800) 513-2467

Lakeshore Learning Materials
www.lakeshorelearning.com
2695 E Domingnez St
Carson, CA 90749
(800) 421-5354
FAX (310) 537-5403
Contact: Charles Kaplan

Learning Services
www.learnserv.com
3895 E 19th Sve
Eugene, OR 97403
(541) 744-0883
FAX (541) 744-2056
Contact: Gerald Schrup (x111)
Geralds@ls.learnserv.com

Micro Warehouse
www.warehouse.com
535 connecticut Ave
Norwalk, CT 06854
(203) 899-4276
FAX (203) 899-4576

Partnership America
www.partnershipamerica.com
1600 East St Andrew Place
Santa Ana, CA 92799
(714) 382-1236
FAX (714) 566-7645

Social Studies School Service
www.socialstudies.com
10200 Jefferson Blvd., Box 802,
Culver City, CA 90232
800-421-4246
FAX (800) 944-5432

Software Express
www.swexpress.com
4128-A South Blvd
Charlotte, NC 28209
(800) 527-7638
FAX (704) 529-1010

Software Plus
www.swpnet.com
1880 Baur Blvd
St. Louis, MO 63132
(888) 251-7638
FAX (314) 692-0856

Simplexis
www.simplexis.com
640 Second Street
San Francisco, CA 94107
(415) 354-2100
FAX (415) 354-2099

Technology Integration Group
www.tigsd.com
7810 Trade Street
San Diego, CA 92121
(858) 566-1900
FAX (619) 566-8794

Technology Resource Center
www.gotrc.com
749 S. 8th St./Rt 31
West Dundee, IL 60118
(800) 517-2320
FAX (847) 426-9894
Contact: susan@gotrc.com

Ventura Educational Systems
www.venturaes.com
P.O Box 425
Grover Beach, CA 93433
800-336-1022
FAX 800-493-7380

Way2Bid, Inc.
www.way2bid.com
3343 E. Montclair
Springfield, MO 65804
(417) 879-2100

Creative Agencies

CD Squared
www.cdsquared.com
212 Post Road West
Westport, CT 06880
(203) 227-9900
FAX (203) 227-9920
Contact: Sharon Streger

Duncan Direct Associates
www.duncandirect.com
16 Elm St
Peterborough, NH 03458
(603) 924-3121
FAX (603) 924-8511
Contact: George Duncan
duncandirect@pobox.com

JMH Communications
1133 Broadway, Suite 1123
New York, NY 10010
(212) 924-2944
FAX (212) 924-3052

LanierWalkington
www.lanierwalkington.com
1410 West Thorn Street
San Diego, CA 92103
Contact: Pat Walkington
(415) 564-2364
planier@home.com
Contact: Peggy Lanier
(619) 260-0974
pat_walkington@phc.net

Lownik Communication Services
www.lcs-impact.com
1719 Monroe St, Ste 201
Madison, WI 53711
(800) 710-3600
FAX (608) 256-6179
Contact: Scott Knicklebine
scottk@lcs-impact.com

MarketingWorks, Inc.
www.marketingworksinc.com
33 South Delaware Ave.
Yardley, PA 19067
(888) MWWORKS4
FAX (215) 321-4249
Contact: Gerry Bogatz
gbogatz@mktgworks.com

Reid Resources
245 E. 24th St.
New York, NY 10010
(212) 685-0190
FAX (212) 685-0144
Contact: W. Kathleen Reid
Wkreid@aol.com

School Market Research Institute
www.school-market.com
PO Box 10
Haddam, CT 06438
(800) 838-3444
FAX (860) 345-3985
Contact: Bob Stimolo (Ext 125)
school.market@snet.net

Winter Group
www.wintergroup.net
1807 S Pearl Street
Denver, CO 80210
(303) 778-0866
FAX (303) 744-9865
Contact: Linda Winter
winterl@wintergroup.net

Public Relations Firms

C. Blohm & Associates, Inc.
4031 Oakhaven
San Antonio, TX 78217
(210) 656-2324
FAX (210) 656-2324
Contact: Charlene Blohm
Charlene@satexas.com

Cheshire Corporation
501 S. Cherry St. Ste 320
Denver, CO 80246
(303) 333-3003, ext. 214
(212) 673-1812
FAX (303) 333-4037
Contact: Mary Kay Jezzini
mary.kay@ix.netcom.com

CommunicationWorks, LLC
www.commworksllc.com
1752 N Street NW, 16th Fl
Washington, DC 20036
(202) 955-9450
FAX (202) 955-5770
Contact: Shep Ranbom (Ext 315)
sranbom@commworksllc.com

Eicher Communications
78 North Street
Naples, FL 34108
(941) 593-6674
FAX (941-593-6685
Contact: Leslie Eicher, APR
leicherpr@aol.com

FanFire Studios
2102 Loquat Place
Oceanside, CA 92054
(760) 722-8041
FAX (760) 722-2546
Contact: Terian Tyre
terian@home.com

KEH Communications
www.kehcomm.com
524 Bowline Rd
Severna Park, MD 21146
(410) 975-9638
FAX (410) 975-9638
Contact: Kati Elliott
kati@kehcomm.com

Terian Tyre
2102 Loquat Place
Oceanside, CA 92054-5719
(760) 722-8041
FAX: (760) 722-254

Wambach & Company, Inc.
162 Skyland Blvd.
Tijeras, NM 87059
(505) 281-5324
FAX (505) 281-4340
Contact: Catherine Wambach
cwambach@aol.com

Publishing Attorneys

Law Office of Lloyd L. Rich, P.C.
www.publaw.com
www.publishingattorney.com
1163 Vine St
Denver, CO 80206
(303) 388-0291
FAX (303) 388-0477
Contact: Lloyd L. Rich
rich@publishingattorney.com

Web Site Developers & Hosts

BookZone
www.bookzone.com
PO Box 9642
Scottsdale, AZ 85252
(800) 536-6162
FAX (480) 481-0103
Contact: Mary Westheimer
mary@bookzone.com

Cognetics Corporation
www.cognetics.com
PO Box 386
51 Everett Drive
Princeton Jct. NJ 08550
(609) 799-5005
Fax 609-799-8555
Contact: Katherine Kish
kish@cognetics.com

Cuesta Technologies
www.cuesta.com
1791 Broadway, Ste 203
Redwood, CA 94063
(650) 298-0250
FAX (650) 298-0257
Contact: Laurie Swiryn
laurie@cuesta.com

Doubleclick'd Publications
www.doubleclickd.com
209 E. Joppa Road
Towson, MD 21286
Contact: Bonnie Raindrop
(410) 337-8644
bonnie@doubleclickd.com

Educational Web Adventures
www.edweb.com
1776 Iglehart Ave
St. Paul, MN 55104
(651) 641-7566
Contact: David Schaller

Winter Group
www.wintergroup.net
1807 South Pearl Street
Denver, CO 80210
(303) 778-0866
FAX (303) 744-9865
Contact: Linda Winter
winterl@wintergroup.net

Telephone Marketing & Sales Support Companies

Marketing Dimensions
748-A Greencrest Dr
Westerville, OH 43081
(614) 890-1510
Contact: Cheryl Cira
mktgpdim@aol.com

MarketingWorks, Inc.
www.marketingworksinc.com
33 South Delaware Ave.
Yardley, PA 19067
(888) MWWORKS4
FAX (215) 321-4249
Contact: Gerry Bogatz
gbogatz@mktgworks.com

Media Management Services
www.edumedia.com
105 Terry Dr, Ste 120
Newtown, PA 18940
(215) 579-8590
Contact: Ed Meell

Peter Li Education Group
www.peterli.com
2621 Dryden Road
Dayton, OH 45439
(800) 523-4625
FAX (937) 293-1310
Contact: Rosemary Walker

Recruitment Services

Boston Search Group
www.bsgweb.com
224 Clarendon Street
Boston, MA 02116
(617) 266-4633
Contact: Ralph Protsik

Meeker & Associates
www.johnmeeker.com
7101 York Avenue, Ste 315
Minneapolis, MN 55435
(952) 921-3262
FAX (952) 921-3299
Contact: John Meeker
john@johnmeeker.com

Solomon-Page Group
www.spges.com
1140 Avenue of the Americas
New York, NY 10036
(212) 403-6190
FAX (212) 764-9690
Contact: Jeannette Gautier-Downes
jdownes@spges.com

Education Publishers Associations & Meetings

Association of American Publishers (AAP) - School Division
www.publishers.org

Members of the AAP School Division publish instructional and assessment materials, in a variety of print and electronic formats, for the elementary and secondary grade levels (kindergarten through 12th grade). They have several meetings throughout the year with an annual meeting in January.

The Association of Educational Publishers
http://www.edpress.org

The Association of Educational Publishers (AEP) supports the growth of educational publishing and its positive impact on learning and teaching. It tracks education and industry information and trends, provides professional development, and promotes quality supplemental materials as essential learning resources. Members include print and digital publishers, educational foundations and associations, and the education and trade press, as well as schools and school districts. They have an annual conference in June of each year and several CEO Roundtables.

Consortium for School Networking (CoSN)

www.cosn.org

CoSN is the premier K-12 education association whose mission is to promote how the Internet and telecommunications can improve learning. CoSN represents a unique partnership of leading decisionmakers from K-12 (local and state) education agencies, business, nonprofits and higher education stakeholders. CoSN has a history of providing vendor eutral analysis and advice to schools regarding technology-related issues and hosts an annual conference that examines the implications for Internet use in K-12 classrooms from the school district, state and national perspective.

EdNET – The Educational Technology and Telecommunications Markets Conference

www.hellerreports.com

The EdNET conference, held in September of each year, is sponsored by The Heller Reports and provides vendors of educational technology and telecommunications the latest information on market trends, business partnering opportunities, funding sources, new technologies, and activities of key market players. A business leadership forum, with peer-to-peer interaction, the meeting attracts senior personnel responsible for marketing, sales, business development and strategic initiatives, top management and financial industry executives, with a minority of education professionals responsible for major educational technology programs. Sessions and networking activities over the three days cover a variety of topics focusing on business strategies as well as educational technology and telecommunications initiatives and trends impacting the K-12, higher education, adult/workplace, and home/consumer markets.

Educational Paperback Association

www.edupaperback.org

Founded in 1975, EPA is known as an innovative voice in the paperback book market, representing both U.S. and Canadian distributors and publishers. The Association holds an annual meeting in January that is educational in nature for both distributors and publishers. An important part of the annual meeting are one-on-one sessions designed to get business discussions going between distributors and publishers.

Market Data Retrieval Seminars

www.schooldata.com

Market Data Retrieval sponsors one-day seminars held around the country on the topic of winning techniques for successful school marketing.

National School Supply & Equipment Association (NSSEA)

www.nssea.org

NSSEA is not-for-profit international trade association, founded in 1916, and is comprised of over 1,400 member companies involved in the school market industry. Members include: suppliers of educational items who market to consumers through a network of distributors; distributors of educational items to consumers; and service providers. NSSEA hosts three primary shows: The NSSEA University, which attracts high quality educational dealers, including retailers and distributors of all sizes – the show is not open to the public or to educators; The School Equipment Show, which is attended by school equipment distributors and anyone responsible for equipment/furniture design, selection and purchasing in schools, colleges, and universities; and Ed Expo, the school market's only Back to School tradeshow, attended by manufacturers, dealers and reps of educational products.

Quality Education Data Forum and Seminars

www.qeddata.com

Each spring and fall, Quality Education Data sponsors one day seminars around the country on successful strategies for direct marketing to schools. They also have a multi-day annual "Forum" usually held in June of each year.

Software & Information Industry Association (SIIA) – Education Division

www.siia.net

Software & Information Industry Association's Education Market Division comprises more than 400 member companies whose common business vocational interest is to publish educational software for the pre-school, K-12, home, special education, post-secondary and adult education markets. The Education Division provides a forum for companies who produce and/or market code, and content. They have an annual conference in March and a Fall conference in September as well as other events and seminars throughout the year.

The World Education Market

www.wemex.com

The World Education Market is an annual marketplace, showcasing educational resources for all levels and ages of learners, for use in the classroom, the workplace or the home, and available on a full range of technologies, from satellites to books and from television to the Internet. Participation is international and multi-sectoral with senior executives from school systems, technical institutes, universities and distance learning, governments and international agencies, the vast training and adult continuing education industries, book publishers, television and video producers, distributors, online and multimedia publishers, satellite, telecommunications and cable companies, and the computer software and hardware industries. The focus of the Market is on commercial transactions — buying and selling products, rights, services and systems as well as finding partners, institutional models and expertise that best respond to specific needs.

Worlddidac

www.worlddidac.org

Worlddidac has 315 corporate members in 47 countries. It is an independent international trade association whose members provide educational products, services and solutions for all levels from early years to lifelong learning and training. The mission of this organization is to provide member companies and organizations with access to information about world markets through exhibitions, seminars, in-country missions, market studies, and information intelligence gathering. They have an annual meeting of members in April and they also sponsor several exhibitions throughout the year in a variety of countries.

Educational Reports and Publications

2000 Education Market Report: K-12

Publisher: Software & Information Industry Association (www.siia.net)

Cost: Free to Members

2000 Report on the Effectiveness of Technology in Schools

Publisher: Software & Information Industry Association (www.siia.net)

Cost: Free to Members

Academic Testing: From the No.2 Pencil to Laptops, Marketing Opportunities in the K-12 Arena

Publisher: SIMBA (www.simbanet.com)

Cost: $495

Annual School Construction Report

School Planning & Management, in partnership with School Construction Alert, a service of Dun and Bradstreet's Market Data Retrieval, provides in this report estimates on construction completed in the current academic year, and projects to be completed and initiated in subsequent years.

Publisher: Peter Li Education Group

Cost: Free

"Best" School Software

Publisher: Education Market Research (www.ed-market.com)

Cost: $595

Building the Net: Trends Report 2000: Trends Shaping the Digital Economy

Analyzes six key trends shaping the digital economy including education technology.

Publisher: Software & Information Industry Association (www.siia.net)

Cost: Free

Building a Successful Internet Commerce Model: Components to Consider for Outsourcing

Publisher: Software & Information Industry Association (www.siia.net)

Cost: Free to Members

Children, Families And The Internet

This report presents findings and analysis from a national survey of student/parent Internet use and attitudes. The survey was conducted with the National School Boards Association, with underwriting from Children's Television Workshop and Microsoft. This survey used a large national random sample of families so that data can be projected to the population as a whole. The report offers hundreds of charts and tables as well as a detailed picture of educational uses of the Internet, media trade-offs, usage habits, and e-commerce possibilities in education.

Publisher: Grunwald Associates (www.grunwald.com)

Cost: $3,850

Current And Projected Use And Expenditures On Education Technology In The Special Education Market (2001)

This survey is designed to identify high demand products and features, and services which are likely to be purchased for use in special education programs whose per pupil allocation of Federal funds has increased from $460 in 1995-1996 to over $1400 in 2000-2001; trend information from 1987 to 1997 to 2001 will be presented.

Publisher: Education TURNKEY Systems, Inc. (www.edturnkey.com)

Cost: $3,000.

The Complete K-12 Report: Market Facts & Segment Analyses 2001

This report analyzes the domestic K-12 school market in all its facets – textbooks, supplementary materials, computer hardware, software/CD-ROM, video, the Internet – and in each of its grade levels and major curriculum areas. In addition, specialized "markets within the market", including Early Childhood, Special Education, ESL/Bilingual, and Standardized Testing, are thoroughly examined. Much of the data presented here comes from original studies conducted by EMR, using a school market information gathering network comprised of tens of thousands of educators at all school levels.

Publisher: Education Market Research (www.ed-market.com)

Cost: $995.

Contenders for the Crown: Six e-Libraries and their Business Models

This report examines the rapidly growing e-library industry.

Publisher: Eduventures.com (www.eduventures.com)

Cost: Available only to Clients

The Customer's Perspective: Survey of Buyers and Users of Educational Technology

A comprehensive survey of 50 educators averaging over 15 years of educational technology experience. Collectively they represent approximately 5% of the U.S. K-12 market, over 13,000 faculty, and over 3,000,000 students. The report covers their views on the educational technology market's (K-12 and Post-Secondary) principal trends, strengths and weaknesses, likes and dislikes about interacting with vendors, and what new products they would like to see.

Publisher: Nelson B. Heller & Associates (www.hellerreports.com)

Cost: $499

Early Childhood Market

Publisher: Education Market Research (www.ed-market.com)

Cost: $595.

Education Channel Partners: A Comprehensive Guide to Channel Options for Selling and Marketing Educational Technology

This report analyzes and profiles over 150 value-added resellers, catalogers, online resellers and distributors focusing on US education institutions. The report provides a blueprint for developing your channel strategy and an effective sales partner program. The detailed company profiles include key contact information, target customer profiles, sales and marketing methodologies, staffing, geographic coverage, product and service offerings, key product lines and more.

Publisher: Nelson B. Heller & Associates (www.hellerreports.com) and The Peak Group, LLC (www.peakgroup.net)

Cost: $1,299

Education Technology Promotion Guide

Publisher: Software & Information Industry Association (www.siia.net)

Cost: $30

The Education Week National Survey of Teachers' Use of Digital Content

Publisher: Education Market Research (www.ed-market.com)

Cost: $595

Electronic Media for the School Market: 2000-2001 Review, Trends & Forecast

This report breaks down the key segments of electronic instructional materials: instructional software, online services and the Internet, satellite TV, comprehensive courseware, multiple media packages and videodiscs and videocassettes. Plus, you get specifics on: market size, structure & hardware installed bases; analysis of major trends - like modular curriculum suites; purchasing patterns and projections; and corporate financial performance rankings and forecasts. Includes comprehensive profiles of the leading electronic education publishers and a chapter on computers and networking systems.

Publisher: SIMBA (www.simbanet.com)

Cost: $1,495

E-Mail Marketing Outlook

A look into how today's K-12 teachers are using e-mail and the Internet. Do teachers respond to e-mail solicitation? Do they use the Internet to find educational products and services? What percentage of teachers have e-mail and Internet access—at home? at school? E-Mail Marketing Outlook provides answers to these and many more questions on this hot topic.

Publisher: Market Data Retrieval (www.schooldata.com)

Cost: $129

The Education Quarterly Investment Report

This report tracks investments in the education industry from venture capital and private equity firms. A summary of investment activity in the education industry is published quarterly.

Publisher: Eduventures.com (www.eduventures.com)

Cost: Available only to Clients

Education is the Import the China Really Wants

As China develops a market-driven economy that is increasingly open to global competition, Chinese government officials are fully aware that education is the key to the nation's success in the global economy.

Publisher: Eduventures.com (www.eduventures.com)

Cost: Available only to Clients

Executive Compensation Basics

Publisher: Meeker & Associates (www.johnmeeker.com)

Cost: Free

Internet Usage in Public Schools, 2000 5th Edition

Quality Education Data's research team went straight to classroom teachers to uncover the extent of Internet usage in America's public schools. The results of this 50 question survey are covered in this informative report. Find out about: teacher use of the Internet, student use of the Internet, Internet blocking software, training and more.

Publisher: Quality Education Data (www.qeddata.com)

Cost: $299

K-6 Supplementary Instructional Materials Survey 2001

This comprehensive report, based on feedback from 6000 principals and teachers nationwide, is a benchmark longitudinal study of the K-6 supplementary market. It covers dollar expenditures in 12 categories (A/V, display, manipulatives, maps and globes, on-line services, periodicals, consumables, books, software, reproducibles, reference, teacher resource materials), funding sources, decision-making, product use, desired product attributes, marketing preferences, trends, and more. Data is broken down by grade level and other factors and is compared to information collected over the past ten years.

Publisher: Lois Eskin Associates (201) 224-8131

Cost: $10,600

K-12 Education Internet Marketplace Report

Profiling and analyzing 100 companies focused on the K-12 market, this dynamic report creates a robust view of the quickly changing online education landscape focusing on the evolving spectrum of products and services, strategic partnership opportunities, evolving business and revenue models, and investments, mergers and acquisitions.

Publisher: Nelson B. Heller & Associates (www.hellerreports.com) and The Peak Group, LLC (www.peakgroup.net)

Cost: $799

K-12 One Book

Publisher: eSchool News (www.eschoolnews.com)

Cost: $199

K-12 School Technology Best Practices

Publisher: eSchool News (www.eschoolnews.com)

Cost: $225

K-12 School Technology Funding Directory

Publisher: eSchool News (www.eschoolnews.com)

Cost: $169

K-12 Special Needs Marketing & Sales Guide 1999

Publisher: Education TURNKEY Systems, Inc. (www.edturnkey.com)

Cost: $595

Making Career Changes

Publisher: Meeker & Associates (www.johnmeeker.com)

Cost: Free

National Survey of Reading

Publisher: Education Market Research (www.ed-market.com)

Cost: $695

National Survey of Mathematics, Grades K-8

Publisher: Education Market Research (www.ed-market.com)

Cost: $695.

New Teachers and Technology

This exclusive report contains the latest information on first- and second-year teachers and their use of technology. Gain insight into how prepared new teachers are to integrate technology into the classroom, how teachers are using the Internet, e-mail, and much, much more.

Publisher: Market Data Retrieval (www.schooldata.com)

Cost: $129

2001 NSSEA Retail Store Report

Profiles the operating characteristics of NSSEA retailers.

Publisher: NSSEA (www.nssea.org)

Cost: Free to Members ($149 Nonmembers)

2001 NSSEA Retail Customer Study

Contains information on the shopping habits of teachers and parents including factors that influence the decision to purchase education products.

Publisher: NSSEA (www.nssea.org)

Cost: Free to Members ($149 Nonmembers)

Print Publishing For The School Market: 1999-2000 Review, Trends & Forecast (5th Edition)

A report on K-12 print publishing that examines the market opportunities for textbooks, supplementary materials and standardized tests. It includs a detailed evaluation of the size and structure of the market and operating characteristics such as revenues and profitability of leading publishers. Provides a perspective on industry productivity; analyzes changing demographics, enrollment, funding and curricula; and provides revenue and growth forecasts through 2001.

Publisher: SIMBA (www.simbanet.com)

Cost: $1,995

Professional Development & Standards-based Education—From the Educator's Perspective

Based on the finding from a nationwide market research study, this objective report examines the attitudes and opinions of K-12 teachers and principals regarding teaching to standards, teacher accountability, and professional development experiences.

Publisher: Market Data Retrieval (www.schooldata.com)

Cost: $129

Research Report on the Effectiveness of Technology in Schools

Publisher: Software & Information Industry Association (www.siia.net)

Cost: Free to Members

Science Market, Grades 4-12

Publisher: Education Market Research (www.ed-market.com)

Cost: $695.

A Second Decade of Technology in K-12 Schools: 1990-2000

Publisher: Software & Information Industry Association (www.siia.net)

Cost: Free to Members ($300 Nonmembers)

Social Studies Market, Grades 3-12

Publisher: Education Market Research (www.ed-market.com)

Cost: $595

Survey of Technology Use in Early Childhood Education Programs 1998

Publisher: Education TURNKEY Systems, Inc. (www.edturnkey.com)

Cost: $995

Survey of Technology Use in Special Education 2001

Publisher: Education TURNKEY Systems, Inc. (www.edturnkey.com)

Cost: $3,000

The State of Technology in Catholic Schools 2000

This special report describes the state of technology in today's Catholic schools, based on data collected by Quality Education Data (QED) through October 1999, in cooperation with the National Catholic Educational Association (NCEA) and Today's Catholic Teacher magazine

Publisher: Peter Li Education Group

Price: Free

State Technology Initiatives Report

Publisher: Software & Information Industry Association (www.siia.net)

Cost: Free to Members ($300 Nonmembers)

Technology Buying Trends: 2000-01 School Year

Publisher: Education Market Research (www.ed-market.com)

Cost: $595

Technology in Education 2001

This annual report reveals the findings of its annual survey of all 87,700 public schools in the United States. Providing an in-depth analysis of significant technology topics, this all-inclusive study offers insight into the current state of technology in schools.

Publisher: Market Data Retrieval (www.schooldata.com)

Cost: $195

Technology Purchasing Forecast, 2000-2001 6th Edition

This annual report contains detailed information to help companies develop plans and projections for the school year ahead. Exclusive information includes: per pupil expenditure comparisons, purchasing plans, technology budgets, and more.

Publisher: Quality Education Data (www.qeddata.com)

Cost: $299

Title I Funding: District Allocations, 2000-2001 3rd Edition

This annual report contains a listing of every U.S. public school's Title I funding for the 1999-2000 school year. It also includes key demographics and enrollment data for all districts, along with their percentages of college bound students.

Publisher: Quality Education Data (www.qeddata.com)

Cost: $199

Title I Survey Report & Marketing Guide

Publisher: Education TURNKEY Systems, Inc. (www.edturnkey.com)

Cost: $995

Top 25 Internet Sites

Publisher: Education Market Research
(www.ed-market.com)

Cost: $595

The Top Twenty States Report: A Guide to Sales and Marketing Educational Technology in the K-12 Market

Co-published with Quality Education Data (QED), this report focuses on providing detailed insight into Federal and State programs that fund educational technology purchases and the important state educational agencies and associations that help manage those funds. The report covers California, Florida, Illinois, New York, Texas and 15 additional top states.

Publisher: Quality Education Data (www.qeddata.com) and The Peak Group, LLC (www.peakgroup.net)

Cost: Pricing range from $499 per state to $4999 for the 20-state bundle.

Education Industry Newsletters

The Complete K-12 Newsletter

This monthly newsletter covers state/district adoptions, government funding, technology initiatives, educator conferences, and company news. Information includes monthly summaries of original market research, Market Data Retrieval Market, Technology Buying Trends, Federal/State Funding Alert and in-depth interviews with opinion leaders and news makers.

Publisher: Open Book Publishing and Education Market Research (www.ed-market.com)

Cost: $595

DataPoints

This quarterly newsletter provides education marketers with timely articles on significant school trends and helpful tips to maximize school marketing programs.

Publisher: Market Data Retrieval (www.schooldata.com)

Cost: Free

The Education Economy

This is a weekly email newsletter read by leading education company executives, investors, academics, policy experts, and education leaders around the globe.

Publisher: Eduventures.com (www.eduventures.com)

Cost: Free

Educational Marketer

Covers upcoming adoptions, mergers and acquisitions, and tested success strategies for K-12 and college markets. Ranks of K-12, college and supplemental publishers by revenues; changes in demographics, enrollment and funding; industry leaders and smaller publishers; what's behind the latest textbook and software publisher alliances, and strategies for non-adoption states.

Publisher: SIMBA (www.simbanet.com)

Cost: $499

Electronic Education Report

Covers opportunities and risks in the growing, multi-billion dollar market for electronic instructional materials. Includes information about the electronic education business with complete revenue, company rankings by revenues, sales and distribution trends; funding and adoptions; enrollment and demographics; trademark and copyright issues; strategic alliances and mergers; legislation; site licensing; and networks; news and analysis from a business perspective about software, multimedia/CD-ROM, videodisc, distance learning, Internet/online services, and educational videocassettes. Coverage includes all major markets – K-12, higher education and consumer.

Publisher: SIMBA (www.simbanet.com)

Cost: $479

Harvard Education Letter

The Harvard Education Letter bridges the worlds of K-12 education research and practice, cutting through the academic blather to help real-world educators stay informed on the most urgent issues facing American schools today.

Publisher: Harvard Education Letter (www.edletter.org)

Cost: $34

The Heller Report: Desktop EdNET Pro

Offers an integrated business information and communication resource. Subscribers receive weekly News Alerts delivered via e-mail and have immediate Web access to the stories behind the headlines. Subscribers also have access to a keyword-searchable database of The Heller Reports archive of industry press releases and news, links to ed tech market news and information sites, and market research.

Publisher: Nelson B. Heller & Associates (www.hellerreports.com)

Cost: $99

The Heller Report: EdNET Week Headlines

This free, weekly e-mail publication brings top educational technology headlines and pertinent information directly to the desktops of industry executives and influencers. Issues are divided into departments with a feature story of the week followed by headlines from top stories in major education market segments. Additional headlines highlight financial and merger information, new product announcements and job market opportunities.

Publisher: Nelson B. Heller & Associates (www.hellerreports.com)

Cost: Free

The Heller Report: Educational Technology Markets

Covers the latest developments in instructional computing, multimedia courseware, CD-ROM, videodisc, video compression, distance learning, fiber optics, networking technologies and more.

Publisher: Nelson B. Heller & Associates (www.hellerreports.com)

Cost: $395

The Heller Report: Internet Strategies for Education Markets

Written for executives developing and marketing Internet-related products and services to schools and the educators exploiting these exciting technologies. Guided by an Advisory Board of distinguished industry leaders, Internet Strategies focuses on actionable information for decision-makers.

Publisher: Nelson B. Heller & Associates (www.hellerreports.com)

Cost: $397

i-Tips Newsletter

A bi-monthly emailed newsletter containing marketing and sales tips for marketing executives selling products and services to schools and libraries.

Publisher: Internet Monitor (www.internet-monitor.com)

Cost: Free

School Marketing Newsletter

This newsletter is the single, easy-to-use, convenient resource that is exclusively devoted to all aspects of marketing to educators. Each month all 12 pages are filled with specific and proven ways to increase sales and deliver improved profits.

Publisher: School Market Research Institute (www.school-market.com)

Cost: $119

School Technology Market Alert

Covers where schools and colleges are spending money on hardware and systems and the steps manufacturers and system installers are taking to win those funds; marketing and sales strategies being used to secure market share; inside look at contracts and market share estimates for leading manufacturers; geographic round-ups of initiatives to equip and wire schools; profiles of leading suppliers and their largest customers; breakdowns of how funds are being allocated for specific products; analysis of important mergers, acquisitions and strategic alliances; and evaluations of district contracts and sales.

Publisher: SIMBA (www.simbanet.com)

Cost: $499

Six Months Six Years

This newsletter, published 5 times a year, covers the pre-school, early childhood, and kindergarten markets.

Publisher: Ross Sackett
(501) 253-8686

Cost: $57.50

Subtext

A bi-weekly newsletter providing comprehensive coverage of trade, educational and professional book publishing and selling, both domestic and international. Each issue offers 8 to 10 pages of comprehensive, timely information and analysis on the global book business.

Publisher: Open Book Publishing (www.subtext.net)

Cost: $398

Technology Monitoring and Information Service (TechMIS)

Published ten times annually, this report addresses Federal policy and funding, state technology initiatives, and identifies targets of opportunities for technology vendors and how to position products.

Publisher: Education TURNKEY Electronic Distribution (www.edturnkey.com)

Cost: Ranges from $2,000-$5,000 including 6-30 hours prepaid consultation depending upon sales/revenue

Publishing Courses

Arizona State University Scholarly Publishing Course

www.asu.edu/clas/history/courses/ScholarlyPublishingCourses.html

Banff Publishing Workshop

www.inforamp.net/%7Ewilber/

Annual two week course held in Banff, Alberta, Canada. Courses in design, book editing, books, magazines and electronic publishing for people just starting out in the industry.

Columbia Publishing Course

www.jrn.columbia.edu/courses/publishing/index.asp

The Publishing Course was originally founded in 1947 at Radcliffe College in Cambridge where it thrived as the Radcliffe Publishing Course. In 2000, the course moved to the Columbia University Graduate School of Journalism. Provids an intensive introduction to all aspects of book and magazine publishing, from evaluations of original manuscripts to sales and marketing of finished products. Students learn from writers, editors, and publishers, design directors and illustrators, advertising experts and publicists-all are leaders in the industry and many are course graduates.

Emerson College

www.emerson.edu

Writing, Literature and Publishing Department.

Undergraduate and graduate publishing courses which encompass book, magazine, and electronic forms.

New York University

www.scps.nyu.edu/pubcenter/

School of Continuing Education

Offers a full complement of courses, workshops, seminars and degrees in book and magazine publishing.

Pace University

www.pace.edu/dyson/graduate/publishi.htm

The Pace University Master of Science in Publishing degree is designed to give you comprehensive, hands-on training in all areas of publishing, including marketing strategies, book and magazine production, financial applications and information systems.

The Publishing Institute at the University of Denver

www.odin.cair.du.edu:80/pi/

Full-time, four-week course that may be taken graduate credit. Covers many aspects of book publishing with a special career session on magazine publishing.

Stanford University

www.publishingcourses.stanford.edu/

Offers experienced publishing professionals an intensive nine-day program on book and magazine publishing presented by over 40 luminaries in publishing and new media.

Books on Marketing to Schools

i-Tips 2000: The Insiders's Guide to School and Library Marketing

by Kathryn Kleibacker, Linda Winter, and Carol Ann Waugh

Publisher: Internet Monitor (www.internet-monitor.com)

Cost: $49.95

Marketing To Schools: A Textbook for the Education Market

by Bob and Lynn Stimolo

Publisher: School Market Research Institute (www.school-market.com)

Cost: $39.95

Educational Product & Company Awards

Apex – Awards for Publication Excellence
Communications Concepts, Inc.
www.apexawards.com

Bologna New Media Prize
Bologna Children's Book Fair and Children's Software Revue
www.bolognanewmediaprize.com

Caldecott Award
American Library Association
www.ala.org/alsc/caldecott.html

Clarion Awards
The Association for Women in Communications
www.womcom.org

Codie Awards
Software and Information Industry Association
www.siia.net/

Distinguished Achievement Awards for Publications
The Association of Educational Publishers
www.edpress.org

Distinguished Achievement Awards for Educational Technology
The Association of Educational Publishers
www.edpress.org

Distinguished Achievement Awards for Instructional Materials
The Association of Educational Publishers
www.edpress.org

Distinguished Marketer Awards Program
The Association of Educational Publishers
www.edpress.org

Districts' Choice Top 100 Products
Curriculum Administrator Magazine
www.ca-magazine.com

Dr. Toy's Awards Program
The Institute for Childhood Resources
www.drtoy.com

EdNET Industry Awards
Nelson B. Heller & Associates, Inc.
www.hellerreports.com

EXCEL Awards
Society of National Association Publications
www.snaponline.com

Golden Lamp Award
The Association of Educational Publishers
www.edpress.org

International ARC Awards
MerComm, Inc.
www.mercommawards.com

Kids First! Endorsement
The Coalition for Quality Children's Media
www.cqcm.org

Media & Methods Awards Portfolio
Media & Methods Magazine
www.media-methods.com

National Magazine Awards
American Society of Magazine Editors
www.asme.magazine.org

The NEMN Apple Awards
National Educational Media Network
www.nemn.org

The New York Festivals
www.nyfests.com

New York International Children's Film Festival
www.gkids.com

Newbery Award
American Library Association
www.ala.org/alsc/newbery.html

NSSEA Ed Tech Awards
National School Supply & Equipment Association (NSSEA)
www.nssea.org

Oppenheim Toy Portfolio
www.toyportfolio.com

Parents' Choice Awards
Parents' Choice Foundation
www.parents-choice.org

Peabody Awards
Henry W. Grady College of Journalism and Mass Communication, University of Georgia
www.peabody.uga.edu

The Teacher's Choice Awards
Learning Magazine
www.theeducationcenter.com

Silver Inkwell Awards Competition
IABC/Washington
www.iabcdc.org

The Webby Awards
The International Academy of Digital Arts and Sciences
www.webbyawards.com

Educational Media Contacts
(In addition to the Educational Associations and Magazines listed in another section)

48 Hours
524 W 57th St
New York, NY 10019
(212) 975-6511
Story Editor: Kathleen O'Connell

ABC News
1717 DeSales St NW
Washington, DC 20036
(202) 222-7300
Education Correspondent: Michele Norris

ABC "Good Morning America"
147 Columbus Ave
New York, NY 10012
(212) 456-6157
Senior Segment Producer: Patty Neger

AFT Catalyst
332 S. Michigan Ave., Suite 500
Chicago, IL 60604-4306
(312) 427-4830

American Teacher
555 New Jersey Ave., NW
Washington, DC 20001
(202) 879-4430
Managing Editor: Roger Glass

Associated Press
50 Rockefeller Pl, 5th Fl
New York, NY 10020
National Writer Newsfeatures: Jerry Schwartz
Education Reporter: Arlene Levinson

Associated Press
2021 St. NW, Room 600
Washington, DC 20006
(202) 776-9400
Education Reporter: Greg Toppo

Boston Globe
135 Morrissey Blvd
Dorchester, MA 02125
(617) 929-2000
Education Editor: Marilyn Garateix

CBS The Early Show
524 W 57th St
New York, NY 10019
Producers: Maureen McFadden, Carol Ann Story, Lyne Pitts

C-Span Booknotes
400 N Capital St, NW, Ste 650
Washington, DC 20001
Interim Producer: Connie Brod

Children's Software Revue
44 Main St.
Flemington, NJ 08822-1411
(908) 284-0404

Chicago Tribune, Washington Bureau
1325 G St., NW, Suite 200
Washington, DC 20005-3104
(202) 824-8200
Bureau Chief: James Warren

Christian Science Monitor
910 16th St, NW
Washington, DC 20006
(202) 785-4400
Education Reporter: Gail Russell Chaddock

Christian Science Monitor
One Norway St
Boston, MA 02115
(617) 450-2440
Education Editor: Amelia Newcomb

Copley News Service
PO Box 120190
San Diego, CA 92112
(619) 293-1818
Education Reporter: Mark Ryan

Cox Newspapers
400 N Capitol St NW
Wahsington, DC 20001
(202) 331-0900
Education Correspondent: Andy Mollison

Creative Classroom
149 Fifth Ave., 12th Floor
New York, NY 10010
(212) 677-4457

Dateline NBC
30 Rockefeller Plaza, #481-E4
New York, NY 10112
(212) 664-7501
Story Editor: Mark Rose

Education Daily
1101 King St., Suite 444
Alexandria, VA 22314-2944
(703) 683-4100

Education Digest
3970 Varsity Drive
Ann Arbor, MI 48108
(734) 975-2800, Ext. 212

Education Economy
20 Park Plaza, Ste 833
Boston, MA 02116
(617) 426-5622

Educational Marketer
PO Box 4234
Stamford, CT 06907-0234
(203) 358-9900

Family Circle
375 Lexington Ave
New York, NY 10017-5514
(212) 463-1346

Family Education Network
20 Park Plaza, Suite 1215
Boston, MA 02116
(617) 542-6500

Gannett News Service
1000 Wilson Blvd
Arlington, VA 22229
(703) 276-5800
Education Correspondent: Fredreka
Schouten

Gifted Child Today Magazine
PO Box 8813
Waco, TX 76714-8813
(254) 756-3337

Harvard Education Letter
349 Gutman Library
6 Appian Way
Cambridge, MA 02138
(617) 495-3432

The Heller Reports
9933 Lawler Avenue, Suite 502
Skokie, IL 60077
(847) 674-6282

Highschool Magazine
1904 Association Drive
Reston, VA 20191-1537
(703) 860-0200

Home Education Magazine
PO Box 1083, 1814 Highway 20 E.
Tonasket, WA 98855-1083
(509) 486-1351

Independent School
1620 L St., NW
Washington, DC 20036-5605
(202) 973-9700

International News Group
8677 Villa La Jolla Dr, #1215
La Jolla, CA 92037
(619) 678-0779
Bureau Chief: Stephen Butler

Language Arts
Boston College School of Education
Campion Hall, 140
Chestnut Hill, MA 02167
(617) 552-4912

Leadership Magazine
1904 Association Drive
Reston, VA 20191-1537
(703) 860-0200

Learning Magazine
3515 W. Market St.
Greensboro, NC 27403
(336) 851-8251

Library Talk
480 E. Wilson Bridge Road, Suite L
Worthington, OH 43085-2372
(614) 436-7107

Los Angeles Times
Times Mirror Square
130 S Broadway
Los Angeles, CA 90012
(213) 237-5000
Education Writer: Louis Sahagan

Los Angeles Times, Washington Bureau
1875 I St., NW, Suite 1100
Washington, DC 20006-5402
(202) 293-4650

Middle School Journal
202 Bailey Hall University Of Kansas
Lawrence, KS 66049
(614) 895-4730

MSNBC
40 Hartz Way
Secaucus, NJ 07094-2479
(201) 583-5000

National Center for Education Reform
4401 Connecticut Ave., NW, Suite 212
Washington, DC 20008
(202) 632-3444

National Public Radio
635 Massachusetts
Washington, DC 20001
(202) 414-2000
Education Reporter: Claudio Sanchez
All Things Considered Producer: Ellen
Weiss
Morning Edition Producer: Ellen
McDonnell

NEA Today
1201 16th St., NW
Washington, DC 20036
(202) 822-7288
Editor: Bill Fisher

Nelson B. Heller & Associates
9933 Lawler Ave., Suite 502
Skokie, IL 60077
(847) 674-6282

New York Times
229 W 43rd St.
New York, NY 10036-3959
(212) 556-8843
Education Editor: Ethan Bronner
Education Life Section: Jane Karr
Education Reporters: Karen Arenson,
Jacques Steinberg, Jodi Wilgoren

Newhouse News Service
1101 Connecticut Ave, NW, Ste 300
Washington, DC 20036
(202) 824-8200

News Hour with Jim Lehrer
3620 27th St South
Arlington, VA 22206-2304
(703) 998-2014
Education Reporter: Alison Sneed

Newsweek
251 W 57th St
New York, NY 10019
Education Reporters: Connie Leslie,
Barbara Kantrowitz
Newsweek Online: Peter McGrath

Reading Today
800 Barksdale Road, P.O. Box 8139
Newark, DE 19714
(800) 336-7323 x2

San Diego Union-Tribune
PO Box 120191
San Diego, CA 92112
(619) 293-2044
Education Editor: John Gilmore

School Marketing Newsletter
PO Box 10
Haddam, CT 06438-0010
(860) 345-8183

Science & Children
1840 Wilson Blvd.
Arlington, VA 22230
703-312-9213

Science Scope
1840 Wilson Blvd.
Arlington, VA 22230
(703) 243-7100

Scripps-Howard
1090 Vermont ?Ave, NW Ste 1000
Washington, DC 20036
(202) 408-2703
Education Correspondents: Jessica
Wehrman, Tom Hargrove

Social Education
3501 Newark St., NW
Washington, DC 20016
(202) 966-7840 ext. 105

Teachers & Writers Magazine
5 Union Square West
New York, NY 10003-3306
(212) 691-6590

Teaching Tolerance
400 Washington Ave.
Montgomery, AL 36104-4344
(334) 241-0726

TECHNOS Quarterly
1800 Stonelake Drive, #A
Bloomington, IN 47404-1517
(800) 457-4509

Theory Into Practice
College Of Education
The Ohio State University
172 Arps Hall,
1945 N. High St.
Columbus, OH 43210
(614) 292-3407

Time Magazine
1271 Ave of the Americas, Ste 2525
New York, NY 10020
Education Editor: Dan Goodgame
Education Reporter: Jodie Morse

Today Show
30 Rockefeller Plaza
New York, NY 10112
(212) 664-2349
Producers: Michael Cowan, Antoinette
Machiaverna

U.S. Department of Education
555 New Jersey Ave., NW, Room 202
Washington, DC 20208-5571
(202) 219-1892

U.S. News & World Report
1050 thomas Jefferson St., NW
Washington, DC 20007-3871
(202) 955-2000
Education Reporters: Ben Wildavasky,
Mary Lord

United Press International
1510 H St., NW
Washington, DC 20005
(202) 898-8000
Education Reporter: Dan Olmstead

USA Today
1000 Wilson Blvd.
Arlington, VA 22209-3901
(703) 558-5641
Education Reporters: Tamara Henry,
Mary Beth Marklein, David Brezing

The Wall Street Journal
1025 Connecticut Ave., NW, Suite 800
Washington, DC 20036-5405
(202) 862-9292
Education Reporter: Dan Golden

**The Wall Street Journal
Classroom Edition**
P.O. Box 300
Princeton, NJ 08543
(609) 520-4296

Washington Post
526 King St., Suite 515
Alexandria, VA 22314
(703) 518-3012
Education Reporter: Jay Matthews

State Departments of Education

Alabama
www.alsde.edu

Alaska
www.educ.state.ak.us

Arizona
www.ade.state.az.us

Arkansas
www.arkedu.k12.ar.us

California
www.goldmine.cde.ca.gov

Colorado
www.cde.state.co.us

Connecticut
www.aces.k12.ct.us

District of Columbia
www.k12.dc.us

Florida
www.firn.edu

Georgia
www.doe.k12.ga.us/

Hawaii
www.k12.hi.us/

Idaho
www.sde.state.id.us/dept/

Illinois
www.isbe.state.il.us/

Indiana
www.ideanet.doe.state.in.us:80/

Iowa
www.state.ia.us/educate

Kansas
www.ksbe.state.ks.us/

Kentucky
www.kde.state.ky.us

Louisiana
www.doe.state.la.us

Maine
www.state.me.us/education/
homepage.htm

Maryland
www.msde.state.md.us/

Massachusetts
www.state.ma.us/govserv.htm#edu

Michigan
www.mde.state.mi.us

Minnesota
www.educ.state.mn.us/

Mississippi
www.mdek12.state.ms.us/

Missouri
www.services.dese.state.mo.us

Montana
www.metnet.state.mt.us

Nebraska
www.nde.state.ne.us

New Hampshire
www.state.nh.us/doe/

New Jersey
www.state.nj.us/education

New Mexico
www.sde.state.nm.us/

New York State
www.nysed.gov

North Carolina
www.dpi.state.nc.us/

North Dakota
www.sendit.nodak.edu/dpi/

Ohio
www.ode.state.oh.us

Oklahoma
www.state.ok.us

Oregon
www.ode.state.or.us/

Pennsylvania
www.pde.psu.edu

Rhode Island
www.ridoe.net

South Carolina
www.state.sc.us/edu/

Tennessee
www.state.tn.us/education/

Texas
www.tea.state.tx.us

Utah
www.usoe.k12.ut.us

Vermont
www.state.vt.us/educ/

Virginia
www.141.104.22.210/

Washington
www.k12.wa.us

West Virginia
www.wvde.state.wv.us/

Wisconsin
www.dpi.state.wi.us/

Wyoming
www.k12.wy.us/wdehome.html

Regional Education Labs

The concept of Regional Educational Laboratories as a national resource for local and state benefit was implemented by Congress over three decades ago under the Elementary and Secondary Education Act. While each Laboratory has distinctive features tailored to meet the special needs of the geographic region it serves, the Laboratories also have common characteristics. Guided by a governing board representing stakeholders in its region—educators, business leaders, state officials, and community members—each Laboratory's work is shaped by the concerns, issues, opportunities, and special attributes of its region.

Appalachia Educational Laboratory (AEL)
www.ael.org
States Served: Kentucky, Tennessee, Virginia, and West Virginia
National Leadership Area: Educational Technology, Rural Education

Mid-Atlantic Laboratory for Student Success (LSS)
www.temple.edu/LSS/
States Served: Delaware, Maryland, New Jersey, Pennsylvania, and Washington, DC
National Leadership Area: Educational Leadership

Mid-continent Research for Education and Learning (McREL)
www.mcrel.org
States Served: Colorado, Kansas, Missouri, Nebraska, North Dakota, South Dakota, and Wyoming
National Leadership Area: Standards-Based Instructional Practice

North Central Regional Educational Laboratory (NCREL)
www.ncrel.org
States Served: Illinois, Indiana, Iowa, Michigan, Minnesota, Ohio, and Wisconsin
National Leadership Area: Educational Technology

Northeast and Islands Laboratory at Brown University (LAB)
www.lab.brown.edu/public/index.shtml
States Served: Connecticut, Maine, Massachusetts, New Hampshire, New York, Rhode Island, Vermont, Puerto Rico, and the Virgin Islands
National Leadership Area: Teaching Diverse Students

Northwest Regional Educational Laboratory (NWREL)
www.nwrel.org
States Served: Alaska, Idaho, Montana, Oregon, and Washington
National Leadership Area: Re-engineering Schools for Improvement

Pacific Resources for Education and Learning (PREL)
www.prel.org
States Served: American Samoa, Commonwealth of the Northern Mariana Islands, Federated States of Micronesia Guam, Hawaii, Republic of the Marshall Islands, and the Republic of Palau
National Leadership Area: Area of Curriculum and Instruction Related to Reading and Language Mastery

SouthEastern Regional Vision for Education (SERVE)
www.serve.org
States Served: Alabama, Florida, Georgia, Mississippi, North Carolina, and South Carolina
National Leadership Area: Expanded Learning Opportunities

Southwest Educational Development Laboratory (SEDL)
www.sedl.org
States Served: Arkansas, Louisiana, New Mexico, Oklahoma, and Texas
National Leadership Area: Family and Community Involvement

WestEd
www.wested.org
States Served: Arizona, California, Nevada, and Utah
National Leadership Area: Assessment of Educational Achievement

Consortia

High Plains Regional Technology in Education Consortium
www.hprtec.org/

Mid-Atlantic Regional Technology in Education Consortium
www.temple.edu/martec/

North Central Regional Technology in Education Consortium
www.ncrtec.org/

Northeast and the Islands Regional Technology in Education Program
www.neirtec.org

Northwest Educational Technology Consortium
www.netc.org

Regional Technology in Education Consortia - Appalachian Region
www.rtec.org/ar_tec.html

Regional Technology in Education Consortium for the Pacific
www.rtec.org/pr_tec.html

Regional Technology in Education Consortium for the Southwest Region
www.westedrtec.org

South Central Regional Technology in Education Consortium
www.southcentralrtec.org

Southeast Initiatives Regional Technology in Education Consortium
www.seirtec.org

Educational Media Centers and Service Centers

National Association of Regional Media Centers
Oneida Herkimer Co. BOCES
Utica, NY 13501-1790
(315) 793-8503
FAX (315) 793-8554

American Association of Educational Service Agencies
www.aaesa.org
1801 North Moore Street
Arlington, VA 22209
(703) 875-0739
FAX (703) 528-2146
Contact: Brian L. Talbott, Executive Director

National Education Associations

American Alliance for Health, Physical Education, Recreation, and Dance
www.aahperd.org

American Association for the Advancement of Science
www.aaas.org

American Association of Physics Teachers
www.aapt.org/main.html

American Association of School Administrators
www.aasa.org

American Council on Education
www.acenet.edu

American Council on the Teaching of Foreign Languages
www.actfl.org

American Counseling Association
www.counseling.org

American Educational Research Association
www.aera.net

American Federation of Teachers
www.aft.org

American Library Association
www.ala.org

American School Health Association
www.ashaweb.org

American Society for Training & Development
www.astd.org

American Speech Language & Hearing Association
www.asha.org

Association for the Advancement of Computing in Education
www.aace.org

Association for Career and Technical Education
www.acteonline.org

Association for Educational Communications and Technologies
www.aect.org

Association Montessori Internationale
www.montessori-ami.org/ami.htm

Association for Supervision & Curriculum Development
www.ascd.org

Consortium for School Networking (CoSN)
www.cosn.org

Council for Exceptional Children
www.cec.sped.org

Council of Chief State School Officers
www.ccsso.org

Distance Learning Resource Network
www.dlrn.org

Educational Theatre Association
www.etassoc.org

Educause
www.educause.edu

INFOCOMM International
www.infocomm.org

International Reading Association
www.reading.org

International Society for Technology in Education
www.iste.org

Learning Disabilities Association of America
www.ldanatl.org

Modern Language Association of America
www.mla.org

Music Teachers National Association
www.mtna.org

National Alliance of Black School Educators
www.nabse.org

National Art Education Association
www.naea-reston.org

National Association for Bilingual Education
www.nabe.org

National Association of Biology Teachers
www.nabt.org

National Association of Child Care Professionals
www.naccp.org

National Association for Education of Young Children
www.naeyc.org

National Association of Elementary School Principals
www.naesp.org

National Association for Gifted Children
www.nagc.org

National Association of Independent Schools
www.nais-schools.org

National Association for Multicultural Education
www.inform.umd.edu/NAME/

National Association for Music Education
www.menc.org

National Association of Secondary School Principals
www.nassp.org

National Association of State Boards of Education
www.nasbe.org

National Association of State Directors of Special Education
www.nasdse.org

National Association for Year Round Education
www.nayre.org

National Business Education Association
www.nbea.org

National Catholic Education Association
www.ncea.org

National Child Care Association
www.nccanet.org

National Council for the Social Studies
www.ncss.org

National Council of Teachers of English
www.ncte.org

National Council of Teachers of Mathematics
www.nctm.org

National Council on
Measurement in Education
www.ncme.org

National Education Association
www.nea.org

National Information Center for
Educational Media
www.nicem.com

National Middle School
Association
www.nmsa.org

National PTA
www.pta.org

National School Boards
Association
www.nsba.org

National Science Teachers
Association
www.nsta.org

National Staff Development
Council
www.nasc.org

The School Building Association
www.cefpi.org

School, Home & Office Products
Association
www.shopa.org

Society for Applied Learning
Technology
www.salt.org

Teachers of English to Speakers
of Other Languages
www.tesol.org

US Distance Learning Association
www.usdla.org

K-12 Education Magazines

American Educator
www.aft.org

American Language Online
www.alr.org

American School Board Journal
www.asbj.com

The Book Report
www.linworth.com

Booklinks
www.ala.org/BookLinks/

Booklist
www.ala.org/booklist/

Cable in the Classroom
www.ciconline.com

Catechist Magazine
www.catechist.com

Children's Software Review
www2.childrenssoftware.com/
childrenssoftware/

Converge
www.convergemag.com

District Administration
www.districtadministration.com

Early Childhood News
www.earlychildhoodnews.com

Early Childhood Today
www.scholastic.com/ect/

Educational Leadership
www.ascd.org/frameedlead.html

Education Week
www.edweek.org

Electronic School
www.electronic-school.com

The English Teacher's Assistant
www.etanewsletter.com

eSchool News
www.eschoolnews.com

ESL Magazine
www.eslmag.com

HomeSchooling Today
www.homeschooltoday.com

Horn Book
www.hbook.com/mag.shtml

Inside Education
www.insideeducation.com

Instructor
www.scholastic.com/instructor/

Learning by Design
www.nsba.org

Learning & Leading with
Technology
www.iste.org/L&L/index.html

Learning Magazine
http://themailbox.com/learning/
lrnhome.html

Library Talk
www.linworth.com

Media & Methods
www.media-methods.com

MultiMedia Schools Magazine
www.infotoday.com/MMSchools/
default.htm

NASSP Bulletin
www.nassp.org

Principal
www.naesp.org/comm/principl.htm

Principal Leadership
www.nassp.org

Scholastic Administrator
www.scholasticadministrator.com

School Administrator
www.aasa.org/SA/contents.htm

School Board News
www.nsba.org

School Library Journal
www.slj.com

School Library Media Activities
www.crinkles.com/schoolmedia.html

School Planning & Management
www.spmmag.com

Social Education
www.socialstudies.org/news/tssp.html

The Social Studies Professional
www.socialstudies.org/news/tssp.html

Social Studies & the Young Learner
www.socialstudies.org/news/tssp.html

Teacher Librarian
www.teacherlibrarian.com

Teacher Magazine
www.edweek.org/button4/

Teaching PreK–8
www.teachingk-8.com

Technology & Learning
www.techlearning.com

Tech Trends
www.aect.org:80/Pubs/techtrends.html

THE Journal
www.thejournal.com

Today's School — Shared Leadership in Education
www.todaysschool.com

Today's Catholic Teacher
www.catholicteacher.com

Education Statistics

AskERIC
http://ericir.syr.edu

This is one of the most comprehensive sites for getting information about education. Besides offering the ERIC database (containing more than one million abstracts of documents and journal articles on education research and practice), this site also offers lesson plans, a database of Internet resources, and maintains the archives for more than 25 discussion groups. But perhaps the most useful service they offer is a question and answer service where you can send in a question and an information specialist will respond personally within two days of receipt.

CEO Forum
www.ceoforum.org

The CEO Forum on Education and Technology was founded in the fall of 1996 to help ensure that America's schools effectively prepare all students to be contributing citizens and productive workers in the 21st Century. They offer annual reports on the state of education and these reports can be downloaded in PDF format.

The Center for Children and Technology
www2.edc.org/CCT/cctweb/index.html

Founded by the Bank Street College of Education in 1980, this organization conducts research into the ways technology affects learning. This site contains many free articles that report the results of their research.

Computer Learning Foundation
www.computerlearning.org

The Computer Learning Foundation is an international nonprofit educational foundation, dedicated to improving the quality of education and preparation of youth for the workplace through the use of technology. This organization is the sponsor of the annual October Computer Learning Month as well as other contests throughout the year. They offer a wide variety of articles on technology in the classroom issues.

EdLiNC
www.edlinc.org

The Education and Libraries Networks Coalition (EdLiNC) was formed to represent the viewpoint of schools and libraries in the FCC proceedings dealing with the implementation of the Telecommunications Act of 1996. This site has a wealth of information about the e-Rate and how it has affected schools and libraries.

Milken Family Foundation
www.mff.org

As a part of its broad-based mission, this nonprofit foundation sponsors educator awards and educational research. A number of helpful research publications are available free of charge on their Web site.

National Center for Education Statistics
www.nces.ed.gov/

This is the primary federal entity for collecting and analyzing data that are related to education in the United States and the world. The annually issued Digest of Educational Statistics is available for free and contains all the information about educational demographics, trends, statistics and funding. This site has hundreds of publications available from the GPO at no cost.

The National Goals Panel

www.negp.gov/

The National Education Goals Panel (NEGP) is a unique bipartisan and intergovernmental body of federal and state officials created in July 1990 to assess and report state and national progress toward achieving the National Education Goals. They offer a free weekly and monthly eZine to keep you up to date with the latest news and information in the field of education. The NEGP publishes an annual report on national and state progress toward the Goals and issues publications on goal-related topics. These publications can be ordered from the Goals Panel free of charge by filling out the electronic publication request form on this web site. You can view and download many other reports from the site as well.

StateLine.org

www.stateline.org

This site is operated by the Pew Center on the States, a research organization administered by the University of Richmond, and funded by the Pew Charitable Trusts. Stateline.org was founded in order to help journalists, policy makers and engaged citizens become better informed about innovative public policies. This site follows the development of major issues as they appear on the public agenda in a critical number of states. One of the issues covered is education—especially the manner in which public schools are financed.

Thomas

www.thomas.loc.gov

Maintained by the Library of Congress, this site offers a comprehensive database of Legislative Information. This is where you can track the educational funding initiatives being discussed in the Congress.

US Department of Education

www.ed.gov/

This site is a huge collection of resources on educational information including grants, publications, federal initiatives, research & statistics, and more. They publish an eZine called EDInfo covering new reports, new initiatives, and funding opportunities from the Department of Education.